Chr
in Sch.

This book investigates scholastic discussions of Christ's wills from Anselm of Canterbury to John Duns Scotus, concentrating on Thomas Aquinas. The work advances understandings of scholastic Christology in two basic ways. First, it traces the development of scholastic discussions of Christ's wills, attending to the contested issues, to the context of debates, to the use of sources and distinctions, and to the larger implications of these discussions for scholastic Christology. Second, the book utilizes this general analysis as a backdrop for examining the role granted to Christ's humanity by Thomas Aquinas. It argues that Aquinas, based upon his highly developed understanding of Christ's wills, his novel use of patristic sources, and his own terminological and conceptual advancements, portrays Christ's humanity as an *instrumentum divinitatis* that, through its free will and operation, acts as the instrumental efficient cause of salvation. In presenting Christ's human will as an instrumental efficient cause of salvation, Thomas developed and extended Anselm's basic soteriological insight by highlighting the Incarnation and Passion as the most fitting means for redemption precisely in their elevation of human dignity in intellect and will. Serious challenges, both medieval and modern, have been directed against Aquinas's Christological formulations. In responding to these challenges, the book demonstrates the enduring value of Aquinas's Christology.

MEDIAEVAL LAW AND THEOLOGY 5

General Editors

Alexander Andrée
University of Toronto

John F. Boyle
University of St Thomas

Joseph Goering
University of Toronto

Giulio Silano
University of Toronto

STUDIES AND TEXTS 178

Christ's Two Wills in Scholastic Thought

The Christology of Aquinas and Its Historical Contexts

COREY L. BARNES

PONTIFICAL INSTITUTE OF MEDIAEVAL STUDIES

Library and Archives Canada Cataloguing in Publication

Barnes, Corey Ladd, author
    Christ's two wills in scholastic thought : the Christology of Aquinas and its historical contexts / Corey L. Barnes.

(Studies and texts ; 178)
(Mediaeval law and theology ; 5)
Reprinted with minor changes.
Reprint of: Christ's two wills in scholastic thought: the Christology of
    Aquinas and its historical contexts / Corey L. Barnes. – Toronto :
    Pontifical Institute of Mediaeval Studies, ©2012.
Includes bibliographical references and index.
ISBN 978-0-88844-424-0 (paperback)

    1. Jesus Christ – Person and offices. 2. Jesus Christ – History of doctrines – Middle Ages, 600–1500. 3. Jesus Christ – Natures. 4. Thomas, Aquinas, Saint, 1225?–1274. I. Pontifical Institute of Mediaeval Studies, issuing body II. Title. III. Series: Studies and texts (Pontifical Institute of Mediaeval Studies) ; 178 IV. Series: Mediaeval law and theology ; 5

BT198.B266 2016   232'.8   C2015-908515-2

Reprinted, with corrections, 2016

© 2012
Pontifical Institute of Mediaeval Studies
59 Queen's Park Crescent East
Toronto, Ontario, Canada M5S 2C4
www.pims.ca

MANUFACTURED IN CANADA

Contents

Acknowledgements   vii

CHAPTER ONE
History and Theological Significance of Christ's Two Wills   1

   Patristic Reflection on Christ's Wills | 6
   Aims of the Present Study | 19

CHAPTER TWO
Foundations of Thirteenth-Century Debates
The *Sentences*, *Summa aurea*, and *Summa fratris Alexandri*   26

   Anselm of Canterbury, Peter Abelard, Hugh of St Victor,
      and the *Summa sententiarum* | 27
   Peter Lombard's *Sentences* | 37
   William of Auxerre's *Summa aurea* | 47
   Summa fratris Alexandri | 56

CHAPTER THREE
Scholastic Debates on Christ's Two Wills
Albert the Great and Bonaventure   69

   Albert the Great | 71
   Bonaventure | 89

CHAPTER FOUR
Thomas Aquinas on Christ's Two Wills
Continuities and Developments between the *Scriptum* and
Summa theologiae   113

   Establishing a Human Will in Christ | 117
   The Will of Sensuality | 132

The Twofold Act of the Will of Reason | 135
  Perfect Knowledge, Perfect Free Choice | 139
  A Human Will Obedient to God | 144
  The Acts of Christ's Will | 158

CHAPTER FIVE
Fitting Means for Redemption
Christ's Human Nature as Instrumental Efficient Cause of Salvation 180

  The Plan of the *Summa theologiae* | 183
  The Incarnation as Fitting Communication of Goodness Itself | 193
  The Mode of Union | 199
  The Nature Assumed | 204
  Christ the Mediator: Christ's Human Will as Cause of Salvation | 224

CHAPTER SIX
Later Treatments of Christ's Wills and Problems of Christological Causation
Giles of Rome, Peter Olivi, and John Duns Scotus   291

  Giles of Rome, Peter Olivi, and Christology after 1277 | 292
  John Duns Scotus on Christ's Wills | 300
  Sorrow, Sadness, and Freedom | 306
  Finite Causality, Finite Merit | 313

Conclusion   329

Bibliography   333

Index   352

Acknowledgements

Without the generous assistance of many people, this project never would have come to fruition. My teachers and mentors at the University of Notre Dame tirelessly provided encouragement, advice, and a scholarly example. Through a variety of formal and informal means, John Cavadini, Brian Daley, Cyril O'Regan, Thomas Prügl, and Joseph Wawrykow were trustworthy guides and inspirations. My good friends Caleb Congrove and Shawn Colberg assisted me at crucial stages of the process. My colleagues in the Department of Religion at Oberlin College also have offered me consistent support, for which I am most grateful. Finally and most importantly, I owe many thanks to my wife, Doris Jankovits, for her patience, friendship, and optimism.

Oberlin, Ohio

CHAPTER ONE

History and Theological Significance of Christ's Two Wills

Respondeo dicendum quod duplex est efficiens: principale, et instrumentale. Efficiens quidem principale humanae salutis Deus est. Quia vero humanitas Christi est divinitatis instrumentum, ut supra dictum est, ex consequenti omnes actiones et passiones Christi instrumentaliter operantur in virtute divinitatis ad salutem humanam. Et secundum hoc passio Christi efficienter causat salutem humanam.

Thomas Aquinas, *Summa theologiae* III, q.48, a.6[1]

Scholastic Christologies devoted remarkable attention to the humanity of Christ, reflecting a broader trend within the medieval world of devotion focused on Christ's humanity and suffering.[2] The scholastic form of this devotion concerned what it meant for Christ to be truly, fully, and perfectly human, a human being free from sin and its diverse effects. Such considerations attempted to balance the gospel portrayals of Jesus of Nazareth with the redemptive purpose of the Incarnation, gathering a host of topics from theological anthropology to soteriology. No one better exemplifies this scholastic concern than Thomas Aquinas, whose *Summa theologiae* completes its treatment of Christological doctrine with treatment of the *acta et passa Christi in carne*, the mysteries of Christ's life and death. The very structure of the *Summa*'s treatise on Christ reminds the reader that, for scholastic theologians, doctrine explicates and clarifies scripture, provid-

---

1 *Summa theologiae*, cura et studio Instituti studiorum medievalium Ottaviensis ad textum S. Pii Papae V iussu confectum recognita, ed altera emendata (Ottawa, 1941–1945), 4: 2739a.
2 For discussions of this general trend, see Giles Constable, *Three Studies in Medieval Religious and Social Thought* (Cambridge, 1995), pp. 143–248 and Richard William Southern, *The Making of the Middle Ages* (New Haven, 1959), pp. 231–240.

ing a lens through which to read profitably scriptural revelation. Even more striking is the soteriological value Thomas granted to Christ's humanity. Aquinas holds that Christ's humanity was the instrumental efficient cause of salvation, that Christ *secundum quod homo* (according as a human being) could produce a divine effect. This radical claim supports and depends upon Thomas's commitment to expounding the Incarnation as the wisest means for human salvation.

The question of Christ's human will provided an open field for fruitful reflection on Christ's human nature, its component parts, and the soteriological function of these parts. Thomas Aquinas, following the interpretive trends of the seventh century, regarded Christ's possession of both a human will and the divine will as a necessary extension of Chalcedonian orthodoxy, with its affirmation of two natures in Christ united without confusion, change, separation, or division.[3] To modern eyes, the Chalcedonian 'Definition of the Faith' and a dyothelite (two wills) Christology can seem divorced from the biblical portrayals of Jesus of Nazareth and can seem to impose a foreign scheme onto the gospel accounts. Examined within their own historical and theological contexts, it is apparent that Christological doctrines or definitions intended not to exhaust the possibility for theological reflection and debate but rather to orient that reflection and debate in meaningful, productive directions. The council of Chalcedon (451) well illustrates this.[4] The council sought to answer the

---

[3] Aaron Riches argues that Constantinople III offers a necessary extension of the basic Chalcedonian logic because the Chalcedonian 'Definition of the Faith' leaves room for an unwarranted parallelism in Christology. See Riches, "After Chalcedon: The Oneness of Christ and the Dyothelite Mediation of His Theandric Unity," *Modern Theology* 24 (2008): 199–224.

[4] Sarah Coakley describes a contextualized and fruitful approach to Chalcedon: "Taking this semantic background into account, and remembering again that the assembled bishops at Chalcedon resisted at one point the emperor's demand for greater 'precision,' we may perhaps begin to see the true intentions of the document. It does not, that is, intend to provide a full systematic account of Christology, and even less a complete and precise metaphysics of Christ's makeup. Rather, it sets a 'boundary' on what can, and cannot, be said, by first ruling out three aberrant interpretations of Christ (Apollinarianism, Eutychianism, and extreme Nestorianism), second, providing an abstract rule of language (*physis* and *hypostasis*) for distinguishing duality and unity in Christ, and, third, presenting a 'riddle' of negatives by means of which a greater (though undefined) reality may be intimated. At the same time, it recapitu-

opposing views of Nestorius, who affirmed multiple hypostases in Christ, and Eutyches, who defended a single nature in Christ, carving out space for a middle way without being overly restrictive. The crucial part of the 'definition' from Chalcedon reads as follows:

> So, following the saintly fathers, we all with one voice teach the confession of one and the same Son, our Lord Jesus Christ: the same perfect in divinity and perfect in humanity, the same truly God and truly man, of a rational soul and a body; consubstantial with the Father as regards his divinity, and the same consubstantial with us as regards his humanity; like us in all respects except for sin; begotten before the ages from the Father as regards his divinity, and in the last days the same for us and for our salvation from Mary, the virgin God-bearer, as regards his humanity; one and the same Christ, Son, Lord, only-begotten, acknowledged in two natures which undergo no confusion, no change, no division, no separation; at no point was the difference between the natures taken away through the union, but rather the property of both natures is preserved and comes together into a single person and a single subsistent being; he is not parted or divided into two persons, but is one and the same only-begotten Son, God, Word, Lord Jesus Christ, just as the prophets taught from the beginning about him, and as the Lord Jesus Christ himself instructed us, and as the creed of the fathers handed it down to us.[5]

This statement strives to balance unity and duality in Christ, admitting two perfect natures with one common subject. Christological debates

---

lates and assumes (a point often forgotten in considering the *horos* in abstraction from the rest of the *Acta*) the acts of salvation detailed in Nicaea and Constantinople; and then it leaves us at that 'boundary,' understood as the place now to which those salvific acts must be brought to avoid doctrinal error, but without any supposition that this linguistic regulation thereby *explains* or *grasps* the reality towards which it points. In this, rather particular sense, it is an 'apophatic' document" (Coakley, "What Does Chalcedon Solve and What Does it Not? Some Reflections on the Status and Meaning of the Chalcedonian 'Definition,'" in *The Incarnation: An Interdisciplinary Symposium on the Incarnation of the Son of God*, ed. Stephen T. Davis, Daniel Kendall, and Gerald O'Collins [Oxford, 2002], pp. 143–163, at p. 161).

5 *Nicaea I to Lateran V*, ed. Norman P. Tanner, vol. 1 of *Decrees of the Ecumenical Councils* (Washington, DC, 1990), p. 86.

continued after the council of Chalcedon, and the controversies that grew out of these debates required new specifications or elaborations of earlier doctrine, continuing the process of explicating what scriptural revelation contains implicitly. The seventh-century monothelite (one will) controversy required such specifications and elaborations; Constantinople III (680–681), as had the Lateran Council of 649, answered this requirement by extending the Chalcedonian logic of two natures in one person to affirm two natural wills and operations in Christ. As with earlier debates, questions of unity and duality in Christ sparked the monothelite controversy.

As the monothelite debate gradually sank into the forgotten past, medieval considerations of Christ's two wills or of Christ's human will responded to new and different questions. Medieval attention to Christ's humanity, together with the emerging methods of scholasticism, yielded systematic engagements with a host of related topics. Divergent approaches to the mode of union in the Incarnation arose, each with its own logic and authoritative sources. New vigor accompanied the efforts to explore the perennial topic of human freedom in its power and weakness. Perhaps most important were the reconsiderations of soteriology. Anselm of Canterbury's satisfaction theory of the atonement, as expressed in the *Cur Deus homo*, stressed the voluntary nature of the passion as crucial to its redemptive aim. While Anselm defended this voluntary nature largely in terms of the divine will, later theologians would extend this Anselmian logic with reference to Christ's human will. Peter Abelard's *Commentaria in epistolam Pauli ad Romanos* highlighted the exemplary character of Christ's sacrifice and so reflected the growing interest in the *imitatio Christi*. Bernard of Clairvaux read Abelard's reflections as thinly veiled Pelagianism but did not succeed in squashing Abelard's basic soteriological insight. Scholastic reflection on Christ's human will developed the impulse underlying these soteriological expressions, and Peter Lombard's *Sentences* in particular provided a catalyst for this reflection. Subsequent theologians worked within the basic framework of the Lombard's *Sentences* while adding new insights and sources. Tracing these additions and the patterns of their general adoption into the scholastic vocabulary reveals much about scholastic Christologies, isolating and highlighting individual contributions to these discussions. These contributions are most notable in William of Auxerre, the *Summa fratris Alexandri*, Albert the Great, Bonaventure, Thomas Aquinas, Giles of Rome, Peter Olivi, and John Duns Scotus.

Examining scholastic presentations of Christ's two wills requires an approach that is both historical and systematic. As a topic of historical theology, these presentations reflect and reveal larger trends in scholastic Christologies. The various medieval discussions display great uniformity in the basic lines of argument. Within this uniformity, subtle developments and disagreements persisted. This is especially true for strategies to defend the conformity, harmony, or non-contrariety of wills in Christ. Weighing out this uniformity and diversity reveals the open but well-defined field of scholastic reflection on Christological topics. This historical approach also has systematic value. Ancient and contemporary debates about the utility of Chalcedon's 'Definition of the Faith' focus on the alien technical vocabulary of *ousia* (nature) and *hypostasis* (metaphysical or grammatical subject). When the conversation becomes bogged down in the propriety of such terminology, the basic insight of Chalcedon becomes obscured. Discussions of Christ's wills – and to a lesser extent, discussions of operations – offer a less alien vocabulary for exploring the unity and duality affirmed at Chalcedon without confusion or division.[6] Reflections on wills also allows for an exploration of Christ's full humanity in more common terms than the metaphysical vocabulary of Chalcedon.

Though the focus of this work will rest exclusively on high medieval considerations of Christ's two wills, a brief and selective summary of patristic debates on this topic will provide a helpful frame of reference for those later debates. It must be kept in mind, however, that medieval theologians knew and read very little of patristic theology. This summary will, accord-

---

6 The charge of dividing Christ applies particularly to Nestorius's view of two hypostases in Christ, one divine and one human. Demetrios Bathrellos points out that Leo's expression in the *Tomus ad Flavianum* (*agit enim utraque forma cum alterius communione*) risks implying two willing or operating subjects. Properly speaking, the natures or forms do not act. The person acts through the natures. Bathrellos provides a useful, critical discussion of Leo's formula and its shortcomings. See Bathrellos, *The Byzantine Christ: Person, Nature, and Will in the Christology of Saint Maximus the Confessor* (Oxford, 2004), pp. 176–189. Interpretations of Leo split between orthodox and heterodox readings, but Maximus the Confessor and Pope Agatho both cite Leo's formula as a statement of the orthodox view. John Duns Scotus argued that individual natures do in fact act, and this contention led Scotus to formulate a view of Christological causality radically different than the view forwarded by Aquinas. See Chapter six below (pp. 313–328) for consideration of Aquinas and Scotus on Christological causality.

ingly, stress those sources most relevant to medieval debates. Such a summary imposes a false unity to what were diverse reflections for varying purposes. The theological context changed frequently; earlier debates were constantly reinterpreted to address new concerns. Scholastic theology serves as a prime example of this re-interpretive process, but earlier sources provided the model. Thirteenth-century knowledge of earlier discussions of Christ's two wills depended very heavily on John Damascene's *De fide orthodoxa*. The Damascene crafted a synthetic and systematic presentation of Christological doctrine and offers a convenient *terminus ad quem* for this summary.

Patristic Reflection on Christ's Wills

The question of Christ's two wills largely begins with Jesus's prayer in the garden of Gethsemane: "My Father, if it is possible, let this cup pass from me; nevertheless not what I will, but what you will" (Matthew 26:39).[7] The subtext of the question was scrutinized, developed upon, and transformed throughout the history of Christological debates. The Arians cited Jesus's prayer as evidence that the *Logos* was not of the same substance as the Father.[8] The Apollinarians argued that the *Logos* took the place of a human

---

7   For a brief history of patristic interpretations of the prayer in Gethsemane, see Bathrellos, *The Byzantine Christ*, pp. 140–147. Equally important are Luke 22:42: "Father, if you are willing (βούλει), remove this cup from me; yet, not my will (θέλημα) but yours be done"; and John 6:38: "For I have come down from heaven, not to do my own will, but the will of him who sent me." Luke 22:42 provided the scriptural *locus classicus* for the distinction between *boulēsis* and *thelēsis*, later designated in Latin as *voluntas ut ratio* (will as reason) and *voluntas ut natura* (will as nature). This distinction was important in the anthropology of Nemesius of Emesa and subsequently for Maximus the Confessor and John of Damascus.

8   Heretical or heterodox interpretations of Christ's will(s) were plentiful. In addition to the Arians and Apollinarians, one could mention Nestorius's presentation of the union in Christ in a manner that seemed reduced to a moral union of wills. Nestorius's view of Christ's unity depended heavily on Theodore of Mopsuestia. There have been recent attempts to read Theodore's views within their historical, intellectual, and exegetical contexts with the possible end of rehabilitating his attention to the salvific role of Christ's humanity. See Frederick G. McLeod, *The Roles of Christ's Humanity in Salvation: Insights from Theodore of Mopsuestia* (Washington, DC, 2005). McLeod must interpret charitably Theodore's statements of one will and operation in Christ to tease

soul in Jesus, which excludes the presence of a true human will. Opponents of such trends had to exegete Matt. 26:39 and John 6:38 in defense of both the full divinity and full humanity of Christ. John Chrysostom reads Matt. 26:39 as revealing Christ's humanity and its harmony with the divine will.[9] Ambrose (*De fide ad Gratianum*) and Augustine (*Contra Maximinum episcopum Arianorum*) respond by distinguishing the human will from the will of divinity in Christ. Ambrose and Augustine tend to stress this distinction of wills.[10] Gregory of Nazianzus, in his fourth *Theological Oration*, writes of Christ's human will as taken into God and interprets Matt. 26:39 as a statement of Christ's identity in will with the Father.[11] Gregory distinguishes Christ's human will, which cannot oppose God, from a sinful human will, which normally struggles against God. Too heavy a stress on unity of wills begins to sound more like a numerical identity. Too heavy a stress on diversity of wills begins to suggest contrariety of wills. A desire to avoid any and all contrariety of wills motivated the seventh-century monothelites to deny

---

out an opposition to monothelitism and monenergism. "When Theodore speaks of 'one will and operation' in Christ, he appears to be referring to how the human and divine wills function as one in their common *prosôpon*. Since Christ is portrayed as one person in the gospel accounts, this must mean that there is present one will internally, that is, that the human will always freely chooses to be one with the divine: 'By preserving the natures unconfused and undivided, the union of good pleasure shows [that there is] one person for both and one will and one operation with the accompanying one authority and absolute rule .... For by being thus conjoined to God the Word by means of His good pleasure, as we have said, that temple who is born from the womb of the Virgin remained undivided, having the same will and the same operation with him in all things, than which nothing can be more conjoined.' In brief, while Christ's humanity derives its power to act because of the Word's initiative and empowerment and forms one will with the Word, still Theodore considers that all this is done in a mysterious free way. Otherwise, Theodore would be espousing a monoenergistic or Monothelite view of the unity in Christ – a view he roundly rejects" (McLeod, *The Roles of Christ's Humanity*, pp. 195–196).

9   John Chrysostom, *Homiliae in Matthaeum 83* (PG 58: 745–747).
10 See Ambrose, *De fide ad Gratianum Augustum*, PL 16 and Augustine, *Contra Maximinum Haereticum Arianorum Episcopum*, PL 42. Ambrose attributes Christ's prayer in the garden to the weakness of his assumed nature (*De fide* II.5), defends the Son's identity in will with the Father (*De fide* II.6), and distinguishes the human will fearing death from the divine will willing the passion (*De fide* II.7).
11 See Gregory of Nazianzus, *Discourses 27–31*, ed. Paul Gallay (Paris, 1978).

two wills in Christ.[12] That is, the monothelites equated diversity of wills with contrariety of wills. They eliminated the former to prevent the latter. While the monothelites' underlying concern was with contrariety of wills, the monothelite debate focused on the number of wills in Christ. This focus had theological and political motivations.

Monothelitism emerged as an alternative to the controversial proposal of *mia energeia* (one energy/action/operation) in Christ.[13] In 633 Emperor Heraclius promulgated the Alexandrian pact of union to promote reconciliation between Chalcedonian and non-Chalcedonian Christians.[14] These non-Chalcedonian Christians, sometimes called monophysites (proponents of a one-nature Christology), rejected the definition of faith from the council of Chalcedon and preferred more literal adherence to Cyril of Alexandria's affirmation of one incarnate nature of God the Logos (μία φύσις τοῦ θεοῦ λόγου σεσαρκωμένην).[15] Heraclius sought religious

---

[12] It seems that no one ever argued for *monon thelēma Christou*, where *monon* indicates one only. The preferred terminology for proponents of a one-will view was *mia thelēma* or *hen thelēma*, where *mia* and *hen* express 'one' in a less exclusive or restrictive manner.

[13] The expression *mia energeia* was attributed to Pseudo-Dionysius (Epistle 4). Debates have long surrounded this expression, questioning both the correct reading of the text – some manuscripts have 'one theandric energy', others have 'new theandric energy' – and the true meaning of the expression 'theandric energy'. See F.-X. Murphy and P. Sherwood, *Constantinople II et III* (Paris, 1974), p. 152.

[14] For discussions of the historical origins of the monothelite controversy, see Bathrellos, *The Byzantine Christ*, pp. 60–66; Andrew Louth, *Maximus the Confessor* (London, 1996), pp. 7–18; and Murphy and Sherwood, *Constantinople II et III*, pp. 133–173. Cyrus, bishop of Phasis (Poti), tailored the pact of union to employ Chalcedonian terminology (two natures) in a manner acceptable to the monophysites. "Mais l'équilibre de Chalcédoine a disparu. La tournure particulièrement maladroite est due, semble-t-il, à la façon dont Cyrus essaie de s'accommoder lui-même au parti monophysite d'Alexandrie. L'accent mis sur l'unité du Christ apparaît maintenant comme concernant le Christ en tant qu'unique agent de l'œuvre entière du salut, et à cet unique agent ne peut correspondre, selon le raisonnement et l'affirmation du Pacte, qu'une seule activité divino-humaine. L'activité, ainsi, est faite attribut de la personne plutôt que de la nature" (Murphy and Sherwood, *Constantinople II et III*, p. 150).

[15] The non-Chalcedonians feared that Chalcedon's affirmation of two natures united in one hypostasis without confusion, change, separation, or division represented an unjustifiable departure from Cyril's teachings. The issue then as in the later monothelite debates was how to strike the proper balance

unity between the Chalcedonian and non-Chalcedonian Christians to consolidate political power in what were very turbulent times for the Byzantine Empire.[16] Sergius, Patriarch of Constantinople, initially supported the Alexandrian pact of union. After its rejection by Sophronius, elder monk and Patriarch of Jerusalem, Sergius suspended his support. Sergius's *Psēphos*, his synodal letter to Pope Honorius in 634, advised silence regarding one or two energies in Christ, lest two opposing wills be expressed.[17] Pope Honorius's enthusiastic reply denied opposing wills in Christ by affirming *hen thelēma* (one will).[18] Sergius used the expression *hen thelēma* in his *Ekthesis* (638), which Heraclius promulgated to end debates about one or two energies in Christ.[19] The *Ekthesis* did not end the debates;

---

between affirmations of unity and diversity in Christ. For a detailed examination of Cyril's Christology and translations of Cyril's Christological texts, see John Anthony McGuckin, *St Cyril of Alexandria: The Christological Controversy: Its History, Theology, and Texts* (Leiden, 1994). Though Cyril largely defined the emerging Christological orthodoxy, he was all but unknown in the high Middle Ages. See N.M. Häring, "The Character and Range of Influence of St Cyril of Alexandria on Latin Theology, 430–1260," *Mediaeval Studies* 12 (1950): 1–19.

16 After decades of attacks from the Avars, Persians, and Slavs, the Byzantine Empire faced the new threat of the rapid expansion of Islam after the Prophet Muhammad's death (632).

17 Bathrellos summarizes the doctrinal contents of the *Psēphos* and *Ekthesis* as follows: "According to these texts, no one is allowed to refer to one energy, even though some of the Fathers had mentioned it, because some people believe that it entails the denial of Christ's two natures and, as a result, are offended by it. Any reference to two energies is also forbidden, because none of the Fathers ever spoke of two energies. In addition acceptance of two energies entails acceptance of two wills opposing one another, as if God the Logos willed to endure the passion and his humanity opposed his will, which would introduce two willers, willing opposing things, which is impious" (Bathrellos, *The Byzantine Christ*, p. 73).

18 Honorius agreed with a ban on mention of either one or two energies in Christ. "Furthermore, after exposing a clumsy version of the communication of idioms, Honorius confessed one will in Jesus Christ, on the grounds that the divinity assumed a sinless and pre-lapsarian human nature. For this reason, the words of Christ's prayer in Gethsemane did not express a different will (from the divine will of the Father), but pertained to the economy of Christ's assumed humanity, and were said because Christ wanted to teach us to prefer the will of God to our own will" (Bathrellos, *The Byzantine Christ*, p. 77).

19 "From a practical point of view, it is indisputable that Honorius contributed to the promotion of monothelitism. Whereas in his first epistle (*Psēphos*)

debate continued long after Constans II ascended to the throne in 641. Constans II issued the *Typos* in 647, withdrawing the *Ekthesis* and preparing the way for the Lateran Council of 649.[20]

The most prominent defender of a dyothelite Christology was Maximus the Confessor (580–662).[21] Maximus had worked for Emperor Her-

---

Sergius had not referred to 'one will', in the *Ekthesis* he did so, adopting Honorius's expression" (Bathrellos, *The Byzantine Christ*, p. 78). "Sergius saisit l'occasion, dressa un large exposé de la foi (d'où le nom d'*Ekthèsis*) où il incorpora la substance du *Psephos*, en l'adaptant de manière à y inclure la confession explicite d'une seule volonté, selon Honorius. Puis il soumit ce texte à la signature d'Héraclius (il l'avait rédigé en son nom) et l'afficha à la porte de Sainte-Sophie. Sergius eut le temps, avant sa mort en décembre, de voir l'*Ekthèsis* approuvée par le synode et dut en envoyer une copie à Cyrus. Pyrrhus, successeur de Sergius, fit une fois de plus approuver l'*Ekthèsis* par le synode; plus tard, il émit une encyclique requérant l'adhésion à l'*Ekthèsis* et faisant usage du nom d'Honorius" (Murphy and Sherwood, *Constantinople II et III*, pp. 163–164).

20 The *Typos* quickly failed to end debate and became itself the subject of further debate. The *Typos* attempted to solve the debate by ending discussion of energies or wills in Christ. For more on the *Typos*, see Murphy and Sherwood, *Constantinople II et III*, pp. 171–173. Constans II threatened severe punishment for violation of the bans instituted in the *Typos*, but Pope Martin violated the ban and convoked the Lateran Council of 649, which affirmed two wills in Christ (Bathrellos, *The Byzantine Christ*, p. 65). For more on the Lateran Council of 649, see Murphy and Sherwood, *Constantinople II et III*, pp. 174–188. The Lateran Council of 649 issued its findings in both Greek and Latin. For issues relating to translation and the Latin text of the council, see Rudolf Riedinger, "In welcher Richtung wurden die Akten der Lateransynode von 649 übersetzt und in welcher Schrift was der lateinische Text dieser Akten geschrieben?" in *Martino I papa (649–653) e il suo tempo: Atti del XXVIII Convegno storico internazionale, Todi, 13–16 ottobre 1991* (Spoleto, 1992), pp. 149–164 and "Sprachschichten in der lateinischen Übersetzung der Lateranakten von 649," *Zeitschrift für Kirchengeschichte* 92 (1981): 180–203. For discussion of the political and theological situation prior to the Lateran Council, see Alexander Alexakis, "Before the Lateran Council of 649: The Last Days of Herakleios the Emperor and Monothelitism," in *Synodus: Beiträge zur Konzilen- und allgemeinen Kirchengeschichte: Festschrift für Walter Brandmüller* (Paderborn, 1997), pp. 93–101.

21 Maximus's works most relevant to the monothelite debate are his *Disputation with Pyrrhus*, *Epistle 15*, and the *Opuscula theologica et polemica*, all contained in PG 91. For more detailed treatments of Maximus and aspects of his thought, see Riches, "After Chalcedon"; Bathrellos, *The Byzantine Christ*; and Louth, *Maximus the Confessor*. See also Hans Urs von Balthasar, *Cosmic Liturgy: The Uni-*

aclius from 610–614/615 and expressed more freedom in his opposition to monothelitism after Heraclius's death. Taking up the mantle of his spiritual master Sophronius, Maximus combated monothelitism using the Trinitarian logic and language of the Cappadocians to develop the implications of Chalcedonian orthodoxy.[22] Maximus carefully distinguished hypostatic properties from natural properties and argued that 'will' and 'energy'/'operation' both pertain to nature.[23] Consequently, the Chalcedonian doctrine

verse according to Maximus the Confessor, trans. Brian E. Daley (San Francisco, 2003) and Peter Hauptmann, "Maximus Confessor," in *Alte Kirche*, ed. Martin Greschat (Stuttgart, 1984), 2: 275–288. On Christ's two wills in Maximus, see Demetrios Bathrellos, "The Relationship between the Divine Will and the Human Will of Jesus Christ according to Saint Maximus the Confessor," *Studia patristica* 37 (2001): 346–352; Vasilios Karayiannis, *Maxime le Confesseur: Essence et énergies de Dieu* (Paris, 1993), pp. 233–276; Marcel Doucet, "La volonté humaine du Christ, specialment en son agonie: Maximus le Confesseur, interprète de l'Ecriture," *Science et espirit* 37 (1985): 123–159; François Marie Léthel, "La prière de Jésus à Gethsémani dans la controverse monothélite," in *Maximus Confessor: Actes du Symposium sur Maxime le Confesseur, Fribourg, 2–5 septembre 1980*, ed. Felix Heinzer and Christoph Schönborn (Fribourg, 1982), pp. 207–214; Jean-Miguel Garrigues, *Maxime le Confesseur: La charité, avenir divine de l'homme* (Paris, 1976), pp. 138–147; and René Antoine Gauthier, "Saint Maxime le Confesseur et la psychologie de l'acte humain," *Recherches de théologie ancienne et médiévale* 21 (1954): 51–100.

22 See George C. Berthold, "The Cappadocian Roots of Maximus the Confessor," in *Maximus Confessor: Actes du Symposium sur Maxime le Confesseur, Fribourg, 2–5 septembre 1980*, ed. Felix Heinzer and Christoph Schönborn (Fribourg, 1982), pp. 51–59. "Maximus follows the Cappadocian tradition, according to which nature is related to what is common, and hypostasis to the particular" (Bathrellos, *The Byzantine Christ*, p. 102).

23 "La perfection de toute essence est sa manifestation avec toutes ses propriétés. Les propriétés ontologiques de toute essence sont la volonté et l'énergie, car, par elles, l'essence manifeste son existence parfaite" (Karayiannis, *Maxime le Confesseur*, p. 237). "La nature humaine du Christ est consubstantielle à la nature de Sa Mère temporelle, la Vierge Marie, de qui Il a reçu la nature humaine, elle est aussi consubstantielle à la nature de tout le genre humain. Il a donc la nature et toutes les propriétés naturelles communes à toute l'humanité. Ainsi la volonté et l'énergie de la nature humaine du Christ sont communes à la nature de tout le genre humain. Mais le Christ a aussi des propriétés hypostatiques propres à Lui seul, qui sont caractéristiques de Sa nature humaine" (Karayiannis, *Maxime le Confesseur*, p. 241). The Cappadocians carefully distinguished 'hypostasis' from 'nature'/'essence.' Hypostasis named what were three in God (Father, Son, and Holy Spirit); nature or essence named what was perfectly one in God. For a discussion of Christological terminology

of two unconfused natures required two natural wills, divine and human, in Jesus Christ. Attributing the faculty of will to hypostasis, Maximus noted, would imply three wills in God, which no one would admit.

In response to the monothelites' critique that duality of wills in Christ would imply contrariety, Maximus countered that alterity need not imply contrariety. Christ's two wills are by nature distinct but are in perfect accord by virtue of the hypostatic union. Maximus distinguished *tropos* and *logos* to clarify Christ's possession of diverse, non-contrary wills. He designated all the natural properties or essential elements with the term *logos*. By *tropos*, Maximus specified the hypostatic mode or mode of existence. It belongs to the *logos* of an intellectual nature to possess will (*thelēma*). This will is naturally in accord with God; nothing natural is opposed to God. The opposition of a sinful human will to God rests not in its nature but in its hypostatic mode. Human beings oppose God not with their natural will but with their *gnomic* will, which must choose actions based upon uncertain means and ends.[24] The *gnomic* will is the *tropic* mode for the will of

---

in Greek patristic debates, see Brian E. Daley, "Nature and the 'Mode of Union': Late Patristic Models for the Personal Unity of Christ," in *The Incarnation*, ed. Davis et al., pp. 164–196. Bathrellos notes that "the teaching of Maximus on the two wills of Jesus Christ cannot be fully understood without reference to his understanding of the notions 'person'/'hypostasis' and 'nature'/'essence' in Christology, and vice versa. Actually, the way in which Maximus conceived these notions, as well as the way in which he employed them in order to denote unity and distinction in Christology, form the necessary theological background against which his theology of the wills finds its place, and against which it can be properly understood" (Bathrellos, *The Byzantine Christ*, p. 99). The same could be said for the theologians examined in the following chapters and particularly for Thomas Aquinas. Aquinas's concern to defend Chalcedonian orthodoxy against Nestorian/*homo assumptus* Christologies forms the backbone of his treatise on Christ in the *Summa theologiae*'s *Tertia pars*.

[24] "If the cause of the opposition were the number of the wills, number must be applied neither to the natures of Christ nor to the persons of the Trinity in order that opposition be avoided. Moreover, in opposition to his adversaries, Maximus claimed that difference does not necessarily imply contrariety. The human natural will is different from the divine, but does not oppose it. It is the gnomic will that opposes the divine will, but only when it moves against the logos of nature. On the contrary, there are times when we will by our gnomic will whatever God wills" (Bathrellos, *The Byzantine Christ*, p. 132). "The result of the Fall is not that natures are distorted in themselves, but rather that natures are misused: the Fall exists at the level not of *logos*, but of *tropos*" (Louth, *Maximus the Confessor*, p. 57). Maximus regards willing as natural, but "with

limited, fallen humanity, which must will from its state of ignorance and uncertainty. Maximus denied such uncertainty in Christ. The *tropos* of Christ's human will is the divine mode of the hypostasis of the Word. Christ willed divinely with his human will. This same logic explains Pseudo-Dionysius's reference to Christ's theandric energy or operation. The divine mode of Christ's human will and operation grants, according to Maximus, a soteriological value to Christ's human actions.[25]

Maximus's efforts to defend Chalcedonian orthodoxy before, during, and after the Lateran Council of 649 led to his trials, mutilation, and exile. After suffering the removal of his tongue and right hand, Maximus was exiled to Lazica, where he died in 662.[26] The Empire persisted in religious and political turmoil for the next fifteen years. The threat of Islamic expeditions against Constantinople diminished after 677/678, and Emperor Constantin IV then concentrated on ending the religious disagreements and divisions between Constantinople and Rome.[27] While Emperor Constantin appointed bishops favorable to reconciliation with Rome, Pope Agatho (678–681) sent a delegation representing the Roman synod to Constantinople. Agatho defined the purpose of this delegation and their theological mandate as defending the orthodoxy of Constantinople II (553). His defense offered a lengthy argument, marshalling Chalcedon, Constantinople II, Athansius, Pseudo-Athanasius, Ambrose, Augustine,

---

fallen creatures, their own nature has become opaque to them, they no longer know what they want, and experience coercion in trying to love what cannot give fulfillment. For, in their fallen state, rational creatures are no longer aware of their true good, which is God. Various apparent goods attract them: they are confused, they need to deliberate and consider, and their way of willing shares in all this. Maximus calls this willing in accordance with an opinion, or intention, or inclination (the Greek word for all these is *gnômê*). Such 'gnomic' willing is our way or mode of willing, it is the only way in which we can express our natural will, but it is a frustrating and confusing business" (Louth, *Maximus the Confessor*, p. 61). See also Lars Thunberg, *Microcosm and Mediator: The Theological Anthropology of Maximus the Confessor* (Lund, 1965), pp. 220–243.

25   Karayiannis writes "que saint Maxime attribue l'accomplissement du mystère de l'économie divine non seulement aux volonté et énergie divines, mais bien aussi aux volonté et énergie humaines du Christ" (Karayiannis, *Maxime le Confesseur*, p. 262). Thomas Aquinas places similar stress on the salvific work of Christ's human nature. See Chapter five below (pp. 193–199).

26   See Louth, *Maximus the Confessor*, p. 18.

27   See Murphy and Sherwood, *Constantinople II et III*, pp. 189–191.

Gregory Nazianzen, Gregory Nyssen, Cyril of Alexandria, Leo, and Pseudo-Dionysius in support of two natural wills and operations in Christ.[28] Two natures necessarily imply two natural wills and operations, and, lest this seem to allow for some contrariety between these wills, Agatho repeatedly portrays Christ as obedient to the will of God according to his human will[29]. The prayer in the garden of Gethsemane provides scriptural warrant for the obedience of Christ's human will.

All of these efforts found their culmination in the sixth ecumenical council, Constantinople III (680–681), which was convened on 7 November 680.[30] The council affirmed two non-contrary, natural wills and operations in Christ:

> And we proclaim equally two natural volitions or wills in him and two natural principles of action which undergo no division, no change, no partition, no confusion, in accordance with the teaching of the holy fathers. And the two natural wills not in opposition, as the impious heretics said, far from it, but his human will following, and not resisting or struggling, rather in fact subject to his divine and

---

[28] "Avec un tel encouragement et dans une perspective désormais plus assurée du succès de la doctrine orthodoxe, Agathon, au printemps de 680, veilla à la préparation finale des documents qui devaient être envoyés à Constantinople et à la composition des délégations. Sa propre lettre, nous l'avons vu, avait expliqué les causes du retard et, en nommant ses légats auprès de l'empereur, Agathon fixa avec précision les limites de leur mandat, à savoir le simple exposé de la tradition du Siège apostolique, y compris, bien sûr, les décrets du Ve synode œcuménique. Il ajoutait un long exposé de la foi, avec des textes orthodoxes et hérétiques, dont beaucoup en provenance directe de Martin, bien que ni lui ni son concile ne fussent mentionnés" (Murphy and Sherwood, *Constantinople II et III*, p. 193).

[29] Agatho argues that wills pertain to nature rather than to person, that Jesus possessed a perfect human nature as well as the divine nature, and that Jesus's freedom from sin allowed for his perfect obedience to the Father through his human will. See Agatho, *Epistle I*, in *Concilium universale Constantinopolitanum tertium*, ed. Rudolf Riedinger, Acta conciliorum oecumenicorum, 2nd ser., vol. 2.1 (Berlin, 1990–1992), pp. 53–123.

[30] Murphy and Sherwood, *Constantinople II et III*, pp. 195–260, present a detailed analysis of the procedures and acts of Constantinople III. For the acts of Constantinople III, see *Concilium universale Constantinopolitanum tertium*, ed. Riedinger.

all powerful will. For the will of the flesh had to be moved, and yet to be subjected to the divine will, according to the most wise Athanasius. For just as his flesh is said to be and is flesh of the Word of God, so too the natural will of his flesh is said to and does belong to the Word of God, just as he himself: *I have come down from heaven, not to do my own will, but the will of the Father who sent me* [John 6:38], calling his own will that of his flesh, since his flesh too became his own. For in the same way that his all holy and blameless animate flesh was not destroyed in being made divine but remained in its own limit and category, so his human will as well was not destroyed by being made divine, but rather was preserved, according to the theologian Gregory, who says: "For his willing, when he is considered as saviour, is not in opposition to God, being made divine in its entirety" [*Oratio XXX*.12]. And we hold there to be two natural principles of action in the same Jesus Christ our lord and true God, which undergo no division, no change, no partition, no confusion; that is, a divine principle of action and a human principle of action, according to the godly-speaking Leo, who says most clearly: "For each form does in a communion with the other that activity which it possesses as its own, the Word working that which is the Word's and the body accomplishing the things that are the body's" [*Tomus ad Flavianum*]. For of course we will not grant the existence of only a single natural principle of action of both God and creature, lest we raise what is made to the level of divine being, or indeed reduce what is most specifically proper to the divine nature to a level befitting creatures; for we acknowledge that the miracles and the sufferings are of one and the same, according to one or the other of the two natures out of which he is and in which he has his being, as the admirable Cyril said. Therefore, protecting on all sides the "no confusion" and "no division," we announce the whole in these brief words: Believing our lord Jesus Christ, even after his incarnation, to be one of the holy Trinity and our true God, we say that he has two natures shining forth in his one subsistence in which he demonstrated the miracles and the sufferings through his entire providential dwelling here, not in appearance but in truth, the difference of natures being made known in the same one subsistence in that each nature wills and performs the things that are proper to it in communion with the other; then in accord with this reasoning we hold that two natural wills and principles of action meet in correspondence for the salvation of the human race.[31]

For the purposes of this introduction, the next important figure in the history of debate on Christ's two wills is John of Damascus (d. c. 750).[32] The Damascene repeatedly defended Christological orthodoxy against monophysites and monothelites in his treatises *On Right Thinking* (*De recta sententia liber*), *On the Two Wills in Christ* (*De duabus in Christo voluntatibus*), and *Exposition on the Orthodox Faith* (*De fide orthodoxa*).[33] Inspired by Maximus the Confessor, John distinguished the faculty of the will, as a natural characteristic of every rational being, from the hypostatic mode of exercising the power of the will.[34] Nothing natural is opposed to God; opposition

---

31   *Exposition of Faith of the Third Council of Constantinople*, in *Nicaea I to Lateran V*, ed. Norman P. Tanner, vol. 1 of *Decrees of the Ecumenical Councils* (Washington, DC, 1990), pp. 128–130.

32   The most complete treatment of John Damascene is Andrew Louth, *St John Damascene: Tradition and Originality in Byzantine Theology* (Oxford, 2002). John of Damascus has been described as a mere compiler of patristic theology who had little – if anything – new to offer. Louth counters this reading, presenting John as a subtle thinker dedicated to defending doctrinal orthodoxy (Louth, *St John Damascene*, p. 8). Louth describes the Damascene as a participant in the process of refining doctrinal orthodoxy. "We should see John not as a remarkable individual who was able to reduce the amorphous mass of traditional Orthodoxy to some kind of 'scholastic' form, but as the culmination of a tradition of definition that had entered on a new phase a decade or so before his birth, and consequently regard his works as the high point of this phase" (Louth, *St John Damascene*, p. 12). For a detailed treatment of John's Christology, see Keetje Rozemond, *La christologie de saint Jean Damascène* (Ettal, 1959). Rozemond discusses Christ's two wills (pp. 34–37) and two energies (pp. 37–40).

33   As for Maximus, proper definition of Christological terms is crucial for the Damascene. "The errors of Christological heresy arise from the confusion of these terms: either confusion between the definitions of nature and person (both Monophysites and Nestorians confuse these terms, and argue that either one person implies one nature, or that two natures imply two persons), or confusion over the natural will and the hypostatic (or personal) or 'gnomic' will, in the case of the Monothelites" (Louth, *St John Damascene*, p. 167). For critical editions of John's works, see *Die Schriften des Johannes von Damaskos*, ed. B. Kotter (Berlin and New York, 1969–1988).

34   Describing John's thought in the *De duabus in Christo voluntatibus*, Louth writes: "Will (*thelêma*) is an ambiguous term; it can mean either the process of

of the human will to God arises from the *gnomic* will willing according to deliberation based upon incomplete or faulty knowledge. John denied deliberation, and hence a *gnomic* will in Christ, on account of Christ's human perfection through the hypostatic mode of the Word.[35]

While John of Damascus wrote after the monothelite controversy and the conciliar determination for two wills in Christ, he played a significant role in the later history of discussions on this topic. Latin translations of the Damascene's *De fide orthodoxa* gained popularity in the first half of the thirteenth century.[36] Access to the *De fide orthodoxa* radically supplemented a very partial knowledge of Christological orthodoxy. This is certainly true for the case of Christ's two wills.[37] The scholastics appropriated the Dam-

---

willing (*thelêsis*), or the thing or action willed (*thelêton*). The process of willing is a matter of nature; only a being with a free rational nature can will. But the act of willing a particular thing or action is hypostatic, or personal, and in the case of human willing, as we know it, it involves a process of deliberation, leading to inclination (*gnômê*). Persons will, and will in a particular way – indeed, they will particular things" (Louth, *St John Damascene*, p. 167). For a detailed comparison of Maximus and John, see Gauthier, "Saint Maxime le Confesseur et la psychologie de l'acte humain," pp. 52–57.

35 See Louth, *St John Damascene*, p. 168. Louth notes that the Damascene occasionally admits a different sense of *gnomic* will. Louth writes that "John makes a distinction between the two ways in which the word *thelêma*, the usual Greek word for will, may be used: to mean willing (*thelêsis*) or the power of willing, in which case it is called the 'natural will,' or to mean the object of willing (*thelêton*), in which case it is called the 'gnomic' (or inclining) will. In Christ there are two natural wills, but only one gnomic will. This distinction helps to clarify Maximos's difficult distinction between natural and gnomic will, though Maximos generally uses the term 'gnomic will' to indicate a deliberative will, which is not present in God or the incarnate Son at all" (Louth, *St John Damascene*, p. 139).

36 On the Latin translations of the *De fide orthodoxa*, see John of Damascus, De fide orthodoxa: *Versions of Burgundio and Cerbanus*, ed. Eloi Marie Buytaert (St Bonaventure, NY, 1955). A partial translation from Hungary, attributed to Cerbanus, was available by 1145. A full translation was undertaken by Burgundio of Pisa at the request of Pope Eugene III. Burgundio's translation became the standard for scholastic theology.

37 Rozemond describes affirmation of two wills in Christ as an essential feature of John's soteriological Christology (Rozemond, *La christologie*, p. 12). According to Rozemond, John stresses the obedience of Christ's human will to the divine will. This obedience serves a soteriological purpose. "La volonté humaine, en obéissant, rétablit la volonté pécherese et retrouve la vraie liberté

ascene's distinction between *thelēsis* and *boulēsis*, but found more problematic the denial of *gnōmē*, rendered in Latin as *electio*, in Christ.[38] The denial of *electio* seemed to involve a denial of free choice in Christ. Thomas Aquinas successfully 'read through' the translation to grasp the Damascene's meaning, though without the benefit of reading Maximus as the Damascene's inspiration.

This brief summary of patristic debates on Christ's two wills aims only to provide a basic orientation to the history and systematic theological import of the topic. Prior to the monothelite controversy, debates about Christ's wills focused on exegesis of Matt. 26:39 and John 6:38. These exegetical debates concerned questions of the full divinity and full humanity of Christ, questions decided at Ephesus and Chalcedon. During the monothelite controversy, defenders of a dyothelite Christology viewed the doctrine of Christ's two wills as a necessary extension of Chalcedonian orthodoxy. The vast majority of medieval theologians knew little or nothing of these earlier debates and wrote for vastly different purposes than the seventh-century defenders of Chalcedon. New concerns guided their treatments of Christ's two wills, but many of their firmly held principles bear a close resemblance to those of earlier thinkers. This summary provides some backdrop for considering the novelty and continuity of later presentations.

---

qu'est la conformité à la volonté de Dieu" (Rozemond, *La christologie*, p. 35). Rozemond also correctly highlights a typical, and novel, aspect of John's discussion of Christ's humanity. Rozemond formulates this insight as a response to the question of Christ's prayer in the garden of Gethsemane. "La réponse que saint Jean Damascène donne souvent à ces difficultés est celle-ci: le Christ Dieu a permis à la nature et à la volonté humaines de faire et de souffrir ce qui lui était propre" (Rozemond, *La christologie*, p. 35). Thomas Aquinas frequently cites this formula and develops it extensively in his examination of the salvific work of Jesus Christ's humanity.

38 Louth describes the distinction between *thelēsis* and *boulēsis* as a development of Maximus's view of the will, itself a development from Nemesius of Emesa. "First, a distinction between willing (*thelêsis*) and wishing (*boulêsis*) is posited: willing is 'natural and rational desire (*orexis*)', whereas wishing is such willing directed towards a particular end. Wishing concerns the end, not the means, the means (*tropos*) to that end being something determined upon (*bouleuton*)" (Louth, *St John Damascene*, p. 138). Burgundio of Pisa, the translator of the *De fide orthodoxa*, also translated Nemesius into Latin. See *Némésius d'Émèse: De natura hominis: Traduction de Burgundio de Pise*, ed. J.R. Moncho and Gérard Verbeke (Leiden, 1975).

Aims of the Present Study

Examining scholastic teachings on Christ's two wills reveals a profound dedication to expressing Christ's perfect human nature, perfect both in the sense of faultlessness and completeness. The following chapters will analyze the writings of Peter Lombard, William of Auxerre, the *Summa fratris Alexandri*, Albertus Magnus, Bonaventure, Thomas Aquinas, Giles of Rome, Peter Olivi, and John Duns Scotus on Christ's two wills. Treating these several thinkers reveals both the substantial agreement on this topic (particularly following the Lombard's *Sentences*) and the few points of (sometimes serious) disagreement. The depth of agreement and the import of disagreement become clear only through detailed textual analysis. For those familiar with the style and structure of scholastic thought, the close attention to individual arguments, authorities, frameworks, and solutions needs no further justification. For those less familiar with scholastic thought, the level of textual detail employed throughout this study deserves a bit more explanation. The broad outlines of seemingly harmonious proposals on Christ's wills by themselves conceal the minutiae through which the specifics of these proposals occasionally oppose one another. Even when divergences of opinion do not amount to serious disagreements, they reveal something about a particular author's thinking. The best – if not the only – way to discern and to highlight the texture of scholastic discussions of Christ's wills is to follow the logic of their presentations, turning a careful gaze not only to the magisterial determinations but also to the arguments *pro et contra* and the sources cited. Examining how these arguments and sources frame each theologian's solution to the question necessarily involves a degree of repetition and requires a good deal of patience and perseverance on the reader's part.

These remarks intend to provide a general justification for scrutinizing closely the technical discussions of this scholastic topic. The specific justification will emerge after the labor of rehearsing these details is complete and when attention will turn to contextualizing Thomas Aquinas's presentation of Christ's two wills within the larger setting of the *Summa theologiae*'s Christology. This contextualizing resists neat summary, uniting as it does a variety of considerations. What can be summarily affirmed is that Thomas crafts his presentation of Christology to rely upon and to complete the anthropological sections of the *Summa*; he shows concern to illuminate the dignity of human nature and the possibility of human merit through the assistance of grace; he stresses the wisdom of salvation as achieved through Christ's human nature; and he conceives this achievement to depend upon the free action of Christ's human will. Aquinas allows that Christ's human will produces a divine effect. This remarkable claim finds much of its reasoning in Thomas's presentation of Christ's two wills.

The above remarks indicate that Thomas Aquinas occupies a singular place in this study. This neither excludes nor trivializes serious attention to his predecessors and contemporaries. It neither reduces scholastic presentations to their historical moment nor strips them of all context and history to be read as dislocated signs answering later questions. Attention to the context and diverse sources, patristic and medieval, of Thomas's thought fosters a more profitable engagement with that thought. Reading Thomas out of context neglects his debt to the habits of mind and to the ideas of his contemporaries. Such readings often fail to appreciate the novel and singular in Aquinas, either attributing all things to his genius or regarding his theology as simply a lifeless artifact. Thomas's contributions to the larger discussion of Christology are best appreciated in tandem with the contributions of his many teachers and in light of the questions and issues fueling scholastic reflection on this topic. This end justifies the means of analysis and provides a foundation in scholastic theology upon which a contribution to contemporary discussion may be constructed.

Two tasks of the present study were earlier identified, one historical and one systematic. The historical task requires a careful examination of medieval debates about Christ's two wills to determine their concerns, logic, and conclusions. This task begins with analyses of Peter Lombard's *Sentences*, William of Auxerre's *Summa aurea*, and the *Summa fratris Alexandri* (*Summa Halensis*). The Lombard's presentations of Christ's two wills depended heavily on earlier sources, particularly the *Summa sententiarum*. Chapter two will discuss relevant aspects of early twelfth-century theology as background both for the Lombard's *Sentences* and for the emerging concerns of scholastic theology more generally. These relevant aspects include developments in soteriology from Anselm of Canterbury and Abelard, and discussions of Christ's wills in Hugh of St Victor and the *Summa sententiarum*. With these aspects noted, attention can turn to the Lombard's presentation of Christ's two wills and its relation to Christ's prayer. Of greatest concern will be those aspects that became more or less standard in subsequent treatments, such as the Lombard's distinction of the disposition (*affectus*) of reason and the disposition of sensuality, according to which the Lombard argues that Christ willed the passion with reason and shunned the passion with sensuality.

William of Auxerre followed the Lombard in distinguishing the wills of sensuality and of reason, and elaborated sensuality's refusal of the passion as willing something proper to itself. This raised the question of whether the will of sensuality was contrary to the divine will, and questions of contrariety became the defining questions for medieval treatments of Christ's two wills. William denied contrariety of wills on the grounds that contrariety must be in wills of the same genus and that contrary objects must be contrary of themselves. The *Summa fratris* adopted and extended William's strategy for denying contrariety of wills, but this task became even more difficult, given the recognition of a distinction within the will of reason in the *Summa fratris*. The *Summa fratris* introduced into this discussion John Damascene's distinction between *boulēsis* and *thelēsis*, and inadvertently introduced what came to be the standard rendering of the division within Latin, *voluntas ut ratio* and *voluntas ut natura*. This distinction made more difficult the task of defending non-contrariety because the *Summa fratris* located Christ's refusal of the passion not only within the will of sensuality but also within the *voluntas ut natura*. The *Summa fratris* explains non-contrariety by honing William's basic argument, stipulating that contrariety must be *circa idem et secundum idem* (through the same and according to the same). This amounts to another way of limiting contrariety to wills of the same genus and to objects contrary of themselves. Influential as the *Summa fratris* and its use of the Damascene were for thirteenth-century theologians, the logic of *circa idem et secundum idem* was ill received.

Chapter three will turn to Albert the Great and Bonaventure, who advanced discussion of Christ's two wills and reflection on questions of contrariety and conformity. Their advancements led to rejection of – or at least some – discomfort with the defense of non-contrariety proposed by William of Auxerre and the *Summa fratris Alexandri*. Albert was the great innovator in these debates. He distinguished contrariety and conformity, arguing that contrariety often preserves conformity. Albert defined conformity of wills according to the four Aristotelian causes: efficient, formal, final, and material. Contrariety of wills, according to Albert, relates only to the material cause (the thing willed). Contrariety need not imply any disorder or sin, because conformity of a human will to the divine will often requires contrariety in the thing willed. Albert further justifies his position by noting that agreement with God in the thing willed can depend upon some wicked intent in the human will, e.g. willing the death of a martyr. Albert's basic point is that conformity of a human will to the divine will is not determined solely by the thing willed but by other causes, such as the reason for willing. In short, Albert shifted attention from contrariety to conformity and in fact allowed for contrariety of wills in Christ to preserve conformity. Albert rejects what he describes as the *circa idem ut idem* argument, noting that under such terms, no human will could be contrary to the divine will, nor could there every be any contrariety between sensuality and reason.

In Bonaventure's treatment of Christ's two wills, the tensions created by divergent authorities and linguistic schemes are evident. Bonaventure followed Albert in shifting the focus from contrariety to conformity and substantially agreed with Albert's critique of the *circa idem et secundum idem* argument. He focused on conformity in the reason for willing and in the thing willed, noting that these two types of conformity are occasionally mutually exclusive. True conformity between a superior and an inferior will rests with conformity in the reason for willing, namely when the inferior will wills in accordance with the superior will. This conformity can take the form either of subjection or of assimilation. Assimilation requires agreement in the thing willed, and subjection allows for disagreement. This disagreement, Bonaventure insists, implies no contrariety in the thing willed but only a non-identity. While Bonaventure elevates the significance of conformity, he opts not to follow Albert's affirmation of some morally insignificant contrariety. Bonaventure's decision rests in part on the authority of Hugh of St Victor, whose *De quatuor voluntatibus Christi* denied any contrariety of wills in Christ. Bonaventure made some attempt to reconcile Hugh's terminology with the Damascene's. This led to difficulties of its own, and as a result Bonaventure remained cautious about whether Christ's reluctance to endure the passion could be at all attributed to reason or should only be attributed to sensuality.

Reflection on Christ's two wills underwent much development from the late twelfth century through the first half of the thirteenth century. This development included increasing attention to questions of contrariety and conformity of wills. Various strategies emerged for denying contrariety or, in Albert's case, allowing contrariety to preserve conformity. These debates were complicated when the *Summa fratris Alexandri* introduced the Damascene's division between *thelēsis* and *boulēsis* into considerations of Christ's human will. The *Summa fratris* took the bold step of allowing for some resistance to the passion on the part of Christ's reason or rational will, a step that seems to make more difficult any attempt to deny contrariety of wills in Christ. By the middle of the thirteenth century, questions of contrariety or conformity became dominant aspects of treatments of Christ's two wills.

Thomas Aquinas's presentations of Christ's two wills must be understood within the context of these thirteenth-century debates. Chapter four will compare Thomas's early (*Scriptum*) and late (*Summa theologiae*) considerations of Christ's two wills, noting the many developments in his thought. These developments emerge only through very detailed analysis; a surface examination would indicate a very traditional presentation, from the division of wills to the arguments against contrariety. The novelty of Thomas's discussion becomes evident only through a careful comparison, revealing shifts in emphasis, conceptual and terminological innovations, and recovery of patristic and conciliar sources as factors explaining the development of Thomas's presentation from the *Scriptum* to the *Summa theologiae*. These factors distinguish the *Summa* not only from the *Scriptum* but also from other thirteenth-century presentations. The most noteworthy addition to the *Summa* is Thomas's knowledge of the acts of Constantinople III, which provided him with details of monothelite arguments and of dyothelite refutations of those arguments. The acts of Constantinople III included Pope Agatho's *Epistle I*, in which Thomas discovered a store of patristic citations woven into the fabric of a dyothelite argument. Another noteworthy feature of the *Summa*'s presentation is its stress on Christ's possession of free choice (*liberum arbitrium*). This stress is noteworthy in part because it seems to go against the Damascene's denial of choice (*electio*) in Christ and in part given the context of Latin Averroism and the ensuing debates about the possibility of free choice. Thomas's stress on Christ's free choice reinforces the integrity and perfection of Christ's human nature.

The *Summa*'s denial of contrariety in Christ follows William of Auxerre and the *Summa fratris Alexandri*. The acts of Constantinople III clearly deny any contrariety between Christ's wills, rendering problematic Albert's admission of contrariety for the sake of conformity. Thomas was sensitive to Albert's critiques and strove to place his denial of contrariety on a firm foundation, one aspect of which was the distinction between power and act. Though there is only one power of the will, there are several species of acts of this one power. This distinction provides some terminological and conceptual grounds for the division between the *voluntas ut natura* (will as nature, natural will) and the *voluntas ut ratio* (will as reason, deliberative will) as well as Thomas's explanation for why these are not contrary with respect to the passion. Aquinas's notion of rational instrumentality also serves to explain the relationship of the divine and human wills in Christ, further supporting his denial of contrariety. This notion of rational instrumentality plays an important role in Thomas's Christology.

Chapter five will continue the examination of Aquinas on Christ's two wills, but from a more systematic perspective. That is, Chapter four considers Aquinas on Christ's two wills within the historical context of thirteenth-century debates; Chapter five will consider the role of Christ's two wills within the larger context of the *Summa theologiae*'s Christology. Structural observations will pervade the chapter, including the placement of Christology within the *Summa*'s overall plan and the placement of topics within the *Tertia pars*. These observations will guide the treatment of specific topics. Apparent immediately will be the importance of fittingness and wisdom as ordering categories within the *Summa*, especially in Christology, where Thomas repeatedly stresses that all the details of the Incarnation were not necessary, but were most fitting. If fittingness establishes the logic for Aquinas's Christological arguments, the hypostatic union serves as the major premise. Thomas's insistence that the one person of the Word assumed to itself in hypostatic union a perfect human nature in the Incarnation informs virtually every aspect of the *Summa*'s Christology.

Investigation of particular topics in the *Summa*'s *Tertia pars* will, of necessity, be very selective. The topics discussed will include Christ's perfection of grace and knowledge; Christ's unique status as simultaneously *viator* and *comprehensor*; the grammar of *secundum quod homo*; and Christ's unity of *esse*, will, and operation. These topics all relate to Thomas's presentation of Christ's two wills and highlight the soteriological value of Christ's free human action. Examination of these various topics also draws out Thomas's view of Christ's human nature as *instrumentum divinitatis* and of his human will as the instrumental efficient cause of salvation. This radical claim, without true parallel in the thirteenth century, grants extraordinary import to Christ's humanity in general and human will in particular. The focus on the instrumental efficient causality of Christ's human will reinforces the import of dyothelitism for Thomas's Christology.

Chapter six will turn to scholastic thinkers in the decades after Aquinas. Brief attention will be given to Giles of Rome and Peter Olivi before turning to a lengthier examination of John Duns Scotus. Giles's early lectures on the *Sentences* bear the faint influence of Aquinas but without any trace of instrumental efficient causality or the larger soteriological significance of Christ's human will. Olivi stresses the assumption of a human will to the person of the Word and distinguishes the causal dependence of Christ's humanity on the whole Trinity causing salvation through it and the personal dependence of Christ's humanity on the Word alone. The purpose of this distinction and other aspects of Olivi's unsystematic reflections on Christ's wills is to explain Christ's infinite merit.

Scotus wrote multiple, sustained treatments of Christ's wills, treatments indebted to thirteenth-century discussions while also independent in particular and interesting ways. In both his *Lectura* and his *Ordinatio* on book III of the *Sentences*, Scotus transfers attention from d.17 on Christ's wills and prayer to d.15 on Christ's sorrow (*dolor*) and sadness (*tristitia*), thereby altering concerns about contrariety and conformity. Scotus demands much less of d.17 than did earlier thinkers, but he does adopt and magnify an insight from Olivi that casts a shadow of grave concern on previous treatments of Christ's wills. The insight is that preservation of Trinitarian unity *ad extra* requires that the Word exercise no special causality in Christ's actions beyond the causality of the whole Trinity. Based upon the presentation of Scotus, the chapter will consider potential challenges to Aquinas's understanding of Christ's wills, instrumental efficient causality, and soteriology.

These chapters work together to paint a picture that is both historical and systematic. The historical framing of this issue indicates the larger contours of medieval reflections on Christ's two wills and highlights the contentious issues within those reflections. The systematic considerations depend upon the historical framing and supplement our appreciation of this topic's import for scholastic Christology.

CHAPTER TWO

Foundations of Thirteenth-Century Debates
The *Sentences, Summa aurea,* and *Summa fratris Alexandri*

At the dawn of scholasticism, relatively little was known of patristic theology or the acts of ecumenical councils. Unaware of earlier debates, medieval theologians often approached the same topics from novel perspectives, changing the content and import of some questions. The original and authoritative source of thirteenth-century debates on Christ's two wills was not the acts of Constantinople III (680–681) or the Lateran Council of 649, but rather Peter Lombard's book of *Sentences*. The Lombard's treatment of Christ's two wills (*Sentences* III, d.17) served as the ground upon which later theologians would build. The early builders included William of Auxerre and the authors of the *Summa fratris Alexandri*. William of Auxerre's *Summa aurea* and the *Summa fratris* inherited and developed the terminology and structure of the Lombard's treatment of Christ's wills, while also moving beyond the Lombard in establishing new strategies for defending the non-contrariety of wills in Christ, strategies which later faced severe criticisms.

Christ's prayer in the garden of Gethsemane occasions the Lombard's discussion of Christ's two wills. The *Sentences* attempts both to defend a human will in Christ and to express the obedience of this human will to God. William of Auxerre shifts the focus entirely to the issue of contrariety, which represents a development on the basic question of obedience. If Christ willed not to die by his will of sensuality and willed to die by reason, does this not imply contrariety of wills? The *Summa aurea* relies entirely on the Lombard's defense and division of Christ's human will but adds to the discussion a strategy for denying contrariety of wills. The *Summa fratris Alexandri* hones this strategy while revisiting the question of the division of Christ's will. Informed by the Damascene's *De fide orthodoxa* (II.22), the *Summa fratris* divides the will of reason into the natural will and, confusingly, the will of reason. This division (though indicated through less confusing names) served as a cornerstone for subsequent discussions of Christ's two wills. These remarks introduce the issues to be explored throughout this chapter using close textual analysis to draw out each author's language and sources, as well as the developments between authors. Attention will be given to how understandings of Christ's wills evolved between the 1150s and 1240s.

Anselm of Canterbury, Peter Abelard, Hugh of St Victor, and the Summa sententiarum

Before delving into the *Sentences*, a few other thinkers and texts deserve at least brief mention. These include Anselm's *Cur Deus homo*, Peter Abelard's *Commentaria in Epistolam Pauli ad Romanos*, *Scito te ipsum*, and *Sic et non*, Hugh of St Victor's *De quatuor voluntatibus Christi*, and the *Summa sententiarum*. These texts, with the exception of Hugh's *De quatuor voluntatibus Christi*, exercised little direct influence on thirteenth-century discussions of Christ's wills but did inform Peter Lombard's treatment in the *Sentences* as well as the larger Christological context in which twelfth- and thirteenth-century discussions developed.[1] Examining these sources enriches the overall presentation in several respects, two of which are worth particular mention. Questions of Christology and soteriology came to frame thirteenth-century considerations of Christ's wills, arising from the labors of twelfth-century theologians and offering one means of tracing the continuity between twelfth- and thirteenth-century sources. Early twelfth-century understandings of Christ's wills also offer an interesting contrast with thirteenth-century equivalents. The twelfth-century discussions, as will be indicated below, were entirely less occupied with investigating and elaborating the requirements and consequences of Christ's possession of a perfect human will than were thirteenth-century treatments of the topic. This contrast indicates the profound developments that did take place.

---

1 Chapter five below (pp. 276–290) discusses Thomas Aquinas's use of Anselm or of an Anselmian logic. The *Cur Deus homo*, however, was not a major source for thirteenth-century Christologies, with the exception of some Franciscans (e.g. the *Summa fratris Alexandri* and Bonaventure). Bonaventure quotes at length from Hugh's *De quatuor voluntatibus Christi*.

Anselm of Canterbury (1033–1109) defended the fittingness and necessity of the Incarnation in his *Cur Deus homo*.[2] The basic outline of Anselm's argument is well known but still worthy of a brief synopsis. Questions regarding the rationality of the Incarnation sparked Anselm's argument. In the search for some rational foundation for the Incarnation, Anselm rejected any notion of humanity's just debt to the devil, acquired through sin and paid through the passion. Servitude to sin cannot be conceived as a state of indenture remedied by a transaction between God and the devil. Anselm's swift rejection of such formulations opened the way to new soteriological paths. His own formulation begins with humanity's absolute dependence on God. Humanity owes every action, every thought, and every moment to God. Failure to render unto God the least of these dishonors God and mires humanity in the unhappiness of sin. In order for humanity to achieve its created end of eternal happiness without violating divine justice, voluntary satisfaction of the debt was required. Humanity, however, already owed everything to God and so lacked any and all resources for repaying an additional debt, particularly an infinite one. From these considerations, Anselm concludes that only the God-man could satisfy this debt. Due to his divinity, the God-man would possess infinite power and worth with which to pay the debt, and due to his humanity, he would fulfill justice in paying that debt on behalf of humanity. The Incarnation uniquely achieves human salvation while preserving divine honor, dignity, justice, and order.

---

2   For an introduction to Anselm, see G.R. Evans, "Anselm of Canterbury," in *The Medieval Theologians: An Introduction to Theology in the Medieval Period*, ed. G.R. Evans (Oxford, 2001), pp. 94–101. For discussions of necessity, freedom, and violence in the *Cur Deus homo* see Brian Leftow, "Anselm on the Necessity of the Incarnation," *Religious Studies* 31 (1995): 167–185; Marilyn M. Adams, "Elegant Necessity, Prayerful Disputation: Method in *Cur Deus homo*," in Cur Deus homo: *Atti del Congresso anselmiano internazionale: Roma, 21–23 maggio 1998*, ed. Paul Gilbert, Helmut Kohlenberger, and Elmar Salmann (Rome, 1999), pp. 367–396; John R. Baker, "Must the God-Man Die?" in Cur Deus homo, pp. 609–620; Paul Gilbert, "Violence et liberté dans le *Cur Deus homo*," in Cur Deus homo, pp. 673–695; and Osvaldo Rossi, "*L'aliquid maius* e la riparazione," in Cur Deus homo, pp. 641–657.

Anselm's argumentation at many points hinges on Christ's freedom in the passion.[3] The *Cur Deus homo* features no focused or sustained treatment of Christ's two wills but does touch upon the subject in several places. Anselm explains that Christ came not to do his own will (John 6:38) because every just will is from God rather than humanity. While this implies a human will in Christ, it minimizes the value of that human will in the plan of salvation. Christ's prayer 'not as I will' indicates the truth of his human flesh, which naturally shunned death.[4] Anselm repeatedly indicates Christ's obedience to the Father's will and must defend the freedom of that obedience.[5] Elsewhere, when Anselm considers the freedom of

---

3   On Anselm's presentation in the *Cur Deus homo* of Christ's death as 'voluntary', see John McIntyre, *St Anselm and His Critics: A Re-interpretation of the* Cur Deus homo (Edinburgh, 1954), pp. 154–167. McIntyre argues that Anselm focuses exclusively on Christ's human will as obedient in *Cur Deus homo* I.8–20, though without answering Boso's concerns, and focuses exclusively on Christ's divine will in II.10, 16–17. Anselm only presents a strong defense of Christ's voluntary death with reference to Christ's omnipotence and divine will.

4   Anselm, *Cur Deus homo* I.9 (in *S. Anselmi Opera omnia*, ed. Franciscus Salesius Schmitt [Edinburgh, 1946], 2: 63–64): "Quod autem ipse ait: 'non venit voluntatem meum facere, sed eius qui misit me', tale est quale est et illud: 'mea doctrina non est mea'. Nam quod quis non habet a se, sed a deo, hoc non tam suum quam dei dicere debet. Nullus vero homo a se habet veritatem quam docet, aut iustam voluntatem, sed a deo. Non ergo venit Christus voluntatem suam facere sed patris, quia iusta voluntas quam habebat, non erat ex humanitate, sed ex divinitate. 'Proprio' vero 'filio suo non pepercit' deus, 'sed pro nobis tradidit illum', non est aliud quam: non liberavit eum. Nam multa in sacra scriptura huiusmodi inveniuntur. Ubi autem dicit: 'pater, si possibile est, transeat a me calyx iste; verumtamen non sicut ego volo, sed sicut tu'; et: 'si non potest hic calyx transire, nisi bibam illum, fiat voluntas tua': naturalem salutis per voluntatem suam significat appetitum, quo humana caro dolorem mortis fugiebat. Voluntatem vero 'patris' dicit, non quoniam maluerit pater filii mortem quam vitam, sed quia humanum genus restaurari nolebat pater, nisi faceret homo aliquid tam magnum, sicut erat mors illa; quia non poscebat ratio quod alius facere non poterat, idcirco dicit filius illum velle mortem suam, quam ipse mavult pati, quam ut genus humanum non salvetur."

5   "Anselm explains this [John 6:38; Matt. 26:39] in terms of obedience: the man Christ owes this to God, and his humanity owes obedience to his divinity. This is a clear statement of a *dyothelite* position (building on the councils of Constantinople and Chalcedon), which presupposes two wills in Christ. We can speak about genuine obedience when one person, from his own free initiative, internalizes someone else's will, in which case the plurality of wills will

Christ's sacrifice, he focuses on the freedom of the immutable divine will willing the passion.[6] Anselm admits a human will in Christ, but displays little concern to explain or to explore that will. Scholastic reflections on Christ's two wills would correct Anselm's troubling lack of concern and investigate Christ's human will as a part of Christ's perfect human nature.[7] The very possibility of these corrections, however, depended upon Anselm's framing of this question. Risto Saarinen indicates this well:

> In *Cur Deus homo* 8 Anselm's opponent Boso holds that Christ was crucified "in a certain sense" (*quodam modo*) against his own will (*invitus*). Boso refers to the Augustinian idea that Christ showed reluctance in Gethsemane (*Matt.* 26:39). When Anselm refutes this theological view, he makes distinctions which pertain as well to our discussion on the strength of human will. It should be further noted here that Anselm's refined analysis of *Matt.* 26:39 can be regarded as the starting-point for the medieval philosophical use of this verse.[8]

Saarinen's careful study affirms Anselm's influence on later discussions based largely upon Anselm's understanding of diverse and seemingly con-

---

be eliminated in their identity" (Dániel Deme, *The Christology of Anselm of Canterbury* [Aldershot, England, 2003], p. 164). Deme stresses Anselm's presumption of two wills in Christ and the radical identity of these wills in Christ's human obedience to counter what he recognizes as Anselm's monothelitic rhetoric. "It is disturbing how Anselm sometimes seems to slip into monothelitism, either *via* a *genus maiestaticum*, or by ascribing a merely divine will to Christ" (Deme, *The Christology of Anselm of Canterbury*, p. 190).

6   *Cur Deus homo* II.17 (*Opera omnia* 2: 124): "Quapropter cum dicimus quia homo ille, qui secundum unitatem personae, sicut supra dictum est, idem ipse est qui filius dei, deus, non potuit non mori, aut velle non mori, postquam de virgine natus est: non significatur in illo ulla impotentia servandi aut volendi servare vitam suam immortalem, sed immutabilitas voluntatis eius, qua se sponte fecit ad hoc hominem, ut in eadem voluntate perseverans moreretur, et quia nulla res potuit illam voluntatem mutare."

7   Thomas affirms in the *Summa theologiae* the basic logic of Anselm's argument but stresses the freedom of Christ's sacrifice according to Christ's human will. Aquinas's elaboration of the freedom and perfection of Christ's human will grants remarkable weight to Christ's human nature as the instrumental efficient cause of salvation.

8   Risto Saarinen, *Weakness of the Will in Medieval Thought: From Augustine to Buridan* (Leiden, 1994), pp. 48–49.

tradictory goals simultaneously willed without contradiction.[9] Thirteenth-century considerations of Christ's two wills relied upon this very notion.

Peter Abelard's (1079–1142) harried career is well known.[10] When Abelard turned his dialectical training to theological topics, many took issue with his methods and conclusions. Despite many and frequent challenges, he retained a high reputation among a loyal group of students. Abelard and his school represent an important stage in the development of reflection on Christ's two wills.

Abelard's *Sic et non* follows many conventions of medieval *florilegia* and sentence collections while still offering a new tool for the emerging scholasticism.[11] In *Quaestio* 83 Abelard collects sources discussing whether Christ and the martyrs willed to die or not. The very form of the question reveals that the Christological or soteriological significance of Christ's two wills was not fully recognized. The sources collected by Abelard, ranging from scriptural citations (John 6:38, Matt. 26:39) to citations from Jerome and Augustine, largely confirm Anselm's basic stress on the voluntary nature of Christ's passion without adding much clarification or specifica-

9 "His first solution claims that seemingly 'unwilled' actions are often cases in which something is willed *propter aliud*. If we say that somebody acts *invitus*, we often mean that two or more actual goal-directed volitions exist; each of them aiming for a different end. If a sick person is said to drink absinthe only unwillingly, this means that he both wills to drink it for the sake of health and wills to avoid drinking for the sake of pleasure. Again, if someone lies unwillingly in order to save his own life, he both seeks to save his life (goal 1) and wants to tell the truth (goal 2). In such cases, according to Anselm, the agent has two different will-acts (*diversas voluntates*). They do not, however, contradict one another directly; for it is one thing to will to give up lying for the sake of truth (goal 2) and another to will to lie for the sake of life (goal 1). In other words, the conflict of the will involves willing two different but compatible *goals*, though the agent cannot actually choose two contradictory *means* at once" (Saarinen, *Weakness of the Will*, pp. 46–47; see Anselm, *Opera omnia* 1: 214.27–215.20).

10 See John Marenbon, "Life, Milieu, and Intellectual Contexts," in *The Cambridge Companion to Abelard*, ed. Jeffrey E. Brower and Kevin Guilfoy (Cambridge, 2004), pp. 13–44.

11 Jean Jolivet provides a helpful summary of the *Sic et non* with particular attention to the hermeneutical principles established by Abelard in the prologue and beyond. See Jean Jolivet, *La théologie d'Abélard* (Paris, 1997), pp. 69–77.

tion.¹² Abelard's own position in his *Scito te ipsum* or *Ethica* reduces the voluntary nature of the passion to Christ's divine will and portrays his human will as enduring, rather than willing, the suffering of the passion. Abelard writes:

> In the weakness which he had assumed of human nature the Lord also said to the Father: 'If it be possible, let this chalice pass from me. Nevertheless, not as I will but as thou wilt.' His soul naturally dreaded the great suffering of death and what he knew to be painful could not be voluntary for him. Although it is written of him elsewhere: 'He was offered because it was his own will,' this is either to be understood according to the nature of the divinity in whose will it was that the assumed man should suffer, or 'it was his will' means 'it was his plan' as it does when the Psalmist says: 'He hath done all things whatsoever he would.'¹³

Abelard's students would better succeed at developing the logic of Christ's two wills, but Abelard's notion of a natural aversion to death would retain a central place in reflections on this topic. The *Ysagoge in theologiam*, a text from the school of Abelard written between 1148 and 1152, explicitly affirms two wills in Christ and, following the *Summa sententiarum*, argues that Christ displayed a natural aversion to death.¹⁴

Before turning to later thinkers, some mention need be made of Abelard's reflections on soteriology. The details of Abelard's proposal in

---

12 Perhaps the most interesting source is Jerome's *Sermo de amore Dei et amore saeculi*. Abelard cites Jerome as follows: "Cruciat te amor carnis, tolle crucem tuam et sequere dominum. Et ipse tibi dominus et salvator tuus quamvis in carne Deus humanum tamen demonstravit affectum, ubi ait: *Pater, si fieri potest, transeat a me calix iste*. Noverat quod calix iste transire non poterat, ad eum bibendum venerat voluntate non necessitate. Pro te vocem hominis, vocem carnis emisit; te in se dignatus est transfigurare. Voluntatem ostendit qua temptari posset, continuo docuit quam voluntatem cui voluntati praeferre deberes. *Pater*, inquit, *si fieri potest, transeat a me calix iste*; vox carnis, non spiritus, vox infirmitatis, non divinitatis" (Peter Abelard, *Sic et non* q.83, ed. Blanche Beatrice Boyer and Richard McKeon [Chicago, 1977], pp. 299–300).

13 Peter Abelard, *Peter Abelard's Ethics*, ed. David Edward Luscombe (Oxford, 1971), p. 11. Saarinen discusses this position as a contradiction of Anselm's (Saarinen, *Weakness of Will*, p. 56).

14 See *Ysagoge in theologiam*, in *Écrits théologiques de l'école d'Abélard*, ed. Artur Michael Landgraf (Louvain, 1934), pp. 63–285, esp. pp. 170–172.

his *Commentaria in epistolam Pauli ad Romanos* were and are a matter of some debate and are less relevant for the present purposes than the very fact that Abelard rejected the notion of humanity's just bondage to the devil. Like Anselm, Abelard sought a 'more reasonable' understanding of atonement; unlike Anselm, Abelard devoted precious little space to expounding this alternative. The Incarnation and the passion show to humanity the highest love "by which we are not only freed from the servitude of sin but even gain the true freedom of sons of God, so that we might fulfill everything through love rather than through fear."[15] Though this has often been labeled exemplarism, several contemporary interpretations dispute the label and note that Abelard argues for the objective accomplishment of deliverance from sin through Christ's passion and for the necessity of grace for salvation.[16]

---

15 Peter Abelard, *Commentaria in epistolam Pauli ad Romanos* II, 3:26 (ed. Eloi Marie Buytaert, Corpus Christianorum Continuatio Mediaevalis 11 [Turnhout, 1969], p. 118): "Redemptio itaque nostra est illa summa in nobis per passionem Christi dilectio quae nos non solum a seruitute peccati liberat, sed ueram nobis filiorum Dei libertatem acquirit, ut amore eius potius quam timore cuncta impleamus, qui nobis tantam exhibuit gratiam qua maior inveniri ipso attestante non potest."

16 "Indeed, Abelard's position, although usually labeled exemplarism, is better understood as a theory of response, for his argument in the Romans commentary stresses less example and *imitatio* than the idea that Christ's self-immolation for us is a stimulus that compels the response of repentance and love. Both Anselm and Bernard in fact agree with Abelard that empathetic participation in Christ's suffering arouses humankind to a love that is the first step toward return and reconciliation" (Caroline Walker Bynum, *Wonderful Blood: Theology and Practice in Late Medieval Northern Germany and Beyond* [Philadelphia, 2007], pp. 197–198). See also Thomas Williams, "Sin, Grace, and Redemption," in *The Cambridge Companion to Abelard*, pp. 258–278. Williams stresses that Abelard's theory requires an 'objective transaction' and so avoids exemplarism while also highlighting the need for grace. Quinn offers a detailed analysis of Abelard's commentary on Romans 3 and strives to offer a constructive Abelardian proposal. See Philip L. Quinn, "Abelard on Atonement: 'Nothing Unintellgible, Arbitrary, Illogical, or Immoral about It,' " in *Reasoned Faith: Essays in Philosophical Theology in Honor of Norman Kretzmann*, ed. Eleonore Stump (Ithaca, 1993), pp. 281–300. Weingart attempts to present Abelard's theory of the atonement in a fully orthodox light; see Richard E. Weingart, *The Logic of Divine Love: A Critical Analysis of the Soteriology of Peter Abailard* (Oxford, 1970).

Hugh of St Victor's (c. 1090–1141) short work *De quatuor voluntatibus Christi* influenced the basic scheme followed by the Lombard in the *Sentences*.[17] This influence is not surprising, since Peter studied under Hugh in Paris. The title of Hugh's work, with its statement of four wills in Christ, might cause some surprise. Against a backdrop of the monothelite controversy, affirmation of four wills seems outrageous. Hugh's concern rests not in challenging monothelitism but in expressing the proper disposition of Christ's human will for our instruction. Hugh writes, "Christ was God, and so the divine will was in him. And because he was also man, similarly a human will was in him."[18] The human will can be considered according to reason, according to tender pity, or according to the flesh, but it is not entirely clear whether these are three different wills or only three aspects of the human will.[19] While Hugh concentrates attention on the will of tender pity (or will of humanity, which wills from compassion), he establishes that the divine will willed the passion according to justice, the will of reason obeyed the divine will according to deference to the truth, and the will of the flesh willed not to die according to its nature. This order of wills implies no contrariety and was ordained by God's just will.[20] Hugh

---

17 Hugh's *De quatuor voluntatibus Christi* was one of roughly twenty short works/letters written in response to questions from an unnamed correspondent (Jean Châtillon, "Hugo von St Viktor," *Theologische Realenzyklopädie* 15 [Berlin, 1986], pp. 629–635, at p. 632). The *De quatuor voluntatibus Christi* is roughly dated between 1130 and 1141 (Roger Baron, "Hugues de Saint-Victor," *Dictionnaire de spiritualité* 7.1 [Paris, 1968], pp. 901–939, at p. 912).

18 *De quatuor voluntatibus Christi* (PL 176: 841): "Christus Deus fuit, et ideo voluntas divina in illo fuit. Et quia etiam homo fuit, similiter voluntas humana in illo fuit."

19 *De quatuor voluntatibus Christi* (PL 176: 841): "Humana autem voluntas tripliciter consideratur; secundum rationem, secundum pietatem, secundum carnem." In rendering *voluntas pietatis* as 'will of tender pity,' I am following Boyd Taylor Coolman's proposal in "Hugh of St Victor on 'Jesus Wept': Compassion as Ideal *Humanitas*," *Theological Studies* 69 (2008): 528–556. Coolman's analysis sets Hugh's reflections on Christ's wills within the larger context of compassion.

20 *De quatuor voluntatibus Christi* (PL 176: 841): "Voluntas divinitatis per justitiam sententiam dictabat; voluntas rationis per obedientiam, veritatem approbat; voluntas pietatis per compassionem in malo alieno suspirabat; voluntas carnis per passionem in malo proprio murmurabat." *De quatuor voluntatibus Christi* (PL 176: 841): "Secundum voluntatem itaque deitatis in dispositione praecedentem, et secundum voluntatem rationis divinae dispositionem

accounts for Christ's prayer in the garden through both the will of the flesh naturally shunning death and the will of tender pity's compassion.[21] The Lombard dispenses with the will of tender pity and focuses instead on reason and sensuality as the two aspects of the human will. This focus prompts the developing concern for non-contrariety of wills in Christ.

Hugh's brief attention to such questions in his *De sacramentis fidei Christianae* produces a similar picture but with a vocabulary of wills taken from Matthew 26:41. He notes a unity of soul and body in Christ such that the soul experienced realities in and for the body but remained superior to it. Christ possessed a will of the flesh that naturally feared pain and death, and possessed a will of the spirit that obediently subjected the will of the flesh to the will of the Father. Hugh explains Christ's prayer at Gethsemane through this subjection of the flesh to the spirit to the Father.[22]

---

approbantem et subsequentem Christus pati voluit. Secundum autem voluntatem carnis, secundum quam naturaliter in quantum homo fuit, eamdem carnem suam quia odio non habuit, pati noluit. Neque in hoc tamen divinae voluntati contrarius fuit, quia et hoc ipsum quod noluit eum nolle divinae voluntatis fuit." *De quatuor voluntatibus Christi* (PL 176: 842): "Justum itaque carni erat, quod passionem suam noluit quia hoc erat secundum naturam, justum Deo erat, quod passionem illius voluit; quia hoc erat secundum justitiam."

21 *De quatuor voluntatibus Christi* (PL 176: 845): "Sicut enim calicem passionis carnis voluntatem a se transferri postulabat, quem non transferendum praesciebat, sic sententiam condemnationis secundum pietatem aliis mitigari orabat, quam immutabiliter praevidebat."

22 *De sacramentis* II, Part I, cap. 11 (PL 176: 404–405): "Similiter cum Christus spiritu exultasse dicitur sive affectum aut desiderium, vel timorem habuisse dicitur, secundum solam animam hoc habuisse intelligitur; quia sola anima hoc habuit, et ipse per animam veraciter habuit cujus divinitati ipsa anima personaliter unita fuit, habuit quippe anima illa secundum affectus naturae cum quibus assumpta fuit, et desiderium et gaudium, et dolorem et timorem passionis, pro carne sua; quae omnia ad tempus rationabiliter admissa sunt, potestate facientis et voluntate patientis. Et cum timuit poenam suae carnis et dolores refugit, secundum affectum naturae fecit, quo nemo carnem suam odio habuit, cujus malum aliquando ex ratione sustinere potest; amare autem nunquam potest. Sic itaque in Christo secundum affectum naturae quem anima in carne et pro carne habuit, voluntas quaedam erat, secundum quam et mortem dolorem, et passionem horruisse et noluisse veraciter dicitur. Quam tamen voluntatem, superior voluntas spiritus quae ad obediedientiam [sic] paternae jussionis prompta fuit, dirigebat. Voluntas quippe spiritus, in Christo quasi medio quodam loco constituta, voluntatem carnis subjectam, per rationem moderabatur, et voluntati Patris superiori per obedientiam subjiciebatur dicens: *Non mea voluntas sed tua fiat* (*Luc.* XXII)."

The authorship of the *Summa sententiarum* has been a matter of much debate. The work was long attributed to Hugh of St Victor, then to Otto of Lucca (d. 1146). Scholars have now largely abandoned attempts to isolate or identify a single author.[23] Regardless of authorship, the *Summa sententiarum* exercised great influence on the Lombard's *Sentences*. The *Summa sententiarum*, based upon a passage from Augustine cited later by the *Ysagoge in theologiam*, asserts that there were two wills in Christ. This by itself is unremarkable. What follows this assertion is remarkable. "That there were two wills in Christ we have from a metropolitan synod, in which archbishop Macarius, who asserted there were not two wills in Christ, was condemned."[24] The nameless reference to Constantinople III derives from Gratian's *Decretum* (d.16, c.6 and c.10) and would be repeated by the Lombard.[25] Not until Thomas Aquinas recovered the acts of Constantinople III would the scholastics know anything more about this metropolitan synod or the condemnation of Macarius.

Immediately following its reference to Constantinople III, the *Summa sententiarum* raises the question of whether Christ willed or desired anything that was not fulfilled. The author notes that some answer in the affirmative, citing in particular the prayer in the garden of Gethsemane. The

---

23 For a discussion of the authorship, dating, and sources of the *Summa sententiarum*, see David Edward Luscombe, *The School of Peter Abelard: The Influence of Abelard's Thought in the Early Scholastic Period* (Cambridge, 1969), pp. 198–213.

24 *Summa sententiarum* I.17 (PL 176: 76): "Quod duas voluntates fuerunt in Christo, habemus a metropolita synodo, in qua fuit Macharius archiepiscopus damnatus; qui asserebat in Christo non fuisse duas voluntates."

25 See Gratian, *The Treatise on Laws (Decretum DD. 1–20)*, trans. Augustine Thompson, with *The Ordinary Gloss*, trans. James Gordley (Washington, DC, 1993). The *Decretum* notes that "the Sixth Synod was convoked under Constantine against those who said that there is one operation and one will in Christ" (d.16, c.6; p. 61) and that the "Sixth [Synod] was at Constantinople, of 150 fathers, against Bishop Macarius of Antioch and his associates who asserted the false proposition that there was only one will and operation in Christ" (d.16, c.10; pp. 63–64). Of particular interest is the anonymous gloss on d.16, c.6, which displays a complete misunderstanding of debates about Christ's wills. It reads, "Some were saying that there was only one will in Christ. But it should be said that insofar as he was man he had two wills, one sensual, according to which he said, 'Father, if it may be done, let it pass from me ...', and the other rational, according to which he said, 'Not as I will, but as you will'" (p. 61).

Summa sententiarum finds this unfitting, but provides no counter-interpretation of the prayer at Gethsemane.[26] Peter Lombard developed the *Summa sententiarum*'s insight by striving to provide a credible interpretation of the Gethsemane prayer. The Lombard framed the topic in line with the *Summa sententiarum*, which effectively determined the shape of most thirteenth-century treatments.

Peter Lombard's Sentences

Peter Lombard (1095/1100–1160) began teaching in Paris in the early 1140s, during a period of theological specialization and professionalization.[27] Nowhere were these trends more evident than in Paris, which was fast emerging as the foremost center for theological inquiry. Professional theologians were offering courses in their own schools and presenting theology in a more structured, if not yet scientific, manner. Peter's own experience as a teacher prompted his *Sentences*. The work would require many years and involve multiple editions, but its aims remained constant.[28] The Lombard wanted a collection of sources organized systematically, rather than following the order of scripture, as the *Glosses* did.[29] This compre-

---

[26] Luscombe notes that this may indicate a preference for Abelard's views on Christ's human will over Hugh's views (Luscombe, *The School of Peter Abelard*, pp. 204–205 and p. 207).

[27] On Peter's life and works, see Marcia L. Colish, *Peter Lombard*, (Leiden, 1994), 1: 15–32; "Peter Lombard," in *The Medieval Theologians: An Introduction to Theology in the Medieval Period*, ed. G.R. Evans (Oxford, 2001), pp. 168–183; and Philipp W. Rosemann, *Peter Lombard* (New York, 2004), pp. 34–53.

[28] "A first version of the *Sentences* was completed after Peter's journey to Rome in 1154, during which he incorporated passages from Burgundio's new translation of John Damascene into his text. He then 'read,' or taught, the *Sentences* in the academic year 1156–1157, releasing a first edition for publication. But he continued to work on the book, as we know from remarks in manuscripts of his students, who frequently distinguish two *editiones* or *lectiones*. The students noticed that when Peter taught his second course on the *Sentences*, in 1157–1158 (the academic year before he returned to the Psalms, which was to be his last), he added numerous notes and *glossae volatiles*, 'flying glosses,' in the margins. The second edition appeared in 1158 ..." (Rosemann, *Peter Lombard*, p. 55).

[29] "Prior to 1155, Peter Lombard wanted to give his students a coherent collection such as would put their intelligence at the service of the truth. This was the first version of the *Sententiae*" (Jacques-Guy Bougerol, "The Church Fathers

hensive and structured presentation of theological topics also gathered authoritative sources, many of which required some effort to reconcile or harmonize. Of particular interest for the purposes of this investigation is the Lombard's knowledge of John Damascene's *De fide orthodoxa*. A partial Latin version from Hungary, attributed to Cerbanus, was available by 1145.[30] A full translation was undertaken by Burgundio at the request of Pope Eugene III. Peter Lombard read portions of Burgundio's translation in Rome, though he only ever quotes portions also translated by Cerbanus.[31] Thus, Peter never cites those portions of the *De fide orthodoxa* treating Christ's wills. The most significant aspect to note is simply Peter's introduction of the *De fide orthodoxa* into the theological discussion, which he justified with reference to Pope Eugene.[32] The thirteenth century would witness the rapid expansion of the Damascene's authority.

---

and the *Sentences* of Peter Lombard," in *Reception of the Church Fathers in the West: From the Carolingians to the Maurists*, ed. Irena Backus, vol. 1 [Leiden, 1997], pp. 113–164, at p. 113). "In the 1150s, after many years of teaching, Peter Lombard became dissatisfied with the limitations that the literary genre of the gloss imposed upon theological reflection. He turned to the composition of a sentence collection, a form of writing that he knew from his contemporaries; from his studies at Lucca, for example, he was familiar with Master Otto's *Summa sententiarum*, a work of Victorine inspiration" (Rosemann, *Peter Lombard*, p. 54).

30 John of Damascus, *De fide orthodoxa*, p. vii. Cerbanus's translation was limited to III.1–8.

31 "The sojourn in the Eternal City (1154) proved most useful to Peter, to whom it afforded the opportunity to acquaint himself with the new translation of John Damascene's *De fide orthodoxa*, which Pope Eugene had commissioned Burgundio of Pisa to prepare. Curiously, however, Peter seems to have taken cognizance of this translation in a rather selective manner" (Rosemann, *Peter Lombard*, p. 38).

32 "Peter Lombard is aware that in introducing John Damascene, he is introducing a completely new 'auctoritas' in the West. He feels the need to support it with pontifical patronage, as he says in I, d.19" (Bougerol, "The Church Fathers and the *Sentences* of Peter Lombard," p. 133). "The second redaction of the *Collectanea* contains revisions informed by the teachings of John Damascene, whom Peter was the first Latin theologian to use in 1154 after his translation from Greek; he draws on this authority even more extensively in the *Sentences*, especially in Trinitarian theology and Christology" (Colish, "Peter Lombard," p. 169). For a dissenting view on the date of the Lombard's use of John Damascene and on Gerhoh's use of the Damascene, see Eloi Marie Buytaert, "St John Damascene, Peter Lombard, and Gerhoh of Reichersberg," *Franciscan Studies* 10 (1950): 323–343.

The Lombard composed the *Sentences* with four books divided into chapters. Alexander of Hales further divided the work into distinctions in the mid-1220s.[33] The first book covers God in essence and persons, the divine names, and God's knowledge and will. The second treats creation, the Fall, and sin. Christology and elaboration of the virtues occupy the third book. The fourth book deals with sacraments. Peter loosely arranges this material according to Augustine's distinction between things and signs (*res et signa*), to which the Lombard refers in the prologue/opening to the *Sentences*. As the *Sentences* became the standard theological textbook in the mid-thirteenth century, this arrangement of topics also became the standard format for theological investigations. The Lombard's influence extended far beyond the architecture of a theological work and into the presentation of the topics themselves. This holds true even where the Lombard was thought to need development or correction, such as in Christology.

Peter Lombard famously enumerates three opinions on how the Word became human (III, d.6).[34] Accurately describing these opinions as they were understood by the Lombard and his contemporaries proves no easy task. These three opinions provided the field of play for later debates, and their relevance for the present purposes derives from this later function.[35]

---

33 On Alexander's division of the *Sentences* into 'distinctions,' see Ignatius Brady, "The Distinctions of Lombard's *Book of Sentences* and Alexander of Hales," *Franciscan Studies* 25 (1965): 90–116.

34 These three opinions are commonly known as the *assumptus* theory or *homo assumptus* (first opinion), the subsistence theory (second opinion), and the *habitus* theory (third opinion). Though there is justification for each name, they will here be designated according to the Lombard's numerical scheme. The names are from Bernhard Barth, "Ein neues Dokument zur Geschichte der früscholastischen Christologie," *Theologische Quartalschrift* 100 (1919): 409–426; and 101 (1920): 235–262. Barth identifies these names on p. 423.

35 N.M. Häring investigates the meaning of these opinions in the twelfth century in "The Case of Gilbert de la Porrée, Bishop of Poitiers (1142–1154)," *Mediaeval Studies* 13 (1951): 1–40. See Lauge Olaf Nielsen, *Theology and Philosophy in the Twelfth Century: A Study of Gilbert of Porreta's Thinking and Theological Expositions of the Doctrine of the Incarnation during the Period 1130–1180* (Leiden, 1982). Nielsen offers a more comprehensive examination of the three opinions as presented by the Lombard and uses that examination to identify sources for each theory and the Lombard's own preference (Nielsen, *Theology and Philosophy*, pp. 243–264). Nielsen attributes the first opinion to Hugh of St Victor's Christology and the second, though filtered through the Lombard's own theological framework, to Gilbert Porreta's (pp. 256–257). This reconfig-

Briefly put, the first opinion holds that a rational soul and human body were united to constitute a true human being, and that this human being began to be God through its assumption to the person of the Word.[36] The second opinion affirms that the human being Jesus Christ is composed of two natures (divine and human) and three substances (divinity, body, and soul). This opinion holds that before the Incarnation the person of the Word was simple, but after the Incarnation was composite.[37] The third

---

uration of Gilbert's Christology, Nielsen argues, reflects the Lombard's preference for the third opinion (pp. 257–264). See Colish, *Peter Lombard* 1: 398–438. Colish disputes Nielsen's findings and maintains that the Lombard did not clearly favor any of the three opinions. "In coming to the conclusion that all three positions, despite their biblical and patristic warrants, were problematic, Peter had before him the arguments of contemporaries who espoused one or another of the positions and whose terminology was so unclear or inconsistent that they did not, in his estimation, succeed in making their case" (Colish, *Peter Lombard* 1: 404). "The vast majority of modern commentators have been able to take Peter at his word here, accepting the fact that he was not a Christological nihilianist and that he was not a proponent of the *habitus* theory or, indeed, of any of the three opinions which he outlines and criticizes. There are, however, a few who make the mistake of believing the twelfth-century opponents of the Lombard who erroneously imputed these views to him. The most typical claim of contemporaries who misconstrued the Lombard's Christology was to associate him with the *habitus* theory, seen, in turn, as the theory of the hypostatic union that leads most easily to nihilianism" (Colish, *Peter Lombard*, 1: 427).

36 *Sententiae* III, d.6, c.2 (*Sententiae in IV libris distinctae*, ed. PP. Collegii S. Bonaventurae [Grottaferrata, 1971–1981], 2: 50): "Alii enim dicunt in ipsa Verbi incarnatione hominem quendam ex anima rationali et humana carne constitutum: ex quibus duobus omnis verus homo constituitur. Et ille homo coepit esse Deus, non quidem natura Dei, sed persona Verbi; et Deus coepit esse homo ille." "The first or so-called *homo assumptus* theory takes as its starting point a fully constituted human substance or man composed of body and soul and teaches that, through the Person of the divine Word, the substance became, i.e. began to be God" (Häring, "The Case of Gilbert," p. 29). "The Lombard finds the characteristic feature of this first theory in its insistence that God really became something, as the human substance or soul and body became the same person as the Word and God" (Nielsen, *Theology and Philosophy*, p. 247).

37 *Sententiae* III, d.6, c.3 (*Sententiae in IV Libris distinctae* 2: 52–53): "Sunt autem et alii, qui istis in parte consentiunt, sed dicunt hominem illum non ex anima rationali et carne tantum, sed ex humana et divina natura, id est ex tribus substantiis: divinitate, carne et anima, constare; hunc Christum fatentur, et unam personam tantum esse, ante incarnationem vero solummodo simplicem,

opinion argues that Christ's body and soul were not united to form a substance but that they were united to the person of the Word in an accidental manner, as clothing is united to a person.[38] Each of these opinions suggests different concerns and approaches regarding Christ's two wills. Before elaborating these concerns, it is first necessary to examine the Lombard's own presentation of Christ's two wills in Bk. III, d.17.

The express topic of *Sentences* III, d.17 is whether Christ willed or prayed for something that was not fulfilled, a formulation indebted to the *Summa sententiarum*. The Lombard answers based upon a distinction between Christ's divine will and human will. In Matthew 26:39 ("Father, if it be possible, let this cup pass from me. Nevertheless, not what I will, but what you will"), Christ seems to distinguish his will from the Father's. Peter concludes that this distinction indicates Christ's possession of both the divine will and a human will.[39] Christ's human will itself admits of a distinction according to the disposition of reason and the disposition of sen-

---

sed in incarnatione factam compositam ex divinitate et humanitate. Nec est ideo alia persona quam prius, sed cum prius esset Dei tantum persona, in incarnatione facta est etiam hominis persona: non ut duae essent personae, sed ut una et eadem esset persona Dei et hominis." On the second opinion, see Nielsen, *Theology and Philosophy*, pp. 248–251.

38 *Sententiae* III, d.6, c.4 (*Sententiae in IV Libris distinctae* 2: 55): "Sunt etiam et alii, qui in incarnatione Verbi non solum personam ex naturis compositam negant, verum etiam hominem aliquem, sive etiam aliquam substantiam, ibi ex anima et carne compositam vel factam diffitentur; sed sic illa duo, scilicet animam et carnem, Verbi personae vel naturae unita esset aiunt, ut non ex illis duobus vel ex tribus aliqua substantia vel persona fieret sive componeretur, sed illis duobus velut indumento Verbum Dei vestiretur ut mortalium oculis congruenter appareret." "They [proponents of the third opinion] denied that Christ's body and soul were ever actually so united to one another as to form a man's substance, because such a union, they thought, would result in a human person. To eliminate Christ's humanity as a substantial component, taught by the second theory, they contended that, if we speak in terms of categories, Christ's human nature is related to the second Divine Person not like substance united to substance, but like a *habitus* united to a substance" (Häring, "The Case of Gilbert," p. 34). For more on the third opinion, see Nielsen, *Theology and Philosophy*, pp. 251–255.

39 *Sententiae* III, d.17, c.1–2 (*Sententiae in IV Libris distinctae* 2: 105–106): "Hoc enim aestimari potest per id quod ipse ait: *Pater, si possibile est, transeat a me calix iste. Verumtamen non quod ego volo, sed quod tu vis.* Hic namque voluntatem suam a Patris voluntate discernere videtur. [Cap. II] Quocirca ambigendum non est, diversas in Christo fuisse voluntates iuxta duas naturas, divinam scilicet voluntatem et humanam."

suality.[40] These are both dispositions of the soul, and both can be called the human will.[41] According to the disposition of reason, Christ willed what the divine will willed (namely to suffer and to die). According to the disposition of sensuality, Christ did not will – but rather shunned – the passion. The Lombard has stated all the essentials of his position in these opening remarks. He marshals authorities in support of this position and then connects it to Christ's prayer in the garden. Correctly understanding Christ's prayer in the garden requires some qualifications.

One qualification is that the flesh did not desire against the spirit or against God.[42] The flesh desires against the spirit only in cooperation with the soul. This occurs when the soul desires with the flesh against the recommendation of the spirit. The Lombard characterizes this situation as a quarrel (*rixa*) or contest (*concertatio*) within the soul, and he denies that this could exist in Christ.[43] Peter holds that Christ's refusal of the passion accord-

---

40   *Sententiae* III, d.17, c.2 (*Sententiae in IV Libris distinctae* 2: 106): "Et humana voluntas est affectus rationis, vel affectus sensualitatis; et alius est affectus animae secundum rationem, alius secundum sensualitatem; uterque tamen dicitur humana voluntas." It is difficult to translate *affectus*. Translating *affectus* as 'disposition' conveys the sense of natural orientation. Christ's reason and sensuality are naturally disposed to opposites in the case of the passion.

41   Later treatments would add distinctions and nuance to the Lombard's view. A basic distinction between the will of reason and the will of sensuality remains, but a further distinction is noted in the will of reason, beginning with the *Summa fratris Alexandri*. With fuller knowledge of John Damascene's *De fide orthodoxa*, theologians parse the will of reason into *thelēsis* and *boulēsis*. *Thelēsis* was first translated as natural will, and *boulēsis* as deliberative will or rational will. The standard translations eventually became will as nature (*voluntas ut natura*) for *thelēsis* and will as reason (*voluntas ut ratio*) for *boulēsis*. Thirteenth-century theologians also qualify affirmation of a will of sensuality. Sensuality can only be said to have a will insofar as it obeys reason. The impulse behind this is the notion that sensuality can participate in reason and so be rational. These developments will be discussed in this chapter and the next.

42   The context of this assertion is Galatians 5:17 as expounded by Augustine in *De civitate Dei* XIX.4 and *De Genesi ad litteram* X.12.

43   Christ's freedom from such internal struggle rests in part upon his freedom from ignorance. "Further, as we have noted above, [Peter Lombard] grants to the human Christ a fullness of knowledge that has the effect of exempting Him from the false judgments that might otherwise incline Him to consent to inappropriate or false goods; and he exempts the human Christ from *passio* in the psychogenesis of His moral choices. In this sense, for Peter the human Christ does not suffer the experience of the divided self. His will is not weak-

ing to the disposition of sensuality was willed by God and pleasing to Christ's reason because it proved the truth of Christ's humanity.[44] These two dispositions exist in the rest of humanity, and so their presence in Christ testifies to the truth of his humanity. Christ's disposition of reason was informed by charity; his disposition of sensuality was joined to the weakness of the flesh. It was only according to the disposition of sensuality that Christ willed not to die, and it was according to this disposition that Christ prayed for the cup to pass.[45] The Lombard labels this the human disposition, which Christ took from Mary.[46] This change of language from 'disposition of sensuality' to 'human disposition' serves to introduce and construe the subsequent quotation from Bede (*In Marci Evangelium Expositio* 14:36). Bede attributes Christ's prayer in the garden to his human will and makes no distinction between reason and sensuality. The Lombard takes Bede to indicate not just two wills in Christ, but also that according to these wills, Christ willed different things.[47] After summoning a long series of authorities, the Lombard confirms two wills in Christ with reference to Macarius's con-

---

ened; His flesh does not lust against His spirit; and the eye of His intellect is not clouded" (Colish, *Peter Lombard* 1: 447).

44 *Sententiae* III, d.17, c.2 (*Sententiae in IV libris distinctae* 2: 106–107): "Talis igitur rixa talisque concertatio in anima Christi nullatenus esse potuit, quia carnalis concupiscentia ibi esse nequit. Dei etiam voluntas erat et rationi placebat, ut id secundum carnem vellet, quatenus veritas humanitatis in eo probaretur. Nam qui hominis naturam suscepit, quae ipsius sunt subire debuit. Ideoque, sicut in nobis duplex est affectus, mentis scilicet et sensualitatis, ita et in eo debuit esse geminus affectus, ut mentis affectu vellet mori, et sensualitatis affectu nollet, sicut in viris sanctis fit."

45 *Sententiae* III, d.17, c.2 (*Sententiae in IV libris distinctae* 2: 107): "Secundum istum affectum [i.e. affectum sensualitatis] Christus mori noluit; nec obtinuit quod secundum istum affectum petit."

46 *Sententiae* III, d.17, c.2 (*Sententiae in IV libris distinctae* 2: 107): "Ex affectu igitur humano, quem de Virgine traxit, volebat non mori, et calicem transire orabat."

47 *Sententiae* III, d.17, c.2 (*Sententiae in IV libris distinctae* 2: 108): "Hic aperte dicit, duas in Christo fuisse voluntates, secundum quas diversa voluit." The Lombard follows this with another quotation from Bede's commentary on Mark, though he falsely attributes it to Jerome, and with a quotation from Augustine (*Ennarrat.* 2, in Ps. 32, serm.1). The quotation from Augustine supports Bede's affirmation that Christ willed different things. The second Bede passage interestingly mentions Eutyches as affirming only one will in Christ. Later theologians will continue to link a denial of two wills with Eutyches. Peter also strings together many quotations from Ambrose (*De fide* II.5–7). The quotations from Ambrose all indicate a human will in Christ beyond the divine will.

demnation at Constantinople III. "By these testimonies it is obviously taught that there were two wills in Christ: because Archbishop Macarius denied this, he was condemned in a Metropolitan Synod."[48]

Peter then returns to the division of the human will and the original question of the fulfillment of Christ's will and prayer. He writes:

> And indeed it was from the human disposition of sensuality, not of reason, that [Christ] willed and petitioned what he did not procure. Thus, neither did he petition that he procure it, because he knew that God was not going to do it: nor did he, by the disposition of reason or by the will of divinity, will that to be done. Why then did he petition? So that he might supply a form [of prayer and acting] to his members in imminent danger by shouting to the Lord, and by subjecting his will to the divine will: so that, if they are saddened by a battering worry, they pray for its removal. But if they are unable to avoid it, they would speak as Christ himself. Therefore it was not for foolishness that Christ is not heard while shouting for bodily deliverance. Indeed, he petitioned for a good, namely that he not die: but it was better that he die, which was accomplished.[49]

---

48 *Sententiae* III, d.17, c.2 (*Sententiae in IV libris distinctae* 2: 109): "His testimoniis evidenter docetur, in Christo duas fuisse voluntates; quod quia negavit Macarius archiepiscopus, in Metropolitana Synodo condemnatus est." Martin Morard argues that the Lombard probably knows of Macarius's condemnation through Gratian; see Morard, "Thomas d'Aquin lecteur des conciles," *Archivum franciscanum historicum* 98 (2005): 211–365, at pp. 306–309. The *Summa sententiarum* would be another possibility. "Peter concludes his discussion of this point by citing a barrage of witnesses against the heresies of Monophysitism and Monothelitism, to which his reading of Damascene has sensitized him and which he clearly sees as a problem in the teaching of many of his own contemporaries on this subject" (Colish, *Peter Lombard* 1: 447).

49 *Sententiae* III, d.17, c.2 (*Sententiae in IV libris distinctae* 2: 109): "Et ex affectu humano sensualitatis quidem, non rationis, illud voluit et petiit, quod non impetravit. Nec ideo petiit ut impetraret, quia sciebat, Deum non esse facturum illud; nec illud fieri volebat affectu rationis, vel voluntate divinitatis. Ad quid ergo petiit? Ut membris formam praeberet, imminente turbatione, clamandi ad Dominum et subiiciendi voluntatem suam divinae voluntati, ut, si pulsante molestia tristantur, pro eiusdem amotione orent; sed si nequeunt vitare, dicant quod ipse Christus. Non ergo ad insipientiam fuit, quod Christus clamans non auditur ad salutem corporalem: bonum quidem petiit, scilicet ut non moreretur, sed melius erat, ut moreretur; quod et factum est."

Christ prayed to avoid the passion from sensuality alone.[50] The Lombard takes this to mean that Christ did not intend that prayer to be fulfilled, for he knew the passion would occur.[51] This demonstrates not simply the rectitude of Christ's human will, but also Christ's freedom from ignorance.[52]

The Lombard's presentation of Christ's two wills balances the merits and weakness of earlier twelfth-century proposals, particularly from the *Summa sententiarum* and from Hugh of St Victor.[53] Peter focuses on Christ's possession of a human will and the natural functioning of that will for our instruction. This basic focus persists in thirteenth-century treatments, though with much development and elaboration. The *Sentences* did more than provide a framework for later commentaries; it also provided an

---

50 "On another occasion, Lombard draws a parallel between Phil. 1:23 and Matt. 26:39. He says that, according to Augustine, Paul in Phil. 1:23 is both willing to die and to live. His wish to die involves his rational soul (*ratio mentis*), but he also has a carnal desire (*sensus carnis, affectus humanus*) to live. Correspondingly, the desire of Christ to avoid crucifixion (Matt. 26:39) is a desire arising from only a part of his human nature, namely the sensual part, whereas the rational part of his human nature obeys God's will" (Saarinen, *Weakness of the Will*, p. 64).

51 Later theologians will specify that Christ prayed with reason on behalf of sensuality. This specification clarifies how Christ offered a prayer without intending it to be fulfilled. The Lombard offers less specification and less clarity on this question.

52 "According to Peter, the human Christ had the full power to choose evil or lesser goods. Indeed, He did not shrink from accepting the evils of physical suffering and death, because He judged them to be compatible with rational goods. Thus, Christ always exercised His human free will in perfect conformity with His divine will. He could be tempted to do otherwise, *pace* Hugh; if not, His temptation by the devil would have been meaningless. And, if not, it is impossible to take seriously His prayer that the chalice might pass from Him, along with His submission to the will of the Father" (Colish, *Peter Lombard* 1: 447).

53 "Peter, in effect, seeks to split the difference between the *Summa sententiarum* and Hugh of St Victor. With the former, he agrees that Christ had two wills, a human and a divine. Also, with the former and against thinkers seeking to assimilate the human to the divine will, he argues that the human will of Christ functions in the same way as the wills of other human beings. At the same time (and here he supports Hugh), he sees the human Christ as having been freed from those consequences of original sin that impede or limit the free exercise of the will in fallen man, adding, as we have seen, concupiscence to ignorance as consequences of sin that He does not take on, and which therefore do not limit His use of free will" (Colish, *Peter Lombard* 1: 446–447).

orientation to the question of Christ's two wills against monophysite and monothelite tendencies. This orientation would not be fully realized until Thomas Aquinas's recovery of the acts of Constantinople III. Thomas's mature presentation on Christ's two wills in the *Summa theologiae* builds upon the Lombard's basic focus, though as expanded upon in the commentary tradition. Before turning to the *Summa aurea* and the *Summa fratris Alexandri*, it will prove useful to discuss briefly the influence of the Lombard's three opinions on presentations of Christ's two wills.

What is the purpose of examining the relationship between the three opinions and Christ's two wills? The purpose is simply to indicate that each opinion raises different concerns or questions about Christ's two wills. The first opinion, with its affirmation of a purely human hypostasis in Christ, allows much room for stressing a human will in Christ and affirming Christ's human will as a moral agent capable of meriting.[54] The difficulty faced by the first opinion is to demonstrate the conformity of Christ's human will and divine will as the two wills of the one person of the Word. That is, if the stress is laid on a purely human hypostasis in Christ possessing its own will, then the task becomes demonstrating the conformity of this will to the divine will. This task is virtually eliminated by the third opinion. The third opinion, in its reaction to the first opinion, jeopardizes the integrity of Christ's human nature. Describing the body and soul as accidentally united to the Word and not truly united to each other, the third opinion faces the difficulty of expressing Christ's human will as a 'source' for his actions and merit. The second opinion (subsistent or composite person) must explain how in Christ there can be two wills but only one 'willer' or one agent, and how Christ could will different things with

---

[54] Some theologians, in their attempt to stress the integrity of each nature in Christ, portray natures as principles of activity. For example, Leo's *Tomus ad Flavianum* argues that "agit enim utraque forma cum alterius communione" (Leo the Great, *S. Leonis Magni Epistolae*, PL 54: 767). John of Damascus, in his *De fide orthodoxa* (III.15), describes both person and nature as working. Infelicitous as Leo's expression may be, it need not imply a Nestorian or two-subject Christology. Leo's letter responds to Eutyches, who acknowledged only one nature in Christ after the union. Given this polemical intent, Leo's insistence on the working of each nature can be read in an orthodox manner. For a discussion of Leo, Maximus Confessor, and John Damascene on this issue, see Demetrios Bathrellos, *The Byzantine Christ: Person, Nature, and Will in the Christology of Saint Maximus the Confessor* (Oxford, 2004), pp. 175–189.

different wills. Again, this does not intend to discern any theologian's 'opinion' based upon the issue of Christ's two wills. It rather provides an indication of different impulses or trends in Christological thinking. A stress on one or another opinion influences the presentation of Christ's two wills.[55]

William of Auxerre's Summa aurea

William of Auxerre (d. 1231) is remembered primarily for his *Summa aurea* and his use of Aristotle and Averroes.[56] The recovery of Aristotle in the Latin West (mediated through Arabic translations and the commentaries of Avicenna and Averroes) met with no small resistance.[57] The University of Paris, where William taught, banned the reading of Aristotle's books on natural philosophy in 1210. In 1231 Pope Gregory IX appointed William to a commission examining and correcting Aristotle's *libri naturales*. William's interest in Aristotle is evident in the *Summa aurea* (1215–1220), which adapts

---

55   Chapter four (pp. 114–115, 118–123) and Chapter five (pp. 199–204, 236–250) below will highlight this influence in Thomas Aquinas's *Summa theologiae*. Thomas's Christology centers upon correct understanding of the hypostatic union (according to the second opinion). This focus on hypostatic union characterizes all of Thomas's Christology, including his discussion of Christ's two wills, which falls under the section on the 'consequences of the union' (*ST* III, qq. 16–26).

56   For what is known of William's life, see Carmelo Ottaviano, *Guglielmo d'Auxerre: La vita, le opere, il pensiero* (Rome, 1931), pp. 7–29. Jules A. St Pierre, "The Theological Thought of William of Auxerre: An Introductory Bibliography," *Recherches de théologie ancienne et médiévale* 33 (1966): 147–155 offers a bibliography of scholarship on William. The growing view of William's *Summa aurea* as an important link between the twelfth century and the thirteenth century occasioned St Pierre's bibliography. "It is becoming increasingly clear that William occupies a key, pivotal position between the earlier scholastic theology of the 12th century and the full flowering of the scholastic genius in the 13th" (St Pierre, "The Theological Thought of William of Auxerre," p. 147). For a more recent bibliography and a concise introduction to William's life, see Boyd Taylor Coolman, *Knowing God by Experience: The Spiritual Senses in the Theology of William of Auxerre* (Washington, DC, 2004). Coolman's detailed analysis of the spiritual senses clarifies not only this central theme in the *Summa aurea* but also the basic tone of William's theology.

57   For discussion of Averroes's reception at the University of Paris, see René Antoine Gauthier, "Note sur les débuts (1225–1240) du premier 'Averroïsme,'" *Revue des sciences philosophiques et théologiques* 66 (1982): 321–374.

aspects of the Lombard's *Sentences* in order to present a rational demonstration of faith.[58] The *Summa aurea*'s wide circulation in the thirteenth century testifies to its influence on the development of scholastic theology. This influence is apparent on the topic of Christ's two wills. William stipulates from the beginning the basic division of wills in Christ argued for by Peter Lombard and the basic orientation of each will toward death. Rather than devote attention to such topics, the *Summa aurea* instead shifts the focus squarely to questions of contrariety. Was Christ's human will contrary to the divine will? Was Christ's will of sensuality contrary to his will of reason? These questions drove William's investigation and led him to deny contrariety of wills in Christ because these wills are not in the same genus, and because the objects of these wills are not contrary in and of themselves.

The *Summa aurea*'s discussion of Christology occupies the first nine tractates of Book III, with discussion of Christ's two wills in Tractate 6.[59] The remainder of the book addresses the virtues as flowing from Christ.[60]

---

58 See Ottaviano, *Guglielmo d'Auxerre*, pp. 37–38. Ottaviano indicates William's view of a triple necessity for this rational demonstration: to confirm the faith, to defend the faith against the attacks of heretics, and to guide the 'simple' (*simplicium*) toward the true faith.

59 Ottaviano's presentation of William's thought includes no sub-section on Christology. Ottaviano mentions William's view of the Incarnation mainly as an illustration of William's presentation of persons as singular (Ottaviano, *Guglielmo D'Auxerre*, pp. 101–102). Ottaviano writes: "Si chiede che cosa sia precisamente il Figlio di Dio (Christo) quanto all'unità dell'essenza e dice che *'non est nisi unum solum, licet sit aliquid secundum quod homo'* perchè l'umanità è sì sostanziale all'Uomo Figlio di Dio, ma è accidentale al Figlio di Dio come tale. Il Figlio assunse l'anima e il corpo unamo non comme parti, ma così che in seguito all'unione fossero parti di Dio; e tale unione fece Dio uomo e l'uomo Dio in guisa inesplicabile, ma in modo che la Persona divina assunse la natura e non la persona umana; onde si dice che nella medesima Persona l'essenza divina si è 'associate' alla natura di carne" (Ottaviano, *Guglielmo d'Auxerre*, p. 102).

60 "William's primary discussion of the virtues constitutes nearly the whole of Book III of the *Summa Aurea*, beginning with Tractate 10. Before examining his views on faith and charity, it will be helpful to locate this discussion within two larger trajectories in that book. First, like Peter Lombard in his *Sentences*, William links the virtues with Christology, which he treats in the first nine tractates. The person and work of Christ are the foundation and starting point for the remainder of Book III, as the salvation made possible in Christ is appropriated and completed by the possession and activity of the virtues" (Coolman, *Knowing God by Experience*, pp. 112–113).

The *Summa aurea* adheres to the basic presentation of Christ's two wills in the *Sentences* but offers some innovations of organization and terminology that advanced scholastic discussion of Christ's two wills. William includes under the heading 'On the Twofold Will' discussion of will, merit, and prayer, combining multiple distinctions from the *Sentences* and changing the order of topics.[61] At least, this is William's description of the three topics included in Tractate 6. As will be discussed below, the treatment of 'merit' consists entirely in a consideration of how fear or fearing seized Christ in the garden of Gethsemane. William's concern with Christ's fear provides a link between will and prayer, particularly in terms of the relationship between sensuality and reason.

William's discussion of Christ's twofold will can be described as either focused or limited. The introduction to Tractate 6 stipulates a remarkable number of points, points that required demonstration, or at least support, in the *Sentences*. William writes:

> What was said about the twofold knowledge of Christ should be said of his twofold will. For there was in Christ a twofold will, namely the created will and the uncreated will. The created will was itself twofold, namely the will of reason (*voluntas rationis*) and the will of sensuality (*voluntas sensualitatis*). The will of reason always willed whatever the uncreated will, which is common to the three persons, wills. The will of sensuality willed something proper to itself (*proprium*), which neither the will of reason nor the uncreated will willed, namely not to die.[62]

---

61 The Lombard treats together will and prayer (*Sententiae* III, d.17) and then treats merit (*Sententiae* III, d.18).
62 William of Auxerre, *Summa aurea* III, tr.6 (*Summa aurea Guillelmi Altissiodorensis*, ed. Jean Ribaillier [Grottaferrata, 1986], 3.1: 77): "Dicto de duplici scientia Christi, dicendum est de duplici voluntate eius. Fuit enim in Christo duplex voluntas, scilicet voluntas creata et voluntas increata. Voluntas creata fuit duplex in eo, scilicet voluntas rationis et voluntas sensualitatis. Voluntate rationis semper voluit quicquid vult voluntate increata que communis est tribus personis. Voluntate sensualitatis voluit aliquid proprium quod non voluit voluntate rationis nec voluntate increata, scilicet non mori." William discusses Christ's twofold knowledge in Tractate 5.

This introduces the three points of inquiry, noted above as will, merit, and prayer. The first inquiry (chapter one) begins with the following question: Was the will of sensuality contrary to the will of reason? Before turning to William's answer, the introduction itself deserves attention.

The *Summa aurea* shows little interest in establishing the presence of two wills in Christ or in defending the division of Christ's created will. Given the history of debate on this question during the seventh-century monothelite controversy, William's lack of any argumentation to support Christ's possession of a created will divided into a will of reason and a will of sensuality is striking. The pressing question for William concerns not Christ's possession of a human will or its divisions, but rather how Christ's will of sensuality relates to his will of reason. The task for William is to deny contrariety of wills in Christ. To this extent the *Summa aurea*'s treatment of Christ's two wills reads like an addition to and clarification of the *Sentences*. William takes for granted the Lombard's defense of Christ's two wills but seeks to provide a stronger justification for non-contrariety of wills in Christ. In the thirteenth century, the issue of non-contrariety of wills partially eclipsed the import of defending two wills in Christ. The context of thirteenth-century discussions was far removed from the seventh-century debates, and this contextual difference influenced the character of thirteenth-century presentations.

The introduction also establishes a framework for discussing non-contrariety by specifying that the will of reason always willed what God willed and the will of sensuality willed something proper to itself. William again offers no justification of these points; they are taken for granted (from the *Sentences*) and prompt the question of contrariety. If Christ, by his will of sensuality, willed not to die, then his will of sensuality seems contrary to his will of reason. William establishes in chapter one a basic logic for explaining non-contrariety of wills that will be extended by the *Summa fratris Alexandri*, challenged by Albert the Great and Bonaventure, and eventually reaffirmed by Aquinas.[63]

Chapter one of Tractate 6 asks 'of the will of sensuality, whether it was contrary to the will of reason'. The chapter opens with a series of objections

---

63 A new layer of complexity was added to the issue with the division of Christ's will of reason into the will as reason (*boulēsis*) and will as nature (*thelēsis*) beginning with the *Summa fratris Alexandri*.

that offer an interesting range of ideas. The first objection takes the ark of Noah as a figure for Christ's soul.[64] As all the animals on the ark were peaceful, so too was every movement within Christ's soul. Christ's soul experienced not even an instinctual movement contrary to reason, for neither did his flesh desire against his spirit nor his spirit against his flesh (see Galatians 5:17). The remaining objections argue against the opposite or presume the opposite and consider its consequences. The first *contra* argument, citing Augustine (*De Trinitate* XI, 6), begins, "that according to diversity of things willed (*volitorum*) diverse species of wills are distinguished, since the thing willed is the proper end of the will."[65] The argument transfers this logic from diversity to contrariety, so contrary things willed indicate contrary wills. The objection concludes, based upon contrariety of things willed, that the will of sensuality was contrary to the will of reason.

The next two arguments *contra* focus not on contrariety between sensuality and reason, but between Christ's will and God's will. Contrariety of this latter type would be sinful. The second *contra* reads: "Christ was bound to conform his will to the divine will; and yet he knowingly willed something contrary to the divine will, namely not to die; therefore he sinned."[66] The third *contra* argument presents a similar logic and concludes that in Christ the movement of the soul against dying was illicit and thus sinful. These arguments do not recognize any distinction within Christ's human

---

64 William attributes this to Augustine's *super Genesim*, but it came rather from Alan of Lille.

65 *Summa aurea* III, tr.6, c.1, *contra* 1 (*Summa aurea* 3.1: 78): "Augustinus dicit, in libro *de Trinitate*, quod secundum diversitatem volitorum disinguuntur diverse species voluntatum, quoniam volitum proprius est finis voluntatis." This passage from Augustine became a standard citation on this topic and introduced themes crucial for later treatments. As will become increasingly clear in this chapter and the next, thirteenth-century considerations of Christ's conformity or contrariety of wills often focused on the thing willed (*volitum*). Are contrary wills determined by contrary things willed? How can contrariety of things willed be affirmed, while contrariety of wills is denied? William's mention of 'species of wills' also prepares for his defense of non-contrariety of wills. Albert the Great and Bonaventure (and to a lesser extent the *Summa fratris*) would defend non-contrariety with reference to the mode of willing or the reason for willing.

66 *Summa aurea* III, tr.6, c.1, *contra* 2 (*Summa aurea* 3.1: 78): "Item, Christo tenebatur conformare voluntatem suam voluntati divine; et scienter voluit contrarium voluntati divine, scilicet non mori; ergo peccavit."

will, and in fact do not even specify the human will. William's replies focus on the distinction between the will of sensuality and the will of reason to undermine the objections.

William's solution concedes the logic (from *contra* 1) that "according to diversity or contrariety of things willed, a diversity or contrariety of wills is discernable," but adds the significant qualification, "not however in just any way nor of just any wills, but only of those that are acknowledged in the same [genus] (*in eodem susceptibili*)."[67] This type of qualification is not found in – and is perhaps not necessary – in the *Sentences*. The Lombard seems content to argue that Christ willed the passion according to reason, shunned it according to sensuality, and that this willing and shunning was ordained by God. William does not rest content with the simple affirmation that God willed Christ to will not to die according to sensuality. Such an affirmation does not by itself suffice to explain non-contrariety of wills, at least not according to the logic of the first objection. William must go beyond the Lombard's assertion and thus concedes the logic of the first objection while qualifying it to avoid contrariety of wills in Christ.

William defends non-contrariety of wills in Christ by locating the will of reason and the will of sensuality in different parts of the soul. The will of reason is in the rational power of the soul or in the rational soul.[68] The will of sensuality is in the irrational power (*vi brutali*) of the soul or in its irrational part. So, the will of reason and the will of sensuality are in different powers or parts of the soul. Based upon this, William can argue that the will of sensuality is not truly a will. A will must be free according to itself (*secundum se*). Sensuality is an irrational appetite and not free according to itself. That is, sensuality reacts to extraneous stimuli and cannot freely determine itself with respect to these stimuli. The will of reason and the will of sensuality are not within the 'same proximate genus' and so, according to William's qualification of contrary wills, cannot be contrary to each other.

William provides a second line of argumentation for non-contrariety, focusing on the 'thing willed for itself' for each will. The will of sensuality

---

67 *Summa aurea* III, tr.6, c.1, *solutio* (*Summa aurea* 3.1: 78): "Ad primo obiectum dicimus quod penes diversitatem vel contrarietatem volitorum attendenda est diversitas vel contrarietas voluntatem; nec tamen quolibet modo nec quarumlibet voluntatum, sed earum tantum que sunt in eodem susceptibili."
68 William offers little clarification here. Perhaps under the influence of Aristotle, William is distinguishing a rational soul, animal soul, and vegetative soul.

only wills something 'for itself' and never for the sake of something else. A human being wills with sensuality not to die 'for itself,' as death is a natural evil. "A human being, however, wills to die by the will of reason, not for itself but on account of an extraneous circumstance, nor for its own sake but for the sake of something else."[69] William explains that Christ, with his will of reason, willed to die not for death itself but for humanity's redemption. He concludes that "because the 'things willed for themselves' by those wills are not contrary according to themselves, it stands that they are not contrary."[70]

In response to the third *contra* argument, William argues that Christ was bound or obligated to will to die according to reason but not according to sensuality. So the movement of shunning death according to sensuality was not illicit, but it would have been illicit on the part of reason. Like the Lombard, William attributes Christ's will not to die entirely to sensuality. Later theologians would extend, with qualifications, the will not to die to Christ's will of reason. This extension rests on a division within the will of reason, enriching consideration of Christ's human will.

The introduction to Tractate 6 specified three topics, the second of which was Christ's merit. Recalling this, the title of chapter two, 'How fearing seized Jesus,' seems puzzling.[71] The body of the chapter does little to remove this puzzlement. While several objections do mention merit or affirm something in Christ as meritorious (objections two to five), the solution makes no mention of merit. However named, the true issue of chapter two is the relationship between reason and sensuality. The question of Jesus's fearing simply provides an occasion for this issue. What caused this fearing or movement of fearing in Christ? The objections (and this is how the question of merit enters the discussion) attribute Jesus's fear to reason, will of reason, free will (*libera voluntas*), or free choice (*liberum arbitrium*). The question is whether to assign the various movements (fear, direction

---

69 *Summa aurea* III, tr.6, c.1, *solutio* (*Summa aurea* 3.1: 79): "Voluntate vero rationis vult homo mori non secundum se sed secundum accidens, nec propter se sed propter aliud."
70 *Summa aurea* III, tr.6, c.1, *solutio* (*Summa aurea* 3.1: 79): "et ideo quia illarum voluntatum secundum se non sunt contraria secundum se volita, patet quod non sunt contrarie." This framework is important for later theologians who specify a division within the will of reason.
71 The issue is raised by Mark 14:34 ("Fearing and worrying seized Jesus").

of the will of sensuality to a good end, the will not to die) to reason, will of reason, free will, or free choice. If these movements can be assigned to reason, they were meritorious.[72]

The solution begins that "fear of or shuddering at death or the will for not dying was in Christ, although from sensuality."[73] This does not exclude reason altogether. The will (of reason) was not the first or primary cause of Christ's fear but the occasion for this fear. The will did not cause this fear through itself but 'through something extraneous.' The sensible, appetitive power caused the fear, with reason as its 'prime occasion.'[74] Through his will of reason as occasion, Christ caused the fear of death to seize him. Christ could have avoided causing the fear through the first occasion. That is, Christ could have avoided the occasion for fear and so avoided the fear itself. After Christ allowed the occasion for fear, then fearing seized him and could no longer be avoided (see *solutio* 2).[75] Finally, William extends

---

[72] This question relates to the Lombard's portrayal of Christ's obedience, demonstrated by Christ's prayer in the garden. Affirming Christ as the moral exemplar requires examining Christ's own words and actions to explain their exemplarity.

[73] *Summa aurea* III, tr.6, c.2, *solutio* (*Summa aurea* 3.1: 80): "Ad primum dicimus quod re vera timor sive horror mortis seu voluntas non moriendi fuit in Christo, tamen ex sensualitate."

[74] William provides two examples. Someone opening a window is not the 'cause' of a room being illuminated. The sun is the cause, but the opening of the window is the occasion. Similarly, when someone wills to fast, the will is not the cause of hunger but its occasion. "Proprie ergo prima voluntas non fuit causa sed occasio illius timoris, quia non per se, sed per accidens fuit causa illius, quando fecit quiddam, quo facto exiit timor ille non ab illa voluntate, sed ab estimatione sensiblili sive ymaginabili, sicut ille qui aperit fenestram non illuminat domum nisi occasionaliter, quia facit aliquid, quo facto domus illuminetur, non ab ipso, sed a sole, sicut et voluntas illius qui vult ieiunare diu et diu ieiuni<at>, non est causa quare ipse appetata comedere. Appetit enim comedere velit nolit; sed est quedam occasio, quia facit aliquid, scilicet diuturnam abstinentiam, quo facto fit ille appetitus, non ab illa prima voluntate, sed a vi appetiva sensibili. Stomachus enim sentiens suam inanitionem naturaliter appetit et necessario. Eodem modo fuit in timore Christi, quia voluntas illius fuit prima occasio sed non fuit causa proprie" (*Summa aurea* III, tr.6, c.2, *solutio* [*Summa aurea* 3.1: 80–81]).

[75] *Summa aurea* III, tr.6, c.2, *solutio* 2 (*Summa aurea* 3.1: 81): "Eodem modo Christus potuit vitare timorem mortis, si placuisset ei, sed postquam voluit quod horribile illud caderet in estimativam, non potuit vitare illud."

this basic logic and allows that Christ's will of reason consented to his will of sensuality willing not to die (*solutio* 5).[76]

The third and final chapter of Tractate 6 addresses Christ's prayer in the garden of Gethsemane. William assigns Christ's prayer to both reason and sensuality, though in different ways (*aliter et aliter*). Christ prayed with reason on behalf of sensuality. The prayer belongs to reason as the one proposing and to sensuality as the one for whom it was proposed. Christ's reason added the condition 'if it is possible' to the prayer. So, the form of the prayer was directed by reason. The purpose of the prayer was also directed by reason, namely for our instruction. William notes two ways of this instruction:

> First, it is because through it we are instructed that we are permitted to will something proper to ourselves because of sensuality, and that martyrs ought not to fear, if they should shudder at death, since the Son of God shuddered at it. Second is so as to instruct us that we ought to submit our will of sensuality to the divine will. Whence he added: *Nevertheless not as I will, but as you will* (Matt. 26:39).[77]

The Lombard held that Christ did not intend this prayer to be fulfilled. William provides necessary support to the Lombard's view by specifying that reason proposed the prayer on behalf of sensuality. Thus reason, though proposing the prayer, never intended its fulfillment.

The *Summa aurea* follows the broad lines of the *Sentences* on the question of Christ's two wills but adds qualifications important for the development of thirteenth-century debates. According to William, in the garden of Gethsemane Christ willed to die with his will of reason and willed not to die with his will of sensuality. This divergence of wills raises questions about the relationship between reason and sensuality in Christ, ques-

---

76 William's rather convoluted reply hinges upon various senses of 'voluntarily' and 'involuntarily'.

77 *Summa aurea* III, tr.6, c.3, *solutio* (*Summa aurea* 3.1: 83): "Prima est quia per illam instruimur quod nobis licet velle aliquid proprium ex sensualitate et quod martires non debent timere, si horreant mortem, cum Filius Dei exhorruerit illam. Secunda est ut nos instrueret quod nos debemus supponere voluntatem sensualitatis voluntati divine. Unde subiungit: *Verumtamen non sicut ego volo, sed sicut tu.*"

tions William investigates in terms of contrariety, fear, and prayer. This focus, particularly in terms of contrariety, came to dominate thirteenth-century discussions of Christ's two wills.

Summa fratris Alexandri

The *Summa fratris Alexandri* or *Summa Halensis* was long attributed to the Franciscan master Alexander of Hales (as the *Summa theologica*).[78] Some initial scholarly dissents from this attribution dated the *Summa fratris* to around 1280, long after Alexander's death (1245). The current consensus separates the first three books of the *Summa fratris* from its fourth book, which must certainly be dated later. The first three books were written or compiled by Alexander himself and his students, including John de la Rochelle (John de Rupella), between 1235 and 1245.[79] Regardless of its authorship, the *Summa fratris* inaugurated a new manner of viewing

---

[78] The history of debate on the authorship and dating of the *Summa fratris Alexandri* is presented in Alexander of Hales (?), *Summa theologica seu sic ab origine dicta "Summa fratris Alexandri"* 4: *Prolegomena* (Quaracchi, 1948). This work is generally referred to now as the *Summa fratris Alexandri* or the *Summa Halensis*. For an assessment of the process followed by the Quaracchi editors, see Ignatius Brady, "The *Summa Theologica* of Alexander of Hales (1924-1948)," *Archivum franciscanum historicum* 70 (1977): 437–447. The best introduction to and treatment of the *Summa fratris* remains Elisabeth Gössmann, *Metaphysik und Heilsgeschichte: Eine theologische Untersuchung der* Summa Halensis *(Alexander von Hales)* (München, 1964). Gössmann offers a brief discussion of Christ's wills and the voluntary nature of the passion on pp. 149–151.

[79] "Ex parte ergo auctorum allegatorum nihil obstat quominus *Summa* I–III compilata exstiterit inter annos 1235–1245, adhuc scilicet vivente Alexandro; omnia immo indicia hactenus reperta hanc eius aetatem innuunt" (*Prolegomena*, p. CXX). "Aetas enim *Summae* I–II, quae ratione citationum superius (p. CXX sq.) assignanda videbatur ad annos immediate praecedentes mortem Alexandri et Rupellensis, hic iterum plene confirmatur. Nonnisi enim scripta exorta ante 1245 qua fontes in eadem adhibentur; scripta vero posteriora et ipsos *Commentarios* Odonis Rigaldi et S. Alberti Magni (1243–1246) rivulos esse comperimus seu *Summa* posteriores ab eaque dependentes" (*Prolegomena*, p. CCVI). On the redactorship of John de la Rochelle, see *Prolegomena*, pp. CCCLXI–CCCLXV. The *Summa fratris Alexandri*'s use of Odo Rigaldus on the topic of Christ's two wills is discussed below. Albert's *Commentarii*, though used by the *Summa fratris* on some topics, was later revised and finished in 1249. Its final version clearly makes use of the *Summa fratris* on the topic of Christ's two wills.

Christ's wills and his rational acceptance of death that influenced all subsequent treatments. The *Summa fratris* advocates a division within the will of reason and allows that Christ willed not to die with one part of the will of reason. This allowance grants even greater force to questions of contrariety, questions that the *Summa fratris* answers by developing William of Auxerre's denial of contrariety.

Alexander of Hales, who had been teaching at the University of Paris since about 1221, became the first Franciscan master of Theology when he joined the friars minor in 1236. He introduced the practice of teaching from the Lombard's book of *Sentences* rather than strictly from scripture, an innovation not universally cheered, and divided the *Sentences* into distinctions.[80] The *Summa fratris*, though heavily indebted to the *Sentences*, departed from its structure and incorporated much from William of Auxerre's *Summa aurea*. Discussing the similarities and differences between the *Summa fratris* and the *Sentences* lies far beyond the scope of this chapter. This consideration of the *Summa fratris* will be limited to its treatment of Christ's two wills (III, inq.1, tr.4, q.1), which owes much to the *Sentences* and to the *Summa aurea*, but advances thirteenth-century debates through terminological specification and its use of John Damascene's *De fide orthodoxa*.

The *Summa aurea* altered the ordering of the topics 'will, prayer, and merit' in the *Sentences* to 'will, merit, and prayer.' The *Summa fratris* returns to the order of topics found in the *Sentences*, with the following justification: "The will consists in the act of the heart; prayer in the act of the heart and mouth; merit in the act of the heart, mouth, and work."[81] The chapter on Christ's wills covers first the issue of diversity (c.1) and then contrariety (c.2), with most attention paid to the issue of contrariety. A short consideration of Paul's statements "I desire to depart and to be with Christ" (Phil. 1:23, quoted in c.1) and "We do not will to be stripped, but to be further clothed, etc." (II Cor. 5:4) is appended to the discussion of contrariety (c.2).

The *Summa fratris* cites the *Sentences* as an authority demonstrating diverse wills in Christ. The quotations from the *Sentences* argue for the

---

80 For information on Alexander's teaching from, commentary on, and division into distinctions of the *Sentences*, see Brady, "The Distinctions."
81 *Summa fratris Alexandri* III, inq.1, tr.4, q.1 (*Summa theologica seu sic ab origine dicta "Summa fratris Alexandri"* [Quaracchi, 1948] 4.1: 176): "Voluntas in actu cordis est; oratio in actu cordis et oris; meritum in actu cordis, oris et operas."

divine will, the will of reason, and the will of sensuality in Christ. The third argument, based upon John 21:18 and Phil. 1:23, holds that human beings have a twofold disposition or affection (of reason and of sensuality) and concludes from this that Christ had diverse wills. The issue of concern in the text is not the presence of a human will in Christ (as it was in the seventh century), but the diversity of the human will in terms of reason and sensuality. The *contra* argument makes this explicit: "If Christ willed to die by the will of reason and was unwilling by the will of sensuality, therefore the *flesh* in Christ *desired against the spirit*, and the converse, according to what is said in Gal. 5:17; but this is false; therefore there were not diverse wills in him."[82] The *contra*'s denial of diverse wills in Christ does not concern the human will itself, but its aspects or divisions. Further, the denial of diverse wills in terms of reason and sensuality is ordered toward the question of contrariety. That is, the *contra* argument presumes that diversity implies contrariety and so denies the former to avoid the latter. The response of the *Summa fratris* consists mainly of quotations from Augustine (*De civitate Dei*, XIX, c.4, n.3) and from the Lombard (*Sententiae* III, d.17, c.2). In this passage from the *Sentences*, the Lombard denies any struggle in Christ's soul. The *Summa fratris* concludes from this that "there were diverse wills, although there was not a rebellion of the flesh against the spirit."[83]

The second chapter of question one denies contrariety of wills in Christ. The notable length of this chapter (over three times longer than c.1) suggests the import of this issue for the *Summa fratris*. The discussion of contrariety builds upon the *Sentences*, the *Summa aurea*, Odo Rigaldus, and John Damascene's *De fide orthodoxa*.[84] Every movement in Christ's soul

---

82 *Summa fratris Alexandri* III, inq.1, tr.4, q.1, c.1, *contra* (*Summa theologica* 4.1: 176b): "Si Christus volebat mori voluntate rationis et voluntate sensualitatis nolebat, ergo *caro* in Christo *concupiscebat adversus spiritum*, et e converso, secundum quod dicitur Gal. 5,17; sed hoc est falsum; non ergo fuerunt in eo diversae voluntates."

83 *Summa fratris Alexandri* III, inq.1, tr.4, q.1, c.1, *respondeo* 1 (*Summa theologica* 4.1: 177b): "Sic ergo patet responsio quod diversae fuerunt voluntates nec tamen fuit rebellio carnis ad spiritum."

84 *Summa fratris* c.2 repeats the Lombard's citations of 'Jerome' [Bede] in *contra* 3 and 4 and *ad* 4, and the Lombard's use of Gal. 5:17 in *ad* 2. From the *Summa aurea*, the *Summa fratris* borrows the citation of 'Augustine' [Alan of Lille] on the ark and of Augustine's *De Trinitate*, XI.6. The *Summa fratris* also reproduces verbatim a passage from the *Summa aurea* in *ad* 3. Odo Rigaldus's strategy for

Foundations of Thirteenth-Century Debates | 59

was peaceful and ordered under the will. The *Summa fratris* begins with this assertion and then turns to the *contra* arguments. The *contra* arguments, all derived from the *Sentences* or the *Summa aurea*, argue not just for contrariety of wills but also that this contrariety implies sin.

The response represents a development in scholastic discussions of Christ's two wills. It begins with "Christ is said to have had diverse wills in four ways."[85] The division of wills begins with the familiar distinction between divine will and human will. The human will can be divided into the will of sensuality and the will of reason. These two distinctions are familiar from the Lombard and William of Auxerre; the third and fourth distinctions are new. The *Summa fratris* holds:

> In the third way, according to reason there are said to be diverse wills in Christ, because reason has a certain will as nature can be united to the body (*quamdam voluntatem ut natura est unibilis corpori*), and has a will as reason is conformed to the divinity in all things (*voluntatem ut ratio est per omnia conformis divinitati*), and according to this these diverse wills are said to be in Christ: the natural will (*voluntas naturalis*) and the will of reason (*voluntas rationis*).[86]

The *Summa fratris* here divides the will of reason (*voluntas rationis*) into the natural will (*voluntas naturalis*) and the will of reason (*voluntas rationis*). Thus, will of reason names both the counterpart to the will of sensuality

---

denying contrariety is noted and rejected, with the solution of the Damascene preferred. The *Summa fratris* introduces the use of the Damascene on this topic. The *De fide orthodoxa* would become an increasingly important source in thirteenth-century Christologies and on the question of Christ's two wills. The *Sentences* restricted its quotations of the *De fide orthodoxa* to those portions translated by Cerbanus (III.1–8). The *Summa fratris* introduces into theological discussion the remainder of the *De fide orthodoxa*'s third book.

85 *Summa fratris Alexandri* III, inq.1, tr.4, q.1, c.2, *respondeo* (*Summa theologica* 4.1: 177b): "Praenotandum est quod Christus dicitur habuisse diversas voluntates quatuor modis."

86 *Summa fratris Alexandri* III, inq.1, tr.4, q.1, c.2, *respondeo* (*Summa theologica* 4.1: 177b): "Tertio modo, dicuntur in Christo secundum rationem diversae voluntates, quia ratio habet quamdam voluntatem ut natura est unibilis corpori, et habet voluntatem ut ratio est per omnia conformis divinitati, et secundum hoc dicerentur diversae voluntates in Christo: voluntas naturalis et voluntas rationis."

and a subdivision of that counterpart. To avoid confusion, later authors will employ the qualifications 'as nature' (*ut natura*) and 'as reason' (*ut ratio*) to indicate the divisions of the will of reason.[87] Will as nature comes to name the natural will; will as reason comes to name the will of reason as a subdivision of the will of reason. Though not indicated as such here, this division within the will of reason depends upon John Damascene's *De fide orthodoxa* II.22, which the *Summa fratris* refers to elsewhere.[88] The fourth division posits diverse wills in Christ by reason of himself (*ratione sui*) and by reason of his members (*ratione membrorum*), for Christ can will in his own person and in the person of his members.[89]

[87] The later use of will as nature (*voluntas ut natura*) and will as reason (*voluntas ut ratio*) clearly derives from the *Summa fratris Alexandri*'s phrases "quamdam voluntatem ut natura est unibilis corpori" and "voluntatem ut ratio est per omnia conformis divinitati" noted above. Sometimes the distinction is named according to the natural will and the deliberative will. The distinction between *ut natura* and *ut ratio* goes back at least to Alexander of Hales's *Quaestiones disputatae 'antequam esset frater*,' in which Alexander distinguishes the superior portion of reason considered *ut natura* and *ut ratio*. "Superior portio rationis consideratur dupliciter: quia ut est 'natura', scilicet ut est quaedam potentia animae in se, secundum se carni unita, et apprehendens ex cognitione innata, secundum quod dicit Philosophus quod omnis homo naturalem habet appetitum disciplinae et sanitatum. Vel dicitur ratio ut 'ratio', scilicet quando apprehendit cum electione et deliberatione" (Alexander of Hales, *Quaestiones disputatae 'antequam esset frater',* q.16, disp.2, m.3, n.48 [*Quaestiones disputatae 'antequam esset frater',* ed. PP. Collegii S. Bonaventurae (Quaracchi, 1960), p. 246]). Alexander also refers to the Damascene's distinction between *boulēsis* and *thelēsis* (q.33, disp.3, m.2, n.67 and q.40, m.4, n.40) but does not connect this to a distinction between *ut ratio* and *ut natura*.

[88] *Summa fratris Alexandri* III, inq.1, tr.5, q.1, c.1, a.3 (*Summa theologica* 4.1: 201b): "Respondeo secundum Ioannem Damascenum [II.22]. Voluntas est rationis et liber appetitus; voluntas non est proprie ex parte sensualitatis, sed solum ex parte rationis, quia est appetitus rationis. Sed appetitus duplex, ideo voluntas duplex: appetitus naturalis et rationalis; sic rationalis voluntas est duplex: naturalis, respondens appetitui naturali rationis, et deliberativae quae respondet appetitui rationali; utraque autem voluntas idem est secundum rem, sed differens secundum rationem."

[89] *Summa fratris Alexandri* III, inq.1, tr.4, q.1, c.2 (*Summa theologica*, 4.1: 178a): "Quarto modo, dicuntur diversae voluntates in Christo ratione sui et ratione membrorum; dicendum ergo quod in Christo fuerunt diversae voluntates, ut quaedam dicatur velle in persona sua, quaedam vero in persona membrorum." This division plays no significant role in subsequent treatments of Christ's wills. The source for this division is Odo Rigaldus (*Lectura super Sententias*, III, d.17) citing Hilary's *De Trinitate* X.

After detailing the divisions of the will, the *Summa fratris* immediately distinguishes diversity from contrariety. There were diverse wills in Christ, but these wills were not contrary. The response states: "the will of sensuality was not contrary to the will of reason, nor was the human will contrary to the divine will, nor the natural will contrary to the will of reason, nor the will by reason of his own person contrary to the will by reason of his members."[90] Some would disagree with such unconditional denial of contrariety.[91] The *Summa fratris* presents Odo Rigaldus's view, though without mentioning his name, that contrariety can be either natural or moral.[92] Moral contrariety "is determined with respect to good and evil."[93] Christ's reason and sensuality both willed something good, for to die and not to die were both good. Thus, there was no moral contrariety between Christ's wills. Natural contrariety, on the other hand, requires contrary dispositions in nature. To live and to die are natural contraries, and so wills for these contraries are contrary wills. Christ's wills, however, were not disordered or sinful, because order is determined according to moral contrariety.[94]

90 *Summa fratris Alexandri* III, inq.1, tr.4, q.1, c.2 (*Summa theologica*, 4.1: 178a): "Dicendum ergo quod in Christo fuerunt diversae voluntates, sed non contrariae: nec voluntas sensualitatis contraria voluntati rationis, nec voluntas humana contraria voluntati divinae, nec voluntas naturalis contraria voluntati rationis, nec voluntas ratione personae suae contraria voluntati ratione membrorum."

91 Albert the Great's commentary on the *Sentences* allows for some contrariety of wills in Christ but denies the contrariety of struggle, recalling the Lombard's own view. Albert's strategy focuses on a distinction between the question of conformity and the question of contrariety.

92 *Summa fratris Alexandri* III, inq.1, tr.4, q.1, c.2 (*Summa theologica*, 4.1: 178a): "Quidam distinguant quod est contarietas naturae duplex: naturalis et moralis."

93 *Summa fratris Alexandri* III, inq.1, tr.4, q.1, c.2 (*Summa theologica*, 4.1: 178a): "Contrarietas moralis est, quae est de contrariis in moribus; contrarietas autem in moribus determinatur secundum rationem boni et mali. Quia ergo in Christo utrumque erat bonum, scilicet vivere et mori, voluntas sensualitatis et rationis non fuerunt contrariorum in moribus, cum utrumque sit bonum."

94 *Summa fratris Alexandri* III, inq.1, tr.4, q.1, c.2 (*Summa theologica*, 4.1: 178a): "Contrarietas vero naturalis est illa, quae est de contrariis in natura; contraria autem in natura attenduntur secundum contrarias dispositiones in natura. Unde secundum hoc vivere et mori sunt contraria; et voluntas sensualitatis et rationis secundum hoc fuerunt contrariorum et secundum hoc voluntates contrariae. Non tamen ex hoc sequitur quod inordinatio fuerit in Christo, quia ordinatio et inordinatio attenduntur secundum rationem moralem, id est secundum rationem boni et mali."

The *Summa fratris* rejects Odo's view and considers preferable the Damascene's view that Christ had diverse but not contrary wills. The mention of John Damascene by name on the topic of Christ's two wills is novel. The citations in the *Sentences* of the *De fide orthodoxa* are limited to III.1–8 (those portions translated by Cerbanus, though the Lombard cites Burgundio's translation). The *Summa fratris* here refers to portions of the *De fide orthodoxa* (III.14, 18) unused by the Lombard. These citations provide an *auctoritas* for denying contrariety of wills in Christ, but the *Summa fratris* argues for this conclusion by using arguments found in William of Auxerre's *Summa aurea*. The *Summa fratris* holds that "contraries must be identified through the same (*circa idem*); because, therefore, the will was not for dying and for living through the same (*circa idem*) nor according to the same (*secundum idem*) in Christ, since one through (*circa*) sensuality, another through (*circa*) reason, there was no contrariety of the will of sensuality and the will of reason."[95] William argued along similar, though less refined, lines in the *Summa aurea* that contrary wills must be in the same [genus] (*in eodem susceptibili*) and that contrary things willed must be contrary 'of themselves.' In response to the first objection, the *Summa fratris* argues that wills of contrary things are not contrary wills unless the wills are in the same genus. The will of reason and the will of sensuality are not from the same genus and so cannot truly be contrary wills.[96]

The reply to the second objection offers a slightly different take on contrariety. Galatians 5:17 ("The flesh desires against the spirit and the spirit against the flesh; for both are opposed to each other") provides the context. The flesh and spirit are opposed when the very desiring of each (not only the object of desire) is contrary to the other. There was no such

---

95 *Summa fratris Alexandri* III, inq.1, tr.4, q.1, c.2 (*Summa theologica*, 4.1: 178a): "Sed dicendum est rectius secundum Ioannem Damascenum quod Christus habuit diversas voluntas, sed non contrarias. Contraria enim nata sunt fieri circa idem; quia ergo non erat circa idem voluntas moriendi et vivendi nec secundum idem in Christo, quia unum circa sensualitatem, aliud circa rationem, non erit contrarietas voluntatis sensualitatis et rationis."
96 *Summa fratris Alexandri* III, inq.1, tr.4, q.1, c.2, *ad* 1 (*Summa theologica* 4.1: 178a): "Ad illud quod obiicit quod 'voluntates sunt contrariae, quae sunt contrariorum' dicendum quod non est verum, nisi ubi sunt eiusdem generis voluntates. Voluntas autem sensualitatis et rationis non sunt eiusdem generis, quia illa habet liberam potestatem respectu sui actus, ista vero habet inditam necessitatem."

opposition in Christ. The *Summa fratris* holds that "in the Lord Jesus, although the very things desired by the spirit and by the flesh were contrary, namely to live and to die, nevertheless the desiring of the flesh was not contrary to the very desiring of the spirit, because the spirit willed that the flesh should desire this."[97]

The division of the will of reason establishes another layer of diversity and so also the potential for contrariety. The *Summa fratris* responds to this concern in reply to the fourth objection:

> To the other it should be said that Jerome [Bede] calls the human will either the will of sensuality or the natural will of reason (*voluntas rationis naturalis*). And it must be granted that that movement was ordered; and the will of reason in one way willed the same as sensuality, in another way not: for it willed for that movement to arise, but it was unwilling for that to come to pass. Furthermore, [the will of reason] willed absolutely or in spirit what sensuality willed, namely to live; but as a condition of our redemption it willed the opposite, namely to die. Therefore, by the natural will he willed the same as sensuality, namely to live; but by the rational will, due to a consideration for our redemption, he willed to die; and the wills are not contrary, but diverse.[98]

97 *Summa fratris Alexandri* III, inq.1, tr.4, q.1, c.2, *ad* 2 (*Summa theologica* 4.1: 178b): "Propter hoc ergo dicuntur adversari in nobis concupiscentia carnis et spiritus, quia concupiscere carnis et spiritus contrariantur, non solum ipsa concupita. In Domino autem Iesu, quamvis ipsa concupita fuerint contraria a spiritu et carne, scilicet vivere et mori, tamen concupiscere carnis non erat contrarium ipsi concupiscere spiritus, quia spiritus volebat quod ipsa hoc concupisceret."

98 *Summa fratris Alexandri* III, inq.1, tr.4, q.1, c.2, *ad* 4 (*Summa theologica* 4.1: 178b): "Ad aliud dicendum quod ab Hieronymo appellatur voluntas humana voluntas sensualitatis vel voluntas rationis naturalis. Et concedendum est quod ille motus fuit ordinatus; et voluntas rationis voluit idem uno modo quod sensualitatis, alio modo non: voluit enim ut motus ille surgeret, sed noluit ut procederet. Praeterea voluit absolute sive in spiritu quod voluit sensualitas, scilicet vivere; cum conditione nostrae redemptionis voluit oppositum, scilicet mori. Voluntate ergo naturali voluit idem cum sensualitate, scilicet vivere; rationali vero voluntate, consideratione nostrae redemptionis, voluit mori; nec sunt voluntates contrariae, sed diversae." The *Summa fratris* takes this Bede reference from the *Sentences*. The Lombard argues that it shows Christ's human will of sensuality willed something different than the divine will willed. The *Summa fratris* goes beyond this.

This specifies that Jesus Christ, according to his natural will (a division of the will of reason), willed to avoid the passion.[99] In the *Sentences* and the *Summa aurea*, any movement in Christ to avoid the passion is attributed to sensuality. The *Summa fratris* goes beyond this and allows that Christ with his will of reason (in the broad sense) willed not to die. The division of the will of reason, based upon the Damascene, provides for this allowance. What we find here is no small step toward a full appreciation of Christ's integral human nature doing and undergoing everything proper to it. Does it not, though, raise a greater difficulty?

Christ's will of reason and will of sensuality are not in the same genus and so cannot be contrary wills. The natural will and the will of reason (rational will) are divisions of the will of reason and so are in the same genus (*circa idem*). Denial of their contrariety cannot depend upon the *circa idem* argument. The response (c.2) notes two conditions for contrariety, *circa idem* and *secundum idem* (according to the same). The condition of *secundum idem* grounds the non-contrariety of the natural will and the rational will. The reply to the fourth objection specifies the rational will as willing the passion "due to a consideration for our redemption." The reply concludes diverse but not contrary wills. The natural will willed absolutely, but the rational will willed conditionally.[100] This difference in the mode of

---

99 The *Summa fratris* mitigates this conclusion by denying that the natural will is properly voluntary. "Motus vero voluntarius improprie dicitur voluntatis naturalis vel sensualitatis, qui est determinatus ad unam partem, et ideo necessarius, et ideo circa illum motum non cadit licitum vel illicitum" (*Summa fratris Alexandri* III, inq.1, tr.4, q.1, c.2, *ad* 5 [*Summa theologica* 4.1: 178b–179a]). Later scholastics will affirm that the movement of the will as nature is voluntary and so does regard the licit and illicit.

100 The *Summa fratris* makes this clear in its treatment of the Apostle's sayings (Phil. 1:23 and II Cor. 5:4) appended to chapter two. "Ad aliud vero quod obiicitur, dicendum quod est voluntas absoluta et est voluntas conditionalis. Voluntas absoluta est, qua aliquid volumus simpliciter; voluntas vero conditionalis est, qua volumus aliquid ratione alicuius causae trahentis vel impellentis. Voluntas vero dissolutionis in Paulo non erat absolute, sed sub conditione, ut esset cum Christo; voluntas vero absoluta erat manere. Tamen secundum determinationem Apostoli neutrum erat absolute volitum, quia manere erat propter utilitatem fratrum, dissolvi erat ut esset cum Christo; et ideo non erant voluntates simpliciter absolutae, quia erant conditionales" (*Summa fratris Alexandri* III, inq.1, tr.4, q.1, c.2.2, *ad* 1–2 [*Summa theologica* 4.1: 179b]).

willing seems to exclude the second condition for contrariety (*secundum idem*) and recalls William's affirmation that contrary things willed must be contrary of themselves.[101]

Throughout its treatment of Christ's passion, the *Summa fratris* refers to Christ's wills and to the voluntary nature of Christ's sufferings.[102] The *Summa fratris* argues that Christ possessed an ability to suffer (*potentia patiendi*) differently than fallen humanity and pre-lapsum humanity. Fallen humanity's ability to suffer is characterized by an inevitability of suffering, a will not to suffer, and the powerlessness to prevent suffering. Pre-lapsum humanity, though also powerless to prevent suffering, did not suffer inevitably, did not have a disposition to suffering, and did not possess a will to suffer. Unlike fallen humanity, Christ's suffering was not inevitable; unlike pre-lapsum humanity, Christ was not indisposed to suffering. The *Summa fratris* continues that Christ's ability to suffer was subject to his will, and so Christ could freely prevent or accept the suffering of the passion.[103]

This insistence on the voluntary character of Christ's passion leads the *Summa fratris* again to explore the constitution of Christ's human will. When considering whether Christ suffered in every will, the *Summa fratris* divides the rational will into the natural will (*voluntas naturalis*) and the deliberative will. Christ did not suffer in the deliberative will, which considered the utility of the passion, but did suffer in the natural will, which

---

101 The language of 'mode of willing' is not found in the *Summa fratris* but taken from later discussions of Christ's two wills. Albert and Bonaventure will introduce a distinction between conformity or contrariety *in volito* and in the mode of willing or in the reason for willing.

102 The *Summa fratris*, showing Alexander of Hales's strong influence, emphasizes the affective dimension of Christ's soteriological activity. On this and several relevant themes, see Boyd Taylor Coolman, "The Salvific Affectivity of Christ according to Alexander of Hales," *Thomist* 71 (2007): 1–38.

103 *Summa fratris Alexandri* III, inq.1, tr.5, q.1, m.1 (*Summa theologica* 4.1: 197b): "Dicendum igitur quod, cum sit potentia activa et passiva, potentia activa in nobis est solum subiecta voluntati, potentia passiva non, sed sequitur conditionem naturae; in Domino vero iesu potentia passiva sicut et potentia activa fuit subiecta voluntati, ut esset domina sui actus et suae passionis, ut sicut voluntas nostra habet dominium sui actus potens prohibere eum vel educere, ita Christi voluntas dominium habuit et potens fuit prohibere passionem a potentia patiendi assumpta vel ipsam ducere in actum patiendi."

sorrowed for the separation of soul and body.[104] The *Summa fratris* goes on to affirm that Christ willed the passion absolutely, rather than conditionally, when absolutely indicates the absence of coercion or when absolutely indicates willing something for itself alone.[105] Christ suffered without coercion and willed that suffering for the sake of human redemption alone. In these reflections, the *Summa fratris* adopts the basic outline of Anselm's satisfaction theory of atonement while enriching Anselm's affirmation of Christ freely willing the passion. This enrichment is evident in the *Summa fratris Alexandri*'s interpretation of Christ's wills at Gethsemane, namely that Christ willed to die according to his will as reason and willed not to die according to his will as nature and will of sensuality. Subsequent authors would follow the *Summa fratris* in recognizing this complex arrangement of wills.

Peter Lombard's *Sentences* provided the foundation for scholastic treatments of Christ's two wills. This is most obvious in the commentaries on the *Sentences* but is evident nonetheless in William of Auxerre's *Summa aurea* and in the *Summa fratris Alexandri*. Christ's prayer in the garden of Gethsemane (Matt. 26:39) indicates a human will, and the Lombard divides this human will according to the disposition of sensuality and the disposition of reason. According to the disposition of sensuality, Christ shunned the passion. Christ, however, willed the passion according to the disposition of reason. Peter qualifies this seeming disagreement to rule out the possi-

---

104 *Summa fratris Alexandri* III, inq.1, tr.5, q.1, m.2, a.3 (*Summa theologica* 4.1: 201b): "Sed appetitus duplex, ideo voluntas duplex: appetitus naturalis et rationalis; sic rationalis voluntas est duplex: naturalis, respondens appetitui naturali rationis, et deliberativa quae respondet appetitui rationali; utraque autem voluntas idem est secundum rem, sed differens secundum rationem. In naturali ergo voluntate fuit passio, sed non in deliberativa. Naturalis autem voluntas est per comparationem ad suum corpus, et dolet et contrario, scilicet de separatione; ideo passio fuit in voluntate naturali. Deliberativa est secundum quam contulit utilitatem passionis, et secundum hanc non fuit passio."

105 *Summa fratris Alexandri* III, inq.1, tr.5, q.1, m.2, a.4 (*Summa theologica* 4.1: 202b): "Est velle absolutum, quo aliquid appetitur, non quo aliqua coactione ex alio; et est velle absolutum, quo aliquid appetitur propter se, sicut volo beatitudinem. Utroque modo fuit voluntas absoluta in Christo, quia a nullo fuit coacta; praeterea, appetebat aliquid propter se, scilicet beatitudinem membris suis."

bility of Christ's flesh desiring against the spirit. Christ's refusal of the passion according to sensuality pleased God and Christ's own reason. That refusal showed the truth of Christ's humanity, though Christ never intended that prayer or disposition of sensuality to be fulfilled. Christ's will and prayer testify to his true humanity and instruct us in obedience to God.

The treatment in the *Summa aurea* of Christ's two wills assumes much from the treatment in the *Sentences*. William offers no defense of Christ's human will or its division into the will of reason and the will of sensuality. He simply stipulates these points and also stipulates that Christ's will of reason was wholly conformed to the divine will, while Christ's will of sensuality willed something proper to itself. This final point raises the issue of contrariety of wills. *The Summa aurea* denies any contrariety of wills on the grounds that contrary wills must be in the same genus and contrary objects of the will must be contrary of themselves. The *Summa aurea* follows the *Sentences* in assigning Christ's will not to die wholly to sensuality. Later theologians, beginning with the authors of the *Summa fratris Alexandri*, would find this view an insufficient expression of Christ's true and perfect human nature.

The *Sentences* was the first theological work to employ Damascene's *De fide orthodoxa* as an authority. The *Summa fratris Alexandri* introduced the Damascene into scholastic discussions of Christ's two wills, formulating a division of Christ's will of reason. The *Summa fratris* notes that "reason has a certain will as nature can be united to the body (*ratio habet quamdam voluntatem ut natura est unibilis corpori*), and has a will as reason is conformed to the divinity in all things (*et habet voluntatem ut ratio est per omnia conformis divinitati*)" (*Summa fratris Alexandri* III, tr. 4, c.2, *respondeo*). These are the natural will and the will of reason. This confusing use of 'will of reason' to designate both the counterpart to the will of sensuality and a division of the will of reason is replaced in subsequent scholastic works. The preferred terminology for the division of the will of reason comes from the *Summa fratris*. The scholastics would pluck from the above-cited passage the phrases 'will as nature' (*voluntas ut natura*) and 'will as reason' (*voluntas ut ratio*). These phrases make no literal sense and were simply excerpted from the *Summa fratris*. This by itself indicates the import of the *Summa fratris* for subsequent works.

The use of Damascene's *De fide orthodoxa* in discussions of Christ's two wills changed the character of those discussions. Allowing for a division within the will of reason opened the way for fuller appreciation of Christ's human psychology. The *Summa fratris* locates Christ's refusal of the passion not only in the will of sensuality but also in the natural will. Christ rationally willed to avoid the passion. This signals a dramatic departure from the position of the Lombard and William of Auxerre; it also heightens the import and difficulty of explaining the non-contrariety of Christ's wills. The *Summa fratris* develops William's line of argumentation, noting that contrariety of wills must be *circa idem et secundum idem*. This argument will come under biting rejection in Albert the Great and Bonaventure. Even those who reject the solution of the *Summa fratris* agree on the basics of the question.

The *Sentences* excluded any struggle from Christ's soul by arguing that sensuality's refusal of the passion was pleasing to God and to reason as ordered to our instruction. The *Summa aurea* adopted the conclusions of the *Sentences* and argued that these conclusions do not imply contrariety of wills in Christ. Between the *Sentences* and the *Summa aurea*, the emergence of contrariety as the question of greatest importance is beyond doubt.[106] This trend would continue in the first half of the thirteenth century. The division of the will of reason in the *Summa fratris* brought new urgency to the question of contrariety and new depth to the fullness of Christ's humanity. The shift in emphasis from Christ's possession of a human will to the non-contrariety of Christ's wills persists in Albert the Great and Bonaventure. Thomas Aquinas's commentary on the Lombard's *Sentences* followed the same pattern, though his later *Summa theologiae* displays a renewed interest in defending a human will in Christ. Thomas's *Summa theologiae* represents a flowering of the concern to present the fullness and perfection of Christ's humanity and human will. Thomas's own teaching rests heavily on the writings of Albert and Bonaventure, to which the next chapter will turn.

---

106 The issue is present already in Hugh of St Victor's *De quatuor voluntatibus Christi*, though without much development. Hugh denies contrariety of wills but articulates no argument for that denial.

CHAPTER THREE

Scholastic Debates on Christ's Two Wills
Albert the Great and Bonaventure

The previous chapter traced the beginnings of scholastic reflections on the topic of Christ's two wills. By the mid-thirteenth century, Peter Lombard's *Sentences* had become the standard theological textbook of the schools and producing a commentary on the *Sentences* was one of the prerequisites for the status of *magister* in theology.[1] The Lombard's presentation of Christ's will and prayer became the normative framework for investigating the topic. The normativity of the *Sentences* did not restrict the innovations of other renowned works, notably William of Auxerre's *Summa aurea* and the *Summa fratris Alexandri*. The *Summa aurea* and *Summa fratris* began a trend of developing the Lombard's view, a trend extended by Albert the Great and Bonaventure. Two of the greatest thirteenth-century theologians, Albert and Bonaventure refined and complicated the ongoing discussion regarding Christ's two wills. They critiqued aspects of earlier views and offered new solutions to the problem of contrariety or conformity of wills in Christ. Their attention to questions of contrariety and conformity testifies to this as the central issue for thirteenth-century considerations of Christ's two wills.

Studying the agreements and disagreements between Albert and Bonaventure on the topic of Christ's two wills reveals much about the developing landscape of debate in the mid-thirteenth century. Early in their careers, Albert and Bonaventure commented on Peter Lombard's *Sentences*.[2] They both represented one of the mendicant orders: Albert the Dominicans, and Bonaventure the Franciscans. By the time of Albert and Bonaventure, the mendicants had become a more firmly established pres-

---

1 On the prerequisites for the status of *magister* in theology, see Marie-Dominique Chenu, *Toward Understanding St Thomas*, trans. Albert M. Landry and Dominic Hughes (Chicago, 1964), pp. 264–269.
2 See Chenu, *Toward Understanding St Thomas*, pp. 264–267.

ence at the University of Paris. Not unanimously appreciated, this presence was directly attacked by the secular masters in what have come to be known as the mendicant controversies.[3] The University of Paris also strained to discern the appropriate place for Aristotle, a question not easily settled.[4] In short, Albert and Bonaventure composed their longest works of scholastic theology while students in an exciting, turbulent time.

On the topic of Christ's two wills, William of Auxerre and the *Summa fratris Alexandri* blazed the trail followed by Albert the Great and Bonaventure. The Universal Doctor and the Seraphic Doctor, respectively, showed interest in exploring the richness of Christ's full and perfect humanity while also relating Christ's psychology and moral life to ours. These two feared that through the elimination of contrariety of wills in Christ, William of Auxerre and the *Summa fratris Alexandri* inadvertently eliminated the possibility for any true contrariety of wills within the rest of humanity. Albert and Bonaventure rejected the *secundum idem* argument of William and the *Summa fratris* on the grounds of this unwelcome, though inevitable, consequence. While Albert and Bonaventure agreed on the problem, they diverged slightly in their solutions. Albert stressed conformity of will and noted that this often demands a certain contrariety. So it was in Christ. Bonaventure seemed on the brink of following Albert but, based upon the authority of Hugh of St Victor, denied any contrariety of wills in Christ. Bonaventure prefered to stress the conformity of Christ's every will despite a non-identity in the things willed. These lines of argumentation offer significant developments over the twelfth- and early thirteenth-century reflections on Christ's two wills. They also set the stage for Thomas Aquinas reflections on Christ's two wills in his *Scriptum* on Peter Lombard's *Sentences* and his *Summa theologiae*.

---

3   On the mendicant controversy, see Jean-Pierre Torrell, *Saint Thomas Aquinas*, vol 1: *The Person and His Work*, trans. Robert Royal (Washington, DC, 1996), pp. 75–95.

4   For a discussion of Bonaventure's use of Aristotle, see Zachary Hayes, "Bonaventure: Mystery of the Triune God," in *The History of Franciscan Theology*, ed. Kenan B. Osborne (St Bonaventure, NY, 1994), pp. 39–125, esp. pp. 47–48.

Albert the Great

Albert the Great (c. 1193/1200–1280) earned the designation 'Universal Doctor' for the breadth and character of his learning.[5] This is evident both in the range of fields Albert mastered and within each discipline. Aristotle served as precursor and inspiration for Albert's universal learning, and so the Stagirite's views found a ready student in Albert. A ready student need not be an uncritical recipient. Albert bent Aristotelian ideas in new directions and for novel purposes, a habit developed by his student Thomas Aquinas. Albert did not write some works as a theologian, others as a philosopher, and others still as a scientist. All of his works were written as quests for more unified understanding. It is with this in mind that his works should be studied.

Albert's direct treatments of Christ's two wills, in the *De incarnatione* and *Commentarii in libros Sententiarum*, come from very early in his long career.[6] The beginnings of this career found Albert as the first German

---

[5] On Albert's life, see Georg Schwaiger, "Albertus Magnus," in *"Nimm und lies": Christliche Denker von Origenes bis Erasmus von Rotterdam*, ed. Hans Freiherr von Campenhausen (Stuttgart, 1991), pp. 171–188. On the character of Albert's 'universal' knowledge, see Marie-Dominique Chenu, "The Revolutionary Intellectualism of St Albert the Great," *Blackfriars* 19 (1938): 5–15. For balanced treatments of Albert's various intellectual pursuits, see Gerbert Meyer and Albert Zimmerman, eds, *Albertus Magnus: Doctor Universalis: 1280/1980* (Mainz, 1980) and Albert Zimmerman, ed., *Albert der Grosse: Seine Zeit, sein Werk, seine Wirkung* (Berlin, 1981). For a very useful guide to sources on Albert, see Irven M. Resnick and Kenneth F. Kitchell, Jr, *Albert the Great: A Selectively Annotated Bibliography (1900–2000)* (Tempe, AZ, 2004). Henryk Anzulewicz presents an impressive orientation to the current state of studies on Albert in Henryk Anzulewicz, "Neuere Forschung zu Albertus Magnus: Bestandsaufnahme und Problemstellungen," *Recherches de théologie et philosophie médiévales* 66 (1999): 163–206.

[6] The scholarly consensus identifies the *De incarnatione* as the earlier work, though this theory has had its share of challengers. On the dating of the *De incarnatione* relative to the *Commentarii*, see Ignaz Backes, "Das zeitliche Verhältnis der *Summa de incarnatione* zu dem dritten Buche des Sentenzenkommentars Alberts des Großen," in *Studia Albertina: Festschrift für Bernhard Geyer zum 70. Geburtstage* (Münster, 1952), pp. 32–51; and Odon Lottin, "Commentaire des *Sentences* et *Somme théologique* d'Albert le Grand," *Recherches de théologie ancienne et médiévale* 8 (1936): 117–153. On Albert's Christology, see Stephen A. Hipp, *"Person" in Christian Tradition and in the Conception of*

Dominican student at Paris. He stayed in Paris from 1243/1244 to 1248, at which point he departed for Cologne.[7] Albert completed the *De incarnatione* in Paris and his commentary on the *Sentences* in 1249 in Cologne.[8] Attention will be given to both works, though the focus will be on the *Commentarii*.[9] The presentation will follow the chronological order of the

---

Saint Albert the Great: A Systematic Study of its Concept as Illuminated by the Mysteries of the Trinity and the Incarnation (Münster, 2001); Marie Lamy de la Chapelle, "L'unité ontologique du Christ selon saint Albert le Grand," *Revue thomiste* 70 (1970): 181–226, 534–589; Vincent-Marie Pollet, "Le Christ d'après S. Albert le Grand," *La Vie spirituelle* 34 (1933): 78–108; and "L'union hypostatique d'après saint Albert le Grand," *Revue thomiste* 38 (1933): 502–532, 689–724.

7   See Schwaiger, "Albertus Magnus," pp. 179–181. Albert founded the first Dominican *studium* in Germany (Cologne) and would later (1260) become bishop of Regensburg.

8   Two questions surround the *De incarnatione* and the *Commentarii*. What is the relative date of each work? Was there more than one redaction or version of the *Commentarii*? Lottin rejects the double redaction theory of the *Commentarii* and explains its curious cross references according to Albert's order of composition and as references to the text of the Lombard or to the *De incarnatione* (see Lottin, "Commentaire," pp. 123–138). Lottin proposes that Albert wrote the *Commentarii* in the following order: Bk.I, d.1–d.8/15, Bk.III, d.1–d.10/11, Bk.I, d.8/15–end, Bk.III, d.10/11–end, Bk.II (1246), Bk.IV (1249) (see Lottin, "Commentaire," p. 138). Under this hypothesis, the *De incarnatione* would be prior not only to the completion of the *Commentarii* but also to the composition of its third book.

9   The majority of Albert's direct treatment of will is found in the *Commentarii*. Michaud-Quantin notes that Albert never defines 'will' in his commentaries on Aristotle (see Pierre Michaud-Quantin, *La psychologie de l'activité chez Albert le Grand* [Paris, 1966]). Albert affirms in the *Commentarii* an Augustinian definition, though with reservations. "Au contraire dans ses œuvres inspirés des *Sentences*, il admet et pose dès le début de son étude la définition augustinienne: 'c'est un mouvement de l'âme sans aucune contrainte pour accepter ou acquérir quelque chose' [*Commentarii in II*, d.26, a.8, ed. Auguste Borgnet (Paris, 1894), p. 457]. Mais cette admission n'est pas sans réserve, Albert n'est pas sans reconnaître la déficience d'une telle formule qui peut bien donner la définition d'une acte, non celle d'une puissance" (Michaud-Quantin, *La psychologie*, p. 137). Albert mainly presents the will as a power. Thomas Aquinas, in the *Scriptum* on Peter Lombard's *Sentences*, follows Albert in focusing on will as power. In the *Summa theologiae*, Thomas makes much of considering the will both as power and as act. On Albert stressing that in divisions of the will there is still only one power, see Michaud-Quantin, *La psychologie*, p. 139. Though Albert offers an Augustinian definition of will, his conception remains Aristotelian. "Pour l'ensemble du problème de la volonté et de l'action volontaire chez l'homme, Aristote reste la principale source utilisée par Albert" (Michaud-Quantin, *La psychologie*, p. 143).

works, noting variations in topics and order. The constant through both texts is Albert's novel approach of acknowledging specific and morally neutral contrariety within Christ's wills, while stressing the conformity of Christ's wills to the divine will in the voluntary accomplishment of salvation. No other scholastic was quite so bold as Albert in treating Christ's wills and the issue of contrariety. Albert's boldness led subsequent theologians to restrain their acceptance of his approach.

De incarnatione

The second question of the *De incarnatione* treats Christ's two wills in three articles: the duality of Christ's wills (a.1), Christ's fear (a.2), and Christ's prayer (a.3). As a preliminary remark, it can be noted that Albert's treatment bears strong resemblance to the discussions in the Lombard's *Sentences* and in William of Auxerre's *Summa aurea*. What is further interesting is that (as in William's treatment) the issues of Christ's fear and Christ's prayer are ordered under the topic of Christ's wills, while in the *Sentences*, the Lombard addresses the question of wills in order to explain Christ's prayer. In other words, the Lombard's focus is on Christ's prayer. After the Lombard, the focus began to shift to Christ's wills. Albert perpetuates this shift and views Christ's wills as the central topic.[10]

The first article of question two establishes two wills in Christ according to Christ's two perfect natures. The first objection argues from Christ as 'one willer' (*unus volens*, based upon the Damascene) to Christ's possession of one will. The second objection argues that Christ's actions display only one will. The objections *contra* defend two powers (*duas potentias*) in Christ. This strategy is particularly interesting given the first authority Albert cites, Pseudo-Dionysius. Albert is perhaps the first scholastic to make use of Pseudo-Dionysius in this context. Pseudo-Dionysius's reference to Christ's theandric energy (see *Epistle* 4) functioned as a locus for seventh-century debates on Christ's wills and energies. Albert provides no

---

10 The third question of the *De incarnatione* concerns the union of act (action) in Christ. The entire question involves only one sentence, which holds that the solution to the question of act is clear from the solution to the questions of wills. Albert's replies to the objections from *De incarnatione* q.2, a.1 discuss act and operation. The question of Christ's two acts or operations grows in import for Thomas Aquinas, largely due to his recovery of the acts of Constantinople III.

indication that this reference requires reverential interpretation but rather takes it as naturally supportive of the orthodox position of two powers in Christ, divine and human. This contention extends to the second *contra* argument. Albert writes that "in Christ there are two perfect natures, as Augustine, the Damascene and all the others say; therefore [the natures] are perfect according to being (*esse*) and capacity (*posse*); therefore both have their distinct powers."[11] Albert responds to the *contra* arguments by teasing out the meaning of Pseudo-Dionysius's theandric energy along the lines provided by the Damascene.[12]

The first objection denies two wills in Christ on the grounds that Christ was only 'one willer.' Albert replies by noting that one hypostasis can possess diverse properties according to diverse parts of its nature.[13] He does not expressly apply the analogy to Christ, but the point is clear enough. Christ is 'one willer' because one hypostasis, but the number of wills in Christ is determined according to nature.[14] As Christ has two natures, so he has two wills. Albert follows a similar line of argumentation in dismissing the second objection, highlighting the diverse powers

---

11   Albertus Magnus, *De incarnatione* q.2, a.1, *contra* (in *Opera omnia*, ed. Bernhard Geyer [Münster, 1958], 26: 207b): "Item, in Christo sunt duae perfectae naturae, ut dicit Augustinus, Damascenus et alii omnes; ergo sunt perfectae secundum esse et posse; ergo utraque habet suas potentias distinctas." It is worth noting here that Albert mentions the Damascene as a well-established authority on these matters.

12   On the Damascene's interpretation of the divine and human actions involved in Christ's healing of a leper, see *De fide orthodoxa* III.15.

13   Albertus Magnus, *De incarnatione* q.2, a.1, *ad* 1 (*Opera omnia* 26: 208a): "Bene enim potest eadem hypostasis a diversis proprietatibus secundum diversas partes naturae suae sibi convenientibus denominari, sicut videmus, quod homo dicitur longus vel brevis a proprietatibus corporis, intellectivus autem et voluntativus a proprietatibus animae."

14   Albert occasionally mentions two hypostases in Christ or a purely human hypostasis. Pollet correctly argues that these seemingly careless references do not amount to a *homo assumptus* view (see Pollet, "Le Christ" and "L'union hypostatique.") It is likely true that Albert used 'hypostasis' both as a name of first imposition and of second intention (Hipp, *"Person" in Christian Tradition*, pp. 246, 259, 466). If such is true, then Albert's references to two hypostases are only meant to combat third opinion. I discuss these issues in Corey L. Barnes, "Albert the Great and Thomas Aquinas on Person, Hypostasis, and Hypostatic Union," *Thomist* 72 (2008): 107–146.

of Christ's acts. These replies prepare for Albert's response to the *contra* argument and Pseudo-Dionysius's indication of a theandric action. Albert isolates this expression to name those actions in which the divine and human powers appear as diverse.[15] The standard (from the Damascene) example is Christ's healing of a leper by touch. Albert identifies a twofold will in such actions: a will of nature and a will of the end.[16] No further specification of this twofold will is provided, and Albert completes his reply with reference to action rather than to will. Nonetheless, this twofold will must indicate the distinction of the will of reason into *thelēsis* and *boulēsis*, the natural will and deliberative will respectively.[17] Albert immediately refers this distinction of will to action or act, writing that "[a]ccording to nature there are multiple (*multae*) actions there," but in "comparison to the end there are not multiple (*plures*) acts there, but

---

15   Albertus Magnus, *De incarnatione* q.2, a.1, *ad* 3 (*Opera omnia* 26: 208a): "Ad id quod obiicitur de beato Dionysio, dicimus, quod ipse dicit hoc propter actiones quasdam, in quibus secundum diversa apparuit potentia humana et potentia divina, sicut fuit cura leprosi ad tactum manus."
16   Albertus Magnus, *De incarnatione* q.2, a.1, *ad* 3 (*Opera omnia* 26: 208a): "Et in talibus actionibus est duplex voluntas, scilicet naturae et finis."
17   "C'est ici [*Summa de homine*, q.65] qu'Albert le Grand introduit la division damascénienne de volonté naturelle (*thelesis*), et volonté délibérée (*bulesis*). La première qui n'a pas besoin de détermination préalable volontaire représente le simple désir naturel de posséder ce qui est nécessaire à l'entretien dans la vie de l'être; la seconde a au contraire besoin de cette détermination, elle peut se porter sur n'importe quel objet, quelque soit son rapport avec les besoins naturels. Le théologien syrien s'en était tenu là mais Albert va plus loin: il réserve le nom de *bulesis* à la volonté se portant vers des choses qui sont à la fois possibles en soi et réalisables par nous, alors qu'il appelle, transformant la division double de Jean en tripartition, volonté délibérative celle qui désire des choses impossibles en soi (comme l'immortalité) ou indépendantes de notre action propre (comme l'obtention de la royauté). Cette division que nous ne retrouvons pas ailleurs a un sens précis: Albert le Grand dans ce passage veut affirmer que la volonté délibérée stricte (*bulesis*) ne s'applique que dans le domaine du choix; celui-ci est nous le verrons un acte intellectuel en même temps qu'appétitif, et la *bulesis* représenterait l'acte proprement appétitif dont l'objet serait défini par les mêmes limites. C'est un effort en vue d'amalgamer Aristote et Jean Damascène en ramenant celui-ci à celui-là" (Michaud-Quantin, *La psychologie*, p. 138). Lottin argues that Albert wrote the *Summa de homine* prior to 1250 (Lottin, "Commentaire," p. 143).

one."[18] Christ's healing of the leper was one act with multiple actions (divine and human).[19]

The second article turns to Christ's fear. Albert's decision to include this topic bears the influence of William of Auxerre's *Summa aurea*, which used the question of fear to investigate the relationship between reason and sensuality. Albert approvingly repeats aspects of William's treatment while developing the question of contrariety and fear in terms of reason.[20] Did Christ fear according to the superior part of reason or only according to the inferior part? This question frames the *De incarnatione*'s treatment of contrariety of wills in Christ. The lengthy *contra* argument develops the basic points of Albert's view. He first extends Aristotle's view that movements or actions follow apprehensions, which can themselves be considered diversely. The intellect apprehends many things as ordered to an end rather than as ends themselves.[21] Albert applies this principle to Christ's reason faced with the passion:

18 Albertus Magnus, *De incarnatione* q.2, a.1, *ad* 3 (*Opera omnia* 26: 208a): "Secundum naturam sunt ibi multae actiones. Contactus enim non est fuga leprae nec e converso. Et secundum hoc intelligitur, quod unius potentiae est actus unus. In comparatione vero ad finem non sunt ibi plures actus, sed unus, quia contactus est propter fugam leprae, secundum dicimus, quod una actio est ire ad ecclesiam et orare." Albert characterizes this unity as ethical rather than natural. Though Albert provides no explanation of this difference, it seems to recall Odo Rigaldus's distinction between natural contrariety and moral contrariety.

19 Albert's description relates to the basic view that persons act through or according to nature. While the act properly belongs to the person, the actions (operations) involved in that act pertain to the nature or natures of the person.

20 The *De incarnatione* describes Christ's reason as truly fearing death. Albert's description represents some advancement in thirteenth-century presentations of Christ's human nature and human psychology in particular. Albert seems to approve the basic lines of William's solution to the question of contrariety but adds Aristotelian language of causality to further defend non-contrariety of wills. In the *Commentarii* Albert rejects the defense of non-contrariety put forth by William and the *Summa fratris* according to the logic of *secundum idem* and *circa idem*.

21 Albertus Magnus, *De incarnatione* q.2, a.2, *contra* (*Opera omnia* 26: 208b): "Dicit autem Philosophus, quod intellectus compositus, qui dicitur ratio, simul apprehendit plura, non ut plures terminos, sed ut unum ordinatum ad alterum, ut videmus, quod in propositione praedicatum ordinatur ad subiectum, in argumento vero ordinantur praemissae ad conclusionem et uniuntur in habitudine medii."

Therefore, since Christ's superior reason apprehended death as ordered to redemption and since it had a full conception of death and a full conception of redemption, from the superior part, which is in reason, a twofold affection necessarily follows: one responding to redemption and the other to death, so that as one is ordered to the other, what saddens according to its nature may be a joy.[22]

Here Albert allows that Christ feared death according to his superior reason insofar as death is a natural evil. This fear does not oppose joy at redemption but only joy at death. Christ's fear and joy are thus not contrary to each other, nor is Christ's reason contrary to itself.[23] Albert's basic logic for denying contrariety in Christ follows the *Summa aurea*, but his presentation of conformity of wills in Christ blazes a new path.

The second objection of article two denies fear on the part of superior reason because Christ's superior reason was conformed to the Father's will and thus willed to die.[24] Albert's reply notes a twofold conformity to the divine will. Causal language indicates the different types of conformity. One type follows the material cause, and this is conformity in the thing willed (*in volito*). Conformity according to the efficient cause exists when we will what God wills us to will. Christ's will was conformed to the divine will in the material cause as Christ willed to die for the sake of redemption. Christ's will was conformed to the divine will in

---

22 Albertus Magnus, *De incarnatione* q.2, a.2, *contra* (*Opera omnia* 26: 208b): "Ergo cum ratio Christi superior apprehenderit mortem ordinatam ad redemptionem et in ipsa fuerit plena conceptio mortis et plena conceptio redemptionis, ex parte superioris, quae est in ratione, de necessitate relinquitur duplex affectio: una respondens redemptioni et altera morti, ita tamen, quod una ad alteram ordinetur, ut sit gaudium, quod contristat secundum naturam."

23 Albertus Magnus, *De incarnatione* q.2, a.2, *ad* 1 (*Opera omnia* 26: 208b): "Solutio: Quod concedimus dicentes, quod dolere de morte et gaudere de redemptione, quae est per mortem, non sunt opposita. Sed dolere de morte et gaudere de morte, ista sunt opposita."

24 Albertus Magnus, *De incarnatione* q.2, a.2, ob.2 (*Opera omnia* 26: 208a): "Item, secundum superiorem conformavit voluntatem suam voluntati patris; ergo secundum superiorem voluit mori; ergo secundum illam non timuit mortem."

the efficient cause as Christ willed not to die.²⁵ The divine will allowed for Christ to will what was proper to human nature, that is, willing to avoid the natural evil of death. This presentation of conformity of wills develops the non-contrariety of wills implied by Albert's reply to the first objection. Albert would extend his use of causal language to explain conformity in the *Commentarii*.

Albert, following the order of topics in the *Summa aurea*, ends his discussion of Christ's wills with consideration of Christ's prayer. His treatment of the prayer reinforces the true presence of fear in Christ's reason. The objection notes that some argue Christ prayed from the inferior part of reason. The logic of this position, according to Albert, begins from Christ's perfect knowledge according to the superior part of reason. If Christ feared death according to the superior reason, this fear would be contemporaneous with Christ's knowledge of death. Christ, however, always knew the time and manner of his death, but did not always fear. The *contra* arguments focus on the relationship between the superior and inferior powers of reason. Specifically, the arguments cite Aristotle to show that some things do descend from the superior to the inferior powers of reason. Albert argues that Christ's fear of the cross involved a descent of knowledge to the sensible imagination. Christ feared death and the cross even before these were sensibly visible, so this fear must derive from Christ's perfect knowledge of his impending death. This does not imply a contemporaneity between knowledge of death and fear, because "the certitude of death is not the cause of fear, but the imminence [of death]."²⁶ Albert's discussion has surprisingly little to say about Christ's prayer itself

---

25 Albertus Magnus, *De incarnatione* q.2, a.2, *ad* 2 (*Opera omnia* 26: 208b): "Ad secundum dicimus, quod duplex est conformitas ad voluntatem divinam. Una secundum causam materialem, quae est in volito, et hac conformavit se Christus voluntati divinae, secundum quod voluit mortem, secundum quod erat ordinata ad redemptionem. Alia est secundum causam efficientem, scilicet quando nos volumus id quod deus vult nos velle, et hac conformavit se Christus voluntati divinae, quando voluit non mori, secundum quod mors contraria est naturae."
26 Albertus Magnus, *De incarnatione* q.2, a.3 (*Opera omnia* 26: 209b): "Si autem quaeritur, quare non ab instanti conceptionis timuerit mortem, respondeo, quod certitudo mortis non causat timorem, sed imminentia. Sicut enim dicit Augustinus, timor est fuga quaedam mali. Nullus autem fugit malum, nisi sit vicinum."

and much more to say about Christ's fear. As was William in the *Summa aurea*, Albert is concerned in the *De incarnatione* with the relationship between the higher and lower parts of the soul. In his *Commentarii*, Albert continues this concern but with fuller attention to questions of will.

Commentarii in III Sententiarum

Albert divides the Lombard's *Sentences* Bk.III, d.17 into four parts. The heart of the distinction rests within the first two parts, while the final two parts clarify certain statements from Ambrose and Hilary. In the first part, the Lombard "shows that there was not a struggle of the flesh against the spirit on account of the two natures and wills in Christ. In the second, he proves there were three wills in Christ, namely [the will] of sensuality, of reason, and of deity."[27] This division specifies that, in Albert's view, the Lombard denied a conflict of wills in Christ based upon the distinction between divine will and human will. The Lombard introduces the distinction between will of sensuality and will of reason only after denying any conflict of wills. Albert, in contrast, immediately introduces a division within Christ's human will into the will of reason and the will of sensuality. This strategy allows Albert to separate questions of conformity of wills and contrariety of wills. The distinction between these questions will become sharper as the presentation progresses. Let it suffice for now to note that conformity can occur in four ways of unequal moral weight and with varying degrees of intentionality. It is not always possible for a will to be conformed to the divine will in all of the four ways. Sinful contrariety of wills, on the other hand, involves an intentional and unnatural struggle. The issues of conformity and contrariety are related and in some instances identical. Albert introduces conformity when asking whether Christ willed something that was not accomplished (a.1) and contrariety when asking whether some will in Christ did not have its proper effect (a.4). He reserves discussion of a division of the will of reason for article five.

27 Albertus Magnus, *Commentarii in III Sententiarum* d.17, divisio textus (ed. Auguste Borgnet, Opera omnia 28 [Paris, 1894], pp. 298a–298b): "Unde ista distinctione dividitur in quatuor partes: in quarum prima ostendit principaliter in Christo propter duas naturas et voluntates non fuisse pugnam carnis adversus spiritum. In secunda, probat triplicem voluntatem fuisse in Christo, scilicet sensualitatis, rationis, et deitatis."

The first objection of article one argues that Christ willed nothing that was not accomplished, a conclusion based on the affirmation that "Christ's will was always conformed to the will of the Omnipotent."[28] Albert's *solutio* begins with a repetition of the Lombard's view: everything Christ willed with the divine will was accomplished. This holds true also for what Christ willed "according to the reason of deliberative will," but not for what he willed "according to the will of natural affection."[29] Albert's response to the fourth objection runs to far greater length than the *solutio*. The *solutio* merely repeats the Lombard; Albert's reply to the first objection develops the causal language of conformity introduced in the *De incarnatione*.

While the *De incarnatione* discussed only material and efficient causality, the *Commentarii* discusses material, formal, final, and efficient. Albert again identifies conformity according to material causality as conformity in the thing willed (*in volito*), but here adds that this type of conformity is of minimal value and produces no merit of itself. He defends this by noting that someone can, from evil motives, will the same thing as what God wills, such as the death of a good person.[30] Conformity in the form of willing

---

28 Albertus Magnus, *Commentarii in III*, d.17, a.1, ob.1 (Opera omnia 28: 299a): "Cujus enim voluntas semper conformis est voluntati Omnipotentis: sicut nihil fit contra voluntatem Omnipotentis, ita nihil fit contra voluntatem suam: sed voluntas Christi semper conformis fuit voluntati Omnipotentis: ergo sicut nihil fit contra voluntatem Dei, ita nihil fit contra voluntatem Christi."

29 Albertus Magnus, *Commentarii in III*, d.17, a.1 (Opera omnia 28: 299a–299b): "Solutio: Sicut Magister dicit in *Littera*, plures sunt voluntates Christi: et quidquid voluit voluntate beneplaciti secundum divinam naturam, hoc consecutus est. Similiter quidquid voluit secundum rationem voluntatis deliberativae, totum est consecutus. Sed non quidquid voluit secundum voluntatem affectus naturalis, ut dicit Magister."

30 Albertus Magnus, *Commentarii in III*, d.17, a.1, *ad* 1 (Opera omnia 28: 299b): "Ad id quod objicitur, dicendum quod conformitas est quadruplex qua voluntas nostra conformatur voluntati divinae, scilicet in volito: et haec secundum materiam est, et est minima, ut velim hoc quod Deus vult: et haec non facit meritum de se, quia quandoque quis male potest velle quod Deus vult, ut alicujus boni mortem." This minimal role of conformity *in volito* is striking given its role in the *De incarnatione*, where Albert argued for Christ's conformity of will *in volito* as Christ willed the passion. The presentation of the *Commentarii* would seem to minimize the moral worth of Christ's conformity of will in willing the passion. As will be discussed below, Albert presents contrariety and non-contrariety wholly in terms of disagreement or agreement in the thing willed. This suggests a growing distinction between questions of conformity and of contrariety from the *De incarnatione* to the *Commentarii*.

requires willing out of charity. This conformity produces merit even if the charitable will is not conformed to the divine will in the thing willed.[31] Conformity in the end of willing occurs when we will what we will for the glory of God. As with conformity in the form of willing, conformity in the end of willing produces merit even when the will is not conformed according to the thing willed.[32] Albert also discusses conformity in the efficient cause of willing (*in causa efficiente volendi*). Simply put, this conformity holds when someone wills what God wills her to will. As with conformity in the form and end of willing, this type of conformity often involves a non-conformity in the thing willed. Albert provides the following illustration. We are meant to pity paupers. If we, however, will a pauper to be pitiful, then we do not pity that pauper. God does will the pauper to be pitiful. In this case, conformity in the efficient cause of willing requires a non-conformity in the thing willed.[33] Albert applies this logic to Christ's will to flee death as a natural evil, for that will to flee was conformed to the divine will in the efficient cause of willing. In this first article, Albert has set forth some of the basic principles of his consideration of Christ's wills. He next turns to describing those wills.

Before he affirms a will of sensuality in Christ, Albert affirms the presence in Christ of sensuality itself (a.2). Christ did posses natural, though not corrupt, sensuality. This natural sensuality desires the health of the nature.

---

[31] Albertus Magnus, *Commentarii in III*, d.17, a.1, *ad* 1 (Opera omnia 28: 299b): "Est etiam conformitas secundum formam volendi, ut ex eadem charitate velimus quod volumus, ex qua Deus vult quod vult: quia illa facit meritum, etiamsi quandoque non velimus quod Deus vult, ut dicit Augustinus: et ponitur in fine primi *Sententiarum*."

[32] Albertus Magnus, *Commentarii in III*, d.17, a.1, *ad* 1 (Opera omnia 28: 299b): "Tertia conformitas est in fine volendi, ut propter idem velimus propter quod Deus vult, id est, propter gloriam suam: et haec iterum est laudabilis, et facit ad meritum, etiamsi sit difformitas in materia voliti: quia ad gloriam Dei possem aliquem velle vivere, quem ipse ad gloriam suam vult mori."

[33] Albertus Magnus, *Commentarii in III*, d.17, a.1, *ad* 1 (Opera omnia 28: 299b): "Quarta conformitas est in causa efficiente volendi, quando scilicet volo id quod Deus vult me velle, ut videndo pauperem, si volo ipsum esse miserum, jam non sum misericors, et tamen Deus vult eum esse miserum: ergo vult me velle quod ipse non vult: et haec non sunt contraria." Albert here indicates that non-conformity in the thing willed does not necessarily produce contrariety. Conformity is a more general category than contrariety. Albert applies the basic rules for conformity of a human will to the divine will set forth in *Commentarii in I* d.45. Thomas Aquinas follows and develops Albert's attempt to present Christology as the perfection of anthropology.

Albert's definition of Christ's sensuality foreshadows sensuality's natural refusal of the passion. The question raised implicitly by article three is whether that natural refusal should be considered as a voluntary movement. The objections, drawing from Aristotle and Augustine, insist that every will must be rational. Albert's *solutio* specifies a broad and a strict interpretation of will. "Strictly," Albert writes, "nothing but the rational movement and appetite is called will. Broadly, the appetite of human sensuality is also called will."[34] Only human sensuality can be called will; brute animals lack that freedom proper to the will. These two senses explain the Damascene's stipulation that the will is rational. The mention of the Damascene in the *solutio* is noteworthy, in part due to his absence in the objections. Albert's decision to mention John Damascene, rather than Aristotle or Augustine, in his *solutio* testifies to the Damascene's growing import as an authority on the question of Christ's two wills.[35]

The next two articles reach to the heart of thirteenth-century debates on Christ's two wills. Article four asks whether some will of reason in Christ did not have its proper effect. Article five questions whether the Lombard's division of Christ's wills is sufficient. Or, to put the matter differently, article five wonders why the Lombard did not discuss the will as nature (*voluntas ut natura*). At first, article four's mention of 'some will of reason' (*aliqua voluntas rationis*) seems curious. Albert has not yet provided any grounds for dividing the will of reason or for assuming there to be multiple wills of reason. The first and only objection indicates a prior determination that every part of the soul, reason included, can be considered as nature (*ut natura*).[36] The objection continues that Christ prayed in the gar-

---

34 Albertus Magnus, *Commentarii in III*, d.17, a.3 (Opera omnia 28: 302b): "Solutio: Dicitur, quod *voluntas* sumitur large, et stricte. Stricte non dicitur voluntas, sicut volunt auctoritates, nisi motus et appetitus rationalis. Large etiam dicitur voluntas appetitus sensualitatis humanae."
35 In article three, there are no replies to the objections. Albert never directly replies to the citations from Aristotle or Augustine, but answers these two authorities through reference to John of Damascus.
36 Albertus Magnus, *Commentarii in III*, d.17, a.4, ob.1 (Opera omnia 28: 302b–303a): "Videtur, quod sic: quia supra determinatum est, quod etiam ratio, et quaecumque pars animae, potest considerari ut natura, et sic dolet incommoda et fugit, ergo cum in Christo ratio in illa consideratione fuerit, videtur quod aliquid rationis voluntate voluerit, quod non voluit voluntate divina: ergo cum cujuslibet appetitus sit hoc petere quod appetit, hoc secundum illam voluntatem petiit, quod tamen non est consecutus."

den for what his will of reason as nature willed, yet this was not willed by the divine will and did not follow.

The *contra* argument rejects such a conclusion based upon a denial of contrariety or deformity of wills in Christ. The argument first denies that contrariety arises from natural contrariety within the soul, as the Manicheans' dualist view held. If contrariety within the soul does not emerge from a natural contrariety of appetites, then it must emerge from 'opposition of things willed' (*ex oppositione volitorum*). Such opposition involves a struggle of flesh against spirit or of inferior against superior parts of the soul. The argument denies these struggles in Christ and so denies any opposition of things willed.[37] Based upon Albert's discussion of conformity in article one, the reader of article four knows that non-conformity in the thing willed often follows of necessity from conformity through the other three modes.

Albert's *solutio* grants and clarifies aspects of the first objection. "In concession to the first objection," he writes, "it should be said that nothing prohibits that 'that human being,' in as much as a human being, desired, according to the will of reason as it is nature, something that did not follow."[38] Albert delays until article five his explanation of the 'will of reason as it is nature.' Here the focus rests on a series of qualifications for how and why some rational will of Christ did not have its proper effect. The rational will in question is the natural will or will as nature (*voluntas ut natura*). Albert allows that Christ, according to a division of the will of reason, willed not to die. As Chapter two has shown, the *Summa fratris Alexan-*

---

37 Albertus Magnus, *Commentarii in III*, d.17, a.4, *sed contra* (Opera omnia 28: 303a): "Contrarietas appetitus in anima non est ex hoc quod ipsi appetitus sunt naturae in nobis contrariae, ut Manichaei dicebant, qui ponebant unum creatum a principe lucis, et alterum a principe tenebrarum: ergo relinquitur, quod ista contrarietas sit ex oppositione volitorum. Haec autem oppositio in nobis inducit pugnam carnis sive inferioris partis animae contra superiorem, id est, contra spiritum: ergo in Christo fuit hujusmodi pugna, quod absurdum est ponere: ergo non fuit in eo talis difformitas voluntatum."

38 Albertus Magnus, *Commentarii in III*, d.17, a.4 (Opera omnia 28: 303a): "Consentiendo primae objectioni, dicendum, quod nihil prohibet, quod secundum voluntatem rationis ut natura est, homo ille in quantum homo, aliquid appetierit quod non est consecutus: et etiam quod non est datum, eo quod non oravit ut ex deliberatione hoc volens, sed potius ut nostram infirmitatem ostendens: sicut ipse dixit discipulis suis: *Spiritus quidem promptus est, caro autem infirma.*"

dri introduced this notion, departing from the earlier view (Peter Lombard's *Sentences* and William of Auxerre's *Summa aurea*) that Christ willed not to die only according to sensuality.

Albert then faces the same problem faced in the *Summa fratris*. If some aspect of Christ's will of reason willed not to die, does this imply a contrariety of wills? The *sed contra*, based upon a denial of contrariety, denies that any aspect of Christ's will of reason lacked its proper effect. Albert responds that "it is not the contrariety of struggle, unless it is a stubborn resistance within, just as in us in whom the will is strengthened from the encouragement of carnal weakness, and at some time from the remnants of sin."[39] Albert denies any such carnal weakness in Christ. Accordingly, "the weakness of the will did not progress beyond the natural, showing itself only in these things for a demonstration of nature, and not for this, that it struggled against reason, but rather that it followed it."[40] William of Auxerre, Albert notes, called this a willingness (*velleitatem*) rather than a complete will (*voluntatem perfectam*).[41] The thrust of the argument here,

---

39 Albertus Magnus, *Commentarii in III*, d.17, a.4, *ad* 1 (Opera omnia 28: 303a): "Ad id autem quod contra objicitur, dico quod non est contrarietas pugnae, nisi inter quae est resistentia pertinax, sicut est in nobis in quibus voluntas infirmitatis carnalis confortatur ex fomite, et quandoque ex reliquiis peccatorum."

40 Albertus Magnus *Commentarii in III*, d.17, a.4, *ad* 1 (Opera omnia 28: 303a): "in Christo autem non fuit talis confortatio: et ideo voluntatis infirmitas progressa non est ultra naturalia, in his tantum ostendens se ad naturae demonstrationem, et non ad hoc quod pugnaret contra rationem, sed potius quod sequeretur."

41 "In his discussion of Aristotle's notion of choice in his second commentary, Albert only briefly mentions the Augustinian analysis of will. In order to distinguish between will and choice, he cites Aristotle's dictum (EN [*Nicomachean Ethics*] 1111b20–22) that the will alone can will even impossible things; but choice cannot relate to impossibles, because rational deliberation (*consilium*) eliminates the impossible alternatives. Albert remarks here about *velleitas*. According to him, some of the former writers (*antiqui*) identify *velleitas* with Aristotle's *impossibilum voluntas*. This is misleading, because *velleitas* in fact refers to a latent conditional desire: one formulation of this is, 'if it were possible to do this, I would do it.' But such *velleitas* presupposes a rational judgment concerning the situation in question. The Aristotelian notion of *voluntas*, however, denotes only the appetitive faculty without any judgment imposed upon it by the reason" (Risto Saarinen, *Weakness of the Will in Medieval Thought: From Augustine to Buridan* [Leiden, 1994], p. 103). See also Andrea A. Robiglio, *L'impossibile volere: Tommaso d'Aquino, i tomisti e la volontà* (Milan, 2002), p. 65.

however, is to deny contrariety of wills in Christ because there was no contrariety of struggle, no stubborn resistance to reason. This does not deny any and all contrariety of wills, only contrariety implying disorder.

Others, Albert notes, deny contrariety of wills on different grounds. These others hold that "contraries must originate concerning the same (*circa idem*), and sensuality and reason, or natural reason (*ratio naturalis*) and reason, are not concerning the same as the same (*circa idem ut idem*)."[42] Defining the contrariety of struggle in this way would preclude such contrariety not only in Christ but also in every other human being. Contrariety could never arise within one will or one aspect of the will. Rather, "the contrariety of struggle is wholly from contrary 'things willed' laboring to drag [the wills] after themselves."[43] While Albert declines to name these others, it is certain that William of Auxerre and the author(s) of the *Summa fratris Alexandri* are implicated. This rejection of the *circa idem* argument might seem surprising, but more surprising is Albert's focus on contrariety as determined by contrary things willed. In article one's discussion of conformity, he argued that conformity in the thing willed provides no merit of itself and often conflicts with conformity according to the other three modes. What is least important for conformity is most important for contrariety. Through this strategy, Albert allows for some contrariety of wills in Christ, although never of a sinful sort and only in order to preserve conformity of wills.

Only after this novel presentation of contrariety does Albert consider the division of wills in Christ. The objections challenge the Lombard's division of Christ's wills and raise questions about the unity of Christ's actions. The authorities for the objections include John Damascene and Pseudo-Dionysius. Albert's use of these authorities in article five parallels his use of them in *De incarnatione* q.2, a.1, obs.1 and 3. His *solutio* defends the Lombard's division of Christ's wills against the objections of too few and of too

42 Albertus Magnus, *Commentarii in III*, d.17, a.4, *ad* 1 (Opera omnia 28: 303b): "Sunt autem qui aliter solvunt, dicentes quod non est contrarietas: quia contraria sunt nata fieri circa idem, et sensualitas et ratio, vel ratio naturalis et ratio, non sunt circa idem ut idem."
43 Albertus Magnus, *Commentarii in III*, d.17, a.4, *ad* 1 (Opera omnia 28: 303b): "Unde contrarietas pugnae est ex contrariis volitis totam post se trahere nitentibus, quae quandoque volita (licet non sunt contraria in substantia) tamen per adjunctum sunt contraria, scilicet per rationem, ita quod unum est volitum ut honestum, alterum vero ut turpe."

many. The *Sentences* consolidates a three-part division into a two-part division. The Lombard, Albert argues, does not refer to the will of reason as it is nature (*ut natura*). The reason is that "according to substance and to the *esse* of the power, it does not differ from the [will] that is of reason as deliberative, but rather is a certain mode of considering the same power."[44] The Lombard, in Albert's view, made no mention of the will as nature. It is interesting that Albert specifies the absence of this will rather than the absence of any division within the will of reason. The specificity of will as nature explains why the Lombard assigned Christ's every voluntary movement not to die as a movement of sensuality. Albert seeks to supplement the Lombard's position while appearing simply to clarify it.

The second objection reasons that there "is not one mode of denominating the same thing by many forms," concluding that multiple wills in Christ would make Christ multiple willers, which the Damascene denies.[45] The reply first distinguishes forms determining the whole and natural powers. Albert concedes the objection's logic in the case of forms determining the whole, but disagrees concerning natural powers, "because natural powers, although they exist according to diverse parts of nature, nevertheless are referred to one which is the subject: thus the thing denominated by those

---

[44] Albertus Magnus, *Commentarii in III*, d.17, a.5 (Opera omnia 28: 304a): "Dicendum, quod Magister ponit trimembrem divisionem voluntatum Christi, quae sic ad bimembrem potest reduci. Voluntas Christi aut divina sive increata est, aut humana et creata. Humana autem aut rationis, aut sensualitatis est. Rationis vero aut est ut natura, aut est ut deliberativa. Sed non facit mentionem de illa quae est rationis ut est natura: quia secundum substantiam et esse potentiae non differt ab illa quae est rationis ut deliberativa, sed potius est quidam modus considerationis ejusdem potentiae." Thomas Aquinas, in his *Scriptum super libros Sententiarum*, follows Albert on this topic and stresses the unity of power of the will of reason. In the *Summa theologiae*, Thomas repeats affirmation of one power of the will of reason but notes also that this power has two species of acts. One species of acts corresponds to the will as reason, the other to the will as nature.

[45] Albertus Magnus, *Commentarii in III*, d.17, a.5, ob.2 (Opera omnia 28: 303b): "Item, A plurimis formis non est unus modus denominationis ejusdem, ut albedo Socratem denominat album, et grammatica grammaticum, et sic de aliis: ergo videtur a simili, quod a pluribus voluntatibus Christi ipse sit pluribus modis volens, vel plures volentes, quod negat Damascenus, qui dicit eum tamen unum esse volentem."

is nothing but one."[46] The number of willers in Christ is not determined by the number of wills or the number of natures grounding the diverse powers of the wills. Christ is one willer because he is one subject, the one subject to whom all the wills are referred. Albert ends his reply by noting that "a diversity of wills is recognized in a diversity of things willed."[47] Article five confirms the solution of article four, namely that the diversity of things willed by Christ was not the contrariety of struggle but simply showed the truth of Christ's human nature.

An objection in article five holds that Christ's every action is composite and many rather than one, a view seemingly supported by Pseudo-Dionysius's expression theandric. The objection argues that "an act that is from many actors, differing according to essence, is many, and not one: moreover those acting wills in Christ differ according to essence: therefore the acts are of themselves many and not one."[48] Albert's reply agrees that there are distinct actions in Christ and clarifies a proper understanding of that distinction. He argues that "there are distinct actions in Christ: not in comparison to the one acting, namely that Christ is many actors: but with respect to the principle of the acting, namely because he sometimes acted as man, sometimes as God."[49] In both cases, Christ acted as the God-man. Albert explains Pseudo-Dionysius's theandric as a reference to Christ as

---

46 Albertus Magnus, *Commentarii in III*, d.17, a.5, *ad* 2 (Opera omnia 28: 304b): "Sed quia potentiae naturales licet insint secundum diversas partes naturae, tamen referuntur ad unum quod est subjectum: ideo denominatum ab eis non est nisi unum: et ideo Christus non est nisi unus volens, licet multis modis possit velle: quia volens dicit eum qui vult, hoc est subjectum, et non radicem in qua fundatur potentia illa: sed diversitas voluntatem cognoscitur in diversitate volitorum."

47 Albertus Magnus, *Commentarii in III*, d.17, a.5, *ad* 2 (Opera omnia 28: 304b): "sed diversitas voluntatum cognoscitur in diversitate volitorum."

48 Albertus Magnus, *Commentarii in III*, d.17, a.5, ob.4 (Opera omnia 28: 304a): "Item, Videtur relinqui ex hoc quod omnis actio Christi sit composita, et non una, sed plures: actus enim qui est a pluribus agentibus differentibus secundum essentiam, est plures, et non unus: istae autem voluntates agentes in Christo differunt secundum essentiam: ergo sunt actus, sui plures, et non unus."

49 Albertus Magnus, *Commentarii in III*, d.17, a.5, *ad* 4 (Opera omnia 28: 304b): "Ad aliud dicendum, quod in Christo sunt actiones distinctae: non in comparatione ad agentem, scilicet quod Christus sit plures agentes: sed quoad rationem agendi, scilicet quia aliquando egit ut homo, aliquando ut Deus."

one actor, the God-man. The Damascene, Albert notes, viewed Christ's actions in terms of the natural powers involved in an act.[50] The one actor Christ acted always as the God-man, exercising both the divine and human natural powers, and thus Christ's every action was as the God-man and so was for salvation.[51]

Albert subsequently turns to the familiar question of Christ's prayer at Gethsemane and whether it was from sensuality or from reason. The *solutio* succinctly responds that Christ's "prayer was from reason as it is nature, and conjoined in the same substance with the sensual affection."[52] Albert previously noted that the Lombard did not discuss the will as nature (*voluntas ut natura*) (d.17, a.5). The Lombard's silence regarding this division of the will of reason explains why he limited Christ's prayer to sensuality. Recognition of the will as nature and its movement not to die provides an avenue through which Albert can explain Christ's prayer as from reason and not simply by reason, extending the basic view of the *Summa fratris Alexandri* and continuing the trend toward recognition of a rational fear of death begun already in the *Summa aurea*.

Albert the Great inherited from William of Auxerre's *Summa aurea* and from the *Summa fratris Alexandri* a trend toward fuller recognition of Christ's rational fear of death and rational movement to avoid death. Albert continued this trend in his *De incarnatione* and *Commentarii in Sententiarum*, allowing that at Gethsemane, Christ willed to die according to his will as reason but willed not to die according to his will as nature and will of sensuality. Most striking is Albert's presentation of contrariety and con-

---

50   The fourth objection made no mention of the Damascene. Albert provides no citation but probably has in mind the Damascene's description of the human and divine actions involved in Christ's healing of a leper (*De fide orthodoxa* III.15).
51   Albertus Magnus, *Commentarii in III*, d.17, a.5, *ad* 4 (Opera omnia 28: 304b): "Et nota, quod hoc ipsum quod agens fuit unus Deus et homo, et inclinantia ad actum duo, scilicet creatum et increatum, facit omnem Christi actionem nobis salutarem: quia etiamsi comedit et dormivit, verum erat quod Deus hoc fecit: et ita pro nobis fecit, qui pro se non habuit quid faceret talium. Et idem est de tristitia, timore, et omnibus aliis." Thomas Aquinas will develop this principle of the salvific value of Christ's every action.
52   Albertus Magnus, *Commentarii in III*, d.17, a.7 (Opera omnia 28: 307b): "Dicendum ad hoc, quod oratio fuit rationis ut est natura, et conjuncta in eadem substantia cum sensuali affectu: et haec bene potest ordinare: et sic cessat objectio prima."

formity as related but separable issues. Through this separation, he can allow for some contrariety of wills in Christ based upon the will as nature willing to avoid death. This contrariety represents no disorder and implies no struggle but simply shows that according to diverse aspects of the will of reason, Christ willed contrary things. The greater conformity of Christ's human will to his divine will required a specific and isolated non-conformity in the thing willed. This non-conformity implies some, though morally insignificant, contrariety. Bonaventure follows Albert in rejecting the *secundum idem* argument for denying contrariety of wills in Christ but does not follow to the end Albert's solution to the issue. Influenced by Hugh of St Victor's *De quatuor voluntatibus Christi*, Bonaventure denies any contrariety of wills in Christ. Despite Bonaventure's divergence from Albert on this point, the Seraphic Doctor follows Albert in stressing conformity as the most meaningful category for judging Christ's wills.

Bonaventure

Giovanni di Fidanza was born in Bagnoregio between 1217 and 1221, taking the name Bonaventure when he entered the Franciscan order around 1243.[53] He studied under Alexander of Hales and John de la Rochelle until their deaths in 1245, continuing then under Odo Rigaldus and William of Meliton.[54] From 1250 to 1252, Bonaventure commented on Peter Lombard's *Sentences*, and from 1254 to 1257 served as regent master for the Franciscans in Paris. Bonaventure's academic career ended with his election as minister general on 2 February 1257. Not long before his death in 1274, Bonaventure was named Cardinal Bishop of Albano in 1273.[55]

Bonaventure's Christology has received substantial attention, for good reason.[56] Christology stands at the center of his theology. According to him

---

53 See Hayes, "Bonaventure" and Jaques-Guy Bougerol, *Introduction to the Works of Bonaventure*, trans. José de Vinck (Paterson, NJ, 1964).
54 For a brief discussion of these four figures and Bonaventure's studies under them, see Bougerol, *Introduction*, pp. 16–18.
55 For a chronology of Bonaventure's life and works, see Bougerol, *Introduction*, pp. 171–177.
56 On Bonaventure's Christology, see Zachary Hayes, *The Hidden Center: Spirituality and Speculative Christology in St Bonaventure* (New York, 1981). Hayes provides an overview of Bonaventure's Christology as well as a discussion of key themes, including Bonaventure's treatment of Christ's wills in the *Commentaria*.

the Word of God is the exemplar of all creation, and in the Incarnation, the Word becomes the exemplar from within creation.[57] All of Christ's actions were for our instruction, though not all were for our imitation.[58] Bonaventure keeps this principle in mind when treating Christ's two wills. The topic of Christ's wills received far less attention from Bonaventure than the topic of Christ's knowledge, which Bonaventure treated several times and in various contexts. Though he perceived investigating Christ's knowledge as the more pressing topic, Christ's knowledge intimately affects Christ's wills.[59] This interest in Christ's human knowledge reveals with particular clarity a great concern to explore the truth and richness of Christ's humanity.[60] Given this great concern and given Albert the Great's

---

[57] On exemplarity in Bonaventure, see Efrem Bettoni, *Saint Bonaventure*, trans. Angelus Gambatese (Westport, CT, 1981). "If, at one level, Bonaventure sums up his metaphysical vision in three words – emanation, exemplarity, return – at another level he argues that there is a sense in which the most basic metaphysical question is simply that of the exemplar, or the original model in whose likeness all things have been shaped. Here the great Platonic tradition is given a specifically Christian content, for, as is clear from Bonaventure's trinitarian theology, the exemplar in a preeminent sense is the Word who lives at the very center of God and who, as incarnate, is the center of all created reality. Here is the key to Bonaventure's conviction that the greatest metaphysical question cannot be answered – and perhaps not even asked – in ignorance of the incarnation. We are here at the core of a vision which involves a truly cosmic Christology. The reality of Christ pertains to the very structure of reality: as Word, to the reality of God; as incarnate Word, to the reality of the universe created by God" (Hayes, "Bonaventure," p. 72).

[58] On the imitation of Christ, see Ignatius Brady, "St Bonaventure's Theology of the Imitation of Christ," in *Proceedings of the Seventh Centenary Celebration of the Death of Saint Bonaventure*, ed. Pascal F. Foley (St Bonaventure, NY, 1975), pp. 61–72.

[59] "Since, in scholastic thought, there is an intrinsic relation between being and knowing, it is inevitable that when the Christ-mystery is approached in terms of its essential structure, theology will be moved, at some point, to reflect on the impact of this most intimate relation with God would have on the human intellect and will of Jesus. In this sense, the question of Jesus' human knowledge and freedom becomes an important matter for speculative theology" (Hayes, "Bonaventure," p. 89). Thomas Aquinas follows Bonaventure in connecting Christ's human intellect and human will.

[60] "It is, therefore, not an abstract or universal human nature that is assumed, but a concrete, individual nature which includes the same essential elements as does any other concrete, individual human nature" (Hayes, *The Hidden Center*, p. 67). "From this it becomes clear why Bonaventure, in his own way, would

confidence in proposing novel interpretations of contrariety of wills in Christ, Bonaventure's treatment of Christ's wills stand out for its calm reservation. Rather than adjudicating between various schemes for dividing Christ's wills or between those who allow and those who deny in Christ a rational voluntary movement not to die, Bonaventure takes pains to indicate the strengths of each view and to stress the conformity of Christ's will to the divine will.

Since Bonaventure studied under Alexander of Hales and John de la Rochelle, it is not surprising that his *Commentaria* bears a heavy debt to the *Summa fratris Alexandri*.[61] More interesting are those points at which Bonaventure diverges from the views of his masters. One such point of divergence occurs in *Commentaria in III*, d.17. Before analyzing Bonaventure's view on contrariety of wills and comparing it to the view of the *Summa aurea* and *Summa fratris Alexandri*, we must investigate his presentation of Christ's two wills in the *Commentaria*.

Bonaventure takes d.17 to inaugurate a new part within the Lombard's discussion of the nature assumed, focusing on the exercise of virtue (*usum virtutis*). He divides this part itself into two. This first treats of will as the source for the exercise of virtue; the second treats merit as the reward for the exercise of virtue. Bonaventure notes that "since the disposition of the will is distinctly recognised through the petition of prayer, hence the Master simultaneously makes his determination about Christ's will and about Christ's prayer."[62] Bonaventure divides consideration of Christ's will and of Christ's prayer. The analysis of Christ's will (a.1) includes three questions: whether there were multiple wills (q.1), the number and sufficiency of the wills (q.2), and the concordance or controversy of these wills (q.3). Article

---

share the common Franciscan concern for the humanity of Jesus. For that humanity, in Bonaventure's view, is the key that unlocks to us the meaning of all reality: created and uncreated. This is not simply a concern for a human nature in the abstract. Rather, it is a concern for the actual shape which the life of Jesus took in history" (Hayes, "Bonaventure," pp. 84–85).

61 Bougerol notes that Bonaventure repeatedly called Alexander his father and master. Bougerol proposes a close friendship between the two. See Bougerol, *Introduction*, p. 4.

62 Bonaventure, *Commentaria in III*, d.17, divisio textus (ed. PP. Collegii Bonaventurae, Opera theologica selecta 3: 356a [Quaracchi, 1934–1964]): "Et quoniam affectus voluntatis dignoscitur per petitionem orationis, ideo Magister simul determinat de voluntate Christi et de oratione Christi."

two on Christ's prayer also has three questions: whether it was proper for Christ to pray (q.1), whether his every prayer was heard (q.2), and whether the prayer in the garden was from sensuality or from reason (q.3). The difference between the structure of Bonaventure's commentary on d.17 and Albert's is striking, although there is much continuity between them otherwise. Bonaventure follows the *Summa fratris Alexandri* in first defending multiple wills in Christ. Four arguments *pro* begin the consideration, followed by four *contra* arguments. The first two *pro* arguments quote John 6:38 (a passage cited by the Lombard in support of diverse wills) and John Damascene (*De fide orthodoxa* III.19, a passage not cited by previous thirteenth-century authors on this topic). The third argument ties multiple wills to multiple intellectual natures. The fourth notes that Christ both merited, which is an action proper to a created will, and created all things, an action proper to the divine will.

The *contra* arguments begin with a quotation from the Damascene. This draws attention not only for the authority but also for the logic. The quotation reads: "Of which things the substance is one and the same, the will of these is also one and the same; and of which things the will is diverse, the substance of those is diverse." The argument continues that "the divine nature and the human nature are united in Christ in unity of hypostasis, which is an individual substance, such that in Christ there are not multiple hypostases, but one: therefore if in Christ multiple hypostases are not found, neither are multiple wills."[63] As this argument denies two wills in Christ because there is only one hypostasis in Christ, Bonaventure replies by clarifying the meaning of hypostatic union and the various senses of substance, and he uses this clarification to defend Christ's possession of two wills. The remaining three *contra* arguments similarly depend upon a misconception of Christ's wills in terms of the hypostatic union and set the stage for later considerations of contrariety.

---

63 Bonaventure, *Commentaria in III*, d.17, a.1, q.1, *contra* 1 (Opera theologica selecta 3: 357a–357b): "Damascenus, in libro III [*De fide orthodoxa* III.14]: 'Quorum substantia est eadem, horum et voluntas est eadem; et quorum diversa voluntas, horum diversa substantia.' Sed divina natura et humana uniuntur in Christo in unitate hypostasis, quae est substantia individua, ita quod in Christo non sunt plures hypostases, sed una: ergo, si in Christo non est reperire plures hypostases, nec plures voluntates."

Bonaventure's response, echoing the *Summa aurea*, affirms multiple wills in Christ "since there are in Christ multiple intellectual natures."[64] Cognition and affection in spiritual natures correspond to light and heat in a noble, corporeal nature. Both must be present in their respective nature. Cognition is the act of reason; affection is the act of the will.[65] These reasons suffice for agreeing with the *pro* arguments, but Bonaventure replies to the *contra* arguments at length. These replies by and large focus on qualifying the union of human and divine in Christ as hypostatic union, grounded in the Lombard's second opinion, and explaining the meaning of hypostatic union for the will.

The first *contra* argument cites the Damascene and links will and substance. Substance, as Bonaventure notes, can name the thing as *nature* or the thing as *supposit*. He does not here explain the distinction but simply relies upon it to separate the Damascene's assertions from the argument's conclusion. The Damascene links will with nature, while the argument draws its conclusion based upon substance as supposit. Bonaventure then

---

64 Bonaventure, *Commentaria in III*, d.17, a.1, q.1 (Opera theologica selecta 3: 357b): "Dicendum quod, cum in Christo sint plures naturae intellectuales, videlicet divina et humana, necesse est in Christo plures esse voluntates. – Sicut enim in una natura corporali nobili ista duo se concomitantur, videlicet lux et calor, sic et in natura spirituali perfecta necesse est duo reperiri his duobus correspondentia, videlicet cognitionem et affectionem; sed cognitio est actus rationis, et affectio voluntatis." Bonaventure here recalls and modifies the *Summa aurea*. William of Auxerre writes, "Dicto de duplici scientia Christi, dicendum est de duplici voluntate eius" (*Summa aurea* III, tr.6, c.1 [William of Auxerre, *Summa aurea Guillelmi Altissiodorensis*, ed. Jean Ribaillier, vol. 3.1 [Grottaferrata, 1986], p. 77]). Bonaventure substitutes 'naturae intellectuales' for 'scientia.' This change reflects Bonaventure's interest in distinguishing the various types of knowledge possessed by Christ. Bonaventure was profoundly interested in Christ's knowledge, and he seems to have changed his opinion (or at least his terminology) during his career. For more on Bonaventure's discussions of Christ's knowledge and the debates about development of his thought, see Hayes, *The Hidden Center*, pp. 112–113, and his introduction to Bonaventure's *Disputed Questions on the Knowledge of Christ*, ed. and trans. Zachary Hayes (St Bonaventure, NY, 2005), pp. 21–67.

65 For more on the connection between intellect and will, see Etienne Gilson, *The Philosophy of St Bonaventure*, trans. Illtyd Trethowan and Frank J. Sheed (New York, 1938), pp. 404–430.

quotes the *De fide orthodoxa* in that will follows nature and not hypostasis or person. If such were not the case, then there would be three wills in God on account of the three persons.[66]

The remaining three *contra* arguments develop along similar lines: since Christ was one willer, had one dominion, or had one personality, there could be only one will in Christ. Bonaventure's reply to the first *contra* argument distinguishes what pertains to nature and what pertains to hypostasis or person. That distinction serves as the foundation for Bonaventure's replies to the remaining *contra* arguments, showing his skill in the plan for this question. To the second objection, Bonaventure replies that the 'will makes a willer' "is, speaking *per se*, understood of nature, but, speaking *per consequens*, it is understood of person; and since multiple natures could be in one person: it is for this reason that from a plurality of wills, even if a plurality of natures follows, nevertheless a plurality of persons does not follow."[67] Multiple wills imply multiple natures but not multiple persons. Again, Bonaventure does not here explain how there can be multiple natures in one person, a task completed in earlier distinctions. Proper

---

66 Bonaventure, *Commentaria in III*, d.17, a.1, q.1, *ad* 1 (Opera theologica selecta 3: 358a): "Ad illud vero quod obiicitur, quod quorum substantia est eadem, et voluntas est eadem, dicendum quod *substantia* dicitur multipliciter: uno modo dicitur substantia idem quod essentia vel natura; alio modo dicitur substantia idem quod suppositum. Damascenus autem in praedicta auctoritate accipit substantiam pro essentia vel natura. Argumentum vero in contrarium adductum procedit de substantia-supposito sive substantia quae est individua; et hoc patet per ipsum Damascenum. Ipse enim dicit sic: 'Naturales, et non hypostaticas, id est personales, aimus voluntates' [*De fide orthodoxa* III.14]; et hoc probat ipse, quia in tribus personis una est voluntas, non propter unitatem in personis, sed propter unitatem in natura."

67 Bonaventure, *Commentaria in III*, d.17, a.1, q.1, *ad* 2 (Opera theologica selecta 3: 358a): "Ad illud quod obiicitur, quod voluntas facit volentem, dicendum quod hoc, per se loquendo, intelligitur de natura, per consequens autem intelligitur de persona; et quoniam plures naturae possunt esse in una persona, hinc est quod ad pluralitatem voluntatum, etsi consequatur pluralitas naturarum, non tamen consequitur personarum pluralitas." Bonaventure confirms his interpretation through a quotation of the Damascene: "Et hoc est quod dicit Damascenus: 'Quia duas naturas Christi duas eius naturales voluntates et naturales actus aimus. Quoniam autem una duarum naturarum est hypostasis, unum aimus et volentem et agentem naturaliter secundum ambas' [*De fide orthodoxa* III.14]" (Bonaventure, *Commentaria in III*, d.17, a.1, q.1, *ad* 2 [Opera theologica selecta, 3: 358a]).

understanding of Christ's two wills depends upon proper understanding of the hypostatic union.

The third *contra* argument holds that one dominion in Christ forbade multiple wills. Bonaventure's reply hinges on distinguishing "exercising authority and dominion through lack of coercion" and "exercising authority and dominion through lack of subjection."[68] Exercising authority and dominion through lack of coercion is synonymous with the will itself. Taken in this sense, there can be more than one dominion in Christ, "just as in Christ free choice is found according to the divine nature and the human nature."[69] Christ can freely act as God and as man. This does not, however, imply multiple dominions through lack of subjection. Exercising authority through lack of subjection "is not proper to every will; for it is not proper to the human will, which ought to be subject to the divine will, but it is proper to that will which has nothing superior to itself."[70] Without compromise to its freedom, the human will ought to be subject to the divine will. This principle returns in Bonaventure's discussion of harmony of wills in Christ (a.1, q.3).

The fourth *contra* argument focuses on will as a property pertaining to dignity and so to personality. This objection should be read in light of the definition of person perhaps first stated by Alexander of Hales: "Person is

---

68   Bonaventure, *Commentaria in III*, d.17, a.1, q.1, *ad* 3 (Opera theologica selecta 3: 358a–358b): "Ad illud obicitur, quod voluntas dicit illud, penes quod residet regimen et imperium eorum quae sunt in ipso volente, dicendum quod est imperans et dominans per privationem coactionis, et est imperans et dominans per privationem subiectionis."

69   Bonaventure, *Commentaria in III*, d.17, a.1, q.1, *ad* 3 (Opera theologica selecta 3: 358b): "Primo modo accipiendo imperans convenit ipsi voluntati generaliter; et hoc modo possibile est plura imperantia reperiri in eodem in quo reperiuntur plura a coactione libera, sicut in Christo est reperire liberum arbitrium secundum divinam naturam et humanam." Defending free choice (*liberum arbitrium*) in Christ became an increasingly important task in the thirteenth century, particularly as the so-called Latin Averroists denied free choice in general.

70   Bonaventure, *Commentaria in III*, d.17, a.1, q.1, *ad* 3 (Opera theologica selecta 3: 358b): "Si autem dicatur imperans et dominans per privationem omnis subiectionis, sic bene concedendum est quod necesse est esse unum solum. Sed tale imperium non competit omni voluntati; non enim competit voluntati humanae, quae debet esse subiecta divinae, sed illi voluntati competit quae nihil habet superius se. Ideo ex hoc non potest argui quod in Christo non sint plures voluntates, sed quod non sint plures voluntates divinae."

a hypostasis distinct through a property pertaining to dignity."[71] If the power of the will is identified with this property pertaining to dignity, then multiple wills in Christ would imply multiple persons. Bonaventure must distinguish the will from the property of dignity marking personhood. He writes:

> I say therefore that personality is taken as belonging to the dignity of excellence in respect of all things that are in the person himself, and thus in one [person] there cannot be but one personality; the will, however, is not so, because it names the noble and perfect power of a rational substance. And thus, just as multiple noble natures can be compatible with each other in the one person in Christ, so also multiple wills.[72]

In broad outline, the next question resembles the fifth article of Albert the Great's commentary on d.17. Bonaventure follows Albert in questioning whether the Lombard recognized too many or too few wills. Question two first presents four arguments critiquing the Lombard's three-part division as superfluous and four *contra* arguments affirming the necessity of a four-part division. The *contra* arguments are particularly interesting for their authorities. The first quotes from Hugh of St Victor's *De quatuor voluntatibus Christi*.[73] Hugh recognizes a threefold division of Christ's human will into the will of reason, the will of tender pity, and the will of the flesh. Bonaventure will quote from Hugh again in his response. The second *contra* argument proposes of will of *synderesis* (moral sense) parallel to the will of sensuality. The third cites the Damascene's division of the will into "*thelē-*

---

71 "Persona est hypostasis distincta proprietate ad dignitatem pertinente" (Alexander of Hales, *Glossa in quatuor libros Sententiarum Petri Lombardi*, ed. PP. Collegii S. Bonaventurae [Quaracchi, 1951–1957], 1: 226, d.23.9).
72 Bonaventure, *Commentaria in III*, d.17, a.1, q.1, *ad* 4 (Opera theologica selecta 3: 358b): "Dico ergo quod personalitas accipitur penes dignitatem excellentiae respectu omnium quae sunt in ipsa persona, et ideo in uno non potest esse nisi una personalitas; voluntas autem non sic, quia dicit potentiam substantiae rationalis nobilem et perfectam. Et ideo sicut plures naturae nobiles possunt se compati in una persona in Christo, sic et plures voluntates."
73 For a brief discussion of the *De quatuor voluntatibus Christi*, see Chapter two (pp. 34–35) above.

sis and *boulēsis*, that is into natural and deliberative."[74] Bonaventure replies to these three arguments together and based upon his response. The final *contra* argument seeks a correspondence between divisions of the will and the four genera of cognitive powers in Christ.[75] The connection between intellect and will established in question one only seems to strengthen this contention.

Bonaventure reconciles these seemingly competing authorities by noting "that the will has to be considered in three ways: either according to nature, or according to power, through which someone wills, or according to mode of willing."[76] Christ's will, considered according to nature, is twofold, divine and human. The Lombard's three-part division suffices according to the "powers through which someone wills," because "in Christ there was the divine power and the created rational power and the sensitive power, through whichever of those [the will] went forth in the act of willing."[77] The created rational power and the sensitive power follow intellective cognition and sensitive cognition respectively. While this supports dividing the human will into rational and sensitive, it seems to support the

---

[74] Bonaventure, *Commentaria in III*, d.17, a.1, q.2, *contra* 3 (Opera theologica selecta 3: 359b): "Item, voluntas secundum Damascenum, dividitur prima divisione in thelesim et bulesim, hoc est in naturalem et deliberativam; istae duae differentiae constat quod fuerunt in Christo, sicut et praedictae: ergo videtur quod Christus habuerit voluntates plures quam tres."

[75] Bonaventure, *Commentaria in III*, d.17, a.1, q.2, *contra* 4 (Opera theologica selecta, 3: 359b): "Item, voluntas sequitur cognitionem; sed in Christo est reperire quatuor genera virtutum cognoscitivarum, quia in ipso cognoscebat sensus exterior, cognoscebat sensus interior, cognoscebat intellectus humanus, cognoscebat intellectus divinus. Si ergo cuilibet cognitioni respondet affectio, et cuilibet affectioni voluntas, videtur quod in Christo fuerit quadruplex voluntatis differentia."

[76] Bonaventure, *Commentaria in III*, d.17, a.1, q.2 (Opera theologica selecta, 3: 359b): "Ad praedictorum intelligentiam est notandum quod voluntas tripliciter habet considerari: aut secundum naturam aut secundum potentiam per quam quis vult aut secundum modum volendi."

[77] Bonaventure, *Commentaria in III*, d.17, a.1, q.2 (Opera theologica selecta, 3: 360a): "Si autem consideretur voluntas secundum potentias per quas quis vult, sic dividi habet divisione trimembri. Nam in Christo fuit potentia divina et potentia rationalis creata et potentia sensitiva, per quarum quamlibet in actum volendi exibat."

final *contra* argument's assertion of a fourfold will following Christ's four genera of cognitive powers.[78]

The response last addresses the will according to the mode of willing, which requires a fourfold division of Christ's will. Bonaventure declines to name the fourfold division in his own words and prefers instead to quote at length from Hugh of St Victor. Again, Hugh divides Christ's will into the will of divinity, the will of reason, the will of tender pity, and the will of the flesh.[79] Hugh's *De quatuor voluntatibus Christi* exercised no discernible influence on scholastic treatments of Christ's will prior to Bonaventure and this extensive quotation of Hugh is interesting beyond its novelty. John Damascene (as noted in *contra* 3) posited a division between *natural* and *deliberative* will. Bonaventure provides no immediate indication of how to reconcile these two schemes of fourfold division, though he attempts to do so in reply to the first three *contra* arguments.

---

78 Bonaventure replies to the fourth *contra* argument by equating the appetite of the exterior and interior sensitive cognition. "Ad illud quod obiicitur, quod quadruplex est in Christo cognitio, et ita quadruplex debet esse affectio, dicendum quod cognitio sensitiva exterior non habet perfectionem absque interiori. Sicut enim vult Augustinus, non est perfecta visio ex concursu organi et obiecti, nisi adsit interior intentio copulans unum cum altero, sicut dicitur in libro De Trinitate, XI. Illam autem intentionem vocat Augustinus sensualitatem, dicens quod sensualitas est illa 'per quam intenditur in corporis sensus'; et penes hanc attenditur appetitus carnis. Et ideo Magister ex parte cognitionis sensitivae unam tantum ponit voluntatem, scilicet voluntatem sensualitatis; si enim acciperet secundum sensus exteriores, iam non una, sed quinque essent voluntates secundum quinque differentias sensuum exteriorum" (Bonaventure, *Commentaria in III*, d.17, a.1, q.2, *ad contra* 4 [Opera theologica selecta 3: 360b–361a]).

79 Bonaventure, *Commentaria in III*, d.17, a.1, q.2 (Opera theologica selecta 3: 360a): "Per comparationem autem voluntatis ad modum volendi habet multiplicari voluntas in Christo divisione quadrimembri; et sic consideravit magister Hugo voluntatem Christi cum eam per quatuor membra divisit. Ait enim sic [*De quatuor voluntatibus Christi*]: 'In Christo fuit voluntas Divinitatis et voluntas rationis et voluntas pietatis et voluntas carnis: voluntas Divinitatis per iustitiam sententiam dictabat, voluntas rationalis per obedientiam veritatem approbabat, voluntas pietatis per compassionem in malo alieno suspirabat, voluntas carnis per passionem in malo proprio murmurabat.'"

Scholastic Debates on Christ's Two Wills | 99

The replies to the objections distinguish a strict sense of will as rational appetite from a broader sense of will as any appetite or disposition.[80] This broad sense of will allows the threefold division of will according to power, a division Bonaventure defends as sufficient despite the division according to modes of willing:

> To that which is objected that there ought to be many more [wills] through the authority of Hugh and on account of synderesis and thelē-sis and boulēsis; it should be said that from these authorities it cannot be argued that in Christ there are more than three wills, unless the division of the will is taken according to the mode of willing; through which mode the rational will has to be multiplied into the will of reason and of tender pity, that is, according to conditional and absolute; also it has to be divided into natural and deliberative. But, it cannot be argued through this that the above-mentioned division is insufficient, because it is taken according to power; for multiple modes of willing can correspond to one power.[81]

Bonaventure here both defends the distinction between power and mode of willing and harmonizes the terminological variations between Hugh of St Victor and John Damascene. He cites Hugh at far greater length than the Damascene and prefers Hugh's language to the Damascene's. Nevertheless,

---

80 Bonaventure, *Commentaria in III*, d.17, a.1, q.2, *ad* 2 (Opera theologica selecta 3: 360a–360b): "Ad illud quod obiicitur de verbo Philosophi, quod voluntas est in sola rationali, dicendum quod Philosophus accipit voluntatem stricte, videlicet pro appetitu ratiocinativo; Magister autem et Sancti accipiunt voluntatem large ad omnem humanum affectum, sive procedat ex ratione sive procedat ex sensu."

81 Bonaventure, *Commentaria in III*, d.17, a.1, q.2, *ad contra* 1, 2, and 3 (Opera theologica selecta 3: 360b): "Ad illud quod obiicitur, quod multo plures deberent esse per auctoritatem Hugonis et propter synderesim et thelesim et bulesim, dicendum quod ex illis auctoritatibus non potest argui quod in Christo sint plures voluntates quam tres, nisi accipiatur divisio voluntatis secundum modo volendi; per quem modum rationalis voluntas multiplicari habet in voluntatem rationis et pietatis, hoc est secundum conditionalem et absolutam, dividi etiam habet in naturalem et deliberativam. Sed per hoc non potest argui quod preadicta divisio sit insufficiens, quia accepta est secundum potentias; uni enim potentiae possunt respondere plures modi volendi."

Hugh's linguistic scheme is explained through the distinction of absolute and conditional, which is the scholastic differentiation between *thelēsis* and *boulēsis*. Bonaventure dances easily between these two schemes and employs both, as they further his argument.

The final question of article one investigates the conformity and concordance of Christ's wills, extending the lines of argumentation developed throughout article one. This question offers an interesting point of comparison and contrast between Bonaventure, on the one hand, and William of Auxerre, the *Summa fratris Alexandri*, and Albert the Great, on the other hand. Bonaventure agrees with Albert in critiquing the *circa idem et secundum idem* argument of William and the *Summa fratris*. His use of Hugh, however, leads his response in a slightly different direction than that taken by Albert, advancing the discussion of conformity of wills while returning to some older lines of thought.

The first three objections deny conformity between Christ's human and divine wills. The second three deny conformity between Christ's sensuality and reason. Two of these objections deserve special attention. Objection one cites Jesus's prayer 'Not as I will, but as you' (Matt. 26:39) to prove the non-conformity of Christ's human will to the divine will.[82] Bonaventure's reply to this objection defends his response and critiques the view forwarded in the *Summa aurea* and in the *Summa fratris Alexandri*. The fourth objection takes Christ's will of reason and will of sensuality to be opposed based upon Augustine's view (*De Trinitate* XI, c.6) that "wills are contrary, which are of contrary things willed."[83] Citation of this principle goes back through the *Summa fratris Alexandri* (III, tr.4, q.1, c.2, *contra* 1) to the *Summa aurea* (III, tr.6, c.1, *contra* 1). Bonaventure fol-

---

82   Bonaventure, *Commentaria in III*, d.17, a.1, q.3, ob.1 (Opera theologica selecta 3: 361a): "Ex ipsa dominica oratione, qua dicebat: *Non sicut ego volo, sed sicut tu vis*. Ergo aliud volebat Christus secundum quod homo, et oppositum secundum quod Deus: ergo voluntas humana non erat conformis divinae."
83   Bonaventure, *Commentaria in III*, d.17, a.1, q.3, ob.4 (Opera theologica selecta 3: 361b): "Item, videtur, quod voluntas rationis et sensualitatis adversentur sibi invicem, quia, secundum quod dicit Augustinus, De Trinitate, voluntates sunt contrariae quae sunt contrariorum volitorum; sed voluntas rationis volebat mori, voluntas sensualitatis volebat vivere: ergo sensualitatis et rationis erant voluntates contrariae."

lows Augustine here in using the qualification 'contrary' for opposing wills.[84]

The *contra* arguments also borrow from the *Summa fratris Alexandri*. The first two *contra* arguments deny any opposition between Christ's human will and the divine will. Opposition, failure of subjection, or movement toward something illicit would imply disorder, fault, and sin. None of these were in Christ, and so all opposition of his human will to the divine will must be denied.[85] The third and fourth *contra* arguments deny any opposition between Christ's will of reason and will of sensuality. The arguments deny any desiring of the flesh against the spirit (Gal. 5:17) and attribute to Christ the harmony of wills characteristic of Adam in the state of innocence.[86]

---

84   Despite the prevalence of the term 'contrary' in the traditional discussions of Christ's two wills, Bonaventure more often writes of repugnant (*repugnantes*) wills or of wills opposing (*adversabantur*) one another. In the response of question three, Bonaventure defends Christ's conformity of wills. From this it is not entirely certain whether or to what extent Bonaventure recognizes Albert the Great's distinction between the questions of conformity and contrariety of wills.

85   Bonaventure, *Commentaria in III*, d.17, a.1, q.3, *contra* 1 (Opera theologica selecta 3: 361b): "Voluntas humana secundum rectum ordinem debet esse subiecta divinae. Ergo, si in Christo repugnabat, videtur quod in Christo erat inordinatio et culpa." Bonaventure, *Commentaria in III*, d.17, a.1, q.3, *contra* 2 (Opera theologica selecta 3: 361b): "Item, omnis motus qui adversatur voluntati divinae est motus ad illicitum; et omnis talis motus est peccatum: ergo, si Christus secundum humanam voluntatem aliquid volebat adversum voluntati divinae, ergo in Christo erat peccatum. Sed hoc est falsum: ergo etc." Both of these arguments recall arguments from the *Summa fratris Alexandri* III, tr.4, c.2.

86   Bonaventure, *Commentaria in III*, d.17, a.1, q.3, *contra* 3 (Opera theologica selecta 3: 361b–362a): "Item, aut voluntas sensualitatis in Christo subiacebat omnino rationi aut adversabatur. Si omnino subiacebat, ergo nulla erat ibi repugnantia. Si adversabatur in aliquo, ergo caro in Christo concupiscebat adversus spiritum. Sed 'nonnullum vitium est, cum *caro concupiscit adversus spiritum*': ergo in Christo fuisset vitium et peccatum." Bonaventure, *Commentaria in III*, d.17, a.1, q.3, *contra* 4 (Opera theologica selecta 3: 362a): "Item, aeque ordinatus vel ordinatior fuit Christus in se ipso sicut Adam in statu innocentiae; sed in statu innocentiae nulla fuit in Adam repugnantia voluntatum: ergo nec in Christo fuit aliqua repugnantia voluntatis sensualitatis ad rationalem nec rationis ad divinam: ergo nulla."

The objections and *contra* arguments borrow heavily from the *Summa fratris Alexandri*. Considering this, it comes as some surprise that the response proposes a scheme reminiscent of Albert's. Bonaventure writes, "It should be noted that conformity of will to will consists in two things, namely in the thing willed and in the reason for willing."[87] Conformity in the thing willed means diverse wills willing "one and the same thing." Bonaventure acknowledges "conformity in the reason for willing when [diverse wills] will the same thing in the same way, or when one of them wills something in the very way in which the superior will willed it to will."[88] Conformity of wills necessarily requires conformity in the reason for willing but requires conformity in the thing willed "sometimes of necessity, sometimes according to fittingness, sometimes beyond necessity and fittingness."[89] Bonaventure justifies his reading of conformity with reference to a superior and inferior will. The inferior will is conformed to the superior will when properly subject to the superior will. This need not consist in agreement in the thing willed, for the superior will might not will the inferior will to agree in the thing willed. In fact, the superior will may will the inferior to will a contrary thing.[90] When Bonaventure applies this scheme to Christ's wills, he writes not of contrary things willed but rather of the non-identity of the things willed:

87 Bonaventure, *Commentaria in III*, d.17, a.1, q.3 (Opera theologica selecta 3: 362a): "Ad praedictorum intelligentiam est notandum quod conformitas voluntatis ad voluntatem in duobus consistit, videlicet in volito et in ratione volendi."
88 Bonaventure, *Commentaria in III*, d.17, a.1, q.3 (Opera theologica selecta 3: 362a): "Conformitatem in volito dico, quando diversae voluntates unum et idem volunt. Conformitatem in ratione volendi dico, quando idem eodem modo volunt vel altera earum vult illud eodem modo quo superior vult eam velle."
89 Bonaventure, *Commentaria in III*, d.17, a.1, q.3 (Opera theologica selecta 3: 362a): "Cum igitur ad perfectam conformitatem ista duo concurrant, alterum eorum est de necessitate conformitatis, videlicet conformitas in modo; alterum vero aliquando de necessitate, aliquando de congruitate, aliquando praeter necessitatem et congruitatem, videlicet conformitas in volito."
90 Bonaventure, *Commentaria in III*, d.17, a.1, q.3 (Opera theologica selecta 3: 362a): "Possibile est enim quod voluntates sint conformes, ita quod una subsit alteri; et tamen non volunt idem, quia voluntas superior non vult inferiorem velle quod ipsa vult, sed magis velle contrarium."

Since, therefore, conformity in the reason for willing was in Christ's every will, because sensuality willed thus, just as reason willed it to will; also Christ's reason willed thus, just as the divine will willed it to will: thus it should be conceded that in Christ there was concordance and consonance of wills, although on the part of the thing willed there was not identity, because each will willed what was proper to it.[91]

Bonaventure again provides a lengthy quotation from Hugh's *De quatuor voluntatibus Christi*, in which Hugh denies any contrariety of wills in Christ.[92] There were diverse wills in Christ, but these diverse wills were consonant. Hugh's authority apparently motivates Bonaventure not to follow Albert any further. Bonaventure's reasoning would seem to allow for contrariety in the thing willed to preserve conformity, but he does not wish to contradict Hugh and so denies all contrariety of wills in Christ. Where Albert allowed some contrariety of wills to maintain conformity, Bonaventure allows only a non-identity in the thing willed.

Bonaventure's distinction between conformity in the thing willed and conformity in the reason for willing or mode of willing resembles Albert's distinction between conformity according to material causality (agreement

---

91 Bonaventure, *Commentaria in III*, d.17, a.1, q.3 (Opera theologica selecta 3: 362a–362b): "Quoniam igitur conformitas in ratione volendi fuit in omnibus voluntatibus Christi, quia sic volebat sensualitas sicut volebat ratio eam velle, sic volebat etiam ratio Christi sicut divina voluntas volebat ipsam velle: ideo concedendum est quod in Christo fuit voluntatum concordia et consonantia, quamvis ex parte voliti non esset identitas, quia unaquaeque voluntas quod suum erat volebat."

92 Bonaventure, *Commentaria in III*, d.17, a.1, q.3 (Opera theologica selecta 3: 362b): "Et hoc est quod dicit magister Hugo: 'Secundum divinam voluntatem quod iustum erat voluit; secundum voluntatem rationis iustitiae consensit et iustitiam approbavit; secundum autem voluntatem pietatis sine odio intime condoluit miseriae, quemadmodum secundum voluntatem carnis iustitiam non accusabat, sed poenam recusabat. Unaquaeque voluntas quod suum erat operabatur et quod ad se pertinebat sequebatur: voluntas divina iustitiam, voluntas rationalis obedientiam, voluntas humanitatis misericordiam, voluntas carnis naturam; neque altera alteri contraria erat. Sicut enim Deitati natura erat iustitiam non deserere, sic carni intererat naturam servare, et pietati alienam miseriam non amare. Iustum itaque carni erat quod passionem suam noluit, quia hoc erat secundum naturam; et iustum Deo erat quod passionem illius voluit, quia hoc erat secundum iustitiam.'"

in the thing willed) and according to efficient causality, though the category of reason for willing or mode of willing seems broader than efficient causality. Conformity in the reason for willing can involve the subjection of an inferior will to a superior will or willing the same thing in the same way (*idem eodem modo*). The latter more economically includes what Albert parses into conformity according to the form of willing (*secundum formam volendi*) and according to the end of willing (*in fine volendi*). Bonaventure jettisons Albert's use of causal language and reduces Albert's fourfold consideration of conformity to a twofold consideration. This reduction effectively broadens one manner of conformity (conformity in the reason for willing) to include two types: subjection and assimilation. Bonaventure distinguishes these types in reply to the objections but in the response argues only that there was conformity of wills in Christ between the will of reason and the will of sensuality and between the will of reason and the divine will. Bonaventure makes this assertion according to conformity in the reason for willing. Furthermore, he here does not address the question of conformity within Christ's will of reason, namely between the natural and deliberative wills.[93]

[93] Hayes presents Bonaventure's denial of contrariety wholly in terms of the rational and sensual wills. "It is necessary to understand the relation between wills in terms of the distinction between assimilation and subjection. Assimilation would mean that there is a full blending of two wills desiring the same good in the same way, while subjection would refer to the harmonious relation of a lower will in its proper relation of subjection to a higher will. In the case of Christ, there is no need to claim a full assimilation on the part of the sensual will so that it would desire precisely what the higher levels of will desire. But there must be a conformity of subjection whereby the sensual will accepts that which God wills it to desire" (Hayes, *The Hidden Center*, p. 120). "The rational will of Christ, in desiring that which is described by the divine will, is both similar to the divine will and subject to it. The sensual will, however, does not naturally desire suffering. Its God-given nature directs it to an object which, while acceptable in normal circumstances, is contrary to the specific requirements of the divine will in this particular instance. Hence, the proper relation of subjection, which is present here, does not exclude tension and struggle in Christ coming to terms humanly with the will of God" (Hayes, *The Hidden Center*, p. 120). "At the level of human will, Bonaventure distinguishes between the sensual will and the rational will. This is basic to his treatment of Christ's acceptance of suffering and death as an act of perfect obedience to God. The sensual will, by reason of its very nature, does not desire suffering. In normal circumstances, this would be quite acceptable. But, in dealing with the suffering involved in the passion and death of Jesus where such suffering

In reply to the first objection, Bonaventure does not so much refute contrariety of wills in Christ as refute previous defenses of non-contrariety:

> And to that which is objected first for the contrary position from the prayer of the Lord: Not as I will, but as you will; others respond that from this it is not concluded that there was contrariety of wills in Christ, in view of the fact that different modes of willing do not introduce contrariety, except as they are considered according to the same (secundum idem). Whence, because different modes of willing are considered through different wills, so they introduce neither contrariety nor repugnance. – But that way of responding is insufficient, since, if two people, who have diverse wills, exercise them in regards to some thing willed but in contrary ways, they are said to have contrary wills.[94]

Bonaventure does not identify the 'others,' but they definitely include William of Auxerre and the authors of the *Summa fratris Alexandri*. His cri-

---

appears to be the consequence of following God's will, this becomes a problem. How is Jesus to be seen as perfectly obedient in these circumstances? It is at the level of the rational will that Jesus accepts what his sensitive nature rejects. It is at this level that his human will is subject to and in harmony with the will of God. Thus, the distinction between a sensual and a rational will makes it possible for Bonaventure to see in Christ a perfect act of subjection to the divine will that does not exclude some form of tension in the human experience of Jesus. Concerning the rational will of Christ, specifically, Bonaventure argues that this will was so deeply conditioned by the grace of the hypostatic union that it was conformed in the good. It would have been impossible for Christ to choose anything contrary to the will of God" (Hayes, "Bonaventure," p. 91). Hayes presents conformity without mention of the will of tender pity or will as nature (natural will), reducing the issue to the relationship between reason and sensuality. This reading of Bonaventure places him in line with Peter Lombard and William of Auxerre, effectively eliminating the developments proposed in the *Summa fratris Alexandri*.

94 Bonaventure, *Commentaria in III*, d.17, a.1, q.3, *ad* 1 (Opera theologica selecta 3: 363a): "Ad illud vero quod primo obicitur in contrarium de oratione Domini: *Non sicut ego volo, sed sicut tu* vis, respondent aliqui quod ex hoc non concluditur contrarietatem voluntatum fuisse in Christo, pro eo quod alius et alius modus volendi non inducunt contrarietatem, nisi prout considerantur secundum idem. Unde, quia alius et alius modus volendi consideratur circa aliam et aliam voluntatem, ideo non inducunt contrarietatem nec repugnantiam. – Sed iste modus respondendi non sufficit, quoniam, si aliqui duo homines, qui habent diversas voluntates, contrario modo se habeant circa aliquod volitum, dicuntur habere voluntates contrarias."

tique of this *secundum idem* logic forwards a view similar to Albert's critique of the same. Both theologians fear that denying contrariety on the grounds of *circa idem* and *secundum idem* eliminates all possible contrariety of wills. Albert maneuvers out of this impasse by separating conformity and contrariety, allowing the latter in Christ in order to preserve the former. Bonaventure, perhaps on account of Hugh's authority, will not admit any contrariety of wills in Christ. Nonetheless, his solution returns to the language of conformity.

Bonaventure continues his reply to the first objection by distinguishing conformity according to *assimilation* and according to *subjection*. Conformity of assimilation requires willing the same thing. Conformity of subjection does not require agreement in the thing willed but only an acceptance of the thing willed by a superior will. Conformity of Christ's will of sensuality was required only according to subjection. Christ's prayer in the garden thus involves both his will of reason and his will of sensuality. Christ's will of reason was both assimilated and subjected to the divine will and in turn subjected the will of sensuality to the divine will. Bonaventure's attempt to tease out this difference faces some difficulties, particularly in light of his subsequent treatment of Christ's prayer. These difficulties arise in part from Bonaventure's use of Hugh to explain Christ's prayer, where he argues that Christ was heard in every prayer from reason but not in every prayer from tender pity or sensuality. Without an express connection between the will of reason and the will of tender pity, Bonaventure seemingly assigns fear of the passion entirely to Christ's sensuality or nonrational faculties. His assimilation of Hugh and the Damascene guards against this conclusion, but his failure to clarify the will of reason and the will of tender pity as two aspects of the one power of the rational will certainly detracts from the presentation.[95]

95 Bonaventure, *Commentaria in III*, d.17, a.1, q.3, *ad* 1 (Opera theologica selecta 3: 363a): "Et propterea potest aliter dici quod conformitas voluntatis ad voluntatem dupliciter attenditur: vel secundum assimilationem vel secundum subiectionem. Dominus autem a voluntate sensualitatis non requirebat conformitatem assimilationis, ut idem vellet, quod ipse vellet; sed conformitatem subiectionis, ut id vellet quod Deus ordinavit eam velle; et Dominus in praedicta petitione tollit conformitatem assimilationis, cum dicit: *Non sicut ego*, et ponit conformitatem subiectionis in hoc quod ostendit se velle divinae voluntati subesse. Unde in praedicto verbo insinuatur duplex voluntas in Christo, una videlicet rationis, quae erat similis et subiecta divinae voluntati; altera vero sensualitatis, quam ratio subiciebat voluntati divinae, licet ipsa sensualitas con-

Bonaventure's reply to the fourth objection attempts to explain further this difference. The objection, following Augustine, identifies contrary wills by contrary things willed. The reply here mimics the reply to objection one with Bonaventure denying contrariety between Christ's will of reason and will of sensuality despite the contrary things willed. Again, the argument resorts to the conformity of subjection and of assimilation. Contrary things willed only yield contrariety of wills when the relevant wills are required to be conformed through both subjection and assimilation. Since Christ's will of sensuality need not be conformed through assimilation, contrary things willed do not result in contrary wills.[96] Bonaventure's logic here seems remarkably similar to the logic of William of Auxerre and the *Summa fratris Alexandri*. That is, his argument no longer rests on the divine will for Christ's sensuality to will something proper to it but rather affirms that sensuality in general is not required to conform to the divine will or to reason through assimilation. This conclusion amounts to denying contrariety because the wills are not in the same genus and not willing for the same reason. Bonaventure, of course, critiques this logic and seeks to avoid it.

He guards against this conclusion with reference to Christ's unique circumstances. The context is whether or not Christ's reason consented to his sensuality and whether such consent would be licit. Christ's reason consented to sensuality in one way and dissented to it in another. A will can consent to another "either by willing the same thing (*volendo idem*) as the other wills, or by willing [the other] to will by itself (*volendo ipsum*

---

trarium appeteret; et ita, quamvis non esset similis, erat tamen subiecta, ac per hoc non erat contraria." In the *Breviloquium* Bonaventure similarly restricts to sensuality Christ's aversion to the passion. "Assumpsit ... nec *qualitercumque*, quia sic necessitatem patiendi suscepit, ut nihil pati posset *invite*, nec secundum voluntatem *Deitatis* nec secundum voluntatem *rationis*, licet passio fuerit contra voluntatem *sensualitatis et carnis*, sicut exprimit oratio Salvatoris, quae dicit: *Non sicut ego volo, sed sicut tu vis*" (*Breviloquium* IV.8 [in *Opera theologica selecta*, ed. PP. Collegii S. Bonaventurae (Quaracchi, 1934–1964), 5: 91b]).

96 Bonaventure, *Commentaria in III*, d.17, a.1, q.3, *ad* 4 (Opera theologica selecta 3: 363b): "Ad illud quod obicitur, quod voluntas sensualitatis repugnabat rationi, quia volebat contrarium, dicendum quod contrarietas ex parte voliti non dicit contrarietatem in voluntate, nisi sint tales voluntates quae non tantum sunt natae conformari per subiectionem, sed etiam per identitatem ex parte voliti."

velle)."⁹⁷ Christ's reason consented to sensuality by willing it to be moved as was proper and natural to it. Such movement was licit to sensuality, yet Christ's reason dissented from sensuality in the thing willed. Consent to sensuality regarding the thing willed would be illicit for reason. Bonaventure relates this scheme to Christ's sinless subjection to the punishment for sin. In prelapsarian human nature, sensuality is perfectly subject to reason; reason then consents to sensuality both in willing it to will by itself and in the thing willed. In fallen nature, there is dissent between reason and sensuality in both manners. This dissent follows from the fault and the punishment. "And," Bonaventure writes, "a middle way exists such that reason consents to sensuality in respect to the act of willing, but not in respect to the thing willed; and this pertains to a nature having the punishment without the fault, such as was the nature assumed by Christ, which had something from the original nature and something from fallen nature."⁹⁸

Bonaventure returns to Hugh's fourfold division when treating Christ's prayer. The second question of article two considers the standard question whether Christ was heard in his every prayer. Prayer proceeds from the will, and so following the divisions of the will prayer can be differentiated according as proceeding from the will of reason, the will of ten-

---

97 Bonaventure, *Commentaria in III*, d.17, a.1, q.3, *ad* 6 (Opera theologica selecta 3: 363b–364a): "Ad illud quod obicitur, quod ratio consentiebat sensualitati aut dissentiebat, dicendum quod quodam modo consentiebat, quodam modo dissentiebat, secundum quod aliquis potest alicui dupliciter consentire, aut volendo idem quod ipse vult aut volendo ipsum velle. Ratio autem sensualitati consentiebat volendo eam sic moveri, et hoc idem erat licitum sensualitati: unde non volebat nisi licitum; non autem consentiebat volendo idem ipsum quod sensualitas: hoc enim esset illicitum voluntati rationis. Et hoc non ponebat carnem concupiscere adversus spiritum sive rebellionem sensualitatis ad rationem: illa enim rebellio ponit utrumque dissensum."

98 Bonaventure, *Commentaria in III*, d.17, a.1, q.3, *ad* 6 (Opera theologica selecta 3: 364a): "Unde notandum quod dissensus potest esse sensualitatis ad rationem et quantum ad volitum et quantum ad actum volendi; et hoc idem pertinet ad naturam lapsam per poenam et culpam. Et est ponere consensum quantum ad utrumque, ita quod sensualitas subiaceat rationi; et hoc pertinet ad naturam institutam. Et est ponere medium, ita quod consentiat ratio sensualitati respectu actus volendi, sed non respectu voliti; et hoc pertinet ad naturam habentem poenam absque culpa, qualis fuit natura a Christo assumpta, quae aliquid habuit de natura instituta, aliquid de natura lapsa."

der pity, or the will of the flesh. After much stress on the Lombard's division of the will, the prominence here of Hugh's division is striking. Bonaventure affirms that every prayer of Christ proceeding from the will of reason was heard in everything. Christ's will of reason agreed with the divine will in every thing willed; every prayer from reason was granted. Christ's prayers emerging from the will of tender pity or the will of sensuality were not always granted. The will of tender pity and will of sensuality did not always agree with the divine will in the thing willed. Prayers from Christ's will of tender pity and will of sensuality were intended for our instruction rather than for fulfillment.[99] Bonaventure here seems to separate the Damascene and Hugh, no longer assimilating Hugh's will of tender pity to the Damascene's *thelēsis*.

Bonaventure weaves together various theological strands in his treatment of Christ's wills. His use of Hugh of St Victor's *De quatuor voluntatibus Christi* provides a different scheme for dividing Christ's wills than those proposed by the Lombard and the Damascene. Bonaventure prefers Hugh's terminology to the Damascene's, but he prefers the Lombard's division of the will according to power to both Hugh's and the Damascene's schemes. This preference for the Lombard's division leads Bonaventure to focus on the relationship between Christ's reason and sensuality, a focus reminiscent of William of Auxerre's *Summa aurea*. Bonaventure interprets Christ at Gethsemane as willing to die according to the will of reason and willing not to die according to the will of sensuality. Treating the agony at Geth-

---

99 Bonaventure, *Commentaria in III*, d.17, a.2, q.2 (Opera theologica selecta 3: 367b): "Dicendum quod, cum oratio sit petitio procedens ex voluntate et desiderio, secundum quod voluntas humana fuit in Christo secundum triplicem differentiam, sic et oratio. Nam quaedam oratio fuit exprimens sive procedens a voluntate rationis, quaedam a voluntate pietatis, quaedam a voluntate carnis. – Oratio procedens a voluntate rationis procedebat a voluntate, quae quidem requirebat exaudiri; et talis oratio in omnibus est exaudita, tum propter hoc quod ista voluntas erat per omnia conformis voluntati divinae; tum etiam quia adeo petebat digne et sancte, quod in omnibus erat exaudienda *pro sua reverentia* [Heb. 5:12] et dignitate. – Oratio autem procedens a voluntate pietatis et voluntate carnis non fuit in Christo exaudita per omnia, tum quia haec voluntate non conformabatur Deo in omni volito, sicut habitum est prius; tum etiam quia illa petitio plus ordinabatur ad nostram instructionem quam ad divinam exauditionem. Magis enim petebat hac voluntate ut nos erudiret quam ut Deum ad suam petitionem inclinaret."

semane in this way leaves open the question of any rational voluntary movement not to die.

Commenting on Peter Lombard's *Sentences* presented interesting challenges and opportunities for thirteenth-century theologians. The parameters set by the *Sentences* established discrete theological topics within a systematically ordered whole and the proper field of discussion for those topics. This provided a context for theological discussion without restraining innovation. Within these limits and based upon the given field of discussion, Albert the Great and Bonaventure furthered scholastic debates on Christ's two wills by developing and blending various lines of thought. On occasion this development amounts to a departure from standard lines. On occasion it amounts to a recovery of neglected sources. Albert and Bonaventure demonstrate both tendencies, though not in equal measure.

It would be no overstatement to label Albert's presentation of Christ's two wills the most innovative of the early thirteenth century. While professing to hold close to Peter Lombard's consideration, he pushes the Lombard's language beyond its intention. The Universal Doctor uses the Lombard's discussion to justify a new framework. Chapter two has argued for an increasing emphasis on the question of contrariety of wills in Christ. Albert preserves the underlying concern of this emphasis but steers attention toward the question of conformity. By separating the question of conformity from the question of contrariety, he could present contrariety as preserving conformity. This represents a significant departure from the parallels in the *Summa aurea* and the *Summa fratris Alexandri*.

In the *De incarnatione*, Albert distinguishes conformity in the thing willed and conformity according to the efficient cause of willing. The *De incarnatione* affirms conformity of wills in Christ because his will of reason willed to die for the sake of redemption and because his will of sensuality willed as the divine will willed it to will. Albert's *Commentarii* adds conformity according to final and formal causality. Conformity according to efficient, final, and formal causality often requires non-conformity according to material causality. The *Commentarii* also notes a distinction between conformity and contrariety. While there are four modes of conformity following the four types of causes, contrariety relates entirely to the thing willed (material cause). From this it is inescapable that conformity of wills according to efficient, final, and formal causality often requires contrariety of wills. Albert finds this to be the case for Christ who, according to his will as nature and will of sensuality, willed not to die. These wills were perfectly conformed to the divine will in the efficient cause of willing, even though they willed something contrary. Albert quickly adds that such contrariety does not imply disorder or sin. Only the contrariety of struggle implies sin and disorder, but there was no such struggle in Christ. There was no stubborn resistance of will to will; there was no attempt by Christ's will as nature or will of sensuality to extend beyond their natural limits.

Tempered though it is, Albert's admission of contrariety of wills in Christ departs significantly from earlier treatments of the question. William of Auxerre and the *Summa fratris Alexandri* deny contrariety of wills in Christ on the grounds that contrariety must be, in Albert's words, *circa idem ut idem*. He rejects their logic and their conclusion, though this does not imply a clean break from previous reflections. Albert follows the *Summa fratris Alexandri* in affirming the Damascene's division of the will of reason into natural and deliberative. Based upon this division, he agrees with the *Summa fratris* that Christ willed not to die with some aspect of his rational will. Bonaventure, in contrast, shies away from this conclusion.

Bonaventure also shifts emphasis from contrariety to conformity. In his *Commentaria*, he distinguishes conformity in the thing willed and conformity in the reason for willing. Like Albert, Bonaventure allows that these two types of conformity are on occasion mutually exclusive. He does not, however, follow Albert beyond this point and allow for contrariety of wills. Bonaventure admits a non-identity in the thing willed between Christ's sensuality and reason, yet this does not amount to contrariety. The justification again focuses on conformity, but now the two types of conformity are subjection and assimilation. God required of Christ's will of sensuality only the conformity of subjection, not of assimilation. This seems to exclude contrariety of wills in Christ because the wills are of different types. In other words, Bonaventure's argument here appears similar to the view of the *Summa aurea* and *Summa fratris Alexandri*.

Hugh of St Victor's *De quatuor voluntatibus Christi* features prominently in Bonaventure's *Commentaria*.[100] Hugh divides Christ's human will into the will of reason, will of tender pity, and will of the flesh. The will of tender pity offers the most interest due to its novelty. Bonaventure attempts

---

100 For a brief description of the school of Saint-Victor as a source for Bonaventure, see Bougerol, *Introduction*, pp. 37–39.

to equate the will of tender pity with the Damascene's *thelēsis*, or will as nature. This equation seems fleeting, however, for Bonaventure divides the will of reason and the will of tender pity when discussing Christ's prayer. Furthermore, when addressing conformity of wills, Bonaventure mentions neither the natural will nor the will of tender pity. On the topic of conformity, he prefers the Lombard's division of the human will into the will of reason and the will of sensuality. Bonaventure seeks to press Albert the Great, Hugh of St Victor, and John of Damascus into the mold of Peter Lombard.

Albert and Bonaventure thus develop the discussion of Christ two wills along notably different lines. Albert breaks with previous treatments by admitting contrariety of wills in Christ. Bonaventure, based at least in part on the authority of Hugh, cannot allow for any contrariety of wills. On this issue Albert and Bonaventure diverge sharply. This contrast makes reception of Albert and Bonaventure more difficult for Thomas Aquinas. Thomas developed elements from both Albert and Bonaventure while returning to the logic of non-contrariety forwarded by William of Auxerre and the *Summa fratris Alexandri*. Thomas also highlights the Damascene's distinction between *thelēsis* and *boulēsis* far more than Albert or Bonaventure. Stressing a distinction within the will of reason only serves to complicate any defense of non-contrariety of wills in Christ. The next chapter analyzes Thomas's presentations of this topic in his *Scriptum* on Peter Lombard's *Sentences* and in his *Summa theologiae*.

CHAPTER FOUR

Thomas Aquinas on Christ's Two Wills
Continuities and Developments between the *Scriptum* and *Summa theologiae*

In the spring of 1272, Thomas Aquinas wrote the first twenty to twenty-five questions of the *Summa theologiae*'s *Tertia pars*.[1] Conceived as a means to better express the truths of the Catholic faith for theological education, the *Summa theologiae* followed a different order than Peter Lombard's *Sentences*. Thomas crafted his commentary on the *Sentences*, the *Scriptum super libros Sententiarum*, from 1252 to 1256.[2] Like other commentaries, Thomas's

---

1 Jean-Pierre Torrell leaves the exact number uncertain but favors the general views of P. Glorieux (25 questions) and I.T. Eschmann (20 questions) over Weisheipl's proposal of two or three. See Jean-Pierre Torrell, *Saint Thomas Aquinas*, vol. 1: *The Person and His Work*, trans. Robert Royal (Washington, DC, 1996), p. 261 and James A. Weisheipl, *Friar Thomas d'Aquino: His Life, Thought and Work* (Garden City, NY, 1974), p. 307. Weisheipl finds it difficult to believe that Thomas could have written so much at the end of his second Parisian regency. The numbers are astounding. Thomas's productivity during his second Parisian teaching period (October 1268 to April 1272) seems incredible, but in the final sixteen months it seems even more so. Torrell writes: "If we only consider the sixteen months of the final period (1271–1272) – keeping in mind the fact that certain works straddle 1 January 1271 – the number rises to around 2747 pages [according to the Marieti manual] composed in 466 days, or a daily average of 5.89 pages, clearly superior to the earlier figure. A final figure will help to visualize the work accomplished: a typical sheet of paper in Europe today will hold around 350 closely typed words. Thomas wrote 12.48 of them a day" (Torrell, *Saint Thomas* 1: 240–241). See also Leonard E. Boyle, "The Setting of the *Summa theologiae*" in *Aquinas's* Summa theologiae: *Critical Essays*, ed. Brian Davies (New York, 2006), pp. 1–24, at 12–14.
2 Thomas followed Albertus Magnus from Cologne to Paris in 1252 to lecture on the *Sentences* of Peter Lombard. In Cologne Thomas probably lectured on Jeremiah, Lamentations, and part of Isaiah (see Weisheipl, *Friar Thomas d'Aquino*, pp. 369–370 and Torrell, *Saint Thomas* 1: 27), took *reportationes* of Albert's lectures on Pseudo-Dionysius's *The Divine Names*, and took Albert's course on Aristotle's *Nicomachean Ethics* (see Torrell, *Saint Thomas* 1: 24–28).

Scriptum followed the order of topics found in the four books of the *Sentences* and their division into distinctions.[3] The *Summa theologiae* provided Aquinas an opportunity, as did the *Summa contra gentiles*, to try different structures for theological topics. Alterations to the structure of the *Sentences* appear on both a grand level of organizing logic and a finer level of pedagogical strategy in the *Summa theologiae*. The expressly Christological section of the *Summa* (*ST* III, qq.1–59) proves no exception. Comparing and contrasting *ST* III, q.18 and *Scriptum, in* III (hereafter referred to as "*in* III"), d.17, both of which treat Christ's two wills, highlights what Thomas sought to preserve from the *Sentences* and what he altered or supplemented.

Thomas's knowledge of earlier engagements with the topic of Christ's two wills clarifies the specific shape of his own teaching. In both the *Scriptum* and the *Summa*, Aquinas integrated different opinions regarding the conformity or contrariety of Christ's wills. Borrowing linguistically and schematically from Albert the Great, Bonaventure, the *Summa fratris Alexandri*, and William of Auxerre, Thomas enjoyed a wealth of expressions for the divisions and workings of Christ's wills. Aquinas's historical research, undertaken in the 1260s, uncovered patristic debates on this subject, most notably the acts of Constantinople III.[4] Among the acts of Constantinople III, Thomas found quotations from Augustine's *Contra Maximinum episcopum Arianorum*, Ambrose's *De fide* and *Super Lucam*, Pseudo-Athanasius's *De incarnatione et Contra Arianos*, and Leo's *Tomus ad Flavianum*. Thomas's knowledge and use of these sources (in *ST* III, qq.9, 13, 18 and 19) comes from Pope Agatho's *Epistle I, Ad Augustos Imperatores*.[5]

---

3   These distinctions were not part of the Lombard's original format but were added by Alexander of Hales (between 1223 and 1227). See Torrell, *Saint Thomas* 1: 40 and Ignatius Brady, "The Distinctions of Lombard's *Book of Sentences* and Alexander of Hales," *Franciscan Studies* 25 (1965): 90–116.

4   See Ignaz Backes, *Die Christologie des hl. Thomas von Aquin und die griechischen Kirchenväter* (Paderborn, 1931), p. 31; Theophil Tschipke, *L'humanité du Christ comme instrument de salut de la divinité*, trans. Philibert Secretan (Fribourg, 2003), pp. 111–174; and Martin Morard, "Thomas d'Aquin lecteur des conciles," *Archivum franciscanum historicum* 98 (2005): 211–365.

5   See *Concilium universale Constantinopolitanum tertium*, ed. Rudolf Riedinger, Acta conciliorum oecumenicorum, 2nd ser., 2.1–2. Bayerische Akademie der Wissenschaften (Berlin, 1990–1992); and *Sancta Synodus sexta Generalis Constantinopolitana tertia*, ed. Joannes Dominicus Mansi, in *Sacrorum conciliorum nova et amplissima collectio* (Florence, 1765; repr. Graz, 1960–1961) 11: 189–

Recovery of these sources produced results for Thomas's teaching parallel to, though perhaps less dramatic than, his recovery of the acts of the councils of Ephesus, Chalcedon, and Constantinople II.[6] The affirmations of these three councils allowed Thomas to equate the first opinion discussed in the *Sentences* with the long-condemned heresy of Nestorianism (see *ST* III, q.2, aa.3, 6).[7] Thomas could then refine his own presentation of the hypostatic union.[8] Similarly, Constantinople III deepened Aquinas's concern with Christ's two wills, enriching this teaching's import for the *Summa*'s Christology, even if not much changing the substance of Thomas's views.[9] Peter Lombard (*Sentences* III, d.17) reported Macarius's condemnation at a metropolitan synod (Constantinople III) for denying two wills in Christ. The Lombard, however, demonstrated no knowledge of the council's arguments. Aquinas's recovery of the acts of Constantinople III brought to light the reasons behind Macarius's condemnation and, perhaps as importantly, the council's affirmation of non-contrariety of wills in Christ.

The present chapter, the first of two on Thomas Aquinas, will investigate the continuous and the novel aspects of Thomas's teaching on Christ's

---

1024. The Riedinger edition of the acts of Constantinople III is the most recent, but as the Mansi edition is the more common, both editions will be referenced throughout. For Pope Agatho's *Epistle I* (actio 4), see Riedinger 2.1: 53–121; Mansi 11: 233–286. On Thomas's knowledge and use of Constantinople III, see Morard, "Thomas d'Aquin lecteur des conciles," pp. 305–316.

6   See Gottfried Geenen, "En marge du Concile de Chalcédonie: Les textes du Quatrième Concile dans les œuvres de saint Thomas," *Angelicum* 29 (1952): 43–59 and "The Council of Chalcedon in the Theology of St Thomas," in *From an Abundant Spring: The Walter Farrell Memorial Volume of the* Thomist, ed. staff of the *Thomist* (New York, 1952), pp. 177–217; and Morard, "Thomas d'Aquin lecteur des conciles," pp. 281–296; and "Une source de saint Thomas d'Aquin: Le deuxième Concile de Constantinople (553)," *Revue des sciences philosophiques et théologiques* 81 (1977): 21–56.

7   See Corey Barnes, "Albert the Great and Thomas Aquinas on Person, Hypostasis, and Hypostatic Union," *Thomist* 72 (2008): 107–146; Joseph Wawrykow, "Hypostatic Union," in *The Theology of Thomas Aquinas*, ed. Rik Van Nieuwenhove and Joseph Wawrykow (Notre Dame, IN, 2005), pp. 222–251 (esp. pp. 232–237); and Joseph Wawrykow, "Hypostatic Union," in *The Westminster Handbook to Thomas Aquinas* (Louisville, KY, 2005), pp. 71–73.

8   See Geenen, "The Council of Chalcedon," pp. 185–190.

9   Backes holds that Thomas was the first scholastic to use Constantinople III. See Backes, *Die Christologie*, p. 25.

two wills between the *Scriptum* and *Summa theologiae*, recalling the findings of previous chapters. This chapter will follow the order of topics in *ST* III, q.18, noting the placement of parallels in the *Scriptum*.[10] The *Summa* and the *Scriptum* follow a nearly identical order in presenting Christ's two wills, but the *Summa*'s presentation adds Christ's free choice (*liberum arbitrium*) as a discrete topic. Developments in Thomas's teaching between the *Scriptum* and the *Summa* are evident. This chapter will describe these developments in terms of shifts in emphasis, recovery of patristic and conciliar sources, terminological and conceptual advancements, and the condemnation of Latin Averroism. Against the backdrop of these developments, Aquinas presents Christ as willing not to die with his will of sensuality and will as nature, while willing to die with his will as reason. There is nothing novel or unusual in such a division of wills, but how Thomas employs these standard divisions reveals his understanding of Christ's perfect human will willing human salvation in full conformity with the divine will.

As in previous chapters, the method utilized will be close, detailed textual analysis. Carefully analyzing the details of Thomas's presentations reveals their nuances in a unique way. With this detailed analysis accomplished, the broader role of Christ's two wills in Thomas's Christology will emerge all the sharper. Chapter five will examine the import of Thomas's teaching on Christ's two wills and its role within the larger context of Christology in the *Summa*. This task requires discussion of some topics not obviously relevant to Christ's two wills, such as questions of fittingness, and brief mention of some more closely connected topics, such as the hypostatic union, unity of operation, prayer, and mediatorship. These topics all contribute to Thomas's distinctive view of Christ's human will as an instru-

10 The basic order of topics is the same in the *Scriptum* and the *Summa theologiae*. The *Summa*, however, adds an article on Christ's free choice (*liberum arbitrium*) (treated only in response to an objection in the *Scriptum*) and combines two *quaestiunculae* from the *Scriptum* (*in* III, d.17, a.2, quae.2 and 3) into one article examining contrariety of wills in Christ (*ST* III, q.18, a.6). Question 18 of the *Summa*'s *Tertia pars* investigates 'Whether there are two wills in Christ' (a.1; *in* III, d.17, a.1, qua.1), 'Whether there was in Christ a will of sensuality beyond the will of reason' (a.2; *in* III, d.17, a.1, qua.2), 'Whether in Christ there were two wills in terms of reason' (a.3; *in* III, d.17, a.1, qua.3), 'Whether there was free choice in Christ' (a.4; *in* III, d.17, a.1, qua.3, *ad* 5), 'Whether Christ's human will was wholly conformed to the divine will in the thing willed' (a.5; *in* III, d.17, a.2, qua.1), and 'Whether there was contrariety of wills in Christ' (a.6; *in* III, d.17, a.2, quae.2–3).

mental efficient cause of salvation. Correctly describing these questions requires framing the description according to Thomas's linguistic scheme for discussing the Word incarnate. Chapter five will utilize the analysis of Christ's two wills provided in this chapter and will clarify the extended implications of Thomas's teaching.

Establishing a Human Will in Christ

Summa theologiae III, q.18, a.1 begins the discussion of Christ's wills by establishing the presence of two wills in Christ. Parallel to this is *in* III, d.17, a.1, qua.1. Though these two considerations begin with the same question and establish the same conclusion, they unfold along interestingly different lines. Apparent immediately is the far greater length of the *Summa*'s discussion. The previous chapters have argued for a shift in emphasis between seventh-century and thirteenth-century discussions of Christ's wills, namely from the number of wills to their conformity or non-contrariety. As the monothelite controversy receded from view, the presence of both a divine and a human will in Christ became a stable, undisputed feature of Christological reflection. The brevity of the *Scriptum*'s discussion testifies to the waning import of this particular question. The waxing import of Christ's conformity of wills occurred simultaneously, prompted by a concern for the functioning of Christ's human will. This concern itself resulted from a combination of factors, including, though not limited to, acquaintance with an Aristotelian understanding of the will, considerations of Christ's merit, and biblical hermeneutics. Broad agreement governed the affirmation of conformity, but the particular strategies for justifying conformity varied greatly. This topic eclipsed the import of the number of Christ's wills. So, given this thirteenth-century disposition, what accounts for the *Summa*'s increased attention to the number of Christ's wills? The historical research undertaken by Thomas in the 1260s offers an answer.[11]

---

11 Thomas's discussion of Christ's two wills and operations in the *Summa contra gentiles* demonstrates no knowledge of Constantinople III. Thomas seems to refer to Constantinople III first in *Quodlibet* IV, q.5, but the first substantial use comes in the *De unione Verbi incarnati* or *ST* III, q.9, a.1. Thomas completed the *Summa contra gentiles* in 1264–1265 and probably did not recover the acts of Constantinople III until his years in Rome (1265–1268), possibly during trips to Viterbo. See Torrell, *Saint Thomas* 1: 101–104, 142–145, 177. On Thomas's use of Constantinople III, see Morard, "Thomas d'Aquin lecteur des conciles," pp. 305–316.

Thomas's recovery of the acts of Constantinople III did more than merely confirm the accepted position; it introduced misunderstandings of Christ's wills that were not reducible to other Christological heresies. Eutyches serves as the sole foil in the *Scriptum* (*in* III, d.17, a.1, qua.1), for his notion of one composite nature implies only one composite will in Christ. The *Summa* adds the heresies of Apollinarius and Nestorius, which, though diversely, misconceive the hypostatic union in ways that compromise Christ's possession of both the divine will and a human will. The absence of Apollinarius and Nestorius from the *Scriptum*'s version is unremarkable, but Thomas's choice not to mention Macarius of Antioch appears more curious. It seems probable that Aquinas, as perhaps his contemporaries, found the Lombard's mention of Macarius's condemnation too obscure to repeat.[12] In the *Summa contra gentiles* (IV.36), Thomas introduces the brief presentation of Christ's two wills and operations with reference to Macarius of Antioch and his affirmation of only one operation and will in Christ. This introduction exhausts Macarius's role in the *Summa contra gentiles*, as he exits this chapter without mention of his condemnation or of his arguments.[13] While writing the *Scriptum* and the *Summa contra gentiles*, Thomas knew neither to which council the Lombard referred nor the logic underlying Macarius's denial of two wills in Christ. When he wrote the *Summa*'s *Tertia pars*, Aquinas knew both of these things. This knowledge influenced the argumentative structure of *ST* III, q.18, a.1.

Thomas's discussions of Christ's two wills in the *Summa theologiae* and the *Summa contra gentiles* differ most notably in the structure of argumentation. Aquinas's true adversaries in *SCG* IV.36 are Eutyches and Apollinarius. Thomas argues that the Eutychian heresy of one composite nature inevitably results from positing only one action in Christ (*SCG* IV.36.1). Denying a human will in Christ excludes a human intellect, and thus

---

12   The Lombard writes: "His testimoniis evidenter docetur, in Christo duas fuisse voluntates; quod quia negavit Macarius archiepiscopus, in Metropolitana Synodo condemnatus est" (Peter Lombard, *Sententiae* III, d.17, c.2 [*Sententiae in IV Libris distinctae*, ed. PP. Collegii Bonaventurae (Grottaferrata, 1971–1981), 2: 109]).

13   The absence of any explication of Macarius's arguments is especially noteworthy given Thomas's intent in the *Summa contra gentiles* to reconstruct ancient heresies (see *SCG* I.2).

arrives at the Apollinarian heresy of the Word taking the place of a human soul in Christ (*SCG* IV.36.3). The *Summa contra gentiles* presents monothelitism as problematic to the extent that it leads to an established heresy. This strategy contrasts with that of the *Summa*, where Thomas argues that Apollinarius, Eutyches, and Nestorius affirmed or implied only one will in Christ, though from diverse motives. Apollinarius "did not posit an intellectual soul in Christ, but posited that the Word was in place of a soul, or even in place of the intellect."[14] From this it follows "that there was not a human will in Christ."[15] Eutyches's postulation of one composite nature entails only one composite will. Finally, he writes of Nestorius, "because he posited that the union of God and man was made only according to disposition and will, posited one will in Christ."[16] These variant argumentative strategies indicate different concerns regarding Christ's wills. The *Summa contra gentiles* emphasizes the consequences of denying two wills in Christ; the *Summa theologiae* stresses instead the motivations behind such a denial.[17] This latter strategy implies a greater concern with the question of wills in and of itself, not as a slippery slope into some other Christological heresy.

After cataloguing the errors of Apollinarius, Eutyches, and Nestorius on the question of wills, the *Summa theologiae* turns to Macarius of Antioch, Cyrus of Alexandria, and Sergius of Constantinople. They and their followers "posited one will in Christ, even though they posited two natures in Christ united according to hypostasis, because they conjectured that the human nature in Christ was never moved by its own, proper motion, but

---

14 *ST* III, q.18, a.1 (*Summa theologiae* [Ottawa, 1941–1945], 4: 2543b): "Appolinarius enim non posuit animam intellectualem in Christo, sed quod Verbum esset loco animae, vel etiam loco intellectus."
15 *ST* III, q.18, a.1 (*Summa theologiae* 4: 2543b): "Sequebatur quod in Christo non esset voluntas humana."
16 *ST* III, q.18, a.1 (*Summa theologiae* 4: 2544a): "Nestorius etiam, quia possuit unionem Dei et hominis esse factam solum secundum affectum et voluntatem, posuit unam voluntatem in Christo."
17 This argumentative shift rests upon Thomas's knowledge of Constantinople III, which provided the 'logic' behind a monothelite view. In this respect, recovery of Constantinople III served a parallel function to Thomas's recovery of Chalcedon. On Chalcedon and Thomas's knowledge of Eutyches, see Geenen, "The Council of Chalcedon," pp. 185–190.

only according as it was moved by the divinity."[18] Macarius, Cyrus, and Sergius appear to uphold an orthodox understanding of the hypostatic union, and thus their error must rest elsewhere, isolated perhaps to the arena of the will. Following the brief description of Macarius's position, Thomas quotes from Constantinople III, affirming two natural wills and operations in Christ. The lead-in to the quotation suggests a conciliar determination of two wills in Christ was necessary in response to this Macarian type of conjecture. The cases of Apollinarius, Eutyches, and Nestorius required no specific determination related to Christ's two wills, because their error in this regard could be traced to a more fundamental error.

While Thomas's quotation from Constantinople III stipulates as necessary the affirmation of two wills in Christ, it omits the logic undergirding this necessity. "It was necessary to say this," Thomas writes, for it is certain "that the Son of God assumed a perfect human nature."[19] Thomas thus grounds this necessity in the orthodox understanding of the hypostatic union and so ultimately categorizes a Macarian position with other Christological heresies, though he does not here label a Macarian position as heretical. In *ST* III, q.5, Thomas argued for the Word's assumption of a perfect, integral human nature, with article three specifying assumption of a human soul and article four of a human intellect. Recalling the discussion of will in *ST* I, qq.82–83,[20] he argues that the will "pertains to the perfection of human nature";[21] hence, "it is necessary to say that the Son of God assumed a human will in human nature."[22] The Incarnation of the Word

---

18   *ST* III, q.18, a.1 (*Summa theologiae* 4: 2544a): "Postmodum vero Macarius Antiochenus Patriarcha, et Ciprus Alexandrinus, et Sergius Constantinopolitanus, et quidam eorum sequaces, posuerunt in Christo unam voluntatem, quamvis ponerent duas naturas in Christo secundum hypostasim unitas, quia opinabantur quod humana natura in Christo numquam movebatur proprio motu, sed solum secundum quod erat mota a divinitate, ut patet ex epistola *Synodica* Agathonis Papae."
19   *ST* III, q.18, a.1 (*Summa theologiae* 4: 2544a): "Et hoc necessarium fuit dici. Manifestum est enim quod Filius Dei assumpsit humanam naturam perfectam, sicut supra ostensum est."
20   In *ST* I, q.83, a.1, Thomas argues that insofar as humanity is rational it necessarily includes a free will.
21   *ST* III, q.18, a.1 (*Summa theologiae* 4: 2544a): "Ad perfectionem autem humanae naturae pertinet voluntas."
22   *ST* III, q.18, a.1 (*Summa theologiae* 4: 2544a): "Unde necesse est dicere quod Filius Dei humanam voluntatem assumpserit in humana natura."

involved no alteration to the divinity (*ST* III, q.1, a.1, *ad* 1), which naturally involves possession of the divine will (*ST* I, q.19, a.1). Therefore, we must affirm two wills in Christ, the divine will and a human will.[23]

Thomas's response to the many heresies rehearsed in *ST* III, q.18, a.1 deserves note for its simplicity and concision. This contrasts slightly with the *Scriptum*'s equivalent (*in* III, d.17, a.1, qua.1), which begins with a compact assertion but develops this diffusely. Aquinas affirms that "a will follows human nature,"[24] in support of which he invokes John Damascene, who proves this assertion through five arguments.[25] The first argument speaks, though without Aquinas's awareness, to the monothelites' view that Christ's human nature never moved by its own, proper movement. The reasoning maintains that "every nature has its own, proper movement: moreover the proper movement of a rational nature is that it tends freely to something, which pertains to the will."[26] The second argument holds that a will is natural to humanity "because no one additionally learns willing."[27] Third, Thomas notes that human beings, unlike non-rational animals, which are directed by their nature, direct their nature, which requires freedom in human beings' proper movement. This freedom pertains to the will. Augustine and the Damascene mingle in the fourth argument, for to the Damascene's affirmation of humanity's creation in God's image, Thomas adds the stipulation that the image consists in memory, understanding, and will. The fifth argument holds simply that a will "is found in

---

23   Though Thomas initially distinguishes a Marcarian denial of two wills from other Christological heresies, he ultimately equates them in a fundamental misconception of the hypostatic union. Christ's possession of both the divine will and a human will follows necessarily from the hypostatic union. Thomas's argumentative structure here highlights the absolute import of a correct conception of the hypostatic union for his Christology.

24   *In* III, d.17, a.1, qua.1 (Thomas Aquinas, *Scriptum super Sententiis Magistri Petri Lombardi*, ed. Maria Fabianus Moos [Paris, 1933], 3: 530): "voluntas consequitur naturam humanam."

25   As Chapter three has indicated, Bonaventure made substantial use of John Damascene on this question. So, while Thomas's use of the *De fide orthodoxa* in the *Scriptum* should startle no one, its absence from the *corpus* of *ST* III, q.18, a.1 merits note. Thomas's use of sources will receive more thorough attention later.

26   *In* III, d.17, a.1, qua.1 (*Scriptum* 3: 530): "quaelibet natura habet motum proprium: motus autem naturae rationalis proprius est ut libere in aliquid tendat, quod voluntatis est."

27   *In* III, d.17, a.1, qua.1 (*Scriptum* 3: 530): "quia nullus addiscit velle."

everyone who has the nature."²⁸ Without development and nuance, the value of this point can be easily missed.

The arguments up to this point in *in* III, d.17, a.1, qua.1 stress the natural and necessary presence of a will in every human nature. With this premise defended, Thomas continues that "since Christ integrally assumed our nature, – otherwise he would not be a true man – it stands that he assumed a will."²⁹ He repeats this second argumentative step in the *Summa*, though the first step, that is, affirming that human nature includes a will, unfolds not in *ST* III, q.18 but in *ST* I, qq.82–83, within the anthropological section of Thomas's discussion of the Trinitarian creation.³⁰ The *Scriptum* concludes from the above points that Christ possessed both the divine will and a human will. In the *Summa* Aquinas adds that through "the assumption of human nature the Son of God underwent no diminution in those things which pertain to the divine nature."³¹ As the divine nature includes a will, "it is necessary to say that in Christ there are two wills, namely one divine and the other human."³² The *Scriptum*'s account introduces here, almost as a postscript, Eutyches's assertion of one composite will, which Thomas reads to imply neither will was truly in Christ. Thomas counters that each will remains distinct in Christ.

The shift in focus between the *Scriptum*'s and the *Summa*'s treatments of this topic is subtle but significant. Thomas labors in the *Scriptum* to prove, through the authority of John Damascene, that integral human nature entails a will. The Word assumed an integral human nature and therefore possessed a human will in addition to the divine will. Thomas's

---

28 *In* III, d.17, a.1, qua.1 (*Scriptum* 3: 530): "quia invenitur in omnibus habentibus naturam."
29 *In* III, d.17, a.1, qua.1 (*Scriptum* 3: 530): "Unde cum Christus nostram naturam integre assumpserit, – alias non esset verus homo – constat quod voluntatem assumpsit."
30 See Gilles Emery, "Trinity and Creation," in *The Theology of Thomas Aquinas*, ed. Rik Van Nieuwenhove and Joseph Wawrykow (Notre Dame, IN, 2005), pp. 58–76 and *La Trinité créatrice: Trinité et création dans les commentaires aux* Sentences *de Thomas d'Aquin et de ses précurseurs Albert le Grand et Bonaventure* (Paris, 1995).
31 *ST* III, q.18, a.1 (*Summa theologiae* 4: 2544a): "Per assumptionem autem humanae naturae nullam diminutionem passus est Filius Dei in his quae pertinent ad divinam naturam."
32 *ST* III, q.18, a.1 (*Summa theologiae* 4: 2544a): "Unde necesse est dicere quod in Christo sunt duae voluntates, una scilicet divina et alia humana."

response focuses on human nature and what pertains to its perfection, and thus on the Word's assumption of a *perfect* human nature. This tone dominates article one and resonates throughout distinction 17. The *Summa*'s version (q.18, a.1) preserves this concern for Christ's perfect human nature while shifting focus to Christ's *assumption* of a perfect human nature, elevating as central a proper understanding of the hypostatic union. Thomas presents misconceptions of Christ's two wills as different types of misconceptions of the hypostatic union. A correct understanding of the hypostatic union (see *ST* III, q.2) guides Thomas's response. Aquinas omits proofs that human nature necessarily involves a will, preferring simply to refer to his earlier demonstration of this point in the *Prima pars* (*ST* I, q.82). Nor need Aquinas here elucidate an orthodox understanding of the hypostatic union. Rather the *Summa* can, following Thomas's design, logically and efficiently build upon itself, referring back to its treatment of the hypostatic union in *ST* III, q.2. The necessary premises are all already well established, and so affirmation of Christ's two wills requires only a *pro forma* argument, as it flows directly from a proper understanding of the hypostatic union.

The dominant themes expressed in *ST* III, q.18, a.1 and in *in* III, d.17, a.1, qua.1 provide keys for Thomas's replies to objections in each work. The *Summa* repeats two of the *Scriptum*'s three objections (*in* III, d.17, a.1, qua.1, obs.1, 2), though in a much expanded form and features two new objections as well. The objections and replies offer clues to the development of Thomas's thought on this issue. The analysis will focus on the *Summa* and draw out comparisons with the *Scriptum* to highlight changes in Thomas's understanding of instrumentality and his use of sources.

The first objection regards the will as the "prime mover and orderer in every willer."[33] In Christ this must be none other than the divine will, "because everything human in Christ was moved according to the divine will."[34] From this, the objection concludes that there was only the divine will in Christ. Aquinas's reply seizes upon the formula "according to" (in distinction from "by") as a means to pry the objection apart. The second objection argues for the absence of a human will due to the human will's

---

33 *ST* III, q.18, a.1, ob.1 (*Summa theologiae* 4: 2543a): "Voluntas enim est primum movens et imperans in unoquoque volente."
34 *ST* III, q.18, a.1, ob.1 (*Summa theologiae* 4: 2543a–2543b): "quia omnia humana in Christo movebantur secundum voluntatem divinam."

role as an instrument.³⁵ "An instrument," the objection begins, "is not moved by its own will, but by the will of the mover."³⁶ The objection argues that as an instrument of the divinity "the human nature in Christ was not moved by its own will, but by the divine [will]."³⁷ Curiously, no mention is made of John Damascene in this objection, perhaps indicating the currency of Christ's humanity as instrument of his divinity (see *De fide orthodoxa* III.15) to be so extensive as to need no reference. It is more likely that this objection develops from Constantinople III, for Thomas's contemporaries do not employ this notion of Christ's instrumentality.³⁸ The conclusions of the *Summa*'s and the *Scriptum*'s corresponding objections differ interestingly. Whereas *in* III, d.17, a.1, qua.1, ob.2 concludes that "the

---

35 The second objection of *in* III, d.17, a.1, qua.1 maintains that it pertains to the will to lead, not to be led. Based upon the Damascene's affirmation (*De fide orthodoxa* III.15) of Christ's human nature, here taken as the human disposition or affection (*affectus humanus*), as the instrument of God, the objection argues that Christ's human affection was led by the divine will and should not be called a will.
36 *ST* III, q.18, a.1, ob.2 (*Summa theologiae* 4: 2543b): "Instrumentum non movetur propria voluntate, sed voluntate moventis."
37 *ST* III, q.18, a.1, ob.2 (*Summa theologiae* 4: 2543b): "Ergo natura humana in Christo non movebatur propria voluntate, sed divina."
38 "Thomas assumes that his readers [of the *Summa*] are roughly as familiar as he is with the disposition of received authorities around standard theological topics. He cuts his references to the minimum, especially when dealing with a famous or reiterated text" (Mark D. Jordan, "The Competition of Authoritative Languages and Aquinas' Theological Rhetoric," *Medieval Philosophy & Theology* 4 [1994]: 71–90, at pp. 73–74). The question remains whether John Damascene's *De fide orthodoxa* III.15 had achieved such status. This does not seem to apply to the present case. Thomas was the first scholastic to cite the Damascene's phrase 'instrumentum divinitatis' (*De fide orthodoxa* III.15); see Tschipke, *L'humanité du Christ*, pp. 105–106. Rather, Thomas takes this objection from Constantinople III's presentation of Apollinaris (actio 11). "Apollinarii heretici de Apori<i>s, id est de difficilibus: <In>strumentum et illud, quod hoc mouet, unam [naturaliter] <solet> [perficit] <perficere> operationem; si enim una est operatio, una et substantia. una igitur substantia facta est uerbi et instrumenti" (Riedinger 2.1: 511). "Apollinarii haeretici de aporiis, id est, de difficilibus: Instrumentum, et illud, quod hoc movet, unam naturaliter perficit operationem. Si ergo una est operatio, una est substantia. Una igitur substantia facta est verbi et instrumenti" (Mansi 11: 515).

human affection ought not to be called a will in Christ,"[39] and thus points to the presence of only the divine will in Christ, the *Summa*'s version holds only that Christ's human nature was not moved by its own will. This bears a strong monothelite cast, the risk of which prompts Thomas to refine his understanding of rational instrumentality. This development owes much to Thomas's knowledge of Constantinople III. The *Scriptum* defended the Damascene; the *Summa* attacks monothelitism. This is a subtle but significant change.

The third objection of *ST* III, q.18, a.1 develops as a misconception of a correct principle, namely that that "alone is multiplied in Christ which pertains to nature."[40] This should not, the objection maintains, include a will, because natural things are from necessity, while the will involves what is not necessary. Again, the logic suggests only one will in Christ, a conclusion shared by the fourth objection. The fourth objection, however, arrives at this conclusion from the opposite direction. A quotation from the Damascene (*De fide orthodoxa* III.14) provides authority that willing in a certain way (*aliqualiter*) is not natural but personal. Further, "every will is a will of a certain type (*aliqualis*),"[41] for everything in a genus must also be in some certain species. The objection jumps from this to affirming that every will pertains to a person, and so there must be only one will in Christ, as "in Christ there was and is only one person."[42] Objections three and four work in tandem by first arguing that the will cannot be natural and then positively defining will as pertaining to person.

The *sed contra* of *ST* III, q.18, a.1 reflects larger differences between the *Summa* and the *Scriptum* on this topic, particularly in terms of authorities cited. The *Scriptum*'s first *sed contra* highlights the soteriological end of the Incarnation. As the human will needed curing, it must have been assumed. Thomas here cites no authority for the presence of a human will in Christ, but only for a principle through which this presence can be concluded.

39 *In* III, d.17, a.1, qua.1, ob.2 (*Scriptum* 3: 527): "Ergo affectus humanus non debet dici voluntas in Christo."
40 *ST* III, q.18, a.1, ob.3 (*Summa theologiae* 4: 2543b): "Illud solum multiplicatus in Christo quod pertinet ad naturam."
41 *ST* III, q.18, a.1, ob.4 (*Summa theologiae* 4: 2543b): "omnis voluntas est aliqualis voluntas."
42 *ST* III, q.18, a.1, ob.4 (*Summa theologiae* 4: 2543b): "in Christo fuit et est una tantum persona."

The *Scriptum*'s second *sed contra* cites the Damascene (*De fide orthodoxa* III.14) and stresses a proportion between will and nature.[43] The *Summa*'s *sed contra*, on the other hand, cites Ambrose, which comes as a surprise. Excerpts from Ambrose's *De fide ad Gratianum Imperatorem* appear in *Sentences* III, d.17 yet hardly play any role in the commentaries. In the *Scriptum* (*in* III, d.17) Aquinas refers, though without a quotation, to Ambrose only in article four, on whether Christ *secundum quod homo* doubted. The Lombard also uses Ambrose in defense of Christ's two wills, citing *De fide* II.5–7.[44] Aquinas here quotes from *De fide* II.7 and from *Super Lucam, Lib. X, super* XXII.42, texts unused by other thirteenth-century authors on this topic. These texts, along with Augustine's *Contra Maximinum episcopum Arianorum*, came to Aquinas's attention through Pope Agatho's *Epistle I*.[45] Though this must suffice for now, Thomas's use of sources in the *Summa* will receive fuller treatment subsequently.

The *sed contra* of *ST* III, q.18, a.1 first quotes Luke 22:42 and then repeats Ambrose's interpretation of this text. Ambrose's commentary on Luke 22:42, as quoted by Aquinas, reads: "His will referred to man; [the will] of the Father to the divinity. For the will of man is temporal; the will

---

43 *In* III, d.18, a.1 (*Scriptum* 3: 555): "*Sicut* se habet unitas actionis ad unitatem naturae, *ita* pluralitas ad pluralitatem" ("*Just as* unity of will entails unity of nature, *so too* plurality entails plurality"). In the case of the Trinity, there are not three wills, one to each person, but one will on account of unity of nature. This logic implies multiple wills in Christ on account of multiple natures.

44 See Peter Lombard, *Sententiae*, III, d.17, c. 2. It is unlikely that the Lombard had the complete text of Ambrose's *De fide*. More likely, the Lombard had passages from Ambrose without the context of the work's argument. On the Lombard's sources, see Jacques-Guy Bougerol, "The Church Fathers and the *Sentences* of Peter Lombard," in *Reception of the Church Fathers in the West: From the Carolingians to the Maurists*, ed. Irena Backus, 2 vols. (Leiden, 1997), 1: 113–164. The Lombard quotes Ambrose sixty-six times, second only – though by a vast margin – to Augustine (see Bougerol, "The Church Fathers," p. 115).

45 Agatho's letter focuses on will and operation but also discusses Christ's knowledge and nativities. Agatho quotes Ambrose (*De fide* and *Super Lucam*) and Augustine (*Contra Maximinum episcopum Arianorum*). Thomas's use of Ambrose and Augustine in *ST* III, q.18 mimics Agatho's use of these sources (see Riedinger 2.1: 69–73, 93, 97; Mansi 11: 246–247, 263, 267). The acts of Constantinople III quote Ambrose's *De fide* and *Super Lucam* in several places: e.g., actio 8 (Riedinger 2.1: 249–250; Mansi 11: 370); actio 10 (Riedinger 2.1: 289–291; Mansi 11: 394–395). Agatho presents a lengthy quotation of Augustine's *Contra Maximinum* (Riedinger 2.1: 71–73; Mansi 11: 247). Thomas repeats portions of this quotation in *ST* III, q.18, a.1, *ad* 1; a.5, *sed contra*.

of divinity, eternal."[46] This *sed contra* more closely resembles the *Sentences* and other theologians' commentaries on the *Sentences* than does the *Scriptum* in arguing for a human will in Christ directly from scripture.

Thomas layers his responses one upon another, erecting a solid foundation for the remaining articles. He concedes to the first objection that everything "in Christ's human nature was moved to the pleasure (*nutu*) of the divine will," but maintains that from this "it does not follow that there was not in Christ a movement of the will proper to human nature."[47] By way of explanation, the response indicates the movements of the saints' individual wills according to the divine will, which possesses the unique ability to move a will interiorly (see *ST* I, q.105, a.4; q.106, a.2; q.111, a.2). "And thus," Aquinas writes, "Christ also, according to his human will, followed the divine will."[48] It merits remark that Thomas here appeals not to the hypostatic union (unity of person) to illuminate the relation between Christ's human and divine wills. Rather, appeal is made to the saints' pious wills and God's interior movement of them. Further, this represents not some general principle establishing an analogue for Christ's human will, but an illustration of the same voluntary mechanics. To put the matter crudely, Thomas endeavors to show that Christ's human will received no special aid from the divine will but was moved by the pleasure of the divine will just like the wills of the saints.[49] Christ's human will possessed its

---

46 *ST* III, q.18, a.1, *sed contra*, quoting *Super Lucam, Lib.* X, *super* XXII.42 (*Summa theologiae* 4: 2543b): "Voluntatem suam ad hominem retulit; Patris, ad divinitatem. Voluntas enim hominis est temporalis; voluntas divinitatis aeterna."

47 *ST* III, q.18, a.1, *ad* 1 (*Summa theologiae* 4: 2544a): "Dicendum quod quidquid fuit in humana natura Christi, movebatur nutu voluntatis divinae, non tamen sequitur quod in Christo non fuerit motus voluntatis proprius naturae humanae." Thomas's use of *nutu* here seems also to derive from Agatho's *Epistle I*.

48 *ST* III, q.18, a.1, *ad* 1 (*Summa theologiae* 4: 2544b): "Et sic etiam Christus secundum voluntatem humanam sequebatur voluntatem divinam."

49 This requires some clarification. There is an obvious difference between Christ and the saints in terms of the person willing, but not in terms of nature. Christ's human will received its determinate mode of willing from the Person of the Word (*ST* III, q.18, a.1, *ad* 4). Thomas aims in *ST* III, q.18, a.1, *ad* 1 simply to show that, by virtue of God's interior movement of a human will, it is proper to a human will to be moved to the pleasure of the divine will. On God's movement of the human will as a secondary cause, see *ST* I, qq.22–23. In the *Secunda pars*, Thomas again discusses God's movement of the human will and adds specification by calling it an instrument of God. "Dicendum

moral perfection through the very same operation of grace that works in other human beings (see *ST* I–II, q.111, a.2; *ST* III, qq.7–8; Chapter five below). In support of this, Thomas cites Psalm 39:9 and Augustine's *Contra Maximinum episcopum Arianorum*, a late anti-Arian work influenced by Ambrose's *De fide*.[50] Thomas begins in this first response a subtle strategy of completing his earlier discussion of the human will (*ST* I, qq.80–83) by showing its perfection in Christ. That is, far from being unnatural, the extraordinary subjection of Christ's human will to the divine will is far more natural than any sinful exercise of human will.[51]

In response to the second objection concerning the instrumentality of Christ's human nature, again no reference to the Damascene appears. The reply distinguishes types of instruments and their proper characteristics. All instruments hold in common being moved by a principal agent. Thomas's insight here highlights the diverse ways a principal agent moves an instrument according to the properties of that instrument's nature. An

---

quod Deus movet hominem ad agendum non solum sicut proponens sensui appetibile, vel sicut immutans corpus, sed etiam sicut movens ipsam voluntatem; quia omnis motus tam voluntatis quam naturae ab eo procedit sicut a primo movente. Et sicut non est contra rationem naturae quod motus naturae sit a Deo sicut a primo movente, inquantum natura est quoddam instrumentum Dei moventis; ita non est contra rationem actus voluntarii quod sit a Deo, inquantum voluntas a Deo movetur. Est tamen communiter de ratione naturalia et voluntarii motus quod sint a principio intrinseco" (*ST* I–II, q.6, a.1, *ad* 3 [*Summa theologiae* 2: 753b]). "Dicendum quod Deus movet voluntatem hominis, sicut universalis motor, ad universale obiectum voluntatis, quod est bonum. Et sine hac universali motione homo non potest aliquid velle. Sed homo per rationem determinat se ad volendum hoc vel illud, quod est vere bonum vel apparens bonum. – Sed tamen interdum specialiter Deus movet aliquos ad aliquid determinate volendum, quod est bonum, sicut in his quos movet per gratiam" (*ST* I–II, q.9, a.6, *ad* 3 [*Summa theologiae* 2: 773b]).

50 On Ambrose's *De fide* and its influence on Augustine, see Brian E. Daley, "The Giant's Twin Substances: Ambrose and the Christology of Augustine's *Contra sermonem Arianorum*," in *Augustine: Presbyter factus sum*, ed. Joseph T. Lienhard, Earl C. Muller and Roland J. Teske (New York, 1993), pp. 477–495. This quotation is taken from Pope Agatho's *Epistle I* (Riedinger 2.1: 71–73; Mansi 11: 247). Thomas quotes the text of the *Contra Maximinum* in the *Secunda pars*, but he identifies the quotation as from Ambrose (*ST* I–II, q.2, a.3, ob.2). This misidentification strengthens the claim that Aquinas draws the *Tertia pars*'s quotations from Agatho.

51 In *ST* I, q.81 Thomas argues that the human will is naturally ordered to God.

agent moves an inanimate instrument only by a corporeal motion. An instrument animated by a sensitive soul is moved through its sensitive appetite. "But," Thomas argues, "an instrument animated by a rational soul is moved through its will."[52] He then turns to Aristotle, who buttresses this argument by affirming a servant moved to do something by the command of his or her master does so as an animate instrument (see I *Pol.*, II.4). Christ's human nature was an instrument of the divinity as a rational instrument, as moved through its own will. This specifies more precisely God's interior movement of Christ's human will (established in *ad* 1) as the movement of a rational instrument through its own will.[53]

---

52 *ST* III, q.18, a.1, *ad* 2 (*Summa theologiae* 4: 2544b): "Dicendum quod proprium est instrumenti quod moveatur a principali agente; diversimode tamen secundum proprietatem naturae ipsius. Nam instrumentum inanimatum, sicut securis aut sera, movetur ab artifice per solum motum corporalem. Instrumentum vero animatum sensibili movetur per appetitum sensitivum, sicut equus a sessore. Instrumentum vero animatum anima rationali movetur per voluntatem eius."

53 The *Scriptum*'s equivalent reply centers on a distinction between compelling and guiding, arguing that the divine will guided Christ's human affection but did not compel it. Thomas's presentation of Christ's human nature as instrument of the divinity changed throughout his works. In the *Summa contra gentiles*, Aquinas first describes Christ's human nature as a conjoined, rational instrument (*SCG* IV.41). This new terminology marks a departure from the purely ministerial or dispositive instrumental causality discussed in the *Scriptum*. In the *Summa*'s *Tertia pars*, Thomas prefers to describe Christ's human nature as an instrument pertaining to unity of hypostasis. This shift in language from the *Summa contra gentiles* no doubt rests on Thomas's concern to combat Nestorianism (see *ST* III, q.2, a.6, *ad* 4). On the instrumentality of Christ's human nature, see Wawrykow, "Instrumental Causality," in *The Westminster Handbook*; pp. 75–76; Tschipke, *L'humanité du Christ*; Paul G. Crowley, "*Instrumentum divinitatis* in Thomas Aquinas: Recovering the Divinity of Christ," *Theological Studies* 52 (1991): 451–475; Nicholas Crotty, "The Redemptive Role of Christ's Resurrection," *Thomist* 25 (1962): 54–106; Humbert Bouëssé, "La causalité efficiente instrumentale et la causalité méritoire de la sainte humanité du Christ," *Revue thomiste* 44 (1938): 256–298; and Edouard Hugon, "La causalité instrumentale de l'humanité sainte de Jésus," *Revue thomiste* 13 (1905): 44–68. Tschipke notes that, despite the heavy use of the Damascene by Albert the Great and Bonaventure, only Thomas offers an account of Christ's human nature as instrument of the divinity (Tschipke, *L'humanité du Christ*, p. 112). Tschipke takes the development in Thomas's own understanding of this instrumentality to have begun already in the *De veritate* (Tschipke, *L'humanité du Christ*, p. 122).

Thomas's response to the third objection specifies more precisely the functioning of this proper will. The third objection argues that natural things are necessary, so a will cannot pertain to nature, e.g. Christ's human nature. Thomas inverts the objection's assertion against its intention by distinguishing the will as power and as act.[54] The "very power of the will is natural, and follows nature from necessity."[55] This indicates that since the Word assumed a human nature, it necessarily includes the assumption of a human will. However, this does not imply that a will's every act is necessary. The act of the power of the will, which itself is also called the will, can itself be regarded in two ways, which Aquinas discusses in *ST* I, qq.82–83. The act or movement of the will naturally and necessarily, in terms of natural necessity or necessity of the end, desires happiness (see *ST* I, q.82, a.1; *ST* I–II, qq.1–5). Happiness remains the natural and necessary end of the will but does not determine the will to specific acts. When the act of the will is considered as the exercise of free choice (*liberum arbitrium*), reason determines the will to specific acts (see *ST* I, q.82, a.2; *ST* I–II, q.10, a.4). Reason itself is natural to humanity, so every instance of human nature must be rational, which entails free choice (*ST* I, q.83, a.1; *ST* I–II, q.13). "And therefore," Thomas concludes, "beyond the divine will, it is necessary to posit a human will in Christ, not only inasmuch as it is a natural power or inasmuch as it is a natural movement, but also inasmuch as it is a rational movement."[56] At first glance, this conclusion seems to add nothing to what was established in response to objection two. Restricting the gains of this response to rationality would be folly, for the aim is not so much Christ's rational will, but its exercise according to free choice, anticipating article four.[57] In other words, *ad* 3 specifies the rational will as nat-

---

54 The *Scriptum* indicates a distinction between power and act but makes little of it. *In* III, d.17, a.1, qua.1, *ad* 3 (*Scriptum* 3: 531): "voluntas dicitur *tribus* modis. Aliquando *ipsa potentia volendi*; aliquando autem *ipse actus volendi*; aliquando, *ipsum volitum*; et quantum ad hoc unitur voluntas sancti hominis voluntati Dei, non autem quantum ad duo prima."

55 *ST* III, q.18, a.1, *ad* 3 (*Summa theologiae* 4: 2544b–2545a): "ipsa potentia voluntatis est naturalis, et consequitur naturam ex necessitate."

56 *ST* III, q.18, a.1, *ad* 3 (*Summa theologiae* 4: 2545a): "Et ideo praeter voluntatem divinam, oportet in Christo ponere voluntatem humanam, non solum prout est potentia naturalis aut prout est motus naturalis, sed etiam prout est motus rationalis."

57 The consequences of a rational will and its movement toward happiness are detailed in *ST* I–II, qq.1–13. Thomas's presentation of Christ's perfect human

urally determined to happiness as an end but free to choose the means by which to achieve this end. Thomas's response to the fourth objection provides clues to Christ's exercise of free choice.

The fourth objection focuses on the Damascene's expression "willing in a certain way (*aliqualiter velle*)." Thomas's dense reply begins that "willing in a certain way" designates a "determinate mode of willing."[58] A determinate mode must be determinate of something. As the will pertains to nature, so too its determinate mode must pertain to nature, "not according as it is considered absolutely, but according as it is in such a hypostasis."[59] A nature and its natural capacities receive a determinate mode from the hypostasis that instantiates them. "Whence," Thomas writes, "Christ's human will also had a determinate mode from the fact that it was in the divine hypostasis, namely that it was always moved according to the pleasure of the divine will."[60] This completes the progressive specification wrought by Thomas's responses to the objections. The process ends rather than begins with reference to the hypostatic union, illuminating the exercise of free choice of this rational, human will as always determined by the divine Word exercising it. Yet, it must be continually stressed that the person of the Word truly exercises a *human* will.[61]

---

    will throughout recalls his discussion of the human will in *ST* I, qq.80–83 and *ST* I–II, qq.6–13. The intention of such parallels is both to show the truth of Christ's human nature and to present the perfection of human nature not just in general but in the concrete. Christology completes anthropology, just as Christ perfects human nature at the most fitting time (*ST* III, q.1, a.5).

58 *ST* III, q.18, a.1, *ad* 4 (*Summa theologiae* 4: 2545a): "Dicendum quod per hoc quod dicitur aliqualiter velle, designatur determinatus modus volendi."

59 *ST* III, q.18, a.1, *ad* 4 (*Summa theologiae* 4: 2545a): "non secundum quod est absolute considerata, sed secundum quod est in tali hypostasi."

60 *ST* III, q.18, a.1, *ad* 4 (*Summa theologiae* 4: 2545a): "Unde etiam voluntas humana Christi habuit quendam determinatum modum ex eo quod fuit in hypostasi divina, ut scilicet moveretur semper secundum nutum divinae voluntatis."

61 This well illustrates Thomas's interest in affirming a full and fully functioning human will in Christ. By virtue of the hypostatic union, that human will has its determinate mode through the Person of the Word. This forms the basis for the possibility of Christ's human nature as instrumental efficient cause of salvation (see Tschipke, *L'humanité du Christ*, p. 139). See also Bernard Catão, *Salut et rédemption chez S. Thomas d'Aquin: L'acte sauveur du Christ* (Paris, 1964). Catão stresses the perfect functioning of Christ's free human will for the work of salvation.

Thomas's recovery of Constantinople III allowed him to provide conciliar authority to affirmation of a human will in Christ. The acts of Constantinople III and Agatho's *Epistle I* in particular also provided Thomas with sources (Ambrose and Augustine) set within an argument. The *Summa*'s discussion of Christ's two wills in many details follows Agatho's logic and sources. This marks a significant difference between the *Summa* (*ST* III, q.18, a.1) and the *Scriptum* (*in* III, d.17, a.1, qua.1). The *Summa*'s version introduces conceptual and terminological specifications (rational instrument; distinction between power and act) that shape the remainder of question 18. The *Summa* also displays a keen interest to present Christ's human will as identical to every other human will. Thomas extends this line of thought throughout question 18 and the *Tertia pars*.

The Will of Sensuality

The *corpus* of article one mentions only a human will, leaving the responses to objections the task of demonstrating this as a rational will. The second article of *ST* III, q.18 argues also for a will of sensuality in Christ, following closely the lines established in the *Scriptum* (*in* III, d.17, a.1, qua.2). Thomas's argument in each work involves two stages, one to establish the presence of sensuality in Christ, the other to explain this as a will. In regard to the first, the *Summa* holds that "the Son of God assumed human nature with all those things which pertain to the perfection of human nature itself."[62] Human nature includes 'animal nature,' and so the Son of God, in assuming human nature assumed the perfections of animal nature, among which is the 'sensitive appetite,' "which is called sensuality."[63] The *Scriptum* contends that "all the things which belong to the perfection of human nature were in Christ."[64] Insofar as human beings are human, the perfection is the rational will, but as human beings are animals, the perfection is the sensitive appetite.[65]

---

62 *ST* III, q.18, a.2 (*Summa theologiae* 4: 2545b): "Filius Dei humanam naturam assumpsit cum omnibus quae pertinent ad perfectionem ipsius naturae humanae."
63 *ST* III, q.18, a.2 (*Summa theologiae* 4: 2545b): "Inter quae est appetitus sensitivus, qui sensualitas dicitur."
64 *In* III, d.17, a.1, qua.2 (*Scriptum* 3: 531): "in Christo fuerunt omnia quae sunt de perfectione humanae naturae."
65 For an excellent analysis of the sensitive appetite, sensuality, and the passions in Christ, see Paul Gondreau, *The Passions of Christ's Soul in the Theology of St Thomas Aquinas* (Münster, 2002).

The second argumentative stage obeys the same logic in both treatments. The *Scriptum*, however, involves an initial step omitted in the *Summa*. The *Scriptum* argues that, while human beings act, other animals "are acted upon by their natural instincts."[66] For this reason the sensual appetite in these animals lacks an element definitive of the will, namely a free movement (*liberum motum*). Both works then labor to justify the designation 'will' for the sensual appetite in human beings, and, with small but significant exceptions, both offer the same argument grounded upon Aristotle (*Nicomachean Ethics* 1.13.18). The *Scriptum* holds that "in man the sensible appetite can also be called a will, inasmuch as it obeys reason."[67] As obedient to reason, Thomas continues, the sensual appetite "in a certain sense participates in the freedom of the will ... and can be called a participative will, as it is called reason through participation."[68] Sensuality, according to the *Summa*, "inasmuch as it is naturally intended (*natus*) to obey reason, is called rational through participation."[69] And, as the will rests in reason and sensuality participates in reason, sensuality can be designated a will through participation.[70]

The *Summa* here repeats some, though not all, of the objections voiced in the corresponding section of the *Scriptum*. Thomas begins the series of objections in the *Scriptum* with a quotation from the Damascene that "will

---

66 *In* III, d.17, a.1, qua.2 (*Scriptum* 3: 531): "Sed iste appetitus in aliis animalibus non habet rationem voluntatis, quia aguntur instinctu naturae potius quam agant." Thomas here cites *De fide orthodoxa* II.22.
67 *In* III, d.17, a.1, qua.2: (*Scriptum* 3: 531) "Tamen appetitus sensibilis potest in homine dici voluntas, inquantum est obediens rationi."
68 *In* III, d.17, a.1, qua.2 (*Scriptum* 3: 531): "et ideo participat aliqualiter libertatem voluntatis ... ut possit dici voluntas participative, sicut et dicitur ratio per participationem."
69 *ST* III, q.18, a.2 (*Summa theologiae* 4: 2545b): "inquantum est natus obedire rationi, dicitur rationale per participationem." Thomas refers here to Aristotle, *Nicomachean Ethics* 1.13.18.
70 "For Thomas, then, the key notion centers on the fact that the lower appetites, possessing their own relative autonomy, *participate in* the life of reason. This active paticipation results from the intimate synergy (or 'ontological uion,' as Chenu calls it) that exists between reason and sensibility, to the point of reason's very penetration into the sense powers themselves; by virtue of this penetration, or what the Master from Aquino calls this 'derivation' (*derivatio*) from reason, the intellectual powers wholly influence, transform, and finalize the very operations of the lower appetites, thereby fostering their capacity for virtue," (Gondreau, *The Passions of Christ's Soul*, p. 280).

follows nature."[71] Since there were only two natures in Christ, the argument continues, there must only be two wills and "not a third [will] beyond the divine will and the will of reason."[72] The *Summa* repeats this objection but offers a slightly different response. In the *Scriptum*, Thomas affirms that "in Christ there are two integral natures, of which one is not part of another."[73] This does not preclude the natures from having parts, though of course the divine nature itself is necessarily simple. Human nature, however, "is divided into multiple natural parts, as into the nature of body and [the nature] of soul, into the sensitive and the rational."[74] Thomas argues that the human will is similarly divided into the will of reason and the will of sensuality as natural parts. In the *Summa*, Thomas counters that "where one is on account of another, there only one is seen to exist."[75] By way of illustration, Thomas notes that a surface or shape is visible through color, but that the surface and the color are only one visible thing. Sensuality is only called a will on account of its participation in the will of reason, and so there is posited only one human will in Christ, though this does not exclude the will of sensuality.

The remaining objections in both works deny either a will of sensuality or sensuality itself in Christ. Objections of the first type link will and reason. Objections of the second type link sensuality and sin. To the objections linking will and reason, Thomas argues that insofar as sensuality obeys reason the name will can be applied to the sensitive part of the soul.[76] The *Scriptum* and *Summa* respond in nearly identical fashion to the second type of objection, restricting the connection with sin to corrupt sensuality.

---

71 *De fide orthodoxa* III.14, quoted in *in* III, d.17, a.1, qua.2, ob.1 (*Scriptum* 3: 528): "voluntas naturam sequitur."
72 *In* III, d.17, a.1, qua.2, ob.1 (*Scriptum* 3: 528): "Ergo non est tertia praeter voluntatem divinam et rationis."
73 *In* III, d.17, a.1, qua.2, *ad* 1 (*Scriptum* 3: 531): "in Christo sunt duae naturae integrae quarum una non est pars alterius ..."
74 *In* III, d.17, a.1, qua.2, *ad* 1 (*Scriptum* 3: 531): "sed tamen altera naturarum, scilicet humana, dividitur in multas partiales naturas, sicut in naturam corporis et animae, in sensitivam et rationalem."
75 *ST* III, q.18, a.2, *ad* 3 (*Summa theologiae* 4: 2546a): "ubi est unum propter alterum, ibi unum tantum esse videtur."
76 The *Scriptum* responds tersely that "voluntas per essentiam, est in ratione per essentiam; et voluntas participative, est in ratione per participationem" (*in* III, d.17, a.1, qua.2, *ad* 3). Thomas replies to *ST* III, q.18, a.2, ob.1 that 'will' named according to its essence resides only in the intellective part of the soul. Thomas adds, "sed voluntas participative dicta potest esse in parte sensitiva, inquantum obedit rationi" (*ST* III, q.18, a.2, *ad* 1 [*Summa theologiae* 4: 2545b]).

Sensuality by its nature bears no taint of sin; its natural presence in Christ implies no sin.[77]

The *Scriptum*'s first *sed contra* regards sensuality as a medium between body and soul (reason). Mediums exist wherever the extremes exist. Christ assumed a human body and a rational soul, and so "it is necessary that sensuality was in him."[78] The second *sed contra* quotes Aristotle (*De anima* II.3) to the effect that the nutritive is in the sensitive, and likewise the sensitive is in the intellective. Since Christ had an intellectual soul, he had sensitivity (the sensitive part) and "a will of sensuality which belongs to the sensitive part."[79]

The *Summa*'s *sed contra* more dramatically departs from the *Scriptum*, quoting Ambrose's *De fide* (II.7). This again comes as some surprise. The Lombard cites Ambrose on Christ's two wills, but the commentators (including Thomas) rarely do. Ambrose holds that Christ, as man, assumed our sadness, "from which," Aquinas interprets, "it is given to understand that sadness pertains to the human will in Christ."[80] Sadness, as argued in the *Secunda pars* (*ST* I–II, q.23, a.1; q.25, a.1), is an aspect of sensuality, and so "it seems that in Christ there is a will of sensuality beyond the will of reason."[81]

The Twofold Act of the Will of Reason

The question next addressed by both works concerns a possible division within the will of reason.[82] As noted in previous chapters, the Lombard

---

77 *In* III, d.17, a.1, qua.2, *ad* 4 (*Scriptum* 3: 532): "sensualitas dicitur serpens et principium peccati, non quantum ad naturam potentiae quam Christus assumpsit."
78 *In* III, d.17, a.1, qua.2, *sed contra* 1 (*Scriptum* 3: 528): "oportet quod in ipso fuerit sensualitas."
79 *In* III, d.17, a.1, qua.2, *sed contra* 2 (*Scriptum* 3: 529): "et voluntas sensualitatis quae est pars sensitivae."
80 *ST* III, q.18, a.2, *sed contra* (*Summa theologiae* 4: 2545b): "ex quo datur intelligi quod tristitia pertinet ad humanam voluntatem in Christo."
81 *ST* III, q.18, a.2, *sed contra* (*Summa theologiae* 4: 2545b): "Ergo videtur quod in Christo sit voluntas sensualitatis praeter voluntatem rationis."
82 Tomas Alvira discusses at length the distinction between *voluntas ut natura* and *voluntas ut ratio* in Thomas, noting the natural inclination to the good and the relationship between the intellectual and voluntary powers, particularly in the *Scriptum* and *De veritate*. See Alvira, *Naturaleza y libertad: Estudios de los conceptos tomistas de* voluntas ut natura *y* voluntas ut ratio (Pamplona, 1985). See also Andrea A. Robiglio, *L'impossibile volere: Tommaso d'Aquino, i tomisti e la volontà* (Milan, 2002), pp. 20–21, 58.

and William of Auxerre acknowledged no division within the will of reason, while the *Summa fratris Alexandri* (based upon John Damascene), Bonaventure, and Albert the Great noted a division, in a certain sense. Thomas was significantly influenced by Albert, both in the manner of recognizing a division and in explaining its absence in the *Sentences*. The substance of Thomas's teaching changes little from the *Scriptum* to the *Summa*, but its presentation changes in interesting ways. To best showcase these changes, the *Scriptum* will receive attention first.

The *Scriptum*'s parallel (*in* III, d.17, a.1, qua.3) concerns a possible plurality within the will of reason. Invoking the Damascene, Aristotle, and Hugh of St. Victor, the objections defend such a plurality. Thomas's response focuses on the will as a power and begins that "a distinction of powers is marked according to diverse reasons."[83] Every will has for its object the good, and precisely according to the definition or meaning of the good. "Whence," Thomas writes, "since that reason is common to all, it cannot be that the appetite of reason is distinguished according to diverse powers."[84] This means that in Christ as in all human beings there is only one power of the will. Thomas here returns to the more proper notion of will as strictly the rational will considered as a power, of which each person has but one. A qualification then follows, allowing the considerations (*respectus*) to be diverse, such as in the distinctions of the will of reason. "The Master, however, attending to the nature of the power, did not distinguish the will of reason in Christ."[85] Aquinas's response ends here, without any mention of how or why the will of reason would be divided, discussion of which occurs only in reply to the first objection. Thomas stresses unity of will first and foremost in the *Scriptum*, though the division of the will of reason provides strategic aid in the second article.

The *Scriptum*'s first objection distinguishes "two wills of reason, namely *thelēsis*, which is the natural will, and *boulēsis*, which is the rational

---

83   *In* III, d.17, a.1, qua.3 (*Scriptum* 3: 532): "distinctio potentiarum attenditur secundum diversas rationes."
84   *In* III, d.17, a.1, qua.3 (*Scriptum* 3: 532): "Unde cum ista ratio sit communis omnibus, non potest esse quod appetitus rationis secundum diversas potentias distinguatur."
85   *In* III, d.17, a.1, qua.3 (*Scriptum* 3: 532): "Magister autem attendens ad naturam potentiae, voluntatem rationis in Christo non distinguit."

will."[86] The argument continues that Christ possessed every perfection of human nature, therefore "in Christ there was a twofold will of reason."[87] It is in responding to this objection that Thomas defines and discusses a division of the will of reason. The *thelēsis*, or natural will, regards the good taken absolutely, while the *boulēsis*, or rational will, regards the good in terms of means.[88] The masters called these the will as nature (*voluntas ut natura*) and the will as reason (*voluntas ut ratio*), "according to which, nevertheless, the power of the will was not diversified, because that very diversity is from this, that we are moved toward something without consideration or with consideration."[89] Considering, that is, applying conditions toward or examining variously, strictly belongs to reason, rather than to the will. Thomas writes, "that division of the will is not of [the will] itself through the essentials, but *through the accidentals*,"[90] that is, through what pertains to reason. Thus, there is only one power of the will, which can differ in comparison to itself either with or without consideration. Thomas concludes from this that Christ possessed both a will as reason and a will as nature, though without compromise to the one power of the will.

The *corpus* of *ST* III, q.18, a.3 describes the division of the will of reason through the conceptual distinction between the will taken as power and taken as act.[91] Thomas utilized this distinction in a.1, *ad* 3 to explain that a will as power naturally and hence necessarily belongs to every

---

86 *In* III, d.17, a.1, qua.3, ob.1 (*Scriptum* 3: 529): "distinguit duas voluntates rationis, scilicet *thelisin*, quae est voluntas naturalis et *boulisin*, quae est voluntas rationalis."

87 *In* III, d.17, a.1, qua.3, ob.1 (*Scriptum* 3: 529): "Ergo in Christo fuit duplex rationis voluntas."

88 Alvira notes that Aquinas's distinction between *voluntas ut natura* and *voluntas ut ratio* is not sufficiently explained as a distinction between a will to ends and a will to means. The *voluntas ut ratio* must also be described as a will to the ultimate end in particular instances or choices. See Alvira, *Naturaleza y libertad*, pp. 74–102.

89 *In* III, d.17, a.1, qua.3, *ad* 1 (*Scriptum* 3: 532): "secundum quae tamen non diversificatur potentia voluntatis, quia ista diversitas ex eo quod movemur in aliquid sine collatione vel cum collatione." The terms *voluntas ut natura* and *voluntas ut ratio* come from the *Summa fratris Alexandri*.

90 *In* III, d.17, a.1, qua.3, *ad* 1 (*Scriptum* 3: 532): "illa divisio voluntatis non est per essentialia ipsius, sed *per accidentalia*."

91 Thomas noted this distinction in *ST* III, q.18, a.1, *ad* 3. He first establishes it in *ST* I, q.83, a.4, where he introduces the distinction between *boulēsis* and *thelēsis*.

rational creature, but that the act of the will remains free. In article three Thomas repeats and further refines this distinction, noting two species of act. This distinction provides the resources for resolutely announcing the absolute unity of will as power, while still allowing breathing space for a real division within the will of reason, and even defending its necessity. The *Scriptum* did not develop a parallel for the will as act and shied away from the stronger affirmations found in the *Summa* concerning this division. This division between power and act serves as the foundation in the *Summa* for Thomas's affirmation that Christ's human will was conformed to the divine will (*ST* III, q.18, a.5).

"If therefore," Thomas writes, "the will be taken for act, it is thus necessary to posit in Christ two wills from the part of reason, that is two species of acts of will."[92] The will concerns, though in different ways, both ends and means (*eorumque sunt ad finem*). Thomas indicates the division of the will of reason along the same line as in *in* III, d.17, a.1, qua.3, *ad* 1. The will is borne toward ends as what is simply and absolutely good in itself, while toward means the will "is borne with a certain comparison, according as it has goodness from its order toward another."[93] Thomas provides the example of health as an end and medicine as a means. The will to ends is the *thelēsis*, or simple will, called by the masters the will as nature (*voluntas ut natura*), and the will to means is the *boulēsis*, or counseling will, called the will as reason (*voluntas ut ratio*) by the masters. Aquinas delays mention of the will's unity of power to this late point in the *corpus*. This delay is curious compared to his frequent and prominent insistence on unity of will in the *Scriptum*. Thomas argues that "the diversity of acts does not diversify the power, because each act concerns (*or* is directed toward) one common reason of object, which is the good."[94] Thus, the power of the human will is essentially one, implying in Christ only one human will. When considered as act, this one power can be distinguished into the will as nature and the will as reason.

---

92 *ST* III, q.18, a.3 (*Summa theologiae* 4: 2546b): "Si ergo voluntas accipiatur pro actu, sic oportet in Christo ex parte rationis ponere duas voluntates, idest duas species actuum voluntatis."
93 *ST* III, q.18, a.3 (*Summa theologiae* 4: 2546b): "fertur cum quadam comparatione, secundum quod habet bonitatem ex ordine ad aliud."
94 *ST* III, q.18, a.3 (*Summa theologiae* 4: 2546b): "diversitas actus non diversificat potentiam, quia uterque actus attendit ad unam communem rationem obiecti, quod est bonum."

Perhaps the difference between the *Scriptum* and the *Summa* on this question seems slight or a simple matter of style or a mere matter of emphasis. Even so, it need not diminish the import of such differences or changes. Thomas's skill as a theologian and writer rests in the control of style, the exchange between subtle and emphatic. Nevertheless, the *Summa*'s treatment of the human will (in Christ and in general) represents discernible conceptual and terminological gains. The *Scriptum* recognizes the one power of the will and admits an accidental division into *boulēsis* and *thelēsis*. The *Summa* adds the category of act, providing a term for comparison with power and so offering a new conceptual and terminological way to explain the division of *thelēsis* and *boulēsis*. The division between will as nature and will as reason grounds Thomas's strategy for explaining the non-contrariety of wills in Christ. Without the distinction between power and act, Thomas has a much harder time defending non-contrariety in the *Scriptum*. The *Summa* bases the difference between will as nature and will as reason on the normal functioning of the will of reason through its two species of acts. This change demonstrates Thomas's concern in the *Summa* both to represent faithfully the scriptural account of Christ and to present Christ in his full and perfect humanity. This second concern serves also to complete the anthropology of the *Prima pars* and *Secunda pars*.

Perfect Knowledge, Perfect Free Choice

The *Summa* also displays marked development on the question of free choice (*liberum arbitrium*) in Christ, devoting an entire article to what received only an objection and response in the *Scriptum*. The *Scriptum*'s treatment falls under the general topic of a division within the will of reason and betrays the preoccupations of that topic as well as of the *Summa fratris*. Thomas responds to the *Scriptum*'s objection (and its reference to Aristotle) by noting that, according to the Philosopher, "the will which is of ends and free choice are not diverse powers."[95] Rather, Thomas argues they differ as *boulēsis* and *thelēsis*, "because it pertains to free choice to elect something in its order to an end, however, the will concerns an end absolutely."[96]

---

95 *In* III, d.17, a.1, qua.3, *ad* 5 (*Scriptum* 3: 533): "voluntas quae est finis et liberum arbitrium, non sunt diversae potentiae."
96 *In* III, d.17, a.1, qua.3, *ad* 5: "quia ad liberum arbitrium pertinet eligere aliquid in ordine ad finem, voluntas autem est de fine absolute."

These responses clarify "how the will in Christ may be distinguished."[97] Aquinas's language comes directly from the *Summa fratris Alexandri* (III, tr.4, q.1, c.2). "For," Thomas holds, "a certain will, *either* is attributed to him by reason of his own person, *or* by reason of his members, whose will carries over into his own person."[98] Despite this distinction, Aquinas then explicates only one side of the equation, namely the will by reason of his own person. This will can be parsed first according to his divine nature and his human nature. Second, the will can be divided in terms of his human nature into the will of sensuality and the will of reason. Third, the will of reason can be divided according to the absolute and according to a consideration (*secundum collectivam*). Thomas finds no need for a will in the person of his members, because he seeks to explain Christ's sadness, fear, agony, and his example wholly in terms of Christ's own human will. The notable absence from the *Scriptum* on this point is John Damascene. As we find later in the *Summa*, Thomas must labor to explain the Damascene's denial of *gnōmē* (opinion) and election in Christ (*De fide orthodoxa* III.14).

Thomas devotes noteworthy attention to free choice already in the *Summa contra gentiles* (IV.36), arguing "it [belonged] to the perfection of human nature that it [had] a will, through which man has free choice."[99] Aquinas repeats and expands this dependence of free choice on the will in *SCG* IV.36.5. If Christ did not assume a human will, he did not assume free choice, which is through the will. "So therefore," the argument goes, "the man Christ did not act in the mode of man, but in the mode of other animals, which lack free choice."[100] This scenario would remove all moral worth from Christ's actions as man, frustrating what is said in scripture (Matt. 11:29; John 13:15). While this treatment of free choice

---

97 *In* III, d.17, a.1, qua.3, *ad* 5: "quomodo distinguatur voluntas in Christo."
98 *In* III, d.17, a.1, qua.3, *ad* 5: "Voluntas enim aliqua, *vel* attribuitur ei ratione suae personae, *vel* ratione membrorum quorum personam in se transfert."
99 *SCG* IV.36.2 (*Liber de veritate Catholicae fidei contra errores infidelium; qui dicitur Summa contra gentiles*, ed. D. Petrus Marc, Ceslas Pera, and D. Pietro Caramello [Turin, 1961], 3: 321, n.3741): "de perfectione humanae naturae est quod habeat voluntatem, per quam est homo liberi arbitrii."
100 *SCG* IV.36.5 (ed. Marc et al., 3: 321, n.3744): "Sic igitur non agebat Christus homo ad modum hominis, sed ad modum aliorum animalium, quae libero arbitrio carent."

might seem sparse, the context undermines this appearance. *SCG* IV.36 defends both Christ's two wills and two operations (to each of which a question is directed in the *Summa theologiae*), accomplishing this dual task in fewer lines than granted most *quaestiunculae* in the *Scriptum* or articles in the *Summa theologiae*. The *Summa contra gentiles* does not even take the time and space to note divisions within the human will, yet it devotes an entire paragraph (one of only eight by number) to free choice in Christ. Even the *Summa contra gentiles*, however, does not address the Damascene's exclusion of election from Christ, a task left for the *Summa theologiae*.

Article four of *ST* III, q.18 addresses free choice in Christ. This article repeats Aristotle's definition of the 'will to ends' as 'free choice' (cf. *in* III, d.17, a.1, qua.3, ob.5 and *ad* 5) but adds points from the Damascene as well as Thomas's notion of will as act. The *corpus* begins with an invocation of the twofold acts of the will; it describes the will as nature to concern things willed in themselves and introduces election, through quotation of Aristotle (*Nicomachean Ethics* 3.2.9), as concerning means. Recalling *ST* I, q.83, a.3, Thomas writes that "election moreover is the same as the will as reason, and is the proper act of free choice."[101] Thus, as the will as reason belonged to Christ, so too did election and consequently free choice. This expands somewhat the *Scriptum*'s defense of free choice and provides the foundation for clarifying and answering the concerns expressed through the Damascene that free choice and election imply ignorance. Thomas answers those concerns by applying the principles of free choice and election established in *ST* I–II, qq.13–14 to Christ. While the principles are identical in the case of Christ and every other human being, Christ's perfect knowledge allows those principles to apply without any ignorance or doubt. In other words, Christ's free choice and election are exactly like those of every other human being, but his knowledge is not.

ST III, q.18, a.4, ob.1 begins with these concerns voiced through the Damascene, who wrote that, properly speaking, there was neither opinion

---

101 *ST* III, q.18, a.4 (*Summa theologiae* 4: 2547b): "electio autem est idem quod voluntas ut ratio, et est proprius actus liberi arbitrii." This builds upon Thomas's earlier discussions. "Sic igitur inquantum motus voluntatis fertur in id quod est ad finem, prout ordinatur ad finem, est electio" (*ST* I–II, q.12, a.4, *ad* 3 [*Summa theologiae* 2: 784b]).

(*gnōmē*) nor election in Christ (see *De fide orthodoxa* III.14).[102] The objection stresses the necessity of speaking properly in matters of faith, and so we must deny election in Christ. As election is the act of free choice, denying election concomitantly excludes free choice in Christ. The second objection extends to an argument from reason what in the first objection was strictly an argument from authority. It begins with Aristotle's wedding of election and deliberation (*Nicomachean Ethics* 3.2.17). "But deliberation," the objection argues, "seems not to have been in Christ, because we do not deliberate concerning matters of which we are certain."[103] Christ was certain concerning all things and so did not deliberate. Aristotle's association of election and deliberation then allows a denial of election, and consequently free choice. The third objection maintains that free choice remains undetermined as toward good or evil. Christ's will, however, was determined to the good, and so the objection denies free choice in Christ.

The responses to these objections together present a picture of Christ's free choice that builds upon earlier distinctions and prepares for subsequent articles. Thomas begins this process by specifying the angle at which the Damascene viewed election, namely from that of an ignorant nature, such as our fallen nature. A small side step and Thomas can gaze at election from an angle unobstructed by the sinful condition of humanity. The Damascene "excludes election from Christ according as he understands doubt to be imported in the name of election."[104] Thomas quotes Ephesians 1:4 ('Elegit nos in ipso') to show that God elects, even though there is absolutely no doubt in God. Election does not require doubt. When in an ignorant nature, however, doubt becomes attached to election, as it does to *gnōmē*. This reasoning shows an appreciation for the Damascene's basic point. While election need not involve doubt, Thomas begins his response to the second objection by conceding that "election presupposes delibera-

---

102 The Damascene here expounds the ideas of Maximus the Confessor. Since the scholastics did not know Maximus on this issue, the task of interpreting the Damascene was complicated. Thomas was able to 'read through' the language and so to grasp the intention of John (and Maximus).
103 *ST* III, q.18, a.4, ob.2 (*Summa theologiae* 4: 2547a): "Sed consilium non videtur fuisse in Christo, quia non consiliamur de quibus certi sumus."
104 *ST* III, q.18, a.4, *ad* 1 (*Summa theologiae* 4: 2547b): "Damascenus excludit a Christo electionem secundum quod intelligit in nomine electionis importari dubitationem."

tion."[105] The next several sentences qualify this concession, noting that election only follows from deliberation when a determination has already been made by judgment. With reference to the Philosopher (*Nicomachean Ethics* 3.3.19), Aquinas holds that we elect something that we judge, after the inquiry of deliberation, ought to be done. Thomas seizes upon judgment as intermediary between deliberation and election in order to reaffirm the finding of *ad* 1. He writes that "if something, apart from doubt and preceding inquiry, is judged as needing to be done, this suffices for election."[106] Doubt and inquiry do not belong to the very nature of election, but to the nature of ignorance. They accrue to election as it is found in ignorant natures. Finally, Aquinas responds to the third objection by arguing that "the will of Christ, although it is determined to the good, is nevertheless not determined to this or that good."[107] Christ elected particular goods through a free choice itself confirmed in the good, yet this confirmation of free choice in the good does not impede the proper functioning of election, which is the act of free choice. Christ's freedom in willing serves an important role in Thomas's Christology and soteriology. Stress on Christ's instrumental efficient causality requires an equal stress on Christ's free choice in willing specific things as means to human salvation. Thomas presents Christology and soteriology to emphasize the active role of Christ's human nature in the work of salvation.

105 *ST* III, q.18, a.4, *ad* 2 (*Summa theologiae* 4: 2547b): "electio praesupponit consilium." Thomas's argument here follows *ST* I–II, q.14, a.1. That article argues that election requires deliberation since we cannot know with certitude the contingent singulars involved in specific actions. "Dicendum quod electio, sicut dictum est, consequitur iudicium rationis de rebus agendis. In rebus autem agendis multa incertitudo invenitur, quia actiones sunt circa singularia contingentia, quae propter sui variabilitatem incerta sunt. In rebus autem dubiis et incertis ratio non profert iudicium absque inquisitione praecedente. Et ideo necessaria est inquisitio rationis ante iudicium de eligendis, et haec inquisitio consilium vocatur" (*ST* I–II, q.14, a.1 [*Summa theologiae* 4: 2:791a]). This principle applies equally to Christ. The results of this application differ between the rest of humanity and Christ due to Christ's perfect knowledge, according to which he knew all things (*ST* III, q.10, a.2; q.11, a.1; q.12, a.1).
106 *ST* III, q.18, a.4, *ad* 2 (*Summa theologiae* 4: 2547b): "si aliquid iudicetur ut agendum absque dubitatione et inquisitione praecedente, hoc sufficit ad electionem."
107 *ST* III, q.18, a.4, *ad* 3 (*Summa theologiae* 4: 2547b): "voluntas Christi, licet sit determinata ad bonum, non tamen est determinata ad hoc vel ad illud bonum."

A Human Will Obedient to God

The next topic considered in each work focuses on the conformity of Christ's human will to the divine will in the thing willed (*in volito*). The previous chapters have highlighted the debates that emerged on this topic in the thirteenth century. These debates form the backdrop for Thomas's own treatment. Even the particular formulation chosen by Thomas foreshadows his evaluation of other solutions. Here too, much development between the *Scriptum* and the *Summa* testifies to Aquinas's growth as a theologian indebted to, though independent from, his predecessors and contemporaries. While Aquinas's position remains relatively stable between these two great works, his presentations adopt different strategies, with the objections of the *Scriptum* affirming conformity in the thing willed and those of the *Summa* denying non-conformity. Affirming conformity and denying non-conformity might amount to the same thing logically, but the tone of each work is rather different. Thomas's knowledge of Augustine's *Contra Maximinum episcopum Arianorum*, which figures into the *sed contra* of *ST* III, q.18, a.5, somewhat explains this shift.[108] Beyond this shift, the style of presentation varies greatly, with the *Summa*'s line of development contrasting with the *Scriptum*'s dense attempt to reconcile viewpoints. The density of the *Scriptum*'s argumentation on this topic makes difficult the task of explication. This task will best be aided by full citation of *in* III, d.17, a.2, qua.1, *corpus*, which can then be carefully dissected and compared closely with the *Summa*. Aquinas writes:

> RESPONSE. It should be said TO THE FIRST QUESTION that since the will follows reason, the process of the will is proportionate to the process of reason.
>
> Reason, moreover, has some principle known through itself, and it reduces what it seeks an understanding of to this principle through a process of resolving; and when it has been able to reduce that [princi-

---

108 This citation repeats portions of Pope Agatho's lengthy quotation in *Epistle I* (Riedinger 2.1: 71–73; Mansi 11: 247). Agatho quotes Augustine to show the presence of a human will in Christ and within the larger context of the obedience of Christ's will. Augustine contends that Christ willed, with his human will, something other than what the Father willed. Agatho relates this to Christ's ultimate obedience. Thomas will follow Agatho in this argumentation.

ple], it has certitude about the matter and judges that it is so. But, before it can reduce to that principle, it is moved by some probabilities; and if it indeed be detained by these as if they were certain, it is deceived and at some point errs; if, however, it not be detained, then it has an estimation of one part with caution about the others.

An end, moreover, as the Philosopher says, VII *Ethics*, stands in matters of the will just as a principle in speculative matters. Whence, when a will reduces something subject to deliberation into an end in which it rests totally, it accepts that something by means of a judgment; if, however, it reduces into an end in which it does not rest totally, it flickers between both.

If we consider what is toward an end without an order to an end, the will is moved into the object according to the goodness or evil that the will finds in it absolutely. And because the will does not set itself into the motion which it has concerning this type of thing, since it was borne into the object as into an end; therefore it does not make a final judgment about that object according to its aforementioned motion, as long as it has not considered the end into which it orders that [object]; whence, the will does not will that object simply, but would will it, if nothing repugnant were found.

Moreover, the will as nature is moved into something absolutely, as was said (preceding article, sol.3). Whence, if it is not ordered to another thing through reason, it will accept the object absolutely and will take that just as an end; if, however, it is ordered into an end, it will not accept absolutely something concerning this until it reaches consideration of an end, which the will as reason does.

It is clear, therefore, that the *will as nature* wills something imperfectly and conditionally, unless it was borne into the object as into an end; but about things which are ordered to an end, the *will as reason* has the ultimate and final decision.

With these things seen, it can be laid plain how the will of reason in Christ is conformed to the divine will in the thing willed; because the *will as nature* in Christ was never moved into something as into an end, unless as God wills. And since the *will as reason* is never moved into something except from the reason of an end, it is clear that the will as reason was always conformed to the divine will in the thing willed.

But the *will as nature*, when moved into something not as into an end – which thing indeed does not stand in the same way in goodness and evil according as it is considered in itself and in its order to an end – was not conformed to the divine will in the thing willed; because thus Christ willed not to suffer. God, however, willed him to die; death, moreover, was an evil according to itself, but, as related to an end, a good. This, however, as was said, is not to will something perfectly, but conditionally; whence it is also called by the masters *velleitas* (willingness).

It is clear therefore that *according to the will of reason* [Christ's human will] was conformed to the divine will in the thing willed with respect to everything it willed perfectly and absolutely, but not with respect to what it willed imperfectly.

Similarly, the *will of sensuality* was also not conformed to the divine will in the thing willed in those things injurious to nature; because it does not pertain to sensuality to order something to an end, but those things injurious to nature were good and acceptable to God from their order to an end. Yet the will of sensuality and the will of reason were conformed to the divine will in the act of willing, although not in the thing willed; because, although God might not will what Christ's will of sensuality or will as nature willed, nevertheless God willed the very act of each, inasmuch as, according to the Damascene (*De fide orthodoxa* III.15) "[God] permitted to each of the soul's parts to undergo and to perform what was natural and proper to it, inasmuch as it was arranged to the end of redemption and to showing the truth of the nature."[109]

---

109 *In* III, d.17, a.2, solutio.1 (*Scriptum* 3: 536–538): "RESPONSIO. Dicendum AD PRIMAM QUAESTIONEM quod cum voluntas sequatur rationem, processus voluntatis proportionatur processui rationis.

Ratio autem habet aliquod principium per se notum, ad quod resolvendo reducit illud cujus cognitionem quaerit; et quando ad illud reducere poterit, habet certitudinem de re et sententiat quod ita est. Sed antequam ad istud principium reducere possit, movetur aliquibus verisimilitudinibus; et si quidem illis detineatur tanquam certis, decipitur et errat quandoque; si autem illis non detineatur, tunc habet opinionem unius partis cum formidine alterius.

Finis autem, ut dicit Philosophus, VII *Eth*., se habet in voluntariis sicut principium in speculativis. Unde quando voluntas reducit aliquod consiliabile in finem in quo totaliter quiescit, sententialiter acceptat illud; si autem reducat in finem in quo non totaliter quiescit, trepidat inter utrumque.

Sed si consideretur hoc quod est ad finem sine ordine ad finem, movetur voluntas in ipsum secundum bonitatem vel malitiam quam absolute in eo

The task now is to explicate this thick argumentation thoroughly, without applying to it an unwarranted sense of clarity and finality. The very contrast of style and lucidity between the *Scriptum* and the *Summa* on this point strongly testifies to a development in Thomas's thought.

The *Scriptum*'s solution begins with an affirmation and exploration of the link between the will and reason. This link provides a framework in which Aquinas can delineate the will as nature and the will as reason as

> inveniet. Sed quia voluntas non sistit in motu quem habet circa hujusmodi, cum non feratur in ipsum sicut in finem; ideo non sentiat finaliter secundum praedictum suum motum de illo, quousque finem in quem ordinat illud, non consideret; unde voluntas non simpliciter vult illud, sed vellet, si nihil repugnans inveniretur.
>
> Voluntas autem ut natura movetur in aliquid absolute, ut dictum est. Unde si per rationem non ordinetur in aliquid aliud acceptabit illud absolute, et erit illius tamquam finis; si autem ordinet in finem, non acceptabit aliquid absolute circa hoc, quousque perveniat ad considerationem finis quod facit voluntas ut ratio.
>
> Patet igitur quod *voluntas ut natura* imperfecte vult aliquid, et sub conditione, nisi feratur in ipsum sicut in finem; sed eorum quae ordinantur ad finem, habet *voluntas ut ratio* ultimum judicium et perfectum.
>
> His visis, potest patere qualiter voluntas rationis, divinae voluntati in Christo conformatur in volito; quia *voluntas ut natura* nunquam in Christo movebatur in aliquid sicut in finem, nisi quod Deus vult. Et cum *voluntas ut ratio* nunquam moveatur in aliquid nisi ex ratione finis, patet quod etiam voluntas ut ratio conformabatur divinae voluntati in volito.
>
> Sed *voluntas ut natura*, mota in aliquid non sicut in finem – quod quidem non eodem modo se habet in bonitate et malitia secundum se consideratum et in ordine ad finem – non conformabatur divinae voluntati in volito; quia sic Christus volebat non pati. Deus autem mori eum volebat; mors autem secundum se mala erat, sed relata ad finem, bona. Hoc autem, ut dictum est, non est perfecte velle aliquid, sed sub conditione; unde et a Magistris *velleitas* appellatur.
>
> Patet igitur quod *secundum voluntatem rationis* conformabatur divinae voluntati in volito quantum ad omne quod perfecte et absolute volebat, non autem quantum ad illud quod volebat imperfecte.
>
> Similiter etiam nec *voluntas sensualitatis* conformabatur divinae voluntati in volito in his quae erant nociva naturae; quia sensualitatis non est ordinare ad finem, ex quo illa habebant quod essent bona et Deo accepta. Tamen sensualitatis voluntas et rationis conformabatur divinae voluntati in actu volendi, quamvis non in volito; quia quamvis Deus non vellet hoc quod sensualitas vel voluntas ut natura volebat in Christo, tamen volebat illum actum utriusque inquantum, secundum Damascenum *permittebat unicuique partium animae pati et agere quod sibi erat naturale et proprium, quantum expediebat ad finem redemptionis et ostensionem veritatis naturae*."

aspects within the process of the will of reason, similar to Albert's approach in *De incarnatione*. Care must be taken to avoid reading Thomas's later distinction of power and act back into the *Scriptum*. The first step must specify what the will parallels. Briefly put, when reason seeks to understand something, it attempts to ground this 'something' in a known and certain principle. In this process, reason must select the correct principle from a group of probable candidates. If it chooses one of the merely probable (instead of certain) principles or a wrong – though certain – principle, reason then errs and does not arrive at an understanding of a thing. When reason discerns the appropriate principle, it can form a judgment with certainty, aware of the fraudulent options.

On the Philosopher's authority, Thomas affirms a parallel between a principle in the process of reason and an end in the process of the will. Whereas reason tries to reduce a potential object of knowledge to a principle, the will tries to reduce something subject to deliberation (*aliquod consiliabile*) into an end. Reason seeks a certain judgment, and the will aims 'to rest totally' in an end, which presumably means to achieve a certainty about the ultimate good of an end in view of other possible ends.[110] If the will does not rest totally in an end, it flickers and flutters between ends or between actions (Thomas does not specify). Up to this point Thomas has written 'into an end' (*in finem*), but in the next paragraph introduces both 'toward an end' (*ad finem*) and 'ordered to an end' (*ordine ad finem*), the latter indicating a means to an end. While the meaning of and distinction between *in finem* and *ad finem* defies obvious answer, it seems likely that Thomas uses *in finem* to express a generic relationship to an end and uses *ad finem* and *ordine ad finem* as specific types of relationships to an end.[111]

In the case of "what is toward an end without an order to an end" (*in* III, d.17, a.2, qua.1), the will is moved according to the qualities found in an object absolutely. The crucial point here regards this type of voluntary motion as not 'into an end' (*in finem*), for this indicates that the will has not set itself in motion and cannot make a final judgment about an action or an end. That is, the will in such motion apparently still flickers, waiting for

---

110 Alvira argues that the relationship between the intellect and will is the same as between the will as nature and the will as reason (Alvira, *Naturaleza y libertad*, p. 49).
111 On the distinction between *in finem* and *ad finem*, see Robiglio, *L'impossibile volere*, p. 58.

a consideration of an end such that the will's object can be ordered as a means to this end or affirmed as the best end relative to the possible ends. Thomas seems to imply that the will is here disposed toward an action but cannot commit to this action until a consideration (parallel to a judgment in the case of reason) determines this action as a good in itself or orders this action toward some end. The will so moved does not will its object simply, but only if no obstructions or undesirable aspects can be found.[112]

With this synopsis of the will's motion, Thomas lays the foundation for dissecting the will of reason into the will as nature and the will as reason. Aquinas previously (*in* III, d.17, a.1, qua.3) argued that the will as nature is moved into something absolutely, and here he specifies this motion in relation to the will as reason. Thomas places a condition on the ability of the will as nature to accept something absolutely, a condition determined by whether reason orders it into an end. If reason does not so order it, the will as nature accepts something absolutely without any mediating step. The will as nature, when ordered into an end by reason, can still accept something absolutely. However, it first requires a "consideration of an end," and this the will as reason accomplishes. The will as reason exercises dominion in matters ordered to an end and so governs the will as nature when it is carried into an end. Without such governance, the will as nature wills imperfectly and conditionally. The will as nature can only regard the inherent value of something and so cannot account for the instrumental good or ill of that thing. The will as nature thus discerns potential objects of the will, based upon their inherent goodness or evil, but cannot in practice evaluate mitigating factors, which would qualify the actual goodness or evil of something.

This concludes a lengthy buildup to the question of conformity of will, specifically how Christ's will of reason "is conformed to the divine will in the thing willed" (*in* III, d.17, a.2, qua.1). Thomas affirms such con-

---

112 For an extended treatment of *velleitas* in Thomas, see Robiglio, *L'impossibile volere*. Robiglio sets Thomas's definition (to will imperfectly or conditionally) within the context of Albert's characterization of *velleitas* as an impossible will (*L'impossibile volere*, pp. 42, 57, 65, 88–89, 187–188). Saarinen points out that Thomas often regards *velleitas* as an incomplete will, a formulation reflecting Albert's view of *velleitas* as a "latent conditional wish" (Risto Saarinen, *Weakness of the Will in Medieval Thought: From Augustine to Buridan* [Leiden, 1994], pp. 103, 130–131).

formity "because the *will as nature* in Christ was never moved into something as into an end, unless as God wills" (*in* III, d.17, a.2, qua.1). The subsequent paragraph completes this assertion's meaning, but first Aquinas turns to the will as reason, which was only moved by reason of an end and was always conformed to the divine will in the thing willed. So, when the will as nature was moved absolutely, it was conformed to the divine will in the thing willed. When the will as nature was ordered to an end, the will as reason, which was always conformed in the thing willed, held ultimate sway and consideration. Thus, even if the will as nature were not conformed to the divine will in the thing willed, Christ's will of reason (*or* human will) would still be conformed due to the will as reason. This offers a reassuring affirmation of conformity guaranteed by the will as reason.

The affirmation reassures because Thomas next discusses the will as nature when "moved into something not as into an end" (*in* III, d.17, a.2, qua.1). Precision requires this specification, because the goodness or evil of something need not be the same in itself and as a means to some end. Moved in this way, the will as nature was not conformed to the divine will in the thing willed, for it willed not to die. Christ's death was an evil in itself but a good as ordered to redemption (for which reason God willed it). Once again, Thomas qualifies the will as nature as willing this imperfectly and conditionally. When willing imperfectly, Christ's will of reason was not conformed to the divine will in the thing willed. However, in everything willed perfectly and absolutely, Christ's will of reason was conformed to the divine will in the thing willed. Thomas's specification of 'perfectly' and 'absolutely' indicates both the will as reason and the will as nature. The will as reason was always conformed (for it always willed perfectly), while the will as nature was conformed only when moved as into an end.

Finally, Thomas extends this logic to Christ's will of sensuality, which was conformed in the thing willed in everything save what was harmful to nature. Those things harmful to nature were goods as ordered to certain ends. Sensuality has not the capacity to order objects to an end and could not discern the instrumental goodness of such natural evils. "Yet," Thomas writes, "the will of sensuality and the will of reason were conformed to the divine will in the act of willing, although not in the thing willed" (*in* III, d.17, a.2, qua.1). When Christ's will of sensuality and will as nature disagreed with the divine will in the thing willed, God willed each of these to do so. A citation of the Damascene authoritatively caps this reasoning, which bears a debt to Bonaventure.[113]

The Bonaventurian reasoning yields to terminological distinctions and logic taken from Albert the Great in Thomas's response to the first objection. Rectitude of a human will, the first objection maintains, is proportionate to that will's conformity to the divine will. Since Christ's human will enjoyed perfect rectitude, it enjoyed perfect conformity, which, even if it encompassed other means of conformity, must have included conformity in every thing willed. Aquinas counters, in what amounts to a long paraphrase of Albert the Great's *Commentarii* (III, d.17, a.1), that conformity in the thing willed does not itself accomplish rectitude of the will. Someone can, from sinful motives, conform to God in the thing willed without thereby achieving rectitude of will. "Rather," Thomas holds, "rectitude of the will is caused from conformity *in the mode of willing*, namely as from charity it wills as God wills; and likewise *in the final cause*, as it wills on account of the same [end]; and likewise *in the efficient cause*, namely as God wills it to will."[114] Thomas's reproduction of arguments from his esteemed teacher Albert offers little surprise, but the manner in which he here does so is interesting. The very closeness of paraphrase could indicate either that Thomas viewed Albert's argument and terminology as difficult to improve upon or that he did not labor to internalize Albert's reasoning within his own solution to the question of conformity. His overall line of argumentation develops along different lines than Albert's. Thomas labors in his solution to explain and defend the conformity of Christ's will of reason to the divine will in the thing willed, and such pains would be extravagant if he were ultimately to undermine the importance of this conformity. Rather, Albert's argument simply affords Thomas some means through which to explain that the isolated non-conformity of Christ's human will to the divine will in the thing willed did not lessen the rectitude of Christ's human will.

---

113 The *Summa contra gentiles* collapses the whole issue into this logic. "Viderunt enim voluntatem humanam in Christo omnino sub voluntate divina ordinatam fuisse, ita quod nihil voluntate humana Christus voluit nisi quod eum velle voluntas divina disposuit" (*SCG* IV.36.8 [ed. Marc et al., 3: 322, n.3748]).

114 *In* III, d.17, a.2, qua.1, *ad* 1 (*Scriptum* 3: 538): "Sed rectitudo voluntatis causatur ex conformitate *in modo volendi*, ut scilicet velit ex caritate sicut Deus; et iterum *in causa finali*, ut propter idem velit; et iterum *in causa efficiente*, ut scilicet Deus velit eum velle."

The second objection links the will of the blessed with Christ's will, as a comprehensor.[115] Since the blessed are conformed to God in the thing willed, and since Christ was a true comprehensor, "with respect to the thing willed, his will was conformed to the divine will."[116] Thomas's response highlights a theme recurrent in his Christology, namely that Christ was both a comprehensor and a wayfarer, bearing similarities to and differences from those who are only one or the other. The blessed, who are only comprehensors, enjoy impassibility and so fear no bodily harm. Thus, "there is not anything in which their sensuality could diverge from the divine will."[117] Though a comprehensor, Christ remained passible and could fear bodily harm. Thomas translates this logic from the will of sensuality to the will as nature. That is, the blessed "are free from every evil,"[118] and so would face nothing evil in itself though good as a means. As a final note, Thomas qualifies the conformity of the blessed's wills to the divine will in the thing willed. The blessed conditionally and imperfectly will for the evils of the damned not to be, thereby conforming to the antecedent divine will for universal salvation, though diverging from the consequent divine will.

The *quaestiuncula*'s final objection provides an exemption for those of us with limited intellects. We are permitted to will something other than what God wills, for we do not know the divine will in all things. Christ, however, knew what God wills in all things, and thus "with respect to every thing willed he conformed his human will to the divine will."[119] Christ, Thomas argues, knew God's will in all things, "yet he did not by his every power apprehend the divine will, nor the reason why God would will something according to its order to a certain end."[120] This removes any

---

115 The blessed are already comprehensors (rather than wayfarers). Thomas argues that Christ was both a wayfarer and a comprehensor (see *ST* III, q.15, a.10; *in* III, d.15, q.2, a.1, qua.3, *ad* 3; d.18, a.2).
116 *In* III, d.17, a.2, qua.1, ob.2 (*Scriptum* 3: 534): "Ergo quantum ad volitum divinae voluntati ejus voluntas conformis erat."
117 *In* III, d.17, a.2, qua.1, *ad* 2 (*Scriptum* 3: 538): "ideo non erit aliquid in quo eorum sensualitas a divina voluntate discordet."
118 *In* III, d.17, a.2, qua.1, *ad* 2 (*Scriptum* 3: 538): "ob omni malo liberati erunt."
119 *In* III, d.17, a.2, qua.1, ob.3 (*Scriptum* 3: 534): "Ergo quantum ad omnia volita voluntatem humanam divinae conformabat."
120 *In* III, d.17, a.2, qua.1, *ad* 3 (*Scriptum* 3: 538): "non tamen qualibet sua vi apprehendebat divinam voluntatem, nec rationem quare Deus id vellet secundum ordinem ad finem aliquem." The Latin for power here is *vis* not *potentia*, so this need not compromise the unity of the *potentia* of the will.

necessity that Christ, in his every power, conform to the divine will in the thing willed. Such necessity only applies to those powers that can apprehend the divine will in all things. This response concludes this lengthy *quaestiuncula*, adding yet one more element to this thick mix of logic.

The *Summa*'s engagement with this topic (*ST* III, q.18, a.5) differs, in its relative simplicity, from the *Scriptum*'s. Another difference immediately stands out in the language of the objections. Whereas the *Scriptum*'s objections argued for conformity in the thing willed, the *Summa*'s deny that Christ's human will willed anything other than the divine will. Both formulations perhaps amount to the same thing logically, but their stylistic variance bears import for the structure and tone adopted by Thomas. The question of *ST* III, q.18, a.5 is 'Whether Christ's human will was wholly conformed to the divine will in the thing willed,'[121] yet the objections mention neither 'conformity' nor 'thing willed' (*volitum*). Thomas can thus counter the objections, affirming that Christ's human will did will something other than the divine will, without denying conformity. This strategy does, however, require a subtle conception of conformity, one that Thomas establishes in *ST* I–II, q.19. His treatment of Christ's conformity and non-contrariety of wills depends heavily on his general presentation of a human will conformed to God in *ST* I–II, q.19.

The objections all conclude that Christ's human will willed nothing other than what the divine will willed. The *Summa*'s objections rework, to varying degrees and to fit this conclusion, those of the *Scriptum*. The first objection in *ST* III, q.18, a.5 quotes Psalm 39:9 as from the person of Christ, where Christ wills to do his God's will.[122] "But," the objection continues, "he who wills to do another's will, wills what that one wills."[123] The second objection defends Christ's perfect charity (*caritas*) on the basis of Ephesians 3:19, and then defines charity as "making man will the same thing as God."[124] The Philosopher (*Nicomachean Ethics* 9.4.1) bolsters this defini-

---

121 *ST* III, q.18, a.5 (*Summa theologiae* 4: 2548a): "Utrum voluntas humana Christi fuerit omnino conformis divinae voluntati in volito."
122 For Thomas's Christological reading of the *Psalms*, see Thomas F. Ryan, *Thomas Aquinas as Reader of the Psalms* (Notre Dame, IN, 2000).
123 *ST* III, q.18, a.5, ob.1 (*Summa theologiae* 4: 2548a): "Sed ille qui vult voluntatem alicuius facere, vult quod ille vult."
124 *ST* III, q.18, a.5, ob.2 (*Summa theologiae* 4: 2548a): "caritas est facere quod homo idem velit quod Deus."

tion. The third objection notes that Christ was a *comprehensor* and continues that "the saints who are comprehensors in heaven will nothing other than what God wills."[125] Quoting Augustine's *De Trinitate* XIII.5, the objection argues that a condition for numbering among the blessed is that one must have everything one wills and will nothing evil.

The *sed contra* provides interest less for its argument than for its source. Aquinas quotes again from Augustine's *Contra Maximinum episcopum Arianorum* (II.20), a novel *auctoritas* on this topic.[126] Augustine argues that Christ, when he said, "'Not as I will, but as you will' (Matt. 26:39), shows himself to have willed something other than the Father."[127] This could only have been with his human will. Therefore, Christ, according to his human will, willed something other than what the divine will willed.

Thomas offers little new material in his response, the majority of which recounts points established in the preceding articles and relies upon the discussion of conformity from *ST* I–II, q.19, a.10. Rather than diminish the value of the *corpus*, this lack of novelty demonstrates Thomas's skill in crafting a question so that the articles build one upon another. He recalls the divisions of Christ's human will, distinguishing first the will of sensuality, which is a will by participation, and the rational will. The rational will may also be considered "through the mode of nature or through the mode of reason."[128] Aquinas then recalls his discussion (*ST* III, q.13, a.3, *ad* 1; q.14, a.1, *ad* 2) of the Damascene's affirmation that "it was permitted to his flesh to do and to suffer those things proper to it" (*De fide orthodoxa* III.19). This permission followed a dispensation before the Son's passion, according to which "it was also permitted to every power of his soul to perform and to undergo which things were proper."[129] In large measure, the *corpus* explores the meaning of this dispensation.

125   *ST* III, q.18, a.5, ob.3 (*Summa theologiae* 4: 2548a): "Sed sancti qui sunt comprehensores in patria, nihil aliud volunt quam quod Deus vult."
126   Thomas draws this quotation from Agatho's *Epistle I*. Agatho's letter provided Thomas with sources previously unused in the thirteenth century. Thomas appropriates the sources cited by Agatho and his basic use of these sources.
127   *ST* III, q.18, a.5, *sed contra*, quoting *Contra Max.* II.20 (*Summa theologiae* 4: 2548a): "In hoc quod Christus ait: 'Non quod volo, sed quod tu,' aliud se ostendit voluisse quam Pater."
128   *ST* III, q.18, a.5 (*Summa theologiae* 4: 2548b): "et voluntas rationalis, sive consideretur per modum naturae, sive per modum rationis."
129   *ST* III, q.18, a.5 (*Summa theologiae* 4: 2548b): "Et similiter etiam permittebat omnibus viribus animae agere et pati quae propria."

"Moreover it is clear," Thomas writes, "that the will of sensuality naturally shuns sensible pains and attacks on the body."[130] The will as nature, since it regards things absolutely according to their inherent goodness or evil, rejects everything contrary to nature and everything evil in itself, which it judges to include death. These two aspects of the dispensation suffice to account for Christ's fear and refusal of death. One might suspect discussion of the powers of Christ's soul doing and suffering what was proper to it to end here. It does not. Thomas also presents Christ's will as reason as following its proper function in electing something from its order to an end. For example, sensuality and the will as nature would shun cauterization, but the will as reason would elect it for the end of health. This inclusion of the will as reason is not trivial but shows Thomas's insistence that 'every power' of Christ's soul functioned as was proper to it. Thus, Christ willed his own passion humanly, through a properly functioning will as reason, just as he shunned and feared the passion through a properly functioning sensuality and will as nature. Christ's free human act of willing the passion for the sake of salvation plays an important role in Thomas's soteriology.[131]

The preceding arguments all serve to frame Aquinas's next assertion and its implications. "Moreover, it was the will of God that Christ suffer distress and pains and death, not that these were things willed by God according to themselves, but from their order to the end of human salvation."[132] Thomas continues that the will of sensuality and the will as nature could indeed will something other than the divine will. Christ's will as reason, however, always willed what the divine will willed. Thomas has here allowed a diversity of things willed to preserve a greater conformity. The divine will recognized Christ's passion as an evil in itself, and as such refused it. Christ's sensuality and will as nature followed the divine will in shunning the passion according to itself. The divine will willed Christ's passion solely as a means to human salvation. To the extent that Christ's human will could

---

130 *ST* III, q.18, a.5 (*Summa theologiae* 4: 2548b): "Manifestum est autem quod voluntas sensualitatis refugit naturaliter dolores sensibiles et corporis laesionem."
131 Thomas also writes of Christ's freely willed obedience to the divine will in the passion despite its repugnance to his natural will (*ST* III, q.47, a.2, *ad* 2).
132 *ST* III, q.18, a.5 (*Summa theologiae* 4: 2548b): "Voluntas autem Dei erat ut Christus dolores et passiones et mortem pateretur, non quod ista essent a Deo volita secundum se, sed ex ordine ad finem humanae salutis."

will something as a means, namely by the will as reason, Christ willed his passion in conformity to the divine will. This act of free obedience serves as cause of salvation. The basic logic of Aquinas's response follows, though in a vastly compressed form, the logic of Agatho's *Epistle I*.

Thomas makes explicit this understanding in response to the first objection, which merits full quotation:

> It should be said that Christ, through his rational will, willed that the divine will be fulfilled; however, not through the will of sensuality, the movement of which does not extend itself up to the will of God; nor through the will which is considered through the mode of nature, which is borne into some object considered absolutely, and not in its order to the divine will.[133]

This response argues that Christ could will something other than the divine will because certain aspects of the human will have not the capacity to reach beyond the object at hand to the divine will. Thus, those aspects functioned naturally in willing something other than the divine will. It would be unnatural for the will of sensuality or the will as nature to overrule the will as reason, thereby doing something other than the divine will. In response to the second objection, Thomas states that conformity of the human will to the divine will takes place in the will of reason. To the third, Aquinas notes that Christ was both a comprehensor and a wayfarer, with a passible body. "And therefore," Thomas concludes, "it was possible on the part of his passible body for something to occur in him which was repugnant to his natural will, and also to his sensitive appetite."[134]

This presentation of Christ's conformity of wills follows the general logic established in *ST* I–II, q.19, where Thomas raises the question of conformity to the divine will in the thing willed. The response begins by

---

133 *ST* III, q.18, a.5, *ad* 1 (*Summa theologiae* 4: 2548b): "Dicendum quod Christus, per voluntatem rationalem, voluit ut divina voluntas impleretur; non autem per voluntatem sensualitatis, cuius motus non se extendit usque ad voluntatem Dei; neque per voluntatem quae consideratur per modum naturae, quae fertur in aliqua obiecta absolute considerata, et non in ordine ad divinam voluntatem."
134 *ST* III, q.18, a.5, *ad* 3 (*Summa theologiae* 4: 2549a): "Et ideo ex parte carnis passibilis poterat in eo aliquid accidere quod repugnaret naturali voluntati ipsius, et etiam appetitui sensitivo."

noting that one and the same object can be good and bad in different respects or for different reasons. This basic point allows for a difference or even opposition of things willed without admitting any contrariety or malice. Thomas extends the point through distinction of the common good and particular goods, a distinction particularly relevant for the conformity of a human will to the divine will. On account of the various considerations of an object's good, "it happens that a certain will is good willing something considered according to a particular reason even when God does not will that thing according to universal reason" (*ST* I–II, q.19, a.10).[135] To this, Aquinas adds the further qualification that willing a particular good only makes a will upright when the particular good "is referred to the common good as into an end" (*ST* I–II, q.19, a.10).[136] This strategy allows the thing willed to be regarded both materially (in terms of the particular good) and formally (in terms of its order to the common good).[137] Even when the object of a human will differs materially from the object of the divine will, this does not imply non-conformity as long as the human will

---

135 *ST* I–II, q.19, a.10 (*Summa theologiae* 2: 830a–830b): "Contingit autem aliquid esse bonum secundum rationem particularem, quod non est bonum secundum rationem universalem, aut e converso, ut dictum est. Et ideo contingit quod aliqua voluntas est bona volens aliquid secundum rationem particularem consideratum, quod tamen Deus non vult secundum rationem universalem, aut e converso."

136 *ST* I–II, q.19, a.10 (*Summa theologiae* 2: 830b): "Non est autem recta voluntas alicuius hominis volentis aliquod bonum particulare, nisi referat illud in bonum commune sicut in finem."

137 *ST* I–II, q.19, a.10 (*Summa theologiae* 2: 830b): "Ex fine autem sumitur quasi formalis ratio volendi illud quod ad finem ordinatur. Unde ad hoc quod aliquis recta voluntate velit aliquod particulare bonum, oportet quod illud particulare bonum sit volitum materialiter, bonum autem commune divinum sit volitum formaliter. Voluntas igitur humana tenetur conformari divinae voluntati in volito formaliter, tenetur enim velle bonum divinum et commune; sed non materialiter, ratione iam dicta. – Sed tamen quantum ad utrumque aliquo modo voluntas humana conformatur voluntati divinae. Quia secundum quod conformatur voluntati divinae in communi ratione voliti, conformatur ei in fine ultimo. Secundum autem quod non conformatur ei in volito materialiter, conformatur ei secundum rationem causae efficientis; quia hanc propriam inclinationem consequentem naturam, vel apprehensionem particularem huius rei, habet res a Deo sicut a causa effectiva. Unde consuevit dici quod conformatur quantum ad hoc, voluntas hominis voluntati divinae, quae vult hoc quod Desu vult eum velle." Thomas makes a similar argument in *ST* II–II, q.104, a.4, *ad* 3.

wills what God wills it to will. Thomas's defense of Christ's conformity of wills provides a concrete and specific example of this general principle.

Thomas's basic understanding of Christ's conformity of will changed little between the *Scriptum* and the *Summa*. His presentation of this basic understanding develops between the two works, with the *Summa* achieving a clarity far lacking in the *Scriptum*. This depends largely on the *Summa*'s distinction of power and act, which provides a conceptual and terminological framework for distinguishing the will as nature and the will as reason. Thomas's presentation of Christ's human will in conformity to the divine will rests squarely upon the will as one power with two acts. Thomas's recovery of Agatho's *Epistle I* with the acts of Constantinople III provided Thomas with sources and an argumentative strategy for affirming both that Christ willed something other than what God willed and that Christ's human will was perfectly obedient to God's.

The Acts of Christ's Will

The next article of *ST* III, q.18 consolidates two *quaestiunculae* from *in* III, d.17, a.2, both of which address contrariety of wills in Christ. Thomas's solution to the question of conformity logically raises that of contrariety. Conformity between Christ's human will and the divine will in the thing willed exists with respect to the will as reason, though not with respect to the will of sensuality and the will as nature. Does this not imply contrariety within Christ's human will? According to Thomas this need not imply contrariety. His justification for non-contrariety, while mindful of the contributions of Albert the Great and Bonaventure, reaches back to William of Auxerre and the *Summa fratris Alexandri*. The differences between the *Scriptum* and the *Summa* are again subtle but important, requiring a high level of detail to draw out.

The first objection of *in* III, d.17, a.2, qua.2 repeats the citation of Augustine's *De Trinitate* handed down through treatments of this topic.[138] The citation argues contrariety of wills derives from contrariety of things

---

138 See William of Auxerre, *Summa aurea* III, tr.6, c.1, ob.1; *Summa fratris Alexandri* III, tr.4, q.1, c.2, *contra* 1 and Bonaventure, *Commentaria in quatuor libros Sententiarum*, Bk.III, d.17, q.3, ob.4. Each of these texts offers some version of the same argument, which is usually attributed to Augustine's *De Trinitate* XI.

willed. The objection continues that "the things willed by sensuality and by reason in Christ were contrary,"[139] and so Christ's will of sensuality was contrary to his will of reason. The second objection turns to the Damascene, who argues it was permitted for Christ's every power to perform what is natural and proper to it. The sensitive appetite naturally desires things delectable to the senses, therefore it desired likewise in Christ. The objection identifies such desire as the root of the "struggle of sensuality against reason in us,"[140] and so extends this struggle to Christ himself. The third objection notes contrariety of will when something both delights and distresses the same person, and, finding this condition satisfied of Christ in Matt. 4:2, declares contrariety of wills in Christ.

After two *sed contra*s, the first linking contrariety to sin and the second repeating a standard authority (spuriously attributed to Augustine),[141] Thomas launches into his response by locating the three causes of contrariety within us. "*First*, [it is caused] from diversity of things willed; *second*, because sensuality is borne without restraint and without the rule of reason into the thing willed; *third*, from this that sensuality tends without restraint into its thing willed, it retards the movement of reason and impedes it either wholly or in part."[142] Of these three, only the first was true of Christ. Thomas argues that reason preordained Christ's every movement of sensuality. Even when sensuality and reason differed in the thing willed, reason and the divine will willed sensuality to be so borne. Thus, the movement of sensuality was never without restraint and never impeded reason.

The *Summa fratris Alexandri* provides Thomas ammunition with which to answer the first objection. Thomas quotes that "contraries naturally

---

139 *In* III, d.17, a.2, qua.2, ob.1 (*Scriptum* 3: 535): "Sed volita sensualitatis et rationis in Christo fuerunt contraria."
140 *In* III, d.17, a.2, qua.2, ob.2 (*Scriptum* 3: 535): "Sed ex hoc est pugna sensualitatis contra rationem in nobis quod sensualitas appetit delectabilia secundum sensum."
141 See William of Auxerre, *Summa aurea* III, tr.6, c.1; *Summa fratris Alexandri* III, tr.4, q.1, c.2. Bonaventure does not cite but alludes to this passage in his *Commentaria in III*, d.17, q.3.
142 *In* III, d.17, a.2, qua.2 (*Scriptum* 3: 539): "*Primo* ex diversitate volitorum; *secundo* quia sensualitas in suum volitum effrenate et sine regimine rationis fertur; *tertio* ex hoc quod sensualitas effrenate tendens in suum volitum, retardat motum rationis et impedit vel in toto vel in parte."

occur concerning the same."[143] This principle becomes a foundation for reiterating the *solutio*'s main points. Although sensuality and reason tend to contrary things, they are not contrary unless sensuality impedes the movement of reason, which can happen in two ways. This occurs "when sensuality is borne without restraint into its object" or "when sensuality retards or extinguishes the movement of reason."[144] As noted in the *solutio*, these two were not in Christ as they are in other human beings. "And so," Thomas concludes, "*in Christ there was no struggle or contrariety of sensuality to reason.*"[145] The response to the second objection specifies that sensuality naturally and properly desires what is delectable to the senses only under the rule and order of reason. The third objection, Thomas holds, proves only diversity of things willed, which does not suffice for contrariety of wills.

Up to this point in the *Scriptum*, Thomas has defended conformity of wills in Christ between human and divine as well as the non-contrariety of sensuality to reason. The final *quaestiuncula* of article two addresses the question of contrariety within the will of reason. The objections defend this contrariety in two ways, the first of which centers upon the will of reason as the medium between the will of sensuality and the divine will. Since a medium "communicates with both of the extremes," the objection holds the will of reason in Christ "was conformed to both [extremes]."[146] As the will of reason willed something contrary to the divine will, the will of reason, conformed both to sensuality and to the divine will, willed contrary things. The second objection argues from conclusions previously established in the *Scriptum*, namely that the will as nature and the will as reason willed contrary things. These are both aspects of the will of reason, and so "in the will of reason there was contrariety in Christ."[147]

---

143 *In* III, d.17, a.2, qua.2, *ad* 1 (*Scriptum* 3: 539): "contraria nata sunt fieri circa idem" (cf. *Summa fratris Alexandri* III, tr.4, q.1, c.2).
144 *In* III, d.17, a.2, qua.2, *ad* 1 (*Scriptum* 3: 535): "et hoc est quando effrenate sensualitas in suum objectum fertur ..., et hoc est quando sensualitas retardat vel extinguit motum rationis."
145 *In* III, d.17, a.2, qua.2, *ad* 1 (*Scriptum* 3: 539): "*Et ideo nulla fuit in Christo pugna vel contrarietas sensualitatis ad rationem.*"
146 *In* III, d.17, a.2, qua.3, ob.1 (*Scriptum* 3: 536): "medium enim communicat cum utroque extremorum. Sed voluntas rationis media erat in Christo inter voluntatem divinam et sensualitatem. Ergo conformabatur utrique."
147 *In* III, d.17, a.2, qua.3, ob.2 (*Scriptum* 3: 536): "Ergo in voluntate rationis erat contrarietas in Christo."

Thomas offers three counter arguments, arguments to which he must himself respond after answering the objections. The first *sed contra* (or third objection) stipulates that contrary things "cannot simultaneously be in the same thing."[148] There cannot, therefore, be contraries in the will of reason, because it is only one power (*potentia*). The fourth maintains that the will of reason follows the apprehension of reason, which was determined to one thing alone in Christ. So the will of reason in Christ was determined to only one thing, not to contrary things. For the fifth objection, Thomas refers to Augustine's contention (*Confessions* VIII.9) that "contrariety of will is caused from an imperfection of will."[149] The objection continues that Christ had no imperfect will, and so his will of reason was not contrary to itself.

The *solutio* of *quaestiuncula* three presents anew the findings of *quaestiuncula* one, stating that "according to the will of reason, Christ willed diverse things, although not in one way, but on the one hand absolutely, on the other, however, conditionally and imperfectly."[150] This implies no contrariety in the will of reason, for contrariety is only "from a contrary reason of the object."[151] The will as reason and the will as nature willed contrary things on account of a reason that possessed no contrariety. Thomas again explains this through divergent modes of considering an object, that is, as an end in itself or as a means. This dispatches the first two objections and any further attempt to ground contrariety simply in a diversity of things willed, and it further dismisses the third objection's attempt to eliminate contrariety at the expense of a contrariety of things willed. However, the lack of distinction between power and act (prominent in the *Summa*) hampers Thomas's attempt to counter the impossibility of contraries in one power. His response to the fourth objection specifies a proportion between reason's determination to one, as a final judgment, and the will's determi-

---

148 *In* III, d.17, a.2, qua.3, ob.3 (*Scriptum* 3: 536): "Contraria non possunt esse in eodem simul."
149 *In* III, d.17, a.2, qua.3, ob.5 (*Scriptum* 3: 536): "contrarietas voluntatis causatur ex imperfectione voluntatis."
150 *In* III, d.17, a.2, qua.3 (*Scriptum* 3: 539): "secundum voluntatem rationis, Christus diversa volebat, non tamen uno modo, sed alterum absolute, alterum autem sub conditione et imperfecte."
151 *In* III, d.17, a.2, qua.3 (*Scriptum* 3: 539–540): "Et ideo non erat contrarietas in voluntate, quia contrarietas in habitu vel in actu est ex contraria ratione objecti."

nation to one, as a final consent. "Nevertheless," Thomas writes, "in reason there was an apprehension of diverse and of contrary reasons about the same thing considered in different ways; and so also it was concerning the movement of the will."[152] Augustine, as cited in the fifth objection, writes about the will pulled between two final consents, and Thomas argues that this was not present in Christ.

Article six of *ST* III, q.18 addresses simply the question of contrariety of wills in Christ, without specifying which wills are under discussion. The objections raised in article six help explain this difference with the *Scriptum*, and, along with the *sed contra*, bear the fruits of Thomas's historical research. The conventional identification of contrary wills with contrary objects opens the first objection. The objection quickly indicates contrary objects in Christ, who with his human will shunned the passion but willed his death with the divine will. The objection now seems misplaced, more properly belonging in article five, or strangely simplistic for not recognizing the divisions of the human will. Aquinas's citation of Pseudo-Athanasius (*De incarnatione et Contra Arianos*, n.21) explains his inclusion of this objection.[153] The quotation from Pseudo-Athanasius prepares for the *sed contra* by implying contrariety of wills in its attempt to discern both a human will and a divine will in Christ. As with works of Ambrose and Augustine, Thomas uncovered in Pseudo-Athanasius's work *Adversus Appolinarium* (*De incarnatione et Contra Arianos*) support for a dyothelite position expressed against the Arians. Agatho repeatedly cites these anti-Arian works to bolster his proof of two wills in Christ. In their attempt to stress plurality of wills in Christ, Augustine and Pseudo-Athanasius sometimes imply contrariety or non-conformity of wills. Thomas follows Agatho in locating this contrariety within a greater scheme of obedience. Christ demonstrates perfect obedience (of sensuality to reason and of the human will to God) in the proper ordering of his natural affections. Thomas uses the contrariety implied by Pseudo-Athanasius and Augustine to show the truth of Christ's human nature and the natural function of every power of that nature. Again, the presentation of Christ's human nature completes

---

152 *In* III, d.17, a.2, qua.3, *ad* 4 (*Scriptum* 3: 540): "Tamen in ratione erat apprehensio diversarum et contrarium rationum circa eamdem rem diversimode consideratam; et sic etiam erat de motu voluntatis."
153 Thomas knows this quotation from Agatho's *Epistle I* (Riedinger 2.1: 71; Mansi 11: 246).

the presentation of anthropology. For Aquinas, it is not merely a matter of demonstrating Christ's true humanity, but of investigating it, plumbing its depths so that we may see our nature as it should be, not as it is deformed by sin. In this context Thomas refocuses these anti-Arian works within the Christological scheme of the *Summa theologiae*.

The second objection defines contrariety of wills as "when the spirit desires one thing, and the flesh another,"[154] referring to Galatians 5:17 for support. The objection argues for such contrariety in Christ. The Holy Spirit directed Christ's will of charity (*or* will of the flesh, as the majority of texts read), but "according to the flesh he shunned the passion."[155] This objection appears only slightly more effective than the former; aside from the explicit mention of contrariety, the main points of the objection have been answered in earlier articles. Scriptural quotation buttresses the third objection as well. The issue presented concerns Christ's agony, mentioned in Luke 22:43, which the objection takes to imply a struggle within Christ's soul between contrary impulses.[156] The conclusion is again contrariety of wills.

The *sed contra*, consisting entirely in quotation of the acts of Constantinople III, further clarifies Thomas's choice of objections.[157] The acts proclaim two natural wills in Christ. There was no contrariety of wills, as the heretics claimed, because Christ's human will was subject to the divine will without reluctance or resistance. Thomas structured and worded the objections to be contradicted by citation of Constantinople III, the previously unused and unknown source now serving as champion of the cause. With the council's affirmation of two natural, non-contrary wills in Christ,

---

154 *ST* III, q.18, a.6, ob.2 (*Summa theologiae* 4: 2549a): "Est igitur contrarietas voluntatum quando spiritus unum concupiscit, et caro aliud."
155 *ST* III, q.18, a.6, ob.2 (*Summa theologiae* 4: 2549a): "nam per voluntatem carnis [*or* caritatis], quam Spiritus Sanctus in eius mente faciebat, volebat passionem, ... secundum autem carnem passionem refugiebat."
156 Thomas quotes Luke 22:42 and Ambrose's commentary on it in *ST* III, q.18, a.1, *sed contra*.
157 *ST* III, q.18, a.6, *sed contra* (*Summa theologiae* 4: 2549b): "Sed contra est quod in determinatione Sextae Synodi, dicitur: 'Praedicamus duas naturales voluntates: non contrarias, iuxta quod impii asserunt haeretici, sed sequentem eius humanam voluntatem, et non resistentem vel reluctantem, sed potius subiectam divinae eius atque omnipotenti voluntati" (see Riedinger 2.2: 775; Mansi 11: 638).

Thomas offers an unambiguous foundation for non-contrariety upon which he can add layers of distinctions and nuance.

Thomas begins his response with the first layer of specification, writing that "there cannot be contrariety, unless opposition is noticed in the same and according to the same."[158] He organizes the *corpus* around this distinction, combining elements from William of Auxerre and the *Summa fratris Alexandri*. Would-be contrariety, when in diverse things and according to diverse things, is properly not contrariety but diversity. Here Thomas develops a logic admitting of two options, contrariety and diversity, rather than contrariety and non-contrariety. Thus, the denial of contrariety serves also to bolster the diversity of wills defended in earlier articles.

Aquinas examines 'according to the same', for which he uses both *secundum idem* and *circa idem*, as the first condition for contrariety of wills.[159] Willing different things does not suffice for contrariety of wills, unless these contrary things are willed according to the same reason (*ratio*), or, more precisely, type of reason. Thomas distinguishes universal and particular reasons, illustrating the point with a robber's execution.[160] A king would will this execution for the universal reason of the public good, but a relative of the robber might will the robber not to be executed for the particular reason of a private good. No true contrariety of wills can be claimed here unless the lower will, namely the will motivated by the particular reason of a private good, endeavors to impede or prevent the higher will. If this were to occur, then "a repugnance of wills is noticed on account of the same (*circa idem*)."[161] The details of this example are well chosen, pitting a higher will, the king's, by whose authority the execution will proceed or be stayed, against a lower will, lower both in authority and capacity. Further, the difference of wills revolves around an execution considered both from the

---

158 *ST* III, q.18, a.6 (*Summa theologiae* 4: 2549b): "Dicendum quod contrarietas non potest esse, nisi oppositio attendatur in eodem et secundum idem."
159 Thomas uses a similar strategy to explain Christ's simultaneous enjoyment of the beatific vision and suffering the pain of crucifixion (*ST* III, q.46, a.8).
160 Aquinas employs the same basic example to illustrate the difference between particular goods and the universal good in *ST* I–II, q.19, a.10.
161 *ST* III, q.18, a.6 (*Summa theologiae* 4: 2549b): "Puta si rex vult suspendi latronem propter bonum publicum, et aliquis consanguineus nolit eum suspendi propter amorem privatum, non erit contrarietas voluntatis; nisi forte in tantum se extendat voluntas hominis privati ut bonum publicum velit impedire ut conservetur bonum privatum; tunc enim circa idem attenditur repugnantia voluntatum."

universal perspective of the benefit to all and from the particulars of a personal attachment.[162] This example serves Thomas well and well prepares for the next condition of contrariety.

"Moreover it is required, second, for contrariety of will that it be through the same will."[163] Thomas explains this point not by discussing the will, but, interestingly, the appetite (*appetitus*), perhaps thereby gesturing back to the *Sentences*. He writes that if "a person wills one thing through the appetite of reason, and wills another through the sensitive appetite, here there is not any contrariety."[164] The exception, already noted with the first condition, is if the sensitive appetite disproportionately exerts itself so as to impede or overpower the appetite of reason. In this case the very movement of the sensitive appetite shows itself contrary to the rational appetite itself, not just to the object willed through the rational appetite.

Neither of these two conditions, outlined in such detail, proves true in the case of Christ's wills. Thomas summarizes the matter with these strong words: "even though the natural will and the will of sensuality in Christ could have willed something other than his divine will and will of reason, there was, nevertheless, not any contrariety of wills."[165] He defends this through the two criteria for contrariety, in the process further detailing these conditions. The case of Christ's wills fails the first test for contrariety because "neither his natural will, nor his will of sensuality, repudiated that reason, namely by which the divine will and the will of human reason in Christ willed the passion."[166] This clarifies the example, for the relative who

---

162 In the case of Christ, the same dynamic exists between the universal good and a personal good. The example of Christ is more dramatic both because of the nature of the universal good and because Christ himself is the one subject to execution.
163 *ST* III, q.18, a.6 (*Summa theologiae* 4: 2549b): "Secundo autem requiritur ad contrarietatem voluntatis, quod sit circa eandem voluntatem."
164 *ST* III, q.18, a.6 (*Summa theologiae* 4: 2549b): "Si enim homo vult unum secundum appetitum rationis, et vult aliud secundum appetitum sensitivum, non est hic aliqua contrarietas."
165 *ST* III, q.18, a.6 (*Summa theologiae* 4: 2550a): "Sic igitur dicendum est quod licet voluntas naturalis et voluntas sensualitatis in Christo aliquid aliud voluerit quam voluntas divina et voluntas rationis ipsius, non tamen fuit aliqua contrarietas voluntatum."
166 *ST* III, q.18, a.6 (*Summa theologiae* 4: 2550a): "neque voluntas eius naturalis, neque voluntas sensualitatis repudiabat illam rationem, scilicet qua divina voluntas et voluntas rationis humanae in Christo, passionem volebat."

wills the robber not to be executed out of personal love can reject or not reject (meaning either not to oppose or to accept) the reason for the execution. Only in the case of such a rejection would the relative's will be contrary to the king's, and even then only if the relative willed to prevent the execution. Such was not the case in Christ, for his will as nature did will the salvation of the human race. The will as nature, however, could not view the passion as ordered to salvation and did not reject the passion as a means. "Moreover, the movement of sensuality did not prevail to extend itself to this,"[167] by which Thomas could mean either that the will of sensuality had not the capacity to accept or reject salvation of the human race or that it had not the capacity to impede the will of reason in willing the passion.[168]

Thomas next turns to the second condition, following the order established by the example. As expected, he denies contrariety of wills on this condition, because neither the natural will nor the appetite of sensuality impeded or retarded the divine will or the will of reason. In what follows, Thomas further specifies what constitutes contrariety, writing that "nor

---

167 *ST* III, q.18, a.6 (*Summa theologiae* 4: 2550a): "Motus autem sensualitatis ad hoc se extendere non valebat."
168 "For Jesus, this 'proper function according to nature' implies that his sense appetite be able to operate spontaneously, or as an *impulse* of affectivity relative to its own sentient object. In the Garden, Christ undergoes an instinctive affective impulse towards the natural good, or, more precisely, away from the natural evil, *before* any kind of awareness on the part of his reason, i.e. before the *imperium* of reason had discerned which specific good – viz. the salvation of the human race – should be elected or chosen. Even such an instinctive impulse of affectivity would however have been finalized by reason, or by a free-willed choice *ut ratio* (as confirmed by Jesus' decision to embrace his violent fate), as all affective movements in Christ operated in harmony with reason's *imperium* in a way that never involved a genuine clash of flesh against spirit; again, all the movements of Jesus' sensate soul were wholly ordered to God. The spontaneous impulse of affectivity on the part of his lower appetite therefore posed no real threat to Jesus' radical integrity and rectification of soul" (Gondreau, *The Passions of Christ's Soul*, pp. 316–317). Gondreau here stresses the incomplete and instinctual nature of Christ's aversion to death in the garden of Gethsemane. This stress interprets the *voluntas ut natura* as an incomplete and imperfect will in the sense of an initial, pre-reflective movement overruled by the *voluntas ut ratio*. Robiglio offers a similar account of the *voluntas ut natura* (Robiglio, *L'impossibile volere*, p. 58). I would agree with this analysis up to a point but would insist that Thomas conceives Christ's aversion to suffering and death according to the *voluntas ut natura* not as a fleeting impulse but as an abiding disposition to a natural evil.

conversely did the divine will, or the will of reason in Christ, refuse or retard the movement of the natural human will, or the movement of sensuality in Christ."[169] Christ willed, through his divine will and his will of reason, that his sensuality and natural will "were moved according to the order of their natures."[170] And so, there was neither repugnance nor contrariety among Christ's wills.[171]

The first objection argued for contrariety of wills based on contrary things willed. Article five already dissected these wills or aspects of the will according to which were conformed to the divine will in the thing willed. Thomas's response to the first objection of article six wastes no time repeating the findings of article five and immediately seizes upon the second condition for contrariety from the *corpus*. He writes that "the very fact that any human will in Christ willed something other than his divine will proceeded from the divine will itself."[172] This focuses on the second aspect of the second condition, highlighting what Bonaventure called concordance or harmony of wills.[173] The same logic answers the second objection. In our fallen state, our flesh not only desires against the spirit but even impedes or retards the desire of the spirit. Christ's perfect human nature permitted no such contrariety, for the desires of his flesh did not impede those of the spirit. Thomas's response to the third objection provides a foretaste of question 21, on Christ's prayer in the garden, for neither his agony

---

169 *ST* III, q.18, a.6 (*Summa theologiae* 4: 2550a): "Similiter etiam e contrario voluntas divina, vel voluntas rationis in Christo, refugiebat aut retardabat motum voluntatis naturalis humanae, et motum sensualitatis in Christo."
170 *ST* III, q.18, a.6 (*Summa theologiae* 4: 2550a): "secundum ordinem suae naturae moverentur."
171 Thomas's distinction between power and act grounds his use of *circa eandem voluntatem* and *in eodem*. Albert the Great argues against those who use *circa idem ut idem* to prevent contrariety of wills in Christ, because, he argues, this condition would remove all "contrariety of struggle within us" (*Commentarii in III*, d.17, a.4). Bonaventure also critiques the logic of *secundum idem* as insufficient to account for non-contrariety in Christ (see *Commentaria in III*, d.17, a.1, q.3, *ad* 1). Thomas appears sensitive to the criticisms of Albert and Bonaventure but employs the distinction of power and act to rehabilitate this terminology and logic.
172 *ST* III, q.18, a.6, *ad* 1 (*Summa theologiae* 4: 2550a): "Dicendum quod hoc ipsum quod aliqua voluntas humana in Christo aliud volebat quam eius voluntas divina, procedebat ex ipsa voluntate divina." This echoes *ST* I–II, q.19, a.10 and its defense of conformity based upon efficient causality.
173 See Bonaventure, *Commentaria in III*, d.17, a.1, q.3.

nor his prayer emanated from reason or the rational soul. The third objection held 'agony' to involve an inner struggle of the will. Aquinas shows this not to be the case in Christ; Christ's human reason never struggled between options. A struggle of wills (*or* within the will) results from the limitations of our rational faculties, which cannot always judge one thing to be simply better than another. As reason wavers from judgment to judgment, so too does the will struggle. "This was not in Christ, because through his reason he judged it to be simply better that through his passion the divine will might be fulfilled concerning the salvation of the human race."[174] There was a struggle in Christ's soul, but Thomas, following the Damascene, locates this in Christ's sensitive soul.

It is now possible to consolidate the findings of this technical textual analysis and so to summarize Aquinas's teaching on Christ's two wills. Many developments are apparent between the *Scriptum* and the *Summa*. 'Developments' rather generally expresses what more specifically range from shifts in emphasis to conceptual and terminological innovations to recovery of authoritative sources. Such shifts in emphasis, though often subtle, reveal changes in approach or orientation. Innovations in concepts of terminology provide Thomas with the precision necessary to better express previously iterated ideas. Finally, Thomas's recovery and use of forgotten sources legitimated commonly held positions and provided insight into the controversies leading up to Constantinople III's determinations. Chapter five will expand upon this discussion as it examines the role of Christ's two wills within the *Summa*'s Christology, and so this summary need do little more than offer a point of departure.

The two most prominent shifts of emphasis between the *Scriptum* and the *Summa* are an increased interest in Christ's free choice (*liberum arbitrium*) in the *Summa* and its focus on the *assumption* of a perfect human nature. More properly, this focus highlights the assumption of a human nature into hypostatic union with the Word; a correct understanding of this assumption yields a correct understanding of the human nature assumed. The question on Christ's two wills in the *Summa* falls within the section on the 'consequences of the union' (qq.16–26). This focus on the

---

174 *ST* III, q.18, a.6, *ad* 3 (*Summa theologiae* 4: 2550b): "Quod in Christo non fuit, quia per suam rationem iudicabat simpliciter esse melius quod per eius passionem impleretur voluntas divina circa salutem generis humani."

assumption of human nature and consequences of this hypostatic union largely depends upon Thomas's historically fueled polemic against Nestorianism and any two-subject Christology. For the present purpose, it will suffice to indicate the difference between the *Scriptum* and the *Summa*.

The *Scriptum*'s consideration of Christ's wills devotes considerable attention to defending the will as a necessary part of the integral human nature assumed by the Word. The *Summa*'s equivalent opens rather differently, resting content in referring to the *Prima pars*' characterization of the will as a necessary attribute of human nature. Aquinas wastes no time in the *Summa* on what occupied so much attention in *in* III, d.17, a.1, qua.1. Rather, the *Summa* catalogues Christological heresies, interrogating these heresies to find the root cause of their denial of two wills in Christ. The *Summa* distinguishes the monothelites proper (Macarius of Antioch, Sergius of Constantinople, Cyrus of Alexandria) from the other heretics, who fundamentally misunderstand the Word's assumption of human nature into hypostatic union. The monothelites seem a different breed; they possess a correct appreciation of the hypostatic union yet deny two wills in Christ. This curious circumstance made necessary a new conciliar determination (Constantinople III), making explicit Christ's possession of two wills. Thomas eventually categorizes monothelitism with the other heresies for misconceiving the hypostatic union, following Agatho's line of argumentation, which argues against the monothelites and monenergists based upon the council of Chalcedon and the second council of Constantinople.

The elevated significance in Thomas's mature thought of Christ's free choice merits extended consideration here. The *Scriptum* discusses free choice in Christ only in response to an objection (*in* III, d.17, a.1, qua.3, *ad* 5) and only briefly. *Quaestiuncula* three's concern over a division within the will of reason sets the context; Thomas's response intends less to defend free choice in Christ than to exclude its importation of a division into the will of reason. Free choice, as regarding means, and the will, as regarding ends, are both aspects of the one power of the will and are distinct only as *boulēsis* and *thelēsis*. The lengthy remainder of the *Scriptum*'s discussion enumerates the ways Christ's wills may be distinguished, without further mention of free choice. Already in the *Summa contra gentiles*, Thomas grants free choice a larger role, both in absolute and in relative terms. The *contra gentiles* argues that absent free choice, Christ would have acted as do irrational animals, and so his actions would have lacked moral worth and exemplary force. This must not be the case; Christ must have had free choice and thus also a human will. In this iteration, free choice is far from an afterthought and serves to defend the presence of a human will in Christ.

Despite the important role of free choice in *Summa contra gentiles* IV.36, Thomas delivers an analysis of Christ's free choice only in the *Summa theologiae*. The *Summa*'s insistence on Christ's free choice responds to certain understandings of Aristotle's practical syllogism and particularly to the so-called Latin Averroism prevalent within the Parisian Faculty of the Arts, most notably Siger of Brabant and Boethius of Dacia.[175] On 10 December 1270 Stephen Tempier, Bishop of Paris, condemned thirteen propositions associated with Averroism. These propositions included "3. That the will of man wills or chooses necessarily," and "9. That free will is a passive power, not an active one; and that it is moved necessarily by the appetible object."[176] Thomas directly combats these propositions in *De malo*, q.6, which labors to establish free choice in human beings. This particular question of the *De malo* must have closely preceded or soon followed the December condemnations of 1270.[177] In the *Prima secundae* of the *Summa*

---

175 "The Aristotelian theory of action caused controversies in Paris during the second half of the thirteenth century. Because the practical syllogism seems to determine the outcome of all human action as a result of intellectual consideration, the traditional Augustinian notion of a 'free decision of the will' was threatened. When the bishop of Paris, Stephen Tempier, in 1277 condemned 219 propositions as heretical, among them were several ethical statements which referred to the Aristotelian practical syllogism. These condemned propositions taught that the will cannot alter a decision made by the intellect" (Saarinen, *Weakness of the Will*, p. 147).

176 These translations are from Weisheipl, *Friar Thomas d'Aquino*, p. 276. For the Latin text, see *Chartularium Universitatis Parisiensis* 1, no. 432, ed. Heinrich Denifle (Paris, 1889) pp. 486–487. For discussions of Latin Averroism, see Abdelali Elamrani-Jamal, "La reception de la philosophie arabe à l'université de Paris au XIIIeme siècle," in *Introduction of Arabic Philosophy into Europe* (Leiden, 1994), pp. 31–39; Fernand Van Steenberghen, "L'averroïsme Latin au XIIIe siècle," in *Multiple Averroès* (Paris, 1978), pp. 283–286; E.-H. Wéber, "Les apports positifs de la noétique d'Ibn Rushd à celle de Thomas d'Aquin," in *Multiple Averroès*, pp. 211–249; and Salvador Gomez Nogales, "Saint Thomas, Averroès et l'averroïsme," in *Aquinas and Problems of his Time*, ed. G. Verbeke and D. Verhelst (Louvain, 1976), pp. 161–177.

177 Many disputes surround the time and place of composition of the *De malo*. Torrell provides a summary of arguments and proposes the two academic years

theologiae Thomas again defends free choice and the freedom of the human will (see *ST* I–II, qq.9 and 13). The *Prima secundae* offers Thomas an opportunity to reflect on these questions with greater distance from the heat of battle and so with more time and calm to develop a layered presentation of the human will's freedom. Thomas's concern for this issue persisted until the spring of 1272, when he began writing the *Summa theologiae*'s *Tertia pars*, and it extends his interest, manifest especially in the *Secunda pars*, in exemplar causality.

Thomas devotes one of the six articles on Christ's human will to defending and explaining free choice in Christ. This task becomes the more crucial and difficult as its main obstacles are presented by John of Damascus and Aristotle. John Damascene, as noted in *ST* III, q.18, a.4, ob.1, denied *gnōmē* and election in Christ. In arguing this line, the Damascene was following Maximus the Confessor and his strategy for presenting Christ's perfect human will.[178] The second objection builds upon Aristotle's linking of election and deliberation, excluding deliberation, and hence election, from Christ. Aquinas's response to these objections develops from the *corpus* and its identification of election and the will as reason. Christ certainly possessed the will as reason, which is election, and so also free choice, which is the act of election. So why would the Damascene exclude election from Christ?

Thomas writes that the Damascene considered election only from the perspective of our ignorant nature, and in this Thomas correctly perceives the motivation behind Maximus's views.[179] In our ignorant nature, election involves doubt, but this doubt adheres to the nature of ignorance rather than to the nature of election. So no contradiction emerges from positing election in Christ while denying doubt. While Thomas affirms the association of election and deliberation, he conditions this association, arguing

---

of 1269–1271 in Paris (Torrell, *Saint Thomas* 1: 201–205, 336). It would thus fall a bit before the *Prima secundae*. The *De malo* can be found in *Quaestiones disputatae et quaestiones duodecim quodlibetales* 2 (Turin, 1931).

178 On Maximus's presentation of Christ's perfect human will, see *Opuscula* 3 and 7 in Louth, *Maximus the Confessor* (London, 1996). Louth also offers a helpful introduction to Maximus and monothelitism, pp. 56–62.

179 Maximus took deliberation as a characteristic of our human, limited knowledge and will. This he designated the *gnomic* will, which Maximus excluded from Christ in light of his human perfection.

that election follows from deliberation only through the intermediary step of judgment. We act upon the judgment that something ought to be done. This judgment (*determinatio per iudicium*) follows (in the case of our ignorant nature) an inquiry and deliberation. Christ, however, could form a judgment regarding what ought to be done without any inquiry or deliberation (see *ST* I–II, q.14, a.4, *ad* 1). Based upon such certain judgment, Christ could elect without any deliberation or doubt.[180] Christ fulfilled all that was natural to humanity, though he exercised it in a way at first strange to our ignorant nature.[181] This offers a glimpse of how Thomas completes the anthropology of the *Prima pars* in his Christology.

There are several secondary developments between the *Scriptum* and the *Summa*. These developments include shifts of emphasis and terminological and conceptual innovations. The *Summa* lays greater stress on God's ability to move a will interiorly. Two points merit discussion in this regard. First, Thomas describes Christ's human will with the same language and logic as every other human will (see *ST* I, qq.22–23; q.105, a.4; q.106, a.2; q.111, a.2; *ST* I–II, q.6, a.1, *ad* 3; q.9, a.6, *ad* 3; q.19). This perhaps sounds unremarkable, but how Aquinas presents Christ's human will as a perfect human will deserves note. Christ's human will receives its determinate mode from the fact that it was in a divine hypostasis (*ST* III, q.18, a.1, *ad* 4); this fact alone could easily serve as the foundation for the rectitude of Christ's human will. Yet this remark Thomas tucks away in response to an objection and highlights instead the same voluntary mechanics at work in Christ's human nature as in ours. The main difference rests less in the person of the Word determining the human will than in Christ's peculiar state as both comprehensor and wayfarer. We lack what Christ in his humanity enjoyed, namely a certitude of the connection between various means and God as the ultimate end in whom is our happiness (see *ST* I, q.82, a.2). This certitude in Christ exhibits a human will in all its promise. Furthermore, Christ's perfection of grace, both habitual grace and the grace of auxilium, perfects Christ's human will in its abolute adherence to the good.

Another development involves the notion of a 'rational instrument' to express Christ's human nature as an instrument of the divine nature while

---

180 This perhaps amounts to the same as what Maximus affirms, just in a different polemical context.
181 Christ had perfect knowledge in several ways (e.g. beatific knowledge, infused knowledge, acquired knowledge).

also moved by its proper will. Being moved by a principal agent belongs to all instruments, but each instrument must be moved in accordance with its nature. Aquinas draws out this point by distinguishing inanimate, animate, and rational instruments (*ST* III, q.18, a.1, *ad* 2).[182] An agent moves inanimate instruments through corporeal motion and animate instruments through the sensitive appetite. A rational instrument, however, is moved through its will.[183] Thomas concludes that "human nature in Christ was an instrument of the divinity as moved through its proper will."[184] We must add this to what Thomas argued earlier, that not only was Christ's human nature an instrument of the divinity, but an instrument united hypostatically (see *ST* III, q.2, a.6, *ad* 4).[185] Thomas's notion of a hypostatically united instrument represents a conceptual and terminological advancement.[186] This advancement changes Thomas's presentation of Christ's will and, more significantly, the role of Christ's human will in the work of salvation.

182 In *De Veritate* q.29, a.1, *ad* 9, Thomas only draws a distinction between inanimate and animate instruments.
183 *ST* I–II, q.6, a.1, *ad* 3 (*Summa theologiae* 2: 753b): "Dicendum quod Deus movet hominem ad agendum non solum sicut proponens sensui appetibile, vel sicut immutans corpus, sed etiam sicut movens ipsam voluntatem; quia omnis motus tam voluntatis quam naturae ab eo procedit sicut a primo movente. Et sicut non est contra rationem naturae quod motus naturae sit a Deo sicut a primo movente; inquantum natura est quoddam instrumentum Dei moventis; ita non est contra rationem actus voluntarii quod sit a Deo, inquantum voluntas a Deo movetur. Est tamen communiter de ratione naturalis et voluntarii motus quod sint a principio intrinseco."
184 *ST* III, q.18, a.1, *ad* 2 (*Summa theologiae* 4: 2544b): "Sic ergo humana natura in Christo fuit instrumentum divinitatis, ut moveretur per propriam voluntatem."
185 In the *Summa contra gentiles*, Thomas describes Christ's human nature as a conjoined and proper instrument (see *SCG* IV.41). Thomas shies away from this wording in the *Summa theologiae* no doubt due to his knowledge of Nestorius and Nestorius's description of the union of divine and human in Christ as a conjunction. In *ST* III, q.18, a.1, *ad* 4, Thomas counters the Nestorian conception of Christ's human nature as a conjoined instrument by referring to Christ's human nature as a hypostatically united instrument. Thomas's basic understanding has changed little between the *Summa contra gentiles* and the *Summa theologiae*, but his terminology changes to reflect the particular concerns of each text.
186 Tschipke argues that Thomas was the first scholastic to use the Latin equivalent of ὄργανον τῆς θεότητος, *instrumentum divinitatis* (Tschipke, *L'humanité du Christ*, p. 136).

Aquinas describes Christ's human nature as the instrumental efficient cause of salvation. This cause is Christ's human will freely willing the passion and resurrection (see the discussion in Chapter five below on pp. 265–283). Another such terminological and conceptual advancement comes in the distinction between power and act, indicated, but hardly developed, in *Prima pars* (*ST* I, q.83, a.4, *ad* 1 and *ad* 2) and utilized more thoroughly in the *Prima secundae* (*ST* I–II, q.8). Aquinas makes much of this distinction in his discussion of Christ's two wills. He resolves questions about the will and necessity, arguing that while human nature necessarily involves a will and this will necessarily desires happiness, the will in its acts remains free and undetermined to specific goods (see *ST* III, q.18, a.1, *ad* 3). Article three repeats that the will may be taken for a power or for an act. The will as act requires a further distinction between two species of acts, one regarding the movement to an end and the other the movement to a means to an end (see *ST* I, q.83, a.4; *ST* I–II, q.8, aa.2, 3). These two species of act explain the 'division' within the will of reason between the will as nature, which regards ends absolutely, and the will as reason, which regards means. This distinction between act and power grounds the *Summa*'s explanation of two species of acts within one united power, providing a surer foundation in the *Summa* for the division of will as nature and will as reason than is found in the *Scriptum*. The *Scriptum* maintains unity of power but without any framework in which to distinguish acts, making tenuous any division between will as nature and will as reason, which, in turn, renders unsteady the very basis for affirming conformity to God in the thing willed and for denying contrariety within the will of reason. The *Summa*'s terminological and conceptual gains make more comfortable the division between will as nature and will as reason and provide a more solid foundation for conformity and non-contrariety of wills in Christ.

The *Summa theologiae* also cites different sources than the *Scriptum* on the topic of Christ's two wills. The *Scriptum* repeats the sources found in Peter Lombard's *Sentences* and in the commentary tradition upon the *Sentences*. The main addition in the commentary tradition is John Damascene's *De fide orthodoxa*, the use and import of which have been discussed in previous chapters.[187] The *Summa* adds the acts of Constantinople III. These

---

187 The Lombard cites the Damascene's *De fide orthodoxa* III.1–8. These were the portions translated by Cerbanus. The Lombard, however, quotes from Burgundio's translation. The *Sentences* do not refer to the Damascene in treating

acts included Pope Agatho's *Epistle I*. Agatho's letter provided Thomas with texts from Augustine's *Contra Maximinum episcopum Arianorum*, Ambrose's *De fide* and *Super Lucam*, and Pseudo-Athanasius's *De incarnatione et Contra Arianos*. These additions and expansions do not so much supplement as replace other sources (with the large and important exception being Aristotle), which results in a markedly different character between the authorities of the *Scriptum* and of the *Summa theologiae*. The most obvious difference centers upon Constantinople III. Theologians from the Lombard to Aquinas had unanimously affirmed two wills in Christ, yet not until Thomas's reintroduction of Constantinople III did this view carry with it the weight of a conciliar determination, suffocating a monothelite view beneath the sentence of anathema.[188] Constantinople III provided Thomas a far greater knowledge of the motivations underlying monothelite and monenergist views, though Aquinas ultimately rejects that they adhered to a correct understanding of the hypostatic union and erred only in the specifics of will or operation. Further, Constantinople III decreed non-contrariety of wills in Christ and the subjection of his human will to the divine will, describing the 'heretics' as defending contrariety. Despite this affirmation of non-contrariety, the acts of Constantinople III provide Thomas with few specifics explaining this non-contrariety. Agatho's letter repeatedly stresses the obedience of Christ's human will to the Father's will. Constantinople III did not revolutionize Thomas's understanding of Christ's two wills or his knowledge of opposing views. The council did place on firmer footing the basic and universally held views (in the thirteenth century) about Christ's two wills. The council, and Agatho's letter in particular, also deepened his account of Christ's human will.

Ambrose's *De fide* and *Super Lucam*, and Augustine's *Contra Maximinum episcopum Arianorum* reflect the heritage of discussion concerning Christ's two wills prior to the monothelite controversy. Consideration of this topic neither began nor ended in the seventh century, an important reminder when not only the first but virtually the only name mentioned

---

Christ's two wills. The *Summa fratris Alexandri* introduces the Damascene into discussion of Christ's two wills. Following the *Summa fratris Alexandri*, Bonaventure, Albert, and Thomas (in the *Scriptum*) use the Damascene as their main source on Christ's two wills.

188 Ephesus and Chalcedon play parallel roles in Thomas's Christology. See Backes, *Die Christologie* and Geenen, "The Council of Chalcedon."

in the context of Christ's two wills is Maximus Confessor. Beyond the time difference separating Ambrose and Augustine from Maximus and the monothelites, the contexts also differ. Ambrose and Augustine wrote against the Arians and their view of the Logos as 'less divine,' or of different substance, than the Father. That Ambrose and Augustine defend Christ's human will in works countering the Arians testifies to their well-balanced Christologies, aware of the dangers greeting all who stray too far in emphasizing Christ's humanity or divinity. Such a balanced Christology finds an eager inheritor in Thomas Aquinas, who happily follows Agatho in calling Ambrose and Augustine to aid.

Thomas quotes *De fide* and *Contra Maximinum episcopum Arianorum* twice each, which, though it may not sound much, is the same number as the acts of Constantinople III. More important than simple frequency is function. Constantinople III figures in the *corpus* of *ST* III, q.18, a.1 as the culminating response to Christological heresies, and in the *sed contra* of article six, authoritatively excluding contrariety of wills in Christ. Ambrose's *De fide* serves as the *sed contra* for both article one, which also quotes Ambrose's commentary on Luke, and article two. The Lombard utilizes Ambrose's *De fide*, though Ambrose's import wanes in the commentary tradition. Thomas does more than simply cite again the texts mentioned by the Lombard. Rather, Thomas offers expanded use of Ambrose as a champion source. Again, the prominence of Ambrose comes directly from Agatho. Agatho's letter provides a model according to which Thomas can defend Christ's two, non-contrary wills based upon classic authorities cited with conciliar approval.

Augustine's *Contra Maximinum episcopum Arianorum* receives first mention in *ST* III, q.18, a.1, *ad* 1, which focuses on God's ability to move a will interiorly.[189] This theme acquires no small significance in Thomas's analysis. Christ's human nature always moved in accordance with the divine will. Far from hindering a human will in Christ or requiring some exception to the normal order, this movement follows perfectly and naturally from God's interior movement of Christ's human will. Thomas quotes *Contra Maximinum episcopum Arianorum* at length and as the last word in response to the first objection. Aquinas's citation of *Contra Maximinum*

---

189 Aquinas quotes the *Contra Maximinum* in *ST* I–II, q.6, a.1, *ad* 3 and q.9, a.6, *ad* 3 without naming the work. He attributes the quotations to Ambrose.

episcopum Arianorum in the *sed contra* of article five bears no less weight. Augustine, as quoted, argues that Christ willed something other than the Father willed. Thomas's answer to the conformity of Christ's human will to the divine will changes little in substance between the *Scriptum* and the *Summa*, but the change in style and language is striking. The *Scriptum* follows the traditional form, considering conformity in the thing willed and laboring to explain and to minimize the dissent of the will of sensuality and the will as nature. Augustine's affirmation justifies serious appreciation of the dissenting wills. In the *Summa* Thomas need not minimize this movement but can instead offer it as testament to the natural operation of Christ's human will, which wills in perfect harmony with the divine will.

Two further points regarding Thomas's use of sources merit mention. Thomas (and this presents no dramatic surprise) quotes Aristotle in *ST* III, q.18 more than any other source, and more times than in *in* III, d.17, aa.1, 2. Aristotle's understanding of the will pervades Thomas's own understanding, as with other high scholastics, yet this is always bent to the divine will. It was during Thomas's second Paris regency (1268–1272) that he labored so assiduously on his Aristotelian commentaries or expositions.[190] This, no doubt, kept citations from Aristotle ready at hand for Aquinas, and he employed those citations to provide aids in the development of his own arguments.[191] The second point concerns John Damascene's waning import in the *Summa*. Thomas quotes *De fide orthodoxa* more often and more extensively in *in* III, d.17, aa.1 and 2 than any other authority. In the *Summa* he only quotes the Damascene in the objections and refers to him only three times outside of the objections (*ST* III, q.18, a.3; a.6, *ad* 1 and *ad* 3). Explaining this change can depend only upon speculation, but a reasonable hypothesis would likely include the following. First, the Damascene had become heavily relied upon in the commentary tradition, including Thomas's *Scriptum*, and thus had become the assumed background to

---

190 Weisheipl argues that Thomas's commentaries on Aristotle were undertaken to provide students with an exegetical guide leading to truth rather than heresy (as the commentaries of Averroes did). With the condemnation of Averroistic principles on 10 December 1270, Weisheipl believes the task of commenting upon Aristotle gained a new urgency for Thomas (Weisheipl, *Friar Thomas d'Aquino*, p. 230).
191 On Thomas's use of Aristotle, see Jordan, "The Competition" and "The Alleged Aristotelianism of Thomas Aquinas," Etienne Gilson Series 15 (Toronto, 1992).

this discussion. Thomas does not reject the Damascene but merely balances use of *De fide orthodoxa* with use of other sources. He can well assume his readers' familiarity with the arguments and terminology of *De fide orthodoxa* on this topic and need only offer an explicit citation when the Damascene is found lacking or unclear. Second, Aquinas's growing concern with Christ's free choice makes the Damascene a problematic source. Thomas must reverentially interpret the Damascene on this point, and this task would not be aided by stressing the Damascene's authority and accuracy on every other issue in q.18.

All of the points so far summarized build upon one another in Thomas's response to the question of contrariety. The human will properly designates the will of reason and participatively designates the will of sensuality, insofar as it obeys reason. The will of reason can be considered both as a power, according to which it is wholly one, and as act, according to which there are two species. As the will of reason is an act regarding ends considered absolutely, it is called the will as nature. The will as reason is the will concerned with means. The latter necessarily involves free choice, though in Christ this stands removed from all doubt and deliberation, which arise only due to ignorance. Christ's free choice benefited from Christ's status as a comprehensor, while his status as wayfarer followed a certain dispensation, according to which every power of Christ's body and soul underwent and performed what was natural to it. Thus Christ's will of sensuality and will as nature shunned the passion, for bodily harm and death are, considered in themselves as ends, natural evils. Christ's will as reason willed the passion as ordered to redemption, and so acted as was natural and proper to it. These disparate natural acts do not, however, imply any contrariety. To defend this position, Aquinas utilizes the logic of William of Auxerre and the *Summa fratris Alexandri*. Thomas argues that contrariety must be in the same and according to the same (*in eodem et secundum idem*). True contrariety must be noticed in one will, otherwise it is not properly contrariety but simply diversity. Second, true contrariety exists when contrary things are willed for the same (type of) reason. These conditions do not apply to Christ's will, and so there was no contrariety of will in Christ.

The non-contrariety of wills in Christ manifests the proper function of a human will, realized to its full potential. Thomas shapes his presentation of this topic with a dual pedagogical purpose. First, Thomas's structuring of the discussion develops scientifically, moving from more basic conclusions to more complex. The movement of articles within the question progressively establishes terminology and principles to ground subsequent arguments. Second, the performance of Christ's human will offers a model for correctly ordering one's own will. Thomas's interest in exemplar causality is most often noted with respect to the *Secunda pars*, yet it plays a prominent role as well in the *Tertia pars*. These twin pedagogical aims of *ST* III, q.18 relate to the larger trends within the *Tertia pars*, to which the next chapter will turn.

CHAPTER FIVE

Fitting Means for Redemption
Christ's Human Nature as Instrumental Efficient Cause of Salvation

The *Summa theologiae*'s treatise on Christ opens with a question on the fittingness of the Incarnation, setting the tone of argumentation employed throughout the treatise. Fittingness (*convenientia*) plays an important role in the *Summa* as a whole, but it is nowhere more important than in Christology and soteriology. Thomas endeavors to demonstrate the fittingness, as opposed to the logical necessity, of the Incarnation as described in the gospel accounts. The Incarnation's fittingness highlights the divine wisdom in accomplishing the salvation of humanity according to the best possible means. Presentation of this fittingness follows the general scientific development of topics, namely the establishment of more fundamental conclusions that serve as principles for subsequent argumentation, favored by Aquinas in the *Summa*. This development appears on the grand scale of division into parts ordered as they are, and on smaller scales within treatises and questions within those treatises, resulting in an edifice at once remarkable as a whole and in its process of construction.

The previous chapters have traced scholastic treatments of Christ's two wills as they developed in the twelfth and thirteenth centuries, noting in particular the increased attention to conformity, harmony, or non-contrariety of wills. Chapter four has focused on Aquinas's increased interest in exploring Christ's free human will. This chapter will examine the same basic theme as it extends through the *Summa theologiae*'s *Tertia pars*. Thomas's understanding of Christ's two wills does not provide the indispensable key to his Christology but certainly provides access to one of its most striking features: the presentation of Christ's humanity as the instrumental efficient cause of salvation. Related themes punctuate the first fifty-nine questions of the *Tertia pars*, requiring any analysis to pick and choose relevant portions without losing sight of the whole. This requirement forbids the level of textual detail favored in previous chapters but demands an equal level of textual support. This demand can most easily be met by following the patterns of emphasis and recapitulation evident in Thomas's Christology, from the initial stress on fittingness to the later affirmation of Christ as mediator *secundum quod homo* (according as an individual human being). These patterns reveal how Thomas's Christology completes his anthropology, highlighting the dignity of human nature, how he presents the Incarnation as the wisest means for human salvation, allowing the possibility of human merit through the assistance of grace, and how these concerns meet in the free action of Christ's human will producing a divine effect.

The *Summa*'s treatise on Christ (*ST* III, qq.1–59) encompasses several smaller sections. The most basic division separates the mystery of the Incarnation itself (qq.1–26) from the *acta et passa Christi in carne*, what Christ as God incarnate did and underwent (qq.27–59).[1] Taken together, these sections establish principles for fruitful reflection on the Incarnation and employ those principles for a profitable engagement with the gospel narratives. These sections admit many subdivisions, and much can be learned from examining these subdivisions and their placement. The systematic arrangement of articles within questions and questions within parts breaks the text up for the reader. The atomic units of scholastic texts are obvious and make topics easily accessible for isolated study. The interpreter faces the task of synthesizing the atoms of a scholastic text into a coherent and meaningful whole. This task presents its own challenges. The basic units of a scholastic text do not fit together as puzzle pieces, where each piece holds

---

[1] See John F. Boyle, "The Twofold Division of St Thomas's Christology in the *Tertia Pars*," *Thomist* 60 (1996): 439–447. Boyle examines this division of the *Tertia pars* against a backdrop of early scholastic theologians' arrangements of Christological topics. He notes in these works (the Lombard's *Sentences*, the *Summa fratris Alexandri*, and Albert the Great's *De incarnatione*) a common task of integrating 'narrative sequence and the categories of intelligibility.' Boyle then rejects Chenu's description of qq.1–26 as a scientific part and qq.27–59 as a biblical part. Recalling Thomas's notion of *sacra doctrina*, Boyle argues that qq.1–26 provide the categories of intelligibility for the narrative sequence (qq.27–59) such that both parts are scriptural and scientific. The two sections allow Thomas to connect revealed truths within a causal arrangement. Boyle's view of the division between the mystery of the Incarnation itself and the *acta et passa Christi in carne* offers insight relevant to the placement and division of topics within the *Summa theologiae* as a whole.

one proper place within the whole. In some sense, every piece of the *Summa* touches every other piece, and this richness of contact and overlap makes difficult the process of discerning meaningful and native patterns. The interpreter risks imposing an alien scheme upon the text and must proceed with caution lest the interpretation reveal more about interpreter than text.

This chapter will offer a synthesis of Thomas's Christology, arguing that it offers a coherent and meaningful account that is itself merely part of a greater edifice. While describing that greater edifice exceeds the scope of this study, some gestures toward proposals for the structure or plan of the *Summa theologiae* will help orient the narrower concern of this chapter. That narrower concern restricts the scope to the *Tertia pars* and particularly to those topics and questions most closely related to Thomas's presentation of Christ's two wills, including fittingness, the human nature assumed, Christ's grace, Christ's human knowledge, the powers and defects of Christ's soul, the grammar of *secundum quod homo*, Christ's unity, and Christ as mediator. These topics by no means encompass or exhaust Aquinas's Christology. The account offered here makes no claim to comprehension or completeness, but it does intend to portray accurately several key features of Thomas's presentation of the Incarnation in a manner that prompts further reflection.

Thomas's express treatment of the mystery of the Incarnation itself culminates with a consideration of Christ as mediator. Nothing appears remarkable about this choice. The notion of Christ as mediator is found in I Timothy 2:5 and can be found in virtually all medieval Christologies. A quick glance at *ST* III, q.26 would reveal what in most respects seems a perfectly typical scholastic engagement with the topic. The novel aspects emerge slowly and only in the details. This question recapitulates the previous twenty-five questions, providing a very dense summary of Thomas's Christological emphases, the most noteworthy of which is Christ's human will as instrumental efficient cause of salvation. As such, Thomas's reflections on Christ as mediator provide an ideal culmination for this chapter and a precisely focused lens for reading the gospel narratives in questions 27 to 59. The investigation will linger on question 26 for these reasons. All of these concerns relate to Christ's humanity as *instrumentum divinitatis*, an idea with a long history but one that received little attention in scholastic thought. Thomas's use of the idea distinguishes his Christology from the Christologies of his peers; it also connects to and clarifies his presentation of Christ's two wills. Thomas's understanding of instrumentality will pervade this chapter, throwing light on several aspects of his Christology.

The Plan of the Summa theologiae

Scholars have long attempted to discern the 'plan' of Thomas Aquinas's *Summa theologiae*. Some such efforts seek an underlying logic to the *Summa*'s structure, that is, its division into three parts arranged as they are. Such an underlying logic would clarify Thomas's reasons, be they intentions or habitual patterns of theological thinking, for constructing the *Summa* as he does.[2] Other efforts highlight an 'innovation' that shapes the overall character of the *Summa*. Various motives inspire such attempts, not the least of which emerges from polemical or apologetic concerns focusing upon the *Summa*'s Christology. Does its placement at the beginning of the *Summa*'s third part make the Christology a less than foundational element of its theology or its very culmination? What role does Thomas's recovery of the acts of early ecumenical councils and patristic texts play in the *Summa*'s Christology? Rehearsing these debates in all but a most cursory fashion lies beyond the scope of this chapter. However, the observations voiced through these debates impact our understanding of the *Summa*'s Christology and accordingly deserve a selective and very brief introduction here.

---

2   It is arguable that the plan and the structure of the *Summa theologiae* are not identical. Thomas's structuring of the *Summa* may or may not reveal his 'plan,' and the *Summa*'s plan might or might not provide insight into its structure. For purposes of economy, questions of the *Summa*'s plan and structure will here be treated together. For a list of sources and a summary of the difference between 'plan' and 'structure,' see Brian V. Johnstone, "The Debate on the Structure of the *Summa theologiae* of St Thomas Aquinas: From Chenu (1939) to Metz (1998)," in *Aquinas as Authority: A Collection of Studies Presented at the Second Conference of the Thomas Instituut te Utrecht, December 14–16, 2000*, ed. Paul van Geest, Harm Goris, and Carlo Leget (Leuven, 2002), pp. 187–200. Johnstone views the majority of scholarship as deficient for its inattention to the *acta et passa Christi* and to the resurrection in particular. He asserts that "the resurrection may be called a theological structure of the *Summa*" (Johnstone, "The Debate," p. 198). Johnstone affirms this based upon a certain reading of the connection between ontology and causality but his main claim perhaps needs more argumentative support.

Any introduction to these debates, however brief, must mention Marie-Dominique Chenu, whose 1939 article "Le plan de la *Somme théologique* de s. Thomas" sparked interest in the topic.[3] Chenu applies a pattern of *exitus a Deo* and *reditus ad Deum* to the *Summa theologiae*. Thomas himself notes such an *exitus-reditus* pattern in his *Scriptum* on the *Sentences* of Peter Lombard.[4] The general prologue to the *Summa* displays a marked concern for God as principle and end of all things, and this similarity to the express pattern of the *Scriptum* provides Chenu a point of departure. Chenu does not uncritically transfer the movement of the *Scriptum* to the *Summa* but rather recognizes the *Summa* as Thomas's masterwork of theological pedagogy, which draws inspiration from many sources. The particular character of the *exitus-reditus* movement of the *Summa*, Chenu argues, reflects Aristotle's scientific method and the Neoplatonic notion of emanation and return, both of which are put to the service of the divine science.[5] In doing so, Thomas reworks two earlier theological methods: Peter Abelard's logical arrangement of topics and Hugh of St Victor's historical ordering.[6]

Chenu's analysis sheds light on Thomas's conception of theology as fundamentally one science. The *Summa*'s *Prima pars* treats of God and the *exitus* of all creation from God; the *Secunda pars* addresses the *reditus* of human beings to God. 'Dogmatic theology' and 'moral theology' together complete the *exitus-reditus* pattern and thus inseparably constitute the one science of God.[7] Chenu's proposal highlights the innovation of the *Secunda pars* as a constitutive element of theology, not to be relegated to moral handbooks. If the *Prima pars* and the *Secunda pars* complete the *exitus-reditus* cycle, then where does this leave the *Tertia pars*? Is the *Summa*'s

---

3   Marie-Dominique Chenu, "Le plan de la *Somme théologique* de S. Thomas," *Revue thomiste* 45 (1939): 93–107. This article is reprinted and expanded in *Toward Understanding St Thomas* .
4   See *in* I, d.2, divisio textus.
5   It is worth noting that Chenu characterizes this *exitus-reditus* as "progression-conversion" (Marie-Dominique Chenu, *Toward Understanding St Thomas*, trans. Albert M. Landry and Domenic Hughes [Chicago, 1964], p. 306). This is an often-overlooked aspect of Chenu's proposal and highlights his connection of *reditus* with the *Secunda pars*. The "moral theology" of the *Secunda pars* constitutes this conversion, but it is only the *Tertia pars* and the Incarnation that provides the means to carry through this conversion to the beatific vision.
6   See Chenu, *Toward*, p. 304.
7   See Chenu, *Toward*, p. 311.

Christology merely a stitched-on adornment to its theological tapestry?[8] According to Chenu, Thomas's placement of Christology, including the sacraments and immortal life, does not lessen its centrality to Aquinas's theology but rather structurally reinforces Thomas's conception of the Incarnation as a wholly gratuitous act of the divine freedom.[9] The Incarnation was not a necessary event within an *exitus-reditus* pattern, but the divinely ordained means to best accomplish the end of humanity's return to God. Christ is humanity's way to the vision of God. Thomas's discussion of this truth in the *Tertia pars* does not compromise its centrality or its integration with the first two parts, but magnifies its gratuitousness. While the *Secunda pars* may address humanity's return to God, the *Tertia pars* specifies the Christian conditions of this return.[10]

Chenu's introduction to the question of the *Tertia pars* and the role of Christology in the *Summa* proves more enduring than his answer to that question. Subsequent scholars, perhaps dissatisfied with the extraordinary status of the *Tertia pars* in Chenu's conception, acknowledged a general *exitus-reditus* movement but sought to revise Chenu's conclusions by analyzing other discernable patterns within the *Summa theologiae*. In some cases this amounts to little more than a shift in emphasis, making primary what was less stressed by Chenu;[11] in others it amounts to a reap-

---

8   Chenu notes that the Incarnation figures into the *exitus-reditus* only as a divinely willed means and that "it is dealt with in a *IIIa Pars* which, judging in the abstract, would seem to play the role of not more than a part added to the whole as an afterthought" (Chenu, *Toward*, p. 310). Chenu utilizes this structural position of the *Tertia pars* as a mark of the Incarnation's contingency and gratuity for Thomas.

9   "The Incarnation is, however, in point of fact, a contingent event, and it enters in the *exitus-reditus* cycle only as an absolutely gratuitous work of God's absolutely free will" (Chenu, *Toward*, p. 314).

10 "The transition from the *IIa* to the *IIIa Pars* is a passage from the order of the necessary to the order of the historical, from an account of structures to the actual story of God's gifts" (Chenu, *Toward*, p. 315).

11 See André Hayen, *Saint Thomas d'Aquin et la vie de l'Église* (Louvain, 1952). Hayen notes that, although Chenu discerned an *exitus-reditus* cycle forecast in the general prologue to the *Summa theologiae* and in the prologues to each part, the prologues themselves do not utilize the language of *exitus-reditus*. Hayen acknowledges the basic warrant for Chenu's notion but finds it more accurately expressed in terms of efficient and final causality. Thomas's commentary on the gospel of John offers a threefold division which Hayen applies

praisal of Thomas's intent manifest in the *Summa*'s arrangement.[12] These revisions highlight other themes prevalent in Thomas's theology as organizing principles in the *Summa*. An initial consideration of these trends can be economically accomplished through discussion of Ghislain Lafont's *Structures et méthode dans la* Somme théologique *de saint Thomas d'Aquin*.[13]

---

to the *Summa* in the following manner: the *Prima pars* concerns *altitudo contemplationis*, the *Secunda pars amplitudo contemplationis*, and the *Tertia pars perfectio contemplationis* (pp. 83–84). This allows a strongly Christological reading of the *Summa* in which Thomas sequentially treats Christ as God, as creator, and as man. Hayen ultimately subsumes this tripartite division within a bipartite model (drawing upon the *Compendium theologiae*) in which the *Prima pars* and the *Secunda pars* are partitioned from the *Tertia pars*. The movement spanning this division is from abstract to concrete. Abstract knowledge involves what is true independently of human knowing; concrete knowledge names what human beings make their own through free consent. Ultimately the latter relates to the concrete life of the church.

12 See Per Erik Persson, "Le plan de la *Somme théologique* et la rapport 'Ratio-Revelatio,' " *Revue philosophique de Louvain* 56 (1958): 545–572. Persson focuses on the *ordo ad Deum* (*ST* I, q.1, a.7) as a foundational principle in the *Summa* and connects it to a Greek impulse to establish knowledge on the more certain and stable. This leads Persson to modify Hayen's causal conception of the *Summa*. Persson notes many aspects of final causality in the *Prima pars* and highlights the role of exemplary causality in the *Secunda pars*. In terms of final causality, he distinguishes *finis cuius*, which is God, and *finis quo*, which consists, at least in part, of human acts as subjectively beatifying. The causal structuring of the *ordo ad Deum* can be encompassed in a consideration of the divine governance and the modes of divine presence. Persson here follows Yves Congar in linking the *Prima pars* with God's presence through creative power, the *Secunda pars* with God's presence through grace, and the *Tertia pars* with divine presence through hypostatic union. Persson also argues that the causal structure of the *ordo disciplinae* as a *scientia* cannot begin with contingent, historical events. He argues that Thomas begins with the abstract scheme (the *Prima pars* and the *Secunda pars*) that then makes the historical events (the *Tertia pars*) comprehensible. Persson thus holds that the placement of the *Tertia pars* is a necessary aspect of Thomas's plan in the *Summa*. This represents an attempt to appreciate the conclusions of Chenu and Hayen while also lessening the extraordinariness of the *Tertia pars*.

13 Ghislain Lafont, *Structures et méthode dans la* Somme théologique *de saint Thomas d'Aquin* (Paris, 1961).

Lafont directs far greater attention to the *Tertia pars* and Thomas's structuring of the treatise on Christ.[14] Developing arguments from Hayen and Persson, Lafont links the *Secunda pars* with the *Tertia pars*.[15] Within this structure Lafont finds the *Prima pars* unified by and intelligible through the mystery of the divine goodness, extending Chenu's characterization of God's gratuitous gift from the Incarnation to creation. Humanity's participation in this divine goodness grounds the *Secunda pars* and its presentation of the complex workings of humanity with a focus on exemplary causality directed toward God as final cause.[16] The *Tertia pars*, in Lafont's view, balances the fittingness of the Incarnation, read through the divine goodness, with the economic necessity of the Incarnation.[17] Lafont's concern for the fittingness of the Incarnation guides his explication of the *Tertia pars* and will inform the analysis developed in this chapter.

14 Lafont's attention to the *Tertia pars* distinguishes sharply his approach from that of Albert Patfoort's *Thomas d'Aquin: Les clés d'une theologie* (Paris, 1983). While Patfoort's conclusions are broadly harmonious with Lafont's, Patfoort holds that we can sufficiently determine the spirit and movement of the entire *Summa* through discussion of the *Prima pars* and the *Prima Secundae*. He offers a Trinitarian reading of the *Summa*, identifying the Father with the *Prima pars*, the Spirit with the *Secunda pars*, and the Son with the *Tertia pars*. Patfoort critiques Chenu's formulation of an *exitus-reditus* cycle on the grounds that the *reditus* begins already in the *Prima pars* and continues through the *Tertia pars*.
15 Lafont generally salutes Persson's efforts but fears he fails to connect the Greek impulse for knowledge with the biblical themes suffusing Thomas's theology. Hayen's use of the prologue to Thomas's commentary on the gospel of John provides Lafont with a 'biblical' scheme, though he critiques Hayen's application of this to the *Summa*. Lafont argues that the *altitudo contemplationis* should more properly be limited to *ST* I, qq.2–43 and that the *amplitudo contemplationis* should more properly be identified with *ST* I, qq.44–119. This approach joins the *Secunda pars* with the *Tertia pars* under the *perfectio contemplationis* and shifts the mark of a bipartite division from the passage of the *Secunda* to the *Tertia pars* to the passage of the *Prima* to the *Secunda pars*. Leo Elders agrees with Lafont's desire to root the plan of the *Summa* in biblical themes and returns to the *exitus-reditus* plan, read through the causal language proposed by Hayen and Persson. On this basis, Elders identifies the *exitus-reditus* of the *Summa theologiae* as less Neoplatonic than biblical. See Leo Elders, "La méthode suivie par saint Thomas d'Aquin dans la composition de la *Somme de théologie*," *Nova et vetera* 66 (1991): 177–192.
16 See Lafont, *Structures*, p. 299.
17 See Lafont, *Structures*, p. 305.

Michel Corbin's *Le chemin de la théologie chez Thomas d'Aquin*, conversant with and dependent upon earlier treatments, sheds different light on the movement within the *Summa*.[18] In broad strokes, Corbin views the *Prima pars* as treating God and God's work of creation, the *Secunda pars* as treating human beings and their works, and the *Tertia pars* as treating Jesus Christ and his works. The *Secunda pars* narrows the focus from all creation to human beings, a move already begun in the *Prima pars*, and examines their works in terms of the ultimate end of beatitude and those acts which aid or retard attainment of this ultimate end. Thomas's continually narrowing scope focuses on Jesus Christ among human beings as the God-man whose proper act leads human beings to the ultimate end of beatitude.[19] Corbin discerns textual warrant for this scheme from the prologues to the various parts of the *Summa* and contrasts this scheme with those of

---

18   Michel Corbin, *Le chemin de la théologie chez Thomas d'Aquin* (Paris, 1974). Corbin's analysis covers far more than the *Summa* alone, including as well the *Scriptum*, the *Summa contra gentiles*, and portions of Thomas's commentary on Boethius's *De Trinitate*. Corbin reads the *Summa* as a culmination of a theological process begun and developed by Thomas in these earlier texts. As important is Corbin's proposal for a speculative reading of these texts that self-consciously resists restricting itself to either a simply historical or a merely theological mode of reading. Corbin's "La Parole devenue chair: Lecture de la première question de la *Tertia pars* de la *Somme théologique*" (*Revue des sciences philosophiques et théologiques* 62 [1978]: 5–40) offers a compressed presentation of his findings on the Christology of the *Summa*. See also Jean-Marc Laporte, "Christ in Aquinas's *Summa theologiae*: Peripheral or Pervasive?" *Thomist* 67 (2003): 221–248. Laporte takes Corbin's approach to involve a "complex pattern of narrowing concentric circles with Christ and his work in the center" ("Christ in Aquinas' *Summa theologiae*," pp. 223–224). Laporte contrasts this pattern with Chenu's cyclical approach and Patfoort's linear approach. Too much need not be made of this contrast, nor does Laporte present this contrast as a matter of irreconcilable differences.

19   Corbin distinguishes this from the *exitus-reditus* pattern of the *Scriptum* and from the pattern of the *Summa contra gentiles*, which is based upon the division of truths accessible to reason and truths not accessible to reason. "La *Tertia* n'a pour objet ni le *Reditus* ou Dieu comme cause finale ni les vérités inaccessibles à la raison mais, dans la mesure où les sacrements constituent l'actualité du Christ dans le temps de l'Eglise et où la résurrection des corps s'effectue dans et per le Christ, *le Christ et son œuvre*. C'est exactement l'objet qu'annonce le prologue de la question 2: *de Christo qui, secundum quod homo, via est nobis tendendi in Deum*" (Corbin, *Le chemin*, p. 801).

the *Scriptum* and the *Summa contra gentiles*, particularly with respect to Christology.[20]

The scientific ordering of the *Summa* involves developing more complex matters from the simpler. Such argumentative development permeates each question and its articles. The articles build upon one another, as do the questions, to draw the reader into the conceptual process. Likewise, the parts of the *Summa* follow this basic rule in treating of God, human beings, and then God incarnate, establishing truths relevant to divine nature and to human nature prior to discussing Jesus Christ as subsisting in both natures. These broad strokes overly simplify what remains a complex matter.[21] Jean-Marc Laporte links the scientificity of *sacra doctrina* to

20 "Désormais la matière christologique n'est plus placée sous l'image du *reditus* (Commentaire des *Sentences*) ni sous la notion de causalité *efficiente* (*Somme contre les gentils*); elle possède la meme amplitude que celle du Dieu un et trine. La personne de Jésus-Christ est au-delà du ternaire *en soi/principe/fin* qui en déploie l'intelligence, ainsi qu'en témoigne la suite du prologue" (Corbin, "La parole devenue chair," p. 14). Corbin's analysis perhaps surpasses Lafont's in recognizing the centrality of the *Tertia pars* for the *Summa*.

21 See John I. Jenkins, *Knowledge and Faith in Thomas Aquinas* (Cambridge, 1997). Jenkins argues, against Chenu, that Thomas presents *sacra doctrina* as a *scientia* fully in accord with the Aristotelian model forwarded in the *Posterior Analytics*. *Sacra doctrina* differs in important and interesting respects from other sciences, but Jenkins maintains all the sciences fall short of the strict ideal. The particularities of *sacra doctrina* pose no challenge to its scientificity; they simply affect the form of its presentation. Jenkins reads the *Summa* as a work of second-level pedagogy, though of a complex sort, which proceeds systematically from causes to effects. As such the *Summa* would be directed to very advanced students in theology, students already acquainted with the principles of the faith and their order of discovery through created effects. "In the initial discovery of difficult truths, tangential discussions and a meticulous consideration of objections are necessary to aid understanding, eliminate confusion and remove doubts. In second-level pedagogy, however, what one needs is a perspicuous presentation of the reasoning which leads from principles to conclusions, so that he will begin to think of the subject in this way. Extraneous or redundant material must be eliminated so that the structure of reasoning in the *scientia* can be better seen. The changes we find in the *Summa theologiae* in comparison to the *Quaestiones disputatae* seem to be directed to this end" (Jenkins, p. 94). Chenu reads the matter in exactly the opposite way. "By the author's own avowal, it [the *Summa theologiae*] was dedicated to the instruction of beginners in theology. The *Disputed Questions* were the book suited to masters, the *Summa* is the book of the pupil" (Chenu, *Toward*, p. 298).

revelation of God's knowledge in scriptural and creedal forms.[22] The preambles of faith, those truths regarding God that are accessible to reason, play no role in Laporte's concise discussion, as he is mainly interested in the systematic (that is, non-creedal) ordering of the articles of faith in the *Summa theologiae* and in the *Compendium theologiae*.[23] The *Summa*'s modification of the *Compendium*'s systematic ordering of articles allows its three parts to cohere with the creedal themes of creation, grace, and glory. Further, the *Summa*'s placement of the treatise on Christ before the sacraments and the work of glory calls attention to Christ as the way to the ultimate end of beatitude.

Jean-Pierre Torrell returns to an *exitus-reditus* pattern, though tempered by a critique of Chenu's views on the *Tertia pars*.[24] Torrell identifies the

---

22 See Laporte, "Christ in Aquinas's *Summa theologiae*," pp. 239–240.

23 The *Compendium theologiae* more strictly obeys this systematic ordering. "Given the scientific intent of Thomas's *Summa*, a study of the articles of the faith in their internal structure and their pattern of derivation will help us grasp the basis of the *Summa*'s structure. What emerges in this article and in the next [*ST* II–II, q.1, aa.7–8] is the statement and expansion of a twofold principle based on Hebrews 11:6 and John 17:3, which serves to distinguish the articles of the creed in a way that coheres with the apparent distinction in the *Summa* between what pertains to God (*Prima pars* and *Secunda pars*) and what pertains to Christ (*Tertia pars*)" (Laporte, "Christ in Aquinas's *Summa theologiae*," p. 233).

24 Jean-Pierre Torrell, *Aquinas's* Summa: *Background, Structure, and Reception*, trans. Benedict M. Guevin (Washington, DC, 2005) and *Saint Thomas Aquinas*, vol. 1: *The Person and His Work*, trans. Robert Royal (Washington, DC, 1996), p. 156. "Many authors have expressed surprise that Thomas waited until the last part of his work to speak of Christ, as if he had forgotten him and now comes back to repair his mistake. This surprise – which is sometimes expressed as a reproach – proceeds from a misunderstanding that is easily clarified if we understand the circular pattern about which I have already spoken. Sometimes this pattern is read simplistically, as if the 'going out from' belongs to the *Prima pars* (which is inexact) and that of the 'return' to the *Secunda pars* (we stop too soon). So we do not know what to do with the *Tertia pars* and that is why it is seen as an irreducible addition" (Torrell, *Aquinas's* Summa, p. 48). "It is a pity that Father Chenu did not have these texts [*in* III, prologue; *Compendium theologiae* c.201] in mind in his first essay, for they show with great clarity that in Thomas's thought not only does the Incarnation not introduce any disruption into the schema *exitus-reditus* but, on the contrary, it is only through the Incarnation that this movement achieves its fruition" (Torrell, *Saint Thomas* 1: 155).

Tertia pars as integral to the circular movement of the *Summa theologiae*. In this sense, Torrell follows Lafont in reading the *Tertia pars* as a balance between the Incarnation's gratuity and economic necessity. This balance of contingency and necessity as expressed by Torrell informs Gilbert Narcisse's *Les raisons de Dieu: Argument de convenance et esthétique théologique selon saint Thomas d'Aquin et Hans Urs von Balthasar*.[25] The 'reconciliation' of contingency and necessity allows Narcisse to propose the following definition: "la convenance est un possible réalisée," or "la convenance est l'unité du possible probable et du réalisée nécessaire."[26] Narcisse's notion of a 'realized possible' combines the necessity of an actual existent with its contingency as a non-necessary occurrence/being, which, in the context of theological inquiry, highlights the freedom and wisdom of the divine design.[27] For Narcisse, fittingness amounts to the specific form of theological necessity.[28]

Narcisse's general analysis of fittingness in Thomas prepares for his consideration of fittingness in Christology. The frequency and the weight of fittingness arguments in Christology suggest their exemplarity for fittingness arguments in general. Various themes converge in Narcisse's presentation of Thomas's Christology, perhaps the two most notable of which are instrumentality and image. A concern for Christ's instrumentality arises easily from an affirmation of a divine person subsisting in a human nature, doing and undergoing everything proper to human nature. The infinite divine efficacy combined with the Word incarnate for the salvation of the human race implies that all of Christ's actions cause our salvation, due to the divine efficacy, and all are fitting in relation to the end of human salvation.[29] What secures the fittingness of Christ's humanity as instrument

---

25 Gilbert Narcisse, *Les raisons de Dieu: Argument de convenance et esthétique théologique selon saint Thomas d'Aquin et Hans Urs von Balthasar* (Fribourg, 1997).
26 Narcisse, *Les raisons*, p. 137.
27 "Le *possible* a été rapporté au libre et sage vouloir de Dieu. Le réalisée s'approchait de l'idée théologique d'Economie en tant que la convenance correspond au meilleur moyen par lequel Dieu a effectué son œuvre de salut" (Narcisse, *Les raisons*, p. 351).
28 See Narcisse, *Les raisons*, p. 292, n.581.
29 "Toutes les actions du Christ causent notre salut et toutes sont en convenance par rapport à la finalité essentielle de l'incarnation, le salut des hommes" (Narcisse, *Les raisons*, p. 368).

of the divinity rests largely on the notion of image, considered both from the perspective of the nature assumed and the person assuming. With respect to the person assuming, the fittingness of the Incarnation of the Word involves the Word, to whom the name *Verum* is appropriated, as image of the Father and as the archetype for humanity's creation in the image of God. Humanity images God, which secures a correspondence and dependence between image and archetype, making fitting the archetype's instrumental use of the image.[30] Christ's instrumentality grounds an exemplarity both on an ontological and on a moral level,[31] and this flows through the *Summa* in the three steps of creation, redemption, and glorification, in which the image comes better to resemble the archetype.[32] Narcisse places Christ, and in particular according to his humanity, as the cosmic and spiritual center of this circular movement.[33] This chapter will continue Narcisse's occupation with Christ's instrumentality but will shift

---

30 "La rapport à ce premier Exemplaire, à l'Archétype, exprime une dependence. Qu'on la pense d'une manière ou d'une autre, cette dependence ouvre une voie possible à la notion d'instrumentalité. La difficulté anthropologique de l'application de l'instrumentalité amène ainsi à insister sur la convenance de l'instrument, d'abord de la notion, ensuite dans le cadre de la mediation chrétienne" (Narcisse, *Les raisons*, p. 409).

31 "L'exemplarité *ontologique*, elle, concerne l'*être* d'une manière plus immédiatement profonde. En elle, s'unissent l'*extériorité* de l'exemplarité morale et d'emblée une certaine *intériorité*" (Narcisse, *Les raisons*, p. 445).

32 "Il est donc prévisible de découvrir une certaine affinité entre le thème de l'exemplarité et celui de la convenance. En effet, si le Créateur est l'Exemplaire, la créature humaine réalise son être, selon tout le réalisme de l'efficience divine, au cours d'un devenir durant lequel divers degrés de convenance s'articuleront dans les ordres de la création, de la rédemption et de la glorification. A chaque étape, l'image acquiert un degré supérieur de ressemblance" (Narcisse, *Les raisons*, p. 318).

33 "Pour les êtres spirituels, ce retour s'effectue par un accomplissement circulaire spirituel, celui de l'intelligence et de la volonté. Cet accomplissement de soi, par l'union à son principe, implique une ressemblance et, pour l'homme, en dépendance des divers états de l'humanité. C'est le Christ, selon son humanité, qui est le centre et le principe de toute circularité des hommes et même du cosmos. La première circularité, dans l'ordre de la manifestation, c'est la création assumée par l'humanité du Christ" (Narcisse, *Les raisons*, p. 533). Narcisse rightly highlights the centrality of Christ's humanity as the instrument of salvation, but he perhaps pushes his interpretation beyond the text of Aquinas in discussing Christ as cosmic center. The overall impression given bears a greater resemblance to Bonaventure than to Thomas, an impression strengthened by Narcisse's concern for Balthasar.

emphasis to Christ as mediator. Question 26 addresses Christ as mediator, capping the 'consequences of the union' (qq.16–26). Before delving into these questions, earlier questions from the *Tertia pars* must be addressed.

This brief and select summary has introduced themes important for a balanced reading of Christology in the *Summa*. The *exitus-reditus* pattern or circular movement of the *Summa* offers a basic framework for interpretation. Within this framework, the Incarnation is gratuitous, fitting, and integral; Christ is *secundum quod homo* the way to God. Another basic schema involves types of causality. This examination will highlight the role of instrumental efficient causality in the work of salvation. Combined with the instrumental causality of the sacraments, instrumental causality can be viewed as an important category for interpreting the role of the *Tertia pars* within the *exitus-reditus* pattern.

The Incarnation as Fitting Communication of Goodness Itself

Thomas's consideration of the Incarnation's fittingness establishes the tone of his entire treatment of Christology.[34] The Incarnation was not logically necessary or necessary for the salvation of the human race, but it accomplishes the end of salvation through a gratuitous display of the divine wisdom. From the bare fact of the Incarnation to the details of Christ's life, death, and resurrection, affirmations of fittingness guide Aquinas's presentation and serve to magnify appreciation of God's gratuity and wisdom. Aesthetic analogies are most ready to hand. The equivalent would be a magnificent painting, which, when viewed as a whole, seems perfectly proportioned and ordered. It gives the impression that not one brushstroke could have been different. When then studied in detail, it is obvious that any given aspect could have differed in numerous ways from the actual painting and that such changes, though individually unimpeachable, would have diminished the beauty of the whole. Fortified with an appreciation of

---

34 Chenu's focus on the gratuity of the Incarnation as a contingent, historical event relates strongly to the fittingness of the Incarnation. Lafont, seeking to move away from the extraordinary status of the *Tertia pars* in Chenu's analysis, links the Incarnation's fittingness to the divine goodness manifest in creation and to the economic necessity of the Incarnation. Narcisse takes fittingness as the particular form of theological necessity that, in the Incarnation, expresses an ontological proportion between creature and creator. See 'Fittingness', in Joseph Wawrykow, *The Westminster Handbook to Thomas Aquinas* (Louisville, KY, 2005), pp. 57–60.

the artistic sense evident in the details, one may then appreciate on a higher level the artistry and beauty of the whole.[35] While beauty perhaps furnishes the most illustrative analogue for judgments of fittingness, Aquinas's operative category remains wisdom. Fittingness arguments express neither a necessity of final causality nor an aesthetic necessity, but rather a sapiential necessity wherein lies a confluent instruction for our intellect and will.[36]

Fittingness answers two basic questions of the Incarnation: 'why?' and 'how?' The question 'why' concerns the rationality or appropriateness of God incarnate. The question 'how' concerns the rationality or appropriateness of the manner of God incarnate. These questions nearly always overlap, but the distinction provides some assistance in specifying Thomas's use of fittingness arguments. The question 'why' takes some logical priority and sets the framework in which to explain and explore the 'how.' The first two articles of the *Tertia pars* question the fittingness or necessity of the Incarnation and establish the basic rules for all subsequent articles. The *sed contra* of article one, citing the Damascene (*De fide orthodoxa* III.1), holds the Incarnation to demonstrate simultaneously God's goodness, wisdom, justice, and power.[37] Aquinas's response concentrates on God as the very essence of goodness (see

---

35 Narcisse argues for some such aesthetic dimension in Aquinas's development of fittingness arguments but concludes that beauty remains for Thomas a secondary category as compared to the proper transcendental 'true.' Much recommends Narcisse' conclusions, and they will be utilized here. This chapter will cultivate a focus, harmonious with this aspect of Narcisse's conclusions, on wisdom as the proper category for considering fittingness.

36 See Joseph Wawrykow, "Wisdom in the Christology of Thomas Aquinas," in *Christ Among the Medieval Dominicans*, ed. Kent Emery, Jr, and Joseph Wawrykow (Notre Dame, IN, 1998), 175–196.

37 The first objection introduces goodness, which will serve as the guiding theme for question one. The *sed contra* discusses goodness, wisdom, justice, and power. These will serve as guiding themes for the *Summa*'s Christology as a whole. "Sed sicut Damascenus dicit in principio III libri, 'per incarnationis mysterium monstratur simul bonitas et sapientia et iustitia et potentia Dei, vel virtus: bonitas quidem, quoniam non despexit proprii plasmatis infirmitatem; iustitia vero, quoniam homine victo, non alio quam homine fecit vinci tyrannum, neque vi eripuit ex morte hominem; sapientia vero, quoniam invenit difficillimi pretii decentissimam solutionem; potentia vero, sive virtus, infinita, quia nihil est maius quam Deum fieri hominem.' Ergo conveniens fuit Deum incarnari" (*ST* III, q.1, a.1, *sed contra* [*Summa theologiae* 4: 2414a–2414b]). Thomas cites this passage in abbreviated form in *ST* III, q.3, a.8, *sed contra*. There he mentions only wisdom and power.

Pseudo-Dionysius's *De divinis nominibus* I.5), the nature of which is to communicate itself to others (*De divinis nominibus* IV.20). As it is fitting to all things to do what is proper to their nature, so it befits the highest good to communicate itself in the highest possible way, which the Incarnation accomplishes.[38]

Even granting the notion of God as self-communicating good, Thomas must still explain the Incarnation's fittingness in light of divine eternity, immutability, impassibility, etc. Thomas's replies to the objections of article one provide initial explanations from the perspective of both the nature assuming and the nature assumed. First, he clarifies that the Incarnation involves no change in God but only a change on the part of mutable creation united to God in a new way. While it befits a creature to exist in a new way, being united to God hypostatically so exceeded the dignity of human nature as to be unfitting. The infinite goodness communicating itself to creation in a new way overshadows any unfittingness from the creaturely side, yet this infinite distance itself seems to render the Incarnation unfitting. Aquinas replies that "every condition according to which any creature whatsoever differs from the Creator was established by God's wisdom and is ordered to God's goodness."[39] This extends to the evil of punishment, which the divine justice implements for the glory of God. The evil of fault (*malum culpae*) occurs as a withdrawal "from the art of the divine wisdom and from the order of the divine goodness."[40] God fittingly assumed a created nature in its order to the divine goodness, including not only mutability and corporeality but also subjection to the evil of punishment. It would not have been fitting, however, for God to assume the evil of fault. Thomas goes to great lengths in exploring these aspects of Christ's humanity.

Thomas's use of the self-communicating good to justify the Incarnation's fittingness raises the further question of the Incarnation's necessity.

---

38 The *corpus* discusses only goodness. Question one's focus on the goodness of the Incarnation will yield to a presentation of its wisdom, in general and in detail. Thomas first addresses the Incarnation's fittingness in response to 'why' and then in response to 'how'.
39 *ST* III, q.1, a.1, *ad* 3 (*Summa theologiae* 4: 2415a): "Dicendum quod quaelibet alia conditio secundum quam creaturam quaecumque differt a Creatore, a Dei sapientia est instituta, et ad Dei bonitatem ordinata."
40 *ST* III, q.1, a.1, *ad* 3 (*Summa theologiae* 4: 2415a): "Malum vero culpae committitur per recessum ab arte divinae sapientiae et ab ordine divinae bonitatis."

Was it necessary given the divine essence as self-communicating good? Was it necessary for the reparation of the human race? Article two notes two types of necessity for an end. The first type names that "without which something cannot be," the second that "through which something comes to its end better and more fittingly."[41] The first necessity expresses a means as a condition for the possibility of the end. The second indicates a means that, while not a condition for the end's possibility, offers the best, most fitting way to that end. The Incarnation was not necessary in the first sense but was in the second. This 'necessity' of fittingness emerges as Thomas presents five ways the Incarnation promotes humanity in the good and five corresponding ways in which it removes evil.[42] Stringing together quotations from Augustine, Aquinas spells out the promotion of good in terms of faith, hope, charity, right operation (correct acting), and fullness of participation in divinity as true beatitude. The withdrawal from evil involves instructing human beings not to prefer the devil to themselves, teaching human beings the dignity of their nature, abrogating human presumption, correcting human pride by healing through humility, and freeing human beings from servitude to sin. Thomas applies an Anselmian logic to this last point, writing that a mere human being "could not make satisfaction for the human race; God, however, had no obligation to make satisfaction; whence it was necessary for Jesus Christ to be God and a human being."[43] Aquinas caps his response with mention that many other things above our capacities of apprehension followed upon the Incarnation. These enumerations provide an introduction, not a limit.

The first two articles of question one debate the fittingness and necessity of the actual dispensation, but the third introduces a series (aa.3, 5, 6) of hypothetical considerations designed to highlight both God's power to

---

41 *ST* III, q.1, a.2 (*Summa theologiae* 4: 2415b): "Dicendum quod ad finem aliquem dicitur aliquid esse necessarium dupliciter: uno modo, sine quo aliquid esse not potest ... ; alio modo, per melius et convenientius pervenitur ad finem."

42 For a discussion of these corresponding ways, see 'Fittingness,' in Wawrykow, *The Westminster Handbook*, pp. 57–60.

43 *ST* III, q.1, a.2 (*Summa theologiae* 4: 2416b): "Homo autem purus satisfacere non poterat pro toto humano genere; Deus autem satisfacere non debebat; unde oportebat Deum et hominem esse Iesum Christum." Satisfaction constitutes one mode of viewing Christ's salvific work (see *ST* III, q.48, a.2). Thomas's use of a satisfaction theory of the atonement hinges on Christ's human will, according to which he wills the passion for salvation.

do otherwise than the actual dispensation and God's wisdom in willing the revealed order.[44] Article three questions whether God would have become incarnate if human beings had not sinned. Opinions on this topic, as evidenced in Aquinas's response, differed during the scholastic period. Some (*quidam*) hold that absent human sin, God would nevertheless have become incarnate. John Duns Scotus would later champion this view, which has become emblematic of differences between the Scotist and Thomist schools. The some (*quidam*) of article three refer not to Scotus but to Thomas's contemporaries, including his teacher Albert the Great (see *Commentarii in III*, d.20, a.4). Aspects of Thomas's theology seem to support Albert's view. Despite these aspects, Thomas counters Albert's view and opts for restraint regarding truths above human reason. He argues that whatever proceeds solely from the divine will can be known by human beings only through revelation, or, more specifically, as it is treated in Holy Scripture. Scripture everywhere designates human sin as the reason God became incarnate to remedy this sin.[45] This does not limit the divine power or freedom, which could ordain the Incarnation apart from human sin, but only situates the human intellect in proper relation to revealed truths.[46]

The speculative concern most germane to this investigation concerns the timing of the Incarnation. The third objection of article five holds that God *ought* to have become incarnate at the beginning of the human race on the premise that the work of grace, as the work of nature, ought to be perfect from the beginning. Aquinas replies that perfection precedes imperfection temporally and naturally in different things, but in one sole thing perfection precedes imperfection naturally but follows it temporally.

---

44 The hypothetical considerations of q.1, aa.3, 5, and 6 parallel such considerations in q.3, aa.5–7 and q.4, aa.4–5. Each of these questions examines the fittingness of the Incarnation from a different perspective. The hypothetical considerations stress the divine freedom and power to have ordained otherwise and the wisdom governing the actual dispensation. As this relates to q.3, see Wawrykow, "Wisdom in the Christology of Thomas Aquinas."
45 Many 'lesser' causes are assigned, just as many other effects are evident, but these all relate to the remedy for sin (see *ST* III, q.1, a.2, *ad* 1).
46 This note of restraint might sound false considering the speculative nature of subsequent topics (e.g. q.1, aa.5–6; q.3, aa.5–7; q.4, aa.4–5). Thomas's aim in all such considerations is to show God's power and freedom to have done otherwise and God's wisdom in ordaining the actual dispensation.

The perfection of human nature in union with God follows humanity's imperfection temporally. Thomas notes a mode in which the imperfect temporally precedes the perfect, namely when something imperfect is perfected, and a mode where the perfect is the efficient cause of an imperfect thing reaching perfection, in which case the perfect temporally precedes the imperfect. Both modes concur in the Incarnation, making both the beginning of the world and its end unfitting times for the Incarnation. The Incarnation itself consummates human nature and so rightly followed its imperfection; the Incarnation also efficiently causes human nature's perfection in beatitude and so rightly precedes that perfection.[47] A long quotation from Ambrosiaster (*Quaestiones Veteris et Novi Testamenti*, II) structures the second line of argumentation based upon the effect of human salvation. The quotation explains the varied effects of the remedy for sin. Aquinas argues that, had this remedy been delayed to the world's end, "knowledge (*notitia*) of God and reverence and honest conduct would have been totally abolished on the earth."[48] This highlights the secondary reasons for the Incarnation. The third argument presents the fittingness of the actual time as a manifestation of the divine power. According to the actual dispensation, God saves human beings through faith not only in future things but also in present and past things. Thomas's response to the second objection well summarizes the *corpus*, arguing that "the work of the Incar-

---

[47] This logic concerning the fitting time for the Incarnation applies as well to the fitting place for its treatment in the *Summa theologiae*. Jesus Christ consummates human nature, and so Thomas's presentation of perfected humanity follows his treatments of humanity in the *Prima pars* and in the *Secunda pars*. Jesus Christ also efficiently causes human nature's perfection in beatitude, and so Thomas's presentation of the Incarnation precedes his (projected, though never begun) treatment of immortal life. This provides a structural clue to the manner in which Thomas's presentation of Jesus Christ's humanity completes his discussions of anthropology. Also relevant here is the instrumental causality of Christ's human nature. This topic will receive greater attention later in this chapter; for now it is worth mentioning that the divine efficient causality of human salvation utilizes the instrumental causality of Christ's human nature as the first mover within the genus of human operation. Christ *secundum quod homo* causes human salvation and the perfection of human nature in beatitude through the passion and resurrection.

[48] *ST* III, q.1, a.6 (*Summa theologiae* 4: 2422b): "Si autem hoc remedium differretur usque in finem mundi, totaliter Dei notitia et reverentia et morum honestas abolita fuisset in terris."

nation should be considered not only as the term of movement from the imperfect to the perfect, but also as the principle of perfection in human nature."[49] Question one begins and ends with the fittingness of the Incarnation, from the very fact of it to its time. Thomas hones these arguments throughout the next twenty-five questions of the *Tertia pars*. This sharpening of argument owes much to *ST* III, q.2 and its specification of the Incarnation in terms of hypostatic union.

The Mode of Union

Question two begins the section on the mode of the union (qq.2–15) with a consideration of the union itself. Sufficient attention cannot here be given to this question, for, perhaps more so than any other question of the *Tertia pars*, question two reaps the benefits of the historical researches undertaken or commissioned by Aquinas in the 1260s.[50] The acts of Ephesus and Chalcedon allowed Thomas to assimilate the first and third Christological opinions set forth in Peter Lombard's *Sentences* to the long-condemned heresy of Nestorius. Christologies were, in Thomas's eyes, slipping toward heretical views, and the clarification wrought by Thomas's recovery of conciliar texts provided the foundation for correcting such unintentional errors. Nor were these errors strictly confined to the twelfth century. The vast majority of thirteenth-century theologians expressly supported the Lombard's second opinion (the subsistent or composite person theory). Aspects from the first opinion, however, crept into many thirteenth-century Christologies. In part, this resulted from terminological confusion regarding *persona* and *hypostasis*; in part, this resulted from ignorance of

---

49 *ST* III, a.1, a.6, *ad* 2 (*Summa theologiae* 4: 2422b): "Dicendum quod opus incarnationis non solum est considerandum ut terminus motus de imperfecto ad perfectum, sed etiam ut principium perfectionis in humana natura." Again, the passion and resurrection are two sides of the same coin.

50 See Ignaz Backes, *Die Christologie des hl. Thomas von Aquin und die griechischen Kirchenväter* (Paderborn, 1931); Torrell, *Saint Thomas* 1: 136–141; Gottfied Geenen, "The Council of Chalcedon in the Theology of St Thomas," in *From an Abundant Spring: The Walter Farrell Memorial Volume of the* Thomist, ed. staff of the *Thomist* (New York, 1952); and Gottfied Geenen, "En marge du Concile de Chalcédonie: Les textes du Quatrième Concile dans les œuvres de saint Thomas," *Angelicum* 29 (1952).

conciliar definitions.[51] Aquinas's tasks in question two include the careful analysis of the first and third opinions, showing them to defend an accidental union between God and human nature.[52] Thomas then equates any view of the Incarnation predicated upon an accidental union with Nestorianism and so implicates the first and third opinions in heresy. A correct understanding of the hypostatic union provides a necessary condition for properly addressing a host of secondary questions, yet the sufficient conditions for such an address are in nowise met without full awareness of the soteriological design of God incarnate as expressed in question one.

The twelve articles of question two offer terminological and conceptual clarifications concerning the union of the divine and human natures in Christ. Briefly put, Aquinas follows the formulations of early church councils and patristic authors, especially Cyril of Alexandria, professing that the person or hypostasis of the Word assumed into union with itself a perfect human nature consisting of a body and rational soul joined together.[53] This act of assumption produced a personal or hypostatic union such that the person of the Word, without any change or loss to self, now subsists in a human nature in addition to the divine nature. Question two extends the transition from the 'why' of the Incarnation, which question one advanced in soteriological terms under the guiding influence of the divine goodness, to the 'how' of the Incarnation. Both the 'why' and the 'how' of the Incarnation follow a certain higher fittingness, but Aquinas's language for discerning this fittingness shifts from the divine goodness to the divine wisdom. Traces of this are evident in question two, but question

---

51 See Corey Barnes, "Albert the Great and Thomas Aquinas on Person, Hypostasis, and Hypostatic Union," *Thomist* 72 (2008): 107–146.

52 On the Lombard's three opinions, see N.M. Häring, "The Case of Gilbert de la Porrée. Bishop of Poitiers (1142–1154)," *Mediaeval Studies* 13 (1951): 1–40. Häring argues that Thomas correctly views the first opinion as a lapse into Nestorianism. He argues Thomas's association of the second opinion with Chalcedonian orthodoxy resulted from a failure to correctly interpret the second opinion (Häring, p. 38). See also Lauge Olaf Nielsen, *Theology and Philosophy in the Twelfth Century: A Study of Gilbert of Porreta's Thinking and Theological Expositions of the Doctrine of the Incarnation during the Period 1130–1180*, trans. Ragnar Christopherson (Leiden, 1982), pp. 214–361.

53 Thomas elaborates this assertion in the next several questions. Question three specifies the person assuming as the Word. Question five enumerates the 'parts' of humanity assumed. Christ's possession of a rational soul is crucial for the salvific work of the Incarnation.

three amplifies these traces to central significance for appreciation of God's gratuitous and wise action in the Incarnation.[54]

Thomas addresses in question three the mode of union from the part of the person assuming.[55] Question three combines the soteriological motivation of the Incarnation with the lessons of question two to appreciate more adequately the wisdom directing the Word's assumption of human nature. At first glance, article one on 'Whether it befits a divine person to assume a created nature' reads as a variant formulation of the question addressed in *ST* III, q.1, a.1, 'Whether it was fitting for God to be incarnate.' Question three, article one, however, investigates a separate and narrower topic. The issue at hand involves the specification of 'incarnation' as 'to assume a created nature,' possible on the grounds of question two, and adds the specification of 'a divine person.' Thomas does not simply reword an earlier article and re-present the same topic but recalls the form of an earlier article on the fittingness of the *reason* for the Incarnation in a new article treating the fittingness of the *mode* of the Incarnation. Aquinas's use of 'to assume' builds upon the findings of q.2, a.8, which distinguishes union from assumption principally insofar as the union designates the relation that results from assumption and assumption names the very action according to which one assumes and another is assumed. The act of assumption involves both a principle and a term.[56] The principle is the 'actor' in the assumption, the moving force behind the act. Term designates the 'recipient' of what is assumed. In the Incarnation, a person assumes both as principle and as term. To act is proper to a person, and so the act of assuming a human nature is proper to a person as principle.[57] Articles one and two

---

54 "In this sense, the movement of the opening questions of the *Tertia pars* is from the communication of the divine goodness to the stress on the sapiential communication of this goodness, thus underscoring the Christic-shape of God's encounters with the world" (Wawrykow, "Wisdom in the Christology of Thomas Aquinas," p. 184).

55 For a careful reading of question three, focusing on the wisdom of the Incarnation, see Wawrykow, "Wisdom in the Christology of Thomas Aquinas." The treatment of question three here draws heavily from Wawrykow's presentation.

56 Thomas grounds this partially on reading 'to assume' (*assumere*) as 'to take to oneself' (*ad se sumere*).

57 *ST* III, q.3, a.1 (*Summa theologiae* 4: 2439a): "Principium quidem, quia personae proprie competit agere; huiusmodi autem sumptio carnis per actionem divinam facta est." Since acting is proper to a person, *ST* III, q.19, a.1, ob.3 will deny two operations in Christ. Thomas responds by qualifying action as pertaining to a person through or according to nature.

of question two specify that the union takes place in a person rather than nature, and so a person is properly also the term of the assuming. "And thus it stands that assuming a nature most properly suits a person."[58]

Articles one and two recast previous gains in a new line of questioning culminating in article eight's affirmation that the actual order of the Incarnation, with the Word assuming one human nature into personal union, was the wisest and most fitting possibility. Thomas places this conclusion at the end of question three to crown the wisdom, as opposed to the necessity, of the revealed order. The fittingness of the actual order is magnified by the divine freedom and power to have ordained otherwise, and Aquinas highlights this in articles five to seven.[59] The momentum of the first articles could carry an incautious reader from a judgment of fittingness to a mistaken notion of necessity. Articles five to seven provide a check on such momentum and, in firmly distinguishing fittingness from necessity, participate in article eight's magnification of the fittingness of the actual order. Article five dispenses with any notion that the Son alone could be incarnate, for the three persons are equal and identical in all but their personal properties.

The first-time reader of scholastic theology encountering articles six and seven would quite likely find its considerations wild and scripturally ungrounded, confirming the worst stereotypes. The final profit of these speculative considerations arrives in the question's return to the Incarnation of the Word. Article six questions whether multiple divine persons could assume numerically one nature. The companion concern of article seven, on whether one divine person could assume two human natures, proceeds along similar lines. These articles address both God's power and freedom to have ordained otherwise than the Word's assumption of one human nature and the grammatical and metaphysical grounds for someone to be one human being. In terms of the first address, article six affirms

---

58 ST III, q.3, a.1 (*Summa theologiae* 4: 2439a): "Et sic patet quod propriissime competit personae assumere naturam."
59 Wawrykow demonstrates this by comparing the arrangement of topics in the *Scriptum* and *Summa*. The *Scriptum* treats the fittingness of the Word becoming incarnate then discusses God's power to have ordained otherwise. The *Summa* re-orders these topics to complete the discussion with the fittingness of the Word becoming flesh. See Wawrykow, "Wisdom in the Christology of Thomas Aquinas," pp. 181–186.

that multiple divine persons could assume one created nature, and article seven grants that one divine person could assume multiple human natures. What would result from such scenarios? Thomas holds that in either scenario, that is, multiple divine persons assuming one nature or one divine person assuming multiple natures, there would be only one human being. There are two grounds for the unity of a human being: singularity of the human nature and unity of supposit. In the case of multiple persons assuming, the first ground confirms one human being; in the case of multiple natures assumed, the unity of supposit confirms one human being. In the actual Incarnation, both of these grounds are present, amplifying its fittingness.

Aquinas opens the *Tertia pars* with the fittingness of God becoming incarnate (q.1, a.1); he hones this line of argumentation by specifying the person assuming as the Son and the mode of Incarnation as the assumption of human nature into personal union (q.3, a.8). Fittingness remains the operative category in *ST* III, q.3, a.8. Between the beginning of question one and the end of question three, Thomas has shifted fittingness from the fact or 'why' of the Incarnation to its mode or 'how.' Question two's specification of the hypostatic union provides a rich vocabulary for the mode of the Incarnation. Thomas exploits this rich vocabulary throughout the *Tertia pars*.

Not only was the Word's assumption of human nature fitting, but most fitting (*convenientissimum*), and so from three perspectives. Thomas discusses this fittingness 'from the part of the union,' 'from the part of the end of the union,' and 'from the sin of the first parents.' Discussion of these three perspectives unfolds through consideration of names for the second person of the Trinity, particularly 'Word' and 'Son.' Wisdom plays a pervasive role, underpinning the treatment of individual names and the treatment as a whole, evidenced already in the *sed contra*'s modified repetition of a John Damascene quotation cited in q.1, a.1, *sed contra*. The quotation concerns divine attributes manifest in the Incarnation. Thomas's earlier and longer citation names goodness, wisdom, justice, and power, but q.3, a.8, *sed contra* notes only wisdom and power. This pair carries special significance for question three, with wisdom the governing category for fittingness arguments and power the governing category for the speculative Christologies, though the divine power remains indifferent to these possibilities and is displayed no more thoroughly in one or the other or the actual dispensation. Both q.1, a.1 and q.3, a.8 address fittingness, but the added specificity of q.3, a.8 carries with it the superlative. Thomas's notion of the Incarnation as the highest expression of the divine wisdom to humanity colors this entire article.

The Nature Assumed

Question four begins a lengthy treatment (qq.4–15) of the nature assumed. Questions four to six discuss what the Word assumed; questions seven to fifteen discuss what was coassumed. These questions cover far more material that can usefully be summarized here, so only select topics will find room for analysis. Before addressing the parts of the assumed nature (q.5) and the order of the assumption (q.6), Aquinas presents the human nature itself (q.4). This presentation focuses on the fittingness of the Incarnation from the part of the nature assumed, with q.4, a.1 well following and complementing q.3, a.8.

In question four, and particularly in articles one and six, Thomas grounds the fittingness of the Word's assumption of human nature in humanity's ability to approach God through intellect and will and in human nature's need for salvation. Article one of question four asks if human nature were more assumable than any other nature (or all of creation as a whole). Something is assumable as "apt to be assumed by a divine person,"[60] though this aptitude cannot be understood as a natural passive potency. Nothing of creation possesses such a natural aptitude for personal union with the Word. "Whence," Thomas writes, "it remains that something is called assumable according to a fittingness to the aforesaid union."[61] Human nature displays both a dignity and a necessity that make it fit for assumption to the Word. This dignity pertains to humanity as rational and as intended, through its operation of knowing and loving, to approach the very Word of God.[62] This argument mirrors the first argument from q.3, a.8

---

60 *ST* III, q.4, a.1 (*Summa theologiae* 4: 2448a): "Dicendum quod aliquid assumptibile dicitur quasi aptum assumi a divina persona."
61 *ST* III, q.4, a.1 (*Summa theologiae* 4: 2448a): "Unde relinquitur quod assumptibile aliquid dicitur secundum congruentiam ad unionem praedictam."
62 *ST* III, q.4, a.1 (*Summa theologiae* 4: 2448a): "Secundum dignitatem quidem quia humana natura, inquantum est rationalis et intellectualis, nata est contingere aliqualiter ipsum Verbum per suam operationem, cognoscendo scilicet et amando ipsum."

on the fittingness of the Word as the person assuming.[63] The third argument of q.3, a.8 develops through consideration of original sin, which likewise grounds the necessity for assumption of human nature as described in q.4, a.1. Human nature alone features both this dignity and this necessity, and so "human nature alone is assumable."[64] This limits assumability to human nature only from the side of the nature assumed and not with respect to the divine nature's power to assume.

Questions one, three, and four all express the fittingness of the Incarnation. Thomas's analyses rotate this notion, considering it from various perspectives. Each viewing reveals further connections to related ideas and offers increasing specification. This specification informs subsequent appraisals and so allows for a process of constant reiteration and refinement. Question one discusses the Incarnation more generally and with attention to its 'why'. The divine goodness communicating itself fully as a remedy for human sin governs the basic content of question one, though not without attention to the wisdom implicit in this divine self-communication. Wisdom plays a more explicit role in questions three and four, which continue examination of the mode or 'how' of the Incarnation begun in question two. Question two hones the notion of God becoming incarnate to God's assumption of human nature into hypostatic union. With this added specification, questions three and four can differently appreciate the fittingness of the Incarnation and can do so from two perspectives. This change of perspective provides greater nuance to the range of ideas reiterated, amplifying the wisdom guiding the Incarnation and so bringing its fittingness into sharper focus. Two examples are ready to hand. Thomas notes (*ST* III, q.1, a.1, *ad* 2) that personal union with God so exceeded the dignity of human nature as to be unfitting from this perspective while wholly fitting according to the divine goodness. Such issues reemerge in question four, where 'assumability' is denied as a natural passive potency of human nature but affirmed as fitting according to human

---

63 Humanity participates in the Word as wisdom. This participation makes the Word the most fitting of the divine persons to assume a human nature. This participation makes human nature the most fitting to be assumed to the Word. Question three, article eight and question four, article one are mirror images, considering the same fittingness from different sides.
64 *ST* III, q.4, a.1 (*Summa theologiae* 4: 2448a): "Unde relinquitur quod sola humana natura sit assumptibilis."

nature's dignity (in intellect and will) and need (due to sin). By altering the stance of reflection upon this topic, the original answer finds a new depth. *ST* III, q.1, a.1, *ad* 3 notes that every difference of creatures from the Creator is ordered by the divine wisdom and that the evil of fault involves a movement away from that wisdom. Question three, article eight's meditation upon Christ as Word and Wisdom magnifies the views of q.1, a.1, *ad* 3 to show not just the fittingness of God becoming incarnate but of God's assumption of human nature to the very person of the Word. Shifting the perspective from the divine nature to the divine person assuming uncovers a more pervasive fittingness. These two examples are introductory rather than exhaustive and serve only as gestures toward the mutually supportive richness of questions one, three, and four.

Discussion of these three questions provides a foundation for examining other aspects of Thomas's treatise on Christ. They also provide clues as to the subsequent questions most productive for the present purposes. Human nature's specific imaging of the Word in intellect and its dignity as intended to approach God through intellect and will mark out questions seven to eight on Christ's grace and nine to twelve on Christ's knowledge as fit for inquiry.[65] Intellect and will are closely connected; dissecting Thomas's presentation of Christ's grace and human knowledge clarifies Aquinas's presentation of Christ's human will. This clarification comes not without raising new questions. Discussion of questions seven to eight and nine to twelve must both remain mindful of earlier gains and aware of the trajectory of the *Tertia pars*. Thomas's consideration of Christ's grace and knowledge may function here as a case study in the application of Christological rules established previously in the *Tertia pars*.

Christ's fullness of grace lays the foundation for all the perfections of Christ's human nature.[66] This holds true for Christ's human knowledge

---

[65] On Christ's human knowledge, see 'Knowledge, Christ's,' in Wawrykow, *The Westminster Handbook*, pp. 80–82; Jean-Pierre Torrell, "Saint Thomas d'Aquin et la science du Christ: Une relecture des questions 9–12 de la *Tertia Pars* de la *Somme théologique*," in *Saint Thomas au XXe siècle: Colloque du centenaire de la "Revue thomiste" (1893–1992): Toulouse, 25–28 mars 1993*, ed. Serge-Thomas Bonino (Paris, 1994), 394–409; and Guy Mansini, "Understanding St Thomas on Christ's Immediate Knowledge of God," *Thomist* 59 (1995): 91–124.

[66] On Christ's merit and grace, see Joseph Wawrykow, "Grace," in *The Theology of Thomas Aquinas*, ed. Rik Van Nieuwenhove and Joseph Wawrykow (Notre Dame, IN, 2005), 192–221; Wawrykow, *God's Grace and Human Action: 'Merit'*

and Christ's human will. Thomas's presentation of Christ's grace also highlights the themes of Christ's instrumentality and mediatorship. In virtue of the hypostatic union, Christ's grace is unique; though unique, Christ's grace is continuous with the grace of other human beings.[67] Examining Christ's grace in its continuities with and differences from the grace of other human beings clarifies both Thomas's Christology and his view of God's grace as operative and cooperative in other human beings as separate instruments.

The *Summa*'s treatise on grace occupies the final six questions of the *Prima Secundae* (qq.109–114). Thomas organizes these questions under three basic headings: the need for grace (qq.109–111), the cause of grace (q.112), and the effects of grace (qq.113–114). Question 109 introduces distinctions crucial for Thomas's mature understanding of grace. He distinguishes the natural from the supernatural and stresses the necessity of grace for humanity's supernatural end of the face-to-face vision of God.[68] Aquinas also specifies two types of grace: habitual grace and the grace of *auxilium*. Habitual grace provides human beings with the potential for supernatural actions. The grace of *auxilium* provides the aid for reducing the potency for the supernatural to act. Thomas lastly distinguishes humanity before the Fall and after the Fall. Sin disorders humanity, making grace necessary not only to elevate humanity to its supernatural end but also to heal and reorder the human soul.[69]

Habitual grace and the grace of *auxilium* admit a further division:

> Each of his two graces can be further distinguished into 'operative' and 'cooperative.' The classic text in the *Summa* for this way of talking about grace is I–II.111.2c. When used of habitual grace, 'operative' refers to being: by operative habitual grace the being of the person, both morally and supernaturally, is enhanced, and the person is ren-

---

in the Theology of Thomas Aquinas (Notre Dame, IN, 1995), pp. 238–247; and Bernard Catão, *Salut et rédemption chez S. Thomas d'Aquin: L'acte sauveur du Christ* (Paris, 1964).

67 Wawrykow argues for the continuity and coherence of Thomas's discussions of predestination (*ST* I, q.23), grace (*ST* I–II, qq.109–114), and the grace of Christ (*ST* III, qq.7–8, 18–19, 24) (Wawrykow, "Grace," pp. 209–211).
68 See Wawrykow, "Grace," p. 193.
69 See Wawrykow, "Grace," pp. 194–195.

dered pleasing to God. 'Cooperative' habitual grace has to do with disposition; by cooperative habitual grace, one is inclined to the meritorious actions that complete the journey to God.[70]

In the infusion of operative *auxilium*, the human being is simply moved by God and does not contribute to the action. In cooperative *auxilium*, the human being is moved and moves, contributing to the graced action.[71] Readers of the *Summa* must approach the treatise on Christ in the *Tertia pars* informed by Thomas's earlier discussion of grace.

Thomas discusses Christ's grace as an individual (q.7) and as head of the Church (q.8). Christ's grace as head of the Church clarifies how Christ can merit for others (q.8, aa.5–6), but even this is founded upon Christ's fullness of grace as an individual. The presentation of Christ's grace begins with Christ's habitual grace (q.7, a.1). Aquinas offers three reasons for positing habitual grace in Christ. The first reason involves the proximity of Christ's soul to God through hypostatic union, which allows Christ's soul to receive the influx of grace to the highest degree.[72] The second reason is that the nobility of Christ's soul required that it reach God in the highest degree through its operations of knowing and loving. Rational natures can reach God in this way only as elevated by grace.[73] The third reason is Christ's relationship to the human race as mediator of God and human

---

70 Wawrykow, "Grace," p. 197.
71 Wawrykow discusses this division of the grace of *auxilium* and the scholarly disputes about which type best describes the various parts of human actions (Wawrykow, "Grace," pp. 197–198). He critiques the readings of operative *auxilium* that limit it to conversion and notes that perseverance in habitual grace also relies upon operative *auxilium*. Limiting operative *auxilium* to conversion would remove this type of grace from Christ, thereby limiting Christ's fullness of grace.
72 *ST* III, q.7, a.1 (*Summa theologiae* 4: 2465b): "Dicendum quod necesse est ponere in Christo gratiam habitualem, propter tria. Primo quidem propter unionem animae illius ad Verbum Dei. Quanto enim aliquod receptivum est propinquius causae influenti, tanto magis participat de influentia ipsius. Influxus autem gratiae est a Deo.... Et ideo maxime fuit conveniens ut anima illa reciperet influxum divinae gratiae."
73 *ST* III, q.7, a.1 (*Summa theologiae* 4: 2465b): "Secundo, propter nobilitatem illius animae, cuius operationes oportebat propinquissime attingere ad Deum per cognitionem et amorem. Ad quod necesse est elevari rationalem naturam per gratiam."

beings. Christ as a human being (*inquantum homo*) is the mediator and so as a human being must possess the grace that flows into others.[74]

These three reasons summarize three aspects of the *Summa*'s Christology, and Thomas elaborates each aspect in response to the objections. The first reason notes Christ's fitting possession of habitual grace on account of the hypostatic union. This again demonstrates Thomas's concern with fittingness and with the hypostatic union as the basis for subsequent assertions about Christ. Even though Christ's soul was united to God hypostatically, the distinction of Christ's human and divine natures remained. Christ's soul was "divine through participation, which is according to grace."[75] The second reason highlights grace as elevating Christ's intellect and will to their highest and proper perfection. Aided by grace, Christ's human will cleaved to God in all things.[76] Christ's human soul

---

74 *ST* III, q.7, a.1 (*Summa theologiae* 4: 2465b): "Tertio, propter habitudinem ipsius Christi ad genus humanum. Christus enim inquantum homo, est 'mediator Dei et hominum', ut dicitur I *ad Tim*. II⁵. Et ideo oportebat quod haberet gratiam etiam in alios redundantem."

75 *ST* III, q.7, a.1, *ad* 1 (*Summa theologiae* 4: 2465b): "Sed quia cum unitate personae remanet distinctio naturarum ... anima Christi non est per suam essentiam divina. Unde oportet quod fiat divina per participationem, quae est secundum gratiam." Thomas will later specify that Christ's habitual grace logically, though not temporally, follows from the grace of union (*ST* III, q.7, a.13).

76 Thomas presents the general framework of a human will aided in terms of operating and cooperating grace in *ST* I–II, q.111, a.2. "Dicendum quod sicut supra dictum est, gratia dupliciter potest intelligi: uno modo, divinum auxilium quo nos movet ad bene volendum et agendum; alio modo, habituale donum nobis divinitus inditum. Utroque autem modo gratia dicta convenienter dividitur per operantem et cooperantem. Operatio enim alicuius effectus non attribuitur mobili, sed moventi. In illo ergo effectu in quo mens nostra est mota et non movens, solus autem Deus movens, operatio Deo attribuitur; et secundum hoc dicitur gratia operans. In illo autem effectu in quo mens nostra et movet et movetur, operatio non solum attribuitur Deo, sed etiam animae; et secundum hoc dicitur gratia cooperans. Est autem in nobis duplex actus. Primus quidem interior voluntatis. Et quantum ad istum actum, voluntas se habet ut mota, Deus autem ut movens; et praesertim cum voluntas incipit bonum velle, quae prius malum volebat. Et ideo secundum quod Deus movet humanam mentem ad hunc actum, dicitur gratia operans. Alius autem actus est exterior; qui cum a voluntate imperetur, ut supra habitum est, consequens est ut ad hunc actum operatio attribuatur voluntati. Et quia etiam ad hunc actum Deus non adiuvat, et interius confirmando voluntatem ut ad actum perveniat, et exterius facultatem operandi praebendo; respectu huiusmodi actus dicitur gratia cooperans" (*ST* I–II, q.111, a.2 [*Summa theologiae* 2: 1369b]).

could not know and love God as the Word does but could reach God through a perfect human operation. This requires grace.[77] The third reason indicates Christ's capital grace and mediatorship. Christ's humanity was a rational instrument that not only is acted upon but also acts through its free will. The perfect operation of a human free will fittingly rests upon habitual grace.[78]

In q.7, a.7 Thomas further specifies Christ's grace in terms of *gratia gratum faciens* and *gratia gratis data*.[79] In the *Prima Secundae pars*, Aquinas presents *gratia gratis data* as ordered to the exterior acts of teaching and persuading.[80] Christ's teaching would only be useful if he possessed the *gratia gratis data* through which that teaching could be expressed.

---

77 ST III, q.7, a.1, *ad* 2 (*Summa theologiae* 4: 2466a): "Dicendum quod Christo, inquantum est naturalis Filius Dei, debetur hereditas aeterna, quae est ipsa beatitudo increata, per increatum actum cognitionis et amoris Dei, eundem scilicet quo Pater cognoscit et amat seipsum. Cuius actus anima capax non erat propter differentiam naturae. Unde oportebat quod attingeret ad Deum per actum fruitionis creatum. Qui quidem esse non potest nisi per gratiam. Similiter etiam inquantum est Verbum Dei, habuit facultatem omnia bene operandi operatione divina. Sed quia praeter operationem divinam oportet poni in eo operationem humanam, ut infra patebit, oportuit in eo esse habitualem gratiam, per quam huiusmodi operatio in eo esset perfecta." Thomas's presentation of Christ's unity of will (*ST* III, q.18) is followed by unity of operation (*ST* III, q.19).

78 ST III, q.7, a.1, *ad* 3 (*Summa theologiae* 4: 2466a): "Dicendum quod humanitas Christi est instrumentum divinitatis, non quidem sicut instrumentum inanimatum, quod nullo modo agit sed solum agitur; sed tanquam instrumentum animatum anima rationali, quod ita agit quod etiam agitur. Et ideo ad convenientiam actionis oportuit eum habere gratiam habitualem." Chapter four has discussed rational instrumentality in connection to Christ's human will (*ST* III, q.18, a.1, *ad* 2). Though Thomas does not mention the grace of *auxilium* here, readers of the *Prima Secundae* know well that the potency of habitual grace must be reduced to act through the grace of *auxilium*. The perfect operation of Christ's human will requires the grace of *auxilium* in addition to habitual grace.

79 *Gratia gratum faciens* is usually translated as 'sanctifying grace.' *Gratia gratis data* is often translated as 'gratuitous grace.' See "Gratuitous Graces," in Wawrykow, *The Westminster Handbook*, pp. 68–69.

80 ST I–II, q.111, a.4 (*Summa theologiae* 2: 1371b): "Dicendum, sicut supra dictum est, gratia gratis data ordinatur ad hoc quod homo alteri cooperetur ut reducatur ad Deum. Homo autem ad hoc operari non potest interius movendo, hoc enim solius Dei est; sed solum exterius docendo vel persuadendo."

"Whence," Thomas argues, "it is clear that every *gratia gratis data* was in Christ most excellently, as in the first and principal Teacher of faith."[81] Furthermore, Christ possessed every *gratia gratis data* in an undivided way as the hypostatically united instrument of God. Christ's fullness of grace granted the efficacy to perform all the works of grace (both interior and exterior) that are divided among others as separate instruments of God.[82] Thomas defends Christ's fullness of grace both according to its intensity (*quantum ad quantitatem eius intensivam*) and according to its power (*secundum virtutem*). Its perfection of intensity results from the proximity of Christ's soul to God as the cause of grace.[83] Christ had the power to operate every effect of grace as the first principle of motion within that genus of action.[84]

Thomas's presentation of Christ's grace as head of the Church builds upon Christ's individual grace. Christ is head of the Church *secundum quod*

---

[81] *ST* III, q.7, a.7 (*Summa theologiae* 4: 2471a): "Unde manifestum est quod in Christo excellentissime fuerunt omnes gratiae gratis datae, sicut in primo et principali fidei Doctore."

[82] *ST* III, q.7, a.7, *ad* 1 (*Summa theologiae* 4: 2471a): "In utraque autem gratia Christus plenitudinem habuit; inquantum enim divinitati unita erat eius anima, plenam efficaciam habebat ad omnes praedictos actus perficiendos. Sed alii sancti, qui moventur a Deo sicut instrumenta non unita, sed separata, particulariter efficaciam recipiunt ad hos vel ad illos actus perficiendos. Et ideo in aliis sanctis huiusmodi gratiae dividuntur; non autem in Christo." It is worth stressing here Thomas's mention of instrumentality. Christ's human nature is an instrument of his divinity. There are two important specifications regarding what type of instrument it is. First, it is a rational instrument, which not only is acted but also acts. Second, it is a hypostatically united instrument. Both of these specifications are important for Thomas's presentation of Christ's human nature.

[83] *ST* III, q.7, a.9 (*Summa theologiae* 4: 2473a): "Utroque autem modo Christus habuit gratiae plenitudinem. Primo quidem quia habuit eam in summo, secundum perfectissimum modum quo haberi potest. Et hoc quidem apparet primo ex propinquitate animae Christi ad causam gratiae. Dictum est enim quod quanto aliquod receptivum propinquius est causae influenti, tanto abundantius recipit. Et ideo anima Christi, quae propinquius coniungitur Deo inter omnes creaturas rationales, maximam recipit influentiam gratiae eius."

[84] *ST* III, q.7, a.9 (*Summa theologiae* 4: 2473a): "Similiter etiam quantum ad virtutem gratiae, plene habuit gratiam, quia habuit eam ad omnes operationes vel effectus gratiae. Et hoc ideo quia conferebatur ei gratia tanquam cuidam universali principio in genere habentium gratiam. Virtus autem primi principii alicuius generis universaliter se extendit ad omnes effectus illius generis."

homo (according as an individual human being) (q.8, a.1).[85] This capital grace allows Christ to merit for others (*ST* III, q.19, a.4), but it also allows Christ *secundum quod homo* to give grace instrumentally. By virtue of the hypostatic union, Christ's human nature is an instrument of his divinity and can instrumentally operate works proper to God. Christ *secundum quod homo* thus causes salvation not just through the mode of merit but also through the mode of efficiency.[86] Thomas's presentation of the efficiency of Christ's human nature represents a distinctive feature of his Christology in the thirteenth-century context. The latter part of this chapter will develop this distinctiveness more fully, particularly in terms of Christ's humanity as an instrument of his divinity.[87]

Questions nine to twelve (on Christ's knowledge) fall under the broad heading of what the Word co-assumed with human nature (qq.7–15), namely its perfections (qq.7–13) and defects (qq.14–15).[88] From questions two and five, readers of the *Tertia pars* already know that the Word assumed a perfect, integral human nature. The issue in questions seven to thirteen thus concerns less whether Christ possessed these perfections than how. Christ assumed the defects of human nature that were conducive to the end of the Incarnation and only those defects.[89] Ultimately this end involves salvation of the human race, but more proximately it involves

---

85 The phrase *secundum quod homo* carries much weight in Thomas's Christology, for it can refer both to the person of the Word as a supposit of human nature and to Christ's human nature itself. Thomas discusses these two senses of *secundum quod homo* in *ST* III, q.16, a.10.
86 *ST* III, q.8, a.1, *ad* 1 (*Summa theologiae* 4: 2479a): "Dicendum quod dare gratiam aut Spiritum Sanctum convenit Christo secundum quod Deus, auctoritative; sed instrumentaliter convenit etiam ei secundum quod homo, inquantum scilicet eius humanitas instrumentum fuit divinitatis eius. Et ita actiones ipsius ex virtute divinitatis fuerunt in nobis causantes et per meritum et per efficientiam quandam." Thomas makes the same distinction between *auctoritative* and *instrumentaliter* in *ST* III, q.26, a.2, *ad* 3 on how Christ *secundum quod homo* bears away sin.
87 See Paul Gondreau, *The Passions of Christ's Soul in the Theology of St. Thomas Aquinas* (Münster, 2002), pp. 152–153.
88 For a concise introduction to the notion of 'co-assumed,' see 'Jesus Christ,' in Wawrykow, *The Westminster Handbook*, pp. 76–80.
89 See Paul Gondreau, "The Humanity of Christ, the Incarnate Word," in *The Theology of Thomas Aquinas*, ed. Rik van Nieuwenhove and Joseph Wawrykow (Notre Dame, IN, 2005), pp. 252–276. Gondreau stresses the defects assumed as contributing to the 'believability' of Christ's human nature.

demonstrating the veracity of Christ's divine nature and human nature. Thomas applies these same basic rules when examining what the Son of God did and underwent in the flesh (qq.27–59). The more 'abstract' discussions of qq.1–26 well prepare for the concrete presentation of the gospel narrative in qq.27–59, offering a 'grammar' for reading the scriptural accounts.[90] Questions nine to twelve add grammatical rules based upon the more general logic of the Incarnation as ordered to human salvation.

Thomas has two basic goals in *ST* III, q.9, a.1. He must show that the perfection of Christ's human nature required human knowledge and explain that such created knowledge was not useless in Christ. The remaining articles in q.9 and qq.10–12 strive for the same basic goals with increasing levels of detail. Thomas's address of the types of Christ's knowledge in question nine and careful elaboration of each type in a later question reflects a scientific organization of material, moving from the general to the specific. Of particular interest here is Christ's infused or imprinted knowledge (q.9, a.3; q.11). After defending Christ's possession of this knowledge, Thomas questions whether it was discursive or collative. He notes two senses of discursive or collative knowledge. The first derives from the acquisition of knowledge, the second from its use. The first sense does not apply to Christ, whose knowledge was divinely imprinted. The second does. Christ's knowledge was discursive in its relation to the will willing the knowledge already possessed. Thomas's arguments here relate closely to those offered in question 18 on Christ's unity of will. Not surprising then is reference to the Damascene's denial of council and election in Christ (*ST* III, q.11, a.3, ob.1; *De fide orthodoxa* III.14). This issue reemerges in *ST* III, q.18, a.4, and the point of both discussions amounts to the same thing. Though Christ knew everything through imprinted knowledge and so could have no doubt due to ignorance, this does not exclude the discursive operation of Christ's practical knowledge manifest in free choice.[91]

---

90 See Boyle, "The Twofold Division."
91 Christ's free choice is important not only in terms of merit but also in terms of sacrifice and satisfaction. Christ freely willed the passion for the sake of salvation. In *ST* III, q.18, a.4, Thomas defends free choice in Christ even though there was no ignorance in him. In *ST* III, q.11, a.3, Thomas defends free choice in Christ despite Christ's lack of ignorance and perfection of imprinted knowledge. The key is Christ's practical knowledge displayed in willing specific acts. Christ willed the passion with full knowledge of its pains and outcome.

Christ's imprinted knowledge, following the mode connatural to humanity, was habitual. *ST* III, q.11, a.5 links habitual knowledge to the will, particularly in *ad* 2. The second objection determines habitual knowledge to be unfitting for Christ, since habitual knowledge of everything cannot be completely reduced to act, just as an infinity cannot be enumerated. Thomas's reply relies on a specification introduced in *ad* 1, where he argues that Christ's knowledge, as it exceeds the mode of human knowing, was perfectly simple and not habitual. As proportioned to the mode of human knowing, Christ's knowledge was perfect in the genus of human knowing. The second type of perfection does not require knowledge to be always in act, an affirmation expanded in *ad* 2. The will reduces habitual knowledge to act, for someone acts by a habit when willing. Habitual knowledge of all things is not useless, for the will, while indeterminate to an infinity of things, exercises a tendency to what fits the actual circumstances. "And so," Aquinas writes, "the habit also is not useless, even though all things subject to the habit are not reduced to act, provided that what befits the proper end of the will according to the exigencies of circumstance and time is reduced to act."[92]

A few remarks on the role of the will in habitual knowledge are prudent. The previous chapter has detailed the divisions of the will accepted by Thomas. Question eleven, article five refers to the will of reason in general. The will of reason itself can regard ends, in which case it is designated the will as nature, or means, in which case it is named the will as reason. This does not represent any division of the one power of the will but simply distinguishes ways of viewing the will. *ST* III, q.18, a.5 holds that Christ's will as nature refused the passion, for taken simply as an end death is a natural evil. Christ's will as reason willed the passion as a means to human salvation, in which sense the passion was good. Thomas's presentation of Christ's infused knowledge enriches consideration of Christ's will. The will reduced certain potencies to act based upon habitual knowledge of all things. Through this habitual knowledge Christ knew every detail of his impending death and every detail of human salvation flowing from the passion. This knowledge included also the non-necessity of the Incarna-

---

92   *ST* III, q.11, a.5, *ad* 2 (*Summa theologiae* 4: 2501a): "Et ideo etiam habitus non est frustra, licet non omnia reducantur in actum quae habitui subiacent, dummodo reducatur in actum id quod congruit ad debitum finem voluntatis secundum exigentiam negotiorum et temporis."

tion and passion for human salvation. These were the fitting means, in accordance with the divine wisdom, to a fitting end, in accordance with the divine goodness. The proper act of the will, however, involved reducing habitual knowledge to act, not willing on account of divine knowledge or blessed knowledge. The point here is to stress Christ's willing of the passion as a human act grounded in human knowledge.[93] These remarks and Thomas's reasoning in these questions foreshadow the discussion of Christ's mediatorship in *ST* III, q.26.

Aquinas's position in the *Summa theologiae* on Christ's acquired knowledge draws attention less for its details and motivations than for its differences from his position in the *Scriptum*. Comparing these positions, beyond noting the obvious that in the *Summa* Aquinas affirms what he denied in the *Scriptum*, exceeds the scope of this chapter. The *Summa*'s treatment of this issue begins in *ST* III, q.9, a.4, where Thomas asserts the perfection of Christ's human nature, which naturally includes not only a possible intellect but also an agent intellect. The *corpus* progresses through several quotations from Aristotle. These quotations afford Thomas a vocabulary of argumentation advancing from the impossibility of God acting uselessly to a thing's definition through its operation.[94] Thomas argues that if the agent intellect in Christ lacked its proper operation it would be

---

[93] Torrell notes in Thomas's treatment of Christ's knowledge a fidelity to the New Testament, to Chalcedon, and to Aristotelian psychology (Torrell, "St Thomas d'Aquin et la science du Christ," p. 408). This threefold fidelity is equally apparent in Thomas's treatment of Christ's two wills, where he maintains fidelity to the New Testament, Constantinople III, and Aristotelian psychology.

[94] In the questions on Christ's knowledge, Thomas more and more frequently employs arguments grounded upon whether or not something is useless or done uselessly. Since the general trend of qq.2–15 concentrates on the 'how' of the Incarnation as the most fitting means to human salvation, something assumed to the Word uselessly or in vain (*frustra*) represents an interesting type of unfittingness. This opposition solidifies the notion of fittingness as wisest means, in which case everything assumed to the Word was so assumed only for a specific reason, purpose, or use. This type of fittingness sets the stage for Thomas's treatment of the consequences of the union (qq.16–26) and in particular for the utility of the proper operation of Christ's human nature as instrument of the divinity working for human salvation. "Deus autem et natura nihil frustra faciunt" (*ST* III, q.5, a.3, ob.2, citing Aristotle, *De caelo* [*Summa theologiae* 4: 2456a]). Thomas's use of arguments regarding utility begins already in his treatment of Christ's grace (see *ST* III, q.7).

useless. "Thus therefore," Thomas argues, "it is necessary to say that in Christ there were some intelligible species received into his possible intellect through the action of the agent intellect."[95] This, indeed, is acquired knowledge, which is proper knowledge according to the human mode of knowing. Acquired knowledge proceeds from the light of the intellectual agent, "which is connatural to the human soul."[96] Thomas expands upon this knowledge in question 12, but before moving on to the subsequent specifications, it is worthwhile to note some possible motivations.

It is possible to mention probable motivations behind Thomas's change of opinion between the *Scriptum* and the *Summa*. Beginning with the most basic, as a young theologian commenting on the *Sentences*, Thomas would likely have been more influenced by the opinions of the masters, who denied acquired knowledge in Christ.[97] Thomas's quotations from Aristotle could signal a source of inspiration or could simply be fresh in Aquinas's mind as he composed his commentaries. The language of operation, though heavily dependent upon Aristotle (e.g. *ST* I, qq.76–79), carries connotations beyond Aristotle. In question nine, article one Thomas refers to Constantinople III.[98] He relies on the acts of Constantinople III in *ST* III, qq.18 and 19 as well as in the roughly contemporary *De unione Verbi incarnati*. The acts of the council, and Thomas's use of it, focus heavily on Christ's perfect human will and operation. It seems not a leap of reasoning to suggest that the arguments in *ST* III, q.9, a.4 relating to perfect operation bear some debt to Constantinople III. This suggestion goes no small way toward offering a compelling motivation for Aquinas to change his opinion and affirm acquired knowledge in Christ.[99] The influence of

---

95 *ST* III, q.9, a.4 (*Summa theologiae* 4: 2490b): "Sic igitur necesse est dicere quod in Christo fuerint aliquae species intelligibiles per actionem intellectus agentis in intellectu possibili eius receptae."

96 *ST* III, q.9, a.4 (*Summa theologiae* 4: 2490b): "Nam talis scientia ponitur in Christo secundum lumen intellectus agentis, quod est animae humanae connaturale."

97 See Bonaventure, *Commentaria in III Sententiarum*, d.14, qq.1 and 2; Albertus Magnus, *Commentarii in III Sententiarum*, d.14.

98 Though he does not specify his reference beyond this, Thomas is certainly indicating Agatho's *Epistle I*. Again, this work provided Thomas with sources linked together in an argumentative sequence. The topics covered include Christ's two knowledges, wills, operations, and nativities.

99 Chapter four has argued for Thomas's pervasive appropriation of Agatho's sources and argumentative structure. This appropriation extends to Christ's human knowledge.

a source often exceeds the impression given solely by explicit citations. Such is the case with the acts of Constantinople III, which broadly influenced Aquinas, perhaps even inspiring his presentation of a secondary *esse* in Christ in the *De unione Verbi incarnati* (a.4).[100]

What Thomas stresses in question 12 holds as much interest as the differences that distinguish it from *Scriptum, in* III (hereafter referred to as "*in* III"), d.14, a.3. Those differences are best summarized by noting that the *Summa* affirms acquired knowledge in Christ and its advancement in terms of habit or essence. The *Scriptum* denies these. Thomas's preferred method for arguing this new case revolves around fittingness. This fittingness itself emerges from Aquinas's insistence upon the proper operation of each agent. If Christ assumed a power, such as the agent intellect, without utilizing that capacity, its assumption would have been useless. This would be out of step with the wisdom directing and manifest in the Incarnation. Rather, Aquinas maintains the fittingness of positing in Christ the proper operation of the agent intellect. In terms of content, it implies acquired knowledge; in terms of mode, it implies advancement in the habit of acquired knowledge commensurate with advancement in age. Given the connection of intellect and will in Aquinas's thought, the discussion of Christ's knowledge provides the backdrop for the discussion of Christ's wills.[101]

100 Thomas alone among thirteenth-century theologians treats of Christ's humanity as instrument of the divinity, citing the Damascene, *De fide orthodoxa* III.15 (Theophil Tschipke, *L'humanité du Christ comme instrument de salut de la divinité*, trans. Philibert Secretan [Fribourg, 2003], p. 112). Thomas's understanding of this instrumentality changes through the course of his writings, due in no small part to his recovery of the acts of Constantinople III. Constantinople III followed the affirmations of Chalcedon to their logical conclusions. Thomas's increasing concern with the instrumentality of Christ's human nature in the work of salvation (based also upon Cyril of Alexandria and John of Damascus) found its expression in Constantinople III's emphasis upon a perfect human will and operation in Christ. Aside from Gerhoh of Reichersberg (d. 1169) and Arno of Reichersberg (d. 1175), Thomas alone among the medievals made use of Cyril in Christology. See Tschipke, *L'humanité du Christ*, pp. 93, 95, 113, 136 and N.M Häring, "The Character and Range of Influence of St Cyril of Alexandria on Latin Theology (430–1260)," *Mediaeval Studies* 12 (1950): 1–19. Knowledge of Cyril, Ephesus, and Chalcedon was regrettably insufficient to prevent monophysitic and monenergistic themes in Gerhoh and Arno.
101 This implies that Thomas preserves in *ST* III, q.18 his concern to exclude anything assumed to the Word uselessly or in vain (*frustra*). This uselessness is particularly unfitting since the Word assumed a human nature for the purpose of achieving humanity's salvation through the human nature assumed.

Before turning to the 'consequences of the union' (qq.16–26), a few points from qq.13–15 deserve brief mention. Question 13 considers the power of Christ's soul and in particular its relation to omnipotence. Thomas first reiterates that "in the mystery of the Incarnation the union was so made in person that the distinction of natures nevertheless remained, namely both natures retaining what is proper to each."[102] Thus, Christ's soul did not possess omnipotence *simpliciter*, for omnipotence is proper to Christ's divine nature. However, by virtue of the hypostatic union, the human being Jesus Christ can be said to possess omnipotence.[103] *ST* III, q.13, a.2 distinguishes the power of Christ's soul according to its proper nature and according as it is an instrument united to the Word. The context of this distinction concerns the power to change creation. According to its proper nature, Christ's soul had the power to do all things fitting to it, from governance of the body to illuminating rational creatures through grace and knowledge. "If however," Thomas writes, "we speak about Christ's soul according as it is an instrument united to the Word itself, thus it has instrumental power for accomplishing every miraculous change that can be ordered to the end of the Incarnation, which is to restore all things."[104]

Article four distinguishes two ways in which Christ's soul willed something, either to be implemented through its own power or through the divine power.[105] Thomas holds that, according to the first way, Christ's soul was capable of whatever it willed, for "it would not befit his wisdom

---

102 *ST* III, q.13, a.1 (*Summa theologiae* 4: 2506b–2507a): "Dicendum quod ... in mysterio incarnationis ita facta est unio in persona quod tamen remansit distinctio naturarum, utraque scilicet natura retinente id quod sibi est proprium."
103 *ST* III, q.13, a.1, *ad* 1 (*Summa theologiae* 4: 2507a): "Dicendum quod homo accepit ex tempore omnipotentiam quam Filius Dei habuit ab aeterno, per ipsum unionem personae, ex qua factum est ut sicut homo dicitur Deus, ita dicatur omnipotens, non quasi sit alia omnipotentia hominis quam Filii Dei, sicut nec alia deitas; sed eo quod est una persona Dei et hominis."
104 *ST* III, q.13, a.2 (*Summa theologiae* 4: 2508b): "Si autem loquamur de anima Christi secundum quod est instrumentum Verbi sibi uniti, sic habuit instrumentalem virtutem ad omnes immutationes miraculosas faciendas ordinabiles ad incarnationis finem, qui est instaurare omnia, sive quae in caelis, sive quae in terris sunt."
105 These two ways of willing follow a division, established in *ST* III, q.13, a.2, of the powers of Christ's soul as proper to human nature and as instrument of the divinity.

that he will to accomplish through himself something that was not subject to his power."[106] According to the second way, Christ's soul willed, as instrument of the divinity, what exceeded its natural powers.[107] Christ's soul was omnipotent as united to the Word. As an instrument of the divinity, Christ's soul could will acts proper to the divine power, a capacity crucial for the instrumental efficient causality of Christ *secundum quod homo*. The power of Christ's soul precedes Thomas's treatment of Christ's unity of will (q.18) and prayer (q.21). Question 13 provides clarifications important for the later questions and for Christ's instrumental causality. It is worth laboring the conclusions of question 13, for they are radical. In virtue of the hypostatic union, the man Jesus Christ is omnipotent. As instrument of the divinity, Christ's soul could will actions brought to effect by the divine power. Thomas's arguments for Christ's mediatorship *secundum quod homo* depend upon the divine power wielded by Christ's human will.

Question 15 discusses the defects of soul assumed by the Word and builds upon question 14's treatment of bodily defects assumed. Thomas's responses in question 14 all obey the logic set forth in article one, which provides three reasons for the fittingness of Christ's assumption of bodily defects. First, this serves the Incarnation's goal of making satisfaction for human sin. Second, it demonstrates the veracity of Christ's human nature.[108] Third, this provides an example for others to follow while suffering. Thomas limits Christ's assumption of bodily defects to those that fittingly serve the end of salvation, and so any bodily defect that would impede perfection of knowledge or grace must be excluded (*ST* III, q.14, a.4). This same logic of affirmation and negation governs question 15,

---

106 *ST* III, q.13, a.4 (*Summa theologiae* 4: 2510b-2511a): "Non enim conveniret sapientiae eius ut aliquid vellet per se facere, quod suae virtuti non subiaceret."
107 *ST* III, q.13, a.4 (*Summa theologiae* 4: 2511a): "Alio modo voluit ut implendum virtute divina, sicut resuscitationis proprii corporis, et alia huiusmodi miraculosa opera. Quae quidem non poterat propria virtute, sed secundum quod erat instrumentum divinitatis."
108 "In brief, the purpose of credibility in the Incarnation means that the human family must have no doubt that Christ is at the same time fully human and true divine savior of the human race. Hence, any perfection that appears to abbreviate his humanity or any defect that undermines his redemptive role or his supreme dignity represents 'unsuitable' features of the Incarnation," (Gondreau, *The Passions of Christ's Soul*, pp. 175-176).

which, along with the entire section on the nature assumed (qq.4–15), culminates in Christ as both a wayfarer and a comprehensor.[109] One might be surprised to find this topic addressed so late in this section, since Thomas relies on Christ as both wayfarer and comprehensor steadily in discussing the nature assumed. When the reader arrives at *ST* III, q.15, a.10, she is well prepared for its conclusion and well aware of its import. In many respects, affirmation that Christ was simultaneously a wayfarer and a comprehensor summarizes the most basic truths expressed diversely throughout qq.4–15.[110] Christ's status as both wayfarer and comprehensor requires certain truths about Christ's human nature, namely that it must be an integral human nature, complete with body and soul, full of grace, perfect in knowledge and power, and passible in body and soul. Thomas's use of *ST* III, q.15, a.10 as a foreshadowed summary of the section on the nature assumed is mirrored by his use of q.26, a.2 on Christ's mediatorship. Question 26 recapitulates and summarizes the section on the consequences of the union, implying its earlier conclusions just as q.15, a.10 did for qq.4–15.

The first three articles of question 15 treat matters related to sin and ignorance, which Aquinas can quickly rule out. Article four affirms Christ's passibility of soul, and articles five to nine examine specific passions of the soul. Article eight allows surprise or wonder (*admiratio*) in terms of Christ's experiential knowledge, an admission possible only due to Thomas's

---

109 "In brief, Aquinas' belief in a Christ who is *simul viator et comprehensor* represents the Dominican's attempt at synthesizing two opposing Medieval theological trends: on the one side, the push to affirm the perfection of all knowledge in Christ, which for the 13th-century scholastics means that Jesus, in his earthly life, enjoys the direct *visio Dei* along with its concomitant supereminent joy; and, on the other side, the need to underscore, contra Hilary of Poitiers, the psychosomatic reality of Christ's suffering and pain, which, again, informs the entire scholastic debate on Christ's passibility of soul. Psychosomatic suffering and supereminent joy do not make good bedfellows, particularly in Aquinas' system of thought, where the hylemorphic notion of *redundantia*, or the redounding effects of the soul's experiences onto the body and of the body's affairs onto the soul, plays a significant role." (Gondreau, *The Passions of Christ's Soul*, p. 443).

110 The placement of this topic also reminds the reader that, while the larger movement of articles, questions, and sections often proceeds along a linear and scientific trajectory, Thomas's arguments in the *Summa* are not solely or strictly linear. Rather, they are shaped to particular aims determined by a given topic.

mature teaching on Christ's acquired knowledge. What more directly concerns the present purpose are articles six and seven, which deal with sadness and fear. Thomas's response to article six begins with the dispensation according to which the divine glory present in the Word did not overwhelm Christ's human nature but rather allowed Christ's body and soul their proper powers and passions. This dispensation provides for such powers and passions while ensuring their ultimate service to the end of salvation. Aquinas distinguishes sadness (*tristitia*) from sorrow (*dolor*) in that sadness concerns an evil interior to apprehension through reason or imagination. "Moreover," Thomas argues, "Christ's soul can apprehend something interior as harmful, both with respect to itself, as was his passion and death; and with respect to others, as the disciples' sin."[111] Thomas's response to the fourth objection treats of sadness in relation to the passion. Its foundation, familiar from the previous chapter's discussion of *ST* III, q.18, concerns how something can be in itself contrary to the will, though willed as a means to some end. Thomas can thus argue that "Christ's death and passion were, considered in themselves, involuntary and causing sadness, although they were voluntary in their order to an end, which is redemption of the human race."[112]

In *ST* III, q.15, a.7 Thomas considers the presence of fear in Christ and, drawing a parallel between sadness and fear, argues that "just as sadness is caused from the apprehension of a present evil, so fear is caused from apprehension of a future evil."[113] A future evil, however, only causes fear in cases where the future evil is not wholly certain and where there can be hope of avoiding it. Christ possessed absolute certainty of future events, so there could be no such fear in Christ. This would seem to be the final word on the matter, but Thomas presents another manner of considering fear.

---

111 *ST* III, q.15, a.6 (*Summa theologiae* 4: 2522a): "Potuit autem anima Christi interius apprehendere aliquid ut nocivum, et quantum ad se, sicut passio et mors eius fuit; et quantum ad alios, sicut peccatum discipulorum."
112 *ST* III, q.15, a.6, *ad* 4 (*Summa theologiae* 4: 2523a): "Et hoc modo mors Christi et eius passio fuit, secundum se considerata, involuntaria et tristitiam causans, licet fuerit voluntaria in ordine ad finem, qui est redemptio humani generis." Christ's sadness and sorrow become increasingly important in John Duns Scotus, a development investigated in Chapter six below (pp. 306–312).
113 *ST* III, q.15, a.7 (*Summa theologiae* 4: 2523a): "Dicendum quod sicut tristitia causatur ex apprehensione mali praesentis, ita timor causatur ex apprehensione mali futuri."

The sensitive appetite naturally flees bodily harm. This natural flight induces sadness when directed to a present harm, but it induces fear when directed to a future harm. Thomas affirms this type of fear in Christ, and thus he can admit fear in Christ without admitting uncertainty. This successfully answers the root worry leading to the Damascene's denial of fear in Christ (*De fide orthodoxa* III.23) and foreshadows the discussion of Christ's will in q.18.[114]

Question 15 ends with a treatment of Christ as wayfarer and comprehensor. A wayfarer strives toward beatitude. A comprehensor has already achieved beatitude. So how can Christ simultaneously be both?[115] Aquinas refers to the *Secunda pars* (*ST* I–II, q.4, a.6), where he argues that perfect beatitude regards both the soul and the body. This perfect beatitude cannot be verified in Christ before his resurrection. Thomas writes: "Before the passion, however, Christ saw God fully according to his mind, and thus he possessed beatitude inasmuch as to what is proper to the soul. But, inasmuch as to other things, he lacked beatitude, because both his soul was passible and his body was passible and mortal."[116] Christ was a comprehensor by virtue of the beatitude proper to his soul, though through a divine dispensation, this beatitude did not overflow to Christ's sensitive soul and body but permitted what was natural to them.[117] With respect to these, Christ tended toward beatitude and so was a wayfarer. Nor does this simultaneous rest in an end and tendency toward that end pose any problem, for these are not according to the same (*ad* 1). Thomas employs the

---

114 Again, the Damascene uniformly rejects whatever would seem to imply ignorance, doubt, or uncertainty in Christ. Thomas finds space to uphold the Damascene's denial of ignorance while admitting what John denies to avoid positing ignorance. Thomas's concern in this effort is to preserve the truth of Christ's human nature and to explain its causality in Christ's salvific work.

115 This question worries many contemporary readers of Aquinas. See Jean Galot, "Le Christ terrestre et la vision," *Gregorianum* 67 (1986): 429–450, especially pp. 433–437.

116 *ST* III, q.15, a.10 (*Summa theologiae* 4: 2526a): "Christus autem ante passionem, secundum mentem plene videbat Deum; et sic habebat beatitudinem quantum ad id quod est proprium animae. Sed quantum ad alia deerat ei beatitudo, quia et anima eius erat passibilis, et corpus passibile et mortale."

117 Thomas refers to this dispensation often. In *ST* III, q.18, a.5, he uses this to explain Christ's will not to die according to sensuality and the will as nature. Leo's *Tomus ad Flavianum* expresses this dispensation, but Thomas prefers the Damascene's formulation. See Gondreau, *The Passions of Christ's Soul*, p. 150.

same logic in discussing the non-contrariety of Christ's will (q.18, a.6).[118] The themes developed in qq.1-15 occupy an equally important role in qq.16-26.

The *Summa theologiae*'s *Tertia pars* stresses the fittingness of the Incarnation. Thomas's presentation of this fittingness develops along two lines. One addresses the 'why' of the Incarnation; the other focuses on the 'how' of the Incarnation. These lines often intersect and always enrich each other. The 'why' of the Incarnation begins with the divine goodness (q.1, a.1) and humanity's need for salvation (q.1, a.3). The divine wisdom governs the 'how' of the Incarnation in general (q.1, a.2) and in particular (qq.2-4 are especially indicative of this, though it is apparent in qq.5-15 as well). Both the 'why' and the 'how' of the Incarnation relate to the dignity of human nature as able to approach God through intellect and will. Thomas's treatment of the 'why' can more easily be summarized than his treatment of the 'how.' He portrays the divine goodness as naturally self-communicative, and there can be no fuller communication of God than in the Incarnation.[119] This theme of self-communication relates equally to creation, which factors into the fittingness of the mode of the Incarnation. The Incarnation befits God's self-communication in terms of the divine goodness but so exceeds the dignity of creation as to be unfitting from the perspective of the creature. Thomas will qualify this somewhat in discussing the mode of the Incarnation in terms of the nature assumed, but, even before that, distills the fittingness of God's self-communication in the Incarnation into a most potent remedy for human sin. These two realities, the self-communicative nature of the highest good and humanity's need for salvation, account for the fittingness of the Incarnation in answer to the question 'why.'

The dignity of human nature in intellect and will introduces a further refinement of fittingness arguments. When discussing Christ's human knowledge, Thomas holds that it would be unfitting for the Word to assume anything uselessly. If anything were assumed without having its

---

118 Thomas inherits this logic from William of Auxerre and the *Summa fratris Alexandri*. Though he uses it in the *Summa*, Thomas avoids this logic in the *Scriptum*.

119 Thomas cites Dionysius (*De divinis nominibus* I.5 and IV.20) to the effect that God is goodness itself and the good naturally communicates itself (*ST* III, q.1, a.1).

proper operation or use, it would be assumed uselessly. Conversely, it is fitting for everything assumed to have its proper operation. A perfect, integral human nature must not only have all the right 'parts' but also have the proper use of those 'parts.'[120]

Fittingness according to the utility of proper operation emerges in the section on the nature assumed as a prime indicator of the wisdom governing the Incarnation and the instrumental role of Christ's humanity in human salvation. The task now is to apply these findings to the consequences of the union, where Thomas advances these same principles in discussing the relation of Christ's two natures to each other in the redemption of humanity. The discussion culminates in consideration of Christ as mediator (q.26, a.2). With the analysis of qq.1-26 complete, it will be possible to revisit the debates concerning the plan of the *Summa theologiae* summarized at the beginning of this chapter. Considerations of the utility of everything assumed carry over into the 'consequences of the union' (qq.16-26). In the section on the consequences, Thomas stresses the utility of Christ's perfect human will and operation as the proper human modes for Christ to achieve human salvation. The analysis will develop these themes, focusing on Christ's human nature as instrument of the divinity exercising instrumental efficient causality in the divine work of redemption.

Christ the Mediator: Christ's Human Will as Cause of Salvation

ST III, q.16 introduces the section on the consequences of the union. In the prologue to this section, Thomas sketches its division into three parts: "first, inasmuch as to these things fitting to Christ according to himself [qq.16-19]; second, concerning those things fitting to Christ in comparison to God the Father [qq.20-24]; third, concerning those things fitting to

---

120 Thomas's discussion of the nature assumed provides all the grounds for affirmation of a human will and operation in Christ. He addresses Christ's human will (q.18) and operation (q.19) not in the section of the nature assumed but in the consequences of the union. The reason behind this placement is that Thomas treats Christ's human will and operation under the heading of unity. Examining Christ's unity of will and unity of operation focuses on the proper use of the 'parts' assumed. That proper use is perfect obedience to God in the work of salvation.

Christ in comparison to us [qq.25–26]."[121] The continued import of fittingness arguments is apparent here. Less immediately obvious is the logic underlying a section on the consequences of the union and the presence of certain topics here rather than in the section on the nature assumed (qq.4–15). These questions will be examined here with particular attention given to the role of q.18 on Christ's unity of will. Due note will also be made of q.26 on Christ as mediator. Questions 16 to 25 all prepare for and are summarized by q.26, a.2 in a movement parallel to the culmination of the section on the nature assumed in q.15, a.10. Beyond that, q.26, a.2 can also be viewed as a culmination of the entire section on the mystery of the Incarnation (qq.1–26), preparing for Thomas's discussion of the *acta et passa Christi in carne* (qq.27–59).

Before discussing specific questions from the section on the consequences of the union, it will prove beneficial to consider this section itself. Why organize these specific questions under the banner of consequences? L.-B. Gillon's "La notion de conséquence de l'union hypostatique dans la cadre de *IIIa*, qq.2–26" offers a point of departure for such considerations.[122] Gillon's study focuses on the relationship of sanctifying grace and the hypostatic union. Thomas, developing themes from earlier thirteenth-century theologians, affirms grace as an effect of the hypostatic union rather than a medium or disposition for the union.[123] Framing the investigation in such terms allows Gillon to question Thomas's division between the *coassumpta* (qq.7–15) and the consequences of the union (qq.16–26). Following Albert the Great,[124] Thomas reads *Sentences*, Bk.III, dd.6–22 as treating the consequences (or conditions) of the union.[125]

---

121 *ST* III, q.16, prologue (*Summa theologiae* 4: 2526b): "Et primo, quantum ad ea quae convenient Christo secundum se; secundo, de his quae convenient Christo per comparationem ad Deum Patrem; tertio, de his quae convenient Christo per comparatione ad nos."
122 L.-B. Gillon, "La notion de conséquence de l'union hypostatique dans la cadre de *IIIa*, qq.2–26," *Angelicum* 15 (1938): 17–34.
123 Insofar as Thomas writes of grace as a medium, it is solely as a *medium congruentiae*, as opposed to a medium of necessity (Gillon, "La notion," pp. 24–25; see also *Quodlibet* IX, q.2, a.2, *ad* 3 and *ST* III, q.7, a.13).
124 Albertus Magnus, *Commentarii in III Sententiarum*, d.6, divisio textus. See also *De incarnatione*. In the *De incarnatione* Albert presents a lengthy section on the consequences of the union.
125 Thomas Aquinas, *in* III, d.6, divisio textus; see Gillon, "La notion," pp. 30–31.

Aquinas divides this section (i.e. *Sent.* III, dd.6–21) into what befits the Word incarnate by reason of the union (dd.6–12) and the consequences of the union according to the nature assumed (dd.13–22). This second consideration is further divided into the *coassumpta* (dd.13–16), the human operations (dd.17–20), and the passion (dd.21–22). Gillon notes that in the *Scriptum* Thomas locates the *coassumpta* within the broader section of the consequences of the union.[126] So, why does the *Summa* address the *coassumpta* in the section on the union itself (qq.2–15) rather than with the consequences?

Gillon finds it possible to distinguish two uses (or a double sense) of "consequences of the union" in the *Summa*, and this fact explains Thomas's positioning of the *coassumpta* in the section on the union itself.[127] In *ST* III, q.17, a.2, Thomas writes that "since human nature is conjoined to the Son of God hypostatically or personally, as said above, and not accidentally, it follows (*consequens est*) that a new personal *esse* did not come to him accord-

---

[126] Gillon, "La notion," p. 31. For a consideration of the consequences of the union in the *Scriptum*, see Francis Ruello, *La christologie de Thomas d'Aquin* (Paris, 1987), pp. 156–238, and Lafont, *Structures*, pp. 387–390. Lafont argues that the consequences are distinct from the *assumpta* and *coassumpta* in the *Summa theologiae* as not central to an explication of Christ. "Nous pensons donc, d'une façon générale, que les *consequentia* peuvent être distingués des *assumpta* et *coassumpta*, parce qu'ils n'appartiennent pas directement à l'élaboration théologique des Mystères centraux du Christ" (Lafont, *Structures*, p. 390). The present study will counter such an interpretation by examining the larger role of Christ's human will and operation (qq.18 and 19) in Christ's mediatorship (q.26). This role characterizes Thomas's presentation of Christ's human nature as efficient instrumental cause of salvation. Thus, the consequences introduce material central to the mystery of Christ.

[127] "Il est cependant possible de distinguer, d'un point de vue purement spéculatif, un double emploi de la notion de conséquence de l'union. La position des perfections coassumées en dehors de la section *De consequentibus unionem* s'en trouvera justifiée par le fait même. Cette distinction d'une double acception du concept de conséquence dans le cadre de la *IIIa Pars*, on peut en découvrir les éléments dans le célèbre article 2 de la q. 17" (Gillon, "La notion," p. 32). Gillon never explicitly defines the first use or sense of 'consequences.' He seems to identify this first usage with the sense of 'conditions' as noted in the *Scriptum*. So, sanctifying grace, as an effect of the union, counts as a consequence in the (first) sense of condition. As such, sanctifying grace serves as an antecedent for the consequences of the union when consequence is taken in the second sense of derivable conclusion.

ing to human nature."[128] The sense of consequence employed here, Gillon argues, involves the necessary connection of a consequence to an antecedent as a logically deducible conclusion.[129] Gillon argues that this sense of consequence as logical conclusion from a premise operates throughout qq.16–26 and that the *coassumpta* function as principles or premises from which to conclude the consequences.[130]

Gillon's analysis seeks to explain the position of the *coassumpta* within the section on the union itself. This task leads Gillon to stress the consequences as logically deducible from the union and the *coassumpta*. A more balanced view must shift emphasis to 'consequences' understood generally as conditions, a use which Gillon notes in the *Scriptum*. More precisely, it is necessary to identify what exactly constitutes the 'consequence.' For example, the perfection of human nature requires a will. Christ's possession of a human will is not the consequence of the union; Christ's unity of will is the consequence (*ST* III, q.18). Similarly, the fact that Christ prayed does not follow upon the union; Christ's manner of prayer (demonstrating the

---

128 *ST* III, q.17, a.2 (*Summa theologiae* 4: 2542b): "Sic igitur cum humana natura coniungatur Filio Dei hypostatice vel personaliter, ut supra dictum est, et non accidentaliter, consequens est quod secundum humanam naturam non adveniat sibi novum esse personale."

129 "Les éléments fondamentaux du mystère, dualité des natures, union hypostatique et pas seulement *in persona*, se trouvent constituer un antécédant, dont le conséquent nous fera atteindre une vérité nouvelle, qui doit en dériver par voie de connexion nécessaire, si nous sommes en présence d'une véritable conclusion scientifique. Aucun doute n'apparaît dans le texte de S. Thomas, sur l'absolue certitude à ses yeux de la conclusion à déduire, l'unique *esse* du Christ" (Gillon, "La notion," p. 32).

130 "Il est curieux de constater que les perfections coassumées deviennent à leur tour *principes* de déduction" (Gillon, "La notion," p. 33). Thomas does not across his works consistently use this sequence of *coassumpta* as principles for the consequences. In *De unione Verbi incarnati*, a.5 (on the number of operations in Christ), Christ's human will is taken to be included in the perfection of the human nature assumed, parallel to the human intellect. Christ's human operation is expressed as a consequence of this human will, insofar as the will not only is acted upon but also acts. Thomas writes that "quia in Christo secundum humanam naturam est creata potentia voluntatis sicut et intellectus creatus, cum nihil ei desit eorum quae pertinent ad perfectionem naturae humanae, consequens est quod motus voluntatis humanae in Christo, actio sit et non solum passio" (*De unione*, a.5, in *Quaestiones disputatae et quaestiones duodecim quodlibetales* (Turin, 1931) 2: 483b]).

perfect operation of his human will and his subjection to the Father) does follow from the union (*ST* III q.21). The consequences do not simply follow from the union abstractly considered but from the union as ordered to salvation. The purpose of the Incarnation leads Thomas to apply the 'grammar' of the Incarnation according to specific conditions. This application occurs in discussion of the consequences. The consequences serve to specify the Incarnation's orientation to salvation and to prepare for the detailed analysis of the *acta et passa Christi in carne* (qq.27–59). The following treatment of the consequences of the union will draw out these aspects.

Performing the Grammar of the Hypostatic Union

Question 16 of the *Tertia pars* addresses those things fitting to Christ in being and in becoming (*in esse et in fieri*). Thomas does so by questioning the proper interpretation and truth of certain statements about Christ, by punctuating this examination with characteristic distinctions that specify the sense in which a statement is true, and by providing a foundation for subsequent questions. In article one Thomas argues for the truth of the statement 'God is a human being' according to both the truth of the terms of predication and the truth of the predication itself.[131] The term 'God' is truly verified of the person of the Word. The term *homo* (a human being) functions as a concrete name for every individual of human nature.[132] The person of the Word is, by virtue of the hypostatic union, a suppositum of

---

[131] *ST* III, q.16, a.1 (*Summa theologiae* 4: 2528a): "Unde supponendo secundum veritatem catholicae fidei ... dicimus hanc propositionem esse veram et propriam: Deus est homo; non solum propter veritatem terminorum, quia scilicet Christus est verus Deus et verus homo; sed etiam propter veritatem praedicationis." Nestorius, in Thomas's view, would affirm the truth of each term but deny the truth of the predication. *ST* III, q.16, a.1 (*Summa theologiae* 4: 2527b): "Alii vero concedunt hanc propositionem cum veritate utriusque termini, ponentes Christum et verum Deum esse et verum hominem; sed tamen veritatem praedicationis non salvant."

[132] On concrete and abstract predication in Christology, see Michael M. Gorman, "Uses of the Person-Nature Distinction in Thomas' Christology," *Recherches de théologie et philosophie médiévales* 67 (2000): 58–79. On concrete and abstract predication as applied to God, see David B. Burrell, *Aquinas: God and Action* (Notre Dame, IN, 1979), pp. 4–7.

human nature.[133] This same logic justifies the statement 'a human being is God,' for *homo* here refers to the person of the Word as a hypostasis of human nature.[134] Both the divine nature and a human nature are predicated of the Word, so what pertains to each nature may truly and properly be predicated of the Word.[135] Though they share one subject, the divine nature and human nature in Jesus Christ remain distinct. While the properties of each nature are truly predicated of the Word, the properties of one nature cannot be predicated of the other nature.[136] These articles cover what is classically termed the *communicatio idiomatum*, the communication of idioms or properties.

A certain equivalence exists between the statements 'God is a human being' and 'a human being is God.' This equivalence disappears when 'was made' substitutes for 'is.' Grammatical analysis provides Thomas with a way to explain the meaning of 'was made' without resort to change. He holds

---

133 An individual or a suppositum of human nature is nothing other than a human person. Thomas can affirm a human person in Christ but not a simply or merely human person. Marie-Vincent Leroy would seem to deny that Thomas can affirm a human person in Christ. Leroy writes: "Cet Homme a une nature humaine: il est le Suppôt d'une nature humaine (*suppositum humanae naturae*), mais il n'est pas une personne humaine. Ce par quoi il est homme ne constitue pas une personne humaine nouvelle, ni ne fait du Verbe une personne humaine (!), elle fait de Jésus le Verbe incarné, Personne divine dans une nature humaine" (Leroy, "L'union selon l'hypostase d'après saint Thomas d'Aquin," *Revue thomiste* 74 [1974]: 205–243, at p. 206). Leroy's denial of a human person intends to show Thomas's difference from Nestorius. He does, however, seem to distinguish *suppositum* and person more strongly than does Thomas. Thomas repeatedly avoids adding qualifications to distinguish person from hypostasis or *suppositum* and views 'person' as simply adding the specification of rational nature (see *ST* III, q.2, a.3).

134 *ST* III, q.16, a.2 (*Summa theologiae* 4: 2529a): "Hoc enim nomen homo potest supponere pro qualibet hypostasis humanae naturae, et ita potest supponere pro persona Filii Dei, quam dicimus esse hypostasim humanae naturae."

135 *ST* III, q.16, a.4 (*Summa theologiae* 4: 2531a–2531b): "Et ideo de homine possunt dici ea quae sunt divinae naturae tanquam de hypostasi divinae naturae; et de Deo possunt dici ea quae sunt humanae naturae tanquam de hypostasi humanae naturae."

136 *ST* III, q.16, a.5 (*Summa theologiae* 4: 2532a): "In mysterio autem incarnationis non est eadem natura divina et humana, sed eadem est hypostasis utriusque naturae." *ST* III, q.16, a.5, *ad* 1 (*Summa theologiae* 4: 2532b): "Et similiter in mysterio incarnationis dicimus quod Filius Dei passus est, non autem dicimus quod divina natura sit passa."

that 'to be made' means to have something newly predicated of the subject. God was not always 'a human being,' so 'human being' is newly predicated of God in the Incarnation. Thus, the affirmation 'God was made a human being' is true and implies no change in God, a point made at the beginning of the *Tertia pars*.[137] In the statement 'a human being was made God,' 'a human being' properly refers in Christ to the divine hypostasis of the Word. Divinity is not newly predicated of the hypostasis of the Word, and so the statement 'a human being was made God' is false.'[138]

Thomas's grammatical analysis of Christ's being and becoming identifies subjects materially with supposits and identifies predicates formally with natures. Article ten introduces a qualification that can be taken for either. This qualification plays a crucial role in the section on the consequences of the union. The statement under consideration in article ten reads, "Christ, *secundum quod homo*, is a creature or began to be." The key phrase here is *secundum quod homo* (according as a human being); the key question is whether to read it materially for the supposit or formally for the nature. The supposit of human nature in Christ neither is a creature nor began to be. Christ's human nature began to be and is a creature. Thomas argues that the *homo* in *secundum quod homo* serves as a term of reduplication and can be taken either for the supposit or for the nature.[139] When *secundum quod homo* reduplicates for the supposit, the statement in question is clearly false. The statement is clearly true when *secundum quod homo* reduplicates for Christ's human nature. Aquinas's subsequent use of the phrase *secundum quod homo* relies on the possibility of both readings. Though he allows for both readings, Thomas holds that reduplicative terms are more properly taken formally for the nature. In the phrase *secundum quod homo*, the word *homo* more properly functions as predicate than as subject. That is, *secundum quod homo* offers a

---

137 *ST* III, q.1, a.1, *ad* 1 (*Summa theologiae* 4: 2414b): "Dicendum quod incarnationis myterium non est impletum per hoc quod Deus sit aliquo modo a suo statu immutatus in quo ab aeterno fuit; sed per hoc quod novo modo se creaturae univit, vel potius eam sibi."
138 *ST* III, q.16, a.7 (*Summa theologiae* 4: 2534a): "Tertio modo, proprie intelligitur, secundum quod hoc participium factus ponit fieri circa hominem in respectu ad Deum ad terminum factionis." *ST* III, q.16, a.7 (*Summa theologiae* 4: 2534b): "Unde non potest dici quod iste homo incoepit esse Deus, vel quod fiat Deus, aut quod factus sit Deus."
139 *ST* III, q.16, a.10 (*Summa theologiae* 4: 2537a): "Dicendum quod cum dicitur: Christus secundum quod homo, hoc nomen homo potest resumi in reduplicatione vel ratione suppositi, vel ratione naturae."

compressed version of *secundum quod est homo* (according as [he] is a human being).[140] The case is different when a demonstrative adjective attaches to *homo*, as in *secundum quod hic homo*. The demonstrative adjective specifies *homo* materially in terms of the supposit.[141] To put the matter otherwise, the word *homo* refers generally or formally to every supposit of human nature. The demonstrative adjective limits the predication to a specific individual and so indicates a particular supposit.

Article eleven illustrates the same grammatical rule of reduplication but from the reverse perspective. Aquinas discusses the statement 'Christ, *secundum quod homo*, is God.' He appeals to the two possible senses of the reduplicative term in explanation of both a true and a false meaning of this statement. Taking *homo* materially for the supposit, the statement must be admitted. The supposit in Jesus Christ is the fully divine Word. In the more proper sense, *homo* designates the nature assumed, making the statement false.[142] Christ's two natures remain distinct in their union. The union does not compromise the distinction, nor does the distinction compromise the unity (as discussed in qq.17–19). Of particular interest here is the second objection, which argues for the truth of the statement 'Christ, *secundum quod homo*, is God' from the fact that Christ, *secundum quod homo*, forgives (*dimittere*) sin. Thomas responds that Christ's power to forgive sin originates in the divine nature but is exercised instrumentally (and ministerially) through Christ's human nature.[143] This foreshadows Aquinas's view of Christ's human nature as instrumental efficient cause of salvation.

---

140 *ST* III, q.16, a.10 (*Summa theologiae* 4: 2537a): "Sciendum tamen quod nomen sic resumptum in reduplicatione magis proprie tenetur pro natura quam pro supposito; resumitur enim in vi praedicati, quod tenetur formaliter; idem enim est dictu: Christus secundum quod homo, ac si diceretur: Christus secundum quod est homo."
141 *ST* III, q.16, a.10 (*Summa theologiae* 4: 2537a): "Si tamen adderetur aliquid per quod traheretur ad suppositum, esset propositio magis neganda quam concedenda, puta si diceretur: Christus, secundum quod hic homo, est creatura."
142 *ST* III, q.16, a.11 (*Summa theologiae* 4: 2538a): "Dicendum quod iste terminus homo, in reduplicatione positus, potest dupliciter accipi. Uno modo, quantum ad naturam. Et sic non est verum quod Christus, secundum quod homo, sit Deus, quia humana natura est distincta a divina secundum differentiam naturae."
143 *ST* III, q.16, a.11, *ad* 2 (*Summa theologiae* 4: 2538a): "Dicendum quod 'Filius Hominis habet in terra potestatem dimittendi peccata,' non virtute humanae naturae, sed virtute naturae divinae, in qua quidem natura consistit potestas dimittendi peccata per auctoritatem; in humana autem natura consistit instrumentaliter et per ministerium."

This efficacious causality in the work of salvation intimately involves Christ's human will.[144]

ST III, q.16, a.12, which considers the statement 'Christ, *secundum quod homo*, is a person,' serves two purposes. Thomas's discussion of this statement reiterates the two senses of *secundum quod homo* and reaffirms his earlier findings on the hypostatic union. When *homo* stands for the supposit, Christ is a person *secundum quod homo*, namely the person of the Word. Thomas offers two interpretations when *homo* is taken formally for human nature. Human nature appropriately exists in a person. Whatever subsists in human nature must be a person. Christ, *secundum quod homo*, subsists in human nature and so is a person, the divine person of the Word. There is no person or personality in Christ derived from the principles of human nature. Christ, *secundum quod homo*, is not a person in this final sense, for the entire personality of Christ derives from the divine person of the Word.[145] Christ's human nature is an individual substance in a certain sense but cannot be counted a person.[146]

---

144 On instrumental efficient causality, see *ST* III, q.8, a.1, *ad* 1; q.22, a.3, *ad* 1; q.36, aa.1 and 2; *Compendium theologiae*, c.239. For discussions of instrumental efficient causality in Thomas, see Humbert Bouëssé, "De la causalité de l'humanité du Christ," in *Problèmes actuels de christologie*, ed. Humbert Bouëssé and Jean-Jacques Latour (Paris, 1965), pp. 147–177; Bouëssé, "La causalité efficiente instrumentale et la causalité méritoire de la sainte humanité du Christ," *Revue thomiste* 44 (1938): 256–298; Bouëssé, "La causalité efficiente instrumentale de l'humanité du Christ et des sacrements chrétiens," *Revue thomiste* 39 (1934): 370–393; Edouard Hugon, *La causalité instrumentale dans l'ordre surnaturel* (Paris, 1924); Hugon, "La causalité instrumentale de l'humanité sainte de Jesus," *Revue thomiste* 13 (1905): 44–68; J. Lécuyer, "La causalité efficiente des mystères du Christ selon saint Thomas," *Doctor communis* 6 (1953): 91–120; P.L. Reynolds, "Philosophy as the Handmaid of Theology: Aquinas on Christ's Causality," in *Contemplating Aquinas: On the Varieties of Interpretation*, ed. Fergus Kerr (London, 2003), pp. 217–245; Jean-Pierre Torrell, "La causalité salvifique de la résurrection du Christ selon saint Thomas," *Revue thomiste* 96 (1996): 179–208; and Tschipke, *L'humanité du Christ*.

145 *ST* III, q.16, a.12 (*Summa theologiae* 4: 2539a): "Alio modo potest intelligi ut naturae humanae in Christo propria personalitas debeatur, causata ex principiis humanae naturae. Et sic Christus, secundum quod homo, not est persona, quia humana natura non est per se seorsum subsistens a divina natura, quod requirit ratio personae."

146 Thomas stipulates that a person must subsist through itself and be separate from others (*ad* 2) and be complete (*ad* 3). Christ's human nature does not subsist through itself but through the Word, and so is neither separate from

If Thomas offers a grammar for the Incarnation in qq.1–15, in question 16 he performs that grammar in a paradigmatic manner. This performance guides qq.17–26 and prepares for Thomas's treatment of the *acta et passa Christi in carne* (qq.27–59). In other words, the grammatical performance of question 16 provides a standard for the application of the grammatical rules for the hypostatic union. Question 16 takes these grammatical rules as a foundation and applies them. The actual application or performance of these rules follows from the rules themselves as effects (consequences) from causes. Here already we can discern the phenomenon discussed by Gillon. Thomas affirms repeatedly that in Jesus Christ there was one person subsisting in two natures that remain distinct. This could be translated as Thomas affirming Christ to be one subject with two distinct categories of predicates.

Christ's Unity in communi

Question 17 introduces the section on "those things that pertain to unity in Christ *in communi*."[147] The meaning of *in communi* is not immediately obvious. Thomas notes that what pertains to "unity or plurality *in speciali*" should be dealt with in its proper place and provides two examples:

---

others nor complete in itself. Thomas employs the analogy of a hand as part of an existing human being. A hand is an individual in a certain sense but does not exist through itself. A hand has its being through the whole to which it belongs. Thomas's language here bears a debt to his teacher Albert the Great. Albert's complex definition of person involves three types of incommunicability, including the incommunicability of assumption. Thomas often backs away from Albert's definition of person (see *ST* III, q.2, aa.2–3; *De potentia* q.9, a.2), but he can employ elements of that definition for a specific point. Aquinas's use of such Albertinian language prepares for *ST* III, q.17, a.2 and the discussion of Christ's *esse*. See Barnes, "Albert the Great and Thomas." On Albertus Magnus, see Stephen A. Hipp, *"Person" in Christian Tradition and in the Conception of Saint Albert the Great: A Systematic Study of its Concept as Illuminated by the Mysteries of the Trinity and the Incarnation* (Münster, 2001).

147 *ST* III, q.17, prologue (*Summa theologiae* 4: 2539a–2539b): "Deinde considerandum est de his quae pertinent ad unitatem in Christo in communi. Nam de his quae pertinent ad unitatem vel pluralitatem in speciali, suis locis determinandum est, sicut supra determinatum est quod in Christo non est una tantum scientia, et infra determinabitur quod in Christo non est una tantum nativitas."

Christ's knowledge (*ST* III, qq.9–12) and Christ's nativities (*ST* III, q.35, a.2).[148] Some editions translate *in communi* as in general and *in speciali* as in detail.[149] However, the relevant questions in the *Tertia pars* seem hardly separable into the general and the detailed. No solution to the puzzle of Thomas's meaning will be offered here, though this need not exclude a suggestion. Let the suggestion begin with a question.

Why organize the questions on unity of *esse*, will, and operation together? Christ's unity of *esse* depends upon there being only one *esse* in Christ (q.17). Christ's unity of will and unity of operation, in contrast, require a human will and operation in addition to the divine will and operation (qq.18 and 19). The unity involved in question 17 seems different from the unity of questions 18 and 19. All of these pertain to unity in Christ *in communi*, but what do they have in common? Thomas's distinction in the prologue to question 17 is not between unity and plurality *in communi* and unity and plurality *in speciali*. Thomas writes of only unity *in communi*. Questions 18 and 19 do not address plurality of wills and operations in Christ but unity of will and operation. This somewhat reveals Aquinas's understanding of the 'interaction' of Christ's human and divine wills. Christ's wills display a unity grounded in the hypostatic union. The same is true of Christ's *esse* and operations. Christ's unity of *esse*, unity of will, and unity of operation follow as a consequence from the hypostatic union. They share in common this characteristic of being consequences. This distinguishes Christ's unity of *esse*, will, and operation from Christ's knowledge and nativities.

Christ's nativities are two as are his natures, for nativity follows nature. Thomas's interest is not in the unity of these nativities in the one hyposta-

---

148 Pope Agatho's *Epistle I* connects the ideas of Christ's two wills and two operations with his two knowledges and two nativities. Thomas recovered Agatho's letter with the acts of Constantinople III and appropriated sources and arguments from it. For Agatho's letter, see actio 4 of *Concilium universale Constantinopolitanum tertium*, ed. Rudolf Riedinger, Acta conciliorum oecumenicorum, 2nd ser., 2.1 (Berlin, 1990), pp. 53–121; and *Sancta Synodus sexta Generalis Constantinopolitana tertia*, ed. Joannes Dominicus Mansi, in *Sacrorum conciliorum nova et amplissima collectio* (Florence, 1765; repr. Graz, 1960–1961) 11: 233–286.

149 *St. Thomas Aquinas:* Summa theologica, Complete English Edition in Five Volumes, trans. Fathers of the English Dominican Province (1911; rev. ed. London, 1920; reissued in 3 vols New York, 1948; repr. Notre Dame, IN, 1981).

sis of the Word, but the duality following the two natures. In other words, Thomas seeks to avoid any and all confusion of Christ's two natures that would result from confusion of his two nativities.[150] Thomas discusses Christ's knowledge in the section on the *coassumpta* (qq.7–15). The *coassumpta* are those things not essential to human nature (that is, which do not follow from its definition) but assumed along with human nature for the end of salvation. Thomas is not discussing Christ's unity of intellect but of his knowledge. A human intellect is part of the definition of a human being, just as is a rational will.[151] The consequence of the union is not simply the presence of a human will in Christ, which is naturally included in the Word's assumption of human nature, but Christ's unity of will.[152] Human nature naturally requires a human intellect but not knowledge. Knowledge is not a consequence of the union but something coassumed. The unity or plurality under discussion in qq.9–12 is different from that of qq.17–19. Thomas affirms a plurality of types of knowledge in Christ; discussion of these types of knowledge is fittingly organized with the other *coassumpta*. The unity or plurality of knowledge and nativities does not follow from the hypostatic union. The unity of *esse*, will, and operation does. This provides little guidance for translating *in communi* and *in speciali* but offers some guidance in how they differ.

150 There is an opposite danger of separating these nativities according to multiple hypostases. The debate between Cyril of Alexandria and Nestorius began with Nestorius's attack on *theotokos* as a proper name for Mary. Thomas, by *ST* III, q.35, has well guarded against a two hypostases view and can focus on other issues.
151 On the Word's assumption of a human intellect, see *ST* III, q.5, a.4. Thomas notes that a rational will is necessarily included in the Word's assumption of an integral human nature (*ST* III, q.18, a.1). If *ST* III, q.18 were rephrased to ask whether Christ assumed a human will, it would more properly belong in the section on the nature assumed in itself (qq.4–6).
152 In *De unione*, a.5, Thomas includes a human will within the perfection of human nature. Following this logic, Thomas uses the assumption of a human will as a premise from which to defend Christ's possession of a human operation. In the *Compendium theologiae*, Thomas presents intellect and will as pertaining to rational nature. "Necesse est ergo in Christo ponere duos intellectus, humanum et divinum, et similiter duas voluntates, duplicem etiam scientiam et iustitiam sive caritatem, creatam scilicet et increatam" (*Compendium theologiae* c.212, Leonine edition [Rome, 1882; repr. Rome, 1979], 42: 165). Thomas connects *esse* to supposit rather than to nature.

Discussion of *ST* III, q.17 often centers on a comparison of its second article with *De unione Verbi incarnati*, a.4. These texts both question and famously provide different answers to the number of *esse* (to be) in Christ.[153] The parallels, however, begin with *ST* III, q.17, a.1 and *De unione* a.3. Before detailing these parallels, it is worth reflecting on the simple presence of such parallels. The *De unione* treats together topics dispersed in the *Summa*'s *Tertia pars*. The first and second articles of the *De unione* teach that the union took place in person, not nature, (a.1) and that there is but one hypostasis or supposit in Christ (a.2). The *Summa*'s discussion of these issues unfolds in *ST* III, q.2, aa.2 and 3, in the section on the union itself. Articles three and four of the *De unione* parallel the two articles of *ST* III, q.17. The fifth and final article of the *De unione* considers Christ's two operations (and to a lesser extent Christ's two wills), treated in the *Summa*'s *Tertia pars* in q.19 (and q.18). The near simultaneity of composition offers a compelling justification for these parallels, but one should not too hastily restrict such justification to reasons of economy and expediency.[154]

The parallels between the *De unione* and the *Summa theologiae* support the suggestion that Thomas groups together questions of *esse*, will, and operation as all directly related to the hypostatic union. The relationship differs between the texts. The *Summa* focuses on Christ's unity of *esse*, will, and operation as a consequence logically derivable from the hypostatic union and *coassumpta*. The *De unione*, without the benefit of any interven-

---

153 For more general treatments of *esse* in Thomas's theology, see Wawrykow, "Esse," in *The Westminster Handbook*, pp. 49–52; Burrell, *Aquinas: God and Action*, pp. 42–54; Etienne Gilson, *The Christian Philosophy of St Thomas Aquinas*, trans. Laurence K. Shook (Notre Dame, IN, 1994); and Albert Patfoort, *L'unité d'être dans le Christ d'après S. Thomas: A la croisée de l'ontologie et de la christologie* (Paris, 1964), pp. 193–309.

154 Torrell briefly recounts the history of debate on authorship and dating of the *De unione* but avoids consideration of the doctrinal debate. Torrell holds it as certain that the *De unione* was disputed in Paris in the spring of 1272 at the end of Thomas's second period of teaching in Paris, nearly contemporaneous with the composition of *ST* III, q.17, a.2 (Torrell, *Saint Thomas* 1: 205–207). The most complete study of the doctrinal differences between the *De unione* and Thomas's other treatments of Christ's *esse* is Patfoort, *L'unité d'être*. Modern concern for the *De unione* and questions of Christ's *esse* were awakened by a series of articles in the *Revue thomiste* by Herman M. Diepen. See Diepen, "La psychologie humaine du Christ," *Revue thomiste* 50 (1950): 515–562 and "L'existence humaine du Christ en métaphysique thomiste," *Revue thomiste* 58 (1958): 197–213.

ing treatment of the *coassumpta*, bases its discussion of *esse* and operation on the hypostatic union, though not under the heading of unity. The *De unione* more strictly considers the number of *esse* and operations in Christ, rather than their unity. While the texts have different organizing schemes and different purposes, they both group together questions of *esse*, will, and operation. Attention to the similarities and differences between the texts clarifies their meaning.

The *De unione* and the *Summa theologiae* utilize different terminological frameworks to argue that Christ is one in the neuter (*unum*). The *De unione* holds that predications based upon accidental *esse* and form predicate *secundum quid* (according to something) and predications based upon substantial *esse* and form predicate *simpliciter* (simply or without qualification). Thomas concludes that Christ can be both one and many, though in different ways (*aliqualiter et aliqualiter*). This affirmation goes far beyond a pure creature being one substantially and many accidentally. Christ is more truly one and many, as one supposit with two natures, than Socrates, as one supposit with many accidents.[155] Thomas's comparison of Christ's (substantial) unity and multiplicity to Socrates's (substantial) unity and (accidental) multiplicity provides a necessary qualification for his return to the language of *simpliciter* and *secundum quid*. He outlines the difference between *simpliciter* and *secundum quid* based upon the distinction of substance and accidents and then transfers this language to Christ, in which case the discussion occurs at the substantial level. To determine what applies to Christ *simpliciter* and what *secundum quid*, Aquinas calls attention to the relationship of whole and part. He writes that "something is properly and *simpliciter* said to be such which is such according to itself."[156] The phrase 'according to itself' (*secundum seipsum*) indicates the whole more than the part. Relating this to the case at hand, Thomas holds that "supposit is signified through the mode of

---

155 *De unione*, a.3 (*Quaestiones disputatae et quaestiones duodecim quodlibetales* 2: 479a): "Sed hoc singulare est in Christo; primum autem est singulare in tribus personis divinis. Manifestum est ergo quod Christus potest dici aliqualiter unum, quia est unum supposito; et aliqualiter multa, vel duo, quia est habens duas naturas. Multo amplius quam Socrates, de quo praedicatur unum, in quantum est unum subiecto; multa, in quantum est album et musicum."
156 *De unione*, a.3 (*Quaestiones disputatae et quaestiones duodecim quodlibetales* 2: 479b): "Sciendum est ergo, quod simpliciter et proprie dicitur aliquid esse tale, quod est secundum seipsum tale."

the whole, but nature [is signified] through the mode of formal part."[157] Christ is thus one (*unum*) *simpliciter* and many (*multa*) *secundum quid*, for *simpliciter* predications refer to the supposit and *secundum quid* predications to the nature. Aquinas illustrates this by noting that the individuals of a species are many *simpliciter* and one *secundum quid*.[158] Predications *secundum quid*, on the substantial level, refer to nature as a formal

---

[157] *De unione*, a.3 (*Quaestiones disputatae et quaestiones duodecim quodlibetales* 2: 479b): "Manifestum est autem quod suppositum significatur per modum totius, natura autem per modum partis formalis." On Thomas's distinction between person and nature, see Gorman, "Uses of the Person-Nature Distinction." Gorman argues that Thomas uses nature to designate only the essential principles of a thing. Any non-essential principles are excluded from the nature. This is nature considered by precision. In the case of human nature, this "results in the concept *humanitas*, humanity, which consists of rational animality and nothing more; everything else is excluded from it" (p. 60). If nature is considered 'not by precision,' then the resultant concept is *homo*, human being, that which possesses animal rationality and other non-essential principles. Gorman views this distinction as problematic for Thomas's Christology. If the Word did not assume a *homo*, then the nature assumed lacks all non-essential principles. Gorman describes the problem as follows: "As a result of the incarnation, Christ is a rational animal. He is not, however, thinking humanly about any particular thing, because human thoughts are accidents and as such are excluded from humanity. By virtue of being human, he possesses flesh and bones, yet he does not possess any particular flesh and bones, but only flesh and bones in general; designated matter, as we have seen, is excluded from humanity" (p. 63). Gorman argues that this is not Thomas's intention but that his distinction between nature and person forces this problem upon his Christology. Gorman further excludes the possibility that Thomas used nature in two senses, one of which "included accidents and individuating principles, but still referred to something non-subsisting" (p. 66). On this proposal, see Richard Cross, "Aquinas on Nature, Hypostasis, and the Metaphysics of the Incarnation," *Thomist* 60 (1996): 171–202. For a critique of both Gorman and Cross, see J.L.A. West, "Aquinas on the Metaphysics of *Esse* in Christ," *Thomist* 66 (2002): 231–250. West holds that Thomas's commentary on Boethius's *De Trinitate* undermines Cross's presentation of the part-whole analogy in the *Summa* (see West, "Aquinas," pp. 238–241).

[158] *De unione*, a.3 (*Quaestiones disputatae et quaestiones duodecim quodlibetales* 2: 479b): "Cuius signum est; quia ea quae differunt supposito et sunt unum in eo quod per se pertinet ad naturam, sunt plura quidem simpliciter, sed unum genere vel specie. Et ideo, e contrario, si unum suppositum habeat multas naturas, erit unum simpliciter et multa secundum quid."

part. The specification of formal part is not insignificant, because *esse* completes the form.[159]

ST III, q.17 develops the same basic point through the distinction of abstract and concrete predication. Article one begins by noting that nature, considered in the abstract, can truly be predicated of a supposit in God alone.[160] Since the supposit in Christ is the divine Word, the divine nature can truly be predicated of Christ both in the abstract and in the concrete, but "human nature cannot be predicated of Christ according to itself in the abstract, but only in the concrete, as it is signified in the supposit."[161] A human being cannot truly be called human nature or humanity, whereas the divine persons are truly identical with the divine nature or divinity. Christ cannot be called human nature but can be called a human being, that is, one having humanity. Calling Christ a human being predicates human nature of Christ in the concrete, but indistinctly. "However," Thomas writes, "the name Peter, or Jesus, introduces having humanity distinctly, namely under determinate individual properties, just as also this name Son of God introduces having deity under a determinate personal property."[162]

---

159 West stresses this point in examining the relationship of a new part to an already existing whole. "This can be clarified further, if we recognize the fact that every form is completed by *esse*. In fact, Aquinas explicitly assigns *esse* the role of completing each thing" (West, "Aquinas," p. 294). "Since *esse* completes each form, it follows that we should expect St Thomas to say that the divine *esse* completes Christ's human nature – and this is precisely what he says" (West, "Aquinas," p. 294). See also James B. Reichmann, "Aquinas, Scotus, and the Christological Mystery: Why Christ is Not a Human Person," *Thomist* 71 (2007): 451–474.

160 See *ST* I, q.29, a.4, *ad* 1; q.40, a.1, *sed contra*; q.50, a.2, *ad* 3; q.75, a.5, *ad* 4 on the identity *in se* of the divine hypostases and the divine nature; Burrell, *Aquinas: God and Action*, pp. 4–6.

161 *ST* III, q.17, a.1 (*Summa theologiae* 4: 2540a): "Sed humana natura non potest praedicari de Christo secundum se in abstracto, sed solum in concreto, prout scilicet significatur in supposito." In *ST* III, q.2, a.2, Thomas makes much the same point, arguing that a human being is not his or her humanity. "Et propter hoc in compositis ex materia et forma natura non praedicatur de supposito; non enim dicimus quod hic homo sit sua humanitas" (*ST* III, q.2, a.2 [*Summa theologiae* 4: 2426a]).

162 *ST* III, q.17, a.1 (*Summa theologiae* 4: 2540a–2540b): "Hoc autem nomen Petrus, vel Jesus, importat distincte habentem humanitatem, scilicet sub determinatis individualibus proprietatibus, sicut et hoc nomen Filius Dei importat habentem deitatem sub determinata proprietate personali."

The response continues with reference to concrete and abstract predication, not distinct and indistinct.[163] Duality applies to Christ solely with respect to his two natures. Granting this, the key becomes the distinction between concrete and abstract predication. Thomas writes that "if both natures were predicated in the abstract of Christ, it follows that Christ would be two."[164] Human nature can be predicated of Christ only in the concrete, and so Christ should be called one in the neuter (*unum*).

In both the *De unione* and the *Summa*, Thomas's strategy for explaining Christ as *unum* shapes his presentation of Christ's *esse*. The *De unione* features prominently the distinction between *simpliciter* and *secundum quid* as applied to *esse*.[165] Christ's human nature does not constitute the

163 Thomas utilizes both the abstract/concrete and distinct/indistinct pairs to explain in what sense Christ is something other than the Father (*ST* III, q.17, a.1, *ad* 4). It should be stressed that nature can be predicated in the abstract of a supposit in God alone. In the case of every other nature, the individual of that nature is not identical to the nature. The nature can only be predicated of individuals in the concrete. Similarly, no supposit possesses a nature indistinctly, but only distinctly. The language of indistinctly possessing a supposit and of abstract considerations of non-divine natures does not indicate the reality of the thing but abstractions considered by the mind. Natures do not exist in the abstract or indistinctly; natures only have real existence concretely in distinct individuals. How do natures exist in concrete individuals? The problem of individuation is not easily settled. Owens suggests a confluence of causes. The act of existence serves as efficient cause. The nature or form (in human beings the soul) functions as formal cause, and matter (determined by the form) serves as material cause, see Joseph Owens, "Thomas Aquinas," in *Individuation in Scholasticism: The Later Middle Ages and the Counter-Reformation (1150–1650)* (Albany, NY, 1994), 173–194.
164 *ST* III, q.17, a.1 (*Summa theologiae* 4: 254ob): "Numerus autem dualitatis in Christo ponitur circa ipsas naturas. Et ideo si ambae naturae in abstracto praedicarentur de Christo, sequeretur quod Christus esset duo."
165 Article four on Christ's *esse* is by far the briefest article of the *De unione*, involving only three objections and one *sed contra* argument. Article one lists 17 objections and two *sed contra* arguments. Article two lists 18 objections and two *sed contra* arguments. Article three has 14 objections and seven *sed contra* arguments. Article five features 14 objections and five *sed contra* arguments. Not only is article four surprisingly concise for the *De unione* but also for the normal style of a disputed question. Despite its brevity, *De unione*, a.4 has sparked much secondary literature. In addition to Patfoort's *L'unité d'être* and Diepen's "L'existence humaine du Christ," see also West, "Aquinas"; Stephen F. Brown, "Thomas Aquinas and His Contemporaries on the Unique Existence in Christ," in *Christ Among the Medieval Dominicans*, ed. Kent Emery, Jr and

substantial *esse* of the Word, and so Christ has but one *esse simpliciter*, the *esse* of the Word. This matches perfectly with Thomas's other treatments on Christ's *esse*, but he continues with what seems to many an aberration.

> There is moreover another *esse* of this supposit, not inasmuch as it is eternal, but inasmuch as it was made a human being in time. This other *esse*, even if it is not accidental *esse* – because human being is not predicated accidentally of the Son of God, as was held above, nevertheless is not the principal *esse* of its supposit, but a secondary *esse*.[166]

Thomas offers no explanantion of secondary *esse*, and the only hint as to its meaning derives from an uncompleted parallel with article three. The parallel affirms that, as Christ is one (*unum*) *simpliciter* but two *secundum quid* (in virtue of the two natures), so too Christ has one *esse simpliciter*. The explicit textual parallel ends there, for Thomas shies away from arguing for two *esse secundum quid* in Christ. The reader can hardly avoid understanding secondary *esse* as parallel to the *secundum quid* predication of Christ as two. Again, this *secundum quid* predication of Christ as two is a substantial rather than accidental predication. Christ's secondary *esse* from his human nature is substantial rather than accidental, though unlike all other substantial *esse* as secondary rather than principal. Aquinas here grapples, per-

---

Joseph Wawrykow (Notre Dame, IN, 1998), pp. 220–237; Cross, "Aquinas"; Etienne Gilson, "L'*esse* du Verbe incarné selon saint Thomas d'Aquin," *Archives d'histoire doctrinale et littéraire du moyen âge* 35 (1968): 23–37; Adrian Hastings, "Christ's Act of Existence," *Downside Review* 73 (1955): 139–159; Thomas V. Morris, "St Thomas on the Identity and Unity of the Person of Christ: A Problem of Reference in Christological Discourse," *Scottish Journal of Theology* 35 (1982): 419–430; Jean-Hervé Nicolas, "L'unité d'être dans le Christ d'après saint Thomas," *Revue thomiste* 65 (1965): 229–260; and M. Corvez, "L'unicité d'existence dans le Christ," *Revue thomiste* 56 (1956): 413–426.

166 *De unione*, a.4 (*Quaestiones disputatae et quaestiones duodecim quodlibetales* 2: 481b): "Est autem et aliud esse huius suppositi, non in quantum est aeternum, sed in quantum est temporaliter homo factum. Quod esse, etsi non sit esse accidentale – quia homo non praedicatur accidentaliter de Filio Dei, ut supra habitum est – non tamen est esse principale sui suppositi, sed secundarium."

haps unsuccessfully, with the linguistic difficulty of expressing the unique reality of the Incarnation.[167]

The *Summa*'s discussion of Christ's *esse* stresses that what pertains to hypostasis is one in Christ. "*Esse* moreover," Thomas writes, "pertains both to nature and to hypostasis; to hypostasis as to that which has *esse*; to nature as to that by which something has *esse*."[168] This recalls the distinction

[167] Cross argues that this account of a secondary *esse* in the *De unione* is coherent but lacks all explanatory value. The alternative, the one *esse* view of the *Summa* and other texts, Cross regards as incoherent (Cross, "Aquinas," pp. 172–173, 198–201). Patfoort regards *De unione*, aa.3–4 as circular and thus incautious if not unsuccessful. He argues that the *De unione* can only justify Christ as two *secundum quid* based upon duality of *esse* and can only justify duality of *esse* based upon Christ as two *secundum quid* (Patfoort, *L'unité d'être*, pp. 168–169). West describes the *De unione*'s two *esse* view as an aberration that leans toward either a *homo assumptus* or *habitus* view (West, "Aquinas," pp. 233–237). West mentions Albert the Great and hints at the connection of Thomas's teaching to Albert's. Albert writes: "Esse autem secundum naturam hanc vel illam, est esse acceptum in comparatione ad naturam facientem esse in hypostasi, et a parte illa geminatur esse in Christo. Est enim in eo esse naturae humanitatis, et esse naturae deitatis. Et si vellemus proprie dicere, tunc diceremus quod haberet tali consideratione non duo esse, sed unum duplex in constituente esse. Esse naturae est esse quod habet natura in se: omnis enim res habet suum esse. Esse naturae humanae in Christo, non est esse naturae Dei, neque illa esse sunt duo sicut naturae" (Albertus Magnus, *Commentarii in III Sententiarum*, d.6, a.5 [Opera Omnia, ed. Auguste Borgnet [Paris, 1890], 28: 132b). Thomas's language in the *De unione* owes much to Albert's attempt to describe one twofold *esse* in Christ. For more on Albert's Christology, see Vincent-Marie Pollet, "L'union hypostatique d'après saint Albert-le-Grand," *Revue thomiste* 38 (1933):505–532, 689–724; and Barnes, "Albert the Great and Thomas Aquinas." Thomas's presentation of Christ's *esse* in the *De unione* recalls Albert's language, but this hardly explains the shift from Thomas's earlier treatments. A possible clue to this shift is Thomas's recovery of the acts of Constantinople III. Aquinas's concern to firmly ground the presence of two operations in Christ could, at least in part, explain his mention of a secondary *esse* in Christ. This contention is strengthened by Thomas's presentation of *esse* and operation in *Compendium theologiae* c.212.

[168] *ST* III, q.17, a.2 (*Summa theologiae* 4: 2542a): "Esse autem pertinet et ad naturam et ad hypostasim; ad hypostasim quidem sicut ad id quod habet esse; ad naturam autem sicut ad id quo aliquid habet esse; natura enim significatur per modum formae, quae dicitur ens ex eo quod ea aliquid est, sicut albedine est aliquid album, et humanitate est aliquis homo." Patfoort argues that the *De unione* strictly adheres to the principle *esse consequitur formam* but that the *Summa* admits of an exception. This marks a key difference between the texts. See Patfoort, *L'unité d'être*, pp. 85–149, 152–153. Thomas's language here again bears a debt to Albert the Great.

between abstract and concrete predication. These types of predication concur in God, for in God there is no distinction between what exists and that by which it exists. The distinction between *simpliciter* and *secundum quid* surfaces here as Thomas characterizes forms or natures that do not pertain to the personal *esse* of a subsistent hypostasis (*esse personalis hypostasis subsistentis*). Accidents are such type of forms, and they can be multiplied in one subject. These forms provide *esse secundum quid*. What pertains to the hypostasis according to itself is *esse simpliciter*, and it cannot be many in one subject. Up to this point, the *Summa*'s consideration of *esse* bears strong resemblance to the *De unione*'s version. What the *Summa* lacks is any notion of substantial predication *secundum quid*. This absence largely determines the presentation of *ST* III, q.17, a.2.[169]

The *Summa*'s consideration of Christ's *esse* recognizes only two types of *esse*. An individual subsistent through or according to itself has one *esse simpliciter*. The same individual can have many accidental forms and so can possess many *esse secundum quid*. Aquinas concludes:

> Since human nature is conjoined to the Son of God hypostatically or personally ... and not accidentally, it follows that no new personal *esse* came to [the Son of God] according to human nature, but only a new relation of the preexistent personal *esse* to human nature, namely so that that person may be said to subsist, not only according to the divine nature, but also according to human [nature].[170]

---

[169] The differences between the texts also concern the part-whole analogy, which Thomas uses in the *Summa* but not in the *De unione*. For a critique of this analogy, see Cross, "Aquinas," pp. 186–191. Patfoort argues that the *Summa* adopts this analogy from earlier treatments of Christ's *esse* and clarifies it (Patfoort, *L'unité d'être*, pp. 107–149). West defends the part-whole analogy (West, "Aquinas," pp. 238–241).

[170] *ST* III, q.17, a.2 (*Summa theologiae* 4: 2542b): "Sic igitur cum humana natura coniungatur Filio Dei hypostatice vel personaliter, ut supra dictum est, et non accidentaliter, consequens est quod secundum humanam naturam non adveniat sibi novum esse personale, sed solum nova habitudo esse personalis praeexistentis ad naturam humanam, ut scilicet persona illa iam dicatur subsistere, non solum secundum divinam naturam, sed etiam secundum humanam." The meaning of *habitudo* is not obvious. I have translated it as 'relation,' but a more common meaning would be 'form' or 'appearance.'

This conclusion differs from that of the *De unione* in not recognizing a secondary *esse* in Christ, and in fact seems to exclude such a possibility.[171]

In response to the second objection, Thomas holds that the eternal *esse* of the Word, which is identical with the divine nature "is the *esse* of a human being, inasmuch as human nature is assumed to the Son of God in unity of person."[172] How can the divine *esse*, identical with the divine nature, be the *esse* of a human being? This question and Aquinas's seeming failure to explain it provide no small prompt for critics of his view in the *Summa*. Further, if the *esse* of Christ's human nature derives wholly from the Word, in what sense is that human nature a created reality? Is Thomas's view even coherent? Whatever its deficiencies, Aquinas takes a one-*esse* view to preserve a single-subject Christology, thereby gaurding against Nestorianism; his stress on the proper functioning of Christ's human will and operation participating in the divine power guards the created reality of Christ's human nature as hypostatically united to the Word.

Questions of Christ as *unum* and of Christ's *esse* prepare for consideration of Christ's wills and operations. The *De unione* emphasizes the substantial reality of the human nature assumed, going so far as to carve out

171 *ST* III, q.17, a.2 thus seems in agreement with Thomas's earlier treatments of Christ's *esse*, which are *in* III, d.6, q.2, a.2; *Quodlibet* IX, q.2, a.3; *Compendium theologiae* c.212. For discussion of these texts, see Patfoort, *L'unité d'être*, pp. 33–84. "Et similiter suo modo unum esse Christi habet duos respectus, unum ad naturam divinam, alterum ad humanam" (*in* III, d.6, q.2, a.2 [*Scriptum* 3: 240]). "Ita etiam dico quod anima in Christo non acquirit proprium esse humanae naturae, sed Filio Dei acquirit respectum secundum esse suum ad naturam humanam, qui tamen respectus non est aliquid secundum rem in divina persona, sed secundum rationem, ut dictum est de unione" (*in* III, d. 6, q.2, a.2, *ad* 1 [*Scriptum* 3: 240]). "Quia ergo in Christo ponimus unam rem subsistentem tantum, ad cujus integritatem concurrit etiam humanitas, quia unum suppositum est utriusque naturae; ideo oportet dicere quod *esse* substantiale, quod proprie attribuitur supposito, in Christo est unum tantum; habet autem unitatem ex ipso supposito, et non ex naturis" (*Quodlibet* IX, q.2, a.3 [*Quaestiones disputatae et quaestiones duodecim quodlibetales* 5: 186a]). "Ea vero quae ad suppositum sive hypostasim pertinent, unum tantum in Christo confiteri oportet: unde si esse accipiatur secundum quod unum esse est unius suppositi, videtur dicendum quod in Christo sit tantum unum esse" (*Compendium theologiae*, c.212 [Leonine ed. 42: 165]).
172 *ST* III, q.17, a.2, *ad* 2 (*Summa theologiae* 4: 2542b): "Dicendum quod illud esse aeternum Filii Dei quod est divina natura, fit esse hominis, inquantum humana natura assumitur a Filio Dei in unitatem personae."

space for substantial predications *secundum quid*. The *Summa* emphasizes that the substantial reality of the human nature assumed exists in hypostatic unity. Lest this seem to veer at all toward monophysitism, Thomas's consistent attention to the truth and integrity of Christ's humanity acts as a counterweight.[173] These various emphases imbue the discussions with different concerns and goals. The theme of Christ's instrumental causality, though present in the *De unione*, finds elaboration most strongly in the *Summa*. Better understanding Thomas's development of this theme clarifies the role of Christ's human will in his Christology.

The *De unione* argues that the unity or plurality of actions or operations can be considered according to the subject acting or according to the "principle by which an agent acts."[174] An agent can work many different actions according to diverse powers, some of which are moved by a superior power and so are both actions and passions.[175] Thomas illustrates this principle with reference to human beings. The rational will is the superior

---

[173] "In addition to his anti-docetism, Thomas also betrays strong anti-Monophysitic currents, particularly in the discussion on Christ's passions. In the analysis of Jesus' human affectivity in the *Sentences* and the *Tertia pars*, Aquinas repeats eight times, *via* Damascene, the celebrated anti-Monophysitic axiom of Leo the Great, viz. that 'Christ's flesh was allowed to suffer and do what is proper to it.' The import that this axiom bears on Christ's passions is that the Person of the Word and the divine nature of Christ allowed the sensitive appetite of his human nature, the facultative grounding of the passions, to operate in a manner completely akin to its nature; the operations of Jesus' sensitive appetite, i.e. the movements of passion, were in no way suppressed through some kind of absorption into Christ's divine element" (Gondreau, *The Passions of Christ's Soul*, p. 150).

[174] *De unione*, a.5 (*Quaestiones disputatae et quaestiones duodecim quodlibetales* 2: 483a–483b): "Respondeo dicendum, quod unitas et pluralitas actionis potest ex duobus considerari. Uno modo ex parte subjecti agentis; et ex hoc consideratur unitas seu pluralitas actionis secundum numerum; sicut et quodlibet aliud accidens habet numeralem unitatem vel pluralitatem ex parte subiecti; haec enim visio vel auditio Socratis est alia numero a visione vel auditione Platonis. Alio modo potest considerari unitas vel pluralitas actiones ex parte principii quo agens operatur; et ex hoc actio dicitur esse una vel plures secundum speciem; sicut visio et auditio sunt operationes specie differentes."

[175] *De unione*, a.5 (*Quaestiones disputatae et quaestiones duodecim quodlibetales* 2: 483b): "Considerandum tamen quod, si virtus quae est actionis principium, ab alia superiori virtute moveatur, operatio ab ipsa procedens non solum est actio, sed etiam passio; in quantum scilicet procedit a virtute quae a superiori movetur."

moving power for all the sensitive powers. For example, seeing is an action and a passion. As an action, seeing is distinct from other actions of the same agent according to its species, which follows from the *ratio* of the power to see. Insofar as the agent proceeds to this action through the movement of the will, seeing is also a passion. "And therefore, although in one man there seem to be many specifically different actions according to diverse potencies and habits; nevertheless, because all proceed from the one first action of the will, there is said to be one action of one man."[176] The 'heretics' draw a strict parallel between the subjection of all human actions to the action of the will and the subjection of Christ's human actions to the divine action. In such an understanding, Christ's human actions would more properly be passions of the divine action, and so there would be but one operation in Christ.

Aquinas provides two lines of argumentation against this conclusion. The first refuses the parallel based upon a fundamental difference between the sensitive powers and the will. The senses do not have dominion over their acts, and so the movement of the senses is acted or operated.[177] The movement of the senses is more a passion than an action and is subject to the movement of the will. In contrast, "the power which has dominion over its acts, namely the will, is moved by a superior, namely by God, such that it is not only acted, but also acts."[178] Thomas takes it for granted that Jesus Christ had a human will as part of his human nature. This human will necessarily had dominion over its acts, and so "it follows that the movement

---

176 *De unione*, a.5 (*Quaestiones disputatae et quaestiones duodecim quodlibetales* 2: 483b): "Et ideo, licet in uno homine secundum diversas potentias et habitus videantur esse plures actiones specie differentes; tamen, quia omnes procedunt ab una prima actione voluntatis, dicitur esse una actio unius hominis."
177 See *ST* I, q.77, a.4; q.81, a.3.
178 *De unione*, a.5 (*Quaestiones disputatae et quaestiones duodecim quodlibetales* 2: 483b): "Sed virtus quae habet dominium sui actus, scilicet voluntas, sic movetur a superiori, scilicet a Deo, quod non solum agitur, sed etiam agit." Thomas notes in *ST* III, q.18, a.1, *ad* 1 that God can move a human will interiorly, referring to *ST* I, q.105, a.4; q.106, a.2; q.111, a.2. The argumentation of *ST* III, q.18 begins with the more general principles according to which free human acts are subject to the divine will and power. The strategy is similar in *De unione*, a.5. Aquinas is not here attempting to explain the possibility of Christ's two operations by reference to the hypostatic union. Rather, Thomas makes use of the general point that all human actions, while remaining free, are subject to the divine action.

of the human will in Christ is an action and not only a passion."[179] This grounds the possibility of Christ meriting.

The second line of argumentation begins with "the operation of whatever thing has its species and unity from a first principle pertaining to its very nature."[180] Human actions have their unity from the will as an intrinsic principle of human nature. Thomas offers no specification of this point, but his intent is to show that an intrinsic principle of a nature provides specific unity to the actions of whatever subject of that nature. This extends his earlier consideration of specific unity from species of power (for example, seeing) to natures. The import of this becomes clear as Thomas rejects the possibility of unity through a first principle of a different nature. If it were possible for actions to have unity from a nature other than that of the actor, "it would follow that all things would be one action, because there is one first principle moving all things, namely God."[181] Thomas concludes that Christ must have two distinct operations following his two natures. The fact that Christ's human operation is moved by God does not compromise its integrity as a human operation.[182] Affirmation of only one

---

179 *De unione*, a.5 (*Quaestiones disputatae et quaestiones duodecim quodlibetales* 2: 483b): "Et quia in Christo secundum humanam naturam est creata potentia voluntatis sicut et intellectus creatus, cum nihil ei desit eorum quae pertinent ad perfectionem naturae humanae, consequens est quod motus voluntatis humanae in Christo, actio sit et non solum passio."
180 *De unione*, a.5 (*Quaestiones disputatae et quaestiones duodecim quodlibetales* 2: 483b–484a): "Secundo, quia operatio alicuius speciem et unitatem habet a primo principio pertinente ad eamdem naturam."
181 *De unione*, a.5 (*Quaestiones disputatae et quaestiones duodecim quodlibetales* 2: 484a): "Non autem aliquae actiones habent unitatem ex hoc quod reducuntur in aliquod primum principium alterius naturae; alioquin sequeretur quod omnium rerum esset actio una, quia est unum primum principium movens omnia, scilicet Deus."
182 Thomas elaborates this point in replying to the objections. These replies focus heavily on Christ's human nature as an instrument of God and what this implies for Christ's unity of operation. Thomas refers to Christ's humanity as an instrument conjoined to his divinity in unity of person (*"instrumentum divinitati coniunctum in unitate personae"*) (*De unione*, a.5, *ad* 1 [*Quaestiones disputatae et quaestiones duodecim quodlibetales* 2: 484]). Christ's human will has dominion over its acts, and so Christ's humanity is an instrument that is both acted upon and acts (*ad* 4). Through its own action, Christ's humanity is used instrumentally by his divinity. These two operations of the one suppoit thus produce the same work, though in different ways.

nature in Christ would concomitantly affirm only one will and one nature. The logic of this argument parallels that of *Summa contra gentiles* IV.36 (on will and operation).

ST III, q.19 completes the section on Christ's unity *in communi* with a consideration of unity of operation.[183] Treatment of this issue in the *Summa theologiae* begins along lines similar to the *De unione*, namely that the first and supreme principle of an action properly possesses an operation, but the "actions and movements of an inferior principle are in some way more operated than operations."[184] The actions can be considered from two perspectives: from the part of the one operating, and from the part of the things operated or accomplished. Informed by the acts of Constantinople III, Thomas notes that the 'heretics' (especially Severus) argued for one operation on the part of the one operating and a diversity of things operated by virtue of the two natures. Aquinas's efforts to plumb the logic of Severus's view sharpen his own presentation of Christ's two natural operations.[185]

Thomas argues that "the action of something that is moved by another is twofold, one indeed that it has according to its proper form; but another that it has according as it is moved by another."[186] Failure to consider this

---

183 In Catão's analysis, qq.3-17 cover Christ in his being and qq.18-59 treat Christ in his actions. Question nineteen would then be read as the second question on Christ's action, establishing the general principles for all particular actions. (Catão, *Salut et rédemption*, pp. 42-43.)

184 *ST* III, q.19, a.1 (*Summa theologiae* 4: 2551b): "Sic igitur actiones et motus inferioris principii sunt magis operata quaedam quam operationes; id autem pertinent ad supremum principium, est proprie operatio."

185 *ST* III, q.19, a.1 presents the example of superior and inferior powers within a human being only as an illustration of Severus's view. Thomas formulates his own view through a discussion of instrumentality, completely abandoning the example of reason to the sensitive powers. The *De unione*, a.5 refuses the parallel between the example of superior and inferior powers within a human being and the case of the divine and human natures in Christ. Thomas's refusal of the parallel rests on the will as the prime mover within a human being (and the assumption of a human will in Christ). Thomas in the *Summa* demonstrates the inadequacy of Severus's understanding and offers an alternative model based upon instrumentality. This marks perhaps the most significant difference between the logic of the arguments in *ST* III, q.19, a.1 and *De unione*, a.5.

186 *ST* III, q.19, a.1 (*Summa theologiae* 4: 2551b): "Quia actio eius quod movetur ab altero, est duplex, una quidem quam habet secundum propriam formam; alia autem quam habet secundum quod movetur ab alio."

double aspect led Severus into heresy. The operation of a hatchet, according to its proper form, is to cut. When a skilled carpenter uses a hatchet, the operation of the hatchet is to make a bench. Thomas explains this example in terms of a mover acting through an instrument. The instrument possesses its own proper form of acting and participates instrumentally in the operation of the mover. In other words, a hatchet cannot make a bench without the operation of a carpenter, but beyond this instrumental participation, the hatchet has an operation according to its own nature or proper form. Thomas writes:

> And therefore wherever the moving and the moved have diverse forms or operative powers, there it is necessary that there is one proper operation of the mover, and another proper operation of the moved; nevertheless the moved participates the operation of the mover, and the mover uses the operation of the moved, and thus each acts in communion with the other.[187]

Aquinas applies this very model in the case of Christ, writing that "therefore in Christ human nature has a proper form and power through which [it/he] operates, and similarly the divine [nature]."[188] Thomas does not prove that Christ's human nature is similar to the hatchet or that it is used instrumentally. The argument proceeds from the assumption that Christ's human nature is the instrument of his divinity and elaborates the nature and operation of instruments to understand Christ's human nature. This logic demonstrates how thoroughly Thomas internalized the notion of Christ's human nature as instrument of his divinity and the extent to which the reader, prepared by q.18, can approach q.19 informed regarding Christ's instrumentality. Based upon the proper form and power of Christ's human nature, Thomas attributes to it a proper operation distinct from the divine operation. The divine operation uses the human operation instrumentally,

---

187 *ST* III, q.19, a.1 (*Summa theologiae* 4: 2552a): "Et ideo ubicumque movens et motum habent diversas formas seu virtutes operativas, ibi oportet quod sit alia propria operatio moventis, et alia operatio propria moti; licet motum participet operationem moventis, et movens utatur operatione moti, et sic utrumque agat cum communione alterius."
188 *ST* III, q.19, a.1 (*Summa theologiae* 4: 2552a): "Sic igitur in Christo humana natura habet propriam formam et virtutem per quam operatur, et similiter divina."

and the human operation participates in the divine operation.[189] Thomas makes no mention here of types of instruments. To understand his meaning, the reader must recall q.18, a.1, *ad* 2, which distinguishes rational instruments from non-rational instruments.[190]

This first and positive stage of argumentation presumes Christ's human nature to be an instrument and argues that an instrument has an operation flowing from its proper form or power. The second stage demonstrates the unacceptable consequences that follow an affirmation of only one operation in Christ. If there were in Christ only one operation, "it would be necessary to say either that the human nature did not have its proper form and power ... or it would be necessary to say that from the divine power and the human [power] there would be one conflated power in Christ."[191] Affirming only one operation either makes the human nature imperfect or confuses the natures, neither of which is acceptable. Note that Thomas does not here mention the human will as a casualty of denying a human operation. That argument features prominently in the *De unione*. The *Summa* has less need to explicitly draw out this point and can rely upon the presentation of the human will in q.18. In both texts the question of a human will in Christ carries import in and of itself, not simply in relation to other questions or concerns as in the *Summa contra gentiles*.

---

189 Thomas quotes here from Leo's *Tomus ad Flavianum* to the effect that each nature does what is proper to it in communion with the other. "Et hoc est quod dicit Leo Papa in epistola *Ad Flavianum*: 'Agit utraque forma,' scilicet tam natura divina quam humana in Christo, 'cum alterius communione, quod proprium est: Verbo scilicet operante quod Verbi est, et carne exequente quod carnis est'" (*ST* III, q.19, a.1 [*Summa theologiae* 4: 2552a]). Agatho repeatedly cites this passage from Leo as a basic formula for understanding Christ's two wills and operations. See Riedinger 2.1: 73–75, 95–99; Mansi 11: 247–250, 266–267.

190 Thomas distinguishes inanimate, animate, and rational instruments in *ST* III, q.18, a.1, *ad* 2. In the *De veritate* (q.29, a.1, *ad* 9) Thomas mentions only inanimate and animate. The *Summa contra gentiles* IV.41 focuses on the difference between conjoined and separate instruments. Thomas's focus on rational instrumentality in the *Summa* highlights the importance of Christ's human will and shapes the presentation of Christ as mediator.

191 *ST* III, q.19, a.1 (*Summa theologiae* 4: 2552a): "Si vero esset una tantum operatio divinitatis et humanitatis in Christo, oporteret dicere vel quod humana natura non haberet propriam formam et virtutem, de divina enim hoc dici est impossibile, ex quo sequeretur quod in Christo esset tantum divina operatio; vel oporteret dicere quod ex divina virtute et humana esset conflata in Christo una virtus."

The differences between the *De unione*, a.5 and *ST* III, q.19, a.1 highlight Thomas's interest with instrumentality in the *Summa*. This interest is present in the *De unione*, though to a lesser degree. The concern of *ST* III, q.19, a.1 with instrumentality extends also into Thomas's responses to the objections. The second objection concluded to one operation in Christ on the grounds that an instrument shares one operation with the principal agent. Thomas responds with reference to the *corpus* and the example of fire, which acts to heat according to its own form but, as a blacksmith's instrument, acts to forge iron. He concludes that the "action of the instrument, inasmuch as it is an instrument, is not other than the action of the principal agent; nevertheless it can have another operation insofar as it is a certain thing."[192] Christ's human nature has its proper operation as a specific nature (a subsisting individual of human nature) and participates instrumentally in the divine operation. As an instrument Christ's human nature shares the operation of the divine nature, "for there is not a different salvation by which Christ's humanity saves, and by which his divinity saves."[193] This repeats and amplifies Thomas's arguments in the *corpus*. The instrument has its own operation not just in terms of its form, but as a specific, individual thing.[194] The *corpus* of article one, due to its focus on instrumental causality, could be misread to portray Christ's human nature as a mere tool for the divine operation. Such a view would ignore Thomas's previous efforts to show the one acting subject as subsisting in two natures. The *De unione*'s treatment of Christ's operations guards far more vigorously against any such danger. What guards against this in the *Summa* is Thomas's rich presentation of Christ's human will. Question 18 detailed the perfect functioning of Christ's human will. Question 19 builds upon

---

192 *ST* III, q.19, a.1, *ad* 2 (*Summa theologiae* 4: 2553a): "Sic igitur actio instrumenti, inquantum est instrumentum, non est alia ab actione principalis agentis; potest tamen habere aliam operationem prout est res quaedam."

193 *ST* III, q.19, a.1, *ad* 2 (*Summa theologiae* 4: 2553a): "Sic igitur operatio quae est humanae naturae in Christo, inquantum est instrumentum divinitatis, non est alia ab operatione divinitatis; non enim est alia salvatio qua salvat humanitas Christi, et divinitas eius."

194 This argument counters both a *habitus* theory of the Incarnation and a monenergist view. Christ's human nature is not simply a mold that gives human shape to the divine operation or power. Human nature cannot be the form of the divine power. The Logos acts through and in his human nature. Christ's human nature is not a lifeless tool but a rational source of activity.

that foundation by portraying this functioning as a true (instrumental) human operation. Thomas's discussion of Christ's two wills also shows the Word as the one subject of the divine will and the human will. That lesson bears heavily upon Christ's unity of operation.

Aquinas's response to the third objection introduces a distinction between the subject of the operation and that by which the subject operates. Thomas's response in *De unione*, a.5 begins with this distinction but proceeds wholly through consideration of the 'by which.' The *Summa*'s discussion links these closely, arguing that "to operate pertains to the subsisting hypostasis, but according to form and nature, from which the operation receives its species."[195] There are diverse species of operation according to diverse natures and forms, but the operation of the species takes its unity from the hypostasis. All of Christ's operations or actions have unity according to the one hypostasis of the Word, yet there are two operations according to the two natures.[196] This echoes Thomas's findings in *De unione*, a.3, that Christ is one *simpliciter* and two *secundum quid*. The *Summa*'s equivalent (q.17, a.1) offers less grounding for affirmation of Christ's two operations. Perhaps *ST* III, q.17, a.2's assertion of only one *esse* in Christ renders attribution of two operations all the more difficult.

These concerns are largely mitigated by Thomas's discussion of Christ's unity of will (*ST* III, q.18). Aquinas's affirmation of a perfect human will in Christ presents this fully functioning will as essential for Christ's human nature as a rational instrument hypostatically united to the Word. The *Summa* leads readers to approach Christ's unity of operation from the perspective of Christ's unity of will. Question 18 clarifies how the divine and human wills in Christ act for one salvation. Question 19 extends this conclusion, particularly in terms of merit. The *De unione* lacks any equivalent to *ST* III, q.18, and this lack necessitates lines of argu-

---

195 *ST* III, q.19, a.1, *ad* 3 (*Summa theologiae* 4: 2553a): "Dicendum quod operari est hypostasis subsistentis, sed secundum formam et naturam, a qua operatio speciem recipit." *ST* III, q.2, a.3 (*Summa theologiae* 4: 2427b): "Tertio, quia tantum hypostasis est cui attribuuntur operationes et proprietates naturae, et ea etiam quae ad naturae rationem pertinent in concreto."
196 Again, the consequence of the union is not simply Christ's possession of two operations, but more importantly his unity of operation. This unity prepares for understanding Christ as mediator.

mentation on Christ as one, Christ's *esse*, and Christ's operation different from those of the *Summa*. Thomas's recovery of Constantinople III and knowledge of the condemnations of Averroistic denials of free choice catapulted the issue of Christ's two wills to greater prominence in the *Summa*. This prominence is not matched in the *De unione*. On the one hand, this lack of specific treatment in the *De unione* might appear as counterevidence to the importance of Christ's two wills. On the other hand, *De unione*, a.5 assumes a human will in Christ and derives a human operation from this assumption. Without this independent treatment of Christ's two wills, the *De unione* stresses the distinction of natures in the questions of Christ as one or two, of Christ's *esse*, and of Christ's operation. Thomas's discussion of will serves this function in the *Summa*, and so his treatment of *esse* and operation can safely stress unity.[197] In the case of operation, Thomas highlights the instrumental (and hypostatic) unity of Christ's operations. Thomas can, through this focus, present Christ's human nature as an instrumental efficient cause of salvation.

The relation of will to operation becomes more explicit in article two, which concludes that there was only one human operation in Christ. What is properly human proceeds from the rational will. Only the operation of the will is properly human. Insofar as the sensitive powers obey the rational will they share in the one human operation. This recalls *ST* III, q.18, a.2 and introduces an element absent from *De unione*, a.5. The *De unione*'s version lacks specificity, indicating only that the will is the first moving principle of human actions. In other human beings, there is only one human operation but other operations not properly human, that is, not obedient to the rational will. Every movement in Christ was in accord with his will, and therefore "there is much more one operation in Christ than in any

---

197 In *ST* III, q.19, a.1, *ad* 4, Thomas argues that "esse et operari est personae a natura, aliter tamen et aliter." What pertains to Christ's unity always involves both the unity of hypostasis and duality of natures. The case of will and operation differs from the case of *esse* in that "esse pertinet ad ipsam constitutionem personae" (*ST* III, q.19, a.1, *ad* 4 [*Summa theologiae* 4: 2553a]). Another way to state the matter is that *esse* pertains more to hypostasis, while will and operation pertain more to nature. Human nature can be predicated of Christ only in the concrete, as an individual. Whatever pertains to Christ's human nature pertains to the person of the Word, though not in the same way as what pertains to the divine nature.

other human being."[198] Once again, Thomas's treatment of the will informs and adds nuance to the *Summa*'s presentation of operation in Christ.[199]

The third and fourth articles address merit.[200] Article three strictly forbids that Christ could merit the hypostatic union, divinity, grace, or the beatific vision. Yet, it is better, when possible, to possess something through oneself than from another. Human beings can cooperate with God and thus merit some good through themselves. "Because moreover," Aquinas argues, "every perfection and nobility should be attributed to Christ, it follows that he himself will have through merit what others have through merit."[201] Granting the aforementioned exclusions, Christ could merit bodily glory and what relates to his outward excellence.[202] Thomas extends

---

198 *ST* III, q.19, a.2 (*Summa theologiae* 4: 2554a): "Sed in homine Iesu Christo nullus erat motus sensitivae partis qui non esset ordinatus a ratione. Ipsae etiam operationes naturales et corporales aliqualiter ad eius voluntatem pertinebant, inquantum voluntatis eius erat ut caro eius ageret et pateretur quae sunt sibi propria, ut dictum est supra. Et ideo multo magis est una operatio in Christo quam in quocumque alio homine."

199 Thomas's presentation of Christ's perfect human nature also completes the anthropology of the *Prima pars* and the *Secunda pars*. In this function of Christology, Thomas's structuring of the *Summa* mimics the actual dispensation. Humanity's perfection, in certain respects, follows its imperfection temporally (*ST* III, q.1, a.5, *ad* 3).

200 On Christ's merit, see Wawrykow, *God's Grace and Human Action*, pp. 238–247. It is worth noting that in the *Summa* Christ's merit is a subtopic of Christ's unity of operation. The case is reversed in the *Scriptum*, where Thomas defends Christ's two operations within the discussion of Christ's merit (*in* III, d.18). See also Catão, *Salut et rédemption*. Catão presents extended discussions of Christ's merit with particular attention to Christ's human will. His helpful study has much to recommend it, though it overly distinguishes the modes of merit and efficient instrumentality in Christ's human act of salvation. Catão argues that Thomas's presentation of the salvific value of Christ's merit develops from theandric activity in the *Scriptum* to the dignity of the person of the Word meriting in the *De veritate* and *Compendium theologiae* to capital grace in the *Summa theologiae* (Catão, p. 138).

201 *ST* III, q.19, a.3 (*Summa theologiae* 4: 2555a): "Quia autem omnis perfectio et nobilitas Christo est attribuenda, consequens est quod ipse per meritum habuerit illud quod alii per meritum habent, nisi sit tale quid cuius carentia magis dignitati Christi et perfectioni praeiudicet quam per meritum accrescat."

202 Catão stresses this aspect of Thomas's presentation. Bodily glory (and what it relates to) does not follow the beatific vision as a consequence, but it follows Christ's unity of will as a consequence. "La gloire du corps, l'immortalité, ne nous est pas présentée comme une simple conséquence de la vision de Dieu,

Christ's merit to others in article four. This article rests heavily on the discussion of Christ's capital grace (*ST* III, q.8, aa.1, 5).[203] As Christ is head of his mystical body, he could merit for his members. This brief presentation of Christ's merit completes the section on what pertains to Christ's unity (qq.17–19).[204]

Christ's Prayer and Priesthood

Questions 20 to 24 discuss the consequences of the union in terms of what befits Christ in comparison to the Father. In these questions Thomas considers Christ's subjection to the Father, his prayer, priesthood, adoption, and predestination. Of particular interest here will be q.21 on Christ's prayer and q.22 on Christ's priesthood. A proper analysis of these questions begins with Christ's subjection. Aquinas begins this section (qq.20–24) by asking whether Christ was subject to the Father (q.20, a.1). In the form of a servant, Christ was subject to the Father (q.20, a.1, *sed contra*). The qualification 'in the form of a servant' excludes an Arian understanding of the Son as less divine than the Father. Christ's subjection to the Father refers only to the form of the servant, or human nature. Thomas then expands upon the threefold subjection of human nature to God. The first manner relates to the grade of goodness. God is goodness itself, "but a created nature has a certain participation of the divine goodness."[205] All creation is subject to the divine operation (the dispensation of the divine power), which constitutes the

---

mais vraiment comme la récompense d'actes auxquels le corps a pris part, comme le couronnement normal des actes humains, qui ont été posés par la volonté, bien sûr, par l'âme, mais qui sont de l'homme tout entier" (Catão, *Salut et rédemption*, p. 76).

203 Catão highlights Christ's capital grace as the reason Christ can merit for others (Catão, *Salut et rédemption*, pp. 137, 144).

204 See *ST* III, q.48, a.1 on Christ causing salvation through the mode of merit. Admirable treatments of Christ's merit and its salvific import exist. This aspect of Christ's human will has been explored. The present study will focus on the less explored aspects.

205 *ST* III, q.20, a.1 (*Summa theologiae* 4: 2557a): "Unam quidem secundum gradum bonitatis, prout scilicet divina natura est ipsa essentia bonitatis … ; natura autem creata habet quandam participationem divinae bonitatis, quasi radiis illius bonitatis subiecta."

second manner.[206] The third mode of subjection is the most interesting because it is specifically human. That is, while all creatures share a subjection in terms of the divine goodness and power, "human nature is specially subject to God in terms of its own proper act, namely inasmuch as by its proper will it obeys [God's] commands."[207] Thomas argues that Christ attributes these three manners of subjection to himself. His description of the third type, the subjection of obedience, references John 8:29 and Philippians 2:8. Thomas quotes Philippians 2:8 in the *sed contra* to q.19, a.3 on Christ's ability to merit for himself. This repetition of Philippians enforces the connection between Christ's subjection to the Father and the unity of Christ's operation, both of which are grounded in the proper obedience of Christ's human will to God.[208]

After questions on *esse* and operation, the question on Christ's prayer (q.21) seems particularly concrete and biblical.[209] In the Lombard's *Sentences*, treatment of Christ's prayer occurs in the same distinction as treatment of Christ's wills (Bk.III, d.17). Thomas's *Scriptum* follows the order of the *Sentences*, with articles one and two of d.17 examining Christ's will and article three examining Christ's prayer. Distinction 18 of the *Sentences* addresses Christ's merit; the *Scriptum*'s treatment addresses operation and merit.[210] Thomas breaks with this order (will, prayer, operation/merit) in the *Summa*, extracting the discussion of prayer and positioning it within a different subsection. The *Summa* also inserts a question on Christ's subjection (cf. *Scriptum, in* III, d.11, a.1, *ad* 2) between questions on operation

---

206 *ST* III, q.20, a.1 (*Summa theologiae* 4: 2557b): "Secundo, humana natura subiicitur Deo quantum ad Dei potestatem, prout scilicet natura humana, sicut et quaelibet creatura, subiacet operationi divinae dispositionis."

207 *ST* III, q.20, a.1 (*Summa theologiae* 4: 2557b): "Tertio modo, specialiter humana natura Deo subiicitur quantum ad proprium suum actum, inquantum scilicet propria voluntate obedit mandatis eius."

208 This again demonstrates the import of the will as what makes human actions properly human. Christ's subjection to the Father involves the very act of a human will in obedience to God that constitutes the cause of salvation (through various modes). This subjection results from Christ's human will.

209 For a more general treatment of Christ's prayer, see Corey Barnes, "Thomas Aquinas on Christ's Prayer," in *A History of Prayer: The First to the Fifteenth Century*, ed. Roy Hammerling (Leiden, 2008), 319–336.

210 The fact of two operations in Christ grounds the possibility of Christ's merit. The order of topics in the *Scriptum* is thus will, prayer, operation, and merit.

and prayer.[211] Given the close connection between scholastic treatments of Christ's will and prayer, why would Thomas separate them thus in the *Summa*? At least in part this separation relates to Thomas's subdivision of the section on the consequences of the union. Questions of *esse*, will, and operation are organized under a heading of unity. Consideration of Christ's prayer unfolds in the section on what befits Christ in comparison to the Father. Such a consideration would be out of place in the section of unity. Positioned as it is, Thomas's discussion of Christ's prayer allows for the reiteration of points established in question 18. Investigation of Christ's prayer demonstrates the obedience of Christ's will as the properly human act of subjection to the Father.

Question 21 first considers whether it was fitting for Christ to pray. The objections deny fittingness on the grounds of Christ's power, his knowledge of the future, and his soul's enjoyment of the beatific vision, all points established previously in the *Tertia pars* (q.13; q.10, a.2; q.9, a.2). Thomas grounds his response in Christ's human will and in prayer as an explication of a will ordered to God. "If therefore," Aquinas writes, "there were only one will in Christ, namely the divine, it would in no way befit him to pray; because the divine will is effective through itself of what it wills."[212] Christ's human will is not effective of whatever it wills in and through itself but only through the divine power. Thomas concludes that "hence it is fitting for Christ, according as he is a human being and has a human will, to pray."[213] Christ's prayer exhibits the proper act of the will's obedience to God, provides for us an example of praying (q.21, a.1, *ad* 1), and exemplifies the role of secondary causality (q.21, a.1, *ad* 2). The *Scriptum* considers Christ's instrumental causality wholly in terms of secondary

---

211 Concerns about Christ's subjection are scattered in the *Scriptum* and distant from discussions of will, operation, prayer, and merit.
212 *ST* III, q.21, a.1 (*Summa theologiae* 4: 2560a): "Dicendum quod, sicut dictum est in Secunda Parte, oratio est quaedam explicatio propriae voluntatis apud Deum, ut eam impleat. Si igitur in Christo esset una tantum voluntas, scilicet divina, nullo modo competeret sibi orare; quia voluntas divina per seipsam est effectiva eorum quae vult."
213 *ST* III, q.21, a.1 (*Summa theologiae* 4: 2560a): "Sed quia in Christo est alia voluntas divina et alia humana; et voluntas humana non est per seipsam efficax ad implendum quae vult, nisi per virtutem divinam; inde est quod Christo, secundum quod est homo et humanam voluntatem habens, competit orare."

causality (whether dispositive or meritorious). The *Summa* develops a more profound notion of Christ's instrumental causality but retains discussion of the more mundane form of secondary causality for our instruction.

Should Christ's prayer be attributed to his sensuality? This attribution has two possible meanings. If it is taken to imply that praying was the act of sensuality, then Thomas denies that Christ prayed according to sensuality.[214] The movement of sensuality cannot transcend the sensible world in ascending to God, nor can it be ordered to seek its fulfillment through God.[215] Another meaning would involve reason praying on behalf of sensuality or praying for the fulfillment of the sensitive appetite.[216] Thomas defends this interpretation of Christ's prayer and explains its fittingness in terms of a threefold instruction for us. First, Christ's prayer shows the truth of his human nature, in all its parts and functions. "Second," Thomas argues, "so that it might show that to will according to natural affection something that God does not will is permitted to man."[217] Third, a human being's proper affection should be subject to God nonetheless, and this Christ's prayer also shows.[218] Christ's

---

214 *ST* III, q.21, a.2 (*Summa theologiae* 4: 2561a): "Uno modo, sic quod ipsa oratio sit actus sensualitatis. Et hoc modo Christus secundum sensualitatem non oravit."

215 *ST* III, q.21, a.2 (*Summa theologiae* 4: 2561a): "Primo quidem, quia motus sensualitatis non potest sensibilia transcendere; et ideo non potest in Deum ascendere, quod requiritur ad orationem. Secundo, quia oratio importat quandam ordinationem, prout aliquis desiderat aliquid quasi a Deo implendum; et hoc est solius rationis."

216 *ST* III, q.21, a.2 (*Summa theologiae* 4: 2561a): "Alio modo potest dici aliquis orare secundum sensualitatem, quia scilicet eius ratio orando Deo proponit quod est in appetitu sensualitatis ipsius. Et secundum hoc Christus oravit secundum sensualitatem, inquantum scilicet oratio eius exprimebat sensualitatis affectum, tanquam sensualitatis advocata."

217 *ST* III, q.21, a.2 (*Summa theologiae* 4: 2561a–2561b): "Secundo, ut ostenderet quod homini licet secundum naturalem affectum aliquid velle quod Deus non vult."

218 *ST* III, q.21, a.2 (*Summa theologiae* 4: 2561b): "Tertio, ut ostendat quod proprium affectum debet homo divinae voluntati subiicere." Thomas follows this third reason with a citation of Augustine in which he explains Matthew 26:39, on Christ's prayer in the garden. Augustine refers this prayer simply to the human will, making no distinction between reason and sensuality. Thomas's careful analysis of Christ's will and prayer equips the reader to reverentially interpret Augustine here.

prayer thus demonstrates the truth and perfection of his human will in all the details established in question 18.

Article three queries whether it was fitting for Christ to pray for himself. Thomas's answer lists two ways Christ prayed for himself. As noted in article two, Christ prayed on behalf of his sensitive affection, which shrank from the passion. Christ's will as nature also shrank from the passion. Through his will of sensuality and will as nature, Christ prayed for himself that the cup of the crucifixion might pass.[219] Christ also prayed for himself according to the affection of his will as reason or deliberative will.[220] With his will as reason, Christ willed the passion. The will as reason serves as the basis upon which Christ prayed for the glory of the resurrection (and for all those things which Christ merited, see *ST* III, q.19, a.3).[221] Thomas construes this as also providing us an example for praying. Christ's prayer through his will of reason further shows "his Father to be the author both from whom he eternally proceeds according to the divine nature, and from whom he possesses whatever good he possesses according to human nature."[222] Christ possesses what-

---

219 *ST* III, q.21, a.3 (*Summa theologiae* 4: 2562a): "Uno modo, exprimendo affectum sensualitatis, ut supra dictum est, vel etiam voluntatis simplicis, quae consideratur ut natura; sicut cum oravit a se calicem passionis transferri." The will of sensuality is not properly speaking a will. Insofar as sensuality obeys reason, the movement of sensuality can be called rational by participation and be called will. Thomas, following early scholastics, used will as nature (*voluntas ut natura*) to translate *thelēsis*. With expanded knowledge of the third book of John Damascene's *De fide orthodoxa*, the scholastics began to use the distinction between *thelēsis* and *boulēsis*, adding nuance to the one power of the rational will. For Thomas's understanding of these, see *ST* III, q.18, aa.2, 3 and Chapter four above (pp. 132–139).

220 Thomas divides the one power of the will of reason according to two species of acts. The will as nature wills its object absolutely as an end. The will as reason wills its object as a means to an end. Christ's will as nature wills to avoid the passion, because death is a natural evil. Christ's will as reason wills the passion as a means to salvation.

221 *ST* III, q.21, a.3 (*Summa theologiae* 4: 2562a): "Alio modo, exprimendo affectum voluntatis deliberatae, quae consideratur ut ratio; sicut cum petiit gloriam resurrectionis."

222 *ST* III, q.21, a.3 (*Summa theologiae* 4: 2562a): "Sicut enim dictum est, Christus ad hoc uti voluit oratione ad Patrem, ut nobis daret exemplum orandi; et ut ostenderet Patrem suum esse auctorem a quo et aeternaliter processit secundum divinam naturam, et secundum humanam naturam ab eo habet quidquid boni habet."

ever good according to human nature from the Father, and whatever good according to human nature he does not yet possess he prays for to the Father.[223] In this way, Christ also provides an example of proper praying, and so even his prayer for himself is for us (q.21, a.3, *ad* 3).

The larger question regarding Christ's prayer concerns its fulfillment. The first objection to article four poses the problem well. Christ prayed in the garden that the cup might be removed from him (Matthew 26:39), yet it was not removed.[224] How should this be understood? Is it fitting for Christ to pray for something he knew would not be and that he did not will to be? How could that instruct us? Thomas's response rests upon his previous discussion of Christ's unity of will, and particularly the conformity and non-contrariety of Christ's will (q.18, aa.5, 6).

The objections deny that Christ's every prayer was granted. Thomas counters by explaining the meaning of having a prayer granted and its relationship to the will. A prayer is granted when the will of the one praying is fulfilled.[225] What at first seemed a simple matter now seems more complex. In order to understand Christ's prayer, we must first understand Christ's unity of will. Aquinas repeats the divisions of the will and explains in what sense Christ's will was fulfilled. Thomas argues that what we will absolutely is what we will according to the deliberation of reason, that is, what we will through the will as reason or deliberative will. In contrast, "what we will according to the movement of sensuality or according to the movement of the simple will, which is considered as nature, we do not will simply, but according to something; namely if something is not found that would be opposed through the deliberation of reason."[226] Thomas again

---

223 Thomas describes this most thoroughly in response to the second objection. "Dicendum quod Christus volebat quidem pati illa quae patiebatur pro tempore illo; sed nihilominus volebat ut post passionem gloriam corporis consequeretur, quam nondum habebat. Quam quidem gloriam expectabat a Patre sicut ab auctore. Et ideo convenienter ab eo ipsam petebat" (*ST* III, q.21, a.3, *ad* 2 [*Summa theologiae* 4: 2562b]).
224 *ST* III, q.21, a.4, ob.1 (*Summa theologiae* 4: 2562b): "Petiit enim a se removeri calicem passionis, ut patet *Matth*. XXVI 39, qui tamen ab eo non fuit translatus. Ergo videtur quod non omnis oratio eius fuerit exaudita."
225 *ST* III, q.21, a.4 (*Summa theologiae* 4: 2563a): "Dicendum quod, sicut dictum est, oratio est quodammodo interpretativa voluntatis humanae. Tunc ergo alicuius orantis exauditur oratio, quando eius voluntas adimpletur."
226 *ST* III, q.21, a.4 (*Summa theologiae* 4: 2563a): "Voluntas autem simpliciter hominis est rationis voluntas; hoc enim absolute volumus quod secundum

describes the movement of the will of sensuality and will as nature as more of a willingness (*velleitas*) than a proper will. Only the movement of the will as reason should properly or absolutely be called a will, for it alone wills without qualifications or conditions. This portrayal of the will as reason and will as nature owes much to q.18, aa. 5 and 6. The most basic distinction between the will as reason and the will as nature involves the mode of willing. The will as reason wills things as means to an end, while the will as nature wills things as ends (which Thomas sometimes confusingly refers to as willing absolutely). Aquinas's rhetoric here diverges somewhat from that of his discussion of the division of the will (q.18, a.3) but recalls starkly the language used to demonstrate the conformity and non-contrariety of Christ's will.

Granting that only the will as reason wills absolutely, Thomas focuses upon this will (referred to as the will of reason) in his response. Christ, according to his will of reason, willed only what God willed.[227] Aquinas concludes that "every absolute will of Christ, even his human, was fulfilled, because it was conformed to God; and as a consequence his every prayer was granted."[228] Thomas's solution hinges upon the conformity of Christ's will to God's will. The ancient writers interpreted Christ's prayer in the garden variously, and Thomas provides a lengthy list of such opinions. The opinions most in accord with his solution view the prayer as made by rea-

---

deliberationem rationis volumus. Illud autem quod volumus secundum motum sensualitatis, vel secundum motum voluntatis simplicis, quae consideratur ut natura, non simpliciter volumus, sed secundum quid; scilicet si aliud non obsistat quod per deliberationem rationis invenitur."

227 Following the Damascene's view that through a certain dispensation it was permitted to Christ's soul to do and suffer those things proper to it, Thomas argues that it was permitted to Christ's every power to do and suffer those things proper to them. It was God's will that Christ's sensuality, following its proper nature, shun the passion as a natural evil. The same can be said about Christ's will as nature, which viewed the passion as an end rather than as a means to salvation. God willed that Christ's will of sensuality and will as nature shun the passion.

228 *ST* III, q.21, a.4 (*Summa theologiae* 4: 2563a): "Secundum autem voluntatem rationis Christus nihil aliud voluit nisi quod scivit Deum velle. Et ideo omnis absoluta voluntas Christi, etiam humana, fuit impleta, quia fuit Deo conformis; et per consequens omnis eius oratio fuit exaudita." Thomas cites Romans 8:27 as proof of the connection between a will conformed to God and the granting of prayers.

son on behalf of sensuality. Reason makes this petition on behalf of sensuality, yet the will as reason does will that it not be fulfilled. Since the granting of a prayer involves the fulfillment of the will, Christ's prayer was granted insofar as it was never willed to be granted. That is, Christ willed that his prayer not come to pass.[229] Rather, the prayer demonstrates the veracity of Christ's human nature, in all its natural powers and passions.[230]

Thomas's consideration of Christ's prayer parallels his treatment of Christ's unity of will. Question 21 begins with Thomas defending the fittingness of Christ praying based upon his possession of a human will (a.1). Article two then introduces Christ's will of sensuality and its relation to his will of reason. This allows Aquinas to indicate in what sense Christ's prayer was from sensuality.[231] Thomas answers the question of whether Christ prayed for himself (a.3) through reference to the division of the will of reason into will as reason and will as nature. Finally, Aquinas formulates the question of article four to be answered according to the conformity of Christ's will. This development mimics Thomas's treatment of Christ's will. In question 18 Thomas first establishes Christ's possession of a human will. This human will is then parsed into the will of reason and the will of sensuality (a.2). Article three presents the will as reason and the will as nature as two species of acts of the one power of the rational will. Thomas explains the conformity of Christ's will to the divine will in article five. The *Summa*'s treatment of Christ's prayer illustrates Christ's unity of will.

229 *ST* III, q.13, a.4 (*Summa theologiae* 4: 2510b–2511a): "Dicendum quod anima Christi dupliciter aliquid voluit. Uno modo, quasi per se implendum. Et sic dicendum quod quidquid voluit, potuit. Non enim conveniret sapientiae eius ut aliquid vellet per se facere, quod suae virtuti non subiaceret. – Alio modo voluit aliquid ut implendum virtute divina, sicut resuscitationis proprii corporis, et alia huiusmodi miraculosa opera. Quae quidem non poterat propria virtute, sed secundum quod erat instrumentum divinitatis, ut dictum est."
230 *ST* III, q.21, a.4, *ad* 1 (*Summa theologiae* 4: 2563b): "Si vero petisse quod non biberet calicem mortis et passionis, vel quod non biberet ipsum a Iudaeis, non quidem est factum quod petiit, quia ratio, quae petitionem proposuit, non volebat ut hoc impleretur; sed ad instructionem nostram volebat demonstrare nobis suam voluntas naturalem, et motum sensualitatis, quem, sicut homo, habebat."
231 In the *Scriptum* Thomas addresses whether Christ prayed for himself and then whether the prayer was from sensuality (*in* III, d.17, a.3, quae. 2 and 3). He switches the order of these topics in the *Summa*. The most obvious explanation is that Thomas changed the order to match the order of q.18. Though Aquinas separated discussion of Christ's will and prayer, the topics remain intimately connected.

One more question from the section on Christ in comparison to the Father deserves mention before moving on. Question 22 examines the priesthood of Christ; this question develops several points important for q.26 on Christ as mediator. Of the six articles in question 22, only the final two have strict parallels in the *Scriptum*. The first three articles have partial parallels only in Thomas's commentary on Hebrews. This paucity of equivalents makes noteworthy Thomas's consideration of these topics and in this place. The discussion of Christ's priesthood will attempt to draw out its import, in itself as well as in relation to question 26.

The consideration begins through the familiar theme of fittingness. The aim is not simply to argue that Christ was a priest (the letter to the Hebrews establishes that point) but to show in precisely which way Christ was a priest and why. Aquinas defines the office of a priest as to be a mediator between the people and God.[232] The priest offers requests or prayers to God on behalf of the people for satisfaction of their sins.[233] This office, Thomas argues, is maximally fitting to Christ. Thomas elaborates Christ's priesthood in terms of his humanity.[234]

Christ was not only a priest but also a host (*hostia*, sacrificial victim). Thomas refers to Augustine (*De civitate Dei* X.5) in arguing that everything which carries the human spirit to God can be called a sacrifice.[235] The human race needs a sacrifice for the remission of sins, to be preserved in a state of grace, and for the human spirit to be perfected in unity with

---

232 *ST* III, q.22, a.1 (*Summa theologiae* 4: 2564b): "Dicendum quod proprie officium sacerdotis est esse mediatorem inter Deum et populum." "Sacerdos enim medius est inter Deum et populum" (*Super Heb.* 7.1, in *Super epistolas S. Pauli lectura*, ed. Raphaele Cai [Turin, 1953], vol. 2, p. 408, n.329; see also *Super Heb.* 9.3–9.4).

233 Thomas writes that the office of a priest is to be a mediator "iterum inquantum preces populi Deo offert, et pro eorum peccatis Deo aliqualiter satisfacit" (*ST* III, q.22, a.1 [*Summa theologiae* 4: 2564b]). These can be viewed as two separate but related tasks. Question 21 addresses the first part of the definition (Christ's prayer). Question 22 then establishes the second element of the definition and prepares for the subsequent treatments of Christ's satisfaction for sin. See also *Super Heb.* 7.1.

234 *ST* III, q.22, a.3, *ad* 3 specifies that Christ was priest *secundum quod homo*, not *secundum quod Deus*. This relates closely to Christ as mediator and the instrumental efficient causality of Christ's human nature.

235 *ST* III, q.22, a.2 (*Summa theologiae* 4: 2565b): "Et ideo omne illud quod Deo exhibetur ad hoc quod spiritus hominis feratur in Deum, potest dici sacrificium."

God.[236] "These moreover," Thomas writes, "have come to us through the humanity of Christ."[237] Christ took away our sin (Romans 4:25), making saving grace (Hebrews 5:9) and the inheritance of glory (Hebrews 10:19) available to us. All of this means that "Christ himself, inasmuch as a human being, was not only a priest, but also a perfect host, simultaneously emerging as host for sin, and peace-making host, and holocaust."[238]

Being both priest and host is a unique situation and raises some difficult questions. Thomas responds by discussing Christ's will. The first objection holds that a priest kills the host. Since Christ did not kill himself, he cannot be called both priest and host.[239] Thomas clarifies that a priest offers a host. Christ willed to die and expose himself to death, thus offering himself as a sacrifice.[240] Christ's free human action of willing the passion makes Christ both priest and sacrifice. Aquinas's response to the second objection distinguishes the will of Christ from the will of those who killed him. Comparing Christ's death to these different wills, Thomas can portray Christ's death as a host only through Christ's own will. Those who killed Christ cannot be said to have offered a sacrifice to God; rather, they committed a grave sin. Christ's death was a host according to his own will as the will of the one suffering.[241] The point

---

236 *ST* III, q.22, a.2 (*Summa theologiae* 4: 2565b): "Uno quidem modo ad remissionem peccati, per quod a Deo avertitur .... Secundo, ut homo in statu gratiae conservetur, semper Deo inhaerens, in quo eius pax et salus consistit .... Tertio, ad hoc quod spiritus hominis perfecte Deo uniatur; quod maxime erit in gloria."
237 *ST* III, q.22, a.2 (*Summa theologiae* 4: 2565b): "Haec autem per humanitatem Christi nobis provenerunt."
238 *ST* III, q.22, a.2 (*Summa theologiae* 4: 2565b): "Et ideo ipse Christus, inquantum homo, non solum fuit sacerdos, sed etiam hostia perfecta, simul existens hostia pro peccato, et hostia pacifica, et holocaustum."
239 *ST* III, q.22, a.2, ob.1 (*Summa theologiae* 4: 2565a): "Sacerdotis enim est hostiam occidere. Sed Christus non seipsum occidit. Ergo ipse non fuit simul sacerdos et hostia."
240 *ST* III, q.22, a.2, *ad* 1 (*Summa theologiae* 4: 2565b–2566a): "Dicendum quod Christus non se occidit, sed seipsum voluntarie morti exposuit .... Et ideo dicitur seipsum obtulisse."
241 *ST* III, q.22, a.2, *ad* 2 (*Summa theologiae* 4: 2566a): "Dicendum quod hominis Christi occisio potest ad duplicem voluntatem comparari. Uno modo, ad voluntatem occidentium. Et sic non habet rationem hostiae; non enim dicuntur occisores Christi hostiam Deo obtulisse, sed graviter deliquisse .... Alio modo potest considerari occisio Christi per comparationem ad voluntatem patientis, qui voluntarie se obtulit passioni. Et ex hace parte habet rationem hostiae." See also *Super Heb.* 9.5.

is that the sacrifice of the cross depends on Christ's will to undergo death for salvation. Christ's human will must will this suffering, and it is this will that makes Christ's death a sacrifice and makes Christ a host. Christ's redeeming work depends upon the perfect functioning of his human will. Christ as a human being (*secundum quod homo*) wills the passion for the sake of salvation. This all relates to Christ's humanity as instrument of his divinity sharing in the divine power for the purpose of salvation.[242]

Christ as Mediator

ST III, qq.25 and 26 examine what is fitting to Christ in comparison to us. Thomas first discusses the adoration owed to Christ and then Christ as mediator between God and human beings. The latter issue is of greater concern here. Christ as both wayfarer and comprehensor (q.15, a.10) recapitulated the entire section on the nature assumed. The final article of question 26 (on Christ as mediator *secundum quod homo*) serves a parallel function, summarizing the whole of the section on the consequences of the union. This summary distills the consequences, demonstrating the value of the entire section and preparing for qq.27–59 on what Christ did and underwent in the flesh (*acta et passa Christ in carne*), otherwise known as the mysteries of the life of Christ.[243]

Subtle but important changes distinguish the *Summa*'s treatment of this topic from that of the *Scriptum*.[244] On the whole, question 26 can be read as a commentary on I Timothy 2:5: "There is one mediator between

---

242 Thomas discusses Christ's sacrifice as efficacious to remove all sins in terms of Christ's humanity. In *ST* III, q.22, a.3, *ad* 1, Thomas first notes that Christ is priest *secundum quod homo* and that the one who is the priest is also God. This allows for his later assertion that "inquantum eius humanitas operabatur in virtute divinitatis, illud sacrificium erat efficacissimum ad delenda peccata" (*ST* III, q.22, a.3, *ad* 1 [*Summa theologiae* 4: 2567a]).
243 If Catão is correct in characterizing qq.18–59 as addressing Christ's actions in principle (qq.18–19), in general (qq.20–26), and in particular (qq.27–59), question 26 completes the general principles of Christ's actions and provides the final rule for interpreting Christ's particular actions.
244 See *in* III, d.19, a.5, qua.2; *De veritate*, q.29, a.5, *ad* 5. Thomas's commentary on I Timothy bears the mark of this development in Thomas's thought, though in an incomplete form (see *in I Tim.* c.2, lectio 1).

God and man, the man Jesus Christ."²⁴⁵ The parallels between Christ as priest and Christ as mediator are important. Thomas argues that Christ was fittingly a priest acting as a mediator between God and humankind (q.22, a.1). This connection grounds a denial that being mediator was proper to Christ (q.26, a.1, ob.1). Aquinas must respond to this and similar objections in affirming Christ as the one mediator. The *sed contra* of article one simply quotes I Timothy 2:5, but Thomas's response unfolds through analysis of what it means to be a mediator.

He stipulates that "it pertains to the office of mediator to conjoin and to unite those between whom the mediator stands, for extremes are united in the middle."²⁴⁶ This office is perfectly fitting to Christ, because humanity is united to God perfectly through the reconciliation of Christ. "And so," Thomas argues, "Christ alone is the perfect mediator of God and human beings, inasmuch as through his death the human race was reconciled to God."²⁴⁷ This does not prohibit others from being mediators in a secondary sense. Thomas describes such a mediatorship as cooperating in Christ's work of uniting humanity with God. The role played by these secondary mediators is purely dispositive or ministerial.²⁴⁸ This final point is of great interest, for in Thomas's early writings he, following his contem-

---

245 I Timothy 2:5: "Unus est mediator Dei et hominum, homo Iesus Christus." The best treatment of Christ as mediator in Aquinas is Gérard Remy, "Le Christ médiateur dans l'œuvre de saint Thomas d'Aquin," *Revue thomiste* 93 (1993): 183–233.
246 *ST* III, q.26, a.1 (*Summa theologiae* 4: 2585a): "Dicendum quod ad mediatoris officium proprie pertinet conjungere et unire eos inter quos est mediator, nam extrema uniuntur in medio."
247 *ST* III, q.26, a.1 (*Summa theologiae* 4: 2585a): "Et ideo solus Christus est perfectus Dei et hominum mediator, inquantum per suam mortem humanum genus Deo reconciliavit."
248 *ST* III, q.26, a.1 (*Summa theologiae* 4: 2585a): "Nihil tamen prohibet aliquos alios secundum quid dici mediatores inter Deum et homines, prout scilicet cooperantur ad unionem hominum cum Deo dispositive vel ministerialiter." Thomas assigns the same role to the angels, whom Pseudo-Dionysius calls mediators as constituted in being below God but above humanity. "Dionysius tamen dicit eos esse medios, quia secundum gradum naturae sunt infra Deum et supra homines constituti. Et mediatoris officium exercent, non quidem principaliter et perfective, sed ministerialiter et dispositive" (*ST* III, q.26, a.1, *ad* 2 [*Summa theologiae* 4: 2585b]).

poraries, limits the causality of Christ's human nature to dispositive and meritorious modes.[249]

Thomas completes the section on the consequences of the union by asking whether Christ was the mediator of God and human beings *secundum quod homo*. At first glance, this article might seem to hold little of interest. Does I Timothy 2:5 not settle the matter definitively? Does *ST* III, q.26, a.2 not express the same opinion as *in* III, d.19, a.5, qua.2 and *De veritate* q.29, a.5, *ad* 5? Is this not the same opinion expressed by Bonaventure and Albert the Great? At first glance it might well appear that the *Summa* repeats the familiar answer to this question handed down by Albert and by Bonaventure,[250] the very answer provided by Thomas in his early works. Under such a reading, this article would make no strong claim to recapitulate the entire section on the consequences of the union. Certainly it would make no claim to express a novel view about the salvific work of Christ's humanity. Such appearances would be deceiving. This article benefits from a slight shift in terminology, which marks a larger conceptual shift regarding the instrumental causality of Christ's humanity.

---

249 In the *Scriptum*, Thomas portrays the salvific causality of Christ's human nature only as meritorious and dispositive, not efficient (see *in* III, d.18, a.6, qua.1). The *De veritate* stresses Christ's possession of habitual grace beyond the grace of union in order to be mediator and head of the church (*De veritate*, q.29, a.5, *ad* 5). For discussions of the shift in Thomas's thought between the *Scriptum* and *Summa*, usually believed to begin with the *De veritate*, see Tschipke, *L'humanité du Christ*, pp. 115–121 and Torrell, "La causalité salvifique," pp. 180–185. Here the difference concerns not only the mode of causality but also the action. Christ is perfect mediator through his freely willed passion.

250 Bonaventure frames the entire question in terms of nature. After asking about a medium, Bonaventure turns to mediator. "Si vero quaeratur qualiter et secundum quam naturam Christus sit mediator, cum mediator dicat officium reconciliationis et mediator debeat differre ab illis quos reconciliat et Christus secundum divinam naturam sit ille cui fit reconciliatio, dicendum quod non potest esse mediator secundum divinam naturam, sed secundum humanam, in qua potest reconciliare secundum diversas proprietates, in quibus communicat cum Deo et cum homine" (*Commentaria in* III *Sententiarum*, d.19, a.2, q.2 [*Opera theologica selecta* 3: 403b]).

In his earlier works, Thomas generally refers to Christ as the one mediator *secundum humanam naturam*.[251] Discerning the meaning of this difference requires us to recall q.16, a.10, where Thomas introduces the phrase

[251] "Christo autem secundum humanam naturam *haec tria* conveniunt. – *Ipse* enim secundum humanam naturam pro hominibus satisfaciens, *homines Deo conjuxit*. – *Ipse* etiam *ab utroque extremorum aliquid participat*, inquantum homo: a Deo quidem beatitudinem, ab hominibus autem infirmitatem. – *Ipse* etiam inquantum homo, *supra homines fuit* per pleniudem gratiarum et unionem, *et infra Deum* propter naturam creatam assumptam. Et ideo, proprie loquendo ratione humanae naturae est mediator" (*in* III, d.19, a.5, qua.2 [*Scriptum* 3: 603]). Thomas's use of *inquantum homo* is not here in all respects equivalent to *secundum quod homo*. That is, the *Scriptum* seems to make no distinction between *secundum humanam naturam* and *inquantum homo*. Thomas does use the phrase *secundum quod homo* in the *Scriptum* (see *in* III, d.10, q.1, aa.1 and 2; d.11, q.1, a.3). Aquinas recognizes the double use of *secundum quod homo* (i.e. for nature and for supposit) with reservation, holding that it properly refers to the supposit only with a demonstrative adjective (*in* III, d.10, a.1, a.1, qua.1). The *Scriptum* also distinguishes abstract and concrete predication and distinct and indistinct predication. The terminological framework already exists in the *Scriptum*, but it is not fully utilized until the *Summa*. "Ad quintum dicendum, quod Christus est mediator Dei et hominum etiam secundum humanam naturam, in quantum cum hominibus habet passibilitatem, cum Deo vero iustitiam, quae est in eo per gratiam: et ideo requiritur praeter unionem habitualis gratia in Christo ad hoc quod sit mediator et caput" (*De veritate* q.29, a.5, *ad* 5 [*Quaestiones disputatae et quaestiones duodecim quodlibetales* 4: 341a]). "Ad nonum dicendum, quod Christus, secundum quod homo, mediator est inter Deum et homines, ut dicitur *I Tim.II, 5*. Unde, sicut Deus *dupliciter* nos iustificare dicitur, *principaliter* scilicet *per actionem suam*, in quantum est causa *efficiens* nostrae salutis, et etiam *per operationem nostram* in quantum est *finis* a nobis cognitus et amatus; ita etiam Christus, secundum quod homo, *dupliciter* nos iustificare dicitur. *Uno modo* secundum suam actionem, in quantum nobis meruit et pro nobis satisfecit; et quantum ad hoc non poterat dici caput Ecclesiae ante Incarnationem. *Alio modo* per operationem nostram in ipsum secundum quod dicimur per fidem eius iustificare; et per hunc modum etiam poterat esse caput Ecclesiae ante Incarnationem secundum humanitatem. *Utroque* autem *modo* est caput Ecclesiae secundum divinitatem, et ante et post" (*De veritate* q.29, a.4, *ad* 9 [*Quaestiones disputatae et quaestiones duodecim quodlibetales* 4: 339a]). These passages from the *De veritate* indicate that Thomas, in his early writings, made no consistent distinction between *secundum quod homo* and *secundum humanam naturam* and that he regarded Christ as mediator *secundum humanam naturam*. Thomas's commentary on *I Timothy* (ca. 1265-1268) already uses the terminology of *secundum quod homo*. "Et potest dici, quod Christus mediator est similis utrique extremo, scilicet Deo et homini inquantum Deus et inquantum homo, quia medium debet

secundum quod homo. Aquinas argues that a reduplicative term can signify either the supposit or (and more properly) the nature. The term *homo* can either be taken materially for the supposit or formally for the nature. Taken formally, *secundum quod homo* differs little from *secundum humanam naturam*. It could be argued that *secundum quod homo* indicates human nature in a more concrete fashion than does *secundum humanam naturam*. *Humanam naturam* expresses the nature purely in the abstract, while *homo* expresses the nature in the concrete, though indistinctly. Taken materially, *secundum quod homo* indicates the supposit as one having human nature distinctly. Both senses are operative in q.26, a.2, and it is through the interplay of the two senses that Thomas can craft his novel presentation of instrumental efficient causality. These two senses of *secundum quod homo* (formally for nature and materially for supposit) will be referred to frequently in the following pages.

The objections offer an interesting series of challenges. The basic problem with each objection is a failure to grasp the double signification of *secundum quod homo*. First it is argued that Christ is mediator as both the Son of God and the son of man. The objection continues that these are affirmed of Christ not only as God or only as a human being but as simultaneously both. The objection reaches the negative conclusion that Christ was not mediator only *secundum quod homo*.[252] The second objection more radically denies the title 'mediator' of Christ. Christ, inasmuch as God, 'fits' with the Father and the Holy Spirit. The *Glossa ordinaria* on I Timothy 2:5 maintains that Christ, inasmuch as God, cannot be a medium; thus, inas-

---

habere aliquid de utroque extremorum. Et haec sunt homo et Deus. Sed quia medium est distinctum ab utroque extremorum, et Filius non est alius Deus a Patre, ideo melius est dicendum quod mediator est secundum quod homo. Sic enim communicat cum utroque extremorum" (*in I Timothy*, c.2, lectio 1, ed. Raphaele Cai [Turin, 1953], 2: 225, n.64). Catão regards Thomas's *Commentary on I Timothy* as an early work. "Cette dernière distinction entre l'effet suffisant et l'effet efficace ou effectué, qu'on ne retrouve que dans les premières œuvres de saint Thomas, nous invite à situer le *commentaire de la première Épître à Timothée* dans la première période de l'enseignement de saint Thomas" (Catão, *Salut et rédemption*, p. 97).

252 *ST* III, q.26, a.2, ob.1 (*Summa theologiae* 4: 2586a): "Sed non est Dei et hominis Filius secundum quod homo, sed simul secundum quod Deus et homo. Ergo neque dicendum est quod sit mediator Dei et hominum solum secundum quod homo."

much as God, Christ fits with God and cannot be a medium or mediator. The objection extends this logic in the opposite direction. Christ, inasmuch as an individual human being, fits with human beings and cannot be called a medium or mediator.[253] Inasmuch as he is an individual human being, Christ is not a middle point between God and human beings but himself a human being, one of the extremes rather than a medium. The final objection holds that Christ was mediator inasmuch as he is God. "Christ is called mediator inasmuch as he reconciled us with God," which involved the remission of sin.[254] The objection continues that "to bear away sin befits Christ not inasmuch as a human being, but inasmuch as God," and so the attribution of mediator should be made of Christ as God.[255]

The *sed contra* features a quotation from Augustine's *De civitate Dei*, IX.15 that identifies Christ as mediator *secundum quod homo*. Thomas's choice of this quotation, which employs *secundum quod homo* rather than *secundum humanam naturam*, testifies to this terminological shift rather than inspires it.[256] This becomes clear in the *corpus*, which first notes two characteristics of a mediator. A mediator must be a medium between extremes and fulfill the office of conjoining. Thomas holds that "it belongs to the definition of medium that it be distant from both of the extremes; however, a mediator conjoins through this, that it confers what belongs to

---

253 *ST* III, q.26, a.2, ob.2 (*Summa theologiae* 4: 2586a): "Sicut Christus, inquantum est Deus, convenit cum Patre et Spiritu Sancto, ita inquantum est homo, convenit cum hominibus. Sed propter hoc quod inquantum est Deus, convenit cum Patre et Spiritu Sancto, non potest dici mediator inquantum est Deus.... Ergo nec etiam inquantum est homo potest dici mediator, propter convenientiam quam cum hominibus habet."
254 *ST* III, q.26, a.2, ob.3 (*Summa theologiae* 4: 2586a): "Christus dicitur mediator inquantum reconciliavit nos Deo; quod quidem fecit auferendo peccatum, quod nos separabat a Deo."
255 *ST* III, q.26, a.2, ob.3 (*Summa theologiae* 4: 2586a): "Sed auferre peccatum convenit Christo non inquantum est homo, sed inquantum est Deus. Ergo Christus inquantum est homo, non est mediator, sed inquantum est Deus."
256 Again, Thomas uses *secundum quod homo* already in the *Scriptum*. The terminology is not novel, but its application in this context is. The *Scriptum* recognizes the possibility of taking *secundum quod homo* for the suppost but regards it as somewhat improper without the addition of a demonstrative adjective. Thomas's use of *secundum quod homo* in the *Scriptum* is very similar to his use of *secundum humanam naturam*. In the *Summa* Thomas still takes *secundum quod homo* to refer more properly to the nature. However, it can refer to suppost even without a demonstrative adjective.

one [of the extremes] to the other."²⁵⁷ These are true of Christ only *secundum quod homo*, not *secundum quod Deus*. Christ *secundum quod Deus* perfectly is the same divine nature as the Father and the Holy Spirit and equally shares the divine power. Christ *secundum quod Deus* does not fit the definition of a medium, for the Word of God is not distant from the extreme of God. Nor, Aquinas argues, do the Father and the Holy Spirit possess anything other than what the Son possesses. Christ *secundum quod Deus* cannot fulfill the office of conjoining; whatever of the divine nature or grace the person of the Word bestows to humanity is not the possession of someone other than the Word.²⁵⁸

Thomas argues that "each befits him inasmuch as he is a human being."²⁵⁹ As a human being, a distance in nature separates Christ from God. Christ's dignity, grace, and glory distance him from other human beings. "Inasmuch as he is a human being," Thomas writes, "it befits him to conjoin human beings to God, by showing the instructions and gifts of God to human beings, and by making satisfaction and entreaties to God for human beings."²⁶⁰ Thomas concludes that Christ is most truly called mediator *secundum quod homo*.²⁶¹ The responses to the objections add some

---

257 *ST* III, q.26, a.2 (*Summa theologiae* 4: 2586a–2586b): "Dicendum quod in mediatore duo possumus considerare: primo quidem rationem medii; secundo, officium coniungendi. Est autem de ratione medii quod distet ab utroque extremorum; coniungit autem mediator per hoc quod ea quae unius sunt, defert ad alterum."
258 Every grace or gift of the divine nature that the person of the Word bestows upon humanity belongs to the Word.
259 *ST* III, q.26, a.2 (*Summa theologiae* 4: 2586b): "Sed utrumque convenit ei inquantum est homo."
260 *ST* III, q.26, a.2 (*Summa theologiae* 4: 2586b): "Inquantum etiam est homo, convenit ei coniungere homines Deo, preacepta et dona Dei hominibus exhibendo, et pro hominibus Deo satisfaciendo et interpellando." It should be stressed that Christ performs the office of mediator through entreaties and making satisfaction. Both of these functions rest upon the perfect obedience of Christ's human will acting with the divine power. See *ST* III, q.7, a.1, where Thomas names Christ as mediator *inquantum homo* in order to defend Christ's habitual grace.
261 Thomas offers a similar line of argumentation when discussing Christ as redeemer. *ST* III, q.48, a.5 (*Summa theologiae* 4: 2738b): "Unde utrumque istorum ad Christum pertinet immediate inquantum est homo; sed ad totam Trinitatem sicut ad causam primam et remotam, cuius erat et ipsa vita Christi sicut primi actoris, et a qua inspiratum fuit ipsi homini Christo ut pateretur

immediate clarifications. Aquinas replies that if the divine nature is taken away from Christ, then he loses all the fullness of grace that makes him a medium between God and human beings.[262] Here the import of the terminological shift from Christ as mediator *secundum humanam naturam* to Christ as mediator *secundum quod homo* comes into view. Removal of the divine nature alters Christ *secundum quod homo* but not *secundum humanam naturam*. That is, removal of the divine nature does not alter Christ's human nature considered in the abstract. This removal drastically alters Christ *secundum quod homo*, for this refers to Christ's human nature in the concrete, as an individual subsists in it. The individual in question is the person of the Word, so removal of the divine nature removes the very constitution of this concrete human individual as well as the ability of that human free will to produce a divine effect through instrumental efficient causality.

The second objection seeks to exclude the title of mediator altogether. Thomas declines the parallel supported by the objection. Though Christ *secundum quod Deus* is in all respects equal to the Father, Christ *secundum quod homo* exceeds every other human being. Christ's relationship to these extremes is not symmetrical. "And therefore," Thomas concludes, "*secundum quod homo*, [Christ] can be mediator; but not *secundum quod Deus*."[263] This also contradicts the third objection's claim that Christ was mediator only *inquantum est Deus*. The reply to the third objection develops a point from the *corpus*, which argued that Christ *secundum quod homo* made satisfaction to God for human beings. Aquinas clarifies that "although to bear away sin as author of the action befits Christ *secundum quod est Deus*, neverthe-

---

pro nobis. Et ideo esse immediate Redemptorem proprium est Christi inquantum est homo, quamvis ipsa redemptio possit attribui toti Trinitati sicut primae causae."

262 *ST* III, q.26, a.2, *ad* 1 (*Summa theologiae* 4: 2586b): "Dicendum quod si subtrahatur divina natura a Christo, subtrahetur per consequens ab eo singularis plenitudo gratiarum.... Ex qua quidem plenitudine habet ut sit super omnes homines constitutus, et propinquius ad Deum accedens."

263 *ST* III, q.26, a.2, *ad* 2 (*Summa theologiae* 4: 2586b): "Dicendum quod Christus, secundum quod Deus, est per omnia aequalis Patri. Sed etiam in humana natura excedit alios homines. Et ideo secundum quod homo, potest esse mediator; non autem secundum quod Deus."

less to make satisfaction for the sin of the human race befits him *secundum quod est homo*. And, according to this, [Christ] is called mediator of God and human beings."[264]

Understanding Thomas's response to the third objection requires a short discursus concerning instrumental efficient causality. John of Damascus described Christ's human nature as an instrument of his divinity (*instrumentum divinitatis*, ὄργανον τῆς θεότητος).[265] Given the import of the *De fide orthodoxa* in scholastic theology, and particularly the import of its third book for thirteenth-century Christology, it is remarkable that Thomas Aquinas was the first scholastic theologian to use the phrase *instrumentum divinitatis* to describe Christ's human nature.[266] Thomas employs the phrase already in the *Scriptum*, but his conception of Christ's instrumental causality developed notably between the *Scriptum* and the

---

264 *ST* III, q.26, a.2, *ad* 3 (*Summa theologiae* 4: 2586b): "Dicendum quod licet auctoritative peccatum auferre conveniat Christo secundum quod est Deus, tamen satisfacere pro peccato humani generis convenit ei secundum quod est homo. Et secundum hoc dicitur Dei et hominum mediator."

265 *De fide orthodoxa* III.15 (De fide orthodoxa: *Versions of Burgundio and Cerbanus*, ed. Eloi Marie Buytaert [Bonaventure, NY, 1955], p. 239): "Instrumentum enim caro deitatis extitit. Et si igitur ex summa conceptione nihil divisum fuit alterutrius formae, sed unius personae omnis temporis actus alterutrius formae facti sunt, tamen ipsa quae indivisibiliter facta sunt, secundum nullum modum confundimus, sed quid cuius fuerit formae ex operum qualitate sentimus."

266 "Si Thomas fut le premier scolastique latin à reprendre l'expression de l'ὄργανον τῆς θεότητος et le seul parmi les maîtres de la haute scolastique à exposer la doctrine de l'efficacité instrumentale de l'humanité du Christ, la théologie occidentale, qui lui était contemporaine ou antérieure, ne pouvait guère le stimuler; il fallut pour cela qu'il retourne aux sources de la théologie" (Tschipke, *L'humanité du Christ*, p. 136; see also pp. 105–106). Tschipke's study remains the best on this topic. See also Reynolds, "Philosophy as the Handmaid of Theology"; Torrell, "La causalité salvifique"; Paul G. Crowley, "*Instrumentum divinitatis* in Thomas Aquinas: Recovering the Divinity of Christ," *Theological Studies* 52 (1991): 451–475; Nicholas Crotty, "The Redemptive Role of Christ's Resurrection," *Thomist* 25 (1962): 54–106; Lécuyer, "La causalité efficiente"; Bouëssé, "La causalité efficiente instrumentale et la causalité méritoire"; and Hugon, "La causalité instrumentale de l'humanité sainte de Jésus." These studies tend to focus on the causality of Christ's resurrection or the physical instrumental causality of healing miracles.

Summa.²⁶⁷ The *Scriptum* describes the instrumental causality of Christ's human nature as only meritorious and dispositive (e.g. *in* III, d.18, a.6, qua.1).²⁶⁸ The *Summa theologiae*, in contrast, depicts Christ's humanity as an instrument participating in the power of the principal cause.²⁶⁹ What is the significance of this change?

Thomas's mature works make the strong and, by thirteenth-century standards, unparalleled claim that Christ's humanity is an instrumental efficient cause of salvation. God remains the principal cause, but Christ's humanity participates as an instrumental efficient cause in the divine power. Christ *secundum quod homo* makes satisfaction for human sin and acts as cause of salvation. Here the grammar of *secundum quod homo* is use-

---

267 Tschipke and Crotty argue convincingly for marked development in Thomas's thought on instrumental efficient causality between his earlier and later works. Reynolds disputes such development, writing that "one may as readily interpret Thomas's mature position as the result of economy and reticence as of theoretical advance" (Reynolds, "Philosophy as the Handmaid of Theology," p. 237). Granting the basic thesis of a development in Thomas's thought, the possible issue of dispute between Crotty and Tschipke becomes the reason for such development. Tschipke, following Backes, views this change as due to the influence of Greek theology mediated by the Damascene. Crotty disagrees and attributes the change to factors internal to Thomas's theological development. It is certainly possible to affirm development both through recovered sources and due to internal theological advancement.

268 On meritorious and dispositive causality in the *Scriptum*, see Lécuyer, "La causalité efficiente," p. 93 and Reynolds, "Philosophy as the Handmaid of Theology," p. 230. Tschipke adopts the language of a physical instrumental cause from M.-Benoît Lavaud, "Saint Thomas et la causalité physique instrumentale de la sainte humanité et des sacrements," *Revue thomiste* 32 (1927): 292–316. See Tschipke, *L'humanité du Christ*, p. 115. Thomas's departure from this early view begins already in the *De veritate* and is seemingly complete by the *Summa contra gentiles* (see Tschipke, *L'humanité du Christ*, pp. 121–126).

269 *ST* III, q.13, a.2 (*Summa theologiae* 4: 2508b): "Si autem loquamur de anima Christi secundum quod est instrumentum Verbi sibi uniti, sic habuit instrumentalem virtutem ad omnes immutationes miraculosas faciendas ordinabiles ad incarnationis finem, qui est instaurare omnia, sive quae in caelis, sive quae in terris sunt." *ST* III, q.19, a.1, *ad* 1 (*Summa theologiae* 4: 2552b): "Dicendum quod Dionysius ponit in Christo operationem 'theandricam', idest divinam virilem, vel divinam humanam, non per aliquam confusionem operationem seu virtutem utriusque naturae, sed per hoc quod divina operatio eius utitur humana, et humana eius operatio participat virtutem divinae operationis." See also *ST* III, q.43, a.2; q.56, a.1, *ad* 3.

ful, for this phrase designates both the principal cause of salvation in the person of the Word and the instrumental efficient cause in Christ's human nature. The person of the Word is the actor in all of Christ's actions. Each of Christ's human actions was the human action of the divine person of the Word and so expressed a theandric activity.[270] Christ's passion caused salvation not simply as a conduit for the divine power but as a freely willed sacrifice of the Word's hypostatically united rational instrument.[271] This particular arrangement was no more necessary for salvation than was the Incarnation itself; the instrumental efficient causality of Christ's human nature was, however, perfectly fitting.

270 *ST* III, q. 19, a. 1, *ad* 1 (*Summa theologiae* 4: 2552b): "Dicendum quod Dionysius point in Christo operationem 'theandricam', idest divinam virilem, vel divinam humanam, non per aliquem confusionem operationum seu virtutum utriusque naturae, sed per hoc quod divina operatio eius utitur humana, et humana eius operatio participat virtutem divinae operationis." "L'humanité du Christ produit instrumentalement le même effet que la divinité" (Tschipke, *L'humanité du Christ*, p. 169). "Because the Humanity was the instrument of the Divinity, its actions and passions not only affected the Humanity itself but exercised in our regard an efficient and salvific activity" (Crotty, "The Redemptive Role," p. 69). "Since according to the formula of John Damascene the Humanity of Christ is the instrument of His Divinity, it follows that the mysteries of that Humanity – all that it did or suffered – exercised a salvific efficiency that reaches out to each one of us, because they act in virtue of the divine power itself" (Crotty, "The Redemptive Role," p. 105). "Toute l'activité humaine du Christ reste humaine; cependant elle est toute divinisée par la divine subsistance et pour ce qui regarde le salut des hommes, elle est tout entière rendue divinement efficiente" (Bouëssé, "La causalité efficiente instrumentale et la causalité méritoire," p. 259).
271 "The Word is the subject as fully incarnate, as the bearer of the humanity. Both natures are in fact crucial to the account of Christ's salvific work. In the union of the two natures in the Word that is the person of Jesus, the God who alone can save and those who need the saving are in effect united. The Word is God; the Word incarnate is human, and as human works on our behalf to bring people to God, their end. The divinity of the Word supplies the efficacy of what Jesus does. God is the principal cause of salvation; what God does is of infinite value and effect. But God does not save apart from humans. Rather, in taking up human nature and making that humanity the Word's own, the Word of God has taken up what is the instrument for the working out of salvation" (Wawrykow, "Cross," in *The Westminster Handbook*, pp. 32–33).

This fittingness develops the basic logic of Anselm's satisfaction theory of atonement.[272] In his *Cur Deus homo*, Anselm argues that humanity owes everything to God always.[273] Sin occasions an infinite debt on top of what is already owed, which is everything. Humanity cannot repay this debt. God can pay the debt but has no obligation to do so. For humanity to achieve its created end of happiness in God, satisfaction must be made for this debt. Anselm deduces that the God-man can satisfy this debt and usher humanity toward the life of blessedness. A sinless God-man would not owe death as a penalty for sin and could sacrifice himself in payment of humanity's debt to God. The actions of the God-man would have the weight of the divine power and the obligation of humanity. This arrangement preserves both God's goodness and justice. Thomas incorporates, in rough outline, Anselm's satisfaction theory as one among many means of explaining the soteriological value of the incarnation, passion, and resurrection.[274]

272 Athanasius establishes a similar line of argumentation in his *On the Incarnation of the Word*, though presented in terms of fittingness rather than necessity. Aquinas cites this work thrice in the Christological questions of the *Tertia pars* (q.46, a.3, *ad* 1 and *ad* 3; q.50, a.1, ob.2), wrongly attributing it to John Chrysostom. Athanasius makes numerous references in *On the Incarnation* to Christ's human nature as 'organon' of his divinity. Thomas demonstrates no knowledge of such passages in the *Tertia pars*. The theory of satisfaction is most associated with Anselm, from whom Thomas draws. Anselm, however, was not the first to develop such lines of thought.

273 For a brief outline of Anselm's theory of satisfaction, see J. Patout Burns, "The Concept of Satisfaction in Medieval Redemption Theory," *Theological Studies* 36 (1975): 285–304; Bernard Sesboüé, *Jésus-Christ, l'unique Médiateur: Essai sur la rédemption et le salut* (Paris, 1988), pp. 329–345. See also Chapter one above.

274 In *ST* III, q.48, Thomas discusses the mode of Christ's passion in terms of its effects. Article two establishes that Christ caused salvation through the mode of satisfaction, though this certainly does not exclude the modes of merit (a.1), sacrifice (a.3), redemption (a.4), and efficiency (a.6). The mode of sacrifice is particularly related to the mode of satisfaction. For a discussion of the similarities and profound differences between Anselm and Aquinas on satisfaction, see Jerry Bracken, "Thomas Aquinas and Anselm's Satisfaction Theory," *Angelicum* 62 (1985): 501–530; Burns, "The Concept of Satisfaction," pp. 298–301; and Sesboüé, *Jésus-Christ, l'unique Médiateur*, pp. 345–350. Bracken emphasizes 'necessity' within Anselm's argument to the exclusion of appeal to fittingness or beauty. See also Caroline Walker Bynum, *Wonderful Blood: Theology and Practice in Late Medieval Northern Germany and Beyond* (Philadelphia, 2007). Bynum stresses that Anselm's theory was not set over and against Abelard's theory in the middle ages but rather both were viewed as aspects of one larger soteriology.

Anselm stresses that the sacrifice made by the God-man must be free to satisfy the debt of sin.[275] Anselm's presentation of this freedom relies on the divine will freely willing the passion and Christ's obedience to the Father's will. Thomas adopts the outline of Anselm's argument but follows out its implications more fully and with a stronger focus on fittingness.[276]

---

275 *Cur Deus homo* I.8–10. Balthasar stresses Anselm's view that human freedom is perfected in its conformity to the divine will. See Hans Urs von Balthasar, *Studies in Theological Style: Clerical Styles*, vol. 2 of *The Glory of the Lord: A Theological Aesthetics*, ed. John Riches, trans. A. Louth, F. McDonagh, and B. McNeil (San Francisco, 1984), especially pp. 237–253; and Balthasar, "La *concordantia libertatis* chez saint Anselme," in *L'homme devant Dieu: Mélanges offerts au Père Henri de Lubac* (Paris, 1963–1964) 2: 29–45.

276 Bracken stresses this point. "This is not the case with Thomas. Christ's death is due to more than a simple willingness to undergo what he was not obliged to undergo. From an analysis of the Passion account in the Gospel of Matthew (1256–1269), Thomas concludes that Christ, unlike other men, died of his own power. He actively engaged the dying process, giving it force and direction so that it turned into a positive act of handing his life over to the Father. Later, in the Easter *Quaestiones quodlibet* of 1269, Thomas explains how this was possible. Christ's power to lay down his life came from his divine nature. Nonetheless, it is a power his human will could call upon, in much the same way that the human will can call upon the power of the body to run faster. Because Christ participated in divine power, he could have kept his soul united to his body by an act of his human will, even though the body's wounds were great enough to dissolve that union. Christ did not just accept death, as other men can and are asked to do; he willed it. For Thomas there is a physical as well as moral force in Christ's willing to die" (Bracken, "Thomas Aquinas and Anselm's Satisfaction Theory," pp. 506–507). Bracken cites *Quodlibet* I, q.2, a.3 in support of this view but stretches this support too far in asserting that 'Christ's power to lay down his life comes from his divine nature.' As *ST* III, q.18, a.5 shows, Christ laid down his life according to his human will. Bracken and Sesboüé both stress Thomas's recasting of Anselm's argument in terms of fittingness rather than necessity. Catão focuses on the moral worth and merit of Christ's action as a freely willed sacrifice. "Saint Thomas ne fait pas appel à une compensation purement objective. La satisfaction n'est pas une 'chose' qu'on offre, indépendamment de la participation volontaire de celui pour qui on l'offre" (Catão, *Salut et rédemption*, p. 94). Catão reduces an Anselmian satisfaction theory to no more than a good analogy in Thomas (p. 79). This relates to Catão's 'personalist' (as opposed to 'juridical') reading of merit. For a critique of this aspect of Catão's argument, see Wawrykow, *God's Grace and Human Action*, pp. 31–32.

Christ serves as host or sacrifice according to his human nature.[277] This sacrifice will be truly free only if it is freely willed according to Christ's human nature. The divine will for the passion does not suffice to render it a free sacrifice. Only Christ's human will can freely will the passion as a sacrifice to make satisfaction.[278]

Thomas's mature position on the instrumental efficient causality of Christ's human nature rests soundly upon his presentation of Christ's human will. Christ freely willed the passion with his human will, and this free human will produced an effect commensurate with the divine power. By virtue of the hypostatic union, Christ is the one person of the Word subsisting in two perfect natures. The one acting subject of the two operations is the person of the Word. When the Word acts through its human operation, the actor is none other than God. The person of the Word, acting through its own human will, can freely will the passion. Discussing Thomas's analysis of instruments highlights the will's import.

Thomas offers two main considerations for an instrument: the type of instrument and its relation to the principal agent. The import of these two

---

[277] *ST* III, q.22, a.2 (*Summa theologiae* 4: 2565b): "Et ideo ipse Christus, inquantum homo, non solum fuit sacerdos, sed etiam hostia perfecta, simul existens hostia pro peccato, et hostia pacifica, et holocaustum." See also *ST* III, q.47, a.3 and a.4, *ad* 2, where Thomas stresses the voluntary character of the passion according to Christ's own will and that the sacrificial nature of the passion depends upon Christ's human will freely willing the passion out of charity.

[278] Reynolds argues against any noteworthy development in Thomas's conception of Christ's instrumental causality. "Whereas in his early work Thomas painstakingly constructs models of instrumentality that approximate to but fall short of efficient causality, in his late work he simply affirms that Christ is an efficient instrumental cause and leaves it at that" (Reynolds, "Philosophy as the Handmaid of Theology," p. 243). Reynolds's argument neglects the role of Christ's human will in this instrumental efficient causality and so fails to recognize Thomas's basic model for explaining instrumental efficient causality. Catão repeatedly stresses the role of Christ's human will in the passion. He recognizes merit and efficiency as two categories through which to examine one reality. *ST* III, q.48, a.6, *ad* 3 supports this. Catão perhaps separates these categories too severely. The presentation here will show that Christ's human will is the instrumental mover of the divine efficacy. This extends the role of Christ's human will beyond the mode of merit. See also J. Mark Armitage, "A Certain Rectitude of Order: Jesus and Justification according to Aquinas," *Thomist* 72 (2008): 45–66.

categories does not remain constant throughout Thomas's writings. In *ST* III, q.18, a.1, Thomas distinguishes inanimate, animate, and rational instruments.[279] Inanimate instruments are moved solely through bodily motion. A principal mover moves an animate instrument through the sensitive appetite. A rational instrument is moved by its will.[280] Aquinas offers a slightly different presentation in the *Summa contra gentiles*. The key distinction introduced in *SCG* IV.41 is between extrinsic, separate, and common instruments on the one hand and proper, united, and conjoined instruments on the other hand. Thomas notes that all human beings are extrinsic and separate instruments in relation to God. Christ's human nature was a proper and conjoined instrument.[281] Aquinas describes an ax as an extrinsic and common instrument, for it can be used by many different agents. A hand, by contrast, is a proper and conjoined instrument of the soul. Christ's human nature, Thomas cautiously affirms, is an instru-

---

279 In *De veritate* q.29, a.1, *ad* 9, Thomas distinguishes inanimate and animate instruments, but does not mention rational instruments. "Ad nonum dicendum, quod duplex est instrumentum: quoddam inanimatum, quod agitur et non agit, ut securis: et tale non indiget habitu; quoddam vero animatum, ut servus, quod agit et agitur: et hoc indiget habitu. Et tale instrumentum est humanitas divinitatis" (*De veritate* q.29, a.1, *ad* 9 [*Quaestiones disputatae et quaestiones duodecim quodlibetales* 4: 331a]).

280 *ST* III, q.18, a.1, *ad* 2 (*Summa theologiae* 4: 2544b): "Dicendum quod proprium est instrumenti quod moveatur a principali agente; diversimode tamen secundum proprietatem naturae ipsius. Nam instrumentum inanimatum, sicut securis aut serra, movetur ab artifice per solum motum corporalem. Instrumentum vero animatum anima sensibili movetur per appetitum sensitivum, sicut equus a sessore. Instrumentum vero animatum anima rationali movetur per voluntatem eius, sicut per imperium domini movetur servus ad aliquid agendum." See also *ST* I-II, q.6, a.1, *ad* 3.

281 Aquinas first describes Christ's humanity as a conjoined and proper instrument in the *Summa contra gentiles*. "C'est ici la première fois que Thomas caractérise l'humanité du Christ comme instrument conjoint et propre, à la différence des instruments extérieurs et maniables par tous" (Tschipke, *L'humanité du Christ*, p. 125). Tschipke argues that this marks a substantial terminological advancement in the *Summa contra gentiles*. This terminological and conceptual advancement signals a development with respect to the *Scriptum*. It remains to be seen whether there is further development in Thomas's thought on this issue between the *contra gentiles* and the *Summa theologiae*. Tschipke seems to regard rational, conjoined instrument as Thomas's mature and final presentation.

ment of his divinity as the body is the proper and conjoined instrument of the soul.[282]

Thomas's discussions of instruments in *ST* III, q.18, a.1, *ad* 2 and *SCG* IV.41 strive for different aims. The *Summa* introduces the distinction of types of instruments to explain how Christ's human nature can both move through its own rational will and be an instrument of his divinity. The *contra gentiles* seeks to illustrate the hypostatic union through the language of the Athanasian Creed. To this end, the *contra gentiles* stresses the relationship of body to soul as one of a proper and united instrument. Thomas must interpret the language of the Athanasian Creed in terms of instrumentality to avoid any misunderstanding that Christ's divinity serves as the form for his humanity, as a soul informs the body.[283] The *contra gentiles* employs the language of rational, conjoined instrument to illustrate the hypostatic union. The *Summa* describes types of instruments largely within the section on the consequences of the union.[284] This section provides rein-

---

282 *Summa contra gentiles* IV.41 (ed. D. Petrus Marc, Ceslas Pera, and D. Pietro Caramello [Turin, 1961], 3: 331, n.3798): "Aliter enim est animae organum corpus et eius partes, et aliter exteriora instrumenta. Haec enim dolabra non est proprium instrumentum, sicut haec manus: per dolabram enim multi possunt operari, sed haec manus ad propriam operationem huius animae deputatur. Propter quod manus est organum unitum et proprium: dolabra autem instrumentum exterius et commune. Sic igitur et in unione Dei et hominis considerari potest. Omnes enim homines comparantur ad Deum ut quaedam instrumenta quibus operatur: ipse *enim est qui operatur in* nobis *velle et perficere pro bona voluntate*, secundum Apostolum, *Philipp.* 2, 13. Sed alii homines comparantur ad Deum quasi instrumenta extrinseca et separata: movetur enim a Deo non ad operationes proprias sibi tantum, sed ad operationes communes omni rationali naturae, ut est intelligere veritatem, diligere bona, et operari iusta. Sed humana natura in Christo assumpta est ut instrumentaliter operetur ea quae sunt operationes propriae solius Dei, sicut est mundare peccata, illuminare mentes per gratiam, et introducere in perfectionem vitae aeternae. Comparatur igitur humana natura Christi ad Deum sicut instrumentum proprium et coniunctum, ut manus ad animam."

283 *SCG* IV.41 (ed. Marc et al., 3: 331, n.3799): "Nec discrepat a rerum naturalium consuetudine quod aliquid sit naturaliter proprium instrumentum alicuius quod tamen non est forma ipsius."

284 This again shows the import of the consequences of the union, of which Christ's theandric activity is one. "Le lien vraiment personnel entre la nature divine et la nature humaine dans l'ordre de l'être, ainsi que la plénitude de grâce de l'humanité du Christ qui en procède, exigent en ultime conséquence une unité correspondante effective des deux natures dans l'ordre de l'efficace,

forcement for Thomas's presentation of the hypostatic union from earlier questions and develops the soteriological import of that union. These different aims shape the presentation of each work; they do not, however, fully account for the differences.

Already in the *Summa contra gentiles* Thomas describes Christ's human nature as instrumentally operating works proper to God.[285] The *contra gentiles* and the *Summa theologiae* share this distinction from the *Scriptum* and *De veritate*. The *Summa* develops the notion of instrumental efficient causality more fully than does the *contra gentiles* and opts for a different terminology.[286] Scholars frequently apply the *Summa contra gentiles*'s terminology of rational, conjoined instrument to Thomas's view in the *Summa*. The *Summa*, however, does not retain this language but prefers the language of Christ's humanity as an instrument hypostatically united to the Word.[287] This terminological shift can be attributed to Thomas's

---

une convergence harmonieuse de leur effets, une inscription véritable de la nature humaine dans l'activité divine, jusqu'aux dernières limites du possible. En tirant ces conséquences de l'union hypostatique, Thomas signale comme plus haute perfection du Christ la puissance qui revient à son humanité en qualité d'instrument conjoint de la divinité" (Tschipke, *L'humanité du Christ*, p. 139). Thomas also notes Christ's humanity as a rational, united instrument in *ST* III, q.7, a.1, *ad* 1 and a.7.

285 *SCG* IV.41 (ed. Marc et al., 3: 331, n.3798): "Sed humana natura in Christo assumpta est ut instrumentaliter operetur ea quae sunt operationes propriae solius Dei, sicut est mundare peccata, illuminare mentes per gratiam, et introducere in perfectionem vitae aeternae."

286 See Tschipke, *L'humanité du Christ*, pp. 130–131.

287 This is not an absolute rule, for Thomas describes Christ's humanity as a conjoined instrument in his treatment of the sacraments. *ST* III, q.62, a.5 (*Summa theologiae* 4: 2862a): "Principalis autem causa efficiens gratiae est ipse Deus, ad quem comparatur humanitas Christi sicut instrumentum coniunctum, sacramentum autem sicut instrumentum separatum." Thomas returns to the language of conjoined instrument only to distinguish Christ's humanity from the sacraments. *De unione*, a.5 features a mixture of these languages. Thomas describes Christ's humanity as an instrument conjoined in unity of person. *De unione*, a.5, *ad* 1 (*Quaestiones disputatae et quaestiones duodecim quodlibetales* 5: 484a): "Et pro tanto dicitur nova actio facta, quia de novo factum est quod humanitas Christi est instrumentum divinitati coniunctum in unitate personae." More representative of the *Summa* are: "instrumentum ad unitatem hypostasis pertinens" (*ST* III, q.2, a.6, *ad* 4 [*Summa theologiae* 4: 2433a]), "instrumentum Verbi Dei sibi personaliter uniti" (*ST* III, q.13, a.2 [*Summa theologiae* 4: 2508b]), and "instrumentum unitum Verbo Dei in persona" (*ST* III, q.13, a.3 [*Summa theologiae* 4: 2510a]).

polemic against Nestorius in the *Summa theologiae*. Aquinas stresses the hypostatic union in contrast to a Nestorian view of two conjoined hypostases. From the acts of Constantinople II, Thomas knows that Nestorius described Christ's human hypostasis as conjoined to the hypostasis of the Word as an instrument in unity of operation.[288] Thomas's response to this view touches upon the distinction stressed in the *contra gentiles*. He writes that "not everything assumed as an instrument pertains to the hypostasis assuming, such as an ax or a sword; yet nothing prohibits what is assumed to unity of hypostasis to be possessed as an instrument" (*ST* III, q.2, a.6, *ad* 4).[289] This demonstrates Thomas's attention to the Nestorian threat and his care to guard the language of instrument against it. He counters the Nestorian portrayal of instrumentality by arguing along with the Damascene that Christ's human nature was an instrument pertaining to unity of hypostasis.[290]

It is worth lingering here on Thomas's presentation of Christ's human nature as a hypostatically united rational instrument. There are several points worth reiterating. Aquinas conceives every human being as a rational instrument of God, serving as a free secondary cause within the providential unfolding of history. God works through the free wills of individual human beings, but what distinguishes Christ's free human will is the identity of the person willing. By virtue of the hypostatic union, the subject of Christ's free human willing is the person of the Word. This enhances the instrumental causality of Christ's human will, granting it an efficient causality wholly superior to its nature.

The elements most relevant to understanding the *Summa*'s presentation of Christ as mediator *secundum quod homo* include the following: Thomas's recovery of patristic texts and acts of councils (particularly Ephesus, Chalcedon, Constantinople II and III), polemic against Nestorianism,

---

288 *ST* III, q.2, a.6 (*Summa theologiae* 4: 2431b): "Tertio secundum operationem, prout scilicet [Nestorius and Theodore of Mopsuestia] dicebant hominem illum esse Verbi Dei instrumentum."

289 *ST* III, q.2, a.6, *ad* 4 (*Summa theologiae* 4: 2432b): "Dicendum quod non omne quod assumitur ut instrumentum, pertinet ad hypostasim assumentis, sicut patet de securi et gladio; nihil tamen prohibet illud quod assumitur ad unitatem hypostasis, se habere ut instrumentum."

290 *ST* III, q.2, a.6, *ad* 4 (*Summa theologiae* 4: 2433a): "Damascenus autem posuit naturam humanam in Christo esse sicut instrumentum ad unitatem hypostasis pertinens."

mature understanding of instrumental efficient causality, heightened interest in Christ's human will and free choice, and the grammar of *secundum quod homo*. The final article of the *Summa*'s consideration of the mystery of the Incarnation summarizes that mystery with impressive success. The one subject in Christ is the hypostasis of the Word, subsisting in two perfect natures. The Word fittingly became incarnate for human salvation.[291] The Incarnation follows the divine goodness and wisdom. God became incarnate for human salvation; the most fitting way to achieve human salvation involved the divine power operating through human nature as an instrumental efficient cause. Prepared by the first twenty-five questions of the *Tertia pars*, readers of the *Summa* can appreciate the richness of Christ as mediator *secundum quod homo*.

With the issue framed thus, we can return to q.26, a.2, *ad* 3. Aquinas argues that "although to bear away sin as author of the action befits Christ *secundum quod est Deus*, nevertheless to make satisfaction for the sin of the human race befits him *secundum quod est homo*."[292] The phrase *secundum quod homo* indicates both Christ's human nature and the person of the Word, and thus includes Christ *secundum quod est homo*. The task of making satisfaction falls to Christ's humanity, through which the Word freely wills the passion as a sacrifice satisfying the debt of sin. This free human act can satisfy the debt of sin because it participates in the divine power. Christ's freely willed human act takes its efficacy from the divine operation (*ST* III, q.43, a.2; q.48, a.6). Since Christ's human will operates in communion with his divine operation (*ST* III, q.19, a.1), that human will wields the divine power (*ST* III, q.13, a.4). This is a remarkable stress on the role of Christ's human will in salvation. A perfect human will in obedience to God is the (instrumental) cause of salvation, crowning the fittingness of the Incarnation as the wisest means for redemption.

---

291 Aquinas describes this fittingness in terms of God becoming incarnate (*ST* III, q.1, a.1), of the Person of the Word assuming (*ST* III, q.3, a.8), and of the nature assumed (*ST* III, q.4, a.1). Fittingness arguments suffuse the *Tertia pars* and are Thomas's preferred way of defending the details of what the Word coassumed.
292 *ST* III, q.26, a.2, *ad* 3 (*Summa theologiae* 4: 2586b): "Dicendum quod licet auctoritative peccatum auferre conveniat Christo secundum quod est Deus, tamen satisfacere pro peccato humani generis convenit ei secundum quod est homo. Et secundum hoc dicitur Dei et hominum mediator."

Attention to fittingness pervades Thomas's Christology and explains its place within the whole of the *Summa theologiae*, following the pattern of scientific development and extending and illustrating the anthropological sections. Aquinas demonstrates remarkable care in exploring the truth and perfection of Christ's human nature. Thomas's extensive treatment of the human nature assumed rests upon his articulation of the hypostatic union, and that articulation safeguards his treatment of the nature assumed from various misinterpretations, chief among which is a two-subject Christology (Nestorius, *homo assumptus*). Aquinas's repeated references to Christ's humanity as *instrumentum divinitatis* avoid Nestorian overtones precisely because he specifes *instrumentum divinitatis* as a hypostatically united rational instrument. This both eliminates a Nestorian interpretation of instrumentality and elevates the soteriological role of Christ's human will.

The person of the Word is the one willer in Christ, but this does not restrict the free operation of Christ's human will. The rectitude of Christ's human will depends upon perfect grace and human knowledge. The centrality of the hypostatic union for Thomas's Christology does not eliminate or minimize the importance of treating Christ's perfection according to principles of human nature. The divine person willing does not force or restrict Christ's human will but provides it with a supernatural efficiency, which in no way obviates the need for grace or severes the connection of intellect and will. Thomas's presentation of Christ's grace and human knowledge make this abundantly clear. The relationship of grace, knowledge, and will reflects the import of Thomas's treatment of Christ's two wills.

The consequences of the union (qq.16–26) apply the grammar of the Incarnation developed in the section on the union itself (qq.2–15). This is most immediately apparent in the grammatical performance of question 16 (on what befits Christ in being and becoming). It is no less true in the remaining questions, where Thomas applies the 'rules' of an orthodox understanding of the hypostatic union under specific conditions. These conditions are not themselves logically deducible consequences of the union. The truth displayed by these circumstances is a consequence. Christ's possession of a human will is not itself the 'consequence', for it is included in the perfection of his human nature. Christ's unity of will, however, follows the union as ordered to salvation. Thus, the consequences apply the grammar of the Incarnation and demonstrate the truth of Christ's human nature in its perfections and defects. As the Incarnation is ordered to human salvation, the section on the consequences ends with consideration of Christ as mediator. Christ's mediatorship rests upon his perfect human nature causing human salvation through its free will as a hypostatically united, rational instrument. Thomas's treatment of Christ as mediator funnels gains from previous questions into a core principle of Christ's salvific work.

Question 16 analyzes the truth of certain statements. The consequence of the union at issue is not the fact but the truth of statements about that fact. The aspect of Thomas's discussion most relevant to the present consideration is the phrase *secundum quod homo* (see *ST* III, q.16, a.10). Thomas notes that the reduplicative term *homo* can be taken formally for nature or materially for supposit. The two senses of this phrase allow Thomas to express the determinate form of Christ's human nature according to the person of the Word. Christ's actions *secundum quod homo* involve the person of the Word acting through its proper human nature.

Christ's human nature receives its determinate form through the person of the Word. This determination by the hypostasis guides the *Summa*'s discussion of Christ's *esse* (q.17, a.2). The *Summa* affirms only one *esse* in Christ, the *esse* of the Word. The *De unione Verbi incarnati*, on the other hand, allows for a secondary *esse* in Christ. The difference between the *De unione* and the *Summa* on Christ's *esse* develops in part from their strategies to explain Christ as one in the neuter (*unum*). But what accounts for these different strategies? Thomas's recovery of the acts of Constantinople III focused his attention on Christ's two wills and operations. The secondary *esse* admitted in the *De unione* serves to ground Christ's perfect human operation. The *Summa* gathers together the topics of *esse*, will, and operation under the category of unity. This shift in focus allows the *Summa* to balance the integrity of Christ's human will and operation with their determinate form in the person of the Word. The *Summa*'s treatment of Christ's unity of will and operation specifies how Christ's human nature is an instrument of his divinity. The instrumental causality of Christ's human nature serves as a guiding theme in the *Summa*'s *Tertia pars*.

Discussion of instrumental causality in the *Summa* often focuses on Christ's resurrection as cause of the general resurrection and on the sacraments as instrumental efficient causes of grace (see *ST* III, q.62, a.1, *ad* 2).²⁹³ The instrumental efficient causality of Christ's human nature in the passion, and in all the *acta et passa*, relates to the resurrection as a willed act. Christ's actions as mediator *secundum quod homo* rely upon Christ's human will and operation. Thomas's presentation of the causality of Christ's resurrection stresses its instrumental efficient causality for the general resurrection (see *ST* III, q.56, a.1, *ad* 2 and *ad* 3; a.2; a.2, *ad* 2)²⁹⁴ and the causality of Christ's human will and operation for his own resurrection. Christ's soul wills the resurrection of his body, and this will instrumentally causes that bodily resurrection (*ST* III, q.13, a.4). Christ also causes his own resurrection through merit by freely willing the passion (*ST* III, q.54, a.4, *ad* 2).²⁹⁵ The instrumental efficient causality in all the *acta et passa Christi* is

---

293 See Liam G. Walsh, "Sacraments," in *The Theology of Thomas Aquinas*, ed. Rik Van Nieuwenhove and Joseph Wawrykow (Notre Dame, IN, 2005), pp. 326–364. Walsh observes that too much attention paid to efficient causality in the sacraments distracts from Thomas's understanding of formal and final causality. Walsh also demonstrates the intimate connection between Thomas's discussion of the sacraments in the *Tertia pars* and the first two parts of the *Summa*. These connections first find their concrete elaboration in Jesus Christ, whose passion causes grace through the sacraments. See Walsh, "Sacraments," pp. 327–328.

294 Thomas employs more ambiguous language here than one might expect, labeling the causality of Christ's resurrection *quasi* instrumental. *ST* III, q.56, a.1, *ad* 2 (*Summa theologiae* 4: 2787b): "Dicendum quod iustitia Dei est causa prima resurrectionis nostrae; resurrectio autem Christi est causa secundaria, et quasi instrumentalis." *ST* III, q.56, a.1, *ad* 3 (*Summa theologiae* 4: 2787b): "Dicendum quod resurrectio Christi non est, proprie loquendo, causa meritoria nostrae resurrectionis; sed est causa efficiens et exemplaris. Efficiens quidem inquantum humanitas Christi, secundum quam resurrexit, est quodammodo instrumentum divinitatis ipsius, et operatur in virtute eius, ut supra dictum est."

295 The instrumental efficient causality of the resurrection is identical to that of the passion. "In the earlier works St Thomas taught that the Death and the Resurrection both act efficiently. He taught also that the one is the exemplary cause of the remission of sin and of the destruction of death, the other the exemplary cause of positive justification and of the newness of life by grace. But obviously while we may distinguish in justification a negative and a positive element, these aspects cannot be separated, so that the efficient cause of the one must be the efficient cause of the other. It is equally obvious that the Passion of Christ must be the efficient cause of eternal life, if it is the efficient cause of the destruction of death, and His Resurrection must destroy death if

the same as the causality of his own bodily resurrection. That is, it all relates to Christ's free human will. The causality for the general resurrection also relies upon Christ freely willing the passion. In the case of the general resurrection, however, Christ's resurrection also operates as first mover within its genus. This involves both Christ's capital grace and exemplar causality. The sacraments, in contrast, are not instruments pertaining to unity of person, but separate instruments (see *ST* III, q.62, a.5). God's instrumental use of the sacraments is categorically different than God's use of Christ's human nature as an instrument hypostatically united to the Word.

The point of these remarks is first to distinguish the instrumental efficient causality of the sacraments from Christ's instrumental efficient causality as mediator. The second point is to stress that Christ's instrumental efficient causality as mediator, who *secundum quod homo* satisfies for sin, operates though Christ's human will.[296] This is not to suggest that proper understanding of Christ's human will is the indispensable key to Thomas's Christology. Proper understanding of Christ's human will, however, magnifies Aquinas's concern with Christ's perfect human nature and its role in the work of salvation. Christ's free human act of willing the passion for the sake of salvation causes (through instrumental efficient causality) that very salvation. Thomas's presentation of Christ's human will and operation provides a concrete demonstration of Christ's perfect human nature. By detailing Christ's human perfection, Thomas simultaneously completes the anthropology of the *Summa* and illustrates the moral exemplar, the fulfillment of the image of God, and humanity's capacity for God.

Thomas's consideration of the consequences of the union ends with Christ as mediator *secundum quod homo*. This mediatorship follows from the hypostatic union and expresses the fittingness of the Incarnation estab-

---

        it is the efficient cause of the newness of life. This difficulty is solved very simply by Thomas in the *Summa Theologiae*. While we distinguish the causality of the two mysteries on the basis of exemplarity, we do not make this distinction in the case of efficiency: under this aspect they act together as one cause – *per modum unius* – and are together the single cause of the two-fold effect" (Crotty, "The Redemptive Role," p. 86).

296 "Ce que le Christ décide de faire et fait, et tant qu'homme, par son *imperium* humain, volontairement donc, peut être un effet que seul Dieu a le pouvoir de produire, une œuvre miraculeuse ou la sanctification par la grace. C'est donc en tant qu'homme que le Christ donne la grace à tous les hommes et réalise le salut du genre humain" (Catão, *Salut et rédemption*, p. 151).

lished in *ST* III, q.1.[297] God became incarnate to redeem humanity from sin. All the consequences of the union lead to this. God could redeem humanity without the Incarnation, yet it was most fitting for salvation to occur through human agency. Thomas's presentation of the consequences of the union builds toward Christ's mediatorship. This in turn prepares for Aquinas's treatment of the *acta et passa Christi incarne* (qq.27–59), which take on new meaning when read as all salvific, as all particular instances of Christ's theandric activity.[298]

The investigation of the role of Christ's human will in Thomas's Christology allows a brief return to the plan or structure of the *Summa* discussed at the chapter's beginning. Chenu's original proposal of a circular *exitus-reditus* plan met with critiques and modified renewal. Modifications included a focus on modes of causality operative in the various parts of the *Summa*, a stronger connection between Incarnation and creation, and a presentation of fittingness that mitigates the extraordinary status of the *Tertia pars* in Chenu's presentation. Lafont, Torrell, and Narcisse sought to temper Chenu's proposal by balancing the gratuity of the Incarnation with its economic necessity.[299] This analysis shows that the Incarnation is the

---

[297] The Incarnation was the most fitting means for human salvation. Aquinas's arguments for this fittingness often repeat the basic lines of Anselm's theory of satisfaction. *ST* III, q.1, a.2, *ad* 2 (*Summa theologiae* 4: 2417a): "Dicendum quod aliqua satisfactio potest dici dupliciter sufficiens. Uno modo perfecte, quia est condigna per quandam adaequationem ad recompensationem culpae commissae. Et sic hominis puri satisfactio sufficiens esse non potuit pro peccato; tum quia tota humana natura erat per peccatum corrupta; nec bonum alicuius personae, vel etiam plurium, poterat per aequiparantiam totius naturae detrimentum recompensare; tum etiam quia peccatum contra Deum commissum quandam infinitatem habet ex infinitate divinae maiestatis; tanto enim offensa est gravior, quanto maior est ille in quem delinquitur. Unde oportuit, ad condignam satisfactionem, ut actus satisfacientis haberet efficaciam infinitam, utpote Dei et hominis existens."

[298] Catão's division of the *Tertia pars* between questions 17 and 18 supports this reading. See Catão, *Salut et rédemption*, pp. 42–43.

[299] Narcisse's definition of fittingness seeks to express this balance through the notion of a 'realized possible'. This definition does not sufficiently identify the role of goodness and wisdom in Thomas's fittingness arguments. The Incarnation was the most fitting means of salvation for the human race. Thomas grounds the 'why' of the Incarnation's fittingness in God's supreme goodness and the 'how' of the Incarnation's fittingness in God's supreme wisdom (though not without attention to God's power and justice).

most fitting means for human salvation also from the perspective of human need. The fittingness of the Incarnation depends not just on divine freedom but also on human freedom. It is fitting for salvation to occur on account of a free human act (parallel or in proportion to the entry of sin). The Incarnation is a contingent event. Its offer of salvation is a contingent event dependent upon Christ's free human will. The perfect obedience of Christ's free human will causes salvation according to instrumental efficient causality.

Discussion of the modes of causality in the *Summa* generally focuses on efficient, exemplar, and final causality. The presentation here has stressed the role of instrumental efficient causality in the *Tertia pars*, to which could be added the instrumental causality of the sacraments. The category of instrumental causality, whether efficient or sacramental, is no less significant in the *Tertia pars* than final or exemplar causality. The instrumental causality of Christ's human nature in the work of salvation supports the wisdom of discussing Christology in the *Tertia pars*. Christ's instrumental causality involves both the divine power and the free operation of the human will. Divine operation and human operation are hypostatically united in Christ. Thomas presents these hypostatically united operations only after first detailing these operations individually in the *Prima pars* and *Secunda pars*.

Thomas's teaching on Christ's two wills underwent development between the *Scriptum* and the *Summa*. Development is noteworthy not only in the details of each work's presentation but also in the role of this teaching within the *Summa*'s Christology. Chapter four has argued for shifts of emphasis, recovery of patristic and conciliar sources, terminological and conceptual advancements, and the condemnation of Latin Averroism as reasons for the development in Thomas's teaching. This chapter has situated Thomas's mature teaching on Christ's two wills within the larger movement of the *Summa*'s Christology, a movement that stresses the fittingness of the Incarnation both in terms of 'why' and 'how' as ordered by the divine goodness and divine wisdom. The divine wisdom orients every detail of the Incarnation toward the end of salvation. This orientation requires the utility of everything assumed or coassumed by the Word as well as the 'consequences of the union.' In the 'consequences,' Thomas applies the 'rules' of an orthodox understanding of the hypostatic union under determinate conditions. Thomas develops a notion of Christ's humanity as instrumental efficient cause of salvation, which requires

Christ's human nature to be a rational instrument operating through its free will. The instrumental efficient causality of Christ's human nature is centered in Christ's perfect human will freely willing salvation. This larger role of Christ's human will in the *Summa*'s Christology highlights the import of the developments noted in Chapter four. Thomas's discussion of Christ's unity of will assigns an awesome role to Christ's human will in the work of salvation.

CHAPTER SIX

Later Treatments of Christ's Wills and Problems of Christological Causation
Giles of Rome, Peter Olivi, and John Duns Scotus

The questions and concerns of scholastic reflections on Christ's wills from the late-thirteenth century, though indebted to earlier treatments, represent a significant shift in approach. Among the scholastics in the decades after Aquinas, John Duns Scotus stands apart for offering a novel, rich, and influential approach to Christ's wills. This is not apparent from a cursory examination of Scotus's *Lectura* III, d.17 and *Ordinatio* III, d.17, which cover a far narrower range of topics than earlier commentaries on III *Sent.* d.17. Questions of contrariety and conformity of wills, central to thirteenth-century discussions of Christ's wills, are absent from Scotus's commentaries on d.17. To the extent that Scotus does address such questions and concerns, he does so while exploring Christ's sorrow (*dolor*) and sadness (*tristitia*) (*Lec.* III, d.15; *Ord.* III, d.15), a context that changes the meaning and significance of contrariety and conformity of wills. Scotus's treatment of d.17 may appear somewhat flat or thin to the reader of thirteenth-century commentaries, who may notice only the topics omitted by the Subtle Doctor rather than the questions and concerns added by him. By the time of Scotus's commentaries on the *Sentences*, many of the pressing questions from thirteenth-century treatments of Christ's wills had lost their novelty or contested status. Scotus thus approached the topic of Christ's wills in a Christological context notably different from the contexts of theologians discussed in earlier chapters. This contextual difference must be kept in mind when analyzing and evaluating Scotus in light of previous thinkers. The present investigation will explore the contours and depth of Scotus's novel approach to Christ's wills, focusing on questions of causality, sorrow and sadness, and inner workings of the will. His understanding of Christological agency differs starkly from Thomas Aquinas's and raises certain important challenges to Aquinas's conception. Analyzing Scotus's treatment of Christ's wills thus provides an interesting term of comparison for earlier developments and isolates with particular clarity the systematic implications of the topic.

Before turning to Scotus on Christ's wills, this chapter will review Giles of Rome and Peter Olivi as significant figures in late thirteenth-century shifts in discussions of Christ's wills. Giles studied under Aquinas and so offers an interesting window into the reception – or lack thereof – of Aquinas's Christological refinements. Though he repeats standard aspects of thirteenth-century treatments of Christ's wills, Giles alters the focus of many arguments and issues while neglecting the larger implications of the topic. Olivi does not offer a sustained investigation of Christ's wills but does provide helpful reflections on Christ's wills in the course of investigating related topics. Most interesting for this chapter are Olivi's discussions of the whole Trinity as the cause of Christ's human actions and of the Word as causing them through the mode of supposit. His thought introduces a concern inherited and magnified by Scotus while preemptively resisting Scotus's own solution to this concern.

Giles of Rome, Peter Olivi, and Christology after 1277

Giles of Rome is thought to have studied with Aquinas in Paris from 1269–1272, slowly developing his own approach to topics and questions in the meantime.[1] The *reportatio* of Giles's lectures on the *Sentences* offers an early window into his theological and intellectual development.[2] Aquinas's influence on Giles's treatment of wills is palpable. Two short but very interesting questions from the *reportatio* on *Sent.* III address Christ's wills: q.28 ('Whether in Christ the irrational human will was conformed to the divine will in the thing willed') and q.29 ('Whether Christ's will of reason as reason was contrary to the will of sensuality'). Given the length and complexity of earlier discussions, Giles's consideration of Christ's wills can seem substantially inadequate and wholly unremarkable. This appearance is mis-

---

[1] For a brief discussion of Giles's life, see John R. Eastman, "Das Leben des Augustiner-Eremiten Aegidius Romanus (c. 1243–1316)," *Zeitschrift für Kirchengeschichte* 100 (1989): 318–339.

[2] Luna argues that Giles lectured on books III and IV of the *Sentences* in 1272–1273. See Concetta Luna, "La *Reportatio* della lettura di Egidio Romano sul libro III delle Sentenze (Clm. 8005) e il problema dell'autenticità dell'*Ordinatio*," in *Documenti e studi sulla tradizione filosofica medievale* 1 (1990): 113–225, 2 (1991): 75–146.

leading. Giles's discussion does not merely repeat earlier views in condensed form; rather, it subtly shifts the focus or meaning of those views.

In q.28 Giles quickly stipulates that as Christ's human will follows deliberative reason, it was conformed to the divine will such that Christ willed to die. When viewing the human will in terms of the natural will following reason as nature (*sequitur rationem ut naturam*), Christ's human will was not conformed to the divine will in the thing willed. An equally brief distinction is offered between the will *simpliciter* and *secundum quid*. The former is ordered to the end, and the latter, here identified with the natural will, regards the good absolutely or without an order to an end. The distinction reveals a larger conformity in the thing willed between Christ's human will and the divine will. Giles writes:

> It must be understood that when uniformly comparing Christ's will to the divine will, namely when comparing *simpliciter* to *simpliciter* and *secundum quid* to *secundum quid*, [Christ's human will] was conformed in the thing willed. God's antecedent will is the will *secundum quid*, by which God wills all to be saved, and by this will [God] willed Christ not to die, because [God] willed the good of human nature absolutely. Similarly, Christ willed not to die by the natural will, which is *secundum quid*. In parallel fashion, God willed Christ to die by [God's] consequent will, and this is the will *simpliciter*; likewise Christ, by the will *simpliciter* and as it is deliberative, willed Christ to die.[3]

Giles here formulates a standard argument for conformity of wills but does so through the non-standard terminology of God's antecedent and consequent wills. This terminological decision relates less to understandings of Christ's wills than to growing attention to questions of divine will and power.

---

3 Aegidius Romanus, *Reportatio* III, q.28 (ed. Concetta Luna, Opera omnia 3.2 [Florence, 2003], p. 426): "Intelligendum tamen quod, comparando uniformiter voluntatem Christi ad voluntatem divinam, conformatur in volito, comparando simpliciter ad simpliciter et secundum quid ad secundum quid, quia voluntas antecedens Dei est voluntas secundum quid, qua vult omnes salvos fieri, et hac voluntate vult Christum non mori, quia humane nature vult bonum absolute, et sic similiter voluntate naturali, que est secundum quid, vult Christus non mori. Similiter voluntate consequente vult Deus Christum mori, et hec est voluntas simpliciter; ita Christus, voluntate simpliciter et ut est deliberabilis, vult Christum mori."

Giles's treatment of contrariety similarly repeats a standard argument, beginning with the assertion that contrariety requires not simply contrary dispositions but rather one thing imposing or producing a contrary disposition in another. Contrariety between the sensitive and intellectual appetites arises when reason, succumbing to a passion of the sense, abandons its proper object and follows instead the contrary desire of the sensitive appetite. Christ's original justice, however, produced "such great obedience that, although sense wills one thing and reason something contrary, nevertheless one was not contrary to the other."[4] Aquinas also appeals to the perfect obedience of Christ's sensuality to reason, and Giles characterizes this obedience as sensuality not impeding reason or the operation of the rational will. Fitting the norms of a *reportatio*, Giles's lectures offer very brief considerations of these topics, focusing on the solution more than on the larger argumentation surrounding the question. Giles inherits and repeats earlier presentations of Christ's wills without dramatically altering them and without highlighting the grander import of the topic. More specifically, Giles's presentation reflects little of the complexity in Aquinas's Christological reflections from the same period.[5]

Peter Olivi's Christological reflections responded to the doctrinal questions raised during the last quarter of the thirteenth century. Stephen Tempier's condemnation of 219 propositions in 1277 offered no direct com-

---

4   Aegidius Romanus, *Reportatio* III, q.29 (Opera omnia 3.2: 426): "Sed in Christo ex originali iustitia tanta fuit obedientia quod, licet sensus vult unum et ratio contrarium, tamen una non contrariatur alteri, quia ratio vult secundum hoc velle, quamvis ipse velit contrarium."
5   For a presentation of Giles as developing Aquinas's understanding of the will in a more voluntarist direction, see. Peter S. Eardley, "Thomas Aquinas and Giles of Rome on the Will," *Review of Metaphysics* 56 (2003): 835–862. Luna argues that the *Ordinatio* on the *Sentences* attributed to Giles is inauthentic (Luna, "La *Reportatio* della lettura di Egidio Romano" 1: 130–157). The *Ordinatio* presents a narrow treatment of Christ's wills and argues that Christ's human will could be perfectly and simultaneously moved to multiple things on account of a divine dispensation. *Quaestiones super III Sententiarum*, d.17, a.1 (*Quaestiones super III Sententiarum* [Rome, 1623; repr. Frankfurt, 1968], 518): "Secundum autem has tres distinctiones, possunt solui tria praefata argumenta. Est enim veritas quaestionis, quod in plura se impedientia secundum naturae cursum, & perfecte non simul voluntas ferri potest: sed in plura se non impedientia, non quidem secundum naturae cursum, seu non perfecte, potest simul voluntas ferri."

mentary on or challenge to presentations of Christ's wills but did influence a host of related topics that ultimately came to bear on them.[6] These related topics include the unicity or plurality of substantial form, and freedom of will and choice from cognitive determinism. Debates about unicity or plurality of substantial form sparked new directions of reflection and, combined with new questions regarding the distinction between essence and *esse*, led to a dramatic shift in approaches to Christ's *esse*. This shift is apparent in Peter Olivi and Matthew of Aquasparta, who both defend a plurality of *esses* in Christ and liken a single-*esse* view to the Lombard's third opinion and to a denial that *Christus secundum quod homo est aliquid* (Christ as a human being was something). In other words, Olivi and Matthew hold that Christ truly "being" human requires an *esse* beyond the divine *esse*. These thinkers tie *esse* to will in similar manners. An argument *contra* from Matthew's *Quaestiones de incarnatione* 9 holds that a plurality of posterior acts in Christ, including *velle, intelligere, posse*, and *operari*, requires a plurality of prior acts, especially *esse*.[7]

Olivi's *Quaestiones de incarnatione et redemptione* (*QDI*) offer no dedicated or sustained discussion of Christ's wills but do contain many reflec-

---

6 The 1277 Condemnations are thought to have had a broad but indirect influence on discussions of the will. For an exploration of how the 1277 Condemnations changed Christological debates, see Joseph Wawrykow, "Thomas Aquinas and Christology after 1277," in *Nach der Verurteilung von 1277: Philosophie und Theologie an der Universität von Paris im letzten Viertel des 13. Jahrhunderts: Studien und Texte*, ed. Jan A. Aertsen, Kent Emery, Jr, and Andreas Speer (Berlin, 2001), pp. 299–319. For a reevaluation of frequent affirmation of a separate investigation against Aquinas, see J.M.M.H. Thijssen, "1277 Revisited: A New Interpretation of the Doctrinal Investigations of Thomas Aquinas and Giles of Rome," *Vivarium* 35 (1997): 72–101.

7 The second *sed contra* of Q.9 reads (*Quaestiones disputatae de incarnatione et redemptione et de lapsu aliaeque selectae de Christo et de eucharistiae*, ed. PP. Collegii S. Bonaventurae [Quaracchi, 1957], p. 174): "Item, plurificatis posterioribus, plurificantur priora. Sed in Christo actus posteriores plurificantur, quia in Christo sunt duo velle, duo intelligere, duo posse, duo operari; ergo plurificantur actus primi. Sed primus actus est esse; ergo pari ratione in Christo sunt plura esse." Matthew responds to the *contra* arguments together, noting that they should be conceded but that some express very little. Zachary Hayes offers a very clear treatment of Matthew on Christ's *esse* in "The Plurality of *Esse* in Christ according to Matthew of Aquasparta," in *Essays Honoring Allan B. Wolter*, ed. William A. Frank and Girard J. Etzkorn (St Bonaventure, NY, 1985), pp. 131–152.

tions directly relevant to the topic.[8] Since these reflections occur in various contexts, sewing them together into a treatment of Christ's wills results in a patchwork whole. Many topics remain unaddressed, and many questions remain unanswered. Despite the scattered and unsystematic nature of Olivi's references to Christ's wills, they provide a bridge from earlier thirteenth-century treatments of Christ's wills to John Duns Scotus's treatment. The foundation for Olivi's discussion of Christ's wills is the affirmation that the Word united a created will to itself personally. The Word is the supposit of the human nature and the human will assumed, yet having an alien supposit in no way undermines the human will's freedom. It is worth quoting Olivi at length:

> It should be said that to act by a person of God as by one's own supposit is not at all contrary to the freedom of rational nature, because a supposit in as much as it is a supposit is not a diverse mover from the nature or the power through which the supposit acts. And, although Christ's human nature does not have dominion over itself as its person does, it nevertheless has dominion over itself in as much as it freely brings about its actions through its own [*propriam*] freedom. Nor is [Christ's human nature] subjected in regards to its power to the power of a *quasi*-other mover, but [it is only subjected] as a nature to its supposit. This subjection of [the human nature's] liberty to [its supposit] provides firmness and stability of being, and consequently also [firmness and stability] of acting, rather than removes or diminishes liberty. Though it is subjected to the power of the three persons of God as to a first and principal mover, this in no way impedes its liberty but rather conserves and aids it. This is so because the condition of common created liberty is naturally and essentially to be subjected to its primary cause.[9]

---

8   On Olivi's life, works, and controversies, see David Burr, *The Persecution of Peter Olivi* (Philadelphia, 1976).

9   *QDI* 1 (*Quaestiones de incarnatione et redemptione: Quaestiones de virtutibus*, ed. Aquilinus Emmen and Ernst Stadter [Grottaferrata, 1981], pp. 31–32): "Ad quartum dicendum quod agi a Dei persona ut a proprio supposito, non est in aliquo contrarium libertati rationalis naturae; quia suppositum in quantum suppositum non habet rationem diversi motoris a natura seu potentia sua, per quam suppositum agit. Et licet natura Christi humana non sit domina sui ut persona sui ipsius, est tamen domina sui in quantum per propriam libertatem

Two points from this quotation deserve comment. Olivi affirms that supposits act through their natures and that natures are naturally subjected to their supposits. Since a free human will is personally united to the Word, the Word can, without loss to created freedom, freely will through its human will. Olivi also affirms that the three Trinitarian persons constitute the first and principal mover of Christ's human nature, a point Olivi reiterates and elaborates elsewhere.

According to Olivi, no created reality can depend causally on one person of the Trinity more than on another, but this does not prevent a created reality from having a personal dependence or a dependence respecting personal properties more on one person than on another. A created reality existing in personal dependence would depend upon the three Trinitarian persons more in one person than in the others. Given the interpenetration of the divine persons, a created reality personally existing in one divine person personally exists in the other divine persons as well. Olivi uses this scheme to explain the difficult reality of distinct personal dependence on one divine person together with personal and causal dependence on the whole Trinity. Christ's human nature personally depends upon the Word and in that personal dependence the Father and the Holy Spirit are equally present and intimate to Christ's human nature, though in a different respect.[10] Olivi thus presents the whole Trinity as performing the whole

---

libere agit actiones suas. Nec est subiecta eius potentiae in quantum est eius potentia quasi alteri motori, sed solum sicut natura suo supposito; quae subiecto suae libertati potius praebet firmitatem et stabilitatem essendi, ac per consequens et agendi, quam auferat vel minuat eam sibi. Licet autem sit subiecta potentiae trium personarum Dei tamquam primo et principali motori, hoc in nullo impedit eius libertatem, immo potius conservat et adiuvat; quia conditio communis creatae libertatis est naturaliter et essentialiter subiecta sua primae causae."

10 Olivi, *QDI*, q.1 (ed. Emmen, pp. 34–35): "Ad septimum dicendum quod, licet nihil creatum possit plus dependere ab una persona Dei quam ab altera, loquendo de dependentia causali, qua scilicet aliquid dependet ab altero tamquam a causa creante et conservante et movente, ac regulante et exemplante ac finiente, nihilominus potest plus dependere ab una personaliter seu tamquam a sua persona. Quod est dicere quod, licet nullo genere causalitatis possit plus esse ab una quam ab altera, secundum tamen quemdam modum essendi potest plus esse in una quam in alia. – Rursus, quantum ad hunc secundum modum sciendum quod, pro quanto quaelibet trium personarum Dei per modum circumincessivae identitatis tantum est in aliis personis quantum in se ipsa, pro tanto persona Patris et Spiritus Sancti ita

work of the satisfaction of Christ *sub ratione principii effectivi* and the Word alone as performing the whole work of satisfaction through the mode of supposit.[11] Olivi clarifies what he means by the Word alone performing or accomplishing satisfaction through the mode of supposit when discussing Christ's merit.

Christ could not sin yet could merit. This possibility for merit is grounded in Christ's freedom to have refused the passion without sin. Because Christ could have licitly refused the passion, he merited in freely willing the passion out of charity for the sake of human salvation. This freedom in willing the passion tempers somewhat Olivi's assertion that the divine will willed Christ's work of redemption from eternity, which could easily be interpreted as removing the freedom of Christ's passion. Olivi admits that Christ's whole soul accepted and willed the passion but qualifies this by noting that Christ's person impressed the will for this on its soul, thus locating Christ's freedom more fundamentally in person than in soul (*QDI*, q.2 [ed. Emmen, p.102]). Christ's soul is subject to the divine person of the Word and necessarily wills according to the free divine will for redemption. The person of the Word "freely performs [the work of redemption] and freely inclines and moves its soul to this" while personally remaining free to will otherwise.[12] Olivi finds this harmonious with the whole Trinity inclining and moving Christ's soul because the relation of Christ's soul to the whole Trinity in causal dependence differs from the relation of Christ's soul to the Word as its person. The meritorious freedom in Christ's willing the passion emanates from the person of the Word

---

    praesentialiter et ita intime attingitur a natura Christi humana – per hoc solum, quod existit in persona Verbi – sicut attingitur ipsamet persona Filii; licet sub alio respectu referatur ad hanc et ad illas propter distinctionem personalium proprietatum."

11 Olivi, *QDI*, q.3 (ed. Emmen, p. 209): "Tota etiam Trinitas sub ratione principii effectivi ita fecit totum opus satisfactionis Christi, sicut et ipsa persona Christi, quamvis ipsa sola hoc fecerit per modum suppositi: solam enim ipsa fuit suppositum illius operis."

12 Olivi, *QDI*, q.2 (ed. Emmen, p. 101): "Quamvis autem anima Christi, inquantum subiecta suae personae et voluntati eius, hoc necessario voluerit, tamen persona eius libere hoc fecit et animam suam ad hoc libere inclinavit et movit, cum, quantum est ex se et sua absoluta libertate, aliud licite posset. – Nec obstat huic dicto quod tota Trinitas inclinavit et movit animam Christi sicut et persona talis animae; et hoc libere fecti, ita quod hoc aliter facere posset."

as the person of Christ's soul. The dignity and nature of the Word grant Christ's merit a transcendent infinity and a certain measure of eternity.[13] Though the meritorious freedom of Christ's actions originates with the Word, this implies no compulsion of human nature by the Word's divine nature but only a proper subjection of human nature to God (*QDI*, q.2 [ed. Emmen, pp.118–119]). Christ's human will enjoyed a perfect subjection to God in willing something not only above its nature but also against its natural inclination (*QDI*, q.2 [ed. Emmen, p. 121]).

What we find in Olivi's *Quaestiones de incarnatione et redemptione* are scattered references to Christ's wills rather than systematic discussions of the topic, yet it remains instructive to compare the picture suggested by these references to earlier treatments of Christ's wills. Stated in the crudest fashion, Olivi's presentation recalls nothing so much as Anselm's considerations of Christ's voluntary acceptance of the passion, which focus heavily on the divine will freely willing the passion. Largely absent from Olivi's account are the standard thirteenth-century reflections on Christ's human will and the standard questions of conformity or contrariety of wills. Olivi touches upon these topics in mentioning the subjection of Christ's human will to the divine will, but his attention is directed primarily to Christ's infinite merit based upon the dignity of the person willing. Furthermore, Olivi insists upon the causality of the whole Trinity in the Incarnation and in Christ's human actions, thereby altering the conversation in notable ways, the full import of which will emerge with greater clarity with John Duns Scotus.[14] Olivi tries to maintain the causality of the whole Trinity and the personal dependence of Christ's human nature upon the Word, a dependence that allows the Word alone to perform Christ's work of salvation through the mode of supposit. The major weaknesses of Olivi's proposal include its fragmentary nature and the absence of specification regarding the causality through the mode of supposit. Scotus seizes upon this latter issue when discussing Christ's causality.

---

13 Olivi, *QDI*, q.2 (ed. Emmen, p. 105): "Secundum hanc autem rationem meritum Christi habet transcendentiam infinitam et quodammodo aeternam; quia, licet Deus fuerit persona hominis ex tempore, id tamen quod realiter ponit habitudo personae Christi ad humanitatem suam, est quid aeternum et increatum et, quantum est ex se, ab aeterno actualiter et preasentialiter eius personam, pro tempore tamen unionis."
14 Olivi also anticipates Scotus in attending to Christ's possession without contradiction of *dolor* and *gaudium* (*QDI*, q.2 [ed. Emmen, p. 126]).

John Duns Scotus on Christ's Wills

John Duns Scotus's presentation of Christ's wills holds great interest for both historical and systematic reasons. The Subtle Doctor inaugurated a new approach to Christ's wills by shifting attention to d.15, thereby elevating the meaning and import of Christ's sorrow (*dolor*) and sadness (*tristitia*). Examining Scotus's commentaries on d.15 provides a helpful window into the shift inaugurated by Scotus, and thus into the historical import of Scotus's commentaries, while examining Scotus's commentaries on dd.17 and 19 further illumines his systematic concerns. The presentation of Scotus offered here will provide a valuable point of contrast with the theologians discussed in earlier chapters. Scotus's *Lectura* and *Ordinatio* will serve as the primary texts for consideration, and, while differences or development between the texts will be indicated on specific issues, they will generally be treated together.[15]

Scotus offers a streamlined presentation of Christ's wills in *Ordinatio* III, d.17, focusing exclusively on the basic question of whether there were two wills in Christ (*utrum in Christo fuerunt duae voluntates*). The presentation repeats and simplifies much from *Lectura* III, d.17, which features a second question whether Christ willed something that did not come about (*utrum Christus aliquid voluit quod non evenit*).[16] In each commentary, Scotus presents two basic objections or types of objection to Christ's possession of two wills. The first denies Christ's possession of two wills on the grounds that only one of the two would have dominion over its acts and so fulfill the definition of will; the second argues for more than two wills in Christ because of the sensitive appetite and natural will (*voluntas naturalis*).[17] Scotus addresses these challenges in reverse order after establishing Christ's possession of two wills.

---

15   For a brief but clear discussion of Scotus on human free will, including in a Christological context, see Antonie Vos, *The Philosophy of John Duns Scotus* (Edinburgh, 2006), pp. 413–430. Vos also presents a lengthy introduction and orientation to Scotus's life and works.

16   The structure of *Lectura* III, d.17 bears some clearer similarities to the Lombard's own presentation than to later commentaries.

17   Scotus does not refer to the *voluntas sensualitatis* but rather to the sensitive appetite, a terminological choice that reflects Scotus's sharp distinction between nature and will while also differentiating Scotus from thirteenth-century discussions of Christ's wills. See Tobias Hoffmann, "The Distinction between Nature and Will in Duns Scotus," *Archives d'histoire doctrinale et littéraire du Moyen Age* 66 (1999): 189–224.

The *Lectura* and the *Ordinatio* defend Christ's possession of two wills with reference to the Damascene: "The Damascene solved that question in ch.60 [*De fide orthodoxa* III.14], saying that just as it should be firmly held according to the faith that there were two natures and one hypostasis in Christ, so also it is necessary to concede – as a consequence from that – that in him there were the natural properties and powers of both natures. The most perfect powers of a rational nature are the intellect and will, and so a created intellect and a created will were in him."[18] Earlier distinctions covered Christ's grace, knowledge, and vision according to the nature assumed (dd.13 and 14), and Scotus asserts that these presuppose a created intellect and will. Arguing for two wills in Christ is not unusual, but it is useful to note what Scotus has preserved or repeated from earlier presentations and how he shapes those standard ideas and arguments.[19] One relevant example is Scotus's mention that intellect and will fall under the umbrella of natural properties and powers that follow as a consequence from the hypostatic union.[20]

Having established the grounds for defending a created will in Christ, Scotus considers whether there could be more than one created will. If will is taken broadly for any appetite, then there are more than two wills in

18 John Duns Scotus, *Ordinatio* III, d.17, n.5 (ed. Barnaba Hechich et al., Opera omnia 9 [Vatican City, 2006], p. 564): "Istam quaestionem solvit Damascenus cap. 60, dicens quod sicut secundum fidem firmiter tenendum est in Christo esse duas naturas et unam hypostasim, ita oportet concedere – sicut consequens ex illo – quod in ipso sint naturales proprietates et potentiae utriusque naturae; sed potentiae perfectissimae rationalis naturae sunt intellectus et voluntas; quare in ipso sunt intellectus creatus et voluntas creata." See also John Duns Scotus, *Lectura* III, d.17, n.5.
19 A particularly intriguing feature from one manuscript of the *Ordinatio* is a reference to Gratian's *Decretum* pars.1, d.16, c.6 and its mention of the sixth synod (i.e. Constantinople III) declaring two wills and operations in Christ. The editors note that there is no precise indication of where the reference should be placed in the text. Knowledge of this text from Gratian would have provided little more concrete or detailed knowledge of the acts of Constantinople III than could be gleaned from the Lombard's passing reference, yet knowledge of this text would signal a greater knowledge of Constantinople III than common in the thirteenth century.
20 In the *Summa*'s section covering the consequences of the union, Aquinas joins questions of *esse*, will, and operation (*ST* III, qq.17–19). Scotus follows Olivi and Matthew of Aquasparta in affirming the relation of these topics and using this relation as ground for defending multiple *esses* in Christ.

Christ on account of the irrational or sensitive appetite. Taken strictly, as is proper, there are but two wills in Christ: the divine and the human free will. This begs the question of the natural will and its relation to the free will. Aware of the many possible meanings of 'natural will,' Scotus tackles the second objection by carefully parsing the possible and proper meanings of natural will. No natural appetite exists as a voluntary power separate from the power of the free will, but the natural will can designate the one power of the free will with respect to the natural perfections proper to it (*Lec.* III, d.17, n.9; *Ord.* III, d.17, n.13). Another usage distinguishes the natural will from every supernatural will or power, including the will as it is informed by the gift of grace (*Ord.* III, d.17, n.14). Natural will can also designate the free will as it elicits acts conformed to the natural inclination (*Lec.* III, d.17, n.11; *Ord.* III, d.17, n.15).[21] Scotus does not settle on a proper meaning of natural will and allows for diverse interpretations, though none imply or allow another human will in Christ beyond the free will.

By far the more difficult and more interesting topic concerns whether or how Christ's free human will has dominion over its acts and so merits the designation 'will.' Scotus grants from the beginning that "every will has dominion over its acts" and that "a will following the movement of another power does not have dominion in its act but is subject," but he argues that Christ's human will does not violate the second premise. The reason is that "the Word had no causality over the acts of the created will in Christ that the entire Trinity did not have, and therefore the created will in Christ did not lack dominion – in respect to its acts on account of the union to the Word – any more than if it were not united [to the Word]."[22] Scotus expresses the same idea more expansively in the *Lectura*:

---

21 In the *Ordinatio*, Scotus specifies that all acts conformed to the natural inclination are according to the *affectio commodi* (*Ordinatio* III, d.17, n.15). For a helpful discussion of Scotus on the will, see Cruz González-Ayesta, "Scotus' Interpretation of the Difference between *voluntas ut natura* and *voluntas ut voluntas*," *Franciscan Studies* 66 (2008): 371–412.
22 John Duns Scotus, *Ordinatio* III, d.17, n.16 (ed. Barnaba Hechich et al., Opera omnia 9: 569): "Ad primum principale, concedo maiorem quod 'omnis voluntas est domina sui actus'. Et cum dicitur in minore quod 'voluntas sequens motum alterius potentiae, in actu suo subditur et non dominatur', dico – sicut alias in prima quaestione huius III – quod Verbum nullam causalitatem habet super actum voluntatis creatae in Christo quam non habeat tota Trinitas; et ideo voluntas creata in Verbo non privatur dominio – respectu actuum suorum propter unionem ad Verbum – magis quam si non uniretur ei."

The Word did not have any causality respecting the union of the nature to it that the other persons did not have but only served as term [of the union] in another way. Every action elicited by Christ's natural power was elicited equally by the three persons. Christ's human and created will was no more deprived [of dominion or freedom] on account of the Word eliciting [its acts] in some manner than on account of the Father and Holy Spirit [eliciting its acts in some manner]. Consequently, union to the Word no more deprived Christ's created will of its liberty with respect to eliciting proper acts than my will or yours.[23]

A commitment to the absolute unity of Trinitarian operations *ad extra* requires, according to Scotus, that the person of the Word exercised no special causality in Christ's actions apart from the causality of the whole Trinity. This commitment and its consequent requirement have far reaching implications for Scotus's Christology and soteriology.[24]

Scotus argues that the divine causality in Christ's human volitions and actions conforms to the standard functioning of such causality in every other human being, though he leaves the exact nature of that functioning

---

23 John Duns Scotus, *Lectura* III, d.17, n.13 (ed. Barnaba Hechich et al., Opera omnia 20 [Vatican City, 2003], p. 426): "Verbum non habet aliquam causalitatem respectu unionis naturae ad ipsum quam non habeant aliae personae, sed tantum alio modo terminat. Sic omnes actiones in Christo, quae eliciuntur a potentia naturali Christi, aequaliter eliciuntur a tribus personis, et sic non plus privatur voluntas Christi humana et creata per hoc quod Verbum aliquo modo elicit, quam per hoc quod Pater aut Spiritus Sanctus, et – per consequens – non plus privatur voluntas libertate sua creata respectu proprii actus eliciendi propter unionem ad Verbum, quam voluntas mea vel tua."

24 For an enlightening treatment of Scotus's soteriology, see Andrew Rosato, *Duns Scotus on the Redemptive Work of Christ*, Ph.D. diss., University of Notre Dame, 2009. Rosato examines Scotus's soteriology as it is informed by his Christology, with the whole investigation set against a backdrop of Anselm's *Cur Deus homo* and the soteriologies of Bonaventure and Richard of Middleton. For debates concerning the infinity, sufficiency, and efficacy of Christ's merit according to Scotus, see Andrew S. Yang, "Scotus' Voluntarist Approach to the Atonement Reconsidered," *Scottish Journal of Theology* 62 (2009): 421–440 and Douglas C. Langston, "Scotus' Departure from Anselm's Theory of the Atonement," *Recherches de théologie ancienne et médiévale* 50 (1983): 227–241.

undetermined.[25] Thus, the objection to Christ's possession of a free human will only succeeds if it similarly deprives all human beings of free will. Christ's human will operates in the same way as every other human will.[26] Scotus is explicit about this in writing "the created will in Christ freely elicited and exercised dominion over its acts in the same way as my will."[27] Denial of any special causality on the part of the Word does not deny that Christ's human actions are attributable to the Word. Scotus explains this attribution through the *communicatio idiomatum*:

> It should be said that the primary communication of properties is in this that 'the Word is a human being,' and other communications of properties follow from that, such as the Son of God 'died,' 'suffered,' etc. Since, therefore, the first denomination did not require any special action [by the Word] that the Word was made a human being apart from what was common to the whole Trinity, the other denominations will not require any special action by the Word that is not common to the whole Trinity.[28]

---

25 John Duns Scotus, *Lectura* III, d.17 and *Ordinatio* III, d.17 both present two opinions for this relationship, options taken from the earlier considerations of II, dd.34–37. The first opinion limits divine causality to creating and maintaining free created wills such that created wills themselves are the sole immediate cause of their actions. The second opinion favors God's immediate co-causality in human actions.

26 For a most useful analysis of Scotus's different views on the functioning of the human will in its relation to the intellect and to the object of the will, see Stephen Dumont, "Did Scotus Change His Mind on the Will?," in *Nach der Verurteilung von 1277: Philosophie und Theologie an der Universität von Paris im letzten Viertel des 13. Jahrhunderts: Studien und Texte.*, ed. Jan A. Aertsen, Kent Emery, and Andreas Speer (Berlin, 2001), pp.719–794.

27 John Duns Scotus, *Ordinatio* III, d.17, n.17 (ed. Barnaba Hechich et al., Opera omnia 9: 570): "tunc dico quod voluntas creata in Christo ita libere elicit et dominatur actui suo sicut voluntas mea modo."

28 John Duns Scotus, *Lectura* III, d.17, n.16 (ed. Barnaba Hechich et al., Opera omnia 20: 427): "dicendum est quod prima communicatio idiomatum est in ista 'Verbum est homo,' et hanc consequuntur ceterae communicationes idiomatum, ut quod Filius Dei sit 'mortuus,' 'passus' etc. Cum ergo propter primam denominationem non habeat specialem actionem quod Verbum factum sit homo quin sit communis toti Trinitati, nec propter alias denominationes erit aliqua actio specialis Verbo quae non sit communis toti Trinitati."

The *Ordinatio* is even clearer in noting "the Word and not the whole Trinity is denominated from the operation of the created will (on account of the union which produces the communication of idioms)."[29] The human actions of Christ denominate the Word rather than the Trinity, for the Word alone among the Trinitarian persons is the subject of human properties in the Incarnation. By this strategy Scotus defends the unity of Trinitarian actions *ad extra* together with the Incarnation of the Word alone among the Trinitarian persons. We will return to this point at some length in comparing Scotus's understanding of Christ's wills to Aquinas's understanding.

Lectura III, d.17 includes a short discussion of whether Christ willed something that did not happen, a discussion omitted from *Ordinatio* III, d.17. The *Lectura*'s treatment allows that Christ's will as nature or natural inclination inclined always toward the personal good and so shunned the Passion. This inclination toward personal benefit relates to Scotus's distinction between *affectio commodi* (affection for the advantageous) and *affectio iustitiae* (affection for justice).[30] The will as nature or natural inclination was not always fulfilled since the opposite of its inclination occurred. Following traditional arguments, Scotus argues that whatever Christ willed simply, which includes everything willed by the superior portion of the will, was fulfilled. The brevity of the discussion and the lack of an equivalent in the *Ordinatio* seems to indicate its slight significance for Scotus, especially when compared to the import of this and related questions for earlier scholastics. Stated more forcefully, it seems as though Scotus completely ignores many of the questions and concerns central to previous discussions of Christ's wills. This impression is misleading.

Scotus is not unconcerned with earlier questions and topics, but he does rework several of them in more and less subtle ways. The preceding chapters have argued that questions of conformity or contrariety came to dominate thirteenth-century scholastic discussions of Christ's wills. Set against that backdrop, the near complete silence of *Lectura* III, d.17 and *Ordinatio* III, d.17 on conformity or contrariety is puzzling to say the least. It is not the case that Scotus simply disregards the previous tradition of

---

29 John Duns Scotus, *Ordinatio* III, d.17, n.17 (ed. Barnaba Hechich et al., Opera omnia 9: 570): "Verbum nullam specialem operationem habet aliam a tota Trinitate, denominatur tamen Verbum et non tota Trinitas ab operatione voluntatis creatae (propter unionem quae facit communicationem idiomatum)."
30 See González-Ayesta, "Scotus' Interpretation," pp. 381–394.

commentaries on the *Sentences* on Christ's wills; rather, he addresses questions of conformity or contrariety in *Lectura* III, d.15 and *Ordinatio* III, d.15 on Christ's sorrow (*dolor*) and sadness (*tristitia*). This shift alters the nature and connotations of the topic.

Sorrow, Sadness, and Freedom

Was there true sorrow in Christ's soul according to the superior portion? This is the central question of *Lectura* III, d.15 and *Ordinatio* III, d.15, and its relevance for discussions of Christ's wills might seem less than obvious. Scotus nevertheless understands sorrow and sadness to be passions of the soul located, at least primarily, in the will, and so his exploration of Christ's sorrow and sadness requires a corresponding exploration of Christ's wills and how Christ willed or shunned the passion. The overlap of Scotus's discussion of sorrow and sadness with earlier theologians' presentation of wills is discernible from the beginning of *Lectura* III, d.15. Scotus presents several arguments to justify the possibility of Christ possessing both the delight of fruition and sadness in the higher part of his soul. One argument is to deny that the delight of fruition and sadness are opposites in Christ's soul "because they are not concerning the same (*circa idem*) (since they are not concerning the same object), and contraries ought to be concerning the same."[31] The *Lectura* preserves other aspects of thirteenth-century discussions on Christ's wills omitted from the *Ordinatio*, and thus the two works represent slightly different stages within the shift of attention from Christ's wills to Christ's sorrow and sadness.

Addressing the presence of sorrow and sadness in Christ requires first specifying what parts of the soul are affected by these sentiments. Properly speaking, sorrow exists in the soul primarily according to the

---

31   John Duns Scotus, *Lectura* III, d.15, n.6 (ed. Barnaba Hechich et al., Opera omnia 20: 361): "quia non sunt circa idem (cum non sint circa idem obiectum), et contraria debent esse circa idem." *Ordinatio* III, d.15, n.2 (ed. Barnaba Hechich et al., Opera omnia 9: 477): "'Contraria non possunt simul inesse in eodem'; gaudium et tristitia sunt huiusmodi, et habuit summum gaudium; ergo etc." William of Auxerre and the *Summa fratris Alexandri* use the *circa idem* argument to deny contrariety of wills in Christ.

sensitive part and from the body, but sadness exists in the soul according to itself, according to the intellective part.[32] Scotus eventually qualifies this proper distinction in his discussion, allowing that in some sense sorrow can exist in the will as a rational appetite, yet this initial distinction provides a point of departure for the investigation. Scotus also reasons that sorrow pertains more to the power of the sensitive appetite than to sensitive apprehension (*Ordinatio* III, d.15, n.43) and that sadness pertains more to the rational appetite or will than to intellect (*Ordinatio* III, d.15, nn.47–48). The parallel between sorrow and sadness breaks down insofar as the sensitive appetite has a natural inclination while the will is free, which means for Scotus that the will is undetermined to opposites.[33]

Scotus grounds his affirmation of true sorrow in Christ on his previous assessments of Christ's knowledge. Christ had perfect knowledge according to his tactile faculty. All the pains of the passion, such as the nails piercing the flesh, were known and present to Christ's sense of touch, the knowledge of which suffices for true sorrow.[34] The presence of true sorrow in Christ's soul raises something of a red flag inasmuch as Scotus accepts the view that true or vehement sorrow normally impedes the use of reason. Though such is normally the case, a supernatural grace prevented

---

32   John Duns Scotus, *Ordinatio* III, d.15, n.25 (ed. Barnaba Hechich et al., Opera omnia 9: 485): "Ex his patet distinctio inter dolorem proprie dictum, qui inest animae a carne et primo secundum partem sensitivam, et inter tristitiam proprie dictam, quae inest animae secundum se et inest animae primo secundum partem intellectivam."

33   Scotus's understanding of synchronic contingency has its roots in Peter Olivi's understanding of the will as undetermined to opposites. See Stephen Dumont, "The Origin of Scotus' Theory of Synchronic Contingency," *The Modern Schoolman* 72 (1995): 149–168.

34   John Duns Scotus, *Lectura* III, d.15, n.49 (ed. Barnaba Hechich et al., Opera omnia 20: 375): "igitur perfectissime secundum suum sensum tactus cognovit illa infligentia et nociva, ut clavos et huiusmodi, et perfectissime apprehendebat et percipiebat. Et per consequens, illa obiecta disconvenientia sensui tactus perfectissime fuerunt praesentia et sensui tactus approximata; et ideo ab illis causabatur verissima passio in sensu tactus Christi, qui fuit verus dolor (secundum modum praedictum, quo ponitur dolor causari in potentia appetitiva sensitiva)." See also *Ordinatio* III, d.15, n.61.

this normal effect of sorrow in Christ.[35] Though Scotus predominantly discusses sadness in the will or rational appetite, he affirms the possibility of locating sorrow in the will as well. The presence of sorrow in the will depends upon either the will's natural inclination to personal preservation or to the union or association of the will with the sensitive appetite.[36]

Sadness presents a far more difficult topic than sorrow, one that requires delicate handling to balance the reality of Christ's human passions with the preservation of Christ's human freedom in the face of suffering. It also raises questions similar to those covered by thirteenth-century treatments of Christ's wills, including the distinction between the natural will or will as nature (*voluntas ut natura*) on the one hand, the free will or will as will (*voluntas ut libera* or *voluntas ut voluntas*) on the other, and the human will's conformity to the divine will. Scotus offers a marginally different take on the natural will in d.15 than in d.17, and this difference depends largely on the different contexts and aims of each distinction. In *Ordinatio* III, d.15, nn.89–91, two understandings of the will as nature are offered: 1) as naturally ordered or inclined to its proper object (that is, the object that perfects it), and 2) as ordered to whatever follows the nature of the will as an intellective appetite pursuing the *affectio commodi*. The natural will according to the first definition relates to the superior portion of the soul or will; according to the second definition it relates to the inferior portion because it is inclined to the object of the sensitive appetite. A further important qualification of the will as nature or natural will is that Scotus conceives it as an inclination rather than a power; the will as nature cannot elicit acts but merely inclines toward that which perfects the will.[37]

---

35 John Duns Scotus, *Lectura* III, d.15, n.53 (ed. Barnaba Hechich et al., Opera omnia 20: 376): "Dico tunc quod naturaliter huiusmodi dolores impedire usum rationis; sed non sic fuit in Christo, quia habuit plenam libertatem respectu cuiuslibet obiecti et usum rationis respectu cuiuslibet, et hoc fuit supernaturale." See also *Ordinatio* III, d.15, n.62.

36 John Duns Scotus, *Ordinatio* III, d.15, n.68 (ed. Barnaba Hechich et al., Opera omnia 9: 509–510): "Sic apparent duae viae quomodo potest poni Christum doluisse in voluntate sive in appetitu rationali: una, propter inclinationem naturalem voluntatis salutem personae, – alia, propter colligationem eius cum appetitu sensitiva."

37 Recall that Aquinas presents the will as one power with two species of acts. While there are clear differences between Aquinas and Scotus on the will, there are some fundamental similarities or overlaps.

The power of the will rests with the will as free (*voluntas ut libera*), which is undetermined toward opposites and can avoid willing at all. The will as free elicits acts.

Sadness pertains to the soul according to the intellective part and exists in the will. So when Scotus turns to the question of sadness in the *Ordinatio*, he must address how and in what parts Christ's soul experienced sadness, which in turn leads to the disposition of Christ's will to the passion. Christ's will as nature refused the passion. Relative to the superior portion, the will as nature sought its personal good according to the *affectio commodi* and so refused the passion as contrary to this personal good. Relative to the inferior portion and as joined to the sensitive appetite, the will as nature refused the passion as contrary to the inclination of the tactile faculty. Though little attention is devoted to the topic, Scotus allows that Christ's will as free refused the passion conditionally but not absolutely. Again, Scotus's concern is with sadness, so the lack of elaboration here is unsurprising. Based upon these refusals of the passion, Christ's whole soul experienced sadness both in the will and in the intellect.[38]

The earlier *Lectura* offers a treatment of sadness exhibiting far more similarities with scholastic discussions of Christ's wills. Scotus presents arguments both that Christ experienced sadness and did not experience sadness according to the inferior portion.[39] The main argument against Christ's sadness treats the inferior and superior portions as the same one power. Powers cannot have opposite acts respecting the same object, and so the power of the will could not both will and refuse the passion. Christ willed the passion according to the superior portion, and so the argument concludes Christ willed the passion according to the inferior portion,

---

38 John Duns Scotus, *Ordinatio* III, d. 15, n. 127 (ed. Barnaba Hechich et al., Opera omnia 9: 530): "Sicque salvatur illa glossa '*Repleta est malis* etc.', id est tristiis sive poenis,' quia tota anima quantum ad voluntatem, secundum utramque portionem tristabatur, et ut natura et ut libera et ex nolitione condicionata, scilicet quantum in ipso fuit, – et quantum ad intellectum, secundum utramque portionem apprehendebat disconveniens et condicionaliter voluntati."

39 The editors take Scotus to favor the view that Christ did not experience sadness according to the inferior portion.

which removes the grounds for sadness.[40] This line of reasoning could be read as an affirmation of Bonaventure's cautious presentation or as a rejection of Aquinas's distinction between the two species of acts within the one power of the will.

The more common response, Scotus notes, affirms sadness in Christ according to the inferior portion, and there are at least four ways to sustain or explain the affirmation. The first way argues that the inferior portion could not regard the passion qualified by all the circumstances relating to the final end and so refused the passion. Thus, the actual happening of the passion sufficed to cause sadness.[41] The second way stresses that the will is naturally inclined toward personal health and happiness and so experiences sadness in the absence of happiness or in the presence of harm.[42] The third way holds that the inferior portion "naturally willed the opposite and naturally refused [the passion] and so experienced sadness." The fourth way posits sadness apart from any act elicited by the will, whether willing or refusing.[43] Before addressing these various ways, Scotus speci-

---

40 John Duns Scotus, *Lectura* III, d.15, n.70 (ed. Barnaba Hechich et al., Opera omnia 20: 380): "Probatur primo sic: eadem potentia respectu eiusdem obiecti non potest habere actus oppositos, quorum alter sit in summo, quia non compatitur secum opposita sic; sed portio superior et inferior sunt eadem potentia, et solum distinguuntur per diversa officia, secundum Augustinum; igitur non possunt habere actus oppositos, quorum alter sit in summo. Cum igitur secundum portionem superiorem summe voluerit passionem suam, ut ostensum est, secundum portionem inferiorem voluit, – et per consequens non tristabatur."

41 John Duns Scotus, *Lectura* III, d.15, n.78 (ed. Barnaba Hechich et al., Opera omnia 20: 382–383): "Quod potest poni uno modo sic: ratio inferior potuit ostendere passionem suam portioni superiori voluntatis, sine omnibus circumstantiis quae pertinent ad finem ultimum (quia ostendere cum talibus circumstantiis pertinet ad portionem superiorem, et sic non est portionis inferioris 'cum circumstantia ultimi finis' ostendere); et sic voluntas secundum portionem inferiorem ipsam noluit, – tamen evenit, ideo secundum portionem inferiorem tristabatur."

42 John Duns Scotus, *Lectura* III, d.15, n.84 (ed. Barnaba Hechich et al., Opera omnia 20: 385): "Alia via potest esse quod voluntas naturaliter inclinatur ad salutem illius personae, et hoc sufficiebat ut esset tristitia. Quod ostenditur, nam voluntas naturaliter inclinatur ad beatitudinem, et ideo si careret beatitudine ad quam naturaliter inclinatur, tristaretur de opposito sequente."

43 John Duns Scotus, *Lectura* III, d.15, n.85 (ed. Barnaba Hechich et al., Opera omnia 20: 385): "Tertia via, quod naturaliter voluit oppositum et illud naturaliter noluit, et ideo tristabatur. Et quarta via potest dici quod sine aliquo actu voluntatis elicito, volendo aut nolendo, tristabatur."

fies that Christ's passion was not one thing *per se* but was one "wholly through the accidental association of many circumstances."⁴⁴ This specification provides some space for regarding the passion in diverse respects and so for possessing diverse inclinations or volitions with respect to it.

Scotus rehearses several strategies for explaining the dispositions of Christ's will toward the passion corresponding to the strategies for explaining sadness according to the inferior portion. Since the passion can be regarded variously, there was nothing illicit or disordered when the will refused it according to the inferior portion. Moreover, this refusal according to the inferior portion actually followed the divine will. God willed Christ to refuse the passion according to the inferior portion, which regarded the passion apart from the larger circumstances related to the ultimate end, and to will it according to the superior portion, which regarded it with the circumstances related to the ultimate end.⁴⁵ The conclusion is that "the will existing in one power according to the superior and inferior portions can refuse and will something according to diverse circumstances."⁴⁶ A second strategy allows for something to be willed *simpliciter* or absolutely and to be refused conditionally such that "Christ willed to die absolutely and nevertheless refused conditionally, from which refusal a great sadness in the will followed."⁴⁷ The third way of experiencing sadness in the inferior portion involved naturally willing one thing and nat-

---

44 John Duns Scotus, *Lectura* III, d.15, n.88 (ed. Barnaba Hechich et al., Opera omnia 20: 386): "Nunc autem passio Christi circumstantionata non erat aliquod per se unum, sicut nec aliquod eligibile morale, sed est unum valde per accidens aggregans multas circumstantias."
45 John Duns Scotus, *Lectura* III, d.15, n.89 (ed. Barnaba Hechich et al., Opera omnia 20: 387): "Nec tamen sequitur quod non recte illam passionem noluit, quia ipse secundum illam portionem noluit quod Deus voluit eum nolle: voluit enim Deus Christum nolle passionem illam nude ostensam, sine illis circumstantiis, – sicut voluit illum velle eam, cum omnibus circumstantiis bonis, secundum portionem superiorem."
46 John Duns Scotus, *Lectura* III, d.15, n.91 (ed. Barnaba Hechich et al., Opera omnia 20: 387): "Sic in proposito, voluntas existens in una potentia secundum portionem superiorem et inferiorem, potest aliquid nolle et velle secundum diversas circumstantias."
47 John Duns Scotus, *Lectura* III, d.15, n.94 (ed. Barnaba Hechich et al., Opera omnia 20: 388): "Ita Christus absolute voluit mori, et tamen habuit nolle condicionatum, quod quidem nolle consequabatur magna tristitia in voluntate."

urally refusing the opposite; if the thing refused happens, sadness ensues. Christ naturally refused his death and passion, and so the opposite occurring suffices for sadness. Scotus continues by noting that this refusal and consequent sadness do not require that the natural willing or refusing elicits an act but only that the natural willing wills the opposite of the elicited act.[48] The fourth way allows sadness according to the inferior portion as it is united with the sensitive appetite. Sorrow in the sensitive appetite causes a passion in the inferior portion experienced as sadness before any volitional act. There is no conflict between Christ's sadness and delight or enjoyment of vision. Delight in Christ's superior reason and will was miraculously prevented from redounding to his sensitive appetite and inferior reason and will, allowing true sorrow in the sensitive appetite and true sadness in the inferior portion (*Lectura* III, d.15, n.110). These four strategies derive from thirteenth-century presentations of Christ's wills and the voluntary character of the passion.

Addressing the disposition of Christ's will toward the passion within a consideration of Christ's sorrow and sadness removes many of the moral connotations at play in thirteenth-century discussions of contrariety and conformity of wills. The underlying concerns of Scotus's presentation seem to reflect his sharp distinction between will and nature and his understanding of the will's freedom. Earlier scholastic theologians approached Christ's prayer at Gethsemane with a desire to explain how Christ willed or refused the passion and how this willing and refusing displayed Christ's obedience to the divine will. Scotus approaches Christ's prayer at Gethsemane with a desire to explain how Christ willed or refused the passion and how this willing and refusing fit with the will's freedom. If sadness exists in the will, how could Christ both freely will the passion and experience sadness in the will? For Scotus, Christ's agony at Gethsemane poses different questions than it did for the theologians examined in previous chapters. Given the differences in his fundamental questions, it is hardly surprising that his answers differ as well.

---

48 John Duns Scotus, *Lectura* III, d.15, n.96 (ed. Barnaba Hechich et al., Opera omnia 20: 389): "Secundum tertiam viam potest dici quod Christus naturaliter noluit mortem et passionem suam; et ideo tristabatur, quia ad tristandum sufficit quod illud accidat cuius oppositum est naturaliter volitum, – nam supremus appetitus est principaliter suppositi, sicut et suprema ratio, ergo Christus naturaliter amabat esse et vitam sui suppositi; hoc autem sufficit ad tristandum de opposito illius."

Finite Causality, Finite Merit

Exploring the sufficiency of Christ's merit (*Lectura* III, d.19; *Ordinatio* III, d.19) provides an opportunity for Scotus to revisit Christ's human will and the question of the Word's causality. One view, to which Scotus takes exception, allows that Christ merits infinitely, either on account of the supposit of the Word eliciting the meritorious acts or on account of the dignity of person meriting.[49] Scotus summarizes the views as follows:

> They say that Christ's merit had a certain infinity from the supposit of the Word, which elicited and exercised the operations of the assumed nature, because it elicited all the operations and acts fitting to both natures, and so – by the life [*or* power] of that supposit – the operations of that supposit were an infinite good: and thus [Christ's] death and passion and other operations have a certain infinity so as to suffice for erasing infinite sins and for conferring grace and glory. Similarly, merit is regarded according to the dignity of the person meriting, who is and was infinite. Therefore he merited infinitely and, with respect to sufficiency, satisfied for all.[50]

These are two related but distinct ways of explaining Christ's capacity for infinite merit. Scotus rejects both, and the logic of his rejection lays bare a

---

49 Scotus's rejection of views such as Aquinas's is more relevant for the purposes of this study than Scotus's own proposal for Christ's merit. On Scotus's soteriology, see Rosato, "Duns Scotus."
50 John Duns Scotus, *Lectura* III, d.19, n.9 (ed. Barnaba Hechich et al., Opera omnia 21 [Vatican City, 2004], pp. 27–28): "Primum probant, quia dicunt quod meritum Christi habuit infinitatem quamdam ex supposito Verbi, quod eliciebat et exercebat operationes huius naturae assumptae, quia eliciebat operationes omnes et actus convenientes utrique naturae, et ideo – vita [*or* virtute] illius suppositi – et operationes illius suppositi fuerunt bonum infinitum: et sic mors et passio et aliae operationes habuerunt infinitatem quamdam, ut sufficerent pro infinitis peccatis delendis, et gratis et gloriis conferendis. Similiter, meritum pensatur secundum dignitatem personae merentis, quae est et fuit infinita; ergo infinite merebatur, et sic quantum ad sufficientiam satisfecit pro omnibus." The manuscripts all have *vita*, but the editors favor the reading of *virtute* based upon Aquinas, *ST* III, q.19, a.1. *Lectura* III, d.19, n.12 commences the response to this position again with reference to *vita Christi fuit ita excellens ut haberet quamdam infinitatem*, and so I favor the reading of *vita* over *virtute*. If *virtute* is the correct reading, then Aquinas would certainly seem to be the target, even if only remotely.

fundamental difference between Scotus and many of his scholastic predecessors regarding the source of volitional activity. The Subtle Doctor rejects any special causality exercised by the Word in Christ's human actions. One justification for this rejection is Trinitarian, but another concerns the causal origin of actions and Scotus's dismissal of the axiom that actions pertain to supposits (*actiones sunt suppositorum*).[51] Disrupting the causal link between supposits and actions requires viewing individual natures as the causal origin of actions and so challenges the basic logic of Aquinas's presentation of Christ's salvific work outlined in the previous chapter.

Richard Cross argues that Aquinas's view of Christ's human actions – caused both in some sense by the Word and by the causal powers of Christ's human nature – results in causal overdetermination.[52] Cross views Scotus

---

51 See Richard Cross, "Accidents, Substantial Forms, and Causal Powers in the Late Thirteenth Century: Some Reflections on the Axiom *actiones sunt suppositorum*," in *Compléments de substance: Études sur les propriétés accidentales offertes à Alain de Libera*, ed. Christophe Erismann and Alexandrine Schniewind (Paris, 2008), pp. 133–146. Cross argues that Scotus identifies powers with forms, writing that the "idea is that causal activity is ascribed properly to things which are singular and *per se* existents but communicable – that is to say, forms" (Cross, "Accidents, Substantial Forms, and Causal Powers," p. 145). Scotus's motivation is to offer a universal account that can cover forms that are not supposits. The axiom that *actiones sunt suppositorum* is traced by de Libera to Aquinas and to Christological debates such as concerns over Christ's wills and actions. See Alain de Libera, "Les actions appartiennent aux sujets: Petite archéologie d'un principe leibnizien," in "Ad ingenii acuitionem": *Studies in Honour of Alfonso Maierù*, ed. Stefano Caroti et al. (Louvaine-la-Neuve, 2006), pp. 199–220. If de Libera's analysis is correct, Aquinas's affirmation of the axiom *actiones sunt suppositorum* does not so much inform his Christology as depend upon it.

52 Scotus himself seems to offer a solution to the worry about causal overdetermination. In *Ordinatio* I, d.3, pars 3, q.2, he introduces a scheme of concurrent causality. This scheme explains how multiple causes concur to the same effect and concentrates on the differences between equal and unequal causes. The description of unequal causes is most relevant to the present case. Sometimes a superior cause moves an inferior cause either by giving the inferior cause the power or form by which it acts or by giving the inferior cause its actual motion for producing the effect. Other times a superior cause neither causes the inferior cause's motion nor gives it the power by which it moves; rather "the superior has of itself a more perfect power of acting, and the inferior has a more imperfect power of acting (*superior de se habet virtutem perfectiorem agendi, et inferior habet virtutem imperfectiorem agendi*")" (John Duns Scotus, *Ordinatio* I, d.3, pars 3, q.2, n.496 [ed. Carolus Balić et al., Opera omnia 3 (Vatican City, 1954), p. 293]). Again, Scotus does not employ this notion of concurrent causality to explore the causality of Christ's wills, but it seems he could have done so.

as approaching the question armed with a distinction between the causal and predicative aspects of actions and causation. The causal origin of Christ's human actions is Christ's human nature, and, by virtue of the *communicatio idiomatum*, these actions can be predicated of the Word. The Word is the predicative subject though not the causal origin of Christ's human actions. By this strategy, Cross argues, Scotus avoids causal overdetermination and navigates a path allowing the truth of Christological predications without reducing the ontological integrity of Christ's human nature.[53] Cross's analysis merits serious attention and, if the argument of the preceding chapter is to be maintained, an informed response.

Cross takes his point of departure from Scotus but formulates a broadly applicable argument respecting Christ's wills, writing that "if (as the medievals assume) the assumed nature is something like an individual substance, then it will not be possible to ascribe properly human activity to the Word unless the assumed nature is itself the *causal origin* of the human actions."[54] The argument begins from the premise that individual substances (or individual substance-like things) possess certain causal powers. Under the assumption that the Word is the causal origin of Christ's human actions, a problem seems to arise. Either the causal powers of the assumed nature are co-causal origins with the causal powers of the Word, which entails causal overdetermination, or the causal powers of the assumed nature are moved by the Word instrumentally and so fail to qualify as causal origins marking Christ's actions as *human* actions. Causal overdetermination pertains when there exists more than one causal origin for an action sufficiently caused or explained by one causal origin. The second strategy avoids causal overdetermination only by limiting the causal origin of Christ's actions to the causal powers of the Word, thereby under-

[53] Richard Cross, *The Metaphysics of the Incarnation: Thomas Aquinas to Duns Scotus* (Oxford, 2002), pp. 218–229. Cross views with caution the characterization offered in Léon Seiller, *L'activité humaine du Christ selon Duns Scot* (Paris, 1944), noting that Seiller stresses a *homo assumptus* reading of Scotus following Déodat de Basly. The overlap between Cross and Seiller regards Scotus's view that the Word is not the causal origin of Christ's human actions but is the predictive subject of them. Cross goes to some length in resisting the *homo assumptus* interpretation of Scotus. Seiller argues that for Scotus the Word did not elicit the acts of Christ's human nature but rather that the *homo assumptus* acted autonomously (Seiller, *L'activité humaine*, pp. 42–3, 56). Seiller also notes that *actio est suppositi ut ultimate denominati*, which guarantees that Christ's autonomous human acts remain predicable of the Word.

[54] Cross, *The Metaphysics of the Incarnation*, p. 218.

mining those actions as truly human actions. Cross presents these as problems faced by Aquinas and as surmounted best, even if not completely, by Scotus.

As was discussed above, Scotus denies that the Word exercised any special causation in Christ's human activity and affirms that Christ's human will was no more subject to or moved by the divine will than is any other human will.[55] Scotus does, however, argue that the Word alone among the Trinitarian persons is denominated by the operation of Christ's human will. Cross explicates this aspect of Scotus's thought through a distinction of the causal and predicative aspects of agency. "In virtue of the communication of properties," Cross writes, "we can predicate human agency of the Word, without this entailing that the Word is the causal originator of the agency ascribed to him."[56] Although the Word is not the causal originator of Christ's human actions, those human actions can be predicated of the Word as of an ultimate subject through the *communicatio idiomatum*.[57] The particular strengths of Scotus's approach, according to Cross, include avoiding the Trinitarian difficulties of any action *ad extra* caused by the Word alone and of conceiving Christ's human will and operation as following the identical causal mechanisms as every other human being's. Further, he suggests that Scouts preserved the ability to denominate the Word as the agent of Christ's human will and actions.[58]

[55] Maria Burger briefly mentions Scotus's treatment of Christ's wills and argues, based upon Scotus's understanding of the hypostatic union, that it allows for Christ's free human will precisely by denying any special causality on the part of the Word. See Burger, *Personalität im Horizont absoluter Prädestination: Untersuchungen zur Christologie des Johannes Duns Scotus und ihrer Rezeption in modernen theologischen Ansätzen* (Münster, 1994), p. 141.
[56] Cross, *The Metaphysics of the Incarnation*, p. 220.
[57] Cross notes that Scotus never addresses Christ's miracles directly but would presumably consider them as caused by the whole Trinity. Seiller does not make special appeal to the *communicatio idiomatum* as a means to explain the denomination of the Word by Christ's human actions. Instead, he appeals to the hypostatic union and the principle that *actio est suppositi ut ultimate denominati* (Seiller, *L'activité humaine*, pp. 42–3).
[58] There appears to be some slight equivocation in Scotus as to whether truths about Christ, such as Christ's human volitions and actions, are true of the Word mediately or immediately. Cross raises this issue and suggests a possible, though potentially *ad hoc*, solution to the difficulty in that "the causal agency is, *qua* causal, immediate to the assumed nature, but, *qua* predication, immediate to the Word" (Cross, *The Metaphysics of the Incarnation*, p. 226). Aquinas

While on the surface these strengths might seem equally applicable to Aquinas, Cross would seem to disagree, holding that Aquinas's use of instrumentality to explain Christ's wills and operations inevitably falls into contradictions or violations of basic principles. Cross perceives a degree of tension in Aquinas's attempt to balance the notion that "the person of the Word brings about human actions 'according to' his human nature – in this case, by using the nature as an instrument" with the notion that "Christ's human nature has its own intrinsic form and power."[59] Instruments, in Cross's reading of Thomas, are normally recipients of the primary agent's causal activity such that the instruments themselves are not the causal origin of the operations worked through them. There is, of course, an important qualification to this claim. Cross adds:

> Aquinas argues that Christ's human nature is an *animate* instrument, and that it therefore is not merely acted upon, but rather 'acts such that it is acted upon'. This account makes the instrumentality of Christ's human nature indistinguishable from a particular sort of secondary causality, and thus hard to see how on this account Christ's human actions are actions of the Word at all – any more than (say) mine are.[60]

The presentation of Aquinas offered in Chapters four and five has stressed a different reading of instrumental causation in Christ's human will and operation. The interpretation has focused on Christ's human nature as a hypostically-united rational instrument, the main points of which bear repeating. It will be most profitable to work backwards. Aquinas distinguishes among inanimate instruments, which are moved solely by corporeal motion, animate instruments, which are moved through the sensitive appetite, and rational instruments, which are moved through the will (*ST* III, q.18, a.1, *ad* 2). Christ's human nature is a rational instrument and so does not simply receive motion but acts through its own free volition, and

---

would no doubt maintain many reservations about any Christology that equivocates on this topic, and such reservations would depend heavily on Thomas's recovery of patristic and conciliar sources.

59 Cross, *The Metaphysics of the Incarnation*, p. 220, referring to *Compendium theologiae* I, 212, *ST* III, q.18, a.1, *ad* 4, and *ST* III, q.19, a.1.
60 Cross, *The Metaphysics of the Incarnation*, p. 221, n.8.

Aquinas goes to great length to explain that the voluntary motion of Christ's human nature follows the same voluntary mechanics as every other human being's. Stated otherwise, Thomas insists that it is proper to a human will to be moved interiorly by the divine will and proper to the wills of the saints to be moved 'according to' the divine will. That Christ's human will is moved interiorly by and according to the divine will poses no danger to Christ's human freedom (*ST* III, q.18, a.1, *ad* 1). The basic structure and aim of Aquinas's argument here parallels, at least roughly, Scotus's argument concerning the integrity of Christ's human causality with respect to the Word.

How, though, can the actions of this human nature be the actions of the Word? Scotus's strategy distinguishes the proximate and remote subjects of Christ's actions, labeling the Word the remote subject through the *communicatio idiomatum*.[61] The answer, for Thomas, rests in the hypostatic union. The instrumentality of Christ's human nature differs from the instrumentality of other human beings as secondary causes operating under the primary divine causality, because Christ's human nature is hypostatically united to the person of the Word. The human nature assumed has the Word as its supposit (person, hypostasis), and it is the supposit that acts in and through the nature. In every other human being, purely human supposits are the origin of all the volitions and actions caused by their natural capacities, and the volitions and actions of the supposits are determined by their natural capacities just as they receive their determinate mode from the willing and acting supposit. In Jesus Christ, the person of the Word is the origin of all the volitions and actions caused by his natural human capacities, and the volitions and actions of Jesus are determined by his natural human capacities just as they receive their determinate mode from the Word as the willing and acting supposit (*ST* III, q.18, a.1, *ad*.4; *ST*

---

61 Scotus, according to Cross, distinguishes or sets up a framework for distinguishing the Word from Christ such that predications of Christ refer to the whole of which the Word is in some sense a part. This should not be read in any Nestorian sense because Scotus maintains that all of Christ's human predicates are predicable of the Word, even if not immediately. Seiller's emphasis on the hypostatic union rather than the *communicatio idiomatum* presents Scotus in a way far closer to Aquinas.

III, q.19, a.1).[62] This contention is crucial to Aquinas's Christology, and its rejection by Scotus represents a fundamental difference of opinion.

Instrumentality, according to Cross, fails to safeguard Christ's human actions as actions of the Word and possibly violates the unity of all divine actions *ad extra*. Cross writes "Augustinianism requires that every action brought about by divine causal powers is undivided since the three persons possess numerically the same causal powers: one intelligence, one will, one creativity, and so on. But, of course, the assumed human nature and the Word's *human* causal powers are possessed merely by the Son – so the Son can on the face of it certainly bring about effects by himself, non-instrumentally, through these causal powers."[63] The specification of 'non-instrumentally' presumably indicates that if the Word causes the action instrumentally, which Cross takes to mean through the primary agent's causal powers rather than through the instrument's causal powers, the action either fails to be an action of the Word or violates the unity of Trinitarian causation by being a divine action brought about by the Word alone. The question of instrumentality and instrumental causation becomes more complicated when one adds the peculiar notion of instrumental efficient causality. Aquinas understands Christ's human will and operation to be instrumental efficient causes of salvation, in which divine efficiency is expressed through the Word's human will and operation to produce an infinite effect.

When discussing causation through instrumental participation, Thomas writes, "the moved participates in the operation of the mover, and the mover uses the operation of the moved, and thus both act in communion with the other" (*ST* III, q.19, a.1). Aquinas's understanding of

62 Aquinas argues that a nature and its natural capacities receive a determinate mode from the hypostasis instantiating them. This contention no doubt rests on Thomas's understanding of *esse* as well as his affirmation that *actiones sunt suppositorum*. Aside from these metaphysical justifications, I take it that Aquinas also means to indicate the common sense observation that while all human beings share the same nature and capacities proper to human nature, every human being instantiates human nature and its proper capacities in an individual mode.
63 Cross, *The Metaphysics of the Incarnation*, p. 219. The quotation does not relate directly to Aquinas but concerns a rejection of Seiller's argument, though the specification of 'non-instrumental' does seem directed at Aquinas.

instrumental causation helps explain his affirmation of Christ's infinite merit. Scotus specifically rejects the infinity of Christ's merit, and the logic of that rejection would extend to all of Christ's human actions.[64] As human actions, they are by definition finite and can only produce finite effects. This relates, as noted above, to Scotus's understanding of individual natures or forms, rather than supposits, as the causal origin or proximate cause of actions. Persons or supposits are instead the predicative subject or the remote cause of actions. Aquinas repeatedly insists that actions pertain to supposits and that supposits or persons act through the capacities and forms of their natures.[65]

The fundamental difference between Aquinas and Scotus concerning the source of causal powers and actions leads to variances in their Christologies. Aquinas insists that supposits act through natures, and so the willer and actor in Christ is none other than the person of the Word. All of Christ's human volitions and actions are proximately volitions and actions of the Word through the Word's human will and operation. Formulated in Cross's terminology, the Word, as a supposit of human nature, is the causal origin of Christ's human volitions and actions, operating through the causal powers of Christ's human nature. Scotus views natures or forms as the possessors of causal powers and as the proximate subjects of volitions and actions. For Scotus, Christ's human volitions and actions only count as truly human if they have Christ's human nature as their proximate subject and causal origin. The Word is the remote subject of Christ's

---

64 Yang argues that in Scotus's account the circumstances of the hypostatic union allow God to regard Christ's intrinsically finite merit as 'quasi-infinite' and that this explains the possibility of Christ's merit having infinite sufficiency and finite efficacy (Yang, "Scotus' Voluntarist Approach" pp. 430–431, 439–440).

65 The background to this difference includes vastly divergent understandings of what constitutes a person or hypostasis as distinct from an individual nature. This topic far exceeds the scope of the present investigation, so it must suffice here to offer only the briefest indications of Aquinas's and Scotus's views. Aquinas defines personhood positively, while Scotus defines it negatively. For Aquinas, persons are individual substances of rational nature where individual substance indicates existence through its own *esse*. For Scotus, persons are distinguished from individual natures and disembodied souls by virtue of lacking actual or aptitudinal dependence. Cross labels these the *esse* theory of subsistence and the negation theory of subsistence. See Cross, *The Metaphysics of the Incarnation*, pp. 246–256, 297–309.

human actions, which can therefore be ascribed to the Word as agent.[66] Aquinas and Scotus thus both attempt to develop a manner of conceiving and speaking about Christ's human volitions and actions that preserves the truth of their human character and their reality as volitions and actions of the Word. Because these similar attempts arise from a contrary premise, they lead to further differences hinting at contradiction.

The point here is not to argue that Aquinas and Scotus formulate the same basic argument and that the divergences in their formulations depend entirely upon competing claims as to the source of actions. Rather, the point is to note that both theologians chase the same goal, or at least very similar goals, though in interestingly different ways. Aquinas and Scotus both seek to explain the perfection and integrity of Christ's human nature with respect to the free motion of its will. To the extent that Scotus would divide or differentiate predicative subjects from causal origins, Aquinas would worry that this risks sliding into an affirmation of two subjects, though vastly different and unequal subjects, in Christ. Scotus insists that Christ's individual human nature must, at least in some logical sense, be the proximate subject of all the things pertaining to Christ's humanity and that the Word is the remote subject, an insistence that intends to guard the Word's immutability together with the integrity and perfection of Christ's humanity. Viewed from Aquinas's understanding of the Lombard's first opinion as veiled Nestorianism, any Christology that allows for a subject in Christ other than the Word risks dividing Christ. Such a division suggests that Christ's human volitions and actions do not sufficiently pertain to the Word but merely denominate the Word through some linguistic sleight of hand such that they are purely and strictly human volitions and actions predicated of the Word accidentally. Aside from rejecting such an approach on the grounds of the mode of union, Thomas would also take exception to it on soteriological grounds. Thomas presents Christ as the one mediator *secundum quod homo* such that Christ's human will and operation act as instrumental efficient causes of salvation, a free human will and operation producing a divine effect. Scotus rejects this type of Christological and soteriological approach.

---

66   Leo's *Tomus ad Flavianum*, with its affirmation that each form in Christ's does what is proper to it in communion with the other, could be taken to support Scotus's position.

Now let us return to the proposed challenges to Aquinas. There seems to be a threefold worry about Aquinas's notion of Christ's instrumental efficient causality. First, the worry that characterizing Christ's human actions through instrumentality reduces them to secondary causes indistinguishable from the actions of other human beings. Under this scenario, there are no specific grounds for predicating these actions of the Word. Second, the worry that characterizing Christ's humanity as an instrument locates the entire causality for Christ's actions in the Word, in which case those actions fail to qualify as properly human actions. This worry seems legitimated when Aquinas and others grant an infinite effect to Christ's actions. Or, if the Word is simply the co-cause along with the nature assumed, causal overdetermination results. Third, if Christ's human actions are caused by the Word to which human nature is hypostatically united, this perhaps violates the unity of Trinitarian actions *ad extra*.

Aquinas's presentation of Christ's humanity as a hypostatically-united rational instrument sufficiently answers the first two challenges. The possible exception might be the charge of causal overdetermination, but the force of this charge seems unclear. Perhaps the argument can be made that causal overdetermination is unfitting since it involves the unnecessary multiplication of causes, but this does not mean that causal overdetermination involves a contradiction or impossibility. Any argument relying on unfittingness appears surmountable by Aquinas, because he could argue that the accomplishment of Christ's salvific act fittingly required a voluntary human action producing an infinite effect. In short, since Thomas would claim the infinite efficacy of Christ's salvific work *secundum quod homo*, presenting Christ's human and divine wills as in some sense co-causes does not necessitate unfitting causal overdetermination. It does, however, raise Trinitarian questions.

The third concern thus offers a more serious challenge to Aquinas's Christology and treatment of Christ's wills and operations. If Christ's human volitions and actions can produce an infinite effect on account of the person of the Word willing and acting, does this mean that the second person of the Trinity acts alone *ad extra*? Aquinas does not expressly address this concern, but he does provide resources for formulating a response. Before investigating those resources, it will be useful to specify responses that, while initially appealing, are ultimately unsuccessful. These unsuccessful strategies depend upon interpretation of *actiones sunt suppositorum* and *instrumentum divinitatis*. Examining how and why these strategies fail clarifies the specific difficulties faced by Aquinas's Christology and soteriology. While this is a generally applicable concern for any Incarnational Christology, Thomas's notion of instrumental efficient causality makes it particularly troubling or difficult.

Aquinas tempers his affirmation that actions pertain to supposits with his insistence that active powers follow forms and that forms (or powers) are the *principium agendi* (e.g. *ST* III, q.13, a.1). Supposits act, but they do so through the active powers determined by their forms or natures. It is tempting to stress that supposits or persons act through the powers proper to their forms or natures such that in Christ's volitions and actions the Word is the sole subject but only with respect to the powers of human nature. The Word alone among the Trinitarian persons would be the subject and origin of Christ's volitions and actions without violating the unity of Trinitarian actions *ad extra* because the Word would cause these volitions and actions strictly as a supposit of human nature. Since the Word alone is the term of the assumption of human nature, the Word alone can cause Christ's human volitions and actions without violating the unity of Trinitarian actions *ad extra*. The *Summa theologiae* offers a remarkably succinct explanation of how one divine person can be incarnate without the others (*ST* III, q.3, a.4), an explanation that reworks the earlier distinction between the act or *principium* of assumption and the term of assumption (*ST* III, q.3, aa.1 and 2).[67] Article one presents assumption as befitting the person in so far as the *principium* of assumption "because acting properly befits the person" (*ST* III, q.3, a.1). Article four notes that "the action of assuming proceeds from the divine power, which is common to the three persons" (*ST* III, q.3, a.4) and relies upon *ST* III, q.2's affirmation of union in person rather than in nature to construe the term of assumption as the

---

67 Aquinas's treatment of this topic in the *Scriptum* (*in* III, d.1, q.2, a.1) is hardly more satisfying. It provides various examples of things united in one respect and diverse in another respect. A human being and an ass are united in genus but diverse in species. Whatever belongs to the genus animal fits both to the human being and to the ass, but whatever belongs to the specific difference of a human being need not belong to the ass. Another example involves viewing souls as united to bodies both as forms and in terms of potencies. Just because the power of sight is an act of the body does not require that the intellect is an act of the body, even though both belong to the soul's essence. Aquinas explicitly likens this last example to the Son being incarnate without the Father.

person. Notably absent is any discussion, substantive or otherwise, of how one divine person can alone be the term of an act of assumption caused by the whole Trinity. This absence is felt when Aquinas turns to questions of Christ's causality.

Shifting the emphasis from *actiones sunt suppositorum* to forms as the *principium agendi* suggests or requires a reinterpretation of Christ's humanity as an *instrumentum divinitatis*. This reinterpretation also offers a convenient and tempting solution to the challenge as it would stress Christ's humanity as an instrument of the divinity such that the entire Trinity utilizes or acts through Christ's humanity to cause salvation. The volitions and actions ascribable to the Word alone are those relating strictly to the active powers of Christ's humanity, which were finite according to the finitude of human nature. Whatever infinite efficacy could be assigned to Christ instrumentally would pertain to the entire Trinity as the undivided actor of an infinite soteriological action. This fits well with Aquinas's discussions of sacramental causality, where he assigns two actions to instruments: "one [action] is instrumental, according to which it operates not in its own power (*in virtute propria*), but in the power of the principal agent (*in virtute principalis agentis*); it has another action that befits it according to its own form" (*ST* III, q.62, a.1, *ad* 2). Christ's humanity would thus have a proper action fitting to human nature and an instrumental action in the infinite power of the Trinity as principal agent. Christ's proper human action would pertain to the Word alone, while his instrumental action would pertain to the whole Trinity. This strategy seems to preserve the unity of Trinitarian actions *ad extra* together with the notion of Christ's instrumentality. Tempting as they seem, these revisions or interpretations cannot be supported from the texts of Aquinas, which indicate a far richer and far more difficult understanding of Christ's volitions and actions.

The key here for Aquinas is the hypostatic union, and it is the hypostatic union that reveals the inadequacy of presenting *instrumentum divinitatis* simply in terms of undivided Trinitarian causality. Limiting Christ's instrumentality to undivided Trinitarian causality undermines the reality of the Incarnation and reduces Christ's humanity to the level of a separate instrument, a secondary cause falling under the primary divine causality. All human beings are separate instruments of the entire Trinity. Presenting Christ's humanity as an instrument of the entire Trinity, though it may helpfully liken Christ's humanity to every other example of humanity in terms of causality, removes the particularity of the Incarnation and hypostatic union. It collapses the significance of distinguishing nature and person where the person provides the determinate mode for the nature. Aquinas cannot accept any presentation of Christ's human actions that overly stresses the causality of Christ's human active powers to the exclusion of their determinate mode through the person of the Word. The particularity of Christ's humanity as determined by the Word through the hypostatic union fulfills a crucial function in Aquinas's Christology and soteriology. Following and developing Anselm's basic insights from the *Cur Deus homo*, Aquinas insists that salvation was most fittingly accomplished through the volitions and actions of the *Deus-homo*. The development consists primarily in specifying the salvific efficacy of Christ's volitions and actions not simply in terms of the *dignity* of the person but rather in terms of the *power* of the person. While profound, this approach also skirts very close to affirming a divided action *ad extra* by one Trinitarian person. This is a general concern for any Incarnational Christology, but it is a specific difficulty for Aquinas's Christology.

Christ *secundum quod homo* causes an infinite effect. The pregnant phrase *secundum quod homo* indicates the Word as a supposit of human nature and Christ's humanity as receiving its determinate mode in the Word. In virtue of the hypostatic union, the person of the Word can humanly will and act with divine efficacy as the instrumental efficient cause of salvation. This differs from presentations of Christ's infinite merit based on the dignity of the person of the Word, because in Thomas's view Christ's efficacy depends on the Word's power rather than simply on the Word's dignity. Insofar as the causality is instrumental, it pertains to the Word alone as the one willer and actor in Christ. In so far as the causality is efficient, it pertains to the Word in concert with the Father and Holy Spirit. Because instrumentality pertains to the Word alone through the Incarnation, instrumental efficient causality pertains to the Word alone. The divine operation in which Christ's humanity participates belongs undividedly to the whole Trinity; the human operation participating the divine operation belongs to the Word alone. This is not a divided divine action *ad extra*, for the whole Trinity most fittingly causes salvation through the Son. This line of reasoning merits expansion both concerning the possibility of this novel type of causality and concerning its fittingness.

The Word shares with the Father and Holy Spirit the unified efficient causality for human salvation. This unity of efficient causality follows necessarily from the absolute unity of Trinitarian actions *ad extra*, neither of which preclude the Incarnation of the Word alone. The distinction of Trinitarian persons allows the whole Trinity to act as principle of the assumption while only the Word serves as term of the assumption and as the suppositum (person, hypostasis) of the assumed nature. A perfect human nature begins to exist in its assumption to the Word in hypostatic union and, as a consequence of the union, becomes a hypostatically-united rational instrument of the divinity in the person of the Word. The Word alone among the Trinitarian persons is the one willer and actor in Christ's volitions and actions, which function instrumentally in virtue of the Word's power and agency.

The question then is how the Word's temporal instrumental causality relates to the Word's eternal efficient causality. The Word's assumption of a perfect human nature into hypostatic union involves no change in the Word; the Word exercises efficient causality for human salvation apart from the Incarnation and continues to do so in the Incarnation. The assumed human nature becomes the 'personal' instrument of the Word and allows a new instrumental form of the Word's efficient causality for salvation. The whole Trinity efficiently causes salvation in and through the Incarnation, but the Word alone exercises that efficiency in and through the instrumental causality of its human will and operation. The causality of Christ's human volitions and actions belongs personally to the Word, participating instrumentally in the Word's primary efficient causality shared with the Father and Holy Spirit. The Word thus exercises instrumental efficient causality without efficient causality being changed into instrumental causality and without the instrumental causality being confused with the unified Trinitarian efficient causality. By the same token, the Word's efficient causality and instrumental causality of human salvation are not separated or divided. These two types of causality are united in the person of the Word, and this union represents the most fitting means for redemption.

The union of divine efficiency and human instrumentality in Christ's instrumental efficient causality is no more and no less possible or explicable than the union of two perfect natures in the one person of the Word. As with the Incarnation itself, Aquinas frames instrumental efficient causality in terms of fittingness. God could bring about human salvation without the Incarnation, but the Incarnation offers the most fitting means for redemption. One framework for the Incarnation's fittingness is provided by Anselm's satisfaction theory of atonement, according to which resolution of the human predicament required a union of divine power with human obligation, weakness, and dignity in the *Deus-homo*. Aquinas extends and enriches this insight by presenting the union as a union of divine and human causality such that Christ *secundum quod homo* can humanly cause an infinite effect, the most fitting remedy for an otherwise intractable disease.

This reading is less an outright rejection of interpreting Christ's humanity as an instrument of the entire Trinity than a refinement. Too much stress on Christ's humanity as an instrument of the whole Trinity compromises the particularity of the Word's Incarnation and causality in Christ. The refinement of this basic view strives for a balance between the undivided Trinitarian causality *ad extra* and the particularity of the Word's Incarnation. If this interpretation is correct, then instrumental efficient causality, which first appeared open to serious criticism for violating the unity of Trinitarian causality, can be read as the starkest guardian against the concern of dividing Trinitarian causality in the Incarnation.

This response to the challenge of dividing Trinitarian causality *ad extra* is far from conclusive. Since Aquinas did not expressly respond to this concern, briefly sketching a response from the available resources should not be taken as limiting Aquinas's possible responses but only gesturing toward them.[68] The absence of any definitive argument settling this concern in Thomas seems like a possible weakness of the Angelic Doctor's Christology and soteriology. Aquinas affirms the unity of Trinitarian actions *ad extra* and seeks to maintain that affirmation together with insistence on the Word alone as incarnate. The various ways to balance these concerns have obvious strengths and weaknesses. Scotus's understanding of individual natures as causal origins represents one such balancing act that offers a well-defined and coherent defense of undivided Trinitarian action. The potential dangers or difficulties of this formulation, especially in light of Scotus's definition of personhood through negation of actual and aptitudinal dependence, include suggestions of a *homo assumptus*

---

68 Gilles Emery notes that Aquinas tempers the absolute unity of Trinitarian actions *ad extra* with the notion that the procession of Trinitarian persons is the reason for the procession of creation (e.g., *ST* I, q.45, a.6). This aspect of Aquinas's understanding of Trinitarian actions *ad extra* offers another potential avenue for developing a response. See Gilles Emery, *Trinity in Aquinas* (Ypsilanti, MI, 2003), pp. 171–175.

Christology.[69] If Christ's human nature is the cause of its volitions and actions and differs from a human person only in virtue of its dependence, this risks slipping into some form of a *homo assumptus* Christology or of affirming a purely human subject in Christ. Aquinas's insistence that actions pertain to supposits and that the Word is the one supposit in Christ carefully guards against any semblance of a *homo assumptus* Christology but leaves itself vulnerable to challenges of violating the absolute unity of Trinitarian actions *ad extra*.

---

69   This is not meant to suggest that Scotus advocated a *homo assumptus* Christology as expounded by Déodat de Basly and Seiller, but only that some of the challenges leveled against a *homo assumptus* Christology could apply to Scotus.

Conclusion

This study has approached scholastic reflections on Christ's wills both historically and systematically, demonstrating that various understandings of Christ's human volitions and actions reflect differing conceptions of the Incarnation and shape differing conceptions of Christ's salvific work. The differences are subtle and easily eclipsed by the substantial agreement among scholastic presentations of Christ's wills. The contextualized textual analysis presented in this investigation has sought to clarify both the substantial agreement and the specific and important disagreements evident in scholastic treatments of Christ's wills. Nothing explains this agreement so much as the dominance of Peter Lombard's *Sentences*, which established the standard framework for scholastic theology, a framework rigid but sufficiently broad to encompass a good deal of debate and development.

The Lombard's *Sentences* did not emerge in a vacuum but reflected questions, concerns, and sources of earlier twelfth-century treatments of Christ's wills, especially the *Summa sententiarum*. The *Sentences* came to dominate thirteenth-century scholastic thought, but this dominance did not silence or erase all other voices. Anselm of Canterbury's *Cur Deus homo* continued to exercise a broad influence in presentations of Christ's wills, based in no small part on its recognition of the passion as a voluntary sacrifice. It was precisely this question of Christ voluntarily willing the passion that occupied the Lombard at length in his discussion of Christ's will and prayer. In highlighting this question and the tension of Christ's agony at Gethsemane, Peter Lombard sparked more than a century of erudite debate concerning the conformity of a human will to the divine will. The *Cur Deus homo* captures none of this tension; thirteenth-century scholastics would compensate by combining a firm stress on the passion as a voluntary sacrifice and a deep sensitivity to Christ's agony at Gethsemane.

This combination raised concerns about the conformity or contrariety of wills in Christ, concerns that consumed ever-greater energies and demanded increasingly subtle responses. William of Auxerre and the authors of the *Summa fratris Alexandri* formulated a denial of contrariety in Christ based on the assumption that true contrariety must be *circa idem et secundum idem* (concerning the same and according to the same). The basic notion is that contrariety of wills requires wills of the same type contrarily disposed to the same object of a voluntary action. Christ's prayer that the cup may pass did not indicate a will contrary to the divine will or any internal contrariety. Instead of indicating contrary wills, the prayer revealed his possession of diverse wills fitting to his two natures and diversely disposed to the same object.

Simple and compelling as this strategy may be, Albert the Great and Bonaventure found it woefully inadequate. Both worried that limiting contrariety to *circa idem et secundum idem* eliminated contrariety in Christ only by removing the very possibility of a created will contrary to the divine will. Emphasizing Christ's true humanity, Albert and Bonaventure sought to explain Christ's will and prayer according to a moral framework equally applicable to every human being. They rejected the *circa idem et secundum idem* argument and shifted the accent from contrariety to conformity or harmony. Albert formulated the more radical proposal by allowing some minimal and morally insignificant contrariety of wills in Christ as a condition for preserving the perfect conformity of Christ's wills. Bonaventure, informed or constrained by Hugh of St Victor, denied all contrariety of wills in Christ and affirmed instead their perfect harmony. Given this sharp rejection of the *circa idem et secundum idem* argument, it comes as some surprise that Thomas Aquinas attempted to retrieve the argument within an enriched consideration of the will. Aquinas wrote the *Summa theologiae*'s treatise on Christ after becoming acquainted with the acts of Constantinople III, which expressly denied any and all contrariety of wills in Christ. Traces of the *circa idem et secundum idem* argument are evident in Scotus, but in discussion of Christ's sorrow and sadness rather than wills. Shifting the topic of contrariety from wills to sorrow and sadness removed or minimized the underlying moral concerns.

Debates about contrariety and conformity of wills were complicated with the introduction of new ways to distinguish aspects of the will, most notably with the *Summa fratris Alexandri*'s introduction of the distinction between will as reason (*voluntas ut ratio*) and will as nature (*voluntas ut natura*). Admitting a distinction within the rational will itself afforded a profound appreciation of Christ's agony at Gethsemane and allowed the possibility of contrariety within Christ's human will. For scholastic theologians from the mid-thirteenth century on, the distinction of *voluntas ut ratio* and *voluntas ut natura* in Christ displayed not contrariety but rather Christ's perfect human obedience to the divine will in spite of an informed natural aversion to the crucifixion as an end in itself. Scholastic theologians presented Christ's obedience as the model for human obedience to the divine will, a modeling that relates to the perfection of Christ's human nature both as an integral nature and as sinless. For thirteenth-century scholastic theologians, Christology completed anthropology.

The medieval stress on Christ's obedience related to discussions of moral theology but in no sense limited Christ to a moral exemplar. While this is generally evident in thirteenth-century Christology, this study highlighted Thomas Aquinas's Christology and its sophisticated presentation of Christ's human will and operation as the instrumental efficient cause of salvation. Aquinas developed traditional presentations of Christ's two wills and operations in new directions. Tracking and explaining that development required attentive comparison of the *Scriptum* on the *Sentences* and the *Summa theologiae* and revealed Aquinas's recovery of patristic and conciliar sources as well as his terminological and conceptual advancements. In the *Summa* Aquinas crafted an intricate Christology, weaving together thirteenth-century understandings of the will, patristic and conciliar affirmations of Christ's two non-contrary wills, a soteriology based upon voluntary acceptance of the passion, and a novel conception of instrumental efficient causality. Emphasizing the causal role of Christ's human will and operation in salvation highlights the dignity of humanity as able to approach God through intellect and will and frames the Incarnation as the wisest and most fitting means for redemption.

Thomas Aquinas's mature presentation of Christ's wills minimally influenced proposals from the end of the thirteenth century and beginning of the fourteenth century, and the topic of Christ's wills itself seems to have diminished in importance. The landscape of Christology was shifting, and new questions or new answers to older questions captivated attention. The most dramatic and important shift appears in John Duns Scotus's Christology, which considered contrariety in terms of sorrow and sadness rather than in terms of will and which employed the absolute unity of Trinitarian actions *ad extra* to reject any special causation by the Word in Christ's human volitions and actions. Scotus charted a new direction for reflections on Christ's sadness, sorrow, and wills while raising a concern that seems disastrous for Aquinas's understanding of Christ's causality. The stance advocated here insists that Aquinas's Christology possesses resources for a sufficient response to challenges concerning instrumental efficient causality. This response notwithstanding, Aquinas's Christology attempts to maintain a precarious balance of the unity of Trinitarian actions *ad extra* with the Word alone as incarnate and as causing salvation through instrumental efficiency.

Throughout their variations, scholastic treatments of Christ's wills explored the integrity and perfection of Christ's human nature. They did so through linguistic and conceptual schemes of great sophistication, yet the utility of scholastic presentations of Christ's wills far exceeds these schemes. The continuing relevance of discussing the topic of Christ's wills rests on both its systematic import for Christology and its reliance on concrete and biblical terminology for examining the complex reality of a simple God incarnate for human salvation.

Bibliography

Abbreviations

PG Patrologiae cursus completus: Series Graeca, ed. J.-P. Migne, 161 vols. (Paris: Migne, 1857–1866)

PL Patrologiae cursus completus: Series Latina, ed. J.-P. Migne, 221 vols. (Paris: Migne, 1844–1864)

Primary Sources

Aegidius Romanus (Giles of Rome). *Reportatio lecturae super III Sententiarum*. Ed. Concetta Luna. Opera omnia 3.2. Florence: Edizioni del Galluzzo, 2003.

— (?). *Quaestiones super III Sententiarum*. Rome: Alexander Zanetti, 1623. Repr. Frankfurt: Minerva, 1968.

Albertus Magnus *Commentarii in II Sententiarum*. Ed. Auguste Borgnet. Opera omnia 27. Paris: Vivès, 1894.

—. *Commentarii in III Sententiarum*. Ed. Auguste Borgnet. Opera omnia 28. Paris: Vivès, 1894.

—. *De incarnatione*. Ed. Ignaz Backes. In *Opera omnia*, ed. Bernhard Geyer, 26: 171–235. Münster: Aschendorff, 1958.

Alexander of Hales. *Glossa in quatuor libros Sententiarum Petri Lombardi*. Ed. PP. Collegii S. Bonaventurae. Bibliotheca franciscana scholastica medii aevi 12–15. Quaracchi: Collegium S. Bonaventurae, 1951–1957.

—. *Quaestiones disputatae 'antequam esset frater'*. Ed. PP. Collegii S. Bonaventurae. Bibliotheca franciscana scholastica medii aevi 19–21. Quaracchi: Collegium S. Bonaventurae, 1960.

— (?). *Summa theologica seu sic ab origine dicta "Summa fratris Alexandri"*. Ed. PP. Collegii S. Bonaventurae. 4 vols text, 2 vols indexes. Quaracchi: Collegium S. Bonaventurae, 1924–1979.

Ambrose. *De fide ad Gratianum Augustum libri quinque*. PL 16: 527–698.

—. *Expositio Evangelii secundum Lucam*. Ed. C. Schenkl. Corpus scriptorum ecclesiasticorum Latinorum 32.4. Vienna: Tempsky, 1902.

Anselm. *Cur Deus homo*. In *S. Anselmi Opera omnia*, ed. Franciscus Salesius Schmitt, 2:37–133. Edinburgh: Thomas Nelson and Sons, 1946.

Augustine. *Contra Maximinum haereticum Arianorum episcopum*. PL 42: 745–814.

Bonaventure. *Breviloquium.* In *Opera theologica selecta,* ed. PP. Collegii S. Bonaventurae, 5:1–175. Quaracchi: Collegium S. Bonaventurae, 1964.

—. *Commentaria in quatuor libros Sententiarum Magistri Petri Lombardi.* Ed. PP. Collegii S. Bonaventurae. Opera theologica selecta 1–4. Quaracchi: Collegium S. Bonaventurae, 1934–1949.

Chartularium universitatis parisiensis 1. Ed. Heinrich Denifle. Paris: Delalain, 1889.

Concilium universale Constantinopolitanum tertium. Ed. Rudolf Riedinger. Acta conciliorum oecumenicorum, 2nd ser., 2.1–2. Bayerische Akademie der Wissenschaften. Berlin: Walter de Gruyter, 1990–1992.

Gratian. *The Treatise on Laws (Decretum DD. 1–20).* Trans. James Gordley and Augustine Thompson. Washington, DC: Catholic University of America Press, 1993.

Gregory of Nazianzus. *Discourses 27–31.* Ed. Paul Gallay. Sources chrétiennes 250. Paris: Cerf, 1978.

Hugh of St Victor. *De quatuor voluntatibus Christi.* PL 176: 841–846.

—. *De sacramentis fidei Christianae.* PL 176: 174–618.

John Chrysostom. *Homiliae in Matthaeum 83.* PG 58: 745–747.

John of Damascus. De fide orthodoxa: *Versions of Burgundio and Cerbanus.* Ed. Eloi Marie Buytaert. St Bonaventure, NY: The Franciscan Institute, 1955.

—. *Die Schriften des Johannes von Damaskos.* Ed. B. Kotter. 5 vols. Berlin and New York: Walter de Gruyter, 1969–1988.

John Duns Scotus. *Lectura* III. Ed. Barnaba Hechich et al. Opera omnia 20–21. Vatican City: Typis Vaticanis, 2003–2004.

—. *Ordinatio* I. Ed. Carolus Balić et al. Opera omnia 3–6. Vatican City: Typis Polyglottis Vaticanis, 1954–1963.

—. *Ordinatio* III. Ed. Barnaba Hechich et al. Opera omnia 9. Vatican City: Typis Vaticanis, 2006–2007.

Leo the Great. *Tomus ad Flavianum.* In *S. Leonis Magni Epistolae,* PL 54: 755–782.

Matthew of Aquasparta. *Quaestiones disputatae de incarnatione et redemptione et de lapsu aliaeque selectae de Christo et de eucharistiae.* Ed. PP. Collegii S. Bonaventurae. Quaracchi: Collegium S. Bonaventurae, 1957.

Maximus Confessor. *Opera omnia.* PG 90–91.

Nemesius of Emesa. *De natura hominis.* In *Némésius d'Émèse:* De natura hominis: *Traduction de Burgundio de Pise.* Ed. J.R. Moncho and Gérard Verbeke. Corpus latinum commentariorum in Aristotelem graecorum, suppl. 1. Leiden: E.J. Brill, 1975.

Nicaea I to Lateran V. Ed. Norman P. Tanner. Vol. 1 of *Decrees of the Ecumenical Councils,* ed. Norman P. Tanner. Washington, DC: Georgetown University Press, 1990.

Peter Abelard. *Commentaria in epistolam Pauli ad Romanos.* Ed. Eloi Marie Buytaert. Corpus Christianorum Continuatio Mediaevalis 11. Turnhout: Brepols, 1969.

—. [*Scito te ipsum* or *Ethica.*] *Peter Abelard's* Ethics. Ed. and trans. David Edward Luscombe. Oxford: Clarendon Press, 1971.

—. *Sic et non.* Ed. Blanche Beatrice Boyer and Richard McKeon. Chicago: University of Chicago Press, 1977.

Peter Lombard. *Sententiae in IV libris distinctae*. Ed. PP. Collegii S. Bonaventurae. Spicilegium Bonaventurianum 4–5. Grottaferrata: Collegium S. Bonaventurae, 1971–1981.

Peter Olivi. *Quaestiones de incarnatione et redemptione; Quaestiones de virtutibus*. Ed. Aquilinus Emmen and Ernst Stadter. Bibliotheca franciscana scholastica medii aevi 24. Grottaferrata: Collegium S. Bonaventurae, 1981.

Sancta synodus sexta generalis Constantinopolitana tertia. In *Sacrorum conciliorum nova et amplissima collectio,* ed. Joannes Dominicus Mansi, 11: 189–1024. Florence, 1965. Repr. Graz: Akademische Druck- u. Verlagsanstalt, 1960–1961.

Summa sententiarum. PL 176: 42–174.

Thomas Aquinas. *Compendium theologiae.* In *Sancti Thomae de Aquino Opera omnia,* Leonis XIII P.M. edita, cura et studio Fratrum Praedicatorum, 42:83–205. Rome: Ex Typographia Polyglotta S.C. de Propaganda Fide, 1882. Repr. Rome: Editori di San Tommaso, 1979.

—. *Liber de veritate Catholicae fidei contra errores infidelium, qui dicitur Summa contra gentiles.* Ed. D. Petrus Marc, Ceslas Pera, and D. Pietro Caramello. 3 vols. Turin: Marietti, 1961.

—. *De unione Verbi incarnati.* In *Quaestiones disputatae et quaestiones duodecim quodlibetales* (Turin: Marietti, 1931) 2: 468–485.

—. *De veritate.* Vols 3–4 of *Quaestiones disputatae et quaestiones duodecim quodlibetales.* Turin: Marietti, 1931.

—. *Quaestiones disputatae et quaestiones duodecim quodlibetales.* 5 vols. Turin: Marietti, 1931.

—. *Quodlibetum nonum.* In *Quaestiones disputatae et quaestiones duodecim quodlibetales* (Turin: Marietti, 1931) 5: 181–202.

—. *Scriptum super Sententiis Magistri Petri Lombardi.* Ed. Maria Fabianus Moos. Vol. 3. Paris: P. Lethielleux, 1933.

—. *Summa theologiae.* Cura et studio Instituti studiorum medievalium Ottaviensis, ad textum S. Pii Pp. V iussu confectum recognita. 5 vols. Ottawa: impensis Studii generalis OP, 1941–1945.

—. *Summa theologica.* Complete English Edition in Five Volumes. Trans. Fathers of the English Dominican Province. Originally published 1911. Rev. ed. London, 1920. Reissued in 3 vols, New York: Benzinger Brothers, 1948. Repr. Notre Dame, IN: Christian Classics from Ave Maria Press, 1981.

—. *Super epistolas S. Pauli lectura.* Ed. Raphaele Cai. 8th ed. 2 vols. Turin: Marietti, 1953.

William of Auxerre. *Summa aurea Guillelmi Altissiodorensis.* Ed. Jean Ribaillier. Vol. 3.1. Spicilegium Bonaventurianum 18A. Grottaferrata: Editiones Collegii S. Bonaventurae ad Claras Aquas, 1986.

Ysagoge in theologiam. In *Écrits théologiques de l'école d'Abélard,* ed. Artur Michael Landgraf, pp. 63–285. Spicilegium sacrum Lovaniense: Etudes et documents. Louvain: Spicilegium sacrum Lovaniense, 1934.

Secondary Sources

Adams, Marilyn M. "Elegant Necessity, Prayerful Disputation: Method in *Cur Deus homo*." In Cur Deus homo, ed. Gilbert et al., pp. 367–396.

Alexakis, Alexander. "Before the Lateran Council of 649: The Last Days of Herakleios the Emperor and Monotheletism." In *Synodus: Beiträge zur Konzilien- und allgemeinen Kirchengeschichte: Festschrift für Walter Brandmüller*, ed. Remigius Bäumer et al., pp. 93–101. Paderborn: Schöningh, 1997.

Alvira, Tomas. *Naturaleza y libertad: Estudio de los conceptos tomistas de* voluntas ut natura *y* voluntas ut ratio. Pamplona: Ediciones Universidad de Navarra, 1985.

Anzulewicz, Henryk. "Neuere Forschung zu Albertus Magnus: Bestandsaufnahme und Problemstellungen." *Recherches de théologie et philosophie médiévales* 66 (1999): 163–206.

Armitage, J. Mark. "A Certain Rectitude of Order: Jesus and Justification according to Aquinas." *Thomist* 72 (2008): 45–66.

Backes, Ignaz. "Das zeitliche Verhältnis der *Summa de incarnatione* zu dem dritten Buche des Sentenzenkommentars Alberts des Großen." In *Studia Albertina: Festschrift für Bernhard Geyer zum 70. Geburtstage*, ed. Heinrich Ostlender, pp. 32–51. Münster: Aschendorff, 1952.

—. *Die Christologie des hl. Thomas von Aquin und die griechischen Kirchenväter.* Paderborn: Schöningh, 1931.

Baker, John R. "Must the God-Man Die?" In Cur Deus homo, ed. Gilbert et al., pp. 609–620.

Balthasar, Hans Urs von. *Cosmic Liturgy: The Universe according to Maximus the Confessor.* Trans. Brian E. Daley. San Francisco: Ignatius Press, 2003.

—. *Studies in Theological Style: Clerical Styles.* Ed. John Riches. Trans. A. Louth, F. McDonagh, and B. McNeil. Vol. 2 of *The Glory of the Lord: A Theological Aesthetics.* San Francisco: Ignatius Press, 1984.

—. "La *concordantia libertatis* chez saint Anselme." In *L'homme devant Dieu: Mélanges offerts au Père Henri de Lubac* 2: 29–45. 3 vols. Paris: Aubier, 1963–1964.

Barnes, Corey L. "Albert the Great and Thomas Aquinas on Person, Hypostasis, and Hypostatic Union." *Thomist* 72 (2008): 107–146.

—. "Thomas Aquinas on Christ's Prayer." In *A History of Prayer: The First to the Fifteenth Century*, ed. Roy Hammerling, pp. 319–336. Leiden: E.J. Brill, 2008.

Baron, Roger. "Hugues de Saint-Victor" [1968]. In *Dictionnaire de spiritualité* 7: 901–939. 17 vols in 20. Paris: Beauchesne, 1932–1995.

Barth, Bernhard. "Ein neues Dokument zur Geschichte der frühscholastischen Christologie." *Theologische Quartalschrift* 100 (1919): 409–426; Archivum franciscanum historicum and 101 (1920): 235–262.

Bathrellos, Demetrios. *The Byzantine Christ: Person, Nature, and Will in the Christology of Saint Maximus the Confessor.* Oxford: Oxford University Press, 2004.

—. "The Relationship between the Divine Will and the Human Will of Jesus Christ according to Saint Maximus the Confessor." *Studia patristica* 37 (2001): 346–352.

Bazán, Bernardo Carlos "Le commentaire de S. Thomas d'Aquin sur le *Traité de l'âme*. Un évènement: L'édition critique de la Commission Léonine." *Revue des sciences philosophiques et théologiques* 69 (1985): 521–547.

—. "Pluralisme de formes ou dualisme de substances: La pensée pré-thomiste touchant la nature de l'âme." *Revue philosophique de Louvain* 67 (1969): 31–73.
Berthold, George C. "The Cappadocian Roots of Maximus the Confessor." In *Maximus Confessor: Actes du Symposium sur Maxime le Confesseur, Fribourg, 2–5 septembre 1980*, ed. Felix Heinzer and Christoph Schönborn, pp. 51–59. Fribourg: Éditions universitaires, 1982.
Bettoni, Efrem. *Saint Bonaventure*. Trans. Angelus Gambatese. Westport, CT: Greenwood Press, 1981.
Biffi, Inos. *I misteri di Cristo in Tommaso d'Aquino. La costruzione della teologia* 1.1. Milan: Jaca, 1994.
Bonnefoy, J. "La place du Christ dans le plan divin de la création." *Mélanges de science religieuse* 4 (1947): 257–284 and 5 (1948): 39–62.
Bouëssé, Humbert. "De la causalité de l'humanité du Christ." In *Problèmes actuels de christologie*, ed. Humbert Bouëssé and Jean-Jacques Latour, pp. 147–177. Paris: Desclée de Brouwer, 1965
—. "La causalité efficiente instrumentale et la causalité méritoire de la sainte humanité du Christ." *Revue thomiste* 44 (1938): 256–298.
—. "La causalité efficiente instrumentale de l'humanité du Christ et des sacrements chrétiens." *Revue thomiste* 39 (1934): 370–393.
Bougerol, Jacques-Guy. "The Church Fathers and the *Sentences* of Peter Lombard." In *Reception of the Church Fathers in the West: From the Carolingians to the Maurists*, ed. Irena Backus, 1: 113–164. 2 vols. Leiden: E.J. Brill, 1997.
—. *Lexique saint Bonaventure*. Paris: Éditions franciscaines, 1969.
—. *Introduction to the Works of Bonaventure*. Trans. José de Vinck. Paterson, NJ: St Anthony Guild Press, 1964.
Bouthillier, D. "Le Christ en son mystère dans les *Collationes* du *Super Isaiam* de saint Thomas d'Aquin." In *Ordo sapientiae et amoris*, ed. Pinto de Oliveira, pp. 37–64.
Boyle, John F. "The Twofold Division of St Thomas's Christology in the *Tertia Pars*." *Thomist* 60 (1996): 439–447.
Boyle, Leonard E. "The Setting of the *Summa theologiae*." In *Aquinas's* Summa theologiae: *Critical Essays*, ed. Brian Davies, pp. 1–24. New York: Rowman and Littlefield Publishers, 2006.
Bracken, Jerry. "Thomas Aquinas and Anselm's Satisfaction Theory." *Angelicum* 62 (1985): 501–530.
Brady, Ignatius. "The *Summa Theologica* of Alexander of Hales (1924–1948)." *Archivum franciscanum historicum* 70 (1977): 437–447.
—. "St Bonaventure's Theology of the Imitation of Christ." In *Proceedings of the Seventh Centenary Celebration of the Death of Saint Bonaventure*, ed. Pascal F. Foley, pp. 61–72. St Bonaventure, NY: Franciscan Institute, 1975.
—. "The Distinctions of Lombard's *Book of Sentences* and Alexander of Hales." *Franciscan Studies* 25 (1965): 90–116.
Bro, Bernard. "La notion métaphysique de tout et son application au problème théologique de l'union hypostatique." *Revue thomiste* 68 (1968): 181–197, 357–380.

Brown, Stephen F. "Thomas Aquinas and His Contemporaries on the Unique Existence in Christ." In *Christ among the Medieval Dominicans*, ed. Kent Emery, Jr and Joseph Wawrykow, pp. 220–237. Notre Dame, IN: University of Notre Dame Press, 1998.

Burger, Maria. *Personalität im Horizont absoluter Prädestination: Untersuchungen zur Christologie des Johannes Duns Scotus und ihrer Rezeption in modernen theologischen Ansätzen*. Beiträge zur Geschichte der Philosophie und Theologie des Mittelalters 40. Münster: Aschendorff, 1994.

Burns, J. Patout. "The Concept of Satisfaction in Medieval Redemption Theory." *Theological Studies* 36 (1975): 285–304.

Burr, David. *The Persecution of Peter Olivi*. Philadelphia: American Philosophical Society, 1976.

Burrell, David B. *Aquinas: God and Action*. Notre Dame, IN: University of Notre Dame Press, 1979.

Buytaert, Eloi Marie. "St John Damascene, Peter Lombard, and Gerhoh of Reichersberg." *Franciscan Studies* 10 (1950): 323–343.

Bynum, Caroline Walker. *Wonderful Blood: Theology and Practice in Late Medieval Northern Germany and Beyond*. Philadelphia: University of Pennsylvania Press, 2007.

Callus, Daniel A. "The Origins of the Problem of the Unity of Form." *Thomist* 24 (1961): 257–285.

Catão, Bernard. *Salut et rédemption chez S. Thomas d'Aquin: L'acte sauveur du Christ*. Paris: Aubier, 1964.

Cessario, Romanus. "Incarnate Wisdom and the Immediacy of Christ's Salvific Knowledge." In *Atti del IX Congresso tomistico internazionale*, ed. Antonio Piolanti, 5: 334–340. Studi tomistici 44. Vatican City: Libreria editrice Vaticana, 1991.

Châtillon, Jean. "Hugo von St Viktor" [1986]. In *Theologische Realenzyklopädie* 15: 629–635. 36 vols. Berlin: Walter de Gruyter, 1977–2007.

Chenu, Marie-Dominique. *Toward Understanding St Thomas*. Trans. Albert M. Landry and Dominic Hughes. Chicago: Henry Regnery Co., 1964.

——. "Le plan de la *Somme théologique* de S. Thomas." *Revue thomiste* 45 (1939): 93–107.

——. "The Revolutionary Intellectualism of St Albert the Great." *Blackfriars* 19 (1938): 5–15.

Coakley, Sarah. "What Does Chalcedon Solve and What Does It Not? Some Reflections on the Status and Meaning of the Chalcedonian 'Definition.'" In *The Incarnation: An Interdisciplinary Symposium on the Incarnation of the Son of God*, ed. Steven T. Davis, Daniel Kendall, and Gerald O'Collins, pp. 143–163. Oxford: Oxford University Press, 2002.

Coffey, David. "The Theandric Nature of Christ." *Theological Studies* 60 (1999): 405–431.

Colish, Marcia L. "Peter Lombard," In *The Medieval Theologians: An Introduction to Theology in the Medieval Period*, ed. Gillian Rosemary Evans, pp. 168–183. Oxford: Blackwell Publishers, 2001.

—. *Peter Lombard*. Brill's Studies in Intellectual History 41. 2 vols. Leiden: E.J. Brill, 1994.
Congar, Yves. "Le moment 'économique' et le moment 'ontologique' dans la *sacra doctrina* (Révélation, Théologie, *Somme théologique*)." In *Mélanges offerts à M.-D. Chenu, maître en théologie*, pp. 135–187. Bibliothèque thomiste 37. Paris: Vrin, 1967.
—. "Le sens de 'l'économie' salutaire dans la 'théologie' de S. Thomas d'Aquin (*Somme théologique*)." In *Festgabe Joseph Lortz*, ed. Erwin Iserloh, 2: 73–122. 2 vols. Baden-Baden: B. Grimm, 1958.
Constable, Giles. *Three Studies in Medieval Religious and Social Thought*. Cambridge: Cambridge University Press, 1995.
Coolman, Boyd Taylor. "Hugh of St Victor on 'Jesus Wept': Compassion as Ideal *Humanitas*." *Theological Studies* 69 (2008): 528–556.
—. "The Salvific Affectivity of Christ according to Alexander of Hales." *Thomist* 71 (2007): 1–38.
—. *Knowing God by Experience: The Spiritual Senses in the Theology of William of Auxerre*. Washington, DC: Catholic University of America Press, 2004.
Corbin, Michel. "La parole devenue chair: Lecture de la première question de la *tertia pars* de la *Somme théologique*." *Revue des sciences philosophiques et théologiques* 62 (1978): 5–40.
—. *Le chemin de la théologie chez Thomas d'Aquin*. Paris: Beauchesne, 1974.
Corvez, M. "L'unicité d'existence dans le Christ." *Revue thomiste* 56 (1956): 413–426.
Cross, Richard. "Accidents, Substantial Forms, and Causal Powers in the Late Thirteenth Century: Some Reflections on the Axiom *actiones sunt suppositorum*." In *Compléments de substance: Études sur les propriétés accidentales offertes à Alain de Libera*, ed. Christophe Erismann and Alexandrine Schniewind, pp. 133–146. Problèmes et controverses. Paris: Vrin, 2008.
—. *The Metaphysics of the Incarnation: Thomas Aquinas to Duns Scotus*. Oxford: Oxford University Press, 2002.
—. "Aquinas on Nature, Hypostasis, and the Metaphysics of the Incarnation." *Thomist* 60 (1996): 171–202.
Crotty, Nicholas. "The Redemptive Role of Christ's Resurrection." *Thomist* 25 (1962): 54–106.
Crowley, Paul G. "*Instrumentum divinitatis* in Thomas Aquinas: Recovering the Divinity of Christ." *Theological Studies* 52 (1991): 451–475.
Daley, Brian E. "'He Himself is Our Peace' (Ephesians 2:14): Early Christian Views of Redemption in Christ." In *The Redemption: an Interdisciplinary Symposium on Christ as Redeemer*, ed. Stephen T. Davis, Daniel. Kendall, and Gerald O'Collins, pp. 149–176. Oxford: Oxford University Press, 2004.
—. "Nature and the 'Mode of Union': Late Patristic Models for the Personal Unity of Christ." In *The Incarnation: An Interdisciplinary Symposium on the Incarnation of the Son of God*, ed. Stephen T. Davis, Daniel Kendall, Gerald O'Collins, pp. 164–196. Oxford: Oxford University Press, 2002.
—. "The Giant's Twin Substances: Ambrose and the Christology of Augustine's

Contra sermonem Arianorum." In *Augustine: Presbyter factus sum*, ed. Joseph T. Lienhard, Earl C. Muller and Roland J. Teske, pp. 477–495. Collectanea Augustiniana. New York: Peter Lang, 1993.

De Amato, Norbert. *Doctrina summae fratris Alexandri de Hales, de ipsa natura a Verbo assumpta: Disquisitio historico-systematica*. Rome: Herder, 1956.

De Clerck, E. "Le dogme de la rédemption: De Robert de Melun à Guillaume d'Auxerre." *Recherches de théologie ancienne et médiévale* 14 (1947): 252–286.

De Libera, Alain. "Les actions appartiennent aux sujets: Petite archéologie d'un principe leibnizien." In *"Ad ingenii acuitionem": Studies in Honour of Alfonso Maierù*. Ed. Stefano Caroti et al., pp. 199–220. Louvaine-la-Neuve: Collège Cardinal Mercier, 2006.

Delaporte, Guy François. *Lecture du commentaire de Thomas d'Aquin sur le* Traité de l'âme *d'Aristote: l'âme souffle de vie*. Paris: Harmattan, 1999.

Deme, Dániel. *The Christology of Anselm of Canterbury*. Aldershot, England: Ashgate, 2003.

Diepen, Herman M. "L'existence humaine du Christ en métaphysique thomiste." *Revue thomiste* 58 (1958): 197–213.

—. "Échange de vues: À propos de la psychologie humaine du Christ." *Revue thomiste* 51 (1951): 465–478.

—. "La psychologie humaine du Christ." *Revue thomiste* 50 (1950): 515–562

Dondaine, H.-D. "À propos d'Avicenne et de saint Thomas: De la causalité dispositive à la causalité instrumentale." *Revue thomiste* 51 (1951): 441–453.

Doucet, Marcel. "La volonté humaine du Christ, spécialement en son agonie: Maxime le Confesseur, interprète de l'Écriture." *Science et esprit* 37 (1985): 123–159.

Dumont, Stephen. "Did Duns Scotus Change His Mind on the Will?" In *Nach der Verurteilung von 1277: Philosophie und Theologie an der Universität von Paris im letzten Viertel des 13. Jahrhunderts: Studien und Texte*, ed. Jan A. Aertsen, Kent Emery, and Andreas Speer, pp. 719–794. Miscellanea mediaevalia 28. Berlin: Walter de Gruyter, 2001.

—. "The Origin of Scotus's Theory of Synchronic Contingency." *The Modern Schoolman* 72 (1995): 149–168.

Eardley, Peter S. "Thomas Aquinas and Giles of Rome on the Will." *Review of Metaphysics* 56 (2003): 835–862.

Eastman, John R. "Das Leben des Augustiner-Eremiten Aegidius Romanus (c.1243–1316)." *Zeitschrift für Kirchengeschichte* 100 (1989): 318–339.

Elamrani-Jamal, Abdelali. "La réception de la philosophie arabe à l'université de Paris au XIIIème siècle." In *The Introduction of Arabic Philosophy into Europe*, ed. Charles E. Butterworth and Blake Andrée Kessel, pp. 31–39. Studien und Texte zur Geistesgeschichte des Mittelalters 39. Leiden: E.J. Brill, 1994.

Elders, Leo. "Le méthode suivie par saint Thomas d'Aquin dans la composition de la *Somme de théologie*." *Nova et vetera* 66 (1991): 177–192.

—. *Autour de saint Thomas d'Aquin: recueil d'études sur sa pensée philosophique et théologique*. 2 vols. Paris: FAC-éditions, 1987.

—. "Les citations de saint Augustin dans la *Somme théologique* de saint Thomas d'Aquin." *Doctor Communis* 40 (1987): 115–167.
Emery, Gilles. "Trinity and Creation." In *The Theology of Thomas Aquinas*, ed. Rik Van Nieuwenhove and Joseph Wawrykow, pp. 58–76. Notre Dame, IN: University of Notre Dame Press, 2005.
—. *Trinity in Aquinas*. Ypsilanti, MI: Sapientia Press of Ave Maria College, 2003.
—. *La Trinité créatrice: Trinité et création dans les commentaires aux* Sentences *de Thomas d'Aquin et de ses précurseurs Albert le Grand et Bonaventure*. Bibliothèque thomiste 47. Paris: Vrin, 1995.
Evans, G. R. "Anselm of Canterbury." In *The Medieval Theologians: An Introduction to Theology in the Medieval Period*, ed. G. R. Evans, pp. 94–101. Oxford: Blackwell, 2001.
Féret, H.M. "Christologie médiévale de saint Thomas et christologie concrète et historique pour aujourd'hui." In *Tomismo e neotomismo*, pp. 107–141. Memorie Domenicane, n.s. 6. Pistoia, Italy: Centro Reviste Padri Domenicani, 1975.
Galot, Jean. "Le Christ terrestre et la vision." *Gregorianum* 67 (1986): 429–450.
Galtier, Paul. "L'union hypostatique et l'entre deux de saint Thomas." *Ephemerides theologicae Lovanienses* 7 (1930): 425–470.
Garrigues, Jean-Miguel. *Maxime le Confesseur: La charité, avenir divin de l'homme*. Théologie Historique 38. Paris: Beauchesne, 1976.
Gauthier, René Antoine. "Note sur le débuts (1225–1240) du premier 'Averroïsme.'" *Revue des sciences philosophiques et théologiques* 66 (1982): 321–374.
—. "Saint Maxime le Confesseur et la psychologie de l'acte humain." *Recherches de théologie ancienne et médiévale* 21 (1954): 51–100.
Geenen, Gottfried. "En marge du Concile de Chalcédoine: Les textes du Quatrième concile dans les œuvres de saint Thomas." *Angelicum* 29 (1952): 43–59.
—. "The Council of Chalcedon in the Theology of St Thomas." In *From an Abundant Spring: The Walter Farrell Memorial Volume of the* Thomist, ed. staff of the *Thomist*, pp. 172–217. New York: P.J. Kenedy, 1952.
—. "The Place of the Tradition in the Theology of St Thomas." *Thomist* 15 (1952): 110–135.
Gilbert, Paul. "Violence et liberté dans le *Cur Deus homo*." In Cur Deus homo, ed. Gilbert et al., pp. 673–695.
Gilbert, Paul, Helmut Kohlenberger, and Elmar Salmann, eds. Cur Deus homo: *Atti del Congresso anselmiano internazionale: Roma, 21–23 maggio 1998*. Studia anselmiana 128. Rome: Centro studi S. Anselmo, 1999.
Gillon, L.-B. "La notion de conséquence de l'union hypostatique dans le cadre de *IIIa* qq. 2–26." *Angelicum* 15 (1938): 17–34.
Gils, P.-M. "Textes inédits de S. Thomas: Les premières rédactions du *Scriptum super Tertio Sententiarum*." *Revue des sciences philosophiques et théologiques* 45 (1961): 201–228; 46 (1962): 445–462, 609–628.
Gilson, Etienne. *The Christian Philosophy of St Thomas Aquinas*. Trans. Laurence K. Shook. Notre Dame, IN: University of Notre Dame Press, 1994.
—. "L'*esse* du Verbe incarné selon saint Thomas d'Aquin." *Archives d'histoire doctrinale et littéraire du moyen âge* 35 (1968): 23–37.

—. *The Philosophy of St Bonaventure*. Trans. Illtyd Trethowan and Frank J. Sheed. New York: Sheed & Ward, 1938.

Glorieux, P. "La christologie du *Compendium theologiae*." *Sciences ecclésiastiques* 13 (1961): 7–34.

Gomez Nogales, Salvador. "Saint Thomas, Averroès et l'averroïsme." In *Aquinas and Problems of His Time*, ed. G. Verbeke and D. Verhelst, pp. 161–177. Mediaevalia Lovaniensia: series 1, studia 5. Louvain: Leuven University Press, 1976.

Gondreau, Paul. "The Humanity of Christ, the Incarnate Word." In *The Theology of Thomas Aquinas*, ed. Rik van Nieuwnhove and Joseph Wawrykow, pp. 252–276. Notre Dame, IN: University of Notre Dame Press, 2005.

—. *The Passions of Christ's Soul in the Theology of St Thomas Aquinas*. Münster: Aschendorff, 2002.

González-Ayesta, Cruz. "Scotus' Interpretation of the Difference between *voluntas ut natura* and *voluntas ut voluntas*." *Franciscan Studies* 66 (2008): 371–412.

Gorman, Michael M. "Christ as Composite according to Aquinas." *Traditio* 55 (2000): 143–157.

—. "Uses of the Person-Nature Distinction in Thomas' Christology." *Recherches de théologie et philosophie médiévales* 67 (2000): 58–79.

Gössmann, Elisabeth. *Metaphysik und Heilsgeschichte: Eine theologische Untersuchung der Summa Halensis (Alexander von Hales)*. Munich: Max Hueber Verlag, 1964.

Häring, N.M. "The Case of Gilbert de la Porrée, Bishop of Poitiers (1142–1154)." *Mediaeval Studies* 13 (1951): 1–40.

—. "The Character and Range of Influence of St Cyril of Alexandria on Latin Theology (430–1260)." *Mediaeval Studies* 12 (1950): 1–19.

Hastings, Adrian. "Christ's Act of Existence." *Downside Review* 73 (1955): 139–159.

Hauptmann, Peter. "Maximus Confessor." In *Alte Kirche*, ed. Martin Greschat, 2: 275–288. 2 vols. Stuttgart: Verlag W. Kohlhammer, 1984.

Hause, J. "Voluntariness and Causality: Some Problems for Aquinas' Theory of Responsibility." *Vivarium* 36 (1998): 55–66.

Hayen, André. "La structure de la *Somme théologique* et Jésus." *Sciences ecclésiastiques* 12 (1960): 59–82.

—. *Saint Thomas d'Aquin et la vie de l' Église*. Louvain: Publications universitaires, 1952.

Hayes, Zachary. "Introduction." In *Disputed Questions on the Knowledge of Christ*, ed. and trans. Zachary Hayes, pp. 21–67. St Bonaventure, NY: Franciscan Institute, St Bonaventure University, 2005.

—. "Bonaventure: Mystery of the Triune God." In *The History of Franciscan Theology*, ed. Kenan B. Osborne, pp. 39–125. St Bonaventure, NY: Franciscan Institute, St Bonaventure University, 1994.

—. "The Plurality of *Esse* in Christ according to Matthew of Aquasparta." In *Essays Honoring Allan B. Wolter*, ed. William A. Frank and Girard J. Etzkorn, pp. 131–152. St Bonaventure, NY: Franciscan Institute, St Bonaventure University, 1985.

—. *The Hidden Center: Spirituality and Speculative Christology in St Bonaventure*. New York: Paulist Press, 1981.

Henninger, Mark Gerald. *Relations: Medieval Theories, 1250–1325*. Oxford: Clarendon Press, 1989.

Héris, Charles Vincent. *Le mystère du Christ*. Paris: Desclée et Cie, 1928.

Hipp, Stephen A. *"Person" in Christian Tradition and in the Conception of Saint Albert the Great: A Systematic Study of its Concept as Illuminated by the Mysteries of the Trinity and the Incarnation*. Beiträge zur Geschichte der Philosophie und Theologie des Mittelalters, n.s. 57. Münster: Aschendorff, 2001.

Hoffmann, Tobias. "The Distinction between Nature and Will in Duns Scotus." *Archives d'histoire doctrinale et littéraire du Moyen Age* 66 (1999): 189–224.

Horst, U. "Über die Frage einer Heilsökonomischen Theologie bei Thomas von Aquin. Ergebnisse und Probleme der neuren Forschung." *Münchener theologische Zeitschrift* 12 (1961): 97–111.

Hugon, Edouard. *La causalité instrumentale dans l'ordre surnaturel*. Paris: Pierre Téqui, 1924.

——. "La causalité instrumentale de l'humanité sainte de Jésus." *Revue thomiste* 13 (1905): 44–68.

Imbach, Ruedi. "L'averroïsme latin du XIIIe siècle." In *Gli studi di filosofia medievale fra otto e novecento. Contributo a un bilancio storiografico: Atti del convegno internazionale, Roma, 21–23 settembre 1989*, ed. Ruedi Imbach and Alfonso Maierù, pp. 191–208. Storia e letteratura 179. Rome: Edizioni di storia e letteratura, 1991.

Jaffa, Harry V. *Thomism and Aristotelianism: A Study of the Commentary by Thomas Aquinas on the Nicomachean Ethics*. Chicago: University of Chicago Press, 1952.

Jenkins, John I. *Knowledge and Faith in Thomas Aquinas*. Cambridge: Cambridge University Press, 1997.

Johnstone, Brian V. "The Debate on the Structure of the *Summa theologiae* of St Thomas Aquinas: From Chenu (1939) to Metz (1998)." In *Aquinas as Authority: A Collection of Studies Presented at the Second Conference of the Thomas Instituut te Utrecht, December 14–16, 2000*, ed. Paul van Geest, Harm Goris, and Carlo Leget, pp. 187–200. Publications of the Thomas Instituut te Utrecht, n.s. 7. Leuven: Peeters, 2002.

Jolivet, Jean. *La théologie d'Abélard*. Paris: Cerf, 1997.

Jordan, Mark D. "The Alleged Aristotelianism of Thomas Aquinas." Etienne Gilson Series 15. Toronto: Pontifical Institute of Mediaeval Studies, 1992. Reprinted in *The Gilson Lectures of Thomas Aquinas*, ed. James P. Reilly, pp. 73–106. Etienne Gilson Series 30. Toronto: Pontifical Institute of Mediaeval Studies, 2008.

——. "The Competition of Authoritative Languages and Aquinas' Theological Rhetoric." *Medieval Philosophy & Theology* 4 (1994): 71–90.

——. "The Modes of Thomistic Discourse: Questions for Corbin's *Le chemin de la théologie chez Thomas d'Aquin*." *Thomist* 45 (1981): 80–98.

Karayiannis, Vasilios. *Maxime le Confesseur: Essence et énergies de Dieu*. Théologie historique 93. Paris: Beauchesne, 1993.

Klima, Gyula. "*Ancilla theologiae* vs. *domina philosophorum*: Thomas Aquinas, Latin Averroism and the autonomy of philosophy." In *Was ist Philosophie im Mittelalter?*

Akten des X. Internationalen Kongresses für mittelalterliche Philosophie der Société Internationale pour l'Étude de la Philosophie Médiévale, 25. bis 30. August 1997 im Erfurt, ed. Jan A. Aertsen and Andreas Speer, pp. 393–402. Miscellanea mediaevalia 26. Berlin: Walter de Gruyter, 1998.

Lafont, Ghislain. *Structures et méthode dans la* Somme théologique *de saint Thomas d'Aquin.* Paris: Desclée de Brouwer, 1961.

Lamy de la Chapelle, Marie. "L'unité ontologique du Christ selon saint Albert le Grand." *Revue thomiste* 70 (1970): 181–226, 534–589.

Landgraf, A.M. "Das Problem *Utrum Christus fuerit homo in triduo mortis* in der Frühscholastik." In *Mélanges Auguste Pelzer: Études d'histoire littéraire et doctrinale de la scolastique médiévale offertes à Auguste Pelzer à l'occasion de son soixante-dixième anniversaire,* pp. 109–158. Université de Louvain: Recueil de travaux d'histoire et de philologie, 3rd ser., 26. Louvain: Bibliothèque de l'université, 1947.

Langston, Douglas C. "Scotus' Departure from Anselm's Theory of the Atonement." *Recherches de théologie ancienne et médiévale* 50 (1983): 227–241.

Laporte, Jean-Marc. "Christ in Aquinas's *Summa theologiae*: Peripheral or Pervasive?" *Thomist* 67 (2003): 221–248.

Lavaud, M.-Benoît. "Saint Thomas et la causalité physique instrumentale de la sainte humanité et des sacrements." *Revue thomiste* 32 (1927): 292–316.

Le Guillou, M.-J. "Quelques réflexions sur Constantinople III et la sotériologie de Maxime." In *Maximus Confessor: Actes du Symposium sur Maxime le Confesseur, Fribourg, 2–5 septembre 1980,* ed. Felix Heinzer and Christoph Schönborn, pp. 235–237. Fribourg: Éditions universitaires, 1982.

Lécuyer, J. "La causalité efficiente des mystères du Christ selon saint Thomas." *Doctor communis* 6 (1953): 91–120.

Leftow, Brian. "Anselm on the Necessity of the Incarnation." *Religious Studies* 31 (1995): 167–185.

Leroy, Marie-Vincent. "L'union selon l'hypostase d'après saint Thomas d'Aquin." *Revue thomiste* 74 (1974): 205–243.

Léthel, François Marie. "La prière de Jésus à Gethsémani dans la controverse monothélite." In *Maximus Confessor: Actes du Symposium sur Maxime le Confesseur, Fribourg, 2–5 septembre 1980,* ed. Felix Heinzer and Christoph Schönborn, pp. 207–214. Fribourg: Éditions universitaires, 1982.

—. *Théologie de l'agonie du Christ: La liberté humaine du Fils de Dieu et son importance sotériologique mises en lumière par saint Maxime Confesseur.* Théologie historique 52. Paris: Beauchesne, 1979.

Lohr, Charles H. *St Thomas Aquinas,* Scriptum super sententiis: *An Index of Authorities Cited.* Avebury: 1980.

Lottin, Odon. *Psychologie et morale au XIIe et XIIIe siècles.* 6 vols in 8. Louvain: Abbaye du Mont César; Gembloux: J. Duculot, 1942–1960.

—. "Commentaire des *Sentences* et *Somme théologique* d'Albert le Grand." *Recherches de théologie ancienne et médiévale* 8 (1936): 117–153.

—. "La pluralité des formes substantielles avant saint Thomas d'Aquin." *Revue néoscolastique* 34 (1932): 449–467.

Louth, Andrew. *St John Damascene: Tradition and Originality in Byzantine Theology*. Oxford: Oxford University Press, 2002.
—. *Maximus the Confessor*. London: Routledge, 1996.
Luna, Concetta. "La *Reportatio* della lettura di Egidio Romano sul libro III delle *Sentenze* (Clm. 8005) e il problema dell'autenticità dell'*Ordinatio*." In *Documenti e studi sulla tradizione filosofica medievale* 1 (1990): 113–225; 2 (1991): 75–146.
Luscombe, David Edward. *The School of Peter Abelard: The Influence of Abelard's Thought in the Early Scholastic Period*. Cambridge: Cambridge University Press, 1969.
Luyten, N.A., ed. *L'Anthropologie de saint Thomas: [8] conférences organisées par la Faculté de théologie et la Société philosophique de Fribourg à l'occasion du 7e anniversaire de la mort de saint Thomas d'Aquin*. Fribourg: Éditions universitaires, 1974.
Madden, John D. "The Authenticity of Early Definitions of Will (*Thelêsis*)." In *Maximus Confessor: Actes du Symposium sur Maxime le Confesseur, Fribourg, 2–5 septembre 1980*, ed. Felix Heinzer and Christoph Schönborn, pp. 61–79. Fribourg: Éditions universitaires, 1982.
Madigan, Kevin. *The Passions of Christ in High-Medieval Thought: An Essay on Christological Development*. Oxford: Oxford University Press, 2007.
Mandonnet, Pierre. *Siger de Brabant et l'averroïsme latin au XIIIe siècle, Ière Partie: Étude critique*. Louvain: Institut supérieur de philosophie de l'université, 1911.
Mansini, Guy. "Understanding St Thomas on Christ's Immediate Knowledge of God." *Thomist* 59 (1995): 91–124.
Manteau-Bonamy, H.-M. "La liberté de l'homme selon Thomas d'Aquin. La datation de la Question disputé *De Malo*." *Archives d'histoire doctrinale et littéraire du moyen âge* 46 (1979): 7–34.
Marenbon, John. "Life, Milieu, and Intellectual Contexts." In *The Cambridge Companion to Abelard*, ed. Jeffrey E. Brower and Kevin Guilfoy, pp. 13–44. Cambridge Companions to Philosophy. Cambridge: Cambridge University Press, 2004.
—, ed. *Medieval Philosophy*. Routledge History of Philosophy. Vol. 3. London: Routledge, 1998.
Margerie, Bertrand de. "Mort sacrificielle du Christ et peine de mort chez saint Thomas d'Aquin, commentateur de saint Paul." *Revue thomiste* 83 (1983): 394–417.
McGuckin, John Anthony. *St Cyril of Alexandria: The Christological Controversy: Its History, Theology, and Texts*. Leiden: E.J. Brill, 1994.
McIntyre, John. *St Anselm and His Critics: A Re-interpretation of the* Cur Deus homo. Edinburgh: Oliver and Boyd, 1954.
McLeod, Frederick G. *The Roles of Christ's Humanity in Salvation: Insights from Theodore of Mopsuestia*. Washington, DC: Catholic University of America Press, 2005.
Metz, Wilhelm. *Die Architektonik des* Summa theologiae *des Thomas von Aquin. Zur Gesamtsicht des thomasischen Gedankens*. Hamburg: Felix Meiner, 1998.
Meyer, Gerbert and Albert Zimmermann, eds. *Albertus Magnus: Doctor universalis: 1280/1980*. Mainz: Matthias-Grünewald-Verlag, 1980.

Michaud-Quantin, Pierre. *La psychologie de l'activité chez Albert le Grand*. Bibliothèque thomiste 36. Paris: Vrin, 1966.
Moloney, Raymond. *The Knowledge of Christ*. London: Continuum, 1999.
Mondin, B. *La cristologia di San Tommaso d'Aquino: Origene, dottrine principali, attualità*. Rome: Urbaniana University Press, 1997.
Morard, Martin. "Thomas d'Aquin lecteur des conciles." *Archivum franciscanum historicum* 98 (2005): 211–365.
—. "Une source de saint Thomas d'Aquin: le deuxième Concile de Constantinople (553)." *Revue des sciences philosophiques et théologiques* 81 (1977): 21–56.
Morris, Thomas V. "St Thomas on the Identity and Unity of the Person of Christ: A Problem of Reference in Christological Discourse." *Scottish Journal of Theology* 35 (1982): 419–430.
Murphy, F.-X. and Sherwood, P. *Constantinople II et III*. Histoire des Conciles Œcuméniques 3. Paris: Éditions de l'Orante, 1974.
Narcisse, Gilbert. *Les raisons de Dieu: Argument de convenance et esthétique théologique selon saint Thomas d'Aquin et Hans Urs von Balthasar*. Studia Friburgensia, n.s. 83. Fribourg: Éditions universitaires, 1997.
—. "Les enjeux epistemologiques de l'argument de convenance selon saint Thomas d'Aquin." In *Ordo sapientiae et amoris*, ed. Pinto de Oliveira, pp. 143–167.
Nicolas, Jean-Hervé. "L'unité d'être dans le Christ d'après saint Thomas." *Revue thomiste* 65 (1965): 229–260.
Nielsen, Lauge Olaf. *Theology and Philosophy in the Twelfth Century: A Study of Gilbert of Porreta's Thinking and Theological Expositions of the Doctrine of the Incarnation during the Period 1130–1180*. Trans. Ragnar Christophersen. Acta theologica danica 15. Leiden: E.J. Brill, 1982.
Ols, D. "Plénitude de grâce et vision béatifique: Une voie peu fréquentée pour établir la vision béatifique du Christ durant sa vie terrestre." In *Atti del IX Congresso tomistico internazionale*, ed. Antonio Piolanti, 1: 315–329. Studi tomistici 40. Vatican City: Libreria editrice Vaticana, 1991.
Ottaviano, Carmelo. *Guglielmo d'Auxerre: La vita, le opere, il pensiero*. Biblioteca di filosofia e scienze 12. Rome: L'Universale tipografia poliglotta, 1931.
Owens, Joseph. "Thomas Aquinas." In *Individuation in Scholasticism: The Later Middle Ages and the Counter-Reformation (1150–1650)*, ed. Jorge J.E. Gracia, pp. 173–194. Albany, NY: State University of New York Press, 1994.
Patfoort, Albert. "Le vrai visage de la satisfaction du Christ selon St Thomas: Une étude de la *Somme théologique*." In *Ordo sapientiae et amoris*, ed. Pinto de Oliveira, pp. 247–265.
—. *Thomas d'Aquin: Les clés d'une théologie*. Paris: FAC-éditions, 1983.
—. "Amorces en S. Thomas de l'idée d'un 'moi humain' dans le Christ." *Revue des sciences philosophiques et théologiques* 48 (1964): 198–204.
—. *L'unité d'être dans le Christ d'après S. Thomas: À la croisée de l'ontologie et de la christologie*. Paris: Desclée, 1964.
Pelzer, A. "Le cours inédit d'Albert le Grand sur la *Morale à Nicomaque* recueilli et rédigé par S. Thomas d'Aquin." *Revue néo-scolastique de philosophie* 14 (1922): 333–361, 478–520.

Persson, Per Erik. "Le plan de la *Somme théologique* et le rapport 'Ratio-Revelatio'." *Revue philosophique de Louvain* 56 (1958): 542–572.
Pesch, Otto H. "Um den Plan der *Summa theologiae* des hl. Thomas von Aquin." *Münchener theologische Zeitschrift* 16 (1965): 128–137.
Pinckaers, Servais. "La conception thomiste de la liberté et ses conséquences en morale." In *Saint Thomas d'Aquin: Somme théologique, 1a–2ae: Tome deuxième: Questions 18–21: Les actes humains*, pp. 249–273. Paris: Cerf, 1966.
Pinto de Oliveira and Carlos-Josaphat, eds. *Ordo sapientiae et amoris: Image et message de saint Thomas d'Aquin à travers les récentes études historiques, herméneutiques et doctrinales.* Studia Friburgensia, n.s.78. Fribourg: Éditions universitaires, 1993.
Pollet, Vincent-Marie. "Le Christ d'après S. Albert le Grand." *La Vie spirituelle* 34 (1933): 78–108.
—. "L'union hypostatique d'après saint Albert-le-Grand." *Revue thomiste* 38 (1933): 505–532, 689–724.
Principe, Walter Henry. "Some Examples of Augustine's Influence on Medieval Christology." In *Collectanea Augustiniana : Mélanges T.J. van Bave*, ed. B. Bruning, M. Lamberigts, and J. van Houtem, pp. 955–974. Bibliotheca ephemeridum theologicarum Lovaniensium 92. Leuven: Leuven University Press, 1990.
—. "St Thomas and the Habitus-Theory of the Incarnation." In *Saint Thomas Aquinas, 1274–1974: Commemorative Studies*, ed. Armand Maurer, 1: 381–418. 2 vols. Toronto: Pontifical Institute of Mediaeval Studies, 1974.
—. *Alexander of Hales' Theology of the Hypostatic Union*. Vol. 2 of Studies and Texts 12. Toronto: Pontifical Institute of Mediaeval Studies, 1967.
—. *William of Auxerre's Theology of the Hypostatic Union*. Vol. 1 of *The Theology of the Hypostatic Union in the Early Thirteenth Century*. Studies and Texts 7. Toronto: Pontifical Institute of Mediaeval Studies, 1963.
Quinn, Philip L. "Abelard on Atonement: 'Nothing Unintelligible, Arbitrary, Illogical, or Immoral about It'." In *Reasoned Faith: Essays in Philosophical Theology in Honor of Norman Kretzmann*, ed. Eleonore Stump, pp. 281–300. Ithaca, NY: Cornell University Press, 1993.
Reichmann, James B. "Aquinas, Scotus, and the Christological Mystery: Why Christ is Not a Human Person." *Thomist* 71 (2007): 451–474.
Remy, Gérard. "Le Christ médiateur dans l'œuvre de saint Thomas d'Aquin," *Revue thomiste* 93 (1993): 183–233.
Resnick, Irven M. and Kenneth F. Kitchell, Jr. *Albert the Great: A Selectively Annotated Bibliography (1900–2000)*. Medieval and Renaissance Texts and Studies 269. Tempe, AZ: Arizona Center for Medieval and Renaissance Studies, 2004.
Reynolds, P.L. "Philosophy as the Handmaid of Theology: Aquinas on Christ's Causality." In *Contemplating Aquinas: On the Varieties of Interpretation*, ed. Fergus Kerr, pp. 217–245. London: SCM, 2003.
Riches, Aaron. "After Chalcedon: The Oneness of Christ and the Dyothelite Mediation of His Theandric Unity." *Modern Theology* 24 (2008): 199–224.
Riedinger, Rudolf. "In welcher Richtung wurden die Akten der Lateransynode von 649 übersetzt und in welcher Schrift was der lateinische Text dieser Akten geschrieben?" In *Martino I papa (649–653) e il suo tempo: Atti del XXVIII Convegno*

storico internazionale, Todi, 13–16 ottobre 1991, ed. Enrico Menestò, pp. 149–164. Atti dei convegni dell'Academia tudertina e del Centro di studi sulla spiritualità medievale, n.s. 5. Spoleto: Centro italiano di studi sull'alto Medioevo, 1992.

———. "Sprachschichten in der lateinischen Übersetzung der Lateranakten von 649." *Zeitschrift für Kirchengeschichte* 92 (1981): 180–203.

Robiglio, Andrea A. *L'impossibile volere: Tommaso d'Aquino, i tomisti e la volontà.* Filosofia: Ricerche. Milan: Vita e Pensiero, 2002.

Rosato, Andrew. "Duns Scotus on the Redemptive Work of Christ." Ph.D. diss., University of Notre Dame, 2009.

Rosemann, Philipp W. *Peter Lombard.* New York: Oxford University Press, 2004.

Rossi, Osvaldo. "L'*aliquid maius* e la riparazione." In Cur Deus homo, ed. Paul Gilbert et al., pp. 641–657.

Rozemond, Keetje. *La christologie de saint Jean Damascène.* Studia patristica et byzantina 8. Ettal: Buch-Kunstverlag Ettal, 1959.

Ruello, Francis. *La christologie de Thomas d'Aquin.* Théologie historique 76. Paris: Beauchesne, 1987.

Ryan, Thomas F. *Thomas Aquinas as Reader of the Psalms.* Notre Dame, IN: University of Notre Dame Press, 2000.

Saarinen, Risto. *Weakness of the Will in Medieval Thought: From Augustine to Buridan.* Leiden: E.J. Brill, 1994.

Salas, Victor, Jr. "Thomas Aquinas on Christ's *Esse*: A Metaphysics of the Incarnation." *Thomist* 70 (2006): 577–603.

Scheffczyk, Leo. "Die Stellung des Thomas von Aquin in der Entwicklung der Lehre von *den Mysteria Vitae Christi*." In Renovatio et Reformatio: *wider das Bild vom "finsteren" Mittelalter: Festschrift für Ludwig Hödl zum 60. Geburtstag überreicht von Freunden sowie Kollegen und Schülern*, ed. Manfred Gerwing and Godehard Ruppert, pp. 44–70. Münster: Aschendorff, 1985.

———. "Die Bedeutung der Mysterien des Lebens Jesu für Glauben und Leben des Christen." In *Die Mysterien des Lebens Jesu und die christliche Existenz*, ed. Leo Scheffczyk, pp. 17–34. Aschaffenburg: Paul Pattloch, 1984.

Schoot, Henk J.M. *Christ the 'Name' of God: Thomas Aquinas on Naming Christ.* Leuven: Peeters, 1993.

———. "The Ineffable Being of Christ according to Thomas Aquinas." In *Atti del IX Congresso tomistico internazionale*, ed. Antonio Piolanti, 5: 273–284. Studi tomistici 44. Vatican City: Libreria editrice Vaticana, 1991.

Schwaiger, Georg. "Albertus Magnus." In *"Nimm und lies": Christliche Denker von Origenes bis Erasmus von Rotterdam*, ed. Hans Freiherr von Campenhausen, pp. 171–188. Stuttgart: Verlag W. Kohlhammer, 1991.

Schweizer, Othmar. *Person und hypostatische Union bei Thomas von Aquin.* Freiburg, Schweiz: Universitätsverlag, 1957.

Seiller, Léon. *L'activité humaine du Christ selon Duns Scot.* Paris: Éditions franciscaines, 1944.

Sesboüé, Bernard. *Jésus-Christ, l'unique Médiateur: Essai sur la rédemption et le salut.* Paris: Desclée, 1988.

Southern, Richard William. *The Making of the Middle Ages*. New Haven: Yale University Press, 1959.

Spatz, N. "Approaches and Attitudes to a New Theology Textbook: The *Sentences* of Peter Lombard." In *Intellectual Climate of the Early University: Essays in Honor of Otto Gründler*, ed. Nancy van Deusen, pp. 27–52. Studies in Medieval Culture 39. Kalamazoo, MI: Medieval Institute Publications, Western Michigan University, 1997.

St Pierre, Jules A. "The Theological Thought of William of Auxerre: An Introductory Bibliography." *Recherches de théologie ancienee et médiévale* 33 (1966): 147–155.

Stump, Elenore. "Aquinas's Account of Freedom: Intellect and Will." In *Aquinas's Summa theologiae: Critical Essays*, ed. Brian. Davies, pp. 203–222. New York: Rowman and Littlefield Publishers, 2006.

—. "Aquinas' Metaphysics of the Incarnation." In *The Incarnation: An Interdisciplinary Symposium on the Incarnation of the Son of God*, ed. Stephen T. Davis, Daniel Kendall, Gerald O'Collins, pp. 197–218. Oxford: Oxford University Press, 2002.

Sweeney, M.J. "Thomas Aquinas's *Quaestiones de anima* and the Difference between a Philosophical and a Theological Approach to the Soul." In *Was ist Philosophie im Mittelalter? Akten des X. Internationalen Kongresses für mittelalterliche Philosophie der Société Internationale pour l'Étude de la Philosophie Médiévale, 25. bis 30. August 1997 im Erfurt*, ed. Jan A. Aertsen and Andreas Speer, pp. 587–594. Miscellanea mediaevalia 26. Berlin: Walter de Gruyter, 1998.

TeSelle, Eugene. *Christ in Context: Divine Purpose and Human Possibility*. Philadelphia: Fortress Press, 1975.

Thijssen, J.M.M.H. "1277 Revisited: A New Interpretation of the Doctrinal Investigations of Thomas Aquinas and Giles of Rome." *Vivarium* 35 (1997): 72–101.

Thiry, André. "Saint Thomas et la morale d'Aristote." In *Aristote et saint Thomas d'Aquin: journées d'études internationales (26–28 avril 1955)*, ed. Paul Moraux, pp. 229–258. Louvain: Publications universitaires de Louvain, 1957.

Thunberg, Lars. *Microcosm and Mediator: The Theological Anthropology of Maximus the Confessor*. Lund: C.K.W. Gleerup, 1965.

Torrell, Jean-Pierre. *Aquinas's Summa: Background, Structure, and Reception*. Trans. Benedict M. Guevin. Washington, DC: Catholic University of America Press, 2005.

—. *Saint Thomas Aquinas*. Vol. 2, *Spiritual Master*. Trans. Robert Royal. Washington, DC: Catholic University of America Press, 2003.

—. *Saint Thomas Aquinas*. Vol. 1, *The Person and His Work*. Trans. Robert Royal. Washington, DC: Catholic University of America Press, 1996.

—. "La causalité salvifique de la résurrection du Christ selon saint Thomas." *Revue thomiste* 96 (1996): 179–208.

—. "St Thomas d'Aquin et la science du Christ: Une relecture des questions 9–12 de la *Tertia Pars* de la *Somme théologique*." In *Saint Thomas au XXe siècle: Colloque du centenaire de la "Revue thomiste" (1893–1992), Toulouse, 25–28 mars 1993*, ed. Serge-Thomas Bonino, pp. 394–409. Paris: Éditions Saint-Paul, 1994.

Tschipke, Theophil. *L'humanité du Christ comme instrument de salut de la divinité*. Trans. Philibert Secretan. Fribourg: Academic Press Fribourg, 2003.

Van Nieuwenhove, Rik and Joseph Wawrykow, eds. *The Theology of Thomas Aquinas*. Notre Dame, IN: University of Notre Dame Press, 2005.

Van Steenberghen, Fernand. "L'averroïseme Latin au XIIIe siècle." In *Multiple Averroès: Actes du Colloque international organisé à l'occasion du 850e anniversaire de la naissance d'Averroès, Paris 20–23 septembre 1976*, ed. Jean Jolivet, pp. 283–286. Paris: Les Belles Lettres, 1978.

Vannest, A. "Nature et grâce dans la théologie de Guillaume d'Auxerre et de Guillaume d'Auvergne." *Ephemerides theologicae Lovanienses* 53 (1977): 83–106.

Verghese, Paul. "Monothelete Controversy: A Historical Survey." *The Greek Orthodox Theological Review* 13 (1968): 196–211.

Vignaux, Paul. "Note sur la considération de l'infini dans les *quaestiones disputatae de scientia Christi*." In *S. Bonaventura: 1274–1974*, ed. Jacques-Guy Bougerol, 3: 107–130. 5 vols. Grottaferrata: Collegio S. Bonaventura, 1972–1974.

Vos, Antonie. *The Philosophy of John Duns Scotus*. Edinburgh: Edinburgh University Press, 2006.

Walsh, Liam G. "Sacraments." In *The Theology of Thomas Aquinas*, ed. Rik Van Nieuwenhove and Joseph Wawrykow, pp. 326–364. Notre Dame, IN: University of Notre Dame Press, 2005.

Wawrykow, Joseph. *The Westminster Handbook to Thomas Aquinas*. Lousiville, KY: Westminster John Knox Press, 2005.

—. "Cross." In *The Theology of Thomas Aquinas*, ed. Rik Van Nieuwenhove and Joseph Wawrykow, pp. 32–34. Notre Dame, IN: University of Notre Dame Press, 2005.

—. "Grace." In *The Theology of Thomas Aquinas*, ed. Rik Van Nieuwenhove and Joseph Wawrykow, pp. 192–221. Notre Dame, IN: University of Notre Dame Press, 2005.

—. "Hypostatic Union." In *The Theology of Thomas Aquinas*, ed. Rik Van Nieuwenhove and Joseph Wawrykow, pp. 222–251. Notre Dame, IN: University of Notre Dame Press, 2005.

—. "Thomas Aquinas and Christology after 1277." In *Nach der Verurteilung von 1277: Philosophie und Theologie an der Universität von Paris im letzten Viertel des 13. Jahrhunderts: Studien und Texte*, ed. Jan A. Aertsen, Kent Emery, Jr, and Andreas Speer, pp. 299–319. Miscellanea mediaevalia 28. Berlin: Walter de Gruyter, 2001.

—. "Wisdom in the Christology of Thomas Aquinas." In *Christ Among the Medieval Dominicans: Representations of Christ in the Texts and Images of the Order of Preachers*, ed. Kent Emery, Jr, and Joseph Wawrykow, pp. 175–196. Notre Dame Conferences in Medieval Studies 7. Notre Dame, IN: University of Notre Dame Press, 1998.

—. *God's Grace and Human Action: 'Merit' in the Theology of Thomas Aquinas*. Notre Dame, IN: University of Notre Dame Press, 1995.

—, ed.: see Van Nieuwenhove, Rik

Wéber, E.H. *La Personne humaine au XIIIe siècle*. Bibliothèque thomiste 46. Paris: Vrin, 1991.

—. *Le Christ selon saint Thomas d'Aquin*. Paris: Desclée, 1988.

—. "Les apports positifs de la noétique d'Ibn Rushd à celle de Thomas d'Aquin." In *Multiple Averroès : Actes du Colloque international organisé à l'occasion du 850e anniversaire de la naissance d'Averroès, Paris 20–23 septembre 1976*, ed. Jean Jolivet, pp. 211–249. Paris: Les Belles Lettres, 1978.

Weinandy, Thomas Gerard. "Aquinas: God *is* Man: The Marvel of the Incarnation." In *Aquinas on Doctrine: A Critical Introduction*, ed. Daniel A. Keating, Thomas G. Weinandy, and John P. Yocum, pp. 67–89. London: T & T Clark, 2004.

—. "Aquinas and the Incarnation as Act: 'Become' as a Mixed Relation." *Doctor Communis* 32 (1979): 15–31.

Weingart, Richard E. *The Logic of Divine Love: A Critical Analysis of the Soteriology of Peter Abailard*. Oxford: Clarendon, 1970.

Weisheipl, James A. *Friar Thomas d'Aquino: His Life, Thought and Work*. Garden City, NY: Doubleday, 1974.

West, J.L.A. "Aquinas on the Metaphysics of *Esse* in Christ." *Thomist* 66 (2002): 231–250.

White, Thomas Joseph. "The Voluntary Action of the Earthly Christ and the Necessity of the Beatific Vision." *Thomist* 69 (2005): 497–534.

Williams, Thomas. "Sin, Grace, and Redemption." In *The Cambridge Companion to Abelard*, ed. Jeffrey E. Brower and Kevin Guilfoy, pp. 258–278. Cambridge Companions to Philosophy. Cambridge: Cambridge University Press, 2004.

Wippel, John F. "Quodlibetal Questions, Chiefly in Theology Faculties." In *Les questions disputées et les questions quodlibétiques dans les facultés de théologie, de droit et de médecine*, ed. Bernardo C. Bazàn, Gérard Fransen, Danielle Jacquart, and John W. Wippel, pp. 151–222. Turnhout: Brepols, 1985.

Yang, Andrew S. "Scotus' Voluntarist Approach to the Atonement Reconsidered." *Scottish Journal of Theology* 62 (2009): 421–440.

Zimmermann, Albert, ed. *Albert der Grosse: Seine Zeit, sein Werk, seine Wirkung*. Miscellanea mediaevalia 14. Berlin: Walter de Gruyter, 1981.

Index

action, Christ's: *see* operation, Christ's
actiones sunt suppositorum ("actions pertain to supposits") 76 n19, 252, 314, 319 n62, 322–324
Agatho 5 n6, 13–14, 14 n29, 23, 126, 132, 156, 175
Albert the Great (Albertus Magnus) 21–23, 69–89, 110–112, 136, 148, 151, 197, 225; actions in Christ 76, 87–88; and Aristotle 71, 76, 78, 82; conformity 73, 77–83; contrariety 73, 79, 83–87; efficient cause 77–78, 80–81; final cause 80–81; formal cause 80–81; and John Damascene 73, 75, 82; and Peter Lombard 73, 79–80; material cause 77–78, 80, 85; rejection of *circa idem ut idem* 22, 85, 111; theandric 73–75, 87; two powers in Christ; 73–74 universal doctor 71; and William of Auxerre 73, 76–79, 84; works: *Commentarii in libros Sententiarum* 79–89, 151; *De incarnatione* 73–79, 148. *See also* conformity; contrariety; operation, Christ's; passion; prayer, Christ's
Alexander of Hales 39, 56, 60, n87, 89, 95–96
Alexandrian pact of union 8–9
Ambrose 7, 126, 128, 162–163; works: *De fide* 7, 7 n10, 126, 128, 135, 175–176; *Super Lucam* 126, 175–176
Ambrosiaster 198
Anselm of Canterbury 4, 27, 28–31, 33; satisfaction theory of atonement 4, 29, 276–278, 325; works: *Cur Deus homo* 4, 27, 28–31, 276–278, 325
Apollonaris/Apollonarius 6, 6 n8, 118–120
Aquinas: *see* Thomas Aquinas
Arians 6, 162, 176
Aristotle 47, 70, 71, 76, 78, 82, 84 n41, 133, 136, 139, 141–143, 145, 148, 153, 170–171, 177, 184, 215–216; *libri naturales* 47; practical syllogism 170; works: *De anima* 135; *De caelo* 215 n94; *Nicomachean Ethics* 113 n2, 133, 142; *Politics* 129
Athanasian Creed 280
Athanasius 13, 276 n272
Augustine 7, 31, 51, 58, 126, 128, 144, 154, 158, 161, 175; cited by Aquinas 144, 154, 158, 161, 162–163, 175–177, 263, 270; works: *Contra Maximinum* 7 n10, 13, 126, 128, 144, 154, 175
Averroes (Ibn Rushd) 47. *See also* Latin Averroism
Avicenna 47

Bede 43, 63
Bernard of Clairvaux 4, 33 n16
Boethius 188 n18, 238 n157
Boethius of Dacia 170
Bonaventure 21–22, 27 n1, 50–51, 68–70, 89–112, 121 n25, 129 n53, 136, 151, 158, 167, 267, 310, 330; assimilation 104–107; Christ's knowledge 90; concordance of wills 91, 103, 167; dominion in Christ 95; effi-

cient cause 104; harmony of wills 95, 101, 105 n93, 167; hypostatic union 92, 95; and Hugh of St Victor 96, 98–99, 103, 106, 108–109; material cause 103–104; subjection 95, 104–108; *synderesis* 96, 99; Word as exemplar 90. *See also* conformity; contrariety; operation, Christ's; passion; prayer, Christ's

boulēsis 6 n7, 18, 21, 23, 42 n41, 50 n63, 60 n87, 75, 97, 99–100, 112, 136–139, 169, 259 n219. *See also* will as reason

Burgundio of Pisa 17 n36, 18 n38, 37 n28, 38

Cappadocians 11. *See also* Gregory Nazianzen; Gregory Nyssen
Cerbanus 38, 59 n84, 62, 174 n87
Chalcedon 2–5, 8–9, 11, 13, 18, 29 n5, 115, 119 n17, 169, 175 n188, 199, 215 n93, 217 n100, 282
Chenu, M.-D. 184–186, 288
circa idem 21–22, 62–65, 68, 76 n20, 85, 100, 105–106, 111, 164, 167 n171, 178, 206, 330
communicatio idiomatum 9 n18, 229, 304–305, 316, 318
conformity (of wills) 5, 23, 46, 277 n275, 329–330; according to Albert the Great 21–22, 23, 61 n91, 65 n101, 69, 73, 77–89, 330; of assimilation 104–108; according to Bonaventure 21–22, 65 n101, 69–70, 91, 100–112, 330; according to Giles of Rome 292; according to John Duns Scotus 25, 291, 302, 305–306, 308, 312; according to Peter Lombard 46; according to Peter Olivi 293; of subjection 104–108; according to the *Summa fratris* 59, 67; according to Thomas Aquinas 23, 114–117, 138, 144–158, 158–162, 167, 174, 177, 180, 261–262; according to William of Auxerre 51, 67

Constans II 10
Constantin IV 13
Constantinople II 13, 115, 169, 282
Constantinople III 2 n3, 4, 14–16, 23, 26, 36, 44, 46, 301 n19; Agatho's *Epistle One* included with, 23, 114, 126 n45, 158, 234 n148; condemnation of Macarius 43–44, 115, 118, 169; Thomas Aquinas's use of 73 n10, 114–115, 117 n11, 118–120, 124–125, 132, 158, 163, 168–176, 215 n93, 216–217, 242 n167, 248, 253, 282, 285

contrariety and non-contrariety (of wills) 5, 7–8, 12, 14, 23, 110, 330; according to Bonaventure 21–22, 69–70, 91–107, 111–112, 330; according to Giles of Rome 292, 294; according to Hugh of St Victor 34–35, 330; according to John Duns Scotus 25, 291, 305–306, 309, 312; according to Peter Lombard 26; according to Peter Olivi 299; according to the *Summa fratris* 21, 23, 26, 56–68, 309 n31, 330–331; according to Thomas Aquinas 23–24, 114–117, 139, 153, 157–180, 221, 223, 260–261, 330–331; according to William of Auxerre 21, 26, 48–56, 309 n31, 330

Corbin, M. 188–189
Cross, R. 314–320
Cyril of Alexandria 8–9, 14, 15, 200, 217 n100, 235 n150

deliberative will: *see* will, deliberative
Dionysius the Aeropagite: *see* Pseudo-Dionysius the Aeropagite
dyothelite 2, 10, 18, 23, 29 n5, 162

electio (election) 18, 23, 140–143, 171–172, 213
Ephesus 18, 115, 175 n188, 217 n100, 282

esse: see Thomas Aquinas
Eugene III 17 n36, 38
Eutyches 3, 43 n47, 118–120, 122
exitus-reditus 184–185, 190, 193, 288

fear in Christ 35, 49, 53–56, 73, 76–79, 88, 106, 140, 152, 155, 221–222
fittingness (*convenientia*): *see* Thomas Aquinas
free choice 18, 23, 53–54, 95, 116, 130–131, 139–143, 168–171, 178, 213, 253, 283. *See also liberum arbitrium*

Galatians 5:17 42 n42, 51, 58, 62, 101, 163
Gerhoh of Reichersberg 38 n32, 217 n100
Gethsemane (prayer in the garden of) 6, 9 n18, 14, 18 n37, 26, 30, 36–37, 49, 55, 66, 82–83, 88, 92, 109, 166, 312, 329, 331. *See also* Luke 22:42; Matthew 26:39
Giles of Rome (Aegidius Romanus) 4, 19, 25, 292–294
Gillon, L.-B. 225–227
gnōmē 13 n24, 17 n34, 18, 140–142, 171
gnomic will 12, 13 n24, 17, 171 n179
grace 20, 44, 33, 128, 181–182, 197, 206, 212, 218–220, 225, 254–255, 263–264, 271–272, 284–287, 301, 302, 307, 313; *auxilium* 172, 207–208; cooperative 207–208; *gratia gratis data* 210–211; *gratia gratum faciens* 210; habitual 172, 207–208, 210, 267 n249; operative 207–208
Gratian 36, 44 n48, 301 n19
Gregory IX 47
Gregory Nazianzen 7, 14
Gregory Nyssen 14

harmony of wills 5, 7, 95, 101, 105 n93, 166 n168, 167, 177, 180, 330
hen thelēma 9
Heraclius 8–9, 11
Hilary of Poitiers 60 n89, 79, 220 n109

homo assumptus 12 n23, 39 n34, 40 n36, 74 n14, 242 n167, 284, 315 n53, 327–328
Honorius 9
Hugh of St Victor 34–36, 39 n35, 45, 70, 100, 106, 108–109, 112, 136, 184, 330; works: *De sacramentis fidei Christianae* 35; *De quatuor voluntatibus Christi* 22, 27, 34–35, 68 n106, 89, 96–99, 103, 108–109, 111
hypostatic union 3, 12, 24, 92–95, 105 n93, 120, 301; Thomas Aquinas's use of 47 n55, 115, 118, 123, 127, 131, 168–169, 175, 186 n12, 200, 203, 207–209, 212, 218–219, 225–228, 236–237, 243–244, 254, 278–301, 318, 322, 324–326
hypostasis 2 n4, 5, 8 n15, 11–13, 46, 74, 92–96, 119, 129 n53, 131, 172, 199–200, 229–230, 236, 242–243, 252–253, 282–283, 285, 301, 318, 326
hypostatically united instrument 173, 211, 252–253, 275, 281, 318, 322, 326

imitatio Christi 4, 90 n58
instrumental causality 123–124, 128–129, 172–174, 198 n47, 245, 249–251, 257, 317–327; instrumental efficient causality 2, 24–25, 30 n7, 131, 143, 174, 180, 182, 193, 224, 226 n126, 231, 253, 272–275, 278–290, 319, 321–327, 331–332. *See also instrumentum divinitatis*
instrumentum divinitatis (instrument of the divinity) 1, 24, 124, 129, 172–173, 182, 191–192, 211 n82, 215 n94, 217–219, 224, 249, 251, 265, 273–275, 278–290, 322–327

Jerome 31, 32 n12, 44 n47, 58 n84, 63
John 6:38 6 n7, 7, 15, 18, 29, 31, 92
John Chrysostom 7, 276 n272
John Damascene 6, 16–18, 22, 26, 58, 301; *boulēsis* 18, 21, 42 n41, 97, 259 n219; Albert the Great's use of 73,

74, 75, 82, 85, 86, 88, 111; Bonaventure's use of 92–93, 96, 98–99, 106, 109, 112; and *electio* 18, 23, 213; Peter Lombard's use of 38, 67; *Summa fratris*'s use of 59 n84, 60, 62, 64, 67; *thelēsis* 16 n34, 17 n35, 18, 21, 42 n41, 96–98, 109, 112, 259 n219; Thomas Aquinas's use of 121–178 *passim*, 194, 203, 213, 222, 261 n227 273, 282; works: *De fide orthodoxa* 6, 17–18, 26, 38, 57, 60, 62, 67–68, 92, 301
John de la Rochelle (John de Rupella) 56, 89, 91
John Duns Scotus 5 n6, 25, 197, 291, 300–321, 327–328; actions pertain to natures 314, 318, 320; *affectio commodi* 305, 308, 309; *affectio iustitiae* 305; on Christ's operations/merit 313–321; on *dolor* and *tristitia* 25, 300, 306–312; *voluntas ut libera* (will as free) 309

Lafont, G. 186–188, 288
Laporte, J.-M. 189
Lateran Council of 649 4, 10, 13, 26
Latin Averroism 23, 116, 170, 289
Leo 5 n6, 14, 15, 46 n54, 114, 222 n117, 245 n173, 250 n189, 321 n66
liberum arbitrium 23, 53, 95 n69, 116, 130, 139. *See also* free choice
Luke 22:42 6 n7, 126, 163 n156. *See also* Gethsemane

Manichean 83
Matthew 26:39 6, 7, 18, 30, 31, 41, 55, 66, 100, 154, 260. *See also* Gethsemane
Matthew of Aquasparta 295, 301 n20
Maximus the Confessor 5 n6, 6 n7, 10–13, 16–18, 46 n54, 142 n102, 171, 176
merit 19, 181, 208; Christ's 25, 46, 49–54, 57, 80–81, 85, 91–92, 117, 208, 212, 247–256, 259, 286, 298–299, 313, 320, 325

mia energeia 8
monenergism 7 n8, 169, 175, 217 n100
monophysite 8, 16 n33, 44 n48, 46, 217 n100, 245. *See also* non-Chalcedonian
monothelite 4, 23, 46, 119 n17, 121, 125, 169, 175–176; controversy 7–16, 17–18, 34, 50, 175

Narcisse, G. 191–193, 288
natural will: *see* will
Nemesius of Emesa 6 n7, 18 n38
Nestorianism 2 n4, 115, 129 n53, 282, 321
Nestorius 3, 5 n6, 6 n8, 118–120, 173 n185, 199, 228 n131, 229 n133, 235 n150, 282, 284
non-Chalcedonian 8–9

Odo Rigaldus 56 n79, 58, 60 n89, 61, 76 n18, 89
one willer in Christ 46, 73–74, 86–87, 94, 284, 320, 325–326
operation, Christ's 4–8, 13–14, 24, 36 n25; Agatho on 126 n45; Albert the Great on 76 n19; John Duns Scotus on 301, 313, 316–317; Thomas Aquinas on 73 n10, 116–120, 141, 175, 198 n47, 201 n57, 210, 216–217, 224, 226–228, 234–237, 244–257, 278, 282–289, 317–32, 325–326, 331. *See also* merit, Christ's; instrumental causality
Otto of Lucca 36, 38 n29

passion: Albert the Great on 76, 80n30, 82; Anselm on 4, 28–31, 329; Bonaventure on 22, 106; Hugh of St Victor on 34; John Duns Scotus on 305–313; Peter Abelard on 32–33; Peter Lombard on 21, 42, 45, 52, 66, 68; *Summa fratris* on 21, 23, 64–66, 68; Thomas Aquinas on 24, 154–156, 162–166, 178, 196 n43, 198 n47, 199 n49, 213 n91, 214–215, 221–222,

226, 259, 216 n227, 264–265, 267 n249, 275, 276–278, 283, 286–287, 298–299, 331
Peter Abelard 4, 27, 31–33. *See also* Ysagoge in theologiam
Peter Lombard 4, 19–21, 37–47, 66–68, 69, 73, 256; Christological opinions 39–41, 46–47, 93, 199–200, 295, 321; disposition of reason (*affectus rationalitatis*) 42, 66; disposition of sensuality (*affectus sensualitatis*) 42, 66; works: *Sentences* 4, 26–27, 39–47, 48–49, 57, 66–68, 69–73, 79–88, 91–97, 109–110, 113–118, 135, 174–176, 184, 256, 321, 329
Peter Olivi 25, 292, 294–299
prayer, Christ's 6; in Albert the Great 73, 78, 82, 88, 330; in Anselm 29; in Bonaventure 91–92, 100, 105–106, 108–109, 112, 330; in Hugh of St Victor 35; in John Duns Scotus 25, 312; in Peter Lombard 20, 26, 42–45, 57, 67, 69, 329; in *Summa fratris* 57, 66, 330; in Thomas Aquinas 116, 167–168, 219, 227, 255–263; in William of Auxerre 49–50, 55–56, 57, 330
Pseudo-Athanasius 13, 114, 162, 175
Pseudo-Dionysius the Aeropagite 8 n13, 13–14, 73–75, 85–87, 113 n2, 195, 223 n119, 266 n248; theandric energy/activity 8 n13, 13, 73–75, 87, 275

sadness (*tristitia*) 25, 135, 140, 221–222, 291–300, 306–312, 330–332
sensuality 35, 45, 52, 76, 92, 258, 294; disposition of 21, 42–44, 58. *See also* will of sensuality
Sergius of Constantinople 9–10, 119–120, 169
Severus 248–249
Siger of Brabant 170
Sophronius 9, 11

sorrow (*dolor*) 25, 66, 221, 291, 300, 306–312, 330–332
soteriology 1, 4, 20, 25, 27, 32, 143, 155, 180, 276 n274, 303, 325, 327, 331
Stephen Tempier 170, 294. *See also* Latin Averroism
Summa fratris Alexandri 19–23, 26–27, 56–66, 83–84, 100–101, 140, 158–160; *voluntas ut natura* in 21, 59–61; *voluntas ut ratio* in 21, 59–61. *See also* conformity; contrariety; operation, Christ's; passion; prayer, Christ's
Summa sententiarum 20, 27, 32, 36–37, 38 n29, 41, 45, 329; citation of Constantinople III, 36; source for Lombard 20, 37, 41, 45

thelēsis 6 n7, 9, 12, 16–18, 21, 23, 42 n41, 50 n63, 60 n87, 75, 96–97, 99–100, 109, 112, 136–139, 169, 259 n219
Theodore of Mopsuestia 6 n8
Thomas Aquinas 1–2, 19–20, 46; *acta et passa Christi in carne* 1, 181, 183 n2, 225, 228, 233, 265, 286, 288; Christ as *comprehensor* 24, 152, 154, 156, 172, 178, 220, 222, 265; Christ's grace 206–212; Christ's knowledge 206–207, 212–217, 221; Christ's *liberum arbitrium* (free choice) 139–143, 168, 178, 213; Christ as mediator 181, 182, 208, 220, 265–267, 269–283, 285–287, 321; Christ's operations 248–255, 256, 286–287, 321–328; Christ as *viator* (wayfarer) 24, 152, 156, 172, 178, 220, 222, 265; Christ's *esse* 217, 236–237, 240–244, 252, 285; *coassumpta* 212, 226–227, 235, 236; consequences of the union 218, 224–228, 234, 267, 280, 284; distinction of power and act 23–24, 130–132, 137–139, 148, 158, 161, 167 n171, 174, 262; fittingness (*convenientia*) 180–182, 191–192, 193–199,

200–203, 205, 209, 219, 223–224, 258–259, 263, 265–266, 271, 275–283, 287–290, 326; rational instrumentality 125, 129, 172–174, 210–211, 249–253, 275, 280, 285, 317; *secundum quod homo* 2, 24, 181, 182, 211–212, 219, 230–232, 265–275, 282–283, 287, 321, 327–328; works: *Compendium theologiae* 186 n11, 190, 232 n144, 235 n152, 242 n167, 244 n171, 254 n200, 317 n59; *in I Tim.* 265 n244, 269 n251; *Quaestiones disputatae de unione Verbi incarnati* 117 n11, 216–217, 227 n130, 235 n152, 236–248, 251–253, 281 n287, 285; *Quaestiones disputatae de veritate* 129 n53, 135 n82, 173 n182, 250 n190, 254 n200, 265 n244, 267 n249, 268 n251, 274 n268, 279 n279, 281; *Quodlibet IX* 225 n123, 244 n171; *Scriptum super libros Sententiarum* 23, 70, 72 n9, 86 n44, 112, 113–177 *passim*, 184, 188, 215–217, 226–227, 244 n171, 256, 263–274, 281, 289; *Summa contra Gentiles* 114, 117–119, 129 n53, 140–141, 151 n113, 169–170, 173 n185, 189, 248, 250, 279–282; *Summa theologiae* 1, 12, 19, 23–24, 46, 68, 70, 113–179 *passim*, 180–290 *passim*, 323, 331; *Super Heb.* 263 n233, 263 n244, 264 n241. *See also* conformity; contrariety; hypostatic union; operation, Christ's; passion; prayer, Christ's

Torrell, J.-P. 190–191, 288

unity of Trinitarian actions *ad extra* 303–305, 316, 322–328

velleitas 84, 146, 149 n112, 261
volitum ("thing willed") 17 n34, 21–22, 51–53, 62, 65, 70, 77, 80–81, 83, 85, 87, 89, 100, 102–11, 116, 141, 144–167, 174, 177–178, 292–293, 311
voluntas ut natura: *see* will as nature
voluntas ut ratio: *see* will as reason

weakness, assumed 7 n10, 32, 327; of flesh 43, 45 n50, 84; of will 84
will: as free (*voluntas ut libera*) 308–309; as nature (*voluntas ut natura*) 6 n7, 24, 50 n63, 59–61, 82–83, 86–88, 135–139, 145–150, 152–161, 166, 174–178, 214, 222, 259–262, 305–309; as reason (*voluntas ut ratio*) 6 n7, 24, 42, 50 n63, 59–61, 87–88, 116, 135–141, 145–158, 161, 171, 174, 178, 214, 259–262; of reason 21, 26–27, 42, 44, 49–68, 75, 79–86, 88–89, 96–101, 104–116, 134–140, 145–151, 156, 159–161, 165–169, 174, 178, 214, 261–262, 292; deliberative 24, 42 n41, 60 n87, 65, 75, 80, 97–99, 104, 111, 259–260, 293; of sensuality 21, 26, 42 n41, 48–55, 58–68, 79–88, 96, 101, 103–112, 132–135, 140, 146, 150, 152, 155–167, 177–178, 222 n117, 259–262, 292; of tender pity 34–35, 96, 98, 99, 106, 109–112
William of Auxerre 20–21, 26, 47–56, 66–68; works: *Summa aurea* 20, 26, 47–56, 66–68. *See also* conformity; contrariety; operation, Christ's; passion; prayer, Christ's
William of Meliton 89

Ysagoge in theologiam 32